EVERY TRICK IN THE BOOK

First published by The Squeeze Press 2010.
An imprint of Wooden Books Ltd.
8A Market Place, Glastonbury BA6 9HW

A CIP catalogue record for this book is available from the British Library.

ISBN: 978-1-906069-07-0

The publishers accept no responsibility for any crashed aircraft, sawn-in-half siblings, angry neighbours, damaged property or any injuries or aggravation to inviduals, animals, plants or objects as a result of owning or reading this book.

Visit www.wiztrix.com for more tricks.

Also visit Wooden Books' web site at www.woodenbooks.com

1 3 5 7 9 10 8 6 4 2

Designed and typeset by Wooden Books Ltd, Glastonbury, UK

Printed and bound in India by Replika Press.

Original illustrations by Charlie Dancey and Matt Tweed.

Some illustrations have previously appeared in *The Encyclopædia of Ball Juggling* or *The Compendium of Club Juggling*, both by Charlie Dancey and published by Butterfingers Books of Glastonbury.

Not everything in this book is true.

EVERY TRICK IN THE BOOK

CHARLIE DANCEY

the

SQUEEZE
PRESS
GLASTONBURY

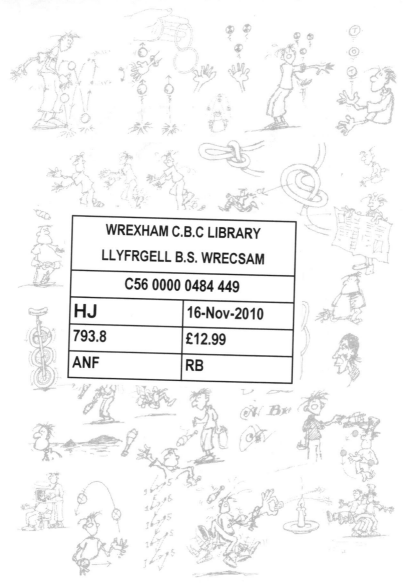

Special thanks to John Martineau for publishing this book, Matt Tweed for assistance with his fine illustrations, Daud Sutton for excellent typographic help and Stephen Parsons for diligent editing.

Other noteable people have been given cameo roles in this book.

Thanks also to Frances Howard-Gordon, Laurie Collard, Suzi Martineau and of course, extra-special thanks to Judith Healey a.k.a. Mrs Dancey.

ABOUT THIS BOOK

To perfect the tautology of the title of this book I should explain that by "*The Book*" I obviously mean *this* book. It would have been quite impossible to complete this work otherwise.

A "*Trick*," for our purposes, is a piece of *magic* that actually *works*.

I have tried to make sure that the most of the tricks in this book are simple to do, once you know *how*, but here and there (and there, and *there...*) I may have stumbled into the deep end of trickdom and described impressive feats of the kind that take hours, days or even years to master. I doubt very much that many readers will *actually* indulge in LION TAMING or master the feat of AUTO ROTATING a crippled helicopter onto the surface of the sea—but I hope they will enjoy knowing *how* these exotic things are done.

If you should happen know a terribly clever trick that you'd like to share with the world, and which I have missed out, then please visit this book's web site at **wiztrix.com** where all contributions are gratefully received and may even be included in future editions of this book.

I'm especially keen to see your illustrations!

Charlie Dancey
Glastonbury
MMX

CONTENTS

ACROBATICS, UNICYCLES & CIRCUS SKILLS

ANIMALS

BALANCING

BAR, CARD, COIN & MATCH TRICKS

BICYCLES, BOATS, VEHICLES & FLYING MACHINES

CODES & CIPHERS, ESPIONAGE & ESCAPOLOGY

DRAWING & SIGNWRITING

EXPLOSIVES, PYROTECHNICS & WEAPONS

Yeast Tablets and Beer, 731; Hydrogen, 331; Flaming Brandy, 240; Orange Peel Flame Thrower, 435; Polyethylene Pyrotechnics, 496; Acetylene, 3; Party Poppers, 456; Flicking Matches, 245; Fire Walking, 228; Elastic Band Sharp-Shooter, 194; Gas Gun, 278; Glove Gun, 290; Sling, 579; Trebuchet, 672; Water Bomb, 706.

FUN WITH SCIENCE

Ball Bearing on Glass, 27; Beanbag Bridge, 38; Blue Roses, 51; Camera Obscura, 74; Chain Twirling Harmonics, 97; Extra Strong Mints, 207; Instant Karaoke Machine, 340; Levitron, 363; Megalilth, 400; Mirrors, 408; Newtonian Super-Bounce, 426; Pinhole Cameras, 483; Self-Sealing Envelopes, 557; Smoke Rings, 582; Sulphur Hexafluoride, 614; Sundials, 615; Supermagnet, 618; Syphon, 627; Thunder and Lightning, 655; Toroidal Bubble, 664; Hydrogen, 331; Mento and Diet Coke, 405; Video Feedback, 700; Fission Pop Bomb, 232; Solar Oven, 587; Helium, 318; Dry Ice, 188; Stereoscopy, 599; Air Cannon, 6; Bubble Within a Bubble, 68.

FILMING, ANIMATION & TECHNICAL WIZARDRY

Contra-Zoom, 135; Crossing the Line, 144; Maguffin, 388; Night Vision Cameras, 427; Aerial Camera Photos, 5; Phenokistoscope, 499; Praxinoscope, 501; Thaumatrope, 639; Zoetrope, 740; Alphabet Backwards, 11; Wine Bottle, opening without a Corkscrew, 722; Ninja Rocks, 429; Wobbly Table Theorem, 724; Pump up the Bass, 505; Drinking Brandy Through Chocolate Fingers, 187.

GEOMETRY & MATHEMATICS

Bisecting an Angle, 48; Dodecahedron, 183; Ellipse, 197; Finding the Centre of a Circle, 218; Geodesic Domes, 279; Golden Section, 291; Hexagon, 318; Icosahedron, 335; Octahedron, 431; Pentagon, 462; Perpendicular Bisector, 467; Platonic Solids, 492; Right Angle, 526; Root Two Rectangle, 538; Tetrahedron, 638; Three-Four-Five Triangle, 649; Reciprocal Frames, 514; Pentagram, 463; Trisecting an Angle, 678; Divisibility Tests, 181; Eleven Times Table, 197; Nineteen Times Table, 428; Pi, 476; Proving That One Equals Two, 502; Parabola, 451; Pythagoras' Theorem, 508; Trigonometry, 676; Nine Times Table, 428; Moebius Strip, 411.

GRIFTING

HAND TRICKS & OBJECT MANIPULATION

JUGGLING

KNOTS

MAGIC

AARDWOLF

ANIMALS

The great geomancer, philosopher and sometime druid *Radical Cheney* declared in the preface to his greatest work that, '*...all things behave according to their True Nature and it is thus that the understanding of the True Nature of Things is also the understanding of the World and all that is in it.*'

The true nature of the Aardwolf is both savage and terrible, quite unlike that of its loveable termite-eating cousin; the *Aardvark**.

The **AARDWOLF** has the look of an overgrown grey fox and howls with a distinctive knuckle-whitening shriek like the sound of a stabbed baby.

The beast can be persuaded to come to heel (without biting off a foot) by tempting it with a mixture of chicken giblets, oxblood and aniseed, all bound together with gelatine. **AARDWOLVES** will do *anything* for a taste of this mixture but take care not to allow the slightest drop onto your skin, lest the creature think that you are made of the stuff.

The **AARDWOLF** appears in this volume for two reasons: firstly, the advice just given regarding the taming of the brute is a *Trick,* something that, once understood, gives one apparently magical powers. Secondly, the animal has remarkable alphabetical precedence and is unlikely to be usurped from its frontmost position in *Every Trick In The Book* in later editions. Hence it can serve as a sort of introduction to what follows.

---

* Which is described in other works by this author.

A
B
C
D
E
F
G
H
I
J
K
L
M
N
O
P
Q
R
S
T
U
V
W
X
Y
Z

A
B
C
D
E
F
G
H
I
J
K
L
M
N
O
P
Q
R
S
T
U
V
W
X
Y
Z

This book is in alphabetical order. Moreover, when you see words or phrases written in **CAPITAL** type it is a pointer to another entry in the book that you can look up. So if I remarked that an understanding of **LION TAMING** might be relevant when dealing with **AARDWOLVES** you'd know that I had taken the trouble to write something about lions and might be curious to find out what it was.

And so I hope the reader will explore this book in a random manner, picking up a trifle here and a secret there, and never knowing if they might have missed some small item whose location could be hidden in the text.

ACCURACY WITH WHIPS

WHIPS

If you need to do target work with whips you'll probably be using the **LION TAMER'S CRACK** or the **WHIP MAN CRACK**, the second being the Zen purist's version of the first. Whatever method you use you need to focus on accuracy, especially if you intending to crack a cigarette out of someone's mouth.

☆ HERE'S *The* TRICK: Whips go where you look! Yes, they do!* The very last thing you need to be doing, while delivering a supersonic cutting crack, is thinking 'I hope I don't hit their nose!'

If your technique is smooth and constant in practice, then you can pretty much rely on your whip going *where you look* when you use it in performance. You must focus *completely* on what you are trying to hit. Work as a Zen archer might: *become* the target.

This will sort out the *direction* of your strike but not the *range!* You absolutely *must* make sure that you know the range of your whip. Be very

---

* So do paragliders. There's a classic type of paraglider accident that happens when a pilot loses lift and 'lands out' in a field. The wing is losing height and the pilot is not thinking straight because they have messed up and will be laughing stock of their friends. They pick a large field that is empty save for one large tree in the middle. 'I hope I don't hit the tree!' thinks the fumbling pilot who is pulling brake-lines and trying to line up a landing. They keep looking at the tree, hoping not to hit it and it starts to exert a magnetic attraction on them. They spiral hopelessly towards disaster and—Wham! It happens all the time.

A
B
C
D
E
F
G
H
I
J
K
L
M
N
O
P
Q
R
S
T
U
V
W
X
Y
Z

careful about this. Whips change length as the **FALL** slowly wears away and the **CRACK** gets re-tied. You may even have replaced the **FALL** and ended up with a whip a few inches longer than the one you were working with last week.

ACETYLENE

PYROTECHNICS / EXPLOSIVES

ACETYLENE, when burnt with oxygen, produces a flame that can melt steel like butter. It is extremely dangerous stuff and should only be used by trained welders.

☆ It therefore follows that you should never even *consider* filling a balloon with the stuff and bursting it with a flame (at a safe distance) because the detonation might be even louder and more dramatic than if you had filled it with **HYDROGEN**.

ACTIVE BOUNCE

JUGGLING

When juggling with **BOUNCING BALLS** the **ACTIVE BOUNCE** is the opposite of the **PASSIVE BOUNCE**. Instead of tossing a ball a little way *up* and letting it drop to the ground you throw the ball *down* at the floor. **PASSIVE BOUNCE** throws are made with the palm of the hand pointing up, **ACTIVE BOUNCE** throws are made palm down.

A
B
C
D
E
F
G
H
I
J
K
L
M
N
O
P
Q
R
S
T
U
V
W
X
Y
Z

When a ball bounces on the floor some energy is lost. If it is to rise to the height it was thrown from it needs some extra momentum. In **PASSIVE BOUNCE** this energy is supplied because it fell from a greater height. In **ACTIVE BOUNCE** it is comes from the force with which you threw the ball at the ground.

PASSIVE BOUNCE is gentle and easy to control. **ACTIVE BOUNCE** is more aggressive and harder to control.

The **ACTIVE BOUNCE** has the advantage of being juggleable on floors with poor bounce, because you can compensate for the low bounces by slamming the balls harder into the ground.

ACTIVE BOUNCE creates more exciting patterns. It's useful when the natural bounce of the balls you are using is poor or when the floor you are working on is a bit "dead". Moreover, by throwing the balls down *really hard* you can get them to bounce back to a far greater height than they were thrown from, which creates opportunities for some great tricks.

☆ Take three balls and try juggling them in an **ACTIVE BOUNCE**. You throw the balls from the *outside* of the pattern, aiming right-hand throws at a point just in front of your right foot, and left-hand throws at the corresponding point in front of your left foot.

Accuracy is everything and it is all going to feel a bit ham-fisted until you get used to the downward-throwing action.

☆ Only attempt a five-ball bounce when you are really solid with three.

☆ A good exercise for the five-ball bouncer is to juggle five balls in the **PASSIVE BOUNCE** style and toss in occasional **ACTIVE BOUNCE** throws; one on the right, one on the left, then some *left-rights* and *right-lefts*. You can drum up some very cool rhythms this way.

☆ If you slam three very hard **ACTIVE BOUNCE** throws into a passively bounced five-ball cascade you can effectively **FLASH** three balls high and then lift the whole pattern into a regular **FIVE BALL CASCADE** juggled in the air.

See also **FIVE BALL BOUNCE, PASSIVE BOUNCE, COLUMN BOUNCE**.

AERIAL CAMERA PHOTOS

TECHNICAL WIZARDRY

Here's how to take photos of yourself *from above*. You need is a camera with a self-timer function which nearly every modern camera has. You'll also require a keen sense of timing and a devil-may-care love of adventure.

☆ Start the self-timer and chuck your camera up high in the air with a little *flat spin* (as if spinning a tray). The gyroscopic effect will keep the camera pointing towards you.

If you time it right (and you'll need some practice) the shot will be taken at the peak of the camera's flight.

Then, obviously, you have to catch it!

Your early attempts will be pictures of a very worried person gazing upwards with hands out-stretched ready to make the catch. But after a while you should be able to relax and look cool for a second or two.

It's a good idea to have the flash on, because the spin on the camera will blur the image radially in low light—but the flash will freeze a moment for you and can make a very nice photo indeed.

Be brave—it's a great way of getting impossible shots! It's no surprise that this trick was invented by a juggler!

A
B
C
D
E
F
G
H
I
J
K
L
M
N
O
P
Q
R
S
T
U
V
W
X
Y
Z

A
B
C
D
E
F
G
H
I
J
K
L
M
N
O
P
Q
R
S
T
U
V
W
X
Y
Z

AGGRESSIVE SWANS

ANIMALS

It is well-known that a swan can break an arm if you get into a tussle with it. These are very big, strong and intimidating birds.

☆ As with all animals, if you approach or threaten them (especially if they have eggs or babies about) then you deserve all you get, so why not just leave the poor creatures alone?

There are times when a *Cob* (a male swan) will get aggressive with you simply in order to impress his true love—a female swan, by the way, is called a *Pen*.

You'll know when they are getting punchy because they will fix you with a stare and approach you while hissing in a very hostile manner, probably raising their wings as well.

☆ Stand your ground and *hiss back* in your best imitation of the swan. Now stop looking at their eyes. This will surprise the swan, who didn't know that you spoke its language and should, defuse the confrontation.

Beware though of approaching young *Cygnets* or a clutch of eggs, the parents will stop at nothing to defend their young.

☆ If you need to capture a swan (remembering that you are *not* allowed to eat the Queen's birds) then you should first grab it *by the beak.*

AIR CANNON

FUN WITH SCIENCE / WEAPONS

An **AIR CANNON** is an easily-made device that shoots an invisible vortex of air for an impressive distance. You can knock someone's hat off at thirty paces with one.

If you fill one of these devices with smoke or **Dry Ice** fog you can shoot great big **Smoke Rings** with them.

☆ You need a large container, perhaps a rubbish bin. Pick a full-size dustbin if you are planning on making a really large weapon. The container needs to be open at one end.

Cut a three-inch round hole in the middle of the closed end and cover the open end with strong plastic sheeting, maybe a plastic tablecloth or a piece of tarpaulin. Wrap the sheet over the opening and tie it on securely as if fitting a lid to a jam jar.

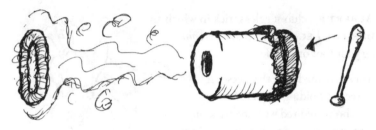

Aim the construction so that the hole points to a suitable test target (a younger brother or sister is best). Whack the plastic sheet on the breach-end of the weapon *hard* with something mallet-like. A pulse of air will shoot invisibly out of the muzzle travelling twenty or thirty feet with ease before smacking the victim harmlessly (but very impressively) in the face.

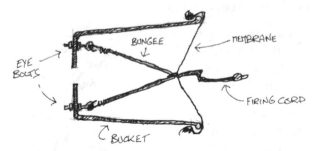

Another design uses an ordinary plastic bucket as the main part of the weapon. A hole is made in the base and a couple of eye bolts are run through, these form anchors for a bungee which is attached to the centre of the membrane that is stretched over the top of the bucket. The

A
B
C
D
E
F
G
H
I
J
K
L
M
N
O
P
Q
R
S
T
U
V
W
X
Y
Z

membrane is therefore pulled down into the bucket by the tension of the bungee forming a depressed conical surface.

Finally a firing cord is attached to the outside of the membrane. When it is pulled back and released the membrane whacks a great pulse of air through the hole producing a powerful vortex.

ALBERT

JUGGLING

An **ALBERT** is a club-juggler's trick in which an **UNDER THE LEG** throw is made *without* lifting your foot off the floor.

The trick is named after the awesome world record-holding juggler *Albert Lucas,* who is credited with the trick on account of performing it very impressively.

☆ This is a difficult move and one that requires a great deal of work to perfect.

In performance it looks very effective if you mix **ALBERTS** with **TREBLAS**—reverse **ALBERTS.** Get it?

☆ A **TREBLA** is a throw under the *opposite* leg—the club is thrown between the legs, from front to back, and rises to a catch at the side.

☆ An extreme variation of the **TREBLA** has the club rising behind the back and up over the shoulder— usually on a double spin.

Continuous *extreme* **TREBLAS** are very difficult to pull off, but impressive as hell.

A
B
C
D
E
F
G
H
I
J
K
L
M
N
O
P
Q
R
S
T
U
V
W
X
Y
Z

ALIEN JUMPER TRICK

SILLINESS

For the benefit of American-speaking readers I should point out the word *jumper* is British-English for *sweater*; the woollen clothing device that has nothing whatever to do with jumping and everything to do with sweating.

The *Alien* reference is from the famous series of horror-space movies. we are comically recalling that moment when a very aggressive creature bursts out of Kane's stomach in the middle of breakfast. Yuk!

You'll need a nice big loose fitting jumper (or sweater) for this one. It's a very funny illusion.

☆ Don the curiously-named garment and then pop one arm out of its sleeve and place the hand belonging to that arm secretly over the stomach. Now take the opposite hand and tuck it into the end of the empty sleeve. Make it look like the empty sleeve has an arm in it.

☆ Now pat your stomach with each hand alternately. it will look like you are about to give birth to an alien.

ALL THE SPOONS IN ALL THE CUPS

OBJECT MANIPULATION

There are two ways of doing this classic manipulation trick, the cheat's *easy* way, and the purists *pure* way.

A
B
C
D
E
F
G
H
I
J
K
L
M
N
O
P
Q
R
S
T
U
V
W
X
Y
Z

☆ The cheat gets a tray and glues or otherwise fixes anything up to a dozen cups along one side.

The same number of teaspoons are laid at the opposite edge of the tray, with the handles pointing towards the cups.

With a deft flick of the tray all the spoons are tossed into the air and they all land in their own cup. It's easier than it looks (don't you just love tricks like that?)

☆ But that is the *cheat's* method. The advantage is that it is very easy to do, the disadvantage being that you need to have a specially prepared tray. The fact is that you *do not need to fix the cups down.*

It takes a little more care, but if you flick the tray just right the cups on the near side will not take off!

The secret to this is revealed here by means of a cross-section. A quick flick of the tray provides the impetus to throw the spoon much as a quick flick of a frying-pan will toss a pancake. In order to prevent the cup from *also* being launched the tray is

manipulated so that it rotates about a centre point located *in the middle of the cup.* Thus the part of the tray lying under the spoon flicks with enough force to send the spoon flying, while the part of the tray under the cup hardly moves at all. This means that the side of the tray nearest you actually moves *downwards* during the toss. It's simple when you know how!

Practice this thoroughly with your own crockery before asking the waiter at a posh restaurant to supply you with china for your amazing after-dinner trick.

ALPHABET BACKWARDS

MNEMONICS

The skill of reciting the **ALPHABET BACKWARDS** is required learning for the trickster.

The trick is simply learned by means of a mnemonic in the form of a reverse *Alphabet Song* and takes but a few minutes practice to learn.

Once memorised the trickster will practice repeating the **ALPHABET BACKWARDS** every day for a full week, after which the sequence will be permanently engraved in the brain.

The following is to be spoken *aloud:*

Z Y X, and W V, U T S, and R Q P,

O N M, and L K J, I H G, and F E D,

And C! B! A!

In certain jurisdictions the test of reciting the **ALPHABET BACKWARDS** is used by the authorities as a test for intoxication. While *Every Trick In The Book* does not condone driving drunk, it can at least help you get away with it.

ALWAYS GET THE MONEY LAID ON THE TABLE

GRIFTING / BAR BETS

If you are going to bet money on something you must **ALWAYS GET THE MONEY LAID ON THE TABLE**—especially if you are betting on a sure thing, like the **BIRTHDAY BET**.

People love to make bets, but they hate to lose and will squirm and wriggle their way out of a promise if they possibly can. So before you do the **MARK** the favour of demonstrating just how foolish they are, get that money laid down.

Otherwise you are just wasting your time.

☆ The bet that has just been won above is the **BEER GLASS BALANCE**.

ANDRUZZI LEVITATION

MAGIC (LEVITATION)

This trick is an improvement on the **BALDUCCI LEVITATION**. It is named after the late magician *Tony Andruzzi*.

The advantage of this trick is that it is is more convincing and less angle-sensitive than the **BALDUCCI LEVITATION**.

The downside is that it requires some preparation, and it will cost you a perfectly good pair of shoes.

☆ HERE'S *The* TRICK: The **ANDRUZZI LEVITATION** is *exactly* like the **BALDUCCI LEVITATION** except that the audience can see the toes of *both* feet rising off the floor. In the **BALDUCCI** they only see the toes of *one* foot lifting (though they see the *heels* of both feet lifting).

In short, the **ANDRUZZI LEVITATION** is less *angle-sensitive* than the **BALDUCCI LEVITATION** and this magic is achieved by using footwear that has been *gimmicked* * beforehand by cutting a special hole in the sole of one shoe.

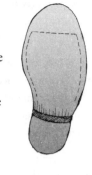

☆ Take a pair of shoes and cut a line right through the sole along the crease of your toes, now cut back along the sides of the shoe so that you end up with a flap running most of the way to your heel.

By keeping your toes on the front "ledge" you can walk more or less normally.

Just before the levitation, sneak your toes out of the shoe and directly onto the ground.

Then carefully transfer your weight to the exposed toes and lift yourself up.

You'll seem to magically rise into the air. You still have to be a little careful about the angles, but nothing like as careful as you would have to with the **BALDUCCI** technique.

ANTI-GRAVITY BALL

JUGGLING

This ball-juggling trick also works very well with a ring of keys.

☆ You hold the object (ball or key ring) low in one hand.

Now cup the other hand over the object and then draw it away and upwards as if *pulling* the object, simultaneously **POPPING A BALL** from the other hand.

---

* *Gimmick* is magicians'-speak for a clever device or prop such as a **THUMB TIP** or double-headed coin.

A
B
C
D
E
F
G
H
I
J
K
L
M
N
O
P
Q
R
S
T
U
V
W
X
Y
Z

Done properly it will look as if the object is rising of its own accord. The key to making it look convincing is to *believe* that the upper hand really is pulling the object up into the air.

This is a very subtle move and it will take a lot of **PRACTICE IN FRONT OF A MIRROR** to get it right. Just remember, any time you are bored or stood in a queue, to get out that bunch of keys and work on it.

In performance you should act as if the trick is something that is *happening to you* rather than something you are deliberately doing. When you get the illusion right people's jaws will drop in amazement.

☆ Another anti-gravity illusion with a ball goes like this:

Place a ball on the flat palm of your hand and lift it quickly, as it rises roll your hand over it. The ball will stay "stuck" to your hand momentarily due to its inertia. Then, as the ball drops roll your palm under it again. So far so good.

Repeat the move a couple of times so your audience get the idea.

Repeat the move once more but as your hand reaches the top trap the ball with your thumb (which will be concealed by the ball) and hold it there for an improbable second or two. Then drop the ball as before, look perplexed and examine the ball for good measure.

One secret of magic, and indeed comedy, is to act as if you don't know that you're deliberately doing anything funny. Make it seem like it's happening to you as a result of forces beyond your control.

ARMPIT FART

SILLINESS

Practice this one in the bath.

☆ Lift one arm and cup the opposite hand over your armpit, endeavouring to trap as much air as possible while making a perfect airtight seal.

No crank your arm up and down and you should be able to create some deliciously noisy farting noises.

ANGELS IN THE SNOW

SILLINESS

This is a popular trick that works in snow or on sand.

☆ Lie down in the snow and then flap your arms like a bird. When you get up you will have left the impression of an angel on the ground.

See also **DINOSAUR FOOTPRINTS**.

ANIMATION

DRAWING

ANIMATION, of the hand-drawn variety, is time-consuming, laborious, fiddly and dull. It can take hours or even days to animate just a few seconds of material but once done the results can be brilliant. You can find out if you are cut out for this sort of work by trying some really simple stuff.

A
B
C
D
E
F
G
H
I
J
K
L
M
N
O
P
Q
R
S
T
U
V
W
X
Y
Z

A
B
C
D
E
F
G
H
I
J
K
L
M
N
O
P
Q
R
S
T
U
V
W
X
Y
Z

☆ To make a two-frame animation all you need is a sheet of paper and a pencil. Start with an A4 sheet, turn it landscape-wise and cut off the bottom third so you end up with a strip about 11 inches wide by 2½ inches high.

Fold it in half and with the fold to your left and draw a little man standing near the right of the "cover page" (but not all the way to the edge). Now open the "book" and draw the same little character doing a star-jump. You can flip the paper open and shut to make sure the two drawings are lined up right.

Now roll up the top page as tight as you can and insert a pencil into the centre of the roll. Slide the pencil from left to right rapidly and your character will come to life.

Watch the little guy go!

☆ An alternative technique, for the more ambitious animator, is the *Flip-* or *Flick-Book Animation*. These were known as *Kineographs* in Victorian times.

Here the successive frames of animation are rendered on the pages of a small book and the animation is viewed by riffling through the pages with the thumb.

School kids commonly mess up their exercise books in this way, usually with highly violent mini-movies that require a great deal of red ink.

The following tips may help.

☆ Hand-drawn animation is almost always developed by starting with a sequence of keyframes; which are the key points in the visual storyline. Keyframes are the expressive moments that are then linked together by a process called tweening; which means drawing the intermediate frames that lie in between the keyframes to smooth things out.

So if your character finds himself at the edge of a chasm and attempts to jump it the keyframes might be: realisation, wind-up, jump, land and scrabble, hang helplessly and finally, fall.

In commercial animation studios the keyframes will be drawn by lead animators, and the duller work of stitching them together will be drawn by lowlier technicians.

☆ The animators work on sheets of paper with specially punched holes which are laid on a peg-bar fitted to their desk to ensure that they line up properly. The paper will often be laid over a light box to assist in tracing.

As they draw they will flick backwards and forwards through the sequence to ensure that things are moving properly.

If you are making a flip-book you won't need to worry about the peg-board since the pages are already bound together.

You will, however, be advised to work in pencil like the professionals do. Inking and colouring is the very last stage in a hand-drawn animation project.

See also **PHENOKISTOSCOPE**, **ZOETROPE**.

A
B
C
D
E
F
G
H
I
J
K
L
M
N
O
P
Q
R
S
T
U
V
W
X
Y
Z

A
B
C
D
E
F
G
H
I
J
K
L
M
N
O
P
Q
R
S
T
U
V
W
X
Y
Z

APPLE PIE BED

SILLINESS

Take care with this trick because you will be victimising somebody at bed time, when they may be tired, grumpy, and unable to see the funny side. The **APPLE PIE BED** has long been a favourite with kids on sleepovers and rock and roll crews on tour.

The victim's bed needs to be one that is made up with a top and bottom sheet. Since most people seem to use duvets these days you may have to save it for a stay in an hotel.

☆ Gain entry to the victim's bedroom and fold back the top covers and top sheet. Yank out the bottom sheet and fold it up over the pillows.

Now replace the top covers and fold both sheets down neatly —everything looks normal except that the bottom half of the bed has been blocked off by folding the bottom sheet in half.

When the victim gets into bed they'll only be able to get their legs halfway down. Quite often they'll kick so hard that their feet rip through the sheet completely—another reason to wait until you are staying in the hotel.

AROUND THE CORNER

YO-YO

☆ Throw a **SPINNER** so the **Yo-Yo** ends up **SLEEPING** at the bottom of the string. Lift your yo-arm so that the string is falling against the back of your yo-bicep and the **Yo-Yo** is **SLEEPING** behind you.

Bring your hand down and your elbow up and the **Yo-Yo** will catch the string and fly over your shoulder and back into your hand.

That's **AROUND THE CORNER**.

AROUND THE WORLD

YO-YO

☆ Throw your **Yo-Yo** out in front of you (as if *Looping the Loop*) but as it reaches the end of the string you let it Sleep.

Now swing the **Yo-Yo** up into the air and let it make a full turn around you before giving it a flick back into your hand.

You've just been **AROUND THE WORLD**.

A B C D E F G H I J K L M N O P Q R S T U V W X Y Z

A
B
C
D
E
F
G
H
I
J
K
L
M
N
O
P
Q
R
S
T
U
V
W
X
Y
Z

ARSE CATCH

JUGGLING

This is the unbelievably cool skill of catching something while reaching behind you between your legs.

It's usually a blind catch which is what makes it so hard, and so cool.

Your best shot at pulling this off is probably in a game of *Frisbee* where looking cool is the name of the game. You have the advantage of catching a horizontally flying object, so there's some chance of watching it in.

Skilled *Ring Jugglers* have been known use this move, but they have to work the trick blind, using *The Force* to guide them.

ASKING PEOPLE FOR FAVOURS

PSYCHOLOGY

Getting people to cooperate with you can be a lot easier if you apply some simple psychology to the way that you ask.

☆ With small children it would be a mistake to say 'do you want to go to bed now or have a smack?' A far more compelling proposition would be to say 'Do you want to go to bed now or have a bath and a story first?'.

Both of these questions are offering alternatives, but the second one uses the trick of offering two alternatives, the *first* of which is deliberately intended not to appeal, but the *second* of which is both attractive and compelling.

☆ With adults you can use the double negative to momentarily short-circuit a brain, as in a request to a partner 'I don't suppose you wouldn't like to take the rubbish out for me now, darling?'

Chances are they'll have picked up the bin bag and reached the back door before they have managed to figure out what you just said.

AUTO ROTATION

FLYING MACHINES

In the event of your helicopter suffering an engine failure (or indeed a tail rotor failure) you will need to make a descent and landing with *no power*. It is crucial that you do not allow the rotor speed to drop much below 100% otherwise the blades will *cone up* to such a point that they will no longer be capable of supporting the aircraft.

If this happens you will suffer what is euphemistically referred to as a *catastrophic hard landing*. In other words you will *crash and burn*—unless you have run out of fuel, in which case you will merely *crash*.

☆ As soon as power is removed the rotor speed will start to drop. Immediately push the collective to the floor, to bring the rotor back up to speed. This works because applying a negative angle of attack causes the blades to work like a sycamore seed, as they fall through the air the updraft pushes them around.

Take care not exceed 100% rotor speed as this will cause extreme stress on the main rotor bearing. You can reduce rotor speed by bringing the collective up a little.

☆ Locate the nearest possible landing spot and fly the aircraft towards it in a steep descent, bear in mind that the aircraft will need to be recovered from wherever it lands, so small islands in rivers or clearings in large forests are to be avoided.

☆ If you are over a large expanse of water you should fire the emergency floats about now. You do have emergency floats don't you?

☆ Now would be a good time to make a mayday call, it won't help *you* much but at least the poor air traffic controller will know why that blip on their screen just vanished.

A
B
C
D
E
F
G
H
I
J
K
L
M
N
O
P
Q
R
S
T
U
V
W
X
Y
Z

A
B
C
D
E
F
G
H
I
J
K
L
M
N
O
P
Q
R
S
T
U
V
W
X
Y
Z

☆ On your final approach you should reduce forward speed to just a few knots and at about twenty feet start to flare the landing by bringing the collective up and pitching back.

☆ Aim to arrive on the ground with a small amount of forward speed remaining, typically you will run forwards on the skids for about ten feet.

☆ If however there is no ground (because you are over water) you have a choice. In *very* calm conditions you can attempt to finish up with the aircraft sitting on its floats. But in rougher conditions you should use the last momentum of the blades to capsize the aircraft onto its side. This is going to happen anyway so it may as well happen in a controlled manner. You then bail out and bob about in a mixture of water, aviation fuel and adrenaline wondering how on earth you are supposed to retrieve the life raft from the cockpit—but help is already on its way since the emergency beacon in your immersion suit will have started transmitting as soon as it hit the water.

You do have an immersion suit don't you?

☆ Bring the rotor to a halt with the rotor brake before leaving the aircraft —we don't want any accidents do we?

Back Crosses

JUGGLING

Juggling **Back Crosses** means juggling clubs
with **Behind the Back** throws.

See **Behind the Back**.

Back Palm

MAGIC (VANISH)

Back Palming is the technique of concealing a card or coin on the back
of your hand. It needs to be **Practiced in Front of a Mirror**.

To **Back Palm** a card (or a really large coin) you clip the edges between
your index and little fingers, while the card itself (or coin) rests behind the
ring and middle fingers. The great trick is getting it in and out of this
position. This is a move which you cannot practice too much.

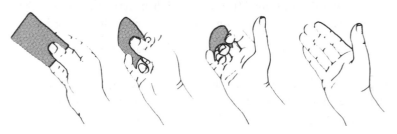

A
B
C
D
E
F
G
H
I
J
K
L
M
N
O
P
Q
R
S
T
U
V
W
X
Y
Z

This trick (run in reverse) is the one that magicians use to pull cards out of thin air. A card is first loaded into the **BACK PALM** position, then the hand is held out as if stopping a bus. A quick movement of the hand is used to obscure the moment at which the card appears.

☆ Gifted magicians will **BACK PALM** a number of cards and pull one into view at a time, before discarding it and producing another. This is tricky, because you need to learn how to peel one card off the stack at a time.

☆ To **BACK PALM** a small coin you should use the **GOSHMAN PINCH** which is very simple and effective.

BAKED ALASKA

KITCHEN TRICKS

This is the famous recipe for baking ice cream *in an oven!*

☆ You will need: a sponge cake base (which you can buy ready-made from a supermarket), a block of ice cream, egg whites and caster sugar plus anything else yummy you want to add (like tinned fruit, maple syrup and stuff like that).

It will help if the ice cream has been seriously frozen, you don't want to be working with stuff that is about to melt!

Heat up an oven to just below nuclear (220°) before you start. Make up loads of meringue mix from the egg whites and sugar (find out how in a recipe book) and get a big baking tray. Cover the base with the sponge cake, plonk the entire block of ice cream onto the sponge base, pour on any yummy stuff (like the tinned fruit etc.) and then encase the entire thing in a thick layer of meringue and slam it in the oven for eight minutes!

While that's cooking I should explain that this is a bit like getting the Space Shuttle back out of orbit only instead of heat-proof ceramic tiles we are using meringue. If there are any defects in the meringue heat-shield there will be a very messy disaster. But if the shield is intact you are in for a treat— lovely hot meringue on the outside and supercool ice cream in the middle!

BALANCING THINGS

JUGGLING AND BALANCING

You can balance all sorts of longish objects on your nose, chin, hand or foot. The trick is to keep the point of support under the centre of gravity. Here we see old Father William from *Alice's Adventures in Wonderland* balancing an eel on the end of his nose as illustrated by *Sir John Tenniel*. Notice William's gaze is firmly fixed upon the fish.

☆ You should always balance things with the heavy end uppermost*. (The other way is far harder).

☆ You'll usually be advised to keep looking at the top of the object by people who don't know any better, but you'll find that your balance is steadier if you look at the centre of gravity instead.

---

* Except, I am reliably informed by *Devil Stick Peat*, when the object being balanced is a Kalashnikov—in which case you want the dangerous end pointing up.

A
B
C
D
E
F
G
H
I
J
K
L
M
N
O
P
Q
R
S
T
U
V
W
X
Y
Z

☆ Tall things are easier to balance than small things. A teaspoon is *very* hard to balance, but a great big broom is easy.

☆ It's pretty easy to balance one thing but *very difficult* to balance two at once—this is a major skill.

☆ Balancing *three* at once is super-human trick.

BALDUCCI LEVITATION

MAGIC (LEVITATION)

The **BALDUCCI LEVITATION** is a very angle-sensitive trick in which you can seem to rise and hover a couple of inches off the ground. This levitation trick was made famous by *David Blaine*.

The great thing about the trick is that it involves no preparation of special equipment. It's weakness is that it really is horribly angle-sensitive and that it needs to be very convincingly performed if you are to get away with it.

☆ HERE'S *The* TRICK: You place both feet and turn your back to the audience so they behind your left shoulder and raise both arı horizontally crucifixion-style. You then rais yourself up on the toes of your right foot, while keeping both feet together and your left foot flat. Because of the angle the audience cannot see that your right toes are still on the ground. Hold the levitation for ⸴ second or two and then collapse back to the ground.

☆ You must set up the levitation dramatically and explain that it is *very* difficult. Give the impression that you are reluctant to do it because of the huge *psychic effort* required. Keep stalling, adjusting your stance, checking that people are not too close (in case they get hurt) and so on. What you are waiting for is the moment at which the people watching you are desperate to see you do it rather than watching to see how you are going to cheat.

Then you lift up, hold it for no more than two seconds and drop to the ground again, feigning sudden exhaustion and looking as much as you can as if you are about to faint.

They'll be amazed!

See also **ANDRUZZI LEVITATION**.

BALL BALANCE ON A STICK

BALANCING

This trick looks as if it might be very difficult indeed, but it isn't.

☆ Get a stick (a piece of smooth dowel about ¾ inch in diameter is best) and balance a football or basketball on it.

☆ A cool trick is to wind the stick a full turn around the ball, without breaking contact, and then go back into the balance.

BALL BEARING ON GLASS

FUN WITH SCIENCE

It turns out that the very best **BOUNCING BALL**, in terms of the height of the bounce, is a **BALL BEARING ON GLASS**.

☆ You need a good-quality steel ball bearing and a nice big thick piece of glass. Drop the thing and watch it go!

See also **SILICONE BALLS ON A PARQUET FLOOR**.

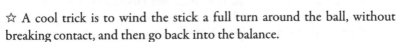

BALL JUGGLING

JUGGLING

"Ooh look! He's playing with his balls." —*Anon.*

Egyptian jugglers from around 1800BC copied from the wall of a tomb. The girl
on the left seems to be juggling a **THREE BALL SHOWER** and is suffering from a
"wardrobe malfunction". The next girl is juggling a **THREE BALL CASCADE**.
The third is juggling a crossed-hand pattern, it could be a cross-arm **CASCADE** or
perhaps an early attempt at a **MILLS' MESS**. The girl on the far right is a beginner.
This is, at the time of writing, the earliest known illustration of juggling.

If you have turned to this entry because you are a beginner, and wish to
learn the basic trick of juggling you should turn to the entry **THREE BALL
JUGGLING** where the first steps are explained.

This entry, on the other hand, explains the various different types of juggling
pattern and is more concerned with
theory than practice.

Let us begin as children in the
playground do, with a ball in each
hand. If one ball is tossed to the
opposite hand then the other
may be *passed* back before the
first ball lands.

When this trick is repeated

continuously it becomes a sort of juggling pattern, which we call a *Two Ball* **SHOWER**.

As will be noted from the **CAUSAL NOTATION** for this pattern—in which the throws are marked as 3's, and the passes (or *feeds*) are 1's—each act of throwing and passing is independent to all the others, hence the juggler can proceed as fast or as slow as they like, there are no pressing issues that need to be resolved by careful timing.

An extension of this pattern is the *Three Ball* **SHOWER** in which *two* balls must be thrown before the first ball can be passed back. This is a lot harder to do and careful timing is important because every throw affects every other throw.

The **SHOWER** patterns can be extended by adding extra balls, each one coming at a higher price to the skill of the juggler. Very few can shower more than five balls.

SHOWER patterns are asymmetrical, one hand always throws, while other **FEEDS**. A useful skill is that of being able to reverse the direction of the **SHOWER** while juggling.

SHOWER patterns can be juggled in two distinct styles, with asynchronous throws, or with synchronous throws. The *natural* pattern is the asynchronous shower—the action of working one side of the body and then the other is called *cross-crawling* and is wired into the reptilian, or limbic, part of the human brain at a low level. This is how you can chew gum and walk at the same time. When both hands work a **SHOWER** in synch, things get harder, because each hand is doing something different, but at the *same* time.

The **FEED** of the ordinary async shower changes to a very low and fast throw when the hands throw in synch. The overall height of the pattern drops considerably—which means that there's a lot more going on in a smaller chunk of air.

A
B
C
D
E
F
G
H
I
J
K
L
M
N
O
P
Q
R
S
T
U
V
W
X
Y
Z

When learning the **SHOWER** patterns it's good to work in both directions, to save becoming too right-handed about things. Changing direction in mid-juggle can produce some interesting effects.

If the juggler reverses direction on *every single throw* of an async **THREE BALL SHOWER** a new pattern emerges—the **THREE BALL CASCADE**.

If a juggler reverses direction, on every throw, in a synch **THREE BALL SHOWER** another new pattern emerges—the **BOX**.

And now we have opened another box, this time belonging to *Pandora*. From here on in, the mountain range of juggling patterns we can reach by changing one small detail or another of what we are doing becomes as infinite as the number of possible melodies you can make from the seven musical notes.

If we wish to juggle four balls, the simplest pattern to juggle is the **FOUR BALL FOUNTAIN** in which each hand juggles **TWO IN ONE HAND** at the same time.

The balls do not cross from hand to hand.

Collisions are avoided by throwing the balls on the inside of the pattern and catching them on the outside.

If instead, you throw on the outside and catch on the inside (which is very much harder) you are juggling a *Reverse* **FOUNTAIN**.

The *Reverse* patterns are not just shape-reversals, they are also time-reversals, so running a film of a *Reverse* **FOUNTAIN** or Cascade backwards will show a normal pattern.

If we add a fifth ball we are obliged to juggle a **CASCADE** once more. The **CASCADE** patterns work for *odd* numbers of objects, while the **FOUNTAINS** work for *even* numbers.

The **FIVE BALL CASCADE** is an achievement for any juggler, being about as hard to master as hovering a helicopter (it is noted that helicopter pilots, like drummers, take well to juggling).

From there we go to the *Six Ball* **FOUNTAIN** (rare) and the *Seven Ball* **CASCADE** (still rarer). Activity in these esoteric areas is known as *Numbers Juggling*.

The limits of normal human ability in juggling are seven clubs, nine balls and eleven rings (but not at the same time obviously). You may occasionally see or hear of people juggling more than this, but they aren't necessarily having *fun*.

Most non-jugglers seem to think that *Numbers Juggling* is what the game is all about, so they will ask you, "how many balls can you juggle?"

The trickster's answer is, "one more than you."

BALLOON GYROSCOPE

SILLINESS

Get an ordinary balloon and squeeze a coin through the neck. A pound coin is a good choice. Now blow up the balloon.

☆ With a shake and a swirl you can get the coin to roll around inside the balloon and then wind it up to great speed. It will make the most fantastic noise and the balloon will go all wobbly and alive in your hands.

You've just created a very weird and wonderful thing—so go and have fun with it!

A B C D E F G H I J K L M N O P Q R S T U V W X Y Z

A
B
C
D
E
F
G
H
I
J
K
L
M
N
O
P
Q
R
S
T
U
V
W
X
Y
Z

BALLOON POP RASPBERRY

SILLINESS

☆ Blow out your cheeks like a balloon and slap them both with your hands to blow a raspberry. It's both big *and* clever.

BALL SPINNING

JUGGLING / OBJECT MANIPULATION

This is the classic basketball player's trick of spinning a ball so that it balances, like a gyroscope, on your finger. The technique can also be applied to hats.

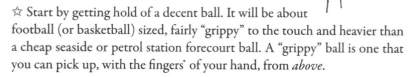

It takes a little while to learn so don't expect to get it in an afternoon.

☆ Start by getting hold of a decent ball. It will be about football (or basketball) sized, fairly "grippy" to the touch and heavier than a cheap seaside or petrol station forecourt ball. A "grippy" ball is one that you can pick up, with the fingers* of your hand, from *above*.

☆ When **BALL SPINNING** it really helps if you arrange matters so that the *heavy end* of the ball is uppermost (at the North Pole if you like). Balls are rarely perfectly balanced.

---

* The word "fingers" is the 100,000th word I have typed in the first draft of *Every Trick In The Book*. My word-processing software does not lie and I keep an eye on such things. It is 9:54pm on Friday the 22nd of September 2006 and I am working late. I'm sat in my obscenely large caravan at the Bristol Juggling Convention where I have come to work on this book and conduct some research into Acrobatics and Poi (neither of which I am very strong on). I have picked up some really great material today! Right now most of the jugglers are enjoying an interval in the Friday night show which I am not attending (though it sounds like a good one). It's taken me longer than I expected to get this far with the manuscript and I have to admit that I'm finding the task more than a little daunting. Right now I am flat broke, low on diesel and desperate for a publishing deal but determined to carry on. Meanwhile, everything is for sale! I'll get there!

If you get the heavy end on the equator your ball will wobble like a poorly balanced wheel on a car. If you get it at the bottom the ball will tend to be more unstable.

☆ **HERE'S** *The* **TRICK:** Drop the ball into water and let it float. The heavy end will rotate to the bottom. Now mark the top of the ball with a pen. That's the light end!

When you spin the ball on your finger this is where your finger should touch it. Think of it as the South Pole.

☆ Grip the ball in the outstretched fingers of your favourite hand (I'll assume this is the right hand) and toss it up while applying massive anti-clockwise spin. Make sure that it is spinning around a perfectly vertical axis with the marked south pole at the bottom. Now catch it on your index finger.

Yes, indeed! This is more easily said than done.

That is why you have to practice for a couple of weeks. In time you'll manage the catch but will have a great deal of trouble keeping the thing upright due to its bizarre gyroscopic behaviour. The trick is *not* to try and balance the thing, let it do that all by itself. The more you *try* to keep it upright the more it will fall over.

☆ To illustrate this bizarre principle get an experienced ball-spinner to transfer an already-spinning ball onto your finger *while you are looking away*. You'll find it stays up perfectly well, but if you look at it and *try* to balance it it will fall off.

☆ Even more extraordinary is the trick of getting a child to hold a long bamboo pole with a spinning ball balanced on top of it. They'll have no trouble at all because the ball *wants* to stay on.

A
B
C
D
E
F
G
H
I
J
K
L
M
N
O
P
Q
R
S
T
U
V
W
X
Y
Z

A
B
C
D
E
F
G
H
I
J
K
L
M
N
O
P
Q
R
S
T
U
V
W
X
Y
Z

BANANA SPLIT

KITCHEN TRICKS

Most people know that a **BANANA SPLIT** is a dish made with ice cream, yummy sauces and a banana. Usually the banana is cut in half lengthways into two long pieces which flank a plateful of ice cream and other goodies.

Very few people realise that a **BANANA SPLIT** is so-called because the banana should really be *split* rather than *cut*. So here's how to split a banana.

☆ Peel a nice ripe banana and then push your finger straight into the middle of the seed end—the last bit to be revealed when you peel it.

You'll find that a banana will naturally split into *three* long pieces.

Lay one on each side of the plate, pile in ice cream and yummy sauces before laying the third piece over the top.

See also **SLICING A BANANA**.

BALLOON KNOT

KNOTS

Blow up a balloon and tie a knot in the neck.

Sounds simple doesn't it? And yet most people do not know how to tie a knot in a balloon.

EVERY TRICK *In The* BOOK

☆ **HERE'S** *The* **TRICK:** Hold the inflated balloon between the thumb and forefinger of your left hand, balloon pointing down. Wind the neck of the balloon over your forefinger. Now place the end of the neck on the end of your forefinger, grip it

there with your thumb and *roll* the loop you have just made over the end of the neck.

Now wasn't that easy?

BANK NOTE AND BOTTLE TRICK

BAR BETS

☆ Lay a bank note flat on the bar and stand an empty bottle upside-down on top of it.

Now bet the **MARK** that you can remove the note *without* touching the bottle or tipping it over. If they can do it, they win the bet.

When they give up, you do this: carefully start to roll up the note like a carpet, this will slowly push the bottle off the note.

BAR BET

TOPIC

A **BAR BET** is a **TRICK** that you pull off in a drinking establishment, usually with the intention of winning money, drinks or just to amuse and impress your drunken companions.

There are plenty of **BAR BETS** sprinkled throughout this book, some are brilliant tricks, others might seem a little lame—but you can be assured that the author has conducted rigorous field research to check that they do work as advertised.

See, for example **DROPPING A MATCHBOX ONTO ITS END**, or **WHICH COIN DID I TOUCH?**

A
B
C
D
E
F
G
H
I
J
K
L
M
N
O
P
Q
R
S
T
U
V
W
X
Y
Z

BASTARD SPLICE

KNOTS

A **BASTARD SPLICE** is a sort of splice made by poking an entire piece of rope through the lay, rather than unravelling the stuff and doing a proper job with nice neat overs-and-unders. This type of splicing is only practical when working with loosely laid material like polypropylene rope (the blue stuff that is very common these days).

☆ You can make a nice secure eye-splice to create a loop in a piece of rope by simply tucking the end through the lay of the standing part three times. Tuck it through every *two* strands to make it really secure. Tucking it through every *three* is not good because you are catching the same strand each time which makes a weak splice.

☆ You can make a nice secure version of the **LINESMAN'S HITCH** without needing any tape.

In a standard **LINESMAN'S HITCH** the end of the rope is secured to the standing part with a piece of tape. In this version you make a **HALF HITCH** and then poke the end *through the lay* of the standing part.

One tuck is enough for most jobs, but two tucks is a lot stronger.

BEANBAG

JUGGLING

The humble **BEANBAG** is the juggler's friend—when they drop they *stay dropped* rather than rolling away; thus they are ideal for learning new tricks.

A good beanbag is about the same size and weight as an orange, made from simulated leather, or a fabric that doesn't collect dirt. They are usually filled with birdseed or something similar.

Jugglers with more money than sense will buy their **BEANBAGS** from a specialist juggling shop or stall. Those with more sense (or indeed time) than money will make their own.

An astonishing amount of ingenuity has been applied to the problem of forming a near-spherical object from flat cloth and many designs have been tried. They are generally based on one of the five **PLATONIC SOLIDS**.

The most common is the four-segment beanbag. For tips on getting the segment profile correct, see **TISSUE PAPER HOT AIR BALLOONS**. The advantage of this design is that only four panels are required. Note that this is almost an **OCTAHEDRON** except that each of the four panels combine two of the eight faces into a single panel.

Beanbags can be made to a **CUBE** pattern, the stretch in the cloth allows them to balloon out nicely. It will help if the six panels are cut with slightly bulged edges, rather than being perfect squares.

An **ICOSAHEDRON** makes a nice beanbag, but you'll need to cut 20 triangular panels, which makes for a lot of sewing.

A
B
C
D
E
F
G
H
I
J
K
L
M
N
O
P
Q
R
S
T
U
V
W
X
Y
Z

The **DODECAHEDRON** is probably a better bet with just 12 pentagonal faces. You'll recognise the pattern as one that is often used for footballs.

When making any of the above shapes it's a good idea to weigh out exactly the same quantity of birdseed for each beanbag in the set. Place each package of seed into a short piece of nylon stocking and tie it off before wrapping it in the outer skin. Beanbags made this way have very nice *squish*.

BEANBAGS are brilliant for learning juggling patterns, but if you want to juggle really *elegantly* you'll use hard round balls or **BOUNCING BALLS** which have the advantage of holding their shape—every throw is made with a perfect sphere, rather than a splodgy lump, and this adds smoothness to your work.

BEANBAG BRIDGE

FUN WITH SCIENCE

People will be surprised and amused when they see you construct a bridge from a set of juggler's **BEANBAGS**. The trick is to keep the *thrust line* within the structure.

☆ Proceed thus: take at least seven beanbags and smack them together one at a time, starting with one foot of the arch and proceeding around the curve. At each stage you support the growing structure with one hand while adding a beanbag with the other.

Arches are amazingly stable structures!

BEHIND THE BACK

JUGGLING

Now here's an impressive and rewarding trick!

Juggling **BEHIND THE BACK** is a tricky thing to learn because your naturally learned hand-eye coordination skills have simply never mapped the region behind your body.

☆ To learn the trick you should start with one **BEANBAG** and practice tossing it behind your back to a catch in the *opposite* hand. It will take you a while to become familiar with the move, so it might be a good idea to practice this a little bit every day to give your subconscious time to get used to the idea (see **LEARNING HOW TO LEARN TRICKS**).

☆ There are two distinct styles of **BEHIND THE BACK** throw. You can either throw the ball low to a side catch, or you can throw it high so that it rises over the opposite shoulder.

☆ Once you have mastered the throw with a single ball it's time to try and work it into a **THREE BALL CASCADE**. You will, almost

certainly, find this hard to pull off at first so here are a couple of tips.

Firstly, when you are about to make a **BEHIND THE BACK** throw you should start the move almost *before you catch the behind-the-back ball* so that the throw is made smoothly and in the rhythm of the main pattern.

Secondly you should look the *wrong way* while making the throw—that is, *not* in the direction of the throw (which is the instinctive thing to do). Instead, keep your eyes on the ball that you are going to catch *immediately after* throwing the behind-the-back ball. You only switch your gaze to the behind-the-back ball *after* that catch.

☆ Once you have managed a few **BEHIND THE BACK** throws from your favourite hand you should start practicing with the other hand, then work your way through the various possibilities in sequence:

☆ Every right hand throw.☆ Every left hand throw.☆ Same ball back and forth☆ And finally: *every* throw **BEHIND THE BACK**.

You'll almost certainly find it easier to juggle *every* throw **BEHIND THE BACK** using high over-the-shoulder throws because you can watch their progress easily by keeping your head craned backwards to see what's going on.

Juggling **BEHIND THE BACK** with clubs can be done using either single-, double- or triple-spins. Each style has its own unique feel.

BEHIND THE BACK throws are commonly referred to by jugglers as **BACK CROSSES**.

☆ Single spin **BACK CROSSES** require the juggler to pay very careful attention to where they are looking. As you throw with your right hand you must also look to the right (which is counter-intuitive) otherwise you will not make the subsequent catch. When your **BACK CROSSES** are up and running your head will be flicking from side to side in an exaggerated manner.

☆ Double-spin **BACK CROSSES** are probably easier to learn because you can see what's going on by simply looking up. Also, the pattern becomes a **SLOW CASCADE** and the reduced tempo makes things a little less frantic.

☆ Triple spin **BACK CROSSES** are great fun and very satisfying to juggle.

☆ If you want to cheat at **BEHIND THE BACK** there's a very convincing trick you can do with just two clubs that *looks* like three-club **BACK CROSSES**.

Hold a club in each hand and make a **BEHIND THE BACK** throw with your right hand and then catch it in the right hand. Now repeat with the left hand. Easy!

Now keep going and *overlap* the two moves as much as you can. It really does look like the real thing.

BENDING FORK ILLUSION

MAGIC / SILLINESS

☆ Hold a fork in your right fist and push the prongs down onto a tabletop so that the handle points upwards nearly vertically.

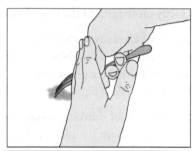

Now place the edge of your left hand, karate-chop style at the lowest point on the handle and mime a really *hard* push downwards with both hands. As you push you release the fingers of your right hand so that the fork is pushed down flat but it will look as if the thing has been bent backwards ninety degrees.

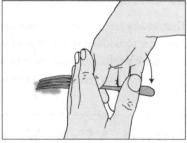

Make a big grunt as you push so they can almost *feel* you bending it.

This looks very realistic and might even get you into trouble—but you can then reveal the completely undamaged fork to everyone's amazement.

A
B
C
D
E
F
G
H
I
J
K
L
M
N
O
P
Q
R
S
T
U
V
W
X
Y
Z

BEER GLASS BALANCE

BAR BETS

Can you balance three beer glasses, each the right way up, in a column?

☆ Beer glasses are designed to stack, like auditorium chairs, so the trick is to place the second and third glasses off-centre, but there's still only one way they will go.

Looking from above, the second glass's centre sits exactly on the rim of the bottom glass at 12 o'clock.

The third glass sits so that its centre is at the 2 o'clock position. Note that the centres of the three glasses end up forming a perfect equilateral triangle.

Another way of thinking about it is that you make arrange the plan of the glasses as a *Venn Diagram*.

That, at any rate, is the guide position, you may have to fiddle just a little bit from here to achieve the balance, but only by a tiny amount. Rest assured that without this knowledge the trick is very hard indeed.

BEER MAT FLIPPING

BAR TRICKS / OBJECT MANIPULATION

☆ Lay a beer mat on the edge of a table so that it is almost toppling off. Put your hand below the mat, palm downwards.

The trick is to strike the beer mat with the back of your fingers so that it flips up, makes a *half-spin* and is caught between your fingers and thumb.

☆ You can play a game by laying a number of beer mats along the edge of the table. You then try to flip each one in turn, keeping the gathered mats in your hand. If you're good at this you could bet someone that you can do seven in a row.

☆ Advanced beer mat flippers should work on making a complete single-spin with each beer mat which looks a lot more dramatic.

BET YOU CAN'T DO WHAT I CAN

GRIFTING / BAR BETS

This is the ultimate bet that you can't lose.

☆ Lay down a bet, "I bet you a pound you can't do what I'm about to do!" Let them lay their money down, then immediately pick it up.

"I won the bet!"—**NEVER GIVE A SUCKER AN EVEN BREAK!**

☆ In a less brutal version you begin with the same bet and then expand on the game by explaining that you're going to do a number of things, and the **MARK** is to copy each one.

Start by touching your nose, turning around, coughing and so on. Each time they'll match the move.

"Hey you're getting pretty good at this!"

If they have any sense they'll repeat the phrase back to you, but if not you can kindly let them get away with it.

Now take a sip from your drink. They will copy.

A B C D E F G H I J K L M N O P Q R S T U V W X Y Z

A
B
C
D
E
F
G
H
I
J
K
L
M
N
O
P
Q
R
S
T
U
V
W
X
Y
Z

Clap your hands again, touch your nose again and then...

☆ HERE'S *The* TRICK: You lift your glass and slowly squirt the sip of beer you took two moves ago *back into your glass.*

They can't follow that!

See also **ALWAYS GET THE MONEY LAID ON THE TABLE.**

BICYCLE PLAYING CARDS

MAGIC

If you pay very close attention to professional magicians performing card tricks you'll notice that they almost always use **BICYCLE PLAYING CARDS**. There is a reason for this, in fact, there are several.

These cards are manufactured by the United States Playing Card Company. You can easily recognise a deck from the famous "Rider back".

These are the "Rolls Royce" of playing cards. They are slightly wider than regular playing cards, being trimmed to just a shade under 2½" by 3½" which makes them *very* close to a perfect **ROOT TWO RECTANGLE**.

They handle superbly well, so they are perfect for learning advanced tricks like the **FARO SHUFFLE**. Once you have used a deck you will know what the fuss is all about.

Serious magicians carry several decks because there are many tricks that involve tearing up or destroying cards and spares are always needed. Also, a tired deck is hard to use when it comes to the precise manipulation that some tricks call for.

Since this is the card of choice for the serious magician, you can get all sorts of modified versions of them. There are giant decks, miniature decks, decks of blank cards, and decks with double faces (two different card designs at each end of the face of a single card) and so on.

In the regular deck "808" deck there are a couple of peculiarities which you can use to good effect in tricks.

☆ The corners of the Jokers are marked with US instead of the JOKER in the corner.

☆ The two Jokers are different, one displays a guarantee message, the other does not.

☆ Both Jokers show a character riding a bicycle, if you look closely you'll see that the character is, in fact, the King of Spades. This can be used to good effect if you **FORCE** the King of Spades onto someone and then reveal the Joker—as if by mistake.

While we are at it, let's get to know a few memorable facts about the face cards (the royal families if you like).

☆ All the face cards (that's Kings, Queens and Jacks to you) look to the *left* except for the royal family of Spades and the Jack of Clubs, who look to the right.

☆ All face cards show two eyes except for the one-eyed King of Diamonds and the two one-eyed Jacks; Hearts and Spades.

A
B
C
D
E
F
G
H
I
J
K
L
M
N
O
P
Q
R
S
T
U
V
W
X
Y
Z

A
B
C
D
E
F
G
H
I
J
K
L
M
N
O
P
Q
R
S
T
U
V
W
X
Y
Z

If you place a one-eyed card next to another card it is easy to imagine that it is looking straight at the card next to it. You can use this to *reveal a card in an interesting way*—an especially charming trick if you flank a "chosen" card with the two one-eyed jacks (Spades to the left and Hearts to the right).

BIRTHDAY BET

GRIFTING / BAR BETS

You are in a bar with the **MARK** and you look around and run a quick calculation in your head, then you lay the bet.

"I bet you there are two people in this room with the same birthday."

This bet is reasonably well-known by tricksters, but the **MARK** will probably never have heard of it. They will look around and see that there are, maybe, thirty people around. This *seems* like pretty good odds ,so you should be able to get them to lay their money down. (**ALWAYS GET THE MONEY ON THE TABLE**).

The thing they don't know is that once there are more than 23 people in the room the odds of you winning are better than 50%. With 30 people present the odds rise to about 75%. If there are 40 people in the room the odds are about 90%. These are very good odds, so make it a large bet if you can.

Now this seems unlikely, which is what makes it a good bet, and without going precisely into the details of how that probability is calculated consider this:

To work out how many ways two people in a group can have the same birthday draw a set of dots, one for each person, and then connect up every dot to every other dot and count the lines. If we start with two people, there is only one way they can have the same birthday, but if there are three there are three ways, with four people there are six ways, if there are five there are ten ways...

From here on it gets harder to work out until you spot something about the series:

1, 3, 6, 10, 15...

It is actually

1, 1+2, 1+2+3. 1+2+3+4, 1+2+3+4+5

Now it turns out that when there are, say, 27 people in the room there are 351 ways to have people with matching birthdays, which makes it a very good bet indeed.

What you now have to do is to carry the bet off, and this requires a little showmanship.

☆ Stand in on a chair and call for everyone's attention.

"Sorry everyone! My friend and I are having a little bet. I'm saying that there are two people in here with the same birthday, and my friend says not, so we've laid some money on it."

They stare back blankly over their drinks. You continue.

"So I'm going to point at each of you in turn and ask you to call out your birthday!"

Now they start to look happy, nobody minds calling out their birthday especially if…

"I don't want the year! After all some of you are women!"

They'll laugh now, this is fun!

"So as I go around I'll point to each of you in turn, sing out your birthday. If you should hear your own birthday being called out by someone else, for goodness' sake shout out and let me know, there's money on this!"

Smiles all round—and off you go!

After pointing to around twenty-three people (on average) you'll hear somebody shout out.

"That's my birthday too!"

Game over!

A
B
C
D
E
F
G
H
I
J
K
L
M
N
O
P
Q
R
S
T
U
V
W
X
Y
Z

Not only have you made some money, but also you have introduced yourself as a fun sort of person. Moreover two people in the bar have just found out that they have something in common with each other.

Everybody wins, except the **MARK**—which is normal.

BISCUIT TOSS

JUGGLING / OBJECT MANIPULATION

☆ Place a biscuit on the back of your hand. Toss it up and catch it using a **SNATCH** catch—easy!

☆ Place two biscuits, one on the back of your hand, and one on your wrist, toss them both up and catch one and then the other.

Still easy?

☆ Here's the killer: place *three* biscuits, one on your hand, one on the wrist and one a little way onto your arm and toss all *three*. Now catch them all one after the other.

BISECTING AN ANGLE

GEOMETRY

Here's a basic geometrical construction that has a hundred uses. It is similar in both effect and technique to the method of constructing a

PERPENDICULAR BISECTOR (dividing a line into two by forming a new line at right angles to it).

☆ You start with two lines that meet at a point, the angle you are going to bisect is the angle between the two lines. Set your compass to a radius and mark off a point on each of the lines. Now place the point of the compass onto each of these points in turn and mark off a small arc in the middle of the angle. Finally connect the point at which these arcs cross to the vertex of the original angle which will now be divided exactly in two.

BLACKWALL HITCH

KNOTS

This is the simplest knot there is and while it looks hideously insecure, when used properly it has all the qualities of a perfect knot: easy to tie, amazingly easy to untie, strong, and secure.

☆ The main use of the **BLACKWALL HITCH** is when lifting things with a crane hook. As long as the weight is bearing down on it the knot will remain secure. As soon as the rope loosens it can quickly be flicked off.

But you'll probably be more interested in this trick: how to climb down a tree on a rope and then recover the rope you just used.

☆ Carefully form a **BLACKWALL HITCH** in around the crook of a branch, make sure it is secure and then make your descent, taking care to keep the rope taught at all times. Once back on the ground you can release your rope with a couple of flicks.

A
B
C
D
E
F
G
H
I
J
K
L
M
N
O
P
Q
R
S
T
U
V
W
X
Y
Z

A
B
C
D
E
F
G
H
I
J
K
L
M
N
O
P
Q
R
S
T
U
V
W
X
Y
Z

BLAKE'S HITCH

KNOTS

BLAKE'S HITCH is a friction hitch, like the
PRUSIK KNOT, that is commonly used by tree
surgeons (*arborists*) for the purpose of
climbing up ropes. **BLAKE'S HITCH** is
formed from the end of the rope, whereas
the **PRUSIK KNOT** is formed from a loop.
Both knots will slide up and down the
main rope when not under load, but lock
fast when weight is put on them.

To form a **BLAKE'S HITCH** you make
four upward spiralling turns around the
main rope then bring the end down over
the standing part, under the main rope, and lead it up
inside the first two turns of the spiral and then out of the knot. A stopper
knot, such as a **FIGURE OF EIGHT KNOT** is then tied in the end for safety.

Once **BLAKE'S HITCH** is drawn up you will find that it
can slide easily up and down that main rope but will seize
fast as soon as a downward load is placed on it.

Unusually, for such an eminently useful knot,
BLAKE'S HITCH is a relatively modern invention,
having first been recorded by *Heinz Prohaska* in 1981.
It was later discovered independently by *Jason Blake*
who published it in 1994 and by whose name it is
now generally known.

The author is grateful to *Matt Lovegrove* for
drawing his attention to this amazing knot during
an animated conversation about tricks on the
occasion of Matt's 41st birthday. Apparently the
arborist *Neil Berry*, a colleague of Lovegrove and
an accomplished expert in such things, trusts his
life to this knot daily.

LOAD

A
B
C
D
E
F
G
H
I
J
K
L
M
N
O
P
Q
R
S
T
U
V
W
X
Y
Z

BLUE ROSES

FUN WITH SCIENCE

Despite years of trying, horticulturists have so far completely failed to produce a blue rose.

But we are not horticulturists, and so we can make one in minutes.

☆ Cut a white rose and stand it in water that is strongly coloured with blue food-colouring. In a few minutes you'll see the petals changing colour, it's actually quite amazing to see just how fast the circulation occurs in a flower!

☆ If you don't want to cut the stem (perhaps you'd like to modify your neighbour's flowers where they stand) you can inject blue food colouring into the stems with a hypodermic syringe. It's best to inject several times from different directions to make sure you hit the right capillaries.

You can also use blue writing inks, but some of them are less soluble to roses, and will leave the flower with a very *veiny* appearance.

Obviously all sorts of other colours are possible too.

BOOBLESS

CALCULATOR TRICKS

Here's a classic **CALCULATOR SPELLING** trick.

> "A woman's boobs weighed 69 pounds, which she thought was too, too, too much..."

So far you've typed 69222 into the calculator.

> "So she went down 51st street to see Doctor X..."

A
B
C
D
E
F
G
H
I
J
K
L
M
N
O
P
Q
R
S
T
U
V
W
X
Y
Z

Now you have typed 6922251 X.

"Who gave her 8 pills which left her..."

You type an 8 and hit the equals button.

55378008!

Which reads, upside-down, as BOOBLESS.

BOOMERANG HATS

JUGGLING / HAT TRICKS

☆ Practically *any* wide-brimmed hat, if thrown like a frisbee upwards at a forty-five degree angle, will fly up and out before returning to the thrower like a boomerang.

In a popular circus trick a juggler runs around the ring and tosses five hats in all directions, over the heads of the audience, before catching them all again on a second circuit.

BOUNCING BALLS

JUGGLING

Jugglers like to start their careers with **BEANBAGS**, which do not bounce or roll away when dropped. They save a lot of time when one is learning a new trick and making a lot of mistakes.

But bouncing balls (which *do* bounce and fly off in all directions when dropped) are a whole lot of fun—once you feel ready for the challenge.

To be truly useful to a juggler a **BOUNCING BALL** needs to rise to at least 75% of the height it was dropped from when working at a height of about a metre off the floor.

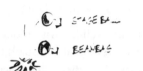

Don't forget that the floor itself plays a part in this: really good floors are polished stone (think airport terminal) or better still, a good-quality wooden parquet floor.

Super high-bounce balls made from synthetic materials of the kind you can find in the shops will bounce up to 85%. The larger ones are good for juggling with, the smaller ones are just annoying.

The "Rolls Royce" of **BOUNCING BALLS** is, without doubt, the *silicone* ball. They don't have the highest bounce, but they feel just perfect!

These balls are specially made for jugglers in precision moulds, so they are incredibly spherical, virtually seamless and, like Rolls Royces, they are *very* expensive.

See that juggler on TV doing that three-ball routine with those big white balls? Those are silicone balls.

Even when jugglers are not doing boun-cing work the true professionals often choose silicone because of their amazing feel.

☆ Here's a cool trick: get a silicone ball and place it next to your ear and give it a tap—it will ring like a bell!

Once you have a set of **BOUNCING BALLS** you'll presumably want to learn to juggle with them.

The basic techniques for juggling a number of balls are, in order of difficulty, the **PASSIVE BOUNCE**, the **COLUMN BOUNCE** and the **ACTIVE BOUNCE**.

A
B
C
D
E
F
G
H
I
J
K
L
M
N
O
P
Q
R
S
T
U
V
W
X
Y
Z

BOUNCING BEAST

JUGGLING

The author boldly claims to have discovered this amazing trick all by himself. He has been persuaded not to apply for a patent or claim copyright on it so you can perform this trick without fear of being sued by anyone. How nice of him.

It's fairly well-known, among **BOUNCING BALL** jugglers that if you make a stack of four silicone balls (they have to be perfectly engineered balls for it to work)—they will roll across a smooth surface *as a unit!*

What is *not* so well known is that you can add two more balls to the stack to create the legendary six-ball **BOUNCING BEAST**. The fifth ball is held against the centre of one of the faces of the little pyramid of four, and the sixth ball is rolled in to support it from underneath.

Assemble your **BOUNCING BEAST** on a smooth surface (marble is good) and then give the creature's back a little stroke and watch it roll off across the floor.

It's the combination of the high surface friction and the utter sphericosity of the balls that makes this work.

BOUNCING HANDKERCHIEF

SILLINESS

Here's a simple throwaway gag.

Get a small high-bounce ball and wrap it into a thin handkerchief to make a **COMET**. Stuff it into the top pocket of your jacket and, at a suitable point in your show remove it to mop your brow.

Now throw it hard at the ground, it will bounce back up. Catch it, pop it back in your pocket and get on with the show.

BOUNCING ROPE

ROPE WALKING

This is one of the great secrets of *Rope Walking* which has been much-used by circus clowns to create great comedy routines.

A **BOUNCING ROPE** is a type of tightrope rig in which the rope or cable is stretched tight by a powerful spring.

Usually a tightrope is stretched as tight as possible so that it ends up feeling pretty much like a solid bar. This can require many tons of tension, especially if the rope is long. With a **BOUNCING ROPE** the tension is supplied by a big spring so it *looks* tight until the artist steps onto it, but then sags alarmingly and bounces up and down under their weight.

☆ HERE'S *The* TRICK:
It turns out that it is *very* easy to balance on a rope like this: it just *looks hard!*

The secret is to work *with* the bounce. By allowing the rope to bounce up and down you'll find it very easy to keep the rope under your centre of gravity. If you are toppling to the right you

A
B
C
D
E
F
G
H
I
J
K
L
M
N
O
P
Q
R
S
T
U
V
W
X
Y
Z

simply kick down and swing the rope to the right. If you topple left, kick down and swing the rope left. If you're perfectly happy just bounce up and down and make out that you're in big trouble!

☆ **BOUNCING ROPE** artists also take advantage of the bounce in the rope to do tricks that could cause serious injury (especially to male performers) such as crutching themselves on the rope deliberately.

BOW

KNOTS

The **Bow** is the knot most commonly used to tie shoelaces. It is actually a double-slipped **REEF KNOT**.

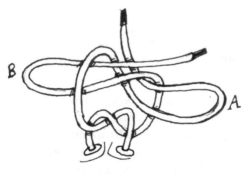

☆ The knot is tied by first making a Half Knot, then forming loop B and passing a *bight* (a loop from the middle of the rope, rather than the ends) through it to form loop A. It's important that the loops are passed through each other in proper Reef Knot fashion (rather than Granny Knot fashion) because the result is a much more secure knot and will also lie elegantly across the shoe. The Granny Knot version sits on the shoe with the loops pointing up and down rather than right to left.

☆ There is a very quick and clever way of tying a **BOW** which is based on the **TOM FOOL KNOT**.

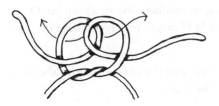

Start with the **HALF KNOT** as before, but then form two loops by twisting the *bights* of the two end *in the same direction*. Overlap the two loops and pull them through each other. WIth a little practice this can be done in one smooth movement and you'll wonder why you were never taught to tie your laces that way.

Even when tied properly the **BOW** is not particularly secure, its principle advantages being that it is very easy to untie and also that spare lace-length can easily be stowed in the loops.

☆ A far more secure version is tied in a similar manner, except that *bight* forming loop A is fed through loop B *twice*. This draws up into a very attractive knot that is far less likely to loosen and yet it can still be untied easily by pulling on the lace ends.

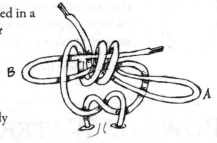

☆ An popular alternative is the *Double Bow* in which a standard **BOW** is tied and then the two loops A and B are further secured by being tied together in a **HALF KNOT**. While this is more secure than a normal **BOW** it is hard to untie and has little to recommend it.

BOWLINE

KNOTS

The **BOWLINE** is just about the best way of forming a loop in the end of a piece of rope. It is easy to tie, easy to untie and very secure.

A
B
C
D
E
F
G
H
I
J
K
L
M
N
O
P
Q
R
S
T
U
V
W
X
Y
Z

☆ The knot is a clever combination of a loop (an O shape) and a bend (a U shape) which combine in a very simple way.

☆ One clever way of tying the knot is to learn the story of the rabbit and the tree.

Make a "rabbit hole" and a "tree" by forming a loop in the rope a little way from the end. The end of the rope is the "rabbit".

The rabbit comes up out the rabbit hole then goes around the tree and finally back down the hole again.

Note that the last part of this metaphorical journey runs *inside* the loop being formed. This is slightly more secure than the other way around. Think of it this way: the rabbit is supposed to end up *inside* the loop you have made rather than *outside* it.

See also **Sheet Bend.**

BOWL OF WATER & BROOM PRANK

SILLINESS / PRACTICAL JOKES

Take a nice big *plastic* bowl (for safety) and fill it nearly to the brim with water. Stand a chair in the middle of the kitchen. Grab a broom and call in the **MARK**.

```
YOU: Hey, come here a second I
want to show you a magic trick!
```

You hand them the broom, climb onto the chair and place the bowl against the ceiling.

YOU: I'm going to make this bowl vanish, just hold it up
with the broom handle for a sec'.

As soon as the broom handle is in position climb down from the chair
and move it away before running off and leaving them stuck there.

BOW TIE

KNOTS

There are many ways to tie a tie, but just two are in common use, the
Windsor Knot and the **Bow**.

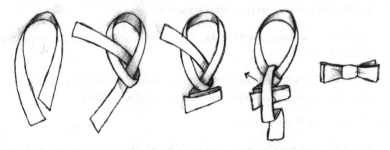

The **Bow** is of course, the knot you use to tie a **BOW TIE** —though the
method of tying is a little different to the one you would use when tying a
shoelace because of the flat nature of the tie itself.

BOX

JUGGLING

The **Box** is a *Square Juggling** pattern for three balls. It is very impressive
trick, albeit a hard one to learn.

---

* *Square Juggling* is juggling with *right angles* rather than the normal natural parabolic curving
paths. The contrast generated by moving balls in straight lines and sharp corners can be amusing,
enthralling or both.

A
B
C
D
E
F
G
H
I
J
K
L
M
N
O
P
Q
R
S
T
U
V
W
X
Y
Z

☆ Both hands throw in together (or *in synch* as some would have it). Each hand is making a different throw at the same time, which is why it's tricky to learn.

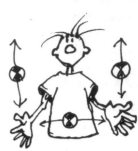

The three balls each play different roles, one rises and falls over the left hand, another rises and falls over the right hand, while the third zips back and forth between the hands.

The combined movement of all three creates a comic and impressive effect.

Here are two ways to learn it:

METHOD ONE (for experts at **SHOWERING**):

☆ Juggle a *synchronous* **THREE BALL SHOWER** and then learn to juggle it in both directions.

Now practice direction changes while the pattern is running. When you can change direction on *every throw* you are juggling a **BOX**.

METHOD TWO (for the rest of us):

☆ Start with just two balls, one in each hand. We're now going to learn how to throw L-shapes. We'll add the third in a minute—right after we complete Basic Training.

Throw the ball in your left hand straight up while *simultaneously* throwing the ball in your right hand sideways into the left.

Yes, I know that feels weird, but there's more, *as soon as that ball hits your left hand you throw it back to the right!*

You *can* do it! Maybe not first time—but you can.

The throw that goes straight up is a 4 in **SITESWAP NOTATION** and the low crossing throw is a 2x (the "x" means that it crosses).

☆ Next you must learn to throw an L-shape the other way around:

Start with one in each hand, throw the right hand ball straight up, while *simultaneously* throwing the left hand ball across. Then throw the cross-ball back.

☆ Basic Training is complete when you can do the two-ball move *both ways* confidently.

Now we put the two L-Shapes together to make a U-shape.

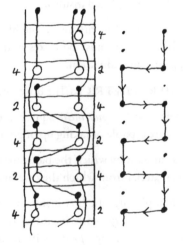

Start with two in the right and one in the left. Toss a right hand ball straight up. Now throw an L-Shape to the left, follow that with an L-Shape to the right...

Keep going and you have cracked it.

☆ The **Box** is a good comedy move, especially if you move your gaze, and your head, from side to side as you juggle. It is funniest if you look *away* from the high ball.

Here's the **Box** in both **LADDER** and **CAUSAL NOTATION**. It's pretty amazing to see just how well the **CAUSAL** diagram conveys the *feel* of the trick.

BOX THAT FITS INSIDE ITSELF

MAGIC

This is a clever mechanical illusion. The idea is that you have a box that will fit inside itself, but obviously (as you explain to your audience) this is a very difficult thing to demonstrate—unless you have *two* of the things.

☆ The performer presents two gift boxes, one is red and one is blue, but otherwise, as anyone can see, they are both the same as each other.

Carefully the lid of the blue box is removed, the red box is placed inside and the lid put back on. As they can now see, the red box fits *inside* the blue box.

Next the red box is removed, opened and the blue box placed inside it.

So if the red box fits inside the blue box, and the blue box fits inside the red box, these must be boxes that can fit inside themselves. Cue much applause and adulation.

☆ HERE'S *The* TRICK: The boxes are made to clever dimensions.

Their bases are *not quite* square and the lids fit on like shoe box lids, so they are capable of taking up or giving out a little slack (so to speak).

The amount by which the bases are not square depends on the thickness of the material from which they are being made.

When placing one box inside another the inner box is placed *sideways* with its lid down tight while the outer box ends up *upright* with its lid up high.

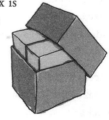

The drawing on the next page can be copied and blown up to about double the printed size and copied onto thin card before being cut, folded and glued up. All the dotted lines are *valley folds*.

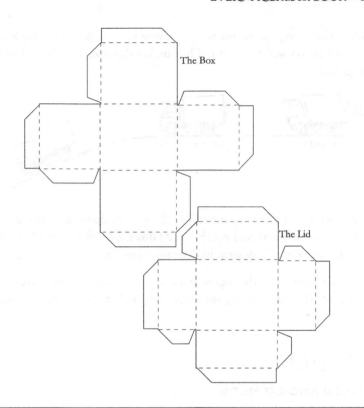

The Box

The Lid

A
B
C
D
E
F
G
H
I
J
K
L
M
N
O
P
Q
R
S
T
U
V
W
X
Y
Z

BRAKES ARE CHEAPER THAN ENGINES AND GEARBOXES

VEHICLES

This is a piece of sound advice to drivers of large and heavy vehicles.

In a car or on a motorcycle, it is perfectly acceptable to use "engine braking" to slow the vehicle down, but in large vehicles it is a bad idea because **BRAKES ARE CHEAPER THAN ENGINES AND GEARBOXES**.

☆ Yes, it is perfectly proper to hold your speed on a hill descent by selecting a low gear and rolling down with the resistance of the engine holding back your speed.

In fact, this is very important because trying to hold the vehicle back with just your brakes will result in red hot brakes that could easily fade or fail altogether.

BRAKES   GEAR CHANGE   DESCENT

☆ But what you *never* do is to slow the vehicle down with the engine. Instead, hit the brakes and get the speed down *first*, then you select a low gear and negotiate the descent under engine braking.

☆ You also *do not* use the engine as a brake when approaching a corner on a flat road. This might be big and clever in a car, but it's a no-no in a truck.

BRAILLE

CODES AND CIPHERS

BRAILLE is a form of writing, designed for the blind, in which letters and other symbols are formed from patterns of raised dots which are read with the fingertips. It was invented in the 1820's by *Louis Braille.*

Braille letters are formed on a matrix of six positions in which a dot may or may not be present, this gives a total of just 64 possible symbols.

Braille comes in several flavours. *Grade 1 Braille* which is easy to learn and simply consists of a set of symbols covering basic letters, numbers and simple punctuation.

Grade 2 Braille which is a rich and very complex typographical tool that can emulate pretty much anything that can be done with the written word. The manual for Grade 2 Braille runs to over 300 pages and takes months to learn.

Grade 3 Braille is another thing again, being a system full of abbreviations and contractions—it is designed as a kind of shorthand.

The basic Braille alphabet is as follows, note that the first ten symbols can re-present letters *or* numbers, we'll deal with how to distinguish them shortly. Notice how the sequence of dots in the top four positions repeats one the second row (where the bottom left dot is set throughout) and would also repeat again on the third row (where both bottom dots are set throughout) if not for a nasty accident at W where the sequence goes wrong.

A 1	B 2	C 3	D 4	E 5	F 6	G 7	H 8	I 9	J 0
K	L	M	N	O	P	Q	R	S	T
U	V	W	X	Y	Z				

In addition to these symbols there are some basic punctuation marks and two *modifiers* which tell you when the next symbol is a capital letter or a number. If you use a modifier twice in a row it indicates that whole of the next "word" is either in capitals, or is a multi-digit number. Note that a question mark is the same as an opening quotation mark.

Capital letter follows	Number follows	Period	Comma	Semicolon	Exclamation
Open quotation	Close quotation	Bracket(open & close)	Hyphen	Question mark	Decimal point

A
B
C
D
E
F
G
H
I
J
K
L
M
N
O
P
Q
R
S
T
U
V
W
X
Y
Z

A
B
C
D
E
F
G
H
I
J
K
L
M
N
O
P
Q
R
S
T
U
V
W
X
Y
Z

BREAKAWAY

YO-YO

☆ Hold your yo-arm up like a body-builder (1) and straighten it out to the side. The **Yo-Yo** will run to the end of the string and **SLEEP**, but allow the string to swing down and out to the opposite side (2) before flicking the **Yo-Yo** back into your hand (3).

This is the **BREAKAWAY**, a nice opening move!

BRIBING A METROPOLITAN POLICE OFFICER

TRICKS OF THE TRADE

The famous punk musician *John Lydon* (Johnny Rotten) said, "You can't arrest me, I'm a rock star."

This is not a good strategy when dealing with the cops.

One must be very careful when offering a bribe to a member of London's police force. In recent years there has been something of a clamp-down on the traditional methods by which these people supplemented their incomes.

☆ Nevertheless there are still many "educated" officers around (that being the word that is used to describe officers whose mercies are available for a price). It is important that you do not risk incriminating yourself when offering a bribe. So here are the correct* words to use:

---

* Upon the word of a Judge no less.

"Can anything be done?"

☆ The self-styled maverick Radical Cheney observed that the Police know only three classes of people:

1. The Force: who are above the Law.
2. The Public: who make complaints and must be tolerated.
3. The Villains: who are to be apprehended and beaten with truncheons.

When dealing with the Police you should take pains to present yourself as if a member of one of the first two classes.

See also the **GREAT HAILING SIGN OF DISTRESS**.

BROKEN NOSE TRICK

SILLINESS

☆ Trap your nose between your palms and tuck one thumb into your mouth so that the nail catches the bottom of your top front teeth.

Push your nose to one side and make a click by 'plucking' your teeth. If you get the movement right it looks as if you are crunching a nasty break in your nose bone. Push it back and forth making a click each time. You can really make people squirm!

A
B
C
D
E
F
G
H
I
J
K
L
M
N
O
P
Q
R
S
T
U
V
W
X
Y
Z

BROKEN SHOELACE KNOT

KNOTS

This knot is about as useful as a knot can ever be. It's just so *clever* and it uses the amazing technique of *capsizing* one knot-shape into another, just as you do when tying the **CRACK** onto your whip.

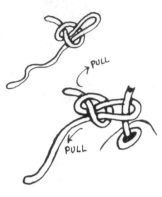

☆ Imagine that you're about to go out through the door and get on with your day, but your shoelace snaps, leaving a very short end poking out through the eye.

Too short, in fact, to tie a regular knot with.

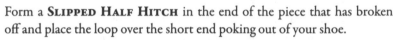

Form a **SLIPPED HALF HITCH** in the end of the piece that has broken off and place the loop over the short end poking out of your shoe.

Grab both ends of the broken piece and pull them tight, this will pull the short end *into* the knot, which will then capsize into a perfect **SHEET BEND**.

You're done!

BUBBLE WITHIN A BUBBLE

FUN WTH SCIENCE

☆ If you blow a nice big bubble and then blow a small jet of air from your mouth *hard* at it (as if blowing out a tiny candle) you can cause a small bubble to appear *inside* the big one—amazing!

BULGING BICEP TRICK

SILLINESS

☆ Forget body-building! It's too much like hard work, instead simply expose your upper arm and use a discretely hidden thumb to push the small amount of flesh in the area into an impressively muscular mound.

BULL-ROARER

SOUND AND MUSIC

A **BULL-ROARER** is a Australian aboriginal communication device.

A shaped aerofoil is carved from wood and attached to the end of a length of cord. The cord is given a couple of twists and is then swung very quickly around the head at a radius of five to eight feet which causes the aerofoil to spin one way, and then the other, causing an impressive buzzing and roaring sound that is enhanced by the doppler effect—it first rises and then drops in pitch once on each revolution.

BULL-ROARERS are are typically between 6 inches and two feet long and are carved into different shapes to produce different sounds. In practice pretty much any aerofoil shape will do, so you could try carving your own from a piece of wood.

A B C D E F G H I J K L M N O P Q R S T U V W X Y Z

The resulting sound, like the song of a whale, can be heard over great distances.

BURNS, TREATMENT OF

FIRST AID

☆ Lavender Oil is an excellent treatment for burns, the type you want is *Lavandula Angustafolia* which you can get from chemists, health food shops and supermarkets. Use only the pure oil, not a blend. If applied immediately and liberally it has truly amazing curative powers.

☆ Of course it is unlikely that you will *have* any lavender oil at the scene of the burn, so the next best thing is cold water applied *immediately*. Immerse the affected part in cold water and keep it there.

☆ Small burns, such as those you may get in the kitchen, can be prevented from causing serious damage by licking them *immediately*.

☆ Smearing a burn with honey (after it has been fully cooled) provides a good antiseptic barrier, burns are very prone to infection and honey is an excellent antiseptic.

☆ If you are practicing any sort of fire juggling it is a good idea to have a bucket of cold water close to hand in case you make any painful mistakes.

If a burn is in any way serious, especially if the skin is charred or broken, you should seek medical attention.

CALCULATOR SPELLING

TYPOGRAPHY

The numbers on an LCD screen, like those on petrol pumps, are made up from a matrix of bars which are turned on and off to represent different numbers.

0 123456789

If you turn these numbers upside-down they can be read as letters, not very well, but legibly enough for tricks like the legendary **BOOBLESS** calculator trick. The numbers translate as follows:

0	1	2	3	4	5	6	7	8	9
O	I	Z	E	h	S	g	L	B	G

With so few letters to work with there is a limit to what you can write and you also have to enter your text backwards. The famous calculator phrase SHELLOIL must be entered as 71011345. If you need to enter a word that ends in an O you must use a decimal point (otherwise the o will drop off the number, hence HELLO is 0.1134.

You could exhaustively search out possible words yourself but that is not what *Every Trick In The Book* is all about. Overleaf therefore, you will find a fairly extensive list, containing pretty much every "proper" word you can spell on the small screen.

A
B
C
D
E
F
G
H
I
J
K
L
M
N
O
P
Q
R
S
T
U
V
W
X
Y
Z

A
B
C
D
E
F
G
H
I
J
K
L
M
N
O
P
Q
R
S
T
U
V
W
X
Y
Z

bees 5338	bosses 535508	hell 7734
bees 5338	bozo 0.208	hellish 4517734
beg................638	bozos 50208	hello 0.7734
begs 5638	ebb 883	hellos 507734
beige 36138	ebbs 5883	hells 57734
belie 31738	eel 733	hes 534
belies 531738	eels 5733	hie 314
bell...............7738	egg 663	hies 5314
belle 37738	eggs 5663	high..............4614
belles 537738	eggshell 77345663	highs 54614
bellies 5317738	eggshells.....577345663	hill 7714
bells 57738	ego 0.63	hillbillies 53177187714
besiege 3631538	egos 5063	hills 57714
besieges 53631538	elegies 5316373	his...............514
bib 818	eligible 37816173	hiss 5514
bible..........37818	ell..................773	hisses 535514
bibles 537818	ells 5773	hob..............804
bibs............5818	else 3573	hobbies 5318804
big..............618	gee 336	hobble 378804
bile 3718	gees 5336	hobbles 5378804
bilge 36718	geese 35336	hobo..........0.804
bilges 536718	gel 736	hoboes.........530804
bill...............7718	gels 5736	hobos 50804
billies 5317718	geologies......531607036	hobs 5804
bills............57718	gibe 3816	hoe 304
bless...........55378	gibes 53816	hoes 5304
blesses 5355378	gig................616	hog..............604
bliss 55178	giggle 376616	hoggish 4516604
blisses 5355178	giggles 5376616	hogs............5604
blob............8078	gigolo 0.70616	hole.............3704
blobs 58078	gigolos.........5070616	holes 53704
bob..............808	gigs..............5616	hollies 5317704
bobbies 5318808	gill 7716	hose.............3504
bobble 378808	gills..............57716	hoses 53504
bobbles 5378808	glee..............3376	ibis..............5181
bobs 5808	glib.............8176	ibises 535181
bog 608	glob 8076	igloos 500761
boggle 376608	globe 38076	ill..................771
boggles 5376608	globes..........538076	illegible 378163771
bogie..........31608	globs 58076	ills 5771
bogies 531608	gloss 55076	isle 3751
bogs............5608	glosses 5355076	isles.............53751
boil.............7108	glossies........53155076	lee 337
boils 57108	gob 806	lees 5337
bole 3708	gobble 378806	leg................637
boles...........53708	gobbles.......5378806	legible 3781637
boll.............7708	gobs 5806	legless 5537637
bolls 57708	goes 5306	legs..............5637
boob 8008	goggle 376606	lei..................137
boobies.......5318008	goggles 5376606	leis 5137
boobs 58008	gollies 5317706	les 537
boogie 316008	goose 35006	less...............5537
boogies 5316008	gooses..........535006	lessee 335537
boos............5008	gos 506	lessees 5335537
booze 32008	gosh.............4506	lib 817
boozes.........532008	goshes 534506	libel..........73817
bosh 4508	heel 7334	libels 573817
boss............5508	heels 57334	libs...............5817

lie...............317	*sigh*.............4615	*Ellie*...........31773
liege...........36317	*sighs* 54615	*Ellis*...........51773
lieges........536317	*sill*...............7715	*Eloise*........351073
lies 5317	*sillies* 5317715	*Elsie*...........31573
lilies 531717	*sills* 57715	*Essie* 31553
lisle 37517	*silo* 0.715	*Geo*............0.36
lob 807	*silos* 50715	*Gibbs* 58816
lobbies 5318807	*sis* 515	*Gil*..............716
lobe 3807	*sises* 53515	*Giles* 53716
lobes 53807	*sisses* 535515	*Gill*............7716
lobs............5807	*sissies* 5315515	*Gish* 4516
log...............607	*size* 3215	*Gobi* 1806
loge 3607	*sizes* 53215	*Goebbels* ...57388306
loges...........53607	*sizzle*...........372215	*Gog*............606
logo 0.607	*sizzles* 5372215	*Gogol*.........70606
logos 50607	*sleigh* 461375	*Google* 376006
logs 5607	*sleighs*........5461375	*HBO*.........0.84
loll 7707	*slob* 8075	*Hebe*...........3834
lolls.............57707	*slobs* 58075	*Hegel*.........73634
loose 35007	*sloe*.............3075	*Helios* 501734
looses 535007	*sloes* 53075	*Hess* 5534
lose.............3507	*slog*.............6075	*Hesse*..........35534
loses...........53507	*slogs* 56075	*Hill*.............7714
loss.............5507	*slosh* 45075	*Hillel*..........737714
losses 535507	*sloshes* 5345075	*Hiss*............5514
obese 35380	*sob*..............805	*Hobbes*......538804
oblige 361780	*sobs* 5805	*Hobbs* 58804
obliges........5361780	*soil*..............7105	*Hollie* 317704
oboe............3080	*soils* 57105	*Hollis* 517704
oboes 53080	*sol*...............705	*Ibo* 0.81
obsess 553580	*sole*..............3705	*Ill*...............771
obsesses 53553580	*soles* 53705	*Isis*..............5151
ogle.............3760	*soli*..............1705	*Lee* 337
ogles...........53760	*solo*..............0.705	*Lego* 0.637
oho.............0.40	*solos* 50705	*Leigh* 46137
ohos 5040	*sols*..............5705	*Leo* 0.37
ohs 540	*zoos* 5002	*Leos* 5037
oil................710	*Beebe* 38338	*Les* 537
oils..............5710	*Belize* 321738	*Leslie* 317537
oleo.............0.370	*Bell*..............7738	*Lessie* 315537
ooze 3200	*Bess* 5538	*Lie*...............317
oozes...........53200	*Bessel*........735538	*Liege* 36317
see 335	*Bessie* 315538	*Lille* 37717
sees...............5335	*Bib*..............818	*Lillie* 317717
seize 32135	*Bible*...........37818	*Liz*...............217
seizes 532135	*Bibles* 537818	*Lizzie* 312217
sell..............7735	*Bilbo*...........0.8718	*Lois*.............5107
sells 57735	*Bill*..............7718	*Ohio* 0.140
she 345	*Billie* 317718	*Oise*.............3510
shell............77345	*Bligh* 46178	*Ollie* 31770
shells 577345	*Bob*..............808	*Oslo*.............0.750
shes 5345	*Bobbi*..........18808	*Ozzie* 31220
shies 53145	*Bobbie* 318808	*Sheol* 70345
shill 77145	*Boise* 35108	*Shiloh*........407145
shills...........577145	*Boole* 37008	*Soho* 0.405
shoe 3045	*Bose* 3508	*Sol*...............705
shoes...........53045	*Elbe* 3873	*Solis* 51705
shoos...........50045	*Eli*...............173	*Zelig*..........61732
siege 36315	*Elise*...........35173	*Zibo* 0.812
sieges 536315	*Eliseo*........0.35173	*Zoe* 302

A
B
C
D
E
F
G
H
I
J
K
L
M
N
O
P
Q
R
S
T
U
V
W
X
Y
Z

Camera Obscura

FUN WITH SCIENCE

A **Camera Obscura** is a sort of camera that you walk inside! They have been around for hundreds of years, having been invented long before the advent of photography itself. They work much like **Pinhole Cameras** except that they are fitted with a lens and a rotating mirror so that one can look in all directions.

Originally a portable **Camera Obscura** was used as a sort of artist's cheating machine, whereby a scene would be projected onto the drawing paper so as to be easily traced.

Other devices were built in the form of rooms that a number of people could walk into, and some survive to this day.

☆ The room is usually small, completely light-proof except for a hole in the top where the lens sits. Light from the outside world is reflected by a mirror that can be turned to point in any direction and which passes light down to the lens which focuses an image onto a white panel or table.

Sometimes this panel takes the form of a dished white tabletop, sometimes it will simply be a round white tray that can be held in position to catch the image. The image is focused by moving the tray closer or further from the lens.

The image is a moving full-colour picture of whatever happens to be outside. It's amazing!

If you want to build your own **CAMERA OBSCURA** then the key component is the lens itself—which can be a hard thing to find.

You need a large lens (to let lots of light through) and a long focal length. The focal length is the distance between the lens and the focused image, and for a walk-in **CAMERA OBSCURA** this will be somewhere around 1–3 meters, depending on your setup.

It turns out that opticians often cut lenses for spectacles from large blanks, which are of a suitable size since typically several lenses will be cut from them. The strength of the lens is measured by opticians in *diopters* and the following formula will come in handy.

$$D = 1/FL$$

...where D is *diopters* and FL is *focal length*.

Lenses are typically available in increments of 0.25 diopters, hence +0.25, +0.5 and +0.75 diopter lenses are commonly available; these have focal lengths of 4m, 2m and 1.3m respectively.

Once a lens has been obtained it only remains to construct a rotating cowl with a tiltable mirror and some clever levers to move the thing around with.

Have fun!

A
B
C
D
E
F
G
H
I
J
K
L
M
N
O
P
Q
R
S
T
U
V
W
X
Y
Z

A
B
C
D
E
F
G
H
I
J
K
L
M
N
O
P
Q
R
S
T
U
V
W
X
Y
Z

CANDY FLOSS VANISHING ROD

MAGIC / SILLINESS (VANISH)

At the fair you may be able to get some candy floss and a cup of coffee.

☆ Make a rod about a foot long from the candy floss by rolling it like plasticene.

☆ Dip the rod into a cup of coffee, it melts to nothing instantly on contact with the hot liquid. You can push it down into the drink pretty much as fast as you like—the cup will seem like a gateway to another dimension.

The coffee will taste a little weird though.

CAN IN SHOE

MAGIC

For a nice piece of business to put in the middle of a show you can do a lot worse than reel out the old CAN IN SHOE gag.

Pre-load one of your shoes with a completely flattened coke can. Have another full can loaded into one of your pockets. Wear something with fat sleeves.

When you're ready to do the trick start looking uncomfortable.

> YOU: Excuse me, I think I have something in my shoe!

Bend down and take off your shoe, as you bend down use the cover to extract the full can from your pocket and slip it up your left sleeve, remove the loaded shoe and hold it in your left hand.

Slide out the flattened can with your right hand and hold it up for all to see while remarking about how it could have got there. This is **MISDIRECTION** to allow the hand holding the shoe to drop down and have the full can slid into it from your sleeve.

> YOU: Mind you, it's a pretty flat can!

You say as you wave the squished can around.

> YOU: Maybe there's something else in here!"

While you are saying that you have brought the shoe back into full view. Now pull out the full can and take your applause.

CANOE AND EIGHTS TRICK

STUNTS

Certain irresponsible members of a canoe club that I belonged to in my schooldays used to do this on the River Thames in Oxford.

The Oxford students would practice rowing on the river in their extremely fast boats which are known a "Eights" because of the eight rowers who all face backwards while a ninth person, the "cox" sits at the back and steers.

These things are like oil tankers in that it takes them a long time to slow down or stop.

A
B
C
D
E
F
G
H
I
J
K
L
M
N
O
P
Q
R
S
T
U
V
W
X
Y
Z

☆ HERE'S *The* TRICK: A brave canoeist in a slalom boat waits at the side of Thames until an eight is approaching at high speed. They paddle into the middle of the river, directly in the boat's path. The terrified cox sees that the canoeist is about to be horribly speared by the ultra-pointy and fast-moving bow of the eight.

Half a second before impact, the brave canoeist capsizes *away* from the eight, which then rides right over the upturned fibreglass hull of the canoe. When the canoeist hears the little rudder bumping over him he completes the manoeuvre with a display of the art of **ROLLING A CANOE**.

There is no possibility of being caught because by the time they have stopped and turned their boat you will be long gone.

CAR WON'T START

VEHICLES

It's perfectly possible that your car is broken, has a flat battery, or is otherwise incapable of running and cannot be fixed but very often this simple trick will work.

If your engine is actually turning over, and if it seems to be "trying" to start—as in it fires occasionally but will not pick up—well you're in with a chance. The engine is probably flooded with petrol.

The author will spare you the lecture about four-stroke engines, fuel-air mixtures and all that jazz and move right on to the trick itself.

☆ If this is a really old car it may have a manual choke. If so push the thing all the way in before trying to start the engine again. If it's a modern car you won't have a manual choke.

Now gently and slowly press the accelerator all the way to the floor and hold it there. Now crank the engine and do not pump the pedal, just let it turn over for a few seconds. With luck all the excess petrol will be flushed out of the engine and it will start to run. As soon as it starts to pick up gently release the pedal and you should be OK.

See also the trick of **STARTING A RELUCTANT DIESEL ENGINE**.

CARD THROUGH WINDOW
MAGIC (PENETRATION / TRANSPORTATION)

Of all the David Blaine tricks mentioned in this book, this one is the one I got asked about most during my research. Now, *I* thought that it was a pretty obvious trick, but the punters were fooled, so it's worth knowing how it works.

☆ The effect is as follows: you get someone to choose a card at random from a deck, which they then shuffle like crazy before handing it back to you. You then go into some sort of deep hypnotic trance and have a card mysteriously appear from the deck—perhaps by rising up from the deck with the back of the card presented to your volunteer. Make a huge show of having them take it and turn it over.

```
YOU: Is that your card?

THEM: Er, well actually no, it isn't!
```

In a horrified fit of rage you fling the entire deck at a nearby window and as the cards hit the floor the card that *they* chose is revealed *sticking to the inside of the glass.*

☆ How is this done? It's all horribly simple. The card inside the window was there all along, and then you simply **FORCED** the *same* card from the deck in your hand before revealing the wrong one and 'losing your temper.'

CARD TRICKS

TOPIC

You may find that there are fewer **CARD TRICKS** in this book than you expected to find. The reason is simple: playing cards are pretty old-fashioned and while they may once have been a major source of entertainment they are hardly used in the twenty-first century outside of bridge clubs. Even the great game of Poker is mostly played on computer screens these days.

A
B
C
D
E
F
G
H
I
J
K
L
M
N
O
P
Q
R
S
T
U
V
W
X
Y
Z

There are literally thousands of card tricks, and many involve fantastic dexterity and a lot of practice, but there are plenty that are just devilishly clever and which can be mastered by mere mortals with less than ten years to spare on their craft.

Probably the most common type of card trick goes like this:

1: **FORCE A CARD** on your volunteer, victim, or **MARK.**

2: Have them either return it to the deck (with a big shuffle) or else destroy it, mark it with a pen, or mail it to Australia.

3: Reveal their original choice *in an interesting way;* perhaps by having an ocean liner sail past at the end of the trick with their card painted 50 feet high on the side.

The secret of all this is simply that the victim has no role in the trick whatsoever apart from being amazed by your skill. You remain in full control at all times.

See also **SVENGALI DECK, CROSS CUT FORCE.**

CARRICK BEND

KNOTS

The **CARRICK BEND** is the King of Knots. It is beautiful, secure, and relatively easy to tie and untie. Nevertheless, you will almost certainly prefer the **SHEET BEND** when joining two ropes together, because it is easier to tie and *almost* as secure.

☆ The knot is formed from two loops, each made in the ends of the two lengths of rope you are joining. The knot has a lovely symmetry.

Arrange the knot as shown and draw it up carefully to keep it well-formed. As it tightens it will take on a different appearance.

If you want to join two ropes in the securest possible manner then this is the knot to use. Seafaring types use this knot to join large cables, such as the ones that are used to tie 200,000 ton liners to the quayside.

All knots will weaken the rope they are tied in to some extent, hence joined ropes will usually break at the knot joining them. The **CARRICK BEND** weakens the rope a good deal less than other knots, hence is preferred for heavy-duty work.

The **CARRICK BEND** is one of the eight most commonly-used knots in **CELTIC KNOTWORK**.

CASCADE

JUGGLING

The normal juggling pattern for *odd* numbers of objects is called a **CASCADE**.

The objects being juggled in a **CASCADE** chase each other around in a figure-of-eight pattern. The pattern is characterised by the following rules:

☆ The hands take it in turns to throw.

☆ Every throw passes from one hand to the other.

☆ The hands throw on the inside and catch on the outside.

☆ All the throws rise to the same height.

☆ The starting point for all *Toss Juggling** is the **THREE BALL CASCADE** which is about as easy to learn as riding a bike.

☆ The same pattern can also be juggled with rings or clubs. This is the starting point for **CLUB JUGGLING** and *Ring Juggling*.

---

* *Toss Juggling* refers to the sort of juggling in which things are thrown and caught, as opposed to things like **YO-YO** and Contact Juggling where they do not.

☆ Advanced jugglers may choose to learn the **FIVE BALL CASCADE** which is an awesome trick which takes a great deal of practice to master.

There are never many jugglers alive in the world who can juggle a seven ball cascade—though there are more now than in former times because of the massive rise in interest in juggling during the last quarter of a century. As far as the author knows, there are less than a dozen people in the world who can manage a cascade of seven clubs.

Although seven clubs is pretty much the limit. You may occasionally see seriously obsessive jugglers attempting cascades of eleven balls or rings.

☆ It's a mathematical fact that **CASCADES** are only possible with *odd* numbers of objects. When juggling *even* numbers the standard patterns are the **FOUNTAIN** or (less commonly) the **WIMPY** pattern.

☆ In a **FOUNTAIN** half of the objects are juggled with one hand and the other half with the other hand. So a *Four Ball* **FOUNTAIN** actually consists of two completely independent **TWO IN ONE HAND** patterns. Because the two patterns are not connected the hands can either throw at the same time or they can throw alternately. Jugglers refer to these styles as "sync" and "async".

Six balls are typically juggled as an async six-ball **FOUNTAIN** which is the same as juggling **THREE IN ONE HAND** in both hands at the same time.

☆ The horribly-named and awkward-to-juggle **WIMPY** patterns are ones in which both hands throw together and every throw goes from one hand to another just like a **Cascade**. There is a collision issue here: if two objects rise to the same height and are thrown in opposite directions to each other it follows that they are likely to meet in the middle. Hence jugglers cheat a little and make the throws from one side a little bit higher.

☆ Any number of objects can (theoretically at least) be juggled in a **Shower** pattern: in which one hand throws to the other while the other **Feeds** back. You are very unlikely to see more than five balls being juggled this way.

Cascade, **Fountain** and **Shower** are all very watery words. The eminent Dr. Colin Wright (who has conducted much interesting research into the math-ematics of juggling) has amusingly noted that another thing you can do while juggling is called a **Drop**.

Catching an Egg on a Plate

OBJECT MANIPULATION

☆ Take a real un-boiled egg, toss it *really* high and catch it on a china plate.

There's an easily-learned technique for pulling this off.

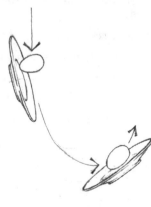

☆ As the egg falls, you hold the plate vertically and arrange matters so that it gently makes contact with the egg from the *side* with a little click.

A B C D E F G H I J K L M N O P Q R S T U V W X Y Z

A
B
C
D
E
F
G
H
I
J
K
L
M
N
O
P
Q
R
S
T
U
V
W
X
Y
Z

Once contact has been made you follow the egg down, turning the plate until it is horizontal. You can easily stop the egg in a couple of feet without breaking it though it looks even more impressive of you carry it all the way to the floor as if you *only just* managed not to break it.

When the comic juggling duo *Cheney & Gold* performed this trick with the clowns of Zippo's Circus it used to go something like this:

SCENE: ONE JUGGLER AND TWO CLOWNS STAND IN A ROW, EACH HAS AN EGG AND A PLATE.

JUGGLER: "Ladies and Gentlemen, the velocity of the egg, falling in a reverse linear motion according to Newton's Law of Flight at an acceleration of ten meters per second per second, thus proving that when the egg hits the plate, the egg will not break!"

TOSSES EGG HIGH, CATCHES IT, THEN BREAKS EGG ON PLATE TO PROVE IT WAS REAL

[APPLAUSE].

FIRST CLOWN: "Ladies and Gentlemen. The perfocity of the egg, falling in a reverse linear motion according to Blewtons, um, at ten meters per second per second per second, thus proving that when the egg hits the plate the egg will not break."

TOSSES EGG HIGH, SHUTS EYES, HOLDS PLATE FLAT, THE EGG (WHICH WAS A WOODEN ONE) HITS PLATE AND BREAKS IT INTO BITS.

[LAUGHTER]

THIRD CLOWN PUSHES FORWARDS.

THIRD CLOWN: "Ladles and Jellyspoons, the velocipede of the eggy weggy, falling in a reverse plinear motion according to Newton's Flaw of Light at a rate of ten meters per second per second per second per second thus proving that the egg will not break!"

TOSSES EGG HIGH, HOLDS OUT PLATE, LOOKS UP, EGG SMASHES ONTO HEAD

[LAUGHTER].

Always give them what they want!

Catching Worms

ANIMALS

When it rains earthworms leave their lowly burrows and come to the surface to avoid being drowned.

Foxes know this, and they also love to eat worms, so here's their trick.

☆ Tap on the ground (in a rainy sort of way) for a minute or so and watch the worms come to the surface!

Very useful if you are going **FISHING FOR TROUT**.

☆ The hi-tech way of doing this is to set a mobile phone to vibrate, lay it on the ground and then call it from another phone.

Cat Smiles

ANIMALS

Cats smile by slowly closing both eyes and opening them again.

Yes they do!

The reason is that if they tried to smile like we do they'd look like they were about to bite.

You can do it back to them.

They'll like it, but being cats they won't let on.

See too **NEVER SHOW A MONKEY YOUR TEETH**.

A B C D E F G H I J K L M N O P Q R S T U V W X Y Z

CAUSAL NOTATION

JUGGLING, MATHEMATICS

CAUSAL NOTATION is the amazing invention of a man called *Martin Frost*.

Unlike the other **JUGGLING NOTATIONS** that tell you where the *objects* are and what they are doing, **CAUSAL NOTATION** tells you where the *problem* is, which turns out to a brilliant map of *what your mind is doing* when you juggle.

Let me explain: when you are juggling three balls, you have a *problem,* specifically:

> *There is one more ball than you have hands to hold balls with.*

This problem is currently located somewhere in front of your face and is heading in the general direction of your right hand. If you don't deal with this problem a ball will shortly be making a forced landing on your kitchen floor.

You *solve* the problem by tossing a ball, in order to free your hand for the catch.

But look! Now we have a new *problem* heading in the general direction of your *right* hand.

And so it goes on.

If we draw a set of little dots down the page to represent the moments at which your hands take turns to throw, and then draw the paths of the problems as arrows, connecting the point at which the problem occurred to the point at

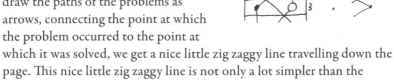

which it was solved, we get a nice little zig zaggy line travelling down the page. This nice little zig zaggy line is not only a lot simpler than the

LADDER NOTATION for the pattern, it also more accurately reflects what your *mind* is doing when you juggle three balls.

☆ If you need more proof of this statement, check out what happens when we draw the **CAUSAL NOTATION** for the **BOX!**

Now here's a secret of **CAUSAL NOTATION:** a mathematician might tell you that **CAUSAL NOTATION** is **SITESWAP NOTATION** *minus two*. What they would mean is that a 4 in siteswap would be drawn as an arrow moving *two* spaces down the chart. A 3 is a line going *one space* down the chart and so on.

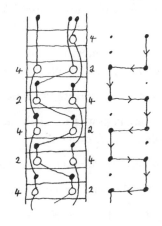

If you examine the **THREE BALL CASCADE** diagram again you'll see that the 3's of the **SITESWAP** pattern translate into arrows moving 1 *beat* down the *Causal Diagram*.

So what happens to 1's and 0's (Feeds and empty hands)—does this mean that they would become minus ones and minus twos?

Yes! That's exactly what it means! And yes, problems can go back in time. Let me explain.

Here's a **TWO BALL SHOWER**. This is 3 1 in **SITESWAP NOTATION**. The right hand is throwing 3's while the left "throwing" 1's back. Note that the 3's become lines moving *one space* down the chart, but the 1's become lines moving one space *backwards*. We can make sense of this if we translate the arrow into a statement in plain english.

*In order to FEED a ball into a hand you have to empty the hand **first**.*

Note also that the chart consists of a set of independent closed loops, each loop describes, graphically, the idea that the right hand throws in order to empty the hand for the **FEED** and the left hand **FEEDS** in order to make room for the right-hand ball. The real point is that you don't actually *have* to juggle when working with two balls because you don;t really have a *problem* in the causal sense. Each closed loop is a little story in itself and has no connection to any of the others.

If a hand is empty (a o in **SITESWAP**) we'll end up with an arrow going back *two spaces*. The plain english translation of this is:

*If you want an empty hand you have to have thrown a ball out of it **first***.

A 2, in **SITESWAP** normally means a *hold* and this translates into an arrow pointing at it's own tail.

If you are holding a ball, it is because you are holding a ball.

It all makes sense, in a perverse sort of way.

☆ The real power of **CAUSAL NOTATION** is in its ability to describe *Passing Patterns*, where there may be an awful lot of objects flying about between many hands. To draw one of these patterns we revert to Martin Frost's original layout and draw the charts horizontally. Here's a *Four Count*⁣* passing pattern for six objects between two people.

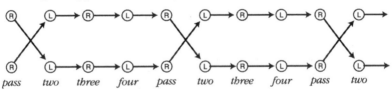

| pass | two | three | four | pass | two | three | four | pass | two |

We draw each juggler's throws as a horizontal row, marking right and left hand throws as appropriate. It's pretty easy to see what's going on.

Here's a *Ten Club Feed* for three people.

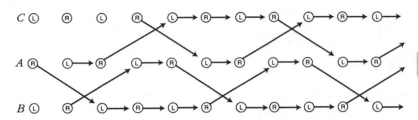

Stand in a V formation with A at the point of the V facing B and C.

A juggles a *Two-Count* passing alternately to B and C.

B and C reply with *Four-Counts*. Every passing throw is a double-spin and the extra time gained in the air makes room for one extra club .

Technically A is juggling 3½ clubs while B and C are juggling 3¼ clubs so we end up with 10 clubs altogether rather than the usual 9.

Notice how *singles* appear as arrows going *one* space along and *doubles* appear as arrows going two spaces along, it's quite neat that it works out that way.

☆ You can always tell how many objects there are in a pattern by adding the number of lines in a chart to the number of hands*—there are four lines in the *Ten Club Feed* chart, and six hands juggling, which adds up to ten—QED.

☆ Finally, and just by way of an example that shows an arrow going *backwards* in time, here's what happens in a *Four Count* when one juggler throws a round of **FOUR FOUR ONE** while passing.

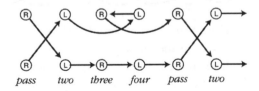

They throw a pass then go *left-self-double, right-self-double, feed, pass*!

Pretty isn't it?

---

* When adding up the lines you count lines going to the right as ones and lines going to the left as minus ones. Trust me!

A
B
C
D
E
F
G
H
I
J
K
L
M
N
O
P
Q
R
S
T
U
V
W
X
Y
Z

CELTIC KNOTWORK

DRAWING

CELTIC KNOTWORK is a descriptive term for the art and craft of forming graphical knots and patterns in the style of certain artists and illuminators who plied their skills during the so-called *Dark Ages* of the more extreme corners of north Western Europe by the people known as the Celts. The finest examples of this type of work are to be found in the amazing *Book of Kells*.

The methods of construction were lost for many centuries and CELTIC KNOTWORK was only reproduced by means of copying, until a gentleman named George Bain, in the mid-twentieth century, published a book called *Celtic Art The Methods of Construction* which showed how they might have been formed, and thus the art, once lost, was found again.

It turns out that there are many ways to construct a celtic knot.

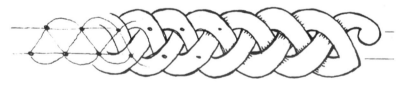

☆ According to George Bain, a Celtic knot based on the shape of a plait of three strands can be made by setting out two rows of dots like footprints across down the page. These dots are then connected by a central zig-zag line and closing curves at each side. These lines are then fattened and finally the drawing in worked over to create the strict over-and-under interlacing that is characteristic of CELTIC KNOTWORK.

It's best to work in pencil when constructing these drawings since a great deal of rubbing out is involved.

The similarity between the grid of lines and certain forms of **JUGGLING NOTATION** will be noticed by the more observant reader.

☆ More interesting knots can be created by using the technique of *breaking and rejoining.* We start again with the simple row of dots, but every so often the lines connecting them miss the dots and join a little short, creating discontinuities in the work. Some care must be taken when placing the breaks to ensure that the knot remains *legal* (a *single strand*).

Here we see that placing a break on every *fifth* dot creates a series of nice **FIGURE-OF-EIGHT KNOTS**.

It turns out that, in traditional Celtic art only a small set of the infinity of possible knots were commonly used by the artists in the Dark Ages—eight to be precise.

 From a plait of three we can make an **OVERHAND KNOT**.

 From a plait of three we can make a **FIGURE-OF-EIGHT KNOT**.

 From a plait of four we can make a **CARRICK BEND**.

 Here two opposing **HALF HITCHES** have been interlaced from a plait of four.

A
B
C
D
E
F
G
H
I
J
K
L
M
N
O
P
Q
R
S
T
U
V
W
X
Y
Z

Two intersecting **Single Hitches** from a plait of four.

Two interlocking *Round Turns*.

Here two crossings have been passed through loops as in chain mail armour, note that this knot breaks the rule of a *single strand*.

Two **Half Hitches,** formed from two strands.

☆ An entirely different method of constructing knots has been proposed that approaches the problem in a slightly more mathematical style. It is capable of generating

extremely complex knots. It takes a little practice to work with, so get your thinking cap on and we'll begin.

The principle of the system is that every knot can be represented by a graph. A simple triangle is a graph and it codes for a *Trefoil Knot*. At first it's not entirely obvious how this works, but notice that each *crossing point* of the trefoil occurs in the middle of one of the sides of the triangle. That's the secret!

☆ Here's what happens if we start with a graph of a square. First the square is marked out and then a clear cross is

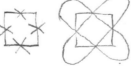

made in the middle of each side. These crosses indicate the direction in which each line will be travelling when it crosses over. Next these crosses have to be joined up. Here's the rule: extend the crossing-lines out of the graph and turn towards their nearest neighbouring crossing-line When all the crossing points have been connected you may fatten the line and finally work in the overs and unders, making sure that they alternate.

This single-square graph results in two separate loops that intersect each other, so it breaks the single-strand rule.

☆ Starting instead with two squares, side by side we end up with a wonderfully complex and pretty knot. This time it's a legal one.

☆ The technique of *breaking and rejoining* is not require by this method of construction. Instead more comples knots are engineered using *blocking lines* that are placed in the graph where lines are not allowed to cross.

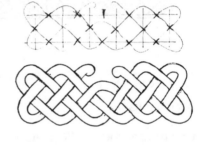

Here a grid has been formed from a row of squares and a single blocking line has been added. The centre line is then drawn by following from crossing point to crossing, but avoiding the block using common sense. With practice very complex patterns can be produced by adding a few blocking lines to a simple grid.

☆ Another type of blocking is achieved by marking the length of an entire line, which prevents it from having a crossing point on it and also prevents lines from passing through it. If you sketch out the drawing yourself you'll see that the centreline takes a sensible route through the crossing points, avoiding the blocked line.

☆ The grids on which knots are based can be of any form you like, they are not limited to closed shapes, squares or triangles. Here a kind of cross has been used as the starting

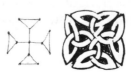

A
B
C
D
E
F
G
H
I
J
K
L
M
N
O
P
Q
R
S
T
U
V
W
X
Y
Z

point, the crossing points are then marked at the centre of each line and the result is shown.

☆ When working the interlacings artists sometimes double up each line, to create more complex images for simple weaves.

CHAIN LETTERS

GRIFTING

CHAIN LETTERS are illegal in most of the civilised world because people need to be protected from their own greed and stupidity. They don't work (as advertised) and anyone that says they do is either a fool or a **GRIFTER** who is trying to persuade you to participate in one for their own evil ends.

Here's the scam.

☆ You receive a letter, probably mostly written in capital letters (which is always a bad sign in advertising material).

The letter tells you how fabulously rich you are about to become —as long as you do not *break the chain*. The let-ter contains a list of four to six names and addresses.

You are asked to make ten to twenty copies of the letter with the first name in the list removed and your name added to the bottom.

You are to send these copies to a whole bunch of people from your address book—oh and you also have to mail a smallish amount of money (say ten pounds) to the name of the top of the list.

You will be presented with some elegant and correct mathematics which may suggest that *if nobody breaks the chain* and if *twenty people* send ten pounds at each stage, by the time your name gets to the top of the list of six people you would receive six hundred and forty *million* pounds.

This is such a staggering amount of money that even if 90% of the people *did* actually break the chain you'd still get sixty four *million* pounds.

In fact if 99% broke the chain you'd *still* get six point four *million* pounds.

It seems to good to be true. And so it is.

The maths looks good, but by the time you are supposed to get your money the chain letter would have had to get copied 20^6 times—which is sixty-four million! That's every single man, woman and child in the whole of the United Kingdom!

It is just barely conceivable that this could work until you consider that by the time the letter arrived in your mailbox it must *already* have been copied sixty-four million times—so we're starting to run out of people! By the time all the *other* people whose names are at the bottom of the millions of letters out there, and if they are all to get paid, we will have needed 20^{12} copies which is just a shade over four *quintillion*!

Since the population of the entire *planet* is a mere six and half *billion* I think we can safely say that these schemes are doomed from the start.

☆ The only way to make money out of **CHAIN LETTERS** (and **GRIFTERS** actually do this) is to *start one yourself* and make sure that *all* the names and addresses on the list are actually *yours*.

Then you keep mailing copies out to people at random, or maybe just poke them through people's doors to save postage and time addressing envelopes. If you're lucky you'll find a few gullible **MARKS** stupid enough to mail you some cash.

See you in jail.

A
B
C
D
E
F
G
H
I
J
K
L
M
N
O
P
Q
R
S
T
U
V
W
X
Y
Z

A
B
C
D
E
F
G
H
I
J
K
L
M
N
O
P
Q
R
S
T
U
V
W
X
Y
Z

CHAINSAW JUGGLING

JUGGLING

CHAINSAW JUGGLING is dangerous.

You might break your chainsaw!

☆ You need a compact, lightweight machine. The *Homelite* brand is popular with jugglers because it is especially compact.

Next you'll need to add a handle to the safe end of the machine. Get a welder to make one up for you.

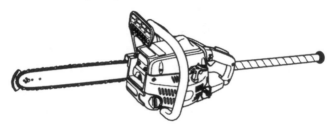

Now here's the most important bit:

The cutting chain on the saw is designed to *pull it into* the material it is cutting, this is why these things are so dangerous.

A chainsaw chain is like a motorcycle chain with special cutting links which have L-shaped knife blades projecting from them. The inside of the blades are are sharpened so that they work like chisels, scooping out wood from the sides and bottom of slot you are cutting and *pulling* the blade into the wood.

If the chain hits flesh while it is running it will pull itself in very deeply and very quickly. The wounds you'll receive will range from severe to life-threateningly gruesome.

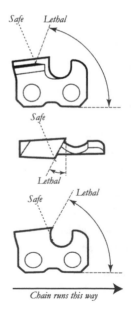

Chain runs this way

This is an unacceptable risk, especially since a chainsaw that is being juggled will have had its dead-man's handle overridden. Normally the machines will only run when both of the operators hands are controlling it—but your chainsaw will be modified so that it continues to run while flying through the air.

☆ HERE'S *The* TRICK: get a rat-tail file and spend two hours carefully sharpening the blade the *wrong way around*. This will result in teeth that still look sharp, but which absolutely will not cut you—no matter how fast the chain is running. You must do this very carefully and then check the entire chain by running your hand along it in the appropriate direction while pressing, gently at first, and then as hard as you can. Make sure you check the chain from every angle, pressing on the top and the sides for the entire length of the chain.

☆ Once the chain has been modified you can start up the saw and test it. You'll find that it will still cut a sheet of hardboard (by battering its way through) but it will not harm human flesh. You can actually lay your hand on the running chain without injury!

☆ The throttle on your chainsaw will be designed to knock back to an idle unless the trigger is kept depressed (for safety reasons) so you'll need to build a mechanical override for that.

☆ As to juggling the thing: you'll need a lot of practice to get used to the weight. You should make up a practice area with a very soft floor (crack a few bales of hay or straw onto the floor) and work with the thing for a few days *without* the engine running.

☆ When you've mastered that you can start 'er up! You'll find that the saw will fly very erratically unless you spin it exactly on the plane of the blade. This is due to the gyroscopic effects of the rotating crankshaft. You'll find that the faster it's running the easier it is to control.

☆ Only when you are quite sure that you can pull off a routine without a drop should you even consider working the trick on the street. Begin by slashing your way through a couple of sheets of hardboard, then go for the big finish.

Good luck!

A
B
C
D
E
F
G
H
I
J
K
L
M
N
O
P
Q
R
S
T
U
V
W
X
Y
Z

CHAIN TWIRLING HARMONICS

FUN WITH SCIENCE

You can do this with a 3 foot length of chain or a piece of heavy but flexible rope.

☆ Hang the chain down and move your hand in a circle. You'll find it is pretty easy to create a *three-quarter* standing wave in the chain. A half wave bend rotates over a stationery point two thirds of the way down the chain and the end swings round below it.

☆ OK now speed up your hand and suddenly you'll end up with a *one and a quarter* standing wave, two half waves and two stationery points above the end.

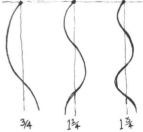

☆ Speed up again and the chain will switch into a *one and three-quarter* standing wave (three stationary points).

3/4   1¼   1¾

☆ With a little practice you can get anything up to five stationary points in the chain.

CHICKEN FROM A NAPKIN

ORIGAMI / SILLINESS

A napkin can be folded into a shape that spookily resembles a comedy rubber chicken.

Take a regular napkin and roll up two opposite sides so they meet in the middle. Turn the work upside-down and fold it in half, next tease out the four corners. Grab two corners in each hand and pull them apart.

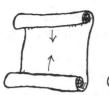

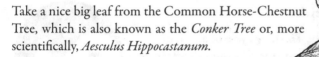

CHESTNUT LEAF FISH SKELETON

SILLINESS

Take a nice big leaf from the Common Horse-Chestnut Tree, which is also known as the *Conker Tree* or, more scientifically, *Aesculus Hippocastanum.*

Rip out the leafy stuff from between the big veins.
You can make a very convincing fish skeleton from it except that it's green!

I suppose that would make it an *Alien Fish.*[*]

CHINESE HOROSCOPE

OCCULT SCIENCE

The **CHINESE HOROSCOPE** is an oriental form of astrology based on the cultural traditions of China. It differs from western astrology in that it is based entirely on the calendar date (which is predictable and regular) rather than the movements of the planets (which is also predictable, but very irregular and complex).

---

[*] The first person who can work out why I might have gone to the trouble of including the phrase Alien Fish in my book and who also manages to post me one with a full explanation will win a prize. Immediate friends, family and former significant others are excluded from the contest.

A
B
C
D
E
F
G
H
I
J
K
L
M
N
O
P
Q
R
S
T
U
V
W
X
Y
Z

A
B
C
D
E
F
G
H
I
J
K
L
M
N
O
P
Q
R
S
T
U
V
W
X
Y
Z

You're probably familiar with people saying things like "I was born in the Year of the Pig" or "This is the Year of the Dragon" but I'll bet that you have no idea how to work out what year is what!

The first thing to realise is that the Chinese New Year is not the same as the western new year. It *usually* happens on the second new moon after the winter solstice. Very occasionally it happens on the third new moon (for reasons similar to the western Leap Year), but this will not happen again until 2033. And since the new year starts at the whim of the lunar calendar it cannot be pinned down to a firm date—but as a rule of thumb it happens between late January and mid-February.

Chinese years are numbered from an earlier starting date than the Gregorian Calendar used by the west; 2,697 years earlier in fact. So the year 2,000AD was the year 4,697 by Chinese reckoning. Chinese Astrology is based on a 60-year cycle, which is the result of the combination of three shorter cycles.

Firstly there is the *Yin-Yang* cycle of alternate years. Even-numbered years (by our calendar) are Yang 阳 and odd-numbered years are Yin 阴.

Next there is the cycle of the *Five Elements* which, according to Chinese tradition, are:

Metal 金, *Wood* 木, *Water* 水, *Fire* 火 *and Earth* 土.

So a *Metal* year is followed by a *Wood* year and so on.

Finally there is the cycle of the *Twelve Animals* which run in the sequence:

Rat 子, *Ox* 丑, *Tiger* 寅, *Rabbit* 卯, *Dragon* 辰, *Snake* 巳, *Horse* 午, *Ram* 未, *Monkey* 申, *Rooster* 酉, *Dog* 戌 and *Pig* 亥.

Rat, Tiger, Dragon, Horse, Monkey and *Dog* years are always *Yang. Ox, Rabbit, Snake, Ram, Rooster* and *Pig* years are always *Yin.*

Here follows the starting date and astrological nature of every Chinese year from 1924 to 2019 which you can use to work out your Chinese astrological sign.

What you do with this knowledge is up to you.

Year	Date	Animal	Element	Polarity		Year	Date	Animal	Element	Polarity
1924	February 5th	Rat	Wood	Yang		1972	February 15th	Rat	Earth	Yang
1925	January 24th	Ox	Water	Yin		1973	February 3rd	Ox	Metal	Yin
1926	February 13th	Tiger	Fire	Yang		1974	January 23rd	Tiger	Wood	Yang
1927	February 2nd	Rabbit	Earth	Yin		1975	February 11th	Rabbit	Water	Yin
1928	January 23rd	Dragon	Metal	Yang		1976	January 31st	Dragon	Fire	Yang
1929	February 10th	Snake	Wood	Yin		1977	February 18th	Snake	Earth	Yin
1930	January 30th	Horse	Water	Yang		1978	February 7th	Horse	Metal	Yang
1931	February 17th	Ram	Fire	Yin		1979	January 28th	Ram	Wood	Yin
1932	February 6th	Monkey	Earth	Yang		1980	February 16th	Monkey	Water	Yang
1933	January 26th	Rooster	Metal	Yin		1981	February 5th	Rooster	Fire	Yin
1934	February 14th	Dog	Wood	Yang		1982	January 25th	Dog	Earth	Yang
1935	February 4th	Pig	Water	Yin		1983	February 13th	Pig	Metal	Yin
1936	January 24th	Rat	Fire	Yang		1984	February 2nd	Rat	Wood	Yang
1937	February 11th	Ox	Earth	Yin		1985	February 20th	Ox	Water	Yin
1938	January 31st	Tiger	Metal	Yang		1986	February 9th	Tiger	Fire	Yang
1939	February 19th	Rabbit	Wood	Yin		1987	January 29th	Rabbit	Earth	Yin
1940	February 8th	Dragon	Water	Yang		1988	February 17th	Dragon	Metal	Yang
1941	January 27th	Snake	Fire	Yin		1989	February 6th	Snake	Wood	Yin
1942	February 15th	Horse	Earth	Yang		1990	January 27th	Horse	Water	Yang
1943	February 5th	Ram	Metal	Yin		1991	February 15th	Ram	Fire	Yin
1944	January 25th	Monkey	Wood	Yang		1992	February 4th	Monkey	Earth	Yang
1945	February 13th	Rooster	Water	Yin		1993	January 23rd	Rooster	Metal	Yin
1946	February 2nd	Dog	Fire	Yang		1994	February 10th	Dog	Wood	Yang
1947	January 22nd	Pig	Earth	Yin		1995	January 31st	Pig	Water	Yin
1948	February 10th	Rat	Metal	Yang		1996	February 19th	Rat	Fire	Yang
1949	January 29th	Ox	Wood	Yin		1997	February 7th	Ox	Earth	Yin
1950	February 17th	Tiger	Water	Yang		1998	January 28th	Tiger	Metal	Yang
1952	February 6th	Rabbit	Fire	Yin		1999	February 16th	Rabbit	Wood	Yin
1952	January 27th	Dragon	Earth	Yang		2000	February 5th	Dragon	Water	Yang
1953	February 14th	Snake	Metal	Yin		2001	January 24th	Snake	Fire	Yin
1954	February 3rd	Horse	Wood	Yang		2002	February 12th	Horse	Earth	Yang
1955	January 24th	Ram	Water	Yin		2003	February 1st	Ram	Metal	Yin
1956	February 12th	Monkey	Fire	Yang		2004	January 22nd	Monkey	Wood	Yang
1957	January 31st	Rooster	Earth	Yin		2005	February 9th	Rooster	Water	Yin
1958	February 18th	Dog	Metal	Yang		2006	January 29th	Dog	Fire	Yang
1959	February 8th	Pig	Wood	Yin		2007	February 18th	Pig	Earth	Yin
1960	January 28th	Rat	Water	Yang		2008	February 7th	Rat	Metal	Yang
1961	February 15th	Ox	Fire	Yin		2009	January 26th	Ox	Wood	Yin
1962	February 5th	Tiger	Earth	Yang		2010	February 14th	Tiger	Water	Yang
1963	January 25th	Rabbit	Metal	Yin		2011	February 3rd	Rabbit	Fire	Yin
1964	February 13th	Dragon	Wood	Yang		2012	January 23rd	Dragon	Earth	Yang
1965	February 2nd	Snake	Water	Yin		2013	February 10th	Snake	Metal	Yin
1966	January 21st	Horse	Fire	Yang		2014	January 31st	Horse	Wood	Yang
1967	February 9th	Ram	Earth	Yin		2015	February 19th	Ram	Water	Yin
1968	January 30th	Monkey	Metal	Yang		2016	February 8th	Monkey	Fire	Yang
1969	February 17th	Rooster	Wood	Yin		2017	January 28th	Rooster	Earth	Yin
1970	February 6th	Dog	Water	Yang		2018	February 16th	Dog	Metal	Yang
1971	January 27th	Pig	Fire	Yin		2019	February 5th	Pig	Wood	Yin

A
B
C
D
E
F
G
H
I
J
K
L
M
N
O
P
Q
R
S
T
U
V
W
X
Y
Z

A
B
C
D
E
F
G
H
I
J
K
L
M
N
O
P
Q
R
S
T
U
V
W
X
Y
Z

CHOP

JUGGLING (CLUBS OR BALLS)

A **CHOP** is a dramatic juggling move, a hand grabs one of the objects being juggled and slices violently *down* through the pattern in an apparently reckless and destructive manner.

CHOPS look best when performed with clubs, but you should master them with balls first. The following instructions will make sense *only* if you actually juggle your way through them; so grab three balls and then read on while actually *doing* what you are reading about.

☆ Start by juggling a **THREE BALL CASCADE** while tossing in a few **UNDER THE HAND** throws.

☆ Notice how the hand you are throwing *under* moves out of the way a little bit. This is a natural move: something you do without thinking about it.

Focus your attention on that move and accentuate it to the extreme. Set your mind on the task of moving the hand out of the way (rather than the task of throwing **UNDER THE HAND**) and make the move as big as you can.

That's the **CHOP**.

☆ Now that you are really focusing on the **CHOP** you should try to catch the chopped ball at the *top* of its flight and pull it *right down* across the pattern as you **CHOP** it. The action of slicing downwards is the thing that makes **CHOPS** look so impressive.

☆ The move takes a good deal of practice to develop, but you should end up being able to **CHOP** every single ball, and when you do the pattern will have changed shape more or less completely—the balls are caught at the top of their flight, and carried downwards.

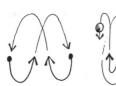

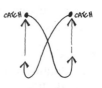

Cascade *Inside Chop* *Outside Chop* *Continuous Chops*

☆ A regular **CHOP** carries a ball down through the middle of the pattern, but you can also **CHOP** to the *far side*. This is called an *outside* **CHOP**.

☆ **CHOPS** really come into their own when juggled with clubs— this is pretty much an essential skill for a club juggler. They are usually juggled with single- or double-spins, and the two styles are very different to watch. Generally, on single spins the aim is to make the move look very aggressive, as if the clubs were three weapons.

☆ With double-spins it's nice to get the pattern as *wide* as you can.

CHOPPING FIREWOOD

SURVIVAL / TRAVELLERS TIPS

There is something fundamentally nasty about the horrible vibrating feeling in your hands as the axe bounces uselessly off the chump of wood you were trying to split.

☆ Use the martial arts technique of aiming *below* the surface of the wood, so that your mind carries the swing right through the wood.

A B C D E F G H I J K L M N O P Q R S T U V W X Y Z

You'll be amazed! This is how people break blocks of concrete with their bare hands.

☆ Sometimes you may want to split some wood into very small pieces to make kindling wood and you'll know, if you have worked with an axe, that it is both difficult and dangerous to hold a small piece of wood with one hand while striking it with an axe held in the other hand.

A mere half-inch out and you could chop off your own fingers!

The trick is to hold the small piece against the axe, and then lift wood together, bringing them both down against the chopping block as one- that way you cannot possibly miss. You can split a chump into matchwood in a minute this way.

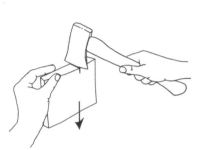

When sawing wood with a bow saw it's handy to work in a trestle, but really small wood, such as you might gather on a walk in the woods, can easily be sawn into stove-sized lengths without a trestle using the *French Method.*

☆ Stand with your feet together and place one end of the the bow saw between your toes with the blade facing forward. Jam the other end of the saw between your knees. This leaves both hands free. Grab a length of wood between both hands and run it up and down the saw to cut it. It feels odd at first to be running the wood up and down instead of running the saw up and down, but it works like a dream! This is just about the best way there is to cut wood up to three or four inches in diameter with a bow saw.

CIGAR BOX JUGGLING

JUGGLING / BALANCING / OBJECT MANIPULATION

CIGAR BOX JUGGLING is a highly energetic form of *Toss Juggling* with a long and interesting history. It was the subject of one of the finest (albeit compact) books on juggling to be published in the 20th century namely *The Juggler's Manual of Cigar Box Manipulation and Balance* by *Reginald Bacon (1983)*.

Bacon gives a concise history of Cigar Box work that takes us right back to the Tang Dynasty in China. The following excerpt is particularly interesting:

A 1914 article in Britain's Strand Magazine tells the tale. Authored by a Japanese juggler, M. Gintaro, the piece explains the origins of selected stunts.

"Some of our most effective feats are very old, and a kind of tradition [is] attached to each of them. Take, for instance, the familiar balancing feat performed with blocks of wood. This is only one of many feats performed with these ordinary blocks. I am able to perform with these blocks for two hours; as a rule, the feats I present to English audiences last five minutes.

"These feats are based on those devised by a Japanese prisoner in the 17th century. In those days the Japanese wore their hair long, and, to protect it during the hours of sleep, very high pillows were used. Even the occupants of the jails had to be provided with pillows; plain wooden blocks, similar to those used today by Japanese jugglers, served the purpose.

"The particular prisoner to whom jugglers will always be grateful suffered from insomnia; at any rate he amused himself by throwing up the blocks in his cell and catching them. Then he devised various simple balancing feats with the blocks, and the exercise he obtained in this way improved his physique.

"His appearance became too good. The authorities could not understand how a man living on little food could contrive to put on flesh. The juggling prisoner was watched, and, being caught in the act, was taken to the governor of the prison. The prisoner was commanded to perform. Tradition does not say what were the actual feats he presented, but they impressed the governor, who had the man taken to the civil authorities of the town. In the end the prisoner was released, because he was appointed Court Entertainer to the Governor of the State."

A
B
C
D
E
F
G
H
I
J
K
L
M
N
O
P
Q
R
S
T
U
V
W
X
Y
Z

Bacon goes on to list some of the more famous Western exponents of this art who include *Harrigan* and *W. C. Fields* and others working in the era of the "Salon Jugglers" (who worked with Top Hats, Canes, Cigars, Billiard Cues and so on) and the "Tramp Jugglers" who aped their more refined peers.

This then, is a style of juggling with a past.

When **CIGAR BOX JUGGLING** migrated to the West the solid wooden blocks were replaced with cigar boxes, which while also wooden, are hollow and therefore a lot lighter, they also fitted nicely into the whole Salon style that was popular at the dawn of the 20th Century. Modern jugglers will use boxes specially made for the purpose, the real things being both practically unobtainable and prone to breaking.

A juggler's cigar box is built to the proportions 1:2:3 with the short side measuring about 2½ inches (or 6 centimetres if you *must*). The proportions are important for the stacking and balancing tricks. The ends of the box are typically covered with suede or some other grippy material.

If you want to be a top Cigar Box Juggler you'll need *nine* boxes, this being the number required for the more impressive balancing tricks. Basic *Toss Juggling* work requires just three.

Stand with a box gripped in each hand and a third pinned between them. This is the rest position.

Most **CIGAR BOX** tricks follow the same basic pattern: the three boxes are lifted as a unit. Then, in the brief zero-G moment that follows, the hands and boxes are rapidly re-arranged in a dextrous manner before being trapped back in the starting position.

If the move is a complicated one the final trap may not happen until the boxes are nearly on the floor.

And so it turns out, to the surprise of most novices, that **CIGAR BOX JUGGLING** is fantastically hard work. The constant lifting and catching will make you very fit indeed!

CIGAR BOX JUGGLING proceeds in a stop-start staccato fashion, punctuated by loud clacks as the boxes come together after each move. A well-designed routine can be very entertaining indeed.

LESSON 1 - RELEASE AND CATCH

Start by lifting all three boxes, releasing them and clapping your hands before catching them again. Simple? OK, try two claps—or even three.

LESSON 2 - GRIP CHANGES

Lift all three boxes, then change the grip on an end box, so that your hand ends up holding it from underneath.

You should work through all the possible combinations of the move. Changing one grip, the other, both at the same time and so on.

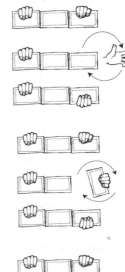

LESSON 3 - END TURNS

Lift all three boxes, then turn one box 180°. Practice all the possible combinations and then add some grip changes.

Turning one end box one way, while turning the opposite one the other way looks cool.

LESSON 4 - SPINS

Lift the boxes and spin the centre box 180°, practice going in both directions. The box spins as if it was a propellor sticking out of your belly.

You can also spin the box helicopter-wise, or lawnmower-wise. These are all useful tricks.

If you start with one end box gripped from underneath and the other from the top you can execute a spin on the centre box while simultaneously doing spins with the end box.

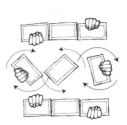

A
B
C
D
E
F
G
H
I
J
K
L
M
N
O
P
Q
R
S
T
U
V
W
X
Y
Z

The end boxes spin one way while the middle box goes the other.

We're starting to get flashy!

LESSON 5 - TAKE-OUTS

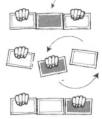

Starting from a normal grip you lift the boxes, release one end box and then grab the middle box.

The middle box is then carried *under* the released box and then used to trap the new middle box.

This is a lot of fun and easier than you might expect. If you want to make it harder you can try picking up the middle box and carrying it to the end by going *over* the end box.

If both boxes are released you can take out the far left box with your right hand, or the far right box with your left hand.

LESSON 6 - FEEDS

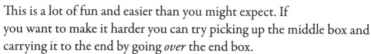

A **FEED** is the action of passing a box directly from one hand to the other. Since both hands are involved in the exchange it follows that two boxes will be in free-fall during the move.

Lift all three boxes, pass the right hand box into the left hand and then trap.

Feeds look particularly dramatic as they are combined with take-outs.

Carry out a **FEED** as before, but after your right hand has handed over its box to the left hand it takes-out the left hand box, carries it under the pattern to the final trap.

If you add a 180° spin to the right hand box you end up with a truly dramatic piece of **CIGAR BOX JUGGLING**.

After just five lessons you already have the basis for an impressive routine!

And yet there is more!

LESSON 7 - BODY MOVES

*Body move*s are common in all types of juggling, we're talking about under the leg, behind the back and so on.

☆ We'll begin with crossed-arm work. The simplest move is simply that of releasing all three boxes and then catching them with your arms crossed. To undo the move you just reverse the action.

It's more interesting to get into this position by *carrying* the right hand box to the left hand side. The left hand has to drop the left box and pick up the middle one while this is happening.

To get *out* again the two hands return to their own sides while carrying their boxes. you get points for style if you spin the middle box during this move.

☆ Under the leg moves are fun, but very hard work. You should practice all of the possible combinations. One box has to go *around* the leg into the trap, while the other two just fall as a unit.

A series of quick leg moves look great, especially if you build up a nice fast rhythm. After about six under-the-leg traps you can finish off by getting comically "stuck" in a behind-the-back trap.

☆ Getting into a behind-the-back is much like getting into the under-the-leg position. Your body cheats itself behind two boxes while the third box is carried around the corner.

Getting out is harder, one way is back the way you came, another is to jump the boxes as if they were a skipping rope.

A
B
C
D
E
F
G
H
I
J
K
L
M
N
O
P
Q
R
S
T
U
V
W
X
Y
Z

A
B
C
D
E
F
G
H
I
J
K
L
M
N
O
P
Q
R
S
T
U
V
W
X
Y
Z

LESSON 8 - NINE BOXES!

If you stack 9 boxes in a pile on the ground you can make a great show of picking them up one at a time with your right hand and passing them to your left. The first two boxes are easy. They end up sandwiched between your hands like two hands like two hands praying.

The third box is a little trickier as you have to let go of the two with your right hand, pick up the third and get back into the trap before you drop anything. As this goes on it looks more and more impossible—but it can be done.

This is one of those tricks that *looks* a lot harder than it is, which makes it a good one to put into a show.

Finally you end up with all nine boxes between your hands and you're ready for the big finale—the *Herring Bone Stack*.

Square up the stack against the ground and kick up the middle box a little with your toe.

Pick up the stack and "fold" it, you'll find that you can interweave the boxes by sliding them judiciously into a pattern like parquet floor tiles. Now you'll be able to see why the 1:2:3 proportions are important.

When you have folded the entire stack you can remove the lowest box and arrange it just-so underneath the stack before balancing the whole thing on your nose.

This is your big applause point!

You can, if you are so inclined, remove the very top box from the stack and place it under the box on your chin, which results in a higher balance. You can then take the next-highest box from the top and place it at the bottom a second time.

At this stage you are unlikely to be able to reach the top box any more (unless you have very long arms), so a good finish, after you have made a couple of valiant attempts, is simply to take a box—which results in the whole lot crashing to the floor and a big laugh.

CIGARETTE PACKET SMOKE RING TRICK

BAR TRICKS

☆ Grab an open cigarette packet and slide the cellophane wrapper down so that you create a sort of glass box at the bottom of the packet. Stand the packet upside-down on the table (or the bar if you happen to be relaxing in an alcoholic manner).

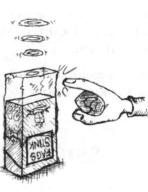

Take a lit cigarette and burn a small hole in the "roof" of the glass box and then slide the cellophane back down.

Now take a puff (do *not* inhale—it's bad for you!) and blow the smoke from your mouth into the hole while sliding the cellophane back up again. The vacuum will pull the thick smoke inside.

Now tap the side of the cellophane gently. Each tap produces a small, but perfectly-formed **SMOKE RING**. Magic!

You have just made a miniature **AIR CANNON**!

A
B
C
D
E
F
G
H
I
J
K
L
M
N
O
P
Q
R
S
T
U
V
W
X
Y
Z

CIGARETTE NOSE VANISH

MAGIC (VANISH)

Hold a cigarette between the tips of your first and ring finger and your thumb. Arrange matters so that the back of your hand is facing your audience.

Now bring your hand up so that the end of the cigarette is touching the "bouncy" bit of the side of your nose —the flare of your nostril.

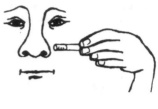

☆ If you tap the cigarette end here and loosen your grip immediately you will bounce the cigarette into a concealed position in your hand faster than anyone can see it.

This is a very effective trick *provided that* you have **PRACTICED IN FRONT OF A MIRROR**.

This is a cool move to pull off right after doing **YOU DON'T WANT TO BE SMOKING THAT!**

CLASSIC FORCE

MAGIC

☆ The **CLASSIC FORCE** is a method of **FORCING A CARD** for dextrous individuals blessed with high self-esteem and untrembling knees. In other words, you need both confidence and skill to pull it off.

If this doesn't sound like you then I suggest you ignore what follows and go out instead and buy yourself a **SVENGALI DECK**.

☆ Start with the card you want to force on the top of the deck and then cut it to the middle leaving a *break* above it. That's card-magician-speak for leaving the pack with a small step in it so you can see the top of the card you are forcing.

Start to fan the cards from one hand to the other, as your volunteer reaches into the fan for their card you fan all the cards *above* the break past their fingers and then fan the force card *into* their fingers. It's a matter of precise timing, you need to get the force card to arrive at their hand just as their hand reaches in to take the card—you have control when they actually take the card by moving the cards towards them to speed things up.

I never said it was easy, just that it was a *classic!*

Cleaning Windows with Newspaper

TRICKS OF THE TRADE

☆ The plain fact is this: newspaper is the very best thing for cleaning windows—slightly damp is best. It cleans the glass to a level of optical perfection that is almost dangerous because it becomes practically invisible to the eye.

So forget chamois leathers and squeegees, grab a newspaper instead. Make some tea, read the thing and *then* clean the windows. This is how work is done in England.

People will walk into glass doors, birds will be concussed as they attempt to fly through apparently empty air, and motorists will think that their windscreens have been stolen.

I think I have made my point.

A
B
C
D
E
F
G
H
I
J
K
L
M
N
O
P
Q
R
S
T
U
V
W
X
Y
Z

CLOVE HITCH

KNOTS

This simple knot isn't the most secure but it is easy to tie and you are welcome to use it for tying your goat or tortoise to a grazing post, provided you don't mind if they escape

If the tethered animal walks *around* the post in one direction the knot will simply work it's way to the end of the rope and fall off completely.

It can be quickly tied in the middle of a rope.

☆ Grab your rope in two places: your left hand should grab the rope from above with the back of your hand facing you. You right hand grabs a piece of rope normally.

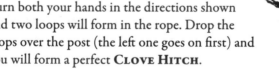

Turn both your hands in the directions shown and two loops will form in the rope. Drop the loops over the post (the left one goes on first) and you will form a perfect **CLOVE HITCH**.

CLOWN STAIRCASE

CIRCUS SKILLS

When this classic clowning trick is done well, the effect is amazing; even though you know it's a trick, and even though you know how it's being done—you can't help being amused and amazed.

The performer will need fit legs, strong knees, a great sense of mime and that special skill of over-acting.

☆ Stand behind a sofa that is in between you and our audience, position yourself at one end, facing the other. Now make your way toward the other end while miming a walk down a staircase; on each pace your head and upper body drop a "step," remaining quite upright as you bend your legs and knees lower and lower.

When you reach the end turn around (as if reaching a turn in the stairs, and work our way back along the sofa until you vanish entirely from view. If it hurts you're probably doing it nearly right!

When done well, the illusion of an invisible staircase going down through the floor is very strong in the eyes of your audience.

☆ Truly great clowns have pulled this trick off using nothing but a suitcase: you open the lid of a large suitcase towards the audience and then step in. Then you make your way down a staircase first one way,  then back the other, until you drop so low that you can shut the lid over yourself. This is a real test of contortionist ability.

A
B
C
D
E
F
G
H
I
J
K
L
M
N
O
P
Q
R
S
T
U
V
W
X
Y
Z

CLUB JUGGLING

JUGGLING

CLUB JUGGLING is a more advanced skill than that of **BALL JUGGLING** because of the added dimension of *spin*.

Clubs are also larger than balls so there is the extra problem of avoiding mid-air collisions.

Juggling clubs are, however, *purpose-designed* throwing objects, and they are terrific fun to play with one the skill has been mastered.

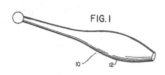

Clubs really come into their own when used in passing patterns because their design lends them to being thrown from one juggler to another.

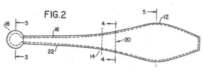

☆ When you set out to learn to juggle clubs you should spend some time working with just one club and practicing single spin throws.

The knack you need to get is that of adjusting the spin on the club to the height you are throwing.

If you're making a low throw you need *fast* spin, whereas a high throw requires a *slow* spin which is counterintuitive as far as your hands are concerned.

☆ You should make catches with your hands low, rather than reaching up for the club.

☆ You'll find that your thumbs suffer a little in the early days of **CLUB JUGGLING** because they keep getting whacked by the club handles. Try not to hurt yourself too much!

☆ Once you have managed a basic **CASCADE** of three clubs you'll probably want to move onto some multi-spin work. Again it might be a good idea to practice with a single club to get used to the feel of double spins, triple spins and beyond.

☆ A useful tip, when trying to catch a fast-spinning club, is to watch the *handle* as it turns in the air, rather than focusing on the entire club. This is, after all, the bit you are trying to catch. By watching the handle you should be able to count the spins easily.

☆ If you throw a club up with *really fast* spin, so it is a mere blur, you should note that the handle of your club projects further from the club's centre of gravity than the nose, so it is possible to catch one of these throws by placing your hand *just inside the blur* from where it should make contact with the handle.

☆ A common problem in club juggling is that of making catches at the *wrong end*. The adept club-juggler is not fazed by this and makes the catch and corrects it when the club is next thrown by making either a *one-and-a-half-spin* or a *half-spin*. This is such a useful skill that it should be at the top of your moves-to-practice-list as soon as you have the regular **CASCADE** solid. Practice deliberately turning a club the wrong way and correcting it in all possible variations:

Juggling with one club reversed and correcting.
Juggling with *two* clubs reversed and correcting (difficult).
Juggling with *all three* reversed and correcting.

☆ When you have mastered all this, and can also juggle three clubs on double-spins you are ready to move on to the really cool stuff.

Have fun!

A B C D E F G H I J K L M N O P Q R S T U V W X Y Z

A
B
C
D
E
F
G
H
I
J
K
L
M
N
O
P
Q
R
S
T
U
V
W
X
Y
Z

COCKNEY RHYMING SLANG

CODES & CIPHERS / LANGUAGE

COCKNEY RHYMING SLANG comes from the East End of London, an area well-known both for open air markets and crime. Some suggest that it appeared at about the same time as Robert Peel introduced his Police Force to the streets of London.

A true Cockney is someone who has been born within earshot of the ringing of Bow Bells which are the bells of St. Mary-le-Bow church, which is in Cheapside.

COCKNEY RHYMING SLANG uses the trick of replacing a word with a short (usually two-word) phrase that rhymes with it and then dropping the actual rhyming word, so *mate* becomes *china plate* which is then shortened to *china*.

Some words from **COCKNEY RHYMING SLANG** have become so ingrained in common English speech that people do not always realise where they came from:

I'm on my *todd—Todd Sloan* - alone. I've got to *scarper—Scapa Flow* - go.

Some examples of the slang are doubled or even tripled up: *Aristotle* means *arse* because *Aristotle* also means *bottle* and *bottle and glass* means *arse*.

The list that follows is far from complete:

Adam and Eve:	believe.
Apples - apples and pears:	stairs.
Apple - apple core	score (twenty pounds)
Bag - bag of sand	grand (a thousand).
Bangers - bangers and mash	cash.
Barnet - Barnet Fair:	hair.
Barney - Barney Rubble	trouble.
Berk - Berkely Hunt	cunt.
Bird - bird lime	time (as in prison).
Brass tacks	facts.

---

* Todd Sloan, 1874–1933 was a famous American jockey who was often seen miles ahead of the field (hence the slang). He was also immortalised as the "Yankee Doodle Dandy" in the well-known Broadway song.

Bread - bread and honey .... money.

Behind with the rent .... bent (gay).

Bangal Lancer .... chancer.

Berlins - Berlin Wall .... balls.

Brassic (a corruption of boracic - boracic lint): .... skint.

Bob Hope .... dope (hashish).

Boat - boat race: .... face.

Bottle - bottle and glass - arse, meaning .... courage.

Brahms and Liszt .... pissed.

Bristols - Bristol City .... titty.

Brown bread .... dead.

Brussel - Brussel sprout .... shout.

Bubble - bubble and squeak .... greek.

Bubble - bubble bath .... laugh (you're having a ...)

Butchers - butcher's hook .... look (have a...).

Chalfonts - Chalfont St. Giles .... piles (haemorrhoids).

Chalk Farms .... arms.

Charlie - Charlie Smirke .... berk (see above).

Charlie Chester .... child molestor.

China - china plate .... mate.

Cobblers - cobbler's awls .... balls.

Cock - cock sparrow - *marrow* - an old word for .... mate.

Creamed - cream crackered .... knackered.

Crust - crust of bread .... head.

Currant Bun .... The Sun (newspaper).

Daisies - daisy roots .... boots.

Daisy Dancers - dancing bears .... stairs.

Dicky - dicky bird .... word (have a...).

Dicky - dicky dirt .... shirt.

Dig - dig in the grave .... shave.

Dipstick .... prick.

Dog - dog and bone .... telephone.

Donald - Donald Duck .... fuck.

Donkey's - donkey's ears .... years.

Dover - Dover Harbour .... barber.

Duke - Duke of Kent .... bent (gay).

Edna - Edna Everage .... beverage.

Elephant & Castle .... asshole.

Farmers - farmer Giles .... piles.

Frog - frog and toad .... road.

Fruit - fruit gum .... chum.

Giggle - giggle and titter .... bitter.

A B C D E F G H I J K L M N O P Q R S T U V W X Y Z

A
B
C
D
E
F
G
H
I
J
K
L
M
N
O
P
Q
R
S
T
U
V
W
X
Y
Z

Ginger - ginger beer..queer (as in gay).

Grasshopper..copper.

Gregory - Gregory Peck...neck (also cheque).

Gyp - gypsy Nell..hell.

Gypsy's - gypsy's kiss..piss.

Haddock - haddock and bloater ....motor (car).

Hampsteads - Hampstead Heath..teeth.

Half Inch ....pinch (steal).

Hampton - Hampton Wick..dick.

Hank Marvin...starving.

Harry - Harry Randall ....candle.

Hearts - hearts of oak...broke (penniless).

Jack - Jack Jones...alone.

Jack & Danny...fanny.

Jam Jar...car.

J. Arthur - J. Arthur Rank..wank.

Jimmy - Jimmy Riddle..piddle.

Jugs - jugs of beer..ears.

Khyber - Khyber Pass...arse.

Lady - Lady Godiva...fiver.

Loaf - loaf of bread...head.

Lucy Lockett...pocket.

Macaroni - pony - pony and trap..crap.

Magic wand..blonde.

Manhole - manhole cover ....brother.

Marbles - marbles and conkers ....bonkers (lost your ...).

Mickey - Micky Bliss...piss (as in taking the...).

Mincers - mince pies ....eyes.

Mutt & Geoff...deaf.

Nelly - Nelly Duff - *puff* - *breath* - breath of life..life.

Nelsons - Nelson Eddy(s) - ....readies (cash in notes).

Niagras - Niagra Falls...balls.

Nobbies - Nobby Stiles...piles.

North - north and south..mouth.

Oily Rag...fag (cigarette).

Ones and Twos..shoes.

Orchestras - orchestra stalls...balls.

Paraffin - paraffin lamp ....tramp.

Peckham Rye ....tie (necktie).

Pen and ink...stink.

Pete Tong...wrong (it's all gone...)

Piccadilly...silly.

Pigs Ears...big beers.

Plaster - plaster of Paris - *aris* - Aristotle - *bottle* - bottle and glass.......arse.

Plates - plates of meat ....feet.

Pony - pony and trap ....crap.

Poppy - poppy red - *bread* - bread and honey ....money.

Porkie - porkie pie..lie.

Porridge - porridge knife................................life (as in prison sentence)

Rabbit - rabbit and pork ....talk.

Radio rental..mental.

Raspberry - raspberry tart..fart.

Richard - Richard the third..turd.

Rosie - Rosie Lee..tea.

Rock & roll..dole.

Round the houses ....trousers.

Rub-a-dub-dub..pub.

Ruby - Ruby Murray..curry.

Scarper - Scapa Flow..go.

Scratch - scratch and itch..rich.

Septic - septic tank ....yank (American).

Sexton - Sexton Blake................................cake (also fake).

Sherbert - sherbert dab..cab.

Skin - skin and blister ....sister.

Sky - sky rocket..pocket.

Sweaty - sweaty sock................................Jock (Scots person).

Sweeny - Sweeny Todd................................flying squad (hence the cops).

Syrup - syrup of figs..wig.

Tea leaf..thief.

Tiddle - tiddly-wink..drink.

Taters - potatoes in the mould..cold.

Three card trick..dick.

Titfer - tit for tat..hat.

Todd - Todd Sloane................................(on one's) own.

Toe rag..slag.

Tom - tomfoolery................................jewellery (or other stolen goods).

Treacle - treacle tart..sweetheart.

Trombone..phone.

Trouble - trouble and strife..wife.

Two and Eight................................state (in a bit of a...).

Uncle Ted..bed.

Veras - Vera Lynn................................skins (cigarette rolling papers).

Weasel - weasel and stoat..coat.

Whistle - whistle and flute..suit.

A
B
C
D
E
F
G
H
I
J
K
L
M
N
O
P
Q
R
S
T
U
V
W
X
Y
Z

A
B
C
D
E
F
G
H
I
J
K
L
M
N
O
P
Q
R
S
T
U
V
W
X
Y
Z

COIN VANISH SURPRISE

MAGIC / COIN TRICKS

Here's a nice variation on a classic vanish. We'll start by learning the classic method, and then add the surprise.

☆ Hold a coin on the palm of your left hand. I'm assuming that you are right-handed and I hope that those more interesting people of the left-handed persuasion will not take offence, instead, just read the rest of these instructions through a mirror.

In your right hand you hold a pen.

Tap the coin once, as if chastising it for chewing on your rug, (or whatever coins do when they are up to no good).

Explain that you are going to make the coin vanish and that you want people to look *very closely* to see if they can spot when it dematerialises.

Tap once...

> YOU: Everybody looking?

Tap twice...

> YOU: Really concentrating?

Tap thrice...

> THEM: Wow!

It vanished right before their very eyes!

What actually happened was that you programmed them to hear the pen clicking on the coin each time you tapped. But the third time, as the pen comes down, you literally *threw* the coin into the fingers of your right hand, so it clicked against the pen, but ended up out of sight.

You can cover the throwing movement easily by making sure, on the first two taps, that the left hand made a small movement *up* as the pen came *down*. The pen strikes an empty palm and the illusion is complete.

Remember that you must always **PRACTICE IN FRONT OF A MIRROR** and refrain from performing the trick until you are completely confident in your ability to pull it off.

Now let's break a rule of magic and move on to the surprise.

The rule is that you should never repeat a simple sleight of hand like this because it is very likely that the audience will be looking for the secret of the trick, rather than waiting for the *effect* and you'll end up destroying the magic you just created.

But this time we have *another* trick up our sleeve.

> ☆ YOU: OK, I'm going to do it again and I want you to *really* watch this time to see how I'm doing it. Ready?

Tap once...

> YOU: Watching carefully?

Tap twice...

> YOU: Really watching?

Tap....

> YOU: Oh my goodness—the pen has vanished!

The pen has been quietly tucked behind your ear just after the second tap.

Whether you reveal the pen's location (to make this a comedy gag) or conceal it (to make it a serious illusion) is up to you.

A
B
C
D
E
F
G
H
I
J
K
L
M
N
O
P
Q
R
S
T
U
V
W
X
Y
Z

COLD READING

PSYCHOLOGY

While psychics can be impressively good at producing general information, they are hopeless at the specific. They may well be able to discern that you were occasionally unfairly treated as a child (weren't you?)—but coming up with the correct choice of six numbers from 1 to 49 to match the lottery draw on a particular date is not so easy.

COLD READING is an interviewing technique used to give the subjects the impression that the reader has intuitive knowledge about them. It is extensively used by faith healers, tarot readers, chiromancers*, hypnotists, psychics, salespeople and **GRIFTERS.**

Dodgy people all.

> *"Here's something to think about: how come you never see a headline like 'PSYCHIC WINS LOTTERY'?"—Jay Leno.*

☆ HERE'S The TRICK: The reader fires off general statements that might apply to pretty much anyone and watches the subject's body language closely. They are counting on the fact that people will tend to try and fit the statements they are hearing to real facts about themselves and will make positive responses when this happens. They will also pay more attention to statements that match the truth and quickly forget the ones that don't.

It helps if the scene is set with special paraphernalia like Tarot cards or crystal balls. The subject is encouraged to work *with* the psychic to reveal the truth.

---

* Palm Readers in case you did not know.

```
READER: I'm getting something about some problems at
work, people close to you have been taking advantage of
you—is that right?

SUBJECT: Well yes, there have been some problems lately.

READER: That's right. I'm sensing some issues with a
senior worker, perhaps your boss?

SUBJECT: Well, actually I am the boss!

READER: Yes, that fits, so the issues must concern
problems with some of your employees, perhaps. I'm
getting a name, it might begin with an S…?

SUBJECT: No…

READER: ..or an M perhaps? [OBSERVES POSITIVE BODY
LANGUAGE IN SUBJECT] Yes, and M. Could be a Mike or a Mm…

SUBJECT: Maria.

READER: Yes, Maria. She works for you and there are some
issues. You feel that you've been understanding but it is
obviously still not resolved and it's causing you
problems. So she's single yes? A little younger than you…
```

It's a safe bet that a male subject will employ a younger woman and also that the subject will consider himself to be understanding, but most likely misunderstood. In another few minutes the reader could well divine that the subject has, or has at least *wanted to have* a relationship with Maria and that this is causing him sleepless nights.

Note that the **COLD READER** usually opens each statement with a positive affirmation of what the subject has just said (yes, that's right etc.). If they have been challenged, as happened above when the wrong initial was guessed, they continue as if they have been interrupted in mid-sentence.

The top topics to explore when **COLD READING** (and some sample probing statements about them) are as follows:

```
WORK: I'm sensing that you are unsatisfied regarding work
at the moment. Is this right? This will apply even if
they are unemployed.

MONEY: You seem to have some issues over money at the
moment which may take some time to resolve perhaps? This
will work even if they have just won the lottery and are
wondering what to do with the loot.
```

A
B
C
D
E
F
G
H
I
J
K
L
M
N
O
P
Q
R
S
T
U
V
W
X
Y
Z

SEX: I'm getting something that happened in the past concerning a relationship which is still with you in some way. Have you experienced difficulties like that lately? *You may expect a 100% hit rate on that one.*

HEALTH: Someone in your immediate family has some health issues, perhaps a male person who suffered in the heart or chest, or maybe the abdomen? *Pretty much guaranteed.*

By phrasing most statements as questions the reader will quickly gain the confidence of the subject who is likely to give a lot of information about themselves away without even realising they have done it.

See also **SHOTGUNNING**.

COLLECTIVE NOUNS

LANGUAGE

A **COLLECTIVE NOUN** is a name given to a group of objects or things, particularly animals—more particularly the sort of animals that people hunt and kill.

One fish is simply a fish, but a many fish together can be a *school* or a *shoal*. You don't get a *shoal* of birds because that would more properly be called a *flock* unless the birds were say, geese, in which case they would be a *gaggle, flock, nide* or *skein*.

Cows have their *herds*, sheep have their *flocks*, wolves roam in *packs* and beauties come in *bevies*.

Well-known **COLLECTIVE NOUNS** include a *murder* of crows and an *exultation* of larks. You are less likely to know that vultures come in *wakes* or that squirrels group in *drays*.

The more flowery **COLLECTIVE NOUNS** are rarely used except in conversations *about* **COLLECTIVE NOUNS**. These are usually competitive events in which the participants strive to show off their superior knowledge.

☆ HERE'S *The* TRICK: It is important to know some **COLLECTIVE NOUNS** which the smarty-pants sitting opposite does not.

The following *effusion* of **COLLECTIVE NOUNS** will supply you with the required ammunition.

A *congregation* of alligators.
A *host* or *chorus* of angels.
A *herd* of antelopes.
A *colony, swarm* or *army* of ants.
A *shrewdness* of apes.
A *pace, drove* or *herd* of asses.
A *raft* of auks.
A *flange* or *troop* of baboons.
A *culture* of bacteria.
A *colony* of badgers.
A *hand* of bananas.
A *wunch* of bankers (a rude pun, think about it!).
A *shoal* of bass.
A *sloth* or *sleuth* of bears.
A *colony* or *lodge* of beavers.
A *bevy* of beauties.
A *swarm, flight, grist* or *hive* of bees.
A *dissimulation, volery, covey* or *flock* of birds.
A *sedge* or *siege* of bitterns.
A *grind* of blackfish.
A *singular, sounder* or *herd* of boar.
A *chatter* of budgerigars.
A *herd* of buffalo.
A *bellowing* of bullfinches.
A *flock* of bustards.

A *flight, rabble, kaleidoscope* or *rainbow* of butterflies.
A *wake* of buzzards.
A *flock* of camels.
A *mews* of capons.
A *tok* of capercaillies.
An *army* of caterpillars.
A *clowder, cluster* or *glaring* of cats.
A *herd* or *drove* of cattle.
A *herd* of chamois.
A *coalition* of cheetas.
A *brood or peep* of chickens.
A *clutch* of chicks.
A *chattering* or *clattering* of choughs.
A *bed* of clams.
An *intrusion* of cockroaches.
A *quiver* of cobras.
A *lap* of cod.
A *rake* or *rag* of colts.
A *cover* or *raft* of coot.
A *flight* of cormorants.
A *sedge* or *siege* of cranes.
A *bask, float, nest, calvacade* or *congregation* of crocodiles.
A *horde, hover, mob, muster, parcel, parliament, storytelling* or *murder* of crows.

A *head* of curlews.

A *host* of daffodils.

A *herd, leash* or *parcel* of deer.

A *pack* of dogs.

A *pod* or *flock* of dolphins.

A *herd* or *drove* of donkeys.

A *trip* of dotterel.

A *dole, dule, piteousness, pitying, prettying* or *flight* of doves.

A *flight, wind* or *weyr* of dragons.

A *dopping* of ducks if they are diving, a *plump* if flying, or a *paddling* if they are afloat. Ducks in general may be a *flush, raft* or *team.* Two ducks, especially if shot, are a *brace.*

A *fling* of dunlins.

A *jubilee, congress* or *convocation* of eagles.

A *fry* or *swarm* of eels.

A *clutch* of eggs.

A *herd* of elephants.

A *gang* of elk.

A *cast* of falcons.

A *business, cast* or *fesnying* of ferrets.

A *charm, trimming* or *trembling* of finches.

A *draught, drift, scale, school* or *shoal* of fish.

A *stand* of flamingoes.

A *swarm* or *business* of flies.

A *skulk, lead* or *leash* of foxes.

An *army, knot* or *colony* of frogs.

A *wedge* or *skein* of geese if they are flying, a *flock, gaggle* or *nide* of geese if they are on the ground, a *plump* if they are on water.

A *tower* or *corps* of giraffes.

A *cloud, clout* or *horde* of gnats.

A *trip, flock, herd* or *hide* of goats.

A *glister, drum, charm* or *troubling* of goldfinches.

A *band* of gorillas.

A *flight* of goshawks.

A *horde* of Goths.

A *bunch* of grapes.

A *cloud* or *cluster* of grasshoppers.

A *covey, lek* or *pack* of grouse. A single family is a *brood.*

A *bazaar* of guillemots.

A *confusion* of guinea fowl.

A *colony, flock, pack, squabble* or *screech* of gulls or seagulls.

A *horde* or hamsters.

A *cast, leash* or *kettle* of hawks.

A *brood* of hens.

A *drove, down, husk, leash, trace* or *trip* of hares.

A *prickle* of hedgehogs.

A *bloat* or *pod* of hippopotami.

A *drift* of hogs.

A *gang* of hoodlums.

A *nest* of hornets.

A *pack* or *mute* of hounds.

A *siege* or *sedge* of herons.

A *glean* of herrings.

A *drove, harass, herd, stable* or *team* of horses.

A *pack, parcel, passel* or *mute* of hounds.

A *shimmer* or *charm* of hummingbirds.

A *mess* of iguanas.

A *wealth* of information.

A *band, party* or *scold* of jays.

A *fluther, smack* or *stuck* of jellyfish.

A *mob* of kangaroos.

A *litter, kendle* or *kindle* of kittens.

A *loveliness* of ladybirds.

A *deceit* or *desert* of lapwings.

A *leap* of leopards.

A *pride, sault, sowse* or *troop* of lions.

A *plague* of locusts.

A *tiding* or *tittering* of magpies.

A *lute* or *sord* of mallards. If they are on land a *flush* or *sute*, on water a *puddling*.

A *stud* of mares.

A *richness* of martins.

A *mob* of meerkats.

A *leash* of merlins

A *mite* of mites.

A *labour, company* or *movement* of moles.

A *bank* of monitors.

A *troop, cartload, tribe* or *mission* of monkeys.

A *range* of mountains.

A *nest* of mice.

A *scourge* of mosquitoes.

A *fleet* of mud-hen.

A *barren, pack* or *rake* of mules.

A *watch* or *match* of nightingales.

A *family* or *bevy* of otters.

A *parliament* or *stare* of owls.

A *team, yoke* or *span* of oxen.

A *bed* of oysters.

A *flock, company* or *pandemonium* of parrots.

A *bew* or *covey* of partridges.

A *muster, ostentation* or *pride* of peacocks.

A *colony, creche, huddle, rookery* or *parcel* of penguins. On water they are a *raft* on land they may be a *waddle*.

A *covey, nest, nide* or *nye* of pheasants. Flushed pheasants are a *bouquet*.

A *peck* of pickles.

A *flight, flock, kit* or *loft* of pigeons.

A *drove, herd* or *sounder* of pigs. Piglets may be a *farrow* or a *litter*.

A *congregation, leash* or *wing* of plovers.

A *chine* of polecats.

A *string* of ponies.

A *school* of porpoises.

A *run* of poultry.

A *covey* of ptarmigans.

A *litter* of puppies.

A *bevy* or *covey* of quail.

A *covey* of quail.

A *bury, colony, down, drove, husk, leash, trace, trip* or *warren* of rabbits. Baby rabbits are a *wrack* or a *nest*.

A *rhumba* of rattlesnakes.

A *colony, horde, pack, plague, swarm* or *mischief* of rats.

A *conspiracy, murder, storytelling* or *unkindness* of ravens.

A *crash* of rhinoceroses.

A *building, clamour* or *parliament* of rooks.

A *hill* of ruffs.

A *bind, school shoal* or *run* of salmon.

A *fling* of sandpipers.

A *cloud* of sea fowl.

A *colony, harem, herd, pod, bob, crash, rookery, team* or *spring* of seals.

A *raft* of sea otters.

A *school* or *shiver* of sharks.

A *flock, drove, hurtle, trip* or *fold* of sheep.

A *dopping* or *doading* of sheldrakes.

A *fleet, flotilla* or *armada* of ships.

A *troupe* of shrimps.

An *exultation, bevy* or *ascension* of skylarks or larks.

A *rout* or *walk* of snails.

A *bed, den, nest, pit* or *slither* of snakes.

A *walk* or *wisp* of snipe, a walk is on the ground, a wisp in the air

A *host, quarrel, tribe* or *ubiquity* of sparrows.

A *cluster* or *clutter* of spiders.

A *dray* of squirrels.

A *murmuration* of starlings.

A *fever* of stingrays.

A *pack* of stoats.

A *muster*, *mustering* or *phalanx* of storks.

A *flight* or *gulp* of swallows.

A *wedge* of swans if they are flying, otherwise a *gaggle*, *bank*, *bevy*, *gargle*, *squadron*, *game*, *drift*, *whiteness* or *eyrar*.

A *flock* of swifts.

A *diving*, *coil*, *knob*, *raft* or *spring* of teal.

A *dread* of terns.

A *streak* or *ambush* of tigers.

A *taint* of tilapia.

A *mutation* of thrushes.

A *knot*, *nest*, *knob* or *lump* of toads.

A *creep* of tortoises.

A *grove*, *copse*, *thicket* or *stand* of trees.

A *book* of tricks.

A *hover* of trout.

A *flock*, *dole*, *dule*, *raffle*, *raft* or *rafter* of turkeys.

A *bale*, *bevy*, *dule*, *nest* or *turn* of turtles.

A *marvel* of unicorns.

A *nest* or *den* of vipers.

A *wake* or *colony* of vultures.

A *herd* or *pod* of walruses.

A *knob* or *plump* of waterfowl.

A *boogle*, *sneak* or *pack* of weasels.

A *school*, *pod*, *herd* or *gam* of whales.

A *company*, *bunch*, *knob* or *coil* of wigeon.

A *trip* of wildfowl.

A *pack*, *herd* or *rout* of wolves.

A *warren* of wombats.

A *fall*, *covey* or *plump* of woodcock.

A *descent* of woodpeckers.

A *clew* or *knot* of worms.

A *herd* of wrens.

A *herd* of yaks.

A *herd*, *dazzle* or *zeal* of zebras.

COLOUR-CHANGING BALLOONS

MAGIC (TRANSFORMATION)

The simple ones can be the best.

☆ Roll up a red balloon and stick it into the neck of a blue balloon. Now blow up both! It's a fiddle but it can be done.

When you pop the blue balloon with a pin it turns red!

COLOUR-CHANGING RINGS

JUGGLING / MAGIC

COLOUR-CHANGING RINGS are simply *Juggling Rings* that are plain on one side (usually white) and coloured on the other (typically a set will have all the colours of the rainbow). You can buy them ready-made or convert a set of white rings with paint or adhesive plastic. They are used to create a truly magical effect.

☆ The best presentation is to have two jugglers, side on to the audience, passing six or seven rings. They will have arranged matters so that the white sides of the rings are facing the audience. Suddenly the audience will see the rings magically change from white to multi-coloured. It's an easy change to make, all you have to do is to get one juggler to make seven consecutive **Reverse Ring Catches** with their incoming rings.

The **REVERSE RING CATCH** causes the ring to turn 180° before it gets thrown again—without the juggler even having to *think* about it.

☆ A solo juggler can achieve almost the same result by juggling four or five rings and switching them. All they have to do is to count off four or five while making **REVERSE RING CATCHES**.

The effect really is quite magical, the audience simply don't notice the switch.

A
B
C
D
E
F
G
H
I
J
K
L
M
N
O
P
Q
R
S
T
U
V
W
X
Y
Z

A
B
C
D
E
F
G
H
I
J
K
L
M
N
O
P
Q
R
S
T
U
V
W
X
Y
Z

COLUMN BOUNCE

JUGGLING

The **COLUMN BOUNCE** is a **BOUNCING BALL** technique that solves the problem of collisions when juggling **TWO IN ONE HAND** off the floor. It's a bit of a knack, but very easy once learnt. It was discovered by *Radical Cheney* in the 1980's while he was searching for the **BOUNCING BALL** equivalent of the *Four Ball* **FOUNTAIN** which was, at that time, either lost or unknown to juggling science.

☆ Grab two **BOUNCING BALLS** and place them in your favourite hand. Now *lift* the first ball a few inches and let it drop vertically to the floor.

Now here's the tricky bit; the *exchange!*

As the dropped ball rises you turn your hand palm-upwards and *lift* the second ball so that it rises *directly over the other ball*. Now let go and flip your hand over to **SNATCH** the rising ball. You quickly pull the snatched ball out of the way and let the second ball bounce on exactly the same spot as the first.

Now just keep it going!

☆ Once you can manage two you can move on to *three* balls. This is ludicrously simple. Start doing a **TWO IN ONE HAND** column bounce while carrying a 'spare' ball in your free hand. Make the balls bounce on a central spot. Now just allow your hands to 'take it in turns' to make the exchange. *Voila!* A **THREE BALL CASCADE** juggled with all the balls hitting the floor in the same place!

See also **FOUR BALL BOUNCE, FIVE BALL COLUMN BOUNCE.**

COMET

JUGGLING

☆ Get three **BEANBAGS** and three juggling scarves or pieces of light silk. Tie the scarves around the beanbags and juggle. You have just made yourself a set of **COMETS**.

It's not exactly rocket science, but it's fun!

☆ You can also make **COMETS** with **BOUNCING BALLS.**

CONSTRICTOR KNOT

KNOTS

The **CONSTRICTOR KNOT** is a super-knot. It is amazingly secure, very useful, and potentially dangerous! It is easy to tie but *almost impossible* to untie. Curiously very few people seem to know about it, unless that is, they have managed to get their hands on a copy of the awesome *Ashley Book of Knots* in which it ranks as one of the most highly-praised knots in a collection of around 11,000 others.

It grips like a boa constrictor—if you tie a sack closed with it you'll have to cut it to get it off again.

Do not test it on parts of your body, or anyone else's for that matter. It *will* be impossible to untie and it *will* cut off the blood supply.

A
B
C
D
E
F
G
H
I
J
K
L
M
N
O
P
Q
R
S
T
U
V
W
X
Y
Z

A
B
C
D
E
F
G
H
I
J
K
L
M
N
O
P
Q
R
S
T
U
V
W
X
Y
Z

☆ Run the end of the rope or cord over and around the item to be constricted *twice* so that the second turn crosses over the first. Finally lead the end *over* the standing part and then *under* the crossing you made between the two turns. Pull tight and every ounce of effort you put in will get locked into the knot.

☆ To remove the knot you have to cut through the top of the crossover with a sharp knife.

COOL WATER UNDER A HOT SUN

TRAVELLER'S TIPS

There's nothing like a glass of ice-cool water when the sun is hot enough to fry eggs on the bonnet of your car (I suppose that's a trick in itself, but somehow I missed it out).

☆ HERE'S *The* TRICK: You can use the power of the sun to cool your water—as unlikely as that might sound.

☆ Water will slowly seep through a terracotta pot and evaporate on the outside. In hot countries you'll often see water stored in terracotta containers standing in the sun.

The water sweats through the pot and cools the water inside. You can make your own water cooler by blocking the hole in the bottom of a flower pot with a cork and covering it with a lid, just make sure that the blazing sun is hitting the sides.

☆ You can also get tightly woven canvas bags that allow water to seep through slowly that achieve the same result.

☆ In Australia, where blokes are blokeish, it is fashionable to stack crates of beer on the roof of your car when 'going bush'. The beer is then covered with petrol-soaked towels. After driving a few miles the evaporation of the petrol will chill the 'tubes of nectar' nicely.

"Hand me another Sheila! And careful your fingers don't freeze to the metal."

CONTRA-ZOOM

FILMING

This cool camera trick is often thought to have originated in the movie *Jaws* (1975) but it was actually first developed by *Irmin Roberts*, a cameraman working with *Alfred Hitchcock* in the film *Vertigo* (1958). It is also called, among other things, a *Dolly Zoom*, a *Vertigo Zoom* or a *Stretch Shot*.

The principle is simple, the camera *dollys* (travels) toward the actor or actors, which would normally make them appear to grow in size, but the camera is simultaneously *zoomed out*. The visual effect is that of the background shrinking while the actors remain the same size.

The psychological effect is very powerful, the actors presence suddenly seems to dominate the screen—as in the moment in *Jaws* when Police Chief *Martin Brody* realises that there really *is* a shark out there and it's about to start gobbling up bit-part actors.

A
B
C
D
E
F
G
H
I
J
K
L
M
N
O
P
Q
R
S
T
U
V
W
X
Y
Z

If the effect is run in reverse then an actor can be made to seem overwhelmed by their surroundings. To achieve these effects in your own movies you'll need a *Dolly* (a stolen shopping trolley is good) and a very steady zoom-hand. Remember to pull the focus at the same time!

COPPER SLUG RINGS

GARDENER'S TIPS

Here's the thing: slugs eat plants and they especially prefer young juicy ones.

Some gardeners resort to horrible chemical methods to get rid of slugs, others construct vile *beer traps* that fill up with sickening bloated slug bodies.

A more elegant solution is based on the fact that slugs do not like "walking" over copper.

☆ Place rings of copper sheet around your baby plants and the slugs will leave them alone. A ring about three inches high will do. Maybe you could find an old copper boiler and slice it up with tin snips.

These things really work.

COVERING THE JOIN

MAGIC

A basic principle of magic and illusion is that of **COVERING THE JOIN**. It's really quite amazing that people put up with it, but they do!

COVERING THE JOIN is the act of concealing your actions at the critical moment of deceit.

☆ For example, when you perform the trick of **REMOVING YOUR THUMB** you conceal the fact that you are actually separating the halves of two *different* thumbs by **COVERING THE JOIN** with one of your fingers on the assumed pretence that it is concealing the gory sight of the flesh of your thumb actually being torn in two.

☆ A common way of presenting a vanish is to drape a cloth briefly over the item that is to be transported into another dimension. The cloth is then suddenly removed to reveal that the item has gone. This subterfuge prevents anyone from actually *seeing* the item vanish—yet they will still accept the illusion that this is what has happened.

Sometimes the cloth merely conceals the method by which the object has been removed from view (such as when it has dropped through a secret trapdoor) but other times the cloth is actually *part of the method itself* (such as when the object is removed *with* or *inside* the cloth).

A
B
C
D
E
F
G
H
I
J
K
L
M
N
O
P
Q
R
S
T
U
V
W
X
Y
Z

A
B
C
D
E
F
G
H
I
J
K
L
M
N
O
P
Q
R
S
T
U
V
W
X
Y
Z

☆ Most traditional theatres, especially the ones that present pantomimes, have at least one trapdoor in the stage that can rapidly drop or raise an actor on or off the stage in under a second by means of a small counterweighted lift that is operated by stage hands. When it is time for the evil baron to appear or vanish, a few pyros are triggered so as to cause a bright flash and a cloud of smoke. The entire audience will blink and when they open their eyes again the area will be obscured by smoke. During the illusion the entire lighting rig will be dimmed for a second. The combined effect of the flash, bang, smoke and lighting change pretty much guarantees that nobody in the audience will see the lift in action.

☆ When you perform the feat of **MAKING THE STATUE OF LIBERTY** vanish you conceal your method by arranging for a great big screen to conceal the statue while you work your craft, only revealing a big empty space *after* the trick has been done. This is another way of **COVERING THE JOIN**.

☆ When you perform a **PALM RETENTION VANISH** you conceal the fact that you never placed the coin in the receiving palm at all by **COVERING THE JOIN** with the fingers of *both* hands.

☆ When using a **SUPERMAGNET** concealed in your sleeve to "suck" a coin off your hand you conceal the jump of the coin by waving your hand over it: cleverly it is this very action that brings the magnet close enough to the coin to capture it.

By fully realising just how readily people will accept this blunt subterfuge you should be able to concoct some amazing feats of your very own.

See also **DIVING INTO A GLASS OF WATER**.

COWBOY'S HORSE HITCH

KNOTS

Here's one of the knots used by cowboys to fix a horse to a rail and still allow for a quick getaway. This particular one was taught to the author by the legendary cowboy *"Mad" Pete McMadden* who actually rides a Harley Davidson.

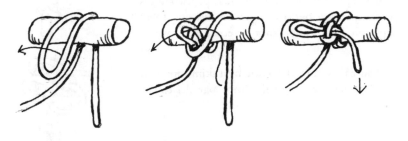

1: The rope from the horse is folded into a *bight* (a loop in the middle of a rope) which is then passed around the rail outside the saloon.

2: A *bight* from the standing part of the rope (the bit attached to the animal) is passed upwards through the loop making a second loop. Then a *bight* from the free end is passed through that loop, which acts as a sort of toggle.

3: The horse is now secured. When it's time for the getaway a quick tug on the end will release the entire knot. Yee-ha!

COW HITCH

KNOTS

The **COW HITCH** is a simple knot but horribly insecure. It's also known as a *Lark's Head*.

A
B
C
D
E
F
G
H
I
J
K
L
M
N
O
P
Q
R
S
T
U
V
W
X
Y
Z

Fold your rope to form a u-bend and pass this around the post your are fixing your cow to.

Now feed the rest of the rope though the loop your have made.

☆ If you pull on *both* parts of the rope the knot is perfectly secure, but if you pull on just one it will slip easily—not a good knot to secure a cow with!

☆ You can secure the knot by taking one end and feeding it through the knot parallel to the post it is secured to.

Once formed in this way the **Cow Hitch** is perfectly secure.

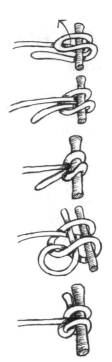

CRACK

WHIPS / KNOTS

The **CRACK** (or *Cracker*) is the small section of twine that is tied to the business end of a whip.

It is a sacrificial component that wears out rapidly from striking things and being hurled through the air at supersonic speeds. The knot that is to hold it fast when travelling through the air a speeds only marginally below 1,000 miles an hour has to be a good one.

☆ You can make a good **CRACK** from thin synthetic material. Paraglider lines are a good source since they are unbelievably strong, but experiment and see what works for you.

☆ First you need to make a loop in the **CRACK** itself. One way is to stitch the material back on itself with an industrial sewing machine.

☆ Another is to fold a piece of line in half and twist both ends in the same direction until the thing winds up like the rubber band on a model aircraft's propellor. When a few inches have wound up you lock in the loops with two **OVERHAND KNOTS**.

Once the **CRACK** is prepared we can tie it on:

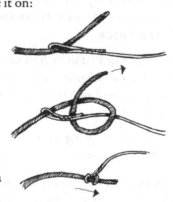

☆ Feed the **FALL** of the whip through the **CRACK** then lay the **FALL** over the standing part of the **CRACK** and feed the end up and through the loop you have just made. This is exactly like tying a **SHEET BEND**.

Now pull the end of the **FALL** against the standing part of the **FALL** and the knot you have made will *capsize* into a new shape.

Slide this knot nearly to the end of the **FALL** and pull it tight.

☆ Crack the whip *gently* at first to tighten up the knot. After the whip has been cracked a few times the knot will become solid and immoveable.

You're done!

A
B
C
D
E
F
G
H
I
J
K
L
M
N
O
P
Q
R
S
T
U
V
W
X
Y
Z

A
B
C
D
E
F
G
H
I
J
K
L
M
N
O
P
Q
R
S
T
U
V
W
X
Y
Z

CROSS & FOLLOW

JUGGLING / POI

A **CROSS AND FOLLOW** is a *Club Swinging* move in which two clubs swing around the body in a figure of eight pattern. In **POI** juggling it is called a *Three-Beat Weave*.

You can also do a **CROSS AND FOLLOW** with ribbons, flags, fire torches, or buckets full of water—see the **UPSIDE DOWN WATER TRICK**.

Take a club or **POI** in each hand and imagine yourself sat in a canoe, ready to paddle off with your *bare hands* (this will make sense in a moment).

Both hands are going to "paddle the boat" and both hands are going to paddle on *both sides*.

☆ Begin with your hands bent forwards at the elbows, palms up. You're holding your **POI,** clubs or whatever, but you're *thinking* bare-handed canoe paddling. The clubs or **POI** are extensions of your hands, so although we describe the movements as if the hands are making them, it's actually your props that are doing the paddling, so the hand movements are quite small:

1: Place your left arm over the right and make a paddling stroke, with your left hand, on the right side of the "canoe".

2: Your right hand now makes a stroke on the right side, but with using the back of the hand.

3: Your left hand makes another stroke on the right side of the canoe.

4: Now your right hand crosses over the left and makes a stroke on the left side of the canoe.

5: Your left hand makes a back-handed stroke on the left.

6: Your right hand makes another stroke on the left side.

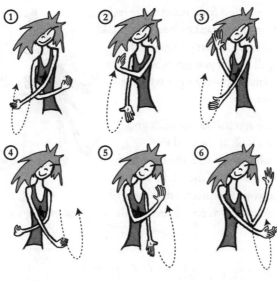

Now just repeat the sequence.

It all boils down to three strokes on one side, and the three strokes on the other.

☆ Skilled tricksters will immediately realise that the whole thing can be done in reverse, as if paddling the canoe *backwards*.

☆ True manipulators will learn to juggle the **CROSS AND FOLLOW** over their heads.

CROSS-CUT FORCE

CARDS / MAGIC

The **CROSS-CUT FORCE** is a method of **FORCING A CARD** that relies on *charisma* rather than manual dexterity.

☆ Prepare the pack by placing the card you want picked on the top. Get your volunteer to cut the pack from your hand, placing the top half on the table. Take the remaining half (which is still in your hand), turn it ninety degrees and place it on top of the cards they cut saying, 'let's mark the cut'.

A
B
C
D
E
F
G
H
I
J
K
L
M
N
O
P
Q
R
S
T
U
V
W
X
Y
Z

Now break the action for a moment by telling them something irrelevant or better still ask them their birthday and try to guess their star sign. It will help if you get it wrong. The idea is to make them forget what has just happened.

Now lift up the top half of the deck and let them have a look at the card they 'chose'—which is, of course, the card that started out on the top of the pack. The trick, as far as you are concerned, is over, all you have to do now is to reveal their choice in an *interesting way*.

CROSSING THE LINE

FILMING

One of the great secrets of film-making is a thing called the *line*. This is one of those things you either get, or you don't get. Plenty of people leave film school with no real understanding of it. The *line* is the *line of sight* between two characters in a dialogue—the eye-line.

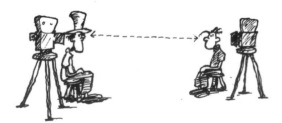

☆ When filming two characters in conversation it is common practice to set up two cameras to record the scene (or set up two shots if you are filming out of sequence). One shot gives a view of character A, the other of character B. In the edit you'll cut from one shot to the other as the dialogue proceeds.

Now it's not immediately obvious to the beginner but *both* cameras must be on the *same* side of the eye-line for this to work. Furthermore, if one character is looking down a little, the other must be looking up a little. It's vital to get the eye-line right in both shots. If you don't they will both look as if they are talking to the scenery rather than each other.

Films typically proceed from *scene to scene* and it's a rule that each scene should be like a miniature story in its own right, thus it should have a beginning, a middle and an end —thus moving the *plot* forward.

For if not, what point in the scene?

If the scene is based mainly on dialogue (as opposed to being a chase scene or something more visually dramatic) then the position of the camera is used to help to suggest the transition from the starting situation in the scene to its resolution.

As this point is reached you may see one of the characters **CROSSING THE LINE**. They will perhaps, get up and literally walk across the line between the two cameras—after which the conversation will continue with the cameras set up *on the other side* of the original line.

Alternatively a camera could move, or there may be a cut to a shot from a camera on the other side of the line.

You see this sort of thing done in soap-operas *all the time* —and now you know the trick you'll have fun spotting it.

☆ **CROSSING THE LINE** is also used to good effect in horror films (always a good choice of genre for the home-movie on a low budget)— especially at the point in the film where *we* all know what's going on but the actors don't. You set up a conversation between two characters sat at the kitchen table with two cameras as usual, but have one of the cameras located way back, actually out of the room looking in through the door and over one of the actors shoulders. Have them talk about something inconsequential while flipping between one camera and the other as the dialogue proceeds.

Suddenly, while on the long through-the-door shot, a hard-to-make-out shape flashes past the camera as if passing by the open door (you add a spooky whooshing sound as it goes past in post-production). The person facing the camera freezes in mid sentence. Now cut to a new camera on the *other side* of the line looking back towards the door. The character with their back to the door says something like "you look like you've just seen a ghost!" and you've just built some real suspense.

☆ The technique of **CROSSING THE LINE** works just as well in cartoon strips or stage performances and every director and cartoonist should master it.

CUP OF COFFEE SIR? OOPS!

SILLINESS

☆ Get a cup, saucer and teaspoon. Stick the teaspoon through the handle of the coffee cup and trap the handle between your thumb and the saucer.

Now walk up to your victim. As you approach you do a **FAKE TRIP** and let the cup fall off the saucer towards their lap—but will get caught by the teaspoon at the last minute.

Oh, and the cup has to be *empty!*

CUP OF TEA ON HEAD

OBJECT MANIPULATION / SILLINESS

Some tricks are just great fun, here's one.

☆ Place all the essentials for a nice cup of English tea on a low table and sit on a chair next to it. I suggest that you let the tea go cold for reasons that will become obvious in a moment.

Balance a cup and saucer on your head.

The milk, as everyone knows, goes in first, pour a dash into the cup.

Now pour in some tea (pretty impressive) you'll have to use your judgement as to when to stop pouring.

Now get a sugar lump (you do have sugar lumps don't you?) and toss a lump of sugar into the cup.

Finally, take a teaspoon and toss that in. You'll have to focus very hard on the problem to pull this off. You hold the spoon in front of your face and gaze at it in a zen-like manner. Then you make a gently half-spin toss into the cup.

Finally, stir the tea and drink it (if there is any left).

With a little practice you will have a fine party piece to impress people with.

A
B
C
D
E
F
G
H
I
J
K
L
M
N
O
P
Q
R
S
T
U
V
W
X
Y
Z

A
B
C
D
E
F
G
H
I
J
K
L
M
N
O
P
Q
R
S
T
U
V
W
X
Y
Z

CUPS AND BALLS

MAGIC

The **CUPS AND BALLS** routine has been played out wherever crowds gather since time began—or very shortly thereafter. It is, therefore, without doubt *The Oldest Trick in The Book*.

The Conjurer—Hieronymus Bosch - Circa 1480
Note the pick-pocket working the small crowd.

Variations of the **CUPS AND BALLS** routine, like the **SHELL GAME** and *Thimblerig* are still performed today by **GRIFTERS** as a means of scamming money from unsuspecting **MARKS** and it is generally agreed that this was the original purpose of the trick.

However, in these more enlightened times it has been discovered that the **CUPS AND BALLS** can be worked as a highly entertaining street illusion for which happy crowds are pleased to pay money by dropping it in a hat after the show. Many magicians will argue that the **CUPS AND BALLS** routine is, quite simply, the *best* magical illusion there is.

There are many different ways of performing the trick but they all work to a common theme. Let's start by examining the kit you'll need:

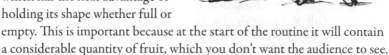

The performer will have a small portable table, a wand, three cups, a hat, some small balls, and around their waist will be hung some sort of apron with a large pocket in the front which is used for storing props and hiding things in. Professionals generally invest in a decent leather *Poacher's Pouch* which has the neat advantage of holding its shape whether full or empty. This is important because at the start of the routine it will contain a considerable quantity of fruit, which you don't want the audience to see.

The cups themselves are held in high regard by exponents of the **CUPS AND BALLS** routine and are sometimes very expensively made from hand-spun copper in matched sets. You can buy them from good magic suppliers. Performers like their cups need to be *clunky* so that you can make a nice loud noise by tapping them with the wand (for **MISDIRECTION** purposes).

They need to have little dips in the bases so that you can place balls or fruit on top of them when they are upturned. They also need to be big enough to hold oranges.

The balls should be big enough to be easy to see yet small enough to palm easily. Three of them should be able to fit easily under a single cup.

The wand should be wooden and a little under a foot long. A short length of wooden dowel or a cannibalised drumstick will do just fine.

Now you must learn a set of moves that you can weave into a smooth performance. You'll need to **PRACTICE IN FRONT OF A MIRROR** until these are all utterly convincing, bearing in mind that the **CUPS AND BALLS** trick is often worked *in the round*—so angle-sensitive moves are out.

A
B
C
D
E
F
G
H
I
J
K
L
M
N
O
P
Q
R
S
T
U
V
W
X
Y
Z

PALMING BALLS

You must become adept at holding a hidden ball in your hand, you may either use a **FINGER PALM** or the more technical method as used when **PALMING A COIN** where the ball is held between the palm and base of the thumb by the limited tenacity of the creases in the skin of your hand.

It's important that the hand appears loose and natural when holding a ball this way. Sometimes you will also need to pick up and hold the wand in the hand that is concealing a ball. You must also be able to pick up (and hold in full view) a second ball while one is already concealed in the hand.

FALSE PASSES

You must also practice moves in which you seem to pass a ball from one hand to the other, yet retain the ball in your passing hand. One method is the the **PALM RETENTION VANISH**.

The ball is offered in full view to the open left hand. *As the hand withdraws the ball is concealed by the right hand's fingers.*

The other is the **FRENCH DROP**. Here the ball is held by the fingertips of the right hand in full view. The left hand closes over the ball which is dropped into a **FINGER PALM** position in the right hand while the left moves away, apparently holding the ball.

Practice these moves until you can actually fool yourself with them in front of a mirror. This may sound odd but you'll understand it better after a few hours spent perfecting these tricks.

LOADS

A load is the act of placing an object in a cup. Sometimes you are actually putting the object into the cup, other times you are retaining the object and simply appearing to place it under, and occasionally you seem to be placing one object under the cup but you are actually placing more than one. Towards the end of your routine you'll need to load cups with fruit without the audience seeing you do it at all.

Tip-over load: Start with an upturned cup with a ball on top of it, a second ball is palmed in the right hand. Place the empty left hand palm up on the table to the north west of the cup. Grab the cup with right hand, lift it a little so the audience can see there is nothing under it and then tip it so the ball on top rolls into the open left hand. Carry the ball up and away from the cup (**MISDIRECTION**) as you secretly push the hidden ball under the cup and place it back on the table.

Scoops: Start with an upturned cup with a ball lying in front of it. Tip the top of the cup towards you with the left hand and scoop the ball under it with the fingers of the right hand. There are three variations of this move.

1: You actually scoop the ball underneath so the audience are seeing what is actually happening.

2: You retain the ball in a **FINGER PALM**, so they think it has gone under the cup but it is actually in your right hand.

A
B
C
D
E
F
G
H
I
J
K
L
M
N
O
P
Q
R
S
T
U
V
W
X
Y
Z

3: You start with an extra ball finger-palmed in the right hand and load it into the cup along with the other ball. They think there is one ball under the cup but actually there are two.

Stack load: three balls lie in a line on the table, you have a fourth ball palmed in your right hand. Lift the cup and place it over two of the balls, simultaneously loading the palmed ball so you end up with three balls under the cup.

Pick up the third ball from the table, place it on top of the cup and then place another cup on top of it. Grab your wand, tap smartly on the cups and lift both cups—it will seem as if the third ball has passed magically through the cup. Remember that you now have one ball trapped between the cups.

Fruit load: at the end of your routine you'll be producing oranges from under your cups. These are too large to palm so instead you'll load them as follows. Your left hand will have gone into the pouch for some perfectly good reason (perhaps to place a ball in there) and it will be sitting there with an orange in it for a moment. Your audience will not see this because they will be watching what your other hand is doing (more on this later).

Your right hand will then pick up an empty, upturned cup and pass it to the left hand, dropping the rim below the edge of the pocket to ensure that the audience do not see a flash or orange. The left hand will push the orange up into the cup and start to return the cup to the table quietly while the right hand returns to the table to get on with the show. Your eyes and attention will be directed to the right during the entire move to complete the **MISDIRECTION**.

Performing a Routine

There are many variations on the **Cups and Balls** routine, the following is intended as an example only, and illustrates most of the basic principles of the trick. Once mastered you may wish to observe the routines of other performers and see if there are any extra tricks and surprises to throw in.

To perform a **Cups and Balls** routine you must have thoroughly practiced it beforehand. You need to apply a great deal of showmanship so as to drive the audience through the routine and get them used to looking where you want them to.

Preamble: Start with your props loaded in the pouch, you'll need four balls, a wand, at least three oranges and possibly a melon—depending on how you aim to finish the show. Start by handing out the cups to three members of the audience. Since this is a street show you need to spend a few minutes arranging your crowd: chalking lines on the ground or laying out a rope to form a nice front row for people to step up to is always a good idea. You may even decide to use a little **Fire and Height** in the form of a pre-show trick to attract a decent crowd.

Once you're ready ask your three cup holders to walk up one at a time and hand over the cups having checked that they are free from secret compartments.

Stand the three cups upturned on the table and grab your wand out of the pouch. Deliver a speech about how you inherited the cups from some great master and count off the cups by tapping each with the wand. Note how the audience will follow the wand with their eyes, you'll be using this for **Misdirection** later on.

Act I: Retrieve three balls from the pouch (you need to get the audience used to seeing you dive into the pouch to retrieve stuff), at the same time grab a fourth ball and keep it **Finger Palmed** in the right hand while you hold the other three in plain sight in the left.

Place a ball on top of each cup and ask the audience to watch closely.

Pick up a ball with your right hand and place it in your left hand.

Pick up a second ball and place it in the left hand, at the same time secretly placing the palmed ball in the left hand. You've now got three balls in the left hand and one left on a cup.

Pick up the last ball and pretend to put it in your pouch, but actually you **FINGER PALM** it again. Pick up the wand, smack your left hand and open it to reveal that there are three balls in there, place them back on the cups.

Some people will miss the trick, so explain that you're going to do it again. Repeat the trick quickly and beg for your first round of applause.

Act II: Place the three balls on top of the three cups and proceed to vanish all three of them as follows.

You have a ball **FINGER PALMED** in the hand right hand.

You now do a *Tip-over Load* on the first cup. Tip the ball on top into your open left hand while secretly loading the palmed ball into it.

Toss the ball in your left hand across and into your right.

Perform a **PALM RETENTION VANISH** with it, pretending to place the ball back in your left hand while actually retaining it in the right.

The right hand then picks up the wand, smacks the left hand which opens to reveal that it is empty.

Repeat the move on the other two cups.

You can, if you like, vary the vanishes a little here. For example one ball could be disposed of into your mouth. To do this you execute a **PALM RETENTION VANISH** as before, but instead of opening your hand to reveal that it is empty mime placing the ball in your mouth and then swallow.

When you have vanished all three balls you can quickly reveal that they have magically ended up under the cups again. Tip each cup back with the wand to reveal what has happened. Demand another round of applause.

Act III: You start with all three balls showing at the mouths of each of the three cups. You're about to use your Scoop Loading skills to great effect.

Start with the a cup at one end, tip it upright with your left hand and scoop into it both the ball on the table and the ball that is still palmed in your right hand.

Next lift up the middle cup, this time retain the ball on the table, so the cup ends up empty.

Finally treat the third cup as you did the first, loading it with two balls. The audience now think there is a ball under each cup, whereas there are actually two under the end cups and none under the middle one.

You now ask an audience member to select a cup. No matter what they do you are going to insist that they choose the middle cup. You can do this as irritatingly as you like but you must insist. This is a great opportunity to inject some real humour into the show. Once the cup is chosen you lift it to reveal that the ball under it has vanished. Now explain that it's actually moved to one of the end cups and lift it to prove that this is what happened.

At this stage the audience will naturally assume that there is a single ball under the third cup, but we know better: there are two under it. We have now gained what chess-players call *tempo*—we are well ahead of the audience. Let's amaze them some more.

Separate the two balls from the end cup, placing one in front of the two cups lying on their sides. Scoop the end ball under the end cup as you lift it back up. Next pretend to scoop the middle ball under the middle cup but actually retain it in a **FINGER PALM**.

Ask how many balls there are under the middle cup. When they say "one" tip the cup to reveal that it has vanished and then tip the third cup, the one you left standing.

Two balls will be revealed suggesting that the ball missing from the middle cup ball has magically found it's way there.

Move the revealed balls to the middle of the table in front of the middle cup. Put down the wand and lift the middle cup with your right hand (loading the palmed ball as you do so). Cover this move by adjusting the position of the two balls with your right hand.

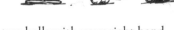

Plonk the now-loaded cup over the two balls (that makes three under the cup) and then remind the audience that there's one more ball.

Lift the end cup that's hiding it. Pick up the ball and place it on the middle cup. Now pick up the end cup and cover the ball with it.

Grab your wand and strike firmly. Lift the two cups and reveal the three balls underneath.

Your audience will be pretty impressed by now,

but it's about to get a whole lot better.

Act IV: This is the final stage of the routine, where we load oranges into the cups and reveal them to everyone's amazement.

Start by placing a ball in front of each cup, and then resting the front lips of the cups each on its ball. You should also arrange matters so as to have the fourth ball palmed in your right hand. Now, using the wand, tip the cups onto the balls. This way there can be no doubt whatsoever that there is a single ball under each cup.

Explain that you are now going to get rid of the balls, there being too many of them to keep track of. Lift the left hand cup with your left hand and pass it to your right hand (loading a ball as you do so). Now pick up the exposed ball with your left hand and replace the cup with your right.

Nicely done! Now it looks as if you have cleared a ball from under the end cup, but actually there is still one there.

Pass the held ball to your right hand and execute yet another **PALM RETENTION VANISH** (or **FRENCH DROP** if you prefer) and then pretend to drop the ball into the pouch with your left hand. Actually you end up with it palmed in the right as usual.

Now do something similar with the right hand cup: lift the right hand cup with your left hand, pass it to your right hand (loading a ball as you do). Pick up the ball on the table with your left hand, and replace the cup with your right.

Now hand the ball to your right hand and execute a vanish, so you end up with your left hand closed around an imaginary ball—which is really palmed in your right hand.

A B C D E F G H I J K L M N O P Q R S T U V W X Y Z

Pick up the wand.

There is still a ball under each cup but the audience think the end ones are empty and that you have a ball in your left hand.

Tap both end cups with the wand explaining that there are no balls under them. Put the wand down and pick up the middle cup, "—just one ball here then!" Put the cup down again (loading the ball in your right hand as you do so).

Now you lower your left hand into the pouch, as if discarding a ball, but really you grab the first piece of fruit and hold it on your hand, waiting to do the load.

Now you pick up the left hand cup with your right hand which reveals an unexpected ball.

Kick it with the base of the cup so it rolls across the table to the right (an important piece of **MISDIRECTION**).

While it rolls across the table drop the cup onto your waiting left hand in the pouch (thus loading a great big orange) and then stop the ball with your right hand. The left hand lifts the now-loaded cup from the pouch and places it on the table—and nobody sees a thing! You now have a ball under each cup and an orange under the leftmost cup.

It gets better!

Now you take a pause and tell the audience that you're going to let them into a secret. Using the ball you've just grabbed off the table you show them how a **FRENCH DROP** works and explain that every time they think a ball is over here it is actually over there and furthermore that every time you lift a cup with nothing underneath it you just cheekily slide in the ball your hiding in your hand.

> YOU: Watch this! We know there is no ball under this cup (pointing to the right cup) but is we lift it up I can make it seem like it was there all along. Now don't get confused here, what you actually do is lift the cup (which really does have a ball under it) but you make it look as if you just put it there.

Now, still holding the cup you very deliberately pick up the ball with your left hand and drop both hand and ball into the pouch, where you immediately pick up the next orange and leave your hand waiting. At the same time you lower the right hand cup to the table, loading it with the palmed ball. Then you pause for a second

> YOU: —but hang on! How come there is still a ball here.

With that you lift the right hand cup again and pass it immediately to your waiting left hand in the pouch (loading another orange). Your right hand returns and picks up the ball that shouldn't be there and holds it up for all to see, while your left hand places the orange-loaded cup back on the table.

Now you have an orange under each end cup and two balls under the middle cup. You're also holding a ball in your right hand. Pretend to place it in your left hand and drop your hand into the pouch and grab the ball you dropped in there a moment before. Bring it out and show it to the audience as you pick up the wand in your right hand.

> YOU: So if I have one ball here, how many balls are here?

Tap the middle cup a couple of times. Anyone who is following closely will say one. But you lift the cup to reveal that there are two. Then you load the cup with the third ball and replace it.

At the same time your left hand gets the third orange into position.

> YOU: We'll try again, how many balls here?

The answer is obviously two, but you lift the cup to reveal three.

Using the surprise as cover, you pass the cup (with your right hand) to your waiting left hand in the pouch, then you pick up the three balls and hold them high as your left hand places the orange-loaded cup in the middle of the table.

> YOU: So if I get rid of all three balls how many will there be under the middle cup?

You pass the three balls to your left hand and lower them into the pouch readying your left hand with the final orange.

> YOU: How many?

The right guess is none, but as you lift the cup the orange will be revealed and the crowd will pretty much go wild. Using this as further cover you transfer the cup to your left hand in the pouch, then pick up the orange. Now place the newly loaded cup in the middle and place the orange on top of it.

> YOU: And how many balls under this cup?

You tap the right hand cup then reveal the second orange.

> YOU: And this one?

You tape the left hand cup and reveal the third one.

> YOU: And of course, this one!

You lift the centre cup to reveal the fourth orange.

And that, dear ladies and gents, is how we do that!

CURL

OBJECT MANIPULATION

A **CURL** is a *body move* that is much-used by jugglers and object manipulators. The classic **CURL** is executed with a **BALL SPINNING** balanced on an index finger—it is an extremely difficult move requiring a great deal of stretch in the arm of the performer.

☆ Here's what you have to do: spin a ball finger and then move it backwards, *under* your arm and then all the way around so it ends up back where it started. If you do this in your right hand the ball will travel in an anti-clockwise circle˙.

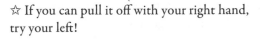

It's not easy because you have to keep your finger vertical throughout the move.

☆ If you can pull it off with your right hand, try your left!

☆ If you can do both try spinning a ball of *both* index fingers and doing a **CURL** on both sides. You'll find it almost impossible to do both at the same time so do one and then the other, letting the moves overlap a little for dramatic effect.

☆ It's possible, though rarely seen, to do *reverse* **CURLS** which go the *other way*.

CURLS can also be done with plates (see **PLATE JUGGLING**) or with trays or even with glasses full of water.

˙ Interestingly, for complex reasons of geometry and anatomy, a Curled object will turn twice before returning to the starting position. That's 720 degrees (even though it seems like a mere 360)—perhaps that's why it looks so cool?

A B C D E F G H I J K L M N O P Q R S T U V W X Y Z

CUSTARD PIES

SLAPSTICK / KITCHEN TRICKS / MARTIAL ARTS

The **SLAPSTICK** artist's **CUSTARD PIE** is never made from *custard*.

You can buy commercially made cans of custard-pie foam from joke shops but the material is a little too light and fluffy for true slapstick work. That shop-made stuff is for *amateurs*.

True professionals make their own foam. It is mixed from shaving sticks; the traditional old-fashioned shaving soap which can be bought from posh shops selling gentlemen's requisites.

The sticks are first grated, as one would a carrot, and then whisked with a small amount of water using a kitchen whisk.

This is a labour-intensive process but the reward is luscious pantomime-grade foam.

Once the foam has been prepared it is usually piled onto paper plates which are set out on a *pie-table*. Spare foam is piled into large bowls on the table which are used to re-load plates as the fight proceeds.

For the more elaborate **CUSTARD PIE** moves you will need two additional bowls containing foam that has been coloured red and blue with food colouring. You'll also need a bowler hat that is a size or two too big. Cut a hole about an inch in diameter in the crown.

For safety reasons, and also to ensure a good effect, these techniques need to be practiced beforehand. It is important that the victims eyes are *shut* at the moment of impact and that they have had time to hold their breath before the blow strikes.

☆ For a full-frontal pie-in-da-face the plate should be slightly *folded* so that the impact does break the victim's nose and the plate should be tilted back at slight angle so that it strikes the chin first. This ensures a nice dramatic splatting effect forcing foam to splash upwards and to the sides.

☆ Alternatively the plate can be *thrown* at the face, though typically at very short range, to ensure it hits the face flat. The throwing gesture should be large and theatrical—which helps to create the illusion of a long trajectory, even though the pie will actually only fly a couple of feet at most.

☆ Two pies can be simultaneously applied to each side of the face. Take care to make contact at neck level first (again to ensure that the foam splatters upwards) and leave them stuck to the face with the two plates meeting over the nose so they look a little like enormous horse-blinkers.

☆ In all cases the plates should be removed by the *victim* in an exaggerated fashion. A single plate is removed with *both* hands. It is placed slowly onto the pie-table. The hands then return to the face and scrape eye-holes through the foam.

The plate can then be re-loaded, slowly and deliberately with absurd amounts of fresh foam before being revenge-slapped into the attacker's face.

☆ The hat moves are extremely funny. Load a hat to the brim with foam and place it on the victim's head. Now firmly pull it down below the ears. A huge fountain of foam will erupt from the hole in the crown.

☆ The victim removes the hat and then reloads it: first with red foam (about a third full) then white foam (another third) and finally with blue foam. The hat is placed on the previous attacker's head and pulled down, producing a patriotically colour-changing fountain!

A
B
C
D
E
F
G
H
I
J
K
L
M
N
O
P
Q
R
S
T
U
V
W
X
Y
Z

Slapstick **CUSTARD PIE** fights typically proceed at a very slow pace, with the protagonists taking it in turn to attack each other—much like one of *John Wayne's* cowboy fist fights in which two big boys take it in turns to ply each other with haymakers pausing, between blows, to examine themselves for chin-damage with wry smiles.

☆ A well-known trick that can be played on a sleeping victim is that of liberally coating their sleeping hand with foam (perhaps whipped cream from the picnic) and then tickling their lip with a blade of grass. The involuntary response is for them to reach up, half asleep and rub their lip with their hand. Hey presto! Self-administered **CUSTARD PIE**!

The two greatest **CUSTARD PIE** fights ever seen on the big screen are to be found in the films *Bugsy Malone* and *The Great Race*.

DARTS

GAMESMANSHIP

The game of **DARTS** is played on a circular board divided into twenty slices, each of which scores between 1 and 20. There is an outer ring that *doubles* the score in that slice and an inner ring that *triples* it. In the centre of the target is the *bull* which scores 25, or 50 if you hit its innermost part which counts as a *double*.

The most popular game of **DARTS** is 501 where two players take it in turns, with three darts each, to score their way *down* from 501 to zero, with the condition that the last throw they make must be a *double*. Thus if you have a remaining score of 22, you can go out by scoring a double 11. If a throw ever takes your score below 2 you lose the entire score for that turn.

The game is great for exercising mental arithmetic skills, as it is easier to hit the doubles that are vertically oriented (like 11 and 6) hence when climbing down through the scores you'll see skilled players moving around the board in intoxicatingly clever ways. You need to know, for example, that the best *out* from a score of 111 is treble-19, single-14, double-20. Actually you'd never say "double twenty" instead you'd say "double top".

Here is a list of *outs* for scores below 170.

170: Triple-top, Triple-top, Double-Bull
169: No way out
168: No way out
167: Triple-top, Triple-19, Double-Bull
166: No way out
165: No way out
164: Triple-top, Triple-18, Double-Bull
163: No way out
162: No way out
161: Triple-top, Triple-17, Double-Bull
160: Triple-top, Triple-top, Double-top
159: No way out
158: Triple-top, Triple-top, Double-19
157: Triple-top, Triple-19, Double-top
156: Triple-top, Triple-top, Double-18
155: Triple-top, Triple-19, Double-19
154: Triple-top, Triple-18, Double-top
153: Triple-top, Triple-19, Double-18
152: Triple-top, Triple-top, Double-16
151: Triple-top, Triple-17, Double-top
150: Triple-top, Triple-18, Double-18
149: Triple-top, Triple-19, Double-16
148: Triple-top, Triple-top, Double-14
147: Triple-top, Triple-17, Double-18
146: Triple-top, Triple-18, Double-16
145: Triple-top, Triple-19, Double-14
144: Triple-top, Triple-top, Double-12
143: Triple-19, Triple-18, Double-16
142: Triple-top, Triple-14, Double-top
141: Triple-top, Triple-19, Double-12
140: Triple-top, Triple-19, Double-10
139: Triple-19, Triple-14, Double-top
138: Triple-top, Triple-18, Double-12
137: Triple-top, Triple-19, Double-10
136: Triple-top, Triple-top, Double-8
135: Triple-top, Triple-17, Double-12
134: Triple-top, Triple-14, Double-16
133: Triple-top, Triple-19, Double-8
132: Triple-top, Triple-16, Double-12
131: Triple-top, Triple-13, Double-16
130: Triple-top, Triple-18, Double-8
129: Triple-19, Triple-16, Double-12
128: Triple-18, Triple-14, Double-16
127: Triple-top, Triple-17, Double-8
126: Triple-top, Triple-15, Double-12
125: Triple-18, Triple-13, Double-16
124: Triple-top, Triple-16, Double-8
123: Triple-19, Triple-14, Double-12
122: Triple-18, Triple-18, Double-7
121: Triple-top, Triple-11, Double-14

120: Triple-top, Single-top, Double-top
119: Triple-19, Triple-12, Double-13
118: Triple-top, Single-18, Double-top
117: Triple-top, Single-17, Double-top
116: Triple-top, Single-16, Double-top
115: Triple-19, Single-18, Double-top
114: Triple-top, Single-14, Double-top
113: Triple-19, Single-16, Double-top
112: Triple-top, Triple-12, Double-8
111: Triple-19, Single-14, Double-top
110: Triple-top, Single-10, Double-top
109: Triple-top, Single-9, Double-top
108: Triple-19, Single-19, Double-16
107: Triple-top, Single-15, Double-16
106: Triple-top, Single-6, Double-top
105: Triple-19, Single-8, Double-top
104: Triple-top, Triple-12, Double-4
103: Triple-17, Single-12, Double-top
102: Triple-top, Single-10, Double-16
101: Triple-17, Single-10, Double-top
100: Triple-top, Double-top
99: Triple-19, Single-10, Double-16
98: Triple-top, Double-19
97: Triple-19, Double-top
96: Triple-top, Double-18
95: Triple-19, Double-19
94: Triple-18, Double-top
93: Triple-19, Double-18
92: Triple-top, Double-16
91: Triple-17, Double-top
91: Triple-17, Double-top
89: Triple-19, Double-16
88: Triple-16, Double-top
87: Triple-17, Double-18
86: Triple-18, Double-16
85: Triple-15, Double-top
84: Triple-top, Double-12
83: Triple-17, Double-16
82: Triple-14, Double-top
81: Triple-19, Double-12
80: Triple-top, Double-10
79: Triple-13, Double-top
78: Triple-18, Double-12
77: Triple-15, Double-16
76: Triple-top, Double-8
75: Triple-17, Double-12
74: Triple-14, Double-16
73: Triple-19, Double-8
72: Triple-16, Double-12
71: Triple-13, Double-16

70: Triple-18, Double-8
69: Triple-19, Double-6
68: Triple-top, Double-4
67: Triple-17, Double-8
66: Triple-14, Double-12
65: Triple-19, Double-4
64: Triple-16, Double-8
63: Triple-13, Double-12
62: Triple-10, Double-16
61: Triple-15, Double-8
60: Single-top, Double-top
59: Single-19, Double-top
58: Single-18, Double-top
57: Single-17, Double-top
56: Triple-16, Double-4
55: Single-15, Double-top
54: Single-14, Double-top
53: Single-12, Double-top
52: Single-12, Double-top
51: Single-11, Double-top
50: Single-10, Double-top
49: Single-9, Double-top
48: Single-8, Double-top
47: Single-15, Double-16
46: Single-14, Double-16
45: Single-13, Double-16
44: Single-12, Double-16
43: Single-11, Double-16
42: Single-10, Double-16
41: Single-9, Double-16
39: Single-7, Double-16
37: Single-5, Double-16
35: Single-3, Double-16
33: Single-1, Double-16
31: Single-7, Double-12
29: Single-13, Double-8
27: Single-11, Double-8
25: Single-9, Double-8
23: Single-7, Double-8
21: Single-5, Double-8
19: Single-3, Double-8
17: Single-13, Double-2
15: Single-7, Double-4
13: Single-5, Double-4
11: Single-3, Double-4
9: Single-1, Double-4
7: Single-3, Double-2
5: Single-1, Double-2
3: Single-1, Double-1
2: Double-1

On the subject of intoxication and skill: the game of **Darts** requires a combination of terrific hand-eye coordination and mental agility, yet the champions of this sport are known to be overweight, unfit, and they play *while they are drunk*!

☆ If you want to win a tenner playing darts here's how:

Explain to your victim that you are really rather good at the game and to give them a fair chance you'll let them score *double* for every throw they make. Remember that you should **Always Get The Money Laid on the Table**, especially when you're conning your **Mark**.

It will take them a while to realise that, because 501 is an odd number, they can't possibly go out.

Days of the Month
MNEMONIC

If you don't already know this, learn it now. You'll be glad you did—for the rest of your life!

> *Thirty days hath September,*
> *April, June and November.*
> *All the rest have thirty one*
> *Excepting February alone,*
> *Which has twenty eight days clear,*
> *And twenty nine in each leap year.*

Defeating a Padlock
ESCAPOLOGY

Defeating a Padlock means smashing the thing open—it's a legal phrase used by bailiffs to explain how they have gained entry to your premises while skirting around the complications of criminal damage.

A
B
C
D
E
F
G
H
I
J
K
L
M
N
O
P
Q
R
S
T
U
V
W
X
Y
Z

☆ A padlock with a brass body is horribly easy to open, and once you know just how easy it is, you'll never buy one again. All you need is a small hammer (bailiffs almost always carry one).

Jam the padlock against the staple (if it is fitted to a hasp and staple) or twist it into its chain (if it is attached to a chain). You need to get it jammed hard against something heavy and immovable.

Now strike the top of the lock downwards nice and hard, you need to hit the lock right next to the U-shaped hardened steel part *on the side that opens.* Obviously it's hard to tell which side this is, but that's no problem— just hit one side and if it doesn't work, hit the other.

When it opens you'll find that the hardened steel U has bitten off the locking piece inside the padlock and the thing will just fly open.

The bailiffs know this, the thieves know this—and now you do too.

DEVIL STICK

JUGGLING

The **DEVIL STICK** is a juggling prop consisting of a stick about two and a half to three feet long. It is usually tapered in such a way that the middle is somewhat thinner than the ends˙.

A **DEVIL STICK** is controlled using two hand-sticks. Traditionally these sticks were plain wood but lately, as juggling has become more of a hi-tech

---

˙ It is best (when turning a Devil Stick on a lathe) to achieve this taper by means of a smooth and shallow curve rather than by means of a shallow V indentation. If you step on a stick made in the second manner it will certainly snap at the centre, whereas the curved stick will not.

activity, they are often sleeved with silicone rubber tubing. This gives incredible grip and is generally preferred by beginners (who need all the help they can get).

Another useful beginner's tip is to work with a **FLOWER STICK: A DEVIL STICK** with air-brakes! It flies considerably slower than the real thing.

The basic technique of devil sticking is to keep the thing aloft by tapping it alternately with one hand-stick and then the other.

☆ Start with the **DEVIL STICK** (or **FLOWER STICK**) resting on the ground in front of you, place one hand-stick under the **DEVIL STICK** about halfway between the end and the centre. Now flip the thing over so that it turns and lands on the other hand stick. It will tend to roll off to the front or back at first but you'll settle down pretty quickly.

Note that the **DEVIL STICK** should make contact with the hand-stick when it is lying horizontally (or close to the horizontal) in the air. The most common beginner's mistake is to try and make contact while the thing is nearly vertical. This doesn't work too well and you'll find that it slips off the hand-sticks.

☆ Now if you start to flip it one way and the other and *keep going* you will find that the thing becomes airborne more or less of its own accord. Pretty soon you'll be able to raise it right up off the ground and keep it going!

A
B
C
D
E
F
G
H
I
J
K
L
M
N
O
P
Q
R
S
T
U
V
W
X
Y
Z

☆ Note that the **DEVIL STICK** is only making half-spins as you juggle it. This leads us on to our first trick— the *full-spin*. All you do is give it an extra whack and then catch the *second* end to approach your hand-stick.

Got it? On Both sides?

Continuously? Good.

☆ You can move on to *One and a Half Spins* or even *Double Spins* as you get more confident.

OK, now for some tricky stuff: *One-Handed Devil Sticking!*

☆ Get the **DEVIL STICK** going and then try keeping it up with just one hand stick. If you are juggling on half-spins you'll need to move your hand very quickly and it will look as if you are doing some delicate sword-fighting.

☆ Some find it easier to use full spins when working one-handed.

☆ Next I'd like you to get your **DEVIL STICK** going and then go into a three club **CASCADE** with the **DEVIL STICK** and the two hand sticks, before dropping back into regular devil-sticking. That should keep you busy for a little while!

☆ For the last part of your basic training I'd like you to learn a very useful little move.

In regular devil-sticking the hand stick strikes the **DEVIL STICK** *above* the centre point at A (*opposite*).

Now just try hitting it *below* instead, at the point B.

This will carry the stick around an extra half-turn before you hit it again in the normal way *with the same hand*. This makes a fine pattern in its own right as you juggle:

...left-left right-right...

It also forms the basis of the trick-everyone-wants-to-get, which is, of course, the *Propellor*.

☆ In the *Propellor* you hit the Devil Stick at point B and let it make a full turn and then hit it at B again. Now just just keep going!

The Devil Stick turns improbably like a propellor under control from just one stick. It's a bit of a knack, but not as hard as you think.

☆ The skills acquired when learning to Devil Stick can be applied to a number or real-world props—like umbrellas and walking sticks. Juggle these objects with the heavy end down—it's a lot easier that way.

DIABOLO, A BLUFFER'S GUIDE

JUGGLING

The name **DIABOLO** derives from the Greek, *"dia bolo"*, where *dia* means "across" and *bolo* means "throw". Naturally enough, this is what a juggler does with a **DIABOLO** (which is a sort of free **YO-YO**, or spinning top). Some dictionaries claim that the word derives:

> ORIGIN early 20th cent.: from Italian, from ecclesiastical Latin *diabolus* 'devil' ; the game was formerly called devil on two sticks.

This truth is more interesting. The word *devil* is actually a corruption of **DIABOLO,** hence *diabolical* means "devil-like" while the "game with two sticks" is, of course, the **DEVIL STICK**. It's easy to see how the two activities might be confused, since both involve manipulating a juggler's prop by means of hand-sticks.

For an explanation of just why this type of juggling became confused with a name for Satan we can take advice from one *Radical Cheney* who

A
B
C
D
E
F
G
H
I
J
K
L
M
N
O
P
Q
R
S
T
U
V
W
X
Y
Z

mentions the topic in his obscure and rambling masterpiece, *The True Nature of Things*.

> In the early days of the Christian Church it was the custom of the Evangelists to make their way to the busier thoroughfares and squares of the cities around the Mediterranean to extoll the virtues of their creed by way of comparing the pleasures of Heaven and the horrors of Hell so to swell the numbers of the faithful. Thus they found themselves in contest with the longer-established street entertainers such as the jugglers and magicians who worked the crowds by flaunting or concealing their hard-learned skills according to their respective crafts.

> Seeking to ridicule their opponents the Evangelists would point out their opponents and loudly decry them by claiming that their unnatural talents must have been won somehow by means of bargaining with the dark force of Satan, an angel of the Lord who had somewhat fallen from grace. And so it was that the name **DIABOLO** and its later corruption DEVIL came to be synonymous with SATAN.

To this day some of the more extreme sects of Christianity hold that jugglers are in league with the Devil, not realising the reason for the derivation.

So much for the history.

DIABOLO is an impressively rich art form, and those who take to it, and then invest plenty of time and trouble in their practice can soon gain dizzying skills.

The purpose of *Every Trick In The Book* however, is to give you just sufficient knowledge and ability to pull off a short, but impressive display.

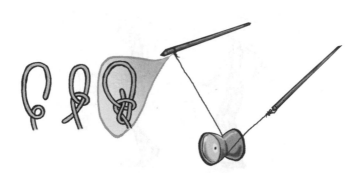

To begin you will need a **DIABOLO** and two handsticks. The string is fixed to each handstick with a **BOWLINE**, lesser knots being unlikely to survive the ravages of earnest work.

The **DIABOLO** is juggled either right-handed or left-handed; most commonly right-handed, in which case the **DIABOLO** will turn anti-clockwise as viewed by the performer.

A right-handed performer lays the diabolo over the string on the ground in front of them, and rolls it to the left to impart a little spin before lifting it from the ground. The gyroscopic action will keep it balanced for as long as it continues to spin. It will however immediately begin to slow down and the first secret of **DIABOLO** is to keep the machine running.

This is done by pulling up on the right stick while repeatedly lifting the diabolo. With a little practice the **DIABOLO** can be made to spin very fast indeed.

It will however, tend to tilt either forward of backward in the manner of a slowly toppling spinning top and so the next trick is to learn how to correct this tilt.

A
B
C
D
E
F
G
H
I
J
K
L
M
N
O
P
Q
R
S
T
U
V
W
X
Y
Z

A
B
C
D
E
F
G
H
I
J
K
L
M
N
O
P
Q
R
S
T
U
V
W
X
Y
Z

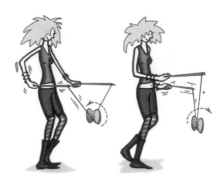

To tip the **DIABOLO** forward (in order to correct the opposite movement) the right handstick is moved forwards, and conversely, to tip the **DIABOLO** backwards the right hand is moved backwards.

If you are juggling a **DIABOLO** either-handed you can remember this easily by noting that it is the *driving* handstick that is moved forwards and backwards to produce forward and backward tilt.

Once spinning, the axis of the **DIABOLO** will point stubbornly in one direction, which may not always be in the usually-desired direction of the audience. So to save the embarrassment or working your show at an unnatural angle to your onlookers you need to learn how to turn the **DIABOLO** to the right or left.

The trick is to move the driving stick down until you can touch the front of back edge of the **DIABOLO** with it, in the manner of a wood-turner applying a chisel to the work. You can touch the stick either on the far cup, which will turn the **DIABOLO** *towards* the

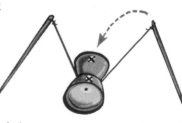

driving hand, or you can touch the stick on the near cup, which will turn the **DIABOLO** *away* from the driving hand.

Thus a right-handed juggler will touch the far cup to turn right, and the near cup to turn left.

With these skills mastered we can move onto some basic tricks, and without doubt the *most* satisfying is the *High Toss*. You will be amazed just how high a **DIABOLO** can be thrown—and so will your audience.

Start by getting some seriously fast spin going and then launch your diabolo high into the air by pulling your hands apart while lunging upward. The **DIABOLO** will take off like a rocket.

Now you need to catch it! Beginners often make the mistake of trying to catch the **DIABOLO** on the centre of the string, when it is actually a lot easier if you catch it on the string *right next to the driving stick*. Point the stick at the falling **DIABOLO** and follow it down for a perfect catch.

Next you can try the *Cat's Cradle* which is just one example of a string-weaving trick.

With the **DIABOLO** spinning fast you take the driving stick, wrap it around the front of the lazy-stick, and then complete the simple knot by taking it around the stick and under the string. You end up with the **DIABOLO** sat on the bottom run of a sort of string ladder.

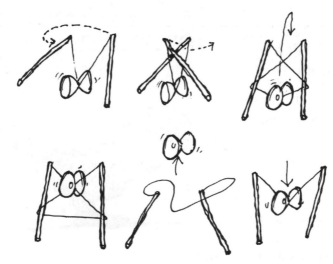

A B C D E F G H I J K L M N O P Q R S T U V W X Y Z

A
B
C
D
E
F
G
H
I
J
K
L
M
N
O
P
Q
R
S
T
U
V
W
X
Y
Z

Now toss the **Diabolo** up a little way and catch it on the crossing point of the string (pause for applause).

Finally toss the **Diabolo** high and pull the sticks apart—the *Cat's Cradle* vanishes in a puff of slip-knot and you catch the **Diabolo** on the string (more applause).

For our last trick in this short introduction we'll do the *Elevator* (also known as *Climb the String*) which is a sweet trick by virtue of the way it looks so impossible to a naive audience.

Start with tons of spin, and then wrap the driving stick over and around the **Diabolo**, while lifting the lazy-stick high so that the string is vertical. You'll find that by tightening the string you have fashioned a sort of clutch, and the **Diabolo** will climb the string! Slacking off the tension will cause the **Diabolo** to fall again.

If you started with enough spin-energy in the **Diabolo** you will be able to make it climb and descend several times.

Finish your routine with a high throw and **Pirouette**.

Dinosaur Footprints

SILLINESS

You can leave **Dinosaur Footprints** in the snow.

Locate an unsullied expanse of virgin snow and proceed as follows:

1: Take a step and make a footprint with your right foot This will be the middle toe of the first **Dinosaur Footprint**.

2: With your left foot, make a second toe (you'll need to lift the heel of your right foot to do this, which makes a nice little dance step).

3: With your right foot make a third toe again lifting the heel of your other foot as you do so— we're getting kinda funky now!

4: With your left toe, make the impression of the fearsome rear talon of the creature's foot and then...

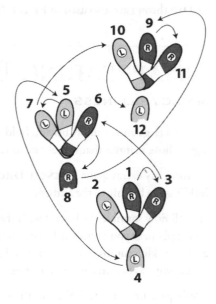

5, 6, 7, 8: Step forwards with your left foot to start the next footprint, which is a mirror image of the first one.

☆ Now just keep going and you'll make great big dinosaur tracks in the snow. It's a kind of dance and you can go really fast after a little practice.

See also **ANGELS IN THE SNOW**.

DIP

JUGGLING

A **DIP** throw is a type of throw made with a juggling club which is thrown sideways, across the front of the body, using a wrist action much like that of opening a door by a handle.

☆ Hold a club in your right hand so the body points to the left, your fingers curled around the handle as if holding a handrail. Now let the club drop under its own weight and then throw it up

again, using the spring of the tendons in your wrist to power it. The club will spin in the same plane as when making **BEHIND THE BACK** throws.

☆ **DIP** throws are also used in **PLATE JUGGLING** and *Ring Juggling.*

DISAPPEARING BISCUIT TRICK

MAGIC / SILLINESS

☆ Get a large and crumbly biscuit, hold it in your left hand and announce in a grandiose manner that it is about to vanish *before their very eyes!*

Perform an extravagant **FRENCH DROP** and present the fist that is *not* holding the biscuit to the audience.

"I shall now sprinkle the biscuit with the *Magic Powder!"* you explain, as you crush the biscuit in the other hand and sprinkle crumbs over the empty hand. This can take a while as biscuits make a lot of, er, *magic crumbs.*

"Perhaps a little more!" You continue in this ludicrous fashion until there are no crumbs left at which point you open you hand and proudly announce "And the biscuit has disappeared!"

DISGUSTING NAPPY TRICK

SILLINESS

Get a disposable nappy (a clean one), a Bourbon biscuit and a pot of coffee. Lay the biscuit in the middle of the nappy and soak it with coffee. When the biscuit gets soggy fold the nappy around it and give it a squeeze. The result is horribly realistic. You're now ready to make somebody throw up!

```
YOU: Look what I found in the kitchen!

Disgusting isn't it!'
```

Pick a small piece of the brown goo off and taste it.

```
'Mind you, it doesn't taste too bad!'
```

Have a sick-bucket ready.

DIVING INTO A GLASS OF WATER

SHOWMANSHIP

This really can be done, but you'll need plenty of charisma. I have seen this trick pulled off outdoors and in the round in front of several hundred people and *nobody* could work out how it was done.

☆ HERE'S *The* TRICK: You are going to do a very very big build-up and when you finally jump off your stepladder and tip the glass of water over your head to make you hair all wet (so it looks as if you might have actually *done* it) absolutely *everybody* in the audience is going to be looking the other way. Your job is to make sure that they do exactly that.

How? Well a stunt like this takes a long time to prepare for. You'll need a stepladder, some goggles, a nose-clip, a towel, at least five child volunteers to pass all this stuff up to you. You'll need some people to fill the glass for you and put it on the right spot. You'll need more people to watch the show— and you can get them in by making your crowd give you huge rounds of applause for no reason at all. In short, you are going to make a complete street-show out of it. Every non-musical busker knows that the best shows contain absolutely no skills whatsoever and a *lot* of audience participation.

As you build the show you must train your audience to look at what you want them to look at. You can, for example, make a big show of picking a big fella from the back of the audience and haranguing him into coming into the middle to do some close-up personal security for you. Get the audience to look at him by commenting on his hat/shirt or fat tummy— anything, just make sure they look.

Then pick on someone and make out that you have fallen in love with them and so on and so forth. Keep pointing out stuff until you're quite sure that the audience are ready for the big finale.

Explain that everybody is going to count down from ten and then give a huge cheer as you dive into the glass of water. Get them to practice it. Interrupt the practice and complain that some people weren't counting right and get them to do it again. Interrupt the countdown again and pick on one person in particular and remonstrate them for not doing it right. By now your crowd will be completely trained to expect interruptions. Let them do one full countdown and a huge cheer and congratulate them on finally getting it right.

Now it's for real and the countdown starts. Just as they hit "two" you shout out "I didn't know they had *elephants* here!" and point into the distance. They'll all turn but the momentum of the countdown will carry it on.

Jump off the stepladder, pour the water over your head, raise your arms in the air and cheer yourself loudly—they'll all turn back around and start cheering too. Everybody will think they were the *only* one to miss it.

But they'd be wrong of course—*everybody* missed it!

DIVISIBILITY TESTS

MATHEMATICS

Albert Einstein remarked, "Do not worry about your difficulties in mathematics. I can assure you that mine are still greater".

Here then, are a set of tricks that might make maths a little easier for you. These tricks focus on the question: "Does *a* go into *b*?".

Everybody knows that any number ending in a 0 is divisible by 10 and that numbers ending with even numbers are divisible by 2, but we can do a lot better than that! Here are some **DIVISIBILITY TESTS** for your edification.

☆ Divisibility by 3: add up all the digits of your number and if the answer is divisible by 3 so is the original number. If you are starting out with a really big number you can repeat the process as many times as you like.

So, for example:

> The digits of the number 678 add up to 21 which, in turn adds up to 3 so 678 is divisible by 3.

☆ Divisibility by 4: if the last two digits of the number are divisible by 4 then so is the original number.

☆ Divisibility by 5: this is an easy one, if the last digit is 5 or 0 then the number is divisible by 5.

☆ Divisibility by 6: use the divisibility test for 3 *and* the divisibility test for 2. So if the last digit is even *and* all the digits add up to a number divisible by 3 then the number is divisible by 6.

☆ Divisibility by 7: remove the last digit, double it and subtract it from the truncated number. If the result is divisible by 7 then so was the original number. As with the test for 3 you can repeat this operation as many times as you like.

> $791 \rightarrow 79 - 2 = 77$ which is clearly divisible by 7.

A
B
C
D
E
F
G
H
I
J
K
L
M
N
O
P
Q
R
S
T
U
V
W
X
Y
Z

☆ Divisibility by 8: if the last three digits of the number form a number that is divisible by 8, then the original number is also divisible by 8. Of course the last three digits could be anything from 0 to 999 and I'll bet you don't know your eight times table that well, so sometimes you need to take the three digit number and divide it by two a couple of times if the result is an even number we know that it was divisible by 8.

> 44904 → 904 is this divisible by 8? Who knows?
> So divide by 2 twice: 904 / 2 = 452 → 452 / 2 = 226 which is still even.
> So yes, 44904 is divisible by 8.

☆ Divisibility by 9: if the sum of the digits is divisible by 9 then so was the original number. Repeat as often as you need to.

☆ Divisibility by 10: If the number ends in 0 it is divisible by 10.

☆ Divisibility by 11: subtract the last digit from the rest of the number, if the result is divisible by 11 then so was the original number. Again you may repeat for as many steps as are required.

> 51458 → 5145 - 8 = 5137 → 513 - 7 = 506 → 50 - 6 = 44!

☆ Divisibility by 12: test for divisibility by 3 *and* divisibility by 4. If the number passes both tests then it is divisible by 12.

☆ Divisibility by 13: Take the last digit, multiply it by 4 and add it to the rest of the number, once again you may repeat as many times as you like and if the final result is divisible by 13 then so was the number you started out with.

> 31902 → 3190 + 8 = 3198 → 319 + 32 = 351 → 35 + 4 = 39!

I could go on—oh all right then...

☆ Divisibility by 14: Use the tests for 2 and 7.

☆ Divisibility by 15: Use the tests for 5 and 3.

☆ Divisibility by 16: If the last *four* digits are divisible by 16 so was the original number. Proceed much as for 8.

☆ Divisibility by 17: Subtract 5 times the last digit from the rest of the number, repeat as many times as necessary and if the number you end up with is divisible by 17 you're in business.

☆ Divisibility by 18: Combine the tests for divisibility by 2 and 9.

☆ Divisibility by 19: Double the last digit and add to the rest of the number. Rinse and repeat.

I will actually stop here.

DODECAHEDRON

GEOMETRY

A **DODECAHEDRON** is one of the five **PLATONIC SOLIDS**. It has twenty vertices, thirty edges and twelve faces, each of which is a regular pentagon.

☆ The **DODECAHEDRON** is the *dual* of the **ICOSAHEDRON**: if you draw a point in the centre of each face of the **DODECAHEDRON** and connect them all together you will have constructed an **ICOSAHEDRON**. Repeat the process and you'll get back to a **DODECAHEDRON**.

☆ The **DODECAHEDRON** is sometimes used as a starting point for designing a **GEODESIC DOME**.

First the faces are *striated,* or turned into five-sided pyramids and then the facets of the shape and further subdivided into a triangular mesh.

☆ The coordinates of a **DODECAHEDRON** can be calculated from first principles very easily using some clever trickery involving the **GOLDEN SECTION**. You start by creating an imaginary cube with a side length of two units, and then add three rectangles each of which has the dimensions:

A
B
C
D
E
F
G
H
I
J
K
L
M
N
O
P
Q
R
S
T
U
V
W
X
Y
Z

Long side: Φ (*Phi*)
Short side: φ (*Phee*)

Which is 1.61803398875 by 0.61803398875 in real money.

These three rectangles are thrust through the origin of the cube in three directions and the resulting twenty corner points precisely locate the vertices of a regular **DODECAHEDRON**. It's quite a surprise to find that a cube fits so nicely into this polyhedron!

The **ICOSAHEDRON** can be constructed by a similar method.

DRAGONFLIES

ANIMALS

These beautiful creatures are the adult form of a very aggressive larva that lives in ponds and savagely kills and eats anything it can find, including (and especially) poor little tadpoles[*].

When the larvae get bored with slaughtering small creatures at the bottom of the pond they climb out and transform into iridescent four-winged miracles. From now on they are pretty much only interested in sex.

The males are aggressive helicopter-like animals and very territorial. They like to take command of interesting vantage points on the bank of their river or pond from where they can keep an eye out for other males to chase off.

☆ HERE'S *The* TRICK: *You* can be one of those interesting places!

---

[*] Actually, tadpoles are also bitey vicious predators who feed in a sharklike manner on smaller prey...

☆ Sit and watch as they fly up and down looking for females to have sex with. Be amazed at the way they couple together and fly in tandem during the sex act itself.

☆ Now hold the back of your hand out and make like a helipad. Pretty soon a male will come along (it may hover in your face and try staring you out for a while) but it will then, gently and deliberately, land on your hand!

Honestly! This really works!

DRIVING A CAR OFF A CLIFF

STUNTS / SPECIAL EFFECTS

You are making a home movie and, as the director, you think the film (which is mostly about your Uncle and Auntie's golden wedding anniversary) might benefit from an action sequence. So you scout out a suitable cliff location and you obtain a cheap car to drive off it.

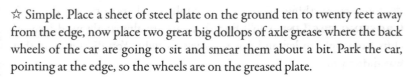

But how do you actually get the car to fly off the cliff without anyone getting hurt?

☆ Simple. Place a sheet of steel plate on the ground ten to twenty feet away from the edge, now place two great big dollops of axle grease where the back wheels of the car are going to sit and smear them about a bit. Park the car, pointing at the edge, so the wheels are on the greased plate.

A
B
C
D
E
F
G
H
I
J
K
L
M
N
O
P
Q
R
S
T
U
V
W
X
Y
Z

The car needs to have a very secure hook mounted on the back, if it has a towing hitch—great! If not you'll have to improvise something. You now tie a rope to a tree (or a secure stake in the ground) and run that over the hook and back to the anchor point where you'll tie it off with a slip knot.

Finally, make up two dummies to represent your relatives, place them in the passenger seat, one sitting on the other's lap.

☆ We're ready. Get all four camera's rolling (you need a lot of cameras because we are only doing this *once*). Your stunt person then gets in the car and starts the engine and (carefully) puts the thing into second gear and lifts the clutch. The wheels will start to spin like crazy, but the car will not move. At least not yet—you've got a good half minute before the grease burns away.

The stunt person then climbs out, moving one of the dummies into the driving seat and swiftly using **GAFFER TAPE** to fix their hands to the steering wheel. As they leave the vehicle they place a stone onto the accelerator and close the door. The car's engine is now roaring and the tail end is gyrating from side to side like a dancer on ecstasy.

Glad to be alive, the stunt person yells "SET!" and gets out of shot.

You yell "ACTION" and the slip knot is released.

Slowly at first, the car starts to move forwards, suddenly picking up speed, and then it rushes headlong towards the edge before flying off just like in the *real* movies.

It flies over the edge, pitches down (revealing just how unrealistic those dummies were) and smashes into the ground, with luck turning over a couple of times before coming to rest.

It absolutely will *not* burst into flames because you forgot to set the pyros.

Shout "CUT!" and then find out how many of your camera people forgot to remove their lens caps.

☆ One more thing. For curious Hollywood reasons to do with **CROSSING THE LINE**, you'll find that cars are almost always driven off cliffs from right to left and not from left to right. You did set it up that way didn't you?

DRINKING BRANDY THROUGH CHOCOLATE FINGERS

TECHNICAL WIZARDY

☆ Get some chocolate fingers, break off each end and use them as straws for drinking brandy.

Oh yeah!

DROPPING A MATCHBOX ONTO ITS END

BAR BET / MATCH TRICKS

☆ Bet you can't drop a matchbox so that it lands standing on its end!

☆ **HERE'S** *The* **TRICK:** Open the box a little and drop it vertically. The closing of the box as it hits the tabletop will absorb the shock of landing and it will remain standing upright instead of bouncing and toppling over like it did when the **MARK** tried the same thing.

DROWNED FLY

ANIMALS

☆ You can, if you are feeling particularly mean, drown a fly in water until it seems to give up its fragile hold on life. If you now cover the tiny corpse in regular table salt it will miraculously come back to life.

There is no end to our cruelty where annoying insects are concerned.

A
B
C
D
E
F
G
H
I
J
K
L
M
N
O
P
Q
R
S
T
U
V
W
X
Y
Z

DRY ICE

FUN WITH SCIENCE / SPECIAL EFFECTS

DRY ICE is solid carbon dioxide. It is a strange material.

Carbon Dioxide freezes from a gas to a *solid* at about -78°C. It has some interesting properties but requires careful handling since contact with bare skin will cause it to adhere by freezing—and will probably result in nasty freeze-burns. At room temperature it will constantly boil off gaseous carbon dioxide which can create a risk of suffocation in a confined space.

So never attempt to handle it with your bare hands, and never use it in a confined space.

☆ It can be used to create **DRY ICE** *fog* which is much used as a theatrical effect. The dry ice is added to hot water and produces huge volumes of cold fog which falls to the floor in a thick white layer and pours down stairs impressively.

☆ If added to a glass of orange juice it produces bubbling and causes fog to pour from the glass in the style of an evil potion. It also chills the drink *and* makes it fizzy! But have a care! Should you drink the "potion" while there is any dry ice left in it you risk death by means of a frozen throat.

☆ You can make small quantities of **DRY ICE** by discharging a CO_2 fire extinguisher into a thick piece of cloth (like a towel) for about a minute. You'll render the extinguisher useless (which is a Bad Thing) but when you open up the towel you'll be rewarded with some lumps of **DRY ICE**.

You must wear gloves and work in an unconfined space to do this.

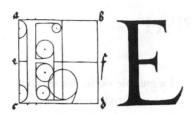

E

EATING AN APPLE WHILE JUGGLING

JUGGLING

This comic trick is an old favourite. There are three techniques that will help here:

☆ Juggle two balls and an apple and take bites out of the fruit while juggling **TWO IN ONE HAND** for a *beat* or two.

☆ While juggling you place the apple in your mouth *instead* of making a throw and take a big bite out as you retrieve it with the opposite hand.

☆ If you have quick hands you can take a bite out of the apple without altering the pattern at all—just slam it in fast and then toss the thing again.

It takes quite a while to consume a whole apple, so make it funny. When just the core is left, throw it high and catch it in your mouth.

A
B
C
D
E
F
G
H
I
J
K
L
M
N
O
P
Q
R
S
T
U
V
W
X
Y
Z

EATING A GOLDFISH

SILLINESS

You'll need a fish tank with goldfish in it and a gullible victim for this one. Don't bother trying this at a pet shop—they are bound to have seen it before.

☆ Prepare by cutting a goldfish-sized piece of carrot and concealing it in your hand.

Walk up to the tank.

'Mmmmm! Fish! And I'm so *hungry!*.'

Whip your hand into the tank (with the carrot) and pull it back out, making it flip and flap by shaking your hand as if trying to lose a piece of Sellotape off your finger.

Quickly pop the "fish" into your mouth and give it a great big crunch and you're done.

EATING GOAT'S EYES

SILLINESS

☆ Obtain a suitably impressionable victim, sit them down and either blindfold them or have them close their eyes.

Take a grape, peel off the skin and place it into their mouth.

```
You: "Don't bite until I tell you what it is."

Them: "OK, what is it?"

You: "It's a goat's eye!"
```

Stand well back, they may provide you with a display of projectile vomiting.

EGG, BALANCING ON ITS END

BALANCING

Here's the story:

After Christopher Columbus had rediscovered the Americas he was dining with some posh and arrogant people and during dinner one vile wag said to him:

'Terrific work Sir! You managed to get in there first and make a name for yourself, but its certain that it was only a matter of time before somebody else found the wretched place.'

Columbus took offence and ordered an egg from the kitchen and asked his critic to see if he could balance it on its end.

After a few attempts the man gave up saying that it was clearly impossible.

☆ HERE'S *The* TRICK: Columbus then made a small pile of salt on the table and balanced the egg on it.

He then carefully blew the salt away and to everyone's amazement the egg remained standing on its end.

The explanation for this seemingly magical effect was that a few almost invisible grains of salt had formed a sort of tripod below the nose of the egg.

'Very clever,' said the man. 'But it's easy once you know how!'

'Which is my point exactly,' replied Columbus.

A B C D E F G H I J K L M N O P Q R S T U V W X Y Z

EGGS, JUGGLING WITH...

JUGGLING

The humble egg is a classic comic prop for the juggler.

☆ Any reasonably competent juggler should practice with eggs It requires the discipline of being both reliable and confident in a way that mere **BEANBAGS** cannot enforce.

Juggling three eggs is no big problem but larger numbers are tricky, especially when it comes to the finish. The most likely cause of a break is that of two eggs striking each other when being gathered in the final catches of the routine.

☆ **BOUNCING BALL** jugglers make use of a clever four-object pattern to combine two balls and two eggs into a single pattern. The trick here is that the two **BOUNCING BALLS** are allowed to make contact with the floor, while the two eggs remain in the air at all times. The pattern is known as a 633 to those who are fluent with **SITESWAP NOTATION**, and the only additional information they need is that the 6's bounce while the 3's remain in the air.

Here are step-by-step instructions for the rest of us:

Start with just three **BOUNCING BALLS.** Juggle a **THREE BALL CASCADE** in the air and then toss one ball straight up and let it hit the floor and return to the pattern to a catch in the same hand.

OK, so far so good. Now try the same trick but *keep the other two balls going* while the ball bounces and returns. You'll find it pretty easy to time matters so that the hand that threw the bounce is empty again by the time the ball returns.

Note that while the ball is away doing the bounce you get a brief **GAP** in the opposite hand.

Practice throwing bounces in this way on both sides until the move feels perfectly natural. When that's done you can pick up the fourth ball.

Now for the full four-ball pattern you proceed as follows:

> Lead with a bounce from the right hand (6)
> Make two non-bouncing throws of a **CASCADE** (33).
> Make a bounce from the left hand (6).
> Make two non-bouncing throws of a **CASCADE** (33).

That sequence now repeats ad infinitum and you're doing a 633!

☆ Before introducing eggs into the pattern you should swap two of the bouncing balls for beanbags and arrange matters so that one beanbag and one **BOUNCING BALL** are held in each hand. In your right hand (which is to lead) the **BOUNCING BALL** should be at the front (so it gets thrown first) but in your left hand it should be at the back.

Now juggle the 633. You'll find that you don't need to concern yourself with what type of ball you are throwing at any moment, the structure of the pattern will take care of that for you. The beanbags will stay in the air and the **BOUNCING BALLS** will bounce.

Once you're completely happy with the pattern you can take the brave step of swapping the beanbags for eggs.

It feels great!

☆ It's really quite easy to shift a gear while juggling a 633 so as to take all four objects up into a Four Ball **FOUNTAIN**. Great!

Changing *down* a gear is trickier since doing so at the wrong moment will send one or both of the eggs crashing to the floor.

Here's how: as you juggle the fountain notice that your hands are juggling the sequence:

> *Egg - egg - ball - ball - egg - egg - ball - ball - egg - egg - ball - ball ...*

A
B
C
D
E
F
G
H
I
J
K
L
M
N
O
P
Q
R
S
T
U
V
W
X
Y
Z

To make the gear-change you lead back into the 633 by throwing one of the *second* ball throws as a bounce—the rest of the change follows naturally.

For another cool egg trick see **CATCHING AN EGG ON A PLATE**.

ELASTIC BAND SHARP-SHOOTER

WEAPONS

Here is the very best way of shooting an elastic band.

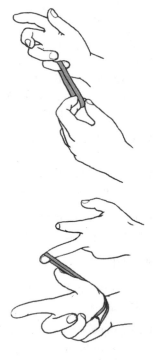

☆ You curl your little finger down onto your palm and hook an elastic band onto it. Now draw the band tight around the heel of your thumb and hook it over the end of your first finger.

Now make like a gun: aim and fire— by straightening your little finger.

Not only does this *look* great, it's also very accurate.

☆ You can set up an elastic band on each hand and get two shots in before reloading.

In fact, you can load each hand with up to *three* elastic bands by using your middle, ring and little finger. You'll need strong hands or weak elastic bands and a lot of perseverance to set this up.

This gives you a theoretical maximum of six shots—just like the real old Wild West.

ELASTIC BAND UP THE NOSE

MAGIC (VANISH) / SILLINESS

Prepare for this trick by placing half-a-dozen elastic bands around your wrist as if saving them for a rainy day.

☆ With your opposite hand draw up the end of an elastic band towards you nose while it remains looped around your wrist. You conceal this with the palm of your hand.

Push the end of the band into your nostril and snort loudly while releasing the band at the nose-end.

It will *twang* back towards your wrist but it will *seem* to have vanished like cocaine up a rock star's nostril.

ELBOW COIN VANISH

MAGIC / COIN TRICKS

☆ Take a coin between the thumb and index finger of your right hand. Do a **FRENCH DROP** or **PALM RETENTION VANISH** so that the coin appears to have been placed in your left hand.

Immediately raise your right arm so as to present the underside of your forearm, your right elbow points at them (your right hand will be over your shoulder).

A
B
C
D
E
F
G
H
I
J
K
L
M
N
O
P
Q
R
S
T
U
V
W
X
Y
Z

Mime the act of placing the coin on your elbow (with your empty left hand) while *actually* dropping it onto the top of your shoulder with your right hand.

Now 'rub it away' and reveal that the coin has vanished.

Your audience will probably want to see that both of your hands are empty —and, or course, they are!

ELEPHANT FROM DENMARK

MIND READING

Here's a classic self-working mind-reading trick.

> YOU: Think of a number from one to ten, then multiply it by nine."

Make sure they get that bit right.

> YOU: Now if you have a two digit number add the digits together. If not, don't do anything."

> YOU: OK, whatever number you have just take away five. Got that? Good remember that number."

> YOU: If A is 1 and B is 2 and C is 3 I bet you can work out what letter your number is. What I want you to do is to think of a country that starts with that letter then I want you to think of the second letter of that country's name and then think of an animal that starts with *that* letter. Finally I want you to think of the colour of that animal. Now write down the colour, the animal and the country but don't let me see."

> YOU: Done that? OK, I reckon you had a *grey elephant from Denmark!*"

And so they did.

The trick is simply that they will always end up with the number 4 (if they get their maths right) and the only countries starting with the letter D are: Denmark, Dominica, The Dominican Republic and the very obscure Djibouti which nobody has ever heard of (Dubai is an *emirate* not a country). Look out therefore for tricksters who might claim to have Brown Owls from Dominica or Black Jaguars from Djibouti.

ELEVEN TIMES TABLE

MATHEMATICS

To multiply by eleven you just multiply by ten, and then add the number you started with.

11 times 145 looks horrible! but 10 times 145 is easy, that's 1450,

Now add 1450 + 145 and you get 1595

Bingo!

See also **NINETEEN TIMES TABLE**.

ELLIPSE

GEOMETRY

An **ELLIPSE** is a simple distortion of a *Circle*.
In one direction, the long or *major* axis,
the shape is stretched and
in another, the short or *minor* axis, is
is squeezed.

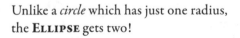

Unlike a *circle* which has just one radius,
the **ELLIPSE** gets two!

The **ELLIPSE** also has two special points called *focii*
(the Latin plural of *focus*). They are called *focii* for a very good reason. If a ray (of light, sound or whatever) is projected in any direction from one focus, it will be reflected by the perimeter toward the other focus.

This trick has been used in architecture to create rooms in which the sound from one point converges and focuses on another, much like the

A B C D E F G H I J K L M N O P Q R S T U V W X Y Z

A
B
C
D
E
F
G
H
I
J
K
L
M
N
O
P
Q
R
S
T
U
V
W
X
Y
Z

way in which the **PARABOLIC** dish of a satellite receiver focuses radio waves at a single point.

The **ELLIPSE** is the shape of a planet or moon's orbit. The thing that is being orbited lies at one of the *focii*.

☆ When doing **PERSPECTIVE DRAWING**, *circles* that are viewed from funny angles *always* present themselves to camera as **ELLIPSES**. Knowing this is the key to getting round things to look right.

☆ Everybody knows that you can draw a neat ellipse using a bit of string, two pins and a pencil (you did know that didn't you?). You'll get a neat shape this way. However precise size and shape of the ellipse will be pretty much random unless you know how far to place the pins apart and what length of string to use.

What if you need to draw an ellipse of a particular width and height?

First establish the dimensions of the long and short axes of your desired ellipse, from this calculate the long radius (B) and the short radius (A). Draw the two axes of the ellipse, at right angles to each other, so that they meet at the centre point (1).

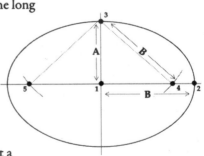

Mark point 2 along the long axis at a distance of B from point 1. Mark point 3 along the short axis at a distance of A from point 1. Set a pair of dividers (or compass, or use a piece of string) to the distance B using points 1 and 2 as a gauge.

Place one point of your dividers (or one end of your string) on point 3 and mark the points of intersection 4 and 5 as shown in the diagram.

Finally, drive nails or pins into points 4 and 5 and tie a loop of string so that it fits exactly around the triangle 3-4-5. Place a pencil inside the loop and you will be able to draw the circumference of your planned ellipse.

☆ You can approximate an ellipse with pencil, ruler and compass using a method that is part of the craft of the type designer.

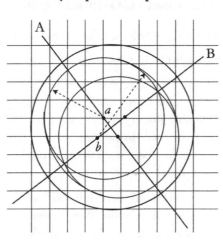

Start, as before, by marking the long and short axes of the desired **ELLIPSE**. Here we are trying to create the elegant thicks and thins of a Roman letter O.

The outside of a Roman O is a perfect *circle*, so we have laid that on a 9x9 grid as a starting point. Now draw in the major axis A and the minor axis B which are at right angles to each other and sloped.

Next make small marks on the axes: two points *a* are marked close to the centre of the major axis, and two points *b* on the minor, you'll find that with a little practice these can be placed by eye.

Take a pair of compasses and by setting a suitable radius from the *a* points you can mark in the steeper curves that define the thinner parts of the letter at the top and bottom. A larger radius is taken from the *b* points and used to mark the shallower curves that define the fatter sides of the letter.

When the marked-up construction is completed with stone chisel of **SIGNWRITER'S** brush you'll have a beautifully formed letter.

The shape of the inside will not be a perfect **ELLIPSE** but it is easily good enough to fool the human eye.

A B C D E F G H I J K L M N O P Q R S T U V W X Y Z

ENGLISH

JUGGLING / GAMESMANSHIP

As *Radical Cheney* said in another book:

> **English** is the *American* term for what the *English* call "spin."

Let me explain further: in the 1820's a keen gambler and billiard player called John Carr (who used to hang out in the billiard rooms at the Assembly Rooms in my home town of Bath) learned that if you applied ordinary chalk to the newly-introduced leather tip of your billiard cue, you could make the cue ball travel across the cloth *in a curve!*

This was revolutionary stuff and had never been seen before. People came from all over the world to see him do it and try to learn the secret.

Never one to miss a financial opportunity, Carr told them that the secret was in the special chalk he used which he marketed as *"Twisting Chalk".*

Of course everybody knows now that any old chalk will do.

ENGLISH is used in all sorts of trick shots on the pool table, as well as providing some interesting fun with high-bounce balls.

☆ Get a **BOUNCING BALL** and toss it up while giving it some furious spin with a flick of the wrist. When it hits the ground it will zoom off to the side. It looks very good if you toss it out to one side and make it come back.

☆ You can throw a **BOUNCING BALL** forwards

with back-spin to bring it back to you.

☆ Then there is the *trouser bounce* where you throw a ball straight at the floor so that it grazes your leg on the way up.

☆ Another nice trick is to throw a ball backwards over your shoulder with back-spin, it will bounce behind you and come back for an easy catch.

See **TABLE BOUNCE**, **WALL BOUNCE**, **KARATE CHOP BOUNCE**.

ENTASIS

SIGNWRITING

ENTASIS is an architectural word that refers to the curve that is applied to classical columns to make them look straight. Signwriters use similar trickery (which they also call Entasis) when carrying out lettering.

The fact is that a perfectly cylindrical column just looks wrong on the front of a building (to the classically trained eye anyway). So columns are typically a little fatter at the bottom than they are at the top, and they bulge slightly as well.

When this is done right, as it is on the Parthenon in Athens, you don't really notice it—the building just looks elegant. Trouble is that once you have ingrained the idea of **ENTASIS** into the brains of young architects, they just can't help over-doing it to *prove* that they know their stuff. Hence you get a lot of columns around the cities of the world that are massively tapered and hideously bulged. The whole point of trying to get things to look right has been utterly missed.

ENTASIS can be a good thing—but only when you don't really notice it. Similar tricks are used in **SIGNWRITING**, and once again, when done right it's not noticeable—the lettering just looks better.

A
B
C
D
E
F
G
H
I
J
K
L
M
N
O
P
Q
R
S
T
U
V
W
X
Y
Z

EVERY

☆ When you are executing block lettering by hand you naturally end up with vertical strokes of varying width. But if you paint the letters with slightly hollow strokes the variation is no longer so noticeable.

☆ It's always tricky **FLICKING THE CORNERS**, but is a little less tricky with hollowed letters, so signwriters often make *all* of the strokes of a letter slightly concave. This style is much-used in traditional narrow boat painting.

The combination of **FLICKING THE CORNERS** and **ENTASIS** in signwriting made a workable and attractive alternative to the more laborious work of executing neat serifs.

Note also that that the letters that meet the top and bottom lines with *curves* (S and O) are always painted a little taller, so that they cut *through* the guidelines, otherwise they look shorter than the other letters. As with **ENTASIS** you sometimes have to make things a little wrong in order to make them look *right*.

EPIDIASCOPE

SIGNWRITING

If you see one of these ancient machines in a junk shop—buy it!

The machines look something like a projector, but are characterised by having a huge lens—much bigger than a regular projector lens. Some **EPIDIASCOPES**, like the one shown here, also double as regular projectors, and may have two projection lenses.

An **EPIDIASACOPE** does something amazing. They are a bit like overhead projectors (the things people used for presentations and lectures before laptop computers and video projectors took over) but instead of shining light *through* transparent film they work by shining light *onto* the artwork.

This means that you can project an image of just about anything onto a screen (or a wall, or a blank sign board, or even the side of a truck).

The artwork is placed inside the machine where a very bright light illuminates it and this light is then reflected off a mirror and sent out through the lens which is enormous, so as to let a lot of light through.

You can take a page from a book, stick it inside the machine, and blow it up until it is ten feet tall—in full glorious colour.

It doesn't take a genius to work out that this could be a great time-saving tool for **SIGN WRITING**.

Most **EPIDIASCOPES** that turn up are 1950's machines and they look a bit like ancient *Magic Lanterns*—the Victorian precursors to slide and movie projectors.

The first thing to do with your machine is to get rid of the ancient and massive 1000 watt bulb in it—these bulbs are unreliable, impossible to

A
B
C
D
E
F
G
H
I
J
K
L
M
N
O
P
Q
R
S
T
U
V
W
X
Y
Z

replace and they run very hot. Even if you get a good one it will only last for about a hundred hours and they will blow at the drop of pin.

Use a modern halogen bulb instead, a car headlight bulb is a good choice (especially because it will run on 12 volts which, with the addition of a battery, makes the thing truly portable).

Once you have the machine running you'll find it invaluable for blowing up interesting artwork to pretty much any size you want.

You'll love this toy.

Eyelid Trick

FIRST AID

Sometimes, when something is stuck in your eye, you can drag it out with your eyelashes.

☆ Work out which eyelid you have an object stuck underneath and pull it away from your eye, then tuck the other eyelid *underneath* it.

Sounds weird, but it doesn't hurt! Now open your eye, with luck the eyelashes from one eyelid will drag out the speck of grit from under the other one.

Expanding Head Illusion

MAGIC

Sometimes, when you travel by train and have been staring out of the window, hypnotised by the tracks flashing by, you'll find yourself stopped at the station with the strange illusion that the carriage is still moving. This works in much the same way that taking off rose-tinted spectacles will cast your world in a shade of green.

And so it turns out that we can use this feature in the human brain to create an impressive illusion.

☆ You need to make a big spinning spiral lollipop. You can draw or paint your own spiral or photocopy the one here and blow it up nice and big. It needs to be bigger than your head. Cut the spiral out and glue it to stiff card or a piece of plywood and punch a hole in the middle, nailing the resulting disc loosely to a handle so that you can hold it up and spin it like a Catherine Wheel.

When you spin the disc it will appear as if constantly expanding, or shrinking, depending on which way it turns. For our trick we shall spin the disc so that it *shrinks*.

You are now ready to blow some minds with one of the greatest parlour tricks of all.

A
B
C
D
E
F
G
H
I
J
K
L
M
N
O
P
Q
R
S
T
U
V
W
X
Y
Z

A
B
C
D
E
F
G
H
I
J
K
L
M
N
O
P
Q
R
S
T
U
V
W
X
Y
Z

"I shall now blow your minds," you say (rather predictably) in a suitably large presentation voice.

"I have in my hand the *Vortex of Awesomeness!'* Or indeed some other suitably pretentious name.

"I ask you to stare at the *Vortex* for a full minute, though those of you with nerves or sensitive dispositions might like to look away lest you become excited or over-stimulated, or perhaps even have a little fun for a change."

You should now spin the disc in the *shrinking direction* and keep it spinning for a full minute while you continue to expostulate in a magical manner.

"Do not look away! Not even for a moment. I realise that, like a minute's silence, holding your gaze on one object is very hard for modern people with their limited attention spans, but nevertheless, for this illusion to work you must keep staring at the centre of the Vortex and listening to my voice. Think of it as a TV set, try to imagine that you are watching a film, it takes a long long time, but you get to the point in the end."

'In a few seconds I am going to ask you all to do something, do not look away until I tell you to. When I count to three I want you all to stop looking at the Vortex and gaze instead directly into my face. Here we go; one... two... three!'

As they look at your face they will see your head expanding and expanding and expanding! It's as if the drugs have suddenly taken hold.

The illusion can last for a quarter of a minute and they will shriek in amazement.

EXTRA STRONG MINTS

FUN WITH SCIENCE

Get an **EXTRA STRONG MINT** and climb under a duvet in a darkened room (OK, you *may* take a friend).

Wait until your eyes have got used to the dark (try not to get bored) and then snap the mint in half.

You get a green flash of light!

Two sugar-lumps rubbed together in the dark also produce a green glow.

See also **SELF-SEALING ENVELOPES**.

A
B
C
D
E
F
G
H
I
J
K
L
M
N
O
P
Q
R
S
T
U
V
W
X
Y
Z

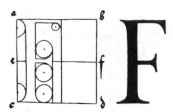

FAKE

JUGGLING

☆ Juggle One-Up Two-Up with three balls and then *carry,* rather than throw, one of the outside balls. This rather silly move is called the **FAKE**.

Effectively you are juggling **TWO IN ONE HAND** in one hand, while *miming* the third ball up and down. The trick is to get the mime-ball moving in perfect unison with its opposite on the far side of the pattern.

☆ Carry the ball right across the pattern and down the other side (keeping in time with the rhythm of the trick) to create a *Square Juggling* move.

☆ You can also carry the ball from left to right and back again *under* the pattern to pile on the agony.

When you have mastered this little bit of comic genius you can pop off and learn to juggle the **MACHINE**.

FAKE LEGS LEVITATION

MAGIC (LEVITATION)

The name of the trick gives it away.

☆ You'll need two old shoes a pair of old socks and two broom handles. Oh yes, and it takes two people to perform the trick.

Fix the shoes and socks onto the broom handles and hide them behind the "Levitation Couch". Place your partner on the couch "hypnotise" them and cover them with a sheet*. As the sheet is being arranged your partner grabs the fake legs and places them in position. You now start to wave your arms, speak in tongues and generally act in a highly mysterious manner. As you do so your partner starts to levitate and ends up hovering several feet off the ground.

☆ You can, if you like, try to make this a serious illusion, but the comedy angle is probably better—suddenly rip that sheet away to reveal the stunt. Your levitating partner should pull a "who me?" face and you should act at first shocked, and then angry.

FAKE SLAP

STAGE FIGHTING

☆ Stand in front of your opponent and place your left hand so that it touches the side of their chin.

Slap your left hand *hard* with your right hand taking care to miss your friend's face.

Your opponent *mimes* receiving a blow to the face

---

* This is, of course, the standard magical practice of **COVERING THE JOIN**.

(and yells for good measure). This move has all the sound and movement of a real slap and is a basic stage-fighting technique.

Fake Trip

SILLINESS

This simple comedy move is a bit of a cliché, but it works, so what the heck!

☆ As you walk onto the stage you deliberately allow the toe of one foot to catch on the heel of the other as you take a step. You'll immediately and very convincingly appear to trip and catch yourself.

☆ Don't forget to look back at the spot where you tripped with a "What the f*ck!" look on your face.

☆ You could then pile on the agony by walking into something (like the mike stand) while you are looking over your shoulder.

And so it goes on...

Fall

WHIPS

The **FALL** of a whip (also known as the *Rat's Tail*) is the un-plaited leather section between the whip itself and the **CRACK**.

It is the semi-sacrificial part of the whip, it will wear out over time as the small end frays from repeated re-tying of the **CRACK**.

A B C D E F G H I J K L M N O P Q R S T U V W X Y Z

A
B
C
D
E
F
G
H
I
J
K
L
M
N
O
P
Q
R
S
T
U
V
W
X
Y
Z

It should be tapered and *tuned* to the length of the whip, the aim being to create a smooth reduction in weight along the entire length of the whip.

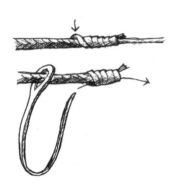

☆ To make a **FALL** you will need a piece of top-quality cow- or kangaroo-hide, it will be cut from the thickest part of the hide and will take the form of a tapered piece of leather about two feet long. An eye will be cut in the fat end so that the whole piece resembles a giant sewing needle.

To replace the **FALL** you very carefully cut through the top of the eye of the old **FALL** on your whip, taking care not to damage the braided knot on the end of the whip. You can then rip it right off the whip. Thread the whip though the eye of the new **FALL** and then tuck the thin end right through the braided knot—it *will* go because it's thinner than the piece you just removed.

Finally pull it tight and you're done.

See also **CRACK**.

FALLING THROUGH THE ICE

SURVIVAL

You're headed for the North Pole and suddenly the ice gives way below you and you are pitched into freezing water.

☆ **HERE'S** *The* **TRICK:** *Turn around* and scrabble back out onto the ice you just walked over. The ice you were heading for was getting thin, too thin to support your weight!

The ice you came from was obviously capable of holding your weight. Turning back could save your life!

FARO SHUFFLE

OBJECT MANIPULATION / MAGIC / MATHEMATICS

The **FARO SHUFFLE** is a very precise method of shuffling a deck of cards. This is not an easy trick by any means, but it is the pinnacle of card manipulation. In a "perfect" Faro Shuffle the deck is split exactly in two and the two halves are riffled together so that cards from each half interleave in perfect alternation.

Expect to work on this for several weeks...

1: Starting with a decent deck of cards your first task is to split the deck exactly in half. It's not as hard as it seems, as long as the deck is in good condition. You can test your work by placing the two stacks side by side on a smooth table and comparing heights.

2: The two halves are squared off perfectly and bent in each hand. The aim here is to get a nice even bevel of around 45° on both halves. You'll be all fingers and thumbs trying to do this, but in time it will come. The two corners closest to you are then put together...

3: ...with the corners laid against each other (and if you have lined them up properly) you will find that rotating the two decks so the end bevels lie against each other will cause the cards to start to interleave. Now, imagining that the two half-decks are the two halves of a partially opened book—you open the book a little more...

A
B
C
D
E
F
G
H
I
J
K
L
M
N
O
P
Q
R
S
T
U
V
W
X
Y
Z

4: ...and as if by magic the cards will start to riffle together from the front to the back.

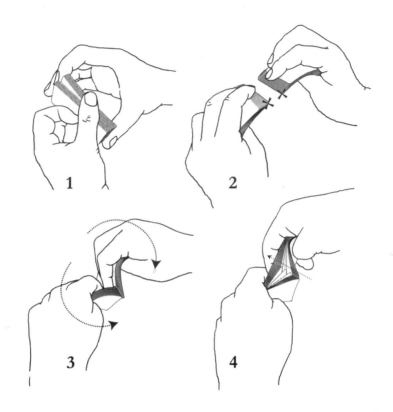

Easy to say, but so hard to do! The motion required is subtle and hard to describe, but once you start to get the feel of it the knack will come.

Your early attempts will be uneven, and you'll find that the cards "clump" sometimes, destroying the perfect alternation you are looking for.

But the natural perseverance of the true trickster will win through in the end and you'll be able to impress people for the rest of your life.

☆ If a perfect **FARO SHUFFLE** is executed *eight times* in a row, a 52 card deck will return its original order. This is a mathematical fact.

FEED

JUGGLING

In ball-juggling a **FEED** is the action of *passing* a ball directly from one hand to the other, as opposed to throwing it.

In **SITESWAP NOTATION** a **FEED** is denoted by a 1, as in 531 (an interesting three-ball pattern—see **FIVE THREE ONE**).

The **SHOWER** patterns are all based on the scheme of one hand making throws, while the other **FEEDS** back. In passing patterns the term **FEED** refers to a pattern in which one juggler passes to several others.

☆ A typical Feed will have three jugglers arranged in a triangular formation.

Each has three balls, clubs or whatever. The *Feeder* passes a *Two-Count**, making right-hand passes to each juggler in turn. The *Feedees* respond by juggling *Four-Counts* (hence they pass half as often).

☆ It is a convention in **FEEDS** that the first pass is always to the *right*.

This saves a lot of confusion before the juggling begins.

☆ Ambidextrous club-passers frown on dexter-centric styles like the *Two-Counts* and *Four-Counts* and prefer more balanced schemes. They might have the *feeder* juggling *Pass-Pass-Self*† while the *feedees* juggle *Three Counts*.

---

* A *Two-Count* is a passing pattern in which every second throw is a pass, typically this means every right-hand throw.

† *Pass Pass Self* is an unusual count in that every third throw is *not* a pass. It's great fun once you get the knack.

A B C D E F G H I J K L M N O P Q R S T U V W X Y Z

A
B
C
D
E
F
G
H
I
J
K
L
M
N
O
P
Q
R
S
T
U
V
W
X
Y
Z

FIGURE OF EIGHT KNOT

KNOTS

The **FIGURE OF EIGHT** knot is a simple *stopper* knot. A stopper knot being one that is tied in the end of a piece of rope to prevent the lay from unreeving or unraveling. It draws up into a nice little button-shape.

You could use an **OVERHAND KNOT** for the same purpose, but the **FIGURE OF EIGHT KNOT** is much easier to untie.

The **FIGURE OF EIGHT KNOT** is one of the eight most commonly found knots in **CELTIC KNOTWORK**. It is easily formed, using pencil and rubber, by breaking and rejoining the strands of a plait of three.

FINDING NORTH & SOUTH

OUTDOORPERSONSHIP / TECHNICAL WIZARDRY

☆ A useful trick for finding north at night (for those that live in the Northern Hemisphere) is that of locating *Polaris*, the North Star.

To do this you must first locate the constellation *Ursa Major* (the Great Bear) which is easy because it consists of bright stars that form the shape of a saucepan in the sky.

In the USA this constellation is known as the *Big Dipper*. The star at the pouring edge of the saucepan is *Dubhe* and below it lies *Merak*.

Project, in your mind's eye, a line from Merak to Dubhe and onwards for about one and a half saucepan-lengths across the void where you'll find *Polaris* which just happens to be on the end of the handle of a smaller saucepan-like constellation which is properly called *Ursa Minor* (The Lesser Bear).

Since Polaris is almost exactly on the celestial north pole it indicates the direction North—a fact that sailors have been using for many years (see **SUNDIALS**).

☆ In the Southern Hemisphere things are not quite so simple, since there is no prominent star at the celestial south pole. There is however a very prominent constellation, *Crux* (The Southern Cross). Nearby is *Triangulum Australis* (The Southern Triangle).

Locate these constellations and in your mind's eye project a line dagger-wise from the cross until it hits another line formed by the **PERPENDICULAR BISECTOR** of the baseline of the triangle. Where the two lines meet lies the celestial south pole and thus the direction South.

In daytime, when you can't see the stars, a brilliant trick to find North and South is to use a watch.

☆ Point the hour-hand of your watch at the Sun.

When you've done done that (or imagined it if you have a digital watch) then halfway between the hour hand and twelve-o-clock is South.

A
B
C
D
E
F
G
H
I
J
K
L
M
N
O
P
Q
R
S
T
U
V
W
X
Y
Z

FINDING THE CENTRE OF A CIRCLE

GEOMETRY

This is something that is very important to wood-turners.

Let's suppose you have a great big chunk of wood, like a piece of telegraph pole, and you want to mount it on a lathe to carve it into a pretty shape.

The wood is round already, but it's very important to set the chuck of the lathe so the piece is centred.

Otherwise, when it starts to spin, the whole rig is likely to shake itself to pieces.

Finding the centre is easy if we make use of some simple geometry.

The well-equipped wood turner will possess a set square onto which has been fitted an additional edge, arranged at 45° and standing proud of the two right-angled legs so that its edge is aligned perfectly on the right-angled joint.

This tool is laid over the end of the work so that the right-angled legs touch the circumference of the wood and the 45° piece lies over the end.

A line is scribed along the 45° piece.

Then the whole assembly is rotated about 90° and a second line is scribed.

The **CENTRE OF THE CIRCLE** lies where the two lines cross.

FINDING THE CENTRE OF BALANCE OF A BROOM

BALANCING

This isn't really a performance trick, but it's a clever little technique for finding the centre of gravity of anything long and thin.

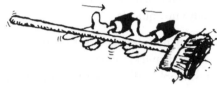

☆ Get a broom and support the shaft horizontally on your two index fingers.

Now simply move your fingers slowly together until they touch. The broom will stay balanced!

Once you have done this you'll see how it works.

FIND THE LADY

GRIFTING

FIND THE LADY is another name for the **THREE CARD MONTE**, a confidence trick in which the **MARK** bets which of three face-down cards is the Queen.

See **THREE CARD MONTE**.

A
B
C
D
E
F
G
H
I
J
K
L
M
N
O
P
Q
R
S
T
U
V
W
X
Y
Z

FINGER CUT WHIP CRACK

WHIPS

☆ Hold your whip up high with your right hand, stick out your left index finger at waist level, now drape the whip over your finger to create a bend in it.

Drop the whip hand down and then bring it up vertically fairly quickly.

As the whip lifts off your finger it will crack. Fold your finger in quickly and make a pained expression and it will look as if you have just cut off your finger.

FINGER PALM

MAGIC / COIN TRICKS

Here is another way of concealing a coin when performing closeup magic. The name is an oxymoron since the coin being hidden from view is being *fingered* rather than **PALMED**.

☆ The coin is hidden in the crook of one of your fingers.

While this is a very angle-sensitive method of hiding a coin, it does allow the hand to appear very relaxed, hence it can be very effective.

See also **THUMB PALM**.

FINGER SPELLING
CODES & CIPHERS / LANGUAGE

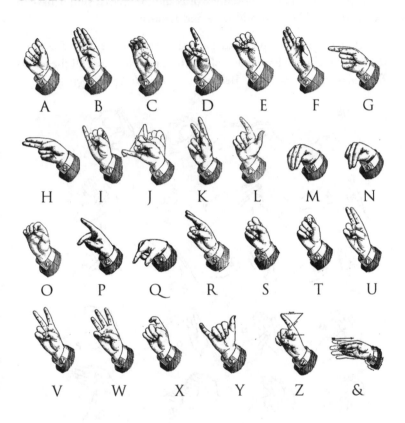

The art of **FINGER SPELLING** is the art of making letter symbols with your hands. It's also a great way of passing secret messages in plain sight, provided you can persuade a friend to learn the same alphabet as you.

Obviously the main application of **FINGER SPELLING** is to provide a means of communication between people who cannot hear or speak, but the primary tool used by such people is proper *Sign Language*.

The sign languages used by people with impaired speech and hearing vary from country to country around the world (a fact which hearing people find surprising for some reason). Sign languages are very rich and expressive languages with complex grammar, just like spoken languages. **FINGER SPELLING** usually forms a part of such languages, but is mostly used for spelling out names, obscure words and things that simply have to be spelt perfectly (like email addresses and acronyms).

☆ The engraving on the previous page shows *American Sign Language (ASL)* finger-spelling which is a cool one to learn. Note that all the letters are formed with just one hand. Below we see *British Sign Language*.

☆ In *British Sign Language* two hands are required. Note how the vowels AEIO and U are formed by pointing at each digit, starting with the thumb. The rest of the signs generally resemble the letters they signify.

Finger Wiggle Woggle

HAND TRICKS

The author confesses to having entirely made that name up since he had no idea what it was *really* called.

This is a simple trick that makes little children smile—and what is wrong with that?

☆ Hold your hands as if praying and fold down your middle fingers.

Now rotate your hands, palms touching all the way, so they lie like sardines against each other (you can only turn one way, depending on which middle finger is in front of the other).

Now bend and unbend your middle fingers in time with each other. You get a nice illusion of a double-ended finger rocking back and forth.

With only a little practice you can do this very smoothly indeed.

See also **Removing your Thumb**.

A B C D E F G H I J K L M N O P Q R S T U V W X Y Z

A B C D E **F** G H I J K L M N O P Q R S T U V W X Y Z

FIRE AND HEIGHT

SHOWMANSHIP

Any seasoned street entertainer will know that **FIRE AND HEIGHT** make for a big crowd. People are naturally attracted by fire, and without the benefit of a stage in the raw street environment it's a good idea to improvise some way of getting higher than your audience—that way more people can see you.

The most impressive fire tricks are **FIRE BLOWING** and fire juggling and methods of gaining height include: riding high **UNICYCLES**, **SLACKROPE WALKING** and acrobatic moves such as standing on your partner's shoulders.

If local architecture provides two conveniently-spaced columns you could use the **STAR JUMP CLIMBING TRICK** to elevate yourself, fire torch in hand, and so draw a large crowd.

On a cautionary note, while the seasoned fire juggler will have almost entirely lost their fear of fire torches, this is not the case with an audience. Most regular sane and normal people have a healthy fear of fire and they will be particularly alarmed if they see anything going wrong, like a fire torch being dropped to the ground for example. So take care to perfect your routines because what is a simple drop to you is a very scary and off-putting moment to most of your audience and your hat will suffer as a consequence.

FIRE BLOWING

CIRCUS SKILLS

FIRE BLOWING is the act of blasting great balls of fire out of your mouth.

☆ Usually this is done with the combustible liquid fuel known as *paraffin* in the UK, *kerosene* in the United States or, rather alarmingly, *petrole* in France. We are talking about lamp-oil, the stuff that does not usually burn on its own, but which requires a wick.

Now this is a dangerous activity for several reasons:

☆ Some varieties of lamp oil contain hideously toxic additives to make the lamps smell nice in use. Whether scented or suspiciously non-odourous these lamp oils are to be avoided at all costs.

☆ Pure paraffin can, it is perfectly true, be drunk without serious ill effects though it will loosen the digestive tract alarmingly[*]. However if *any* paraffin gets into your lungs it will cause very serious problems indeed. The oily liquid will spread out over the inner surface of the lungs like oil on a pond resulting in a life-threatening condition known as *pleurisey*.

☆ There is also the very unpleasant possibility of *blowback* in which the paraffin ignites *inside* your body explosively like a car exhaust backfiring. It has been known for circus performers to actually explode in mid-show with horrific results.

Still with me?

☆ OK, the fire-blower learns their craft under the instruction of a skilled practitioner and they start by working with water, practicing the art of taking gulps and blowing them out a powerful and fine spray using the full force of the lungs to blast the liquid into a nicely aerated from a thin gap between the lips. At the end of the blast the mouth must be clamped tight shut and you should not breathe in again for a second or two. This ensures, when working with actual combustible fuel, that blowback does not occur.

---

[*] This is a medical euphemism for "giving you the shits".

A B C D E F G H I J K L M N O P Q R S T U V W X Y Z

A
B
C
D
E
F
G
H
I
J
K
L
M
N
O
P
Q
R
S
T
U
V
W
X
Y
Z

☆ Once mastered with water the novice should practice the same activity with actual fuel, but not with fire just yet. Get used to the taste and feel of the stuff.

☆ Finally you can move on to work with actual fire. A small firestick is held in the hand and a gulp of fuel taken. A blast is made into the flame which will ignite the aerated fuel.

The fire torch is now removed from the stream of fuel which will now burn on its own (this is one of the refinements of elegant fire-blowing).

The artiste continues to push out a stream of fuel, keeping the flame away from the mouth by keeping the jet fast and narrow and regulating the amount of fuel by the opening and closing of their lips.

The stream is them cut off by *closing the mouth* in mid-blow, and turning away from the flame. The fireball will roll on up into the air and die.

Every Trick In The Book would like to stress, once more, the importance of learning this under instruction.

☆ Alternative fuels can be used, once surprising possibility is *cocoa powder*. Most powdered organic materials will burn, sometimes explosively, when mixed with air. It is not unknown for flour mills to blow themselves to bits for this reason.

Cocoa powder burns very well if sprayed out of the mouth properly and has the comic advantage of leaving the teeth blackened and covering performer's face with black soot.

Oh, and it doesn't give you pleurisy!

FIRE EATING

CIRCUS SKILLS

Extinguishing flames in the mouth is known as **FIRE EATING**. It is a much safer activity than **FIRE BLOWING** and is almost stupidly easy to do. Performers therefore resort to all sorts of serious airs and graces while eating fire to make out that they are doing something dangerous and skilled.

The fact is that the inside of your mouth is coated in a layer of saliva that protects it from burning, though part of the **FIRE EATER'S** technique is to ensure that the flames do not spend any appreciable length of time actually licking the roof of their mouth.

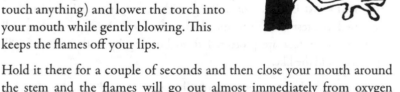

Typically **FIRE EATERS** work with small fire torches which consist of a handle (aluminium please and *never* steel). On the end of the torch is a small wick that will fit easily in the mouth. You light it, tip your head back so your mouth points upwards (thus ensuring that the flames don't actually touch anything) and lower the torch into your mouth while gently blowing. This keeps the flames off your lips.

Hold it there for a couple of seconds and then close your mouth around the stem and the flames will go out almost immediately from oxygen starvation. Remove the now-smouldering torch and you're done.

☆ If you have a big mouth, like the celebrated juggler *Haggis 'Gobby' McLeod,* you can do this with a juggler's fire torch. Normal human beings will prefer to work with smaller torches.

☆ To pile on the agony you can lower the torch into your mouth and grip the wick with your front teeth, letting go completely with your hand. Hold the torch there for a few seconds (until your teeth start to warm up) remembering to keep blowing gently. Then complete the move as before.

A B C D E F G H I J K L M N O P Q R S T U V W X Y Z

A
B
C
D
E
F
G
H
I
J
K
L
M
N
O
P
Q
R
S
T
U
V
W
X
Y
Z

☆ If you secrete a small container packed with cotton wool soaked in lighter fluid in your pocket you can moisten a finger with it, pop the now flammable finger into the burning torch flame where it will immediately ignite. If you keep your finger upright you have a few seconds before it will start to actually hurt or do damage. Carry the small finger-flame to your mouth and pop it in as if to check the taste of the flame before eating the torch.

☆ Real **FIRE EATING** poseurs tend to work with plenty of bare flesh exposed and make a great play of dragging the hot ends of burning torches slowly over their flesh as if they are being terribly brave and somehow immune to the flesh-searing properties of fire.

The fact is that a slowly-dragged flaming wick doesn't hurt or burn for toffee. If you stop for a while you'll quickly be reminded (by your nervous system) that keeping the thing moving is a good idea.

And that is about it!

FIRE WALKING

OCCULT SCIENCES / PYROTECHNICS

FIRE WALKING is the act of walking, with bare feet, over hot coals. It is often used as a test of faith by merchants of the occult. Typically they will claim that your feet are protected from burning by faith, force of will, hypnotism and the like.

If this was really the case then these occulticians would be able to hold their fingers in a candle flame and survive, without burning, by the same means. They can't and they don't.

They might suggest that repeating the mantra "Cool moss, cool moss!" while walking will parascientifically protect your feet. However, in a practical experiment it was found that you can pass over just as safely while repeating "Hot coals, hot coals!"

It just happens that *if* the coals are set up right, and *if* your feet are bone dry, then you *can* walk over hot coals without being burned.

It's quite a common activity and *usually* it goes off without incident.* But it can go horribly wrong, so this book does not encourage the practice.

☆ The coals (note *coals* not wood) must be well burned down and ashy so that when spread out in a thin layer you can see the red hot bits glowing out from a surrounding shroud of white/grey ash.

You must be quite sure that there are no foreign items like stones or pieces of metal lurking in the mix. Typically the bulk of your red-hot carpet will actually be dead ash blocks with a few glowing pieces mixed in.

It is vital that your feet are bone dry, so stepping off wet grass into the fire pit is an absolute no-no.

Once correctly set up you can walk quickly and positively over this material without being instantly burned. Stopping halfway to take a phone call is not a good idea.

The reason you don't get burned is that you are actually walking on ash which is a very poor conductor of heat. Moreover the red-hot bits, while they really are red-hot, do not contain a great *quantity* of heat, so the small amount they do contain is easily absorbed by the hard skin on your feet which quickly cools down the hot material.

It's one of those things that people do *because they can* and because it gives them the confidence of thinking that they have somehow triumphed, with mind, over matter.

☆ A far more amusing activity is walking over a bath of **OOBLECK**.

---

* A notable accident happened to a group of Australian Kentucky Fried Chicken executives in 2002 who were attending a "Management Development Conference" which is newspeak meaning "Tragic party games for business people with more money than sense". About 30 people received serious burns to the feet after walking on hot embers from burnt timber (note the above remarks concerning coals). It's easy to see how one person could get injured in such an exercise, but our confidence in the intelligence of the other 29 KFC bosses is severely challenged by their lemming-like behaviour. The Australian newspaper The Age covered the story under the headline "KFC Bosses aren't chicken, but they sure are tender."

FIREMAN'S LIFT

FIRST AID

When the bold fireman needs to carry an unconscious or incapacitated rescuee down a ladder they will use the **FIREMAN'S LIFT**. It's fun to practice!

Get a pal to pretend to be all wobbly and useless, stand them up (or lean them against a wall if they are acting *really* well). Now, facing them, pick up their right wrist with your right hand and bend forwards. Pull them over your bent back while reaching between their legs with your left hand.

Now balance their apparently lifeless body (no giggling now) across your shoulders and stand up.

Adjust them for balance and then pass their right wrist to your left hand.

You now have your victim (sorry, patient) securely on your shoulders and you still have one hand free! Thus you can safely climb or descend a ladder. Despite the informative illustration, flared trousers are not recommended for emergency work since it is all to easy to snag a toe and trip over in them.

It helps if you are bigger and stronger than your victim—but that's why firemen have to be so big and strong!

FIREWOOD POEM

TRAVELLERS TIPS

In this age of miracle and wonder, when the houses in the developed world are heated by oil, gas and electricity, the humble traveller still relies on firewood for heat in the cold months of winter.

Here is an old poem to remind you which wood is worth gathering. It has been passed around, in one form or another, for many years and usually takes the form of two verses of doggerel roughly as follows:

> Beech wood fires burn bright and clear
> If the logs are kept a year.
> Store your Beech for Christmas tide
> With new cut Holly laid beside.
> Chestnut's only good they say
> If for years it's stored away.
> Birch and Fir wood burn too fast
> Blaze too bright and do not last.
> Flames from Larch will shoot up high
> Dangerously the sparks will fly.
> But Ash wood green and Ash wood brown
> Are fit for a Queen with a golden crown.
>
> Oaken logs logs if dry and old
> Keep away the winters cold.
> Poplar gives a bitter smoke
> Fills your eyes and makes you choke.
> Elm wood burns like churchyard mould
> E'en the very flames are cold.
> Hawthorn bakes the sweetest bread
> So it is in Ireland said.
> Apple wood will scent the room.
> Pear wood smells like flowers in bloom,
> But Ash wood wet and Ash wood dry
> A King can warm his slippers by.

A
B
C
D
E
F
G
H
I
J
K
L
M
N
O
P
Q
R
S
T
U
V
W
X
Y
Z

A
B
C
D
E
F
G
H
I
J
K
L
M
N
O
P
Q
R
S
T
U
V
W
X
Y
Z

FISHING FOR TROUT

POACHING

This trick works in fast-flowing rocky streams.

☆ Use worms as bait. It's like velcro for trouts. You don't need a rod or a float, just a line and a hook and some sort of **PRIEST**.

This is so horribly effective that it is practically illegal and is considered deeply unsportsmanlike by true fisher-folk.

Something I am perfectly happy to discuss with them *after* breakfast.

☆ Alternatively, if you can locate a rocky pool with some nice fish in it, just chuck in a liberal helping of rock salt. This is obviously a very nasty thing to do and will cause the trout some severe problems, in particular their buoyancy will get messed up so that they will float to the surface in a distressed state, but that's nothing!

Next you are going to hoik them out, kill the poor things and eat them!

So not a very nice thing to do, but acceptable as a survival technique.

FISSION POP BOMB

FUN WITH SCIENCE / KITCHEN TRICKS / EXPLOSIVES

☆ Get some vinegar and some bicarbonate of soda. Add roughly equal volumes to each other and a massive chemical reaction will take place releasing large quantities of carbon-dioxide bubbles from a frothy goo. This is both smelly and messy—so keep an eye out for mum!

If you can find a container with a cork lid you can arrange matters (by placing vinegar in a small cup on a bed of bicarb) so that the reaction can start *after* you have rammed the cork in really hard.

Stand back and after a while the cork will blow off with a loud pop releasing a shower of stuff that stains badly and is horrible to clean up.

What fun! See also **MENTO AND DIET COKE**.

FIVE BALL CASCADE

JUGGLING

Now we're getting serious.

Juggling a **FIVE BALL CASCADE** is going to take you a while to learn. The jump from three to four balls is not too bad, but the jump from four to five is a big one. You'll need to put in plenty of hours, but anyone sufficiently determined can get it. There's no particular route to this trick, so take the following as a guide, not a rule book.

☆ Start by getting really good at *Three Ball Flashes* out of a regular **THREE BALL CASCADE.** Juggle normally then make three consecutive high throws that give you enough time to clap your hands underneath. This helps to prepare you for the tempo of throwing to five-ball height.

☆ Next get in plenty of practice doing five-ball **FLASHES** (that's just five throws to a clean catch).

☆ When you are happy with that you can start to pile on a few more throws. You'll find that you get to the 8–12 throw stage pretty easily but will, most likely get stuck there for a while. This is because you have not yet learned to correct a pattern when it is going out of shape. When you get the occasional run of 12–16 throws it will be because you were lucky enough to create a pattern so clean that it *didn't need* to be corrected.

☆ Read the entry on **LEARNING HOW TO LEARN TRICKS** which has some useful tips on keeping your subconscious mind happy while working.

You have to realise that it is the unconscious part of your mind that needs to learn to juggle, not the rational part that thinks it knows perfectly well what to do. Always finish on a high note (i.e. make sure that your last three attempts at the pattern go to a clean finish rather than a drop. Stay relaxed, don't forget to breathe, and don't poke your tongue out!

☆ When you have managed a run of 50 throws you have cracked it.

FIVE BALL COLUMN BOUNCE

JUGGLING

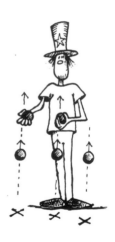

Here's a masterpiece of **COLUMN BOUNCE** technology, invented by *Radical Cheney*.

☆ Take five **BOUNCING BALLS** and place three in the *left* hand and two in the right. That's not a typo, I really mean three in the left.

Now imagine three columns in front of you, a right column, a middle column and a left column. Got that? Good.

To start juggling, lift two balls simultaneously— one from each hand—into the right and middle columns and as they fall move your hands to the left and middle column positions.

As the balls rise you lift a ball into the left column and *at the same time* make an exchange in the middle column.

Let the balls fall and move to the middle and right column position.

As the balls rise make exchanges in the middle and right columns.

Now move to the left and middle position…

… and so it goes.

The balls rise and fall in *three* columns, your hands make exchanges in the left-middle and then middle-right pairs of columns alternately. You'll notice that the outer balls bounce *twice* while the middle balls bounce *once*.

The effect is surreal.

Technically, that is in **SITESWAP NOTATION**, the pattern is:

$(6, 4x)(4x, 6)$

In **CAUSAL NOTATION** the pattern looks like it *feels!* The bounces are marked with little x's and you can see how on every other *beat* of the pattern three balls hit the ground at the same time.

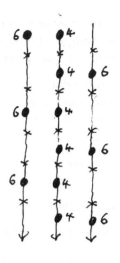

You can extend this technique to juggle six balls in *four* columns, so that four balls hit the floor together on each bounce.

I've heard that people have worked, with limited success on a seven-ball version in which there are *five* columns.

See also **SIX BALL COLUMN BOUNCE, FOUR IN ONE HAND BOUNCE**.

FIVE BALL GAP

JUGGLING

☆ A **FIVE BALL GAP** is a **FIVE BALL CASCADE** juggled with a missing ball.

This often happens accidentally (you've dropped a ball) but it can also happen deliberately, when a juggler *chooses* to juggle a five-ball pattern with just four balls.

Now let's get a little mathematical.

A B C D E F G H I J K L M N O P Q R S T U V W X Y Z

A
B
C
D
E
F
G
H
I
J
K
L
M
N
O
P
Q
R
S
T
U
V
W
X
Y
Z

☆ The most obvious **FIVE BALL GAP** pattern is 55550, where the hands just keep going as normal, but every five throws there is nothing to juggle with, so we get a 0 (an empty hand).

☆ If you think about it you'll realise that the throw *immediately before* the **GAP** is unnecessary because you don't have to clear the hand—there's nothing about to arrive in it, so you can **HOLD THROUGH THE GAP** instead.

If you hold through *every* gap you'll end up juggling the curious pattern 552! This feels like:

right, left-hold-left, right-hold-right, left-hold-left...

This is a much easier pattern to juggle than the **FIVE BALL CASCADE**.

☆ Another trick is to **FEED** a ball into every **GAP** which results in the pattern 5551. Note that all the feeds will go the same way, unlike the related pattern **FOUR FOUR ONE** where the **FEEDS** alternate.

FIVE BALL SPLITS

JUGGLING

This is a cool way of juggling five balls, especially if you have not yet mastered the **FIVE BALL CASCADE**. It is also the easiest way of juggling fave balls, short of sewing beanbags together.

☆ Start with five balls, three in your favourite hand and two in the other.

You lead off with a split **MULTIPLEX** from the favourite hand. Both balls need to go quite high, make it top-of-the-head height.

You then reply with a split **MULTIPLEX** from your other hand, the throw should take the balls up through the middle of the previous **MULTIPLEX**. And so you continue, making **MULTIPLEX** throws from one hand after the other, always up through the middle.

It just kind of works itself out.

This is one of those tricks that makes a big deal out of a little skill. It's easier than juggling four balls—so what are you waiting for?

FIVE-O-FOUR (504)

JUGGLING

There are an infinity of **SITESWAP** patterns so it's good to know which ones are worth doing!

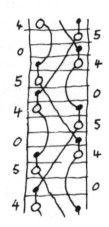

☆ **FIVE-O-FOUR (504)** is one such pattern. It is a *Five Three Four* pattern with the three-ball (or club) missing. That won't help you much if you're not an adept four-object juggler.

The great thing about this pattern is that it keeps everything up high, and it's very satisfying to juggle.

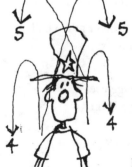

Start by juggling a **SLOW CASCADE** with three balls (that's 522 for those with mathematical minds). Now notice the long holds and see if you can make little self throws (4's) *underneath* the high crossing throws.

Notice that the throwing order is *right-right, left-left*.

☆ In **CAUSAL NOTATION** the pattern *looks* how it *feels* to juggle. Note the bizarre backward lines which are a result of the o's (or empty hands). All this is explained under **CAUSAL NOTATION**.

☆ The pattern works just as well with rings or clubs.

With clubs the 5's are crossing triples and the 4's are self-doubles.

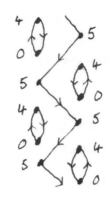

☆ This is an *Excited State* pattern, which is maths-speak for a pattern that you cannot start from cold. So you can't actually lead straight off into it: a typical starting sequence would be 524504504...

When learning **SITESWAPS** you may find that it help to speak the names of the throws out loud as you go.

Once this habit is learned you can develop a skill akin to that of a musician who can sight-read music.

If you stay within the scope of your juggling skill you should be able to juggle pretty much any **SITESWAP** sequence by chanting the sequence as you go.

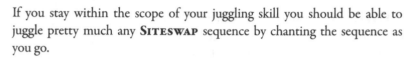

FIVE THREE ONE (531)

JUGGLING

Here's another nice little Siteswap for three objects.

☆ Grab three balls, throw a 5, then reply with a 3 then **FEED** a ball across. To complete the sequence you'll need to do six throws altogether.

If you need a cool way of *thinking* about it, just juggle a **SLOW CASCADE** and toss in one round of a **TWO BALL SHOWER** underneath each high throw. The *Causal diagram* should explain that (unless of course you are deeply offended by juggling notation).

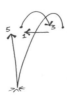

☆ The **FIVE THREE ONE** works brilliantly as a **BOUNCING BALL** pattern. The 5's are **PASSIVE BOUNCES** while the 3's are air throws. The 1's (**FEEDS**) are simply passed from hand to hand as usual.

This is a very busy pattern—but easy to juggle.

☆ You can have a lot of fun with it by letting one of the 5's bounce several times while you run a little **Two Ball Shower**. When the bouncing ball starts to get tired you scoop it back up and resume the regular 5 3 1 sequence.

Flamboyant Enamels

SIGNWRITING

Flamboyant Enamels are used by **Signwriters** in show-painting to produce the candy-wrapper effect you may see on the gallopers or other richly decorated fairground rides. They are simple coloured varnishes, using the more brilliant transparent pigments.

Flamboyant Enamels are usually painted over silver metallic paint, though sometimes over silver or gold leaf. They produce much the same visual effect that coloured cellophane wrappers over silver foil do in the packaging of certain sweets and chocolates.

Flaming Baguettes

JUGGLING / PYROTECHNICS

When one has forgotten one's fire torches it is well to bear in mind that a loaf of french bread, one end dipped in combustible fuel, makes a handy replacement. They are also naturally funny and would work well in the **Frying Pan, Egg and Fire Torch** routine.

Real French Bread becomes nicely stiff and stale if not consumed within a few hours of leaving the bakery. The disgusting English version of this fine food contains hideous preservatives and additives that cause the stuff to become limp and plasticy as time goes on. A limp loaf your neither want nor need and I wish these people would stop pouring stupid chemicals into our food.

Limp loaves are especially dangerous if one end of them is on fire. So work with English-French bread when it is *fresh* but French-French bread when it is *stale*.

FLAMING BRANDY

PYROTECHNICS

The best way to pour **FLAMING BRANDY** onto a Christmas Pudding is to take a ladle and pour into it the amount of brandy required. Hold the ladle over a low gas flame until you judge the brandy to be hot, but do not boil it (for fear of evaporating the alcohol).

Now tip the ladle until the liquid reaches the edge and allow the flame to lick it. It will ignite.

Pour onto the pudding, dim the lights, and present your masterpiece.

FLAPPING BIRD

ORIGAMI

The **FLAPPING BIRD** is the impressive **ORIGAMI** trick of making a bird whose wings will flap for the delight of your audience.

It counts as an essential skill for the trickster.

To make this creature we will first make a *Bird Base* which is one of the basic chords of **ORIGAMI** since it is the starting point for many constructions.

As always one begins with a perfect square of paper.

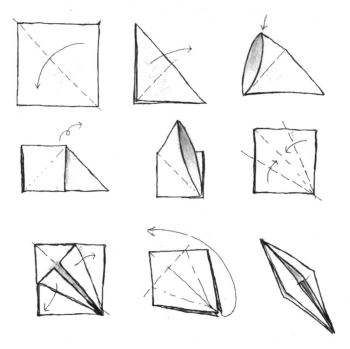

1: make a diagonal valley fold, northwest to southeast, to halve the sheet.

2: Make a valley crease and lift the northwest corner.

3: Squish the corner flat down onto the southwest corner.

4: Turn over the sheet.

5: Squish the opposite corner as before.

6: Fold the northeast and southwest corners of the top sheet into the middle.

7: Open them out again.

8: Make a crease toward the northwest corner, lift up the southwest corner and open it out.

9: When you've done this on both sides you have a *Bird Base.*

A
B
C
D
E
F
G
H
I
J
K
L
M
N
O
P
Q
R
S
T
U
V
W
X
Y
Z

You need to carry out those steps carefully, neatly and in a Zen-like state of oneness with your paper, otherwise you'll now be looking at a horrible tatty mess, which is not exactly the Japanese style.

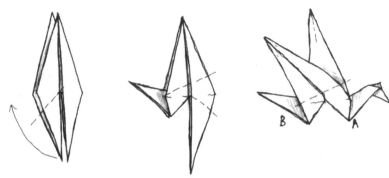

Making the **FLAPPING BIRD** is now simple. First fold out the tail. Next comes the head, which is exactly the same except for an extra fold to form the head.

Finally fold the two wings down a little on a line that starts low by the tail and rises a little toward the head.

Grasp the base of the bird's neck at A and then tug the tail at B—the wings will flap.

FLASH

JUGGLING

A **FLASH**, in juggle-speak, is the act of throwing every object in a juggling pattern once and catching them all again.

☆ You can throw a **FLASH** from a cold start (with all the balls in your hands) as a practice move.

☆ A successful **FLASH** of a large number of balls is an ego-satisfying substitute for being able to actually juggle that many:

'How's your juggling going?'

'Fine, I'm **FLASHING** five balls!'

☆ You can also throw a **FLASH** in a running juggling pattern.

If you juggle three balls and throw all three up high so that both hands are empty for a moment it is called a **FLASH**. It's a good practice move. Sometimes jugglers will clap their hands together during a **FLASH** to confirm that both hands are really free.

FLASH BOX

JUGGLING / FUN WITH SCIENCE

Jugglers love to stay up all night and play with their luminous props, but luminous props fade quickly in the dark and need recharging.

☆ A **FLASH BOX** is a big box lined with aluminium foil that you chuck a pile of luminous juggling equipment into when it starts to go dull. You then more or less close the lid and fire a flash gun into it a couple of times —the stuff is instantly recharged!

☆ Another neat way of keeping these props glowing brightly is to flood the juggling area with invisible light from a couple of UV tubes.

FLASH PIROUETTE

JUGGLING

☆ A juggler does a three ball or club pattern, **FLASHES** all three and turns a **PIROUETTE** before catching and continuing the pattern.

This is a pretty advanced trick. If you are working with clubs you'll probably be throwing **TRIPLES** out of the regular pattern to make the trick.

To achieve a fast pirouette the juggler should remember to pull their arms into their body during the turn, which accelerates the rotation.

They should also note that it can be *very* uncomfortable to be looking upwards during the turn, you can wrench your neck badly doing that.

☆ On catching the **FLASH** it looks very cool to throw one object high and turn again before resuming the regular pattern.

☆ Obviously a **FLASH PIROUETTE** is possible with four, five or more objects, but it gets a lot harder.

More often they will throw, say, three clubs high out of a five club pattern and hang onto the other two as they go around.

FLAT BATTERY

TRICKS OF THE TRADES

You can squeeze a little extra life out of a dry-cell battery (the sort you use in torches and personal stereos) by cooking the battery for a little while.

Do not try this with any type of rechargeable battery!

Take your flat batteries and heat them up to around 80°C for ten minutes or so. Placing them on a hot radiator works, or perhaps a very low oven. You should aim to get them hot all the way through, but not too hot to touch.

Now stick them into the appliance and they'll work just fine for a little while.

You only get about 5%–10% of the original charge but this trick can really get you out of trouble in an emergency.

FLICKING THE CORNERS

SIGNWRITING

FLICKING THE CORNERS is a sleight of hand technique used by signwriters to make lettering look sharper than it actually is.

☆ Instead of a attempting to properly square off the corner of a block letter the signwriter finishes off each corner with a tight little flick of the brush—effectively adding minute *serifs*.

When well-executed it looks very crisp and conceals a multitude of sins.

See also **ENTASIS**

FLICKING MATCHES

PYROTECHNICS / MATCH TRICKS

Never *ever* play with fire. Oh, all right then!

☆ Arrange a match and matchbox in your left hand so that your thumb presses the head of the match into the strike. Aim the line of the strike towards your target (which should for safety's sake, be empty air).

Lean the match slightly in the direction your are aiming.

Now flick the head of the match hard with your other hand.

The match will ignite and fly off like a little incendiary rocket.

FLICKING TOWELS

MARTIAL ARTS

Schoolboys know, only too well, the pain of an adroitly flicked towel. One corner is grasped in the palm of the right (or favourite) hand and the towel is wrapped once around and gripped firmly.

The weapon is used much like a **WHIP**, the opposite corner to the one being held plays the part of the **CRACK** and is often wetted to increase the severity of the injuries caused.

To fire the weapon the right hand is aimed toward the victim and the left hand holds the crack-end

The towel is launched toward your opponent's fleshy parts, usually the upper thigh and, just before the wet end hits, the right hand pulls back, causing the crack-end to turn over, inflicting a nasty blow.

Battles usually take place in the shower-room, where targets of naked flesh are plentiful.

The trickster will ensure that they are more dressed than their opponent before indulging in a first strike.

FLOURISH

JUGGLING / OBJECT MANIPULATION

A **FLOURISH** is rapid twirl of a juggling club between the fingers. It's easy enough to learn with one club, but you'll need to work on it a little before you can pop it into a juggling pattern.

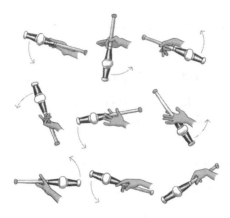

☆ Hold a club nose down in your hand between your thumb and index finger. The hand is palm downwards.

This is called a *Reverse Grip* because the club sits in the opposite direction to the *Normal Grip*.

Swing the club up so that it points forwards and up a bit, leaning back on your index finger. This is the starting position.

Now shove it back down and allow the momentum of the club to carry it a full 360°, passing *inside* your wrist. Your hand turns over as you do this.

Still letting the momentum of the club carry it on, let it fall between your index and middle fingers and keep going for another 360° · this time passing *outside* your wrist. It ends up pointing down in something like a Normal Grip.

Work on this until it is smooth.

☆ OK, now learn to do the move with a club you have just caught out of the air.

Toss a club from left to right on a single spin and catch it a little early between your index finger and thumb with your palm downwards.

This is a *Reverse Catch*—your hand is the wrong way up!

Now go straight into the **FLOURISH**.

You'll find that the first bit of momentum can be quickly applied by slamming the handle upwards as you make the catch.

Practice this on both sides until it is solid.

☆ The next step is to pull off a **FLOURISH** in a running pattern.

Juggle three clubs in the normal **CASCADE** pattern and then throw a **TRIPLE** with your right hand to buy you some time.

The next club to reach your right hand is caught in a *Reverse Catch* and **FLOURISHED** before resuming the **CASCADE**.

☆ You can pull off two **FLOURISHES** at more or less the same time.

Juggle three and then make a left hand reverse catch *at the same time* as you throw the **TRIPLE** in the right.

The left-hand club is already starting to **FLOURISH** as you make a reverse catch in the right and do the same thing over there. You should have time to complete *both* **FLOURISHES** before the **TRIPLE** lands.

☆ You can **FLOURISH** *every* club in a **CASCADE** by juggling on double-spins and making every catch a reverse catch. This is pretty advanced!

☆ At the end of a **FLOURISH** you can let the club keep going and release it as a **OVER THE SHOULDER** throw—very impressive!

☆ In a passing pattern you can add **FLOURISHES** by using *Early Doubles*[*] to buy you the time you need. In a *Four Count* for instance you toss an *Early Double* with your left hand while you make a reverse catch in the right and **FLOURISH** the club.

At the end of the move you toss the **FLOURISHED** club to your partner on the *pass beat*.

You can make that pass an **OVER THE SHOULDER** or **SLAPOVER** style for extra points.

FLOWER STICK

JUGGLING

A **FLOWER STICK** is a type of **DEVIL STICK** for the beginner. They are highly recommended for those who are still working on the basics since they have built-in *air brakes*.

They look a little medieval in a court jester sort of way.

Thus they will suit earthy folk-music loving horse-drawn juggling types (and there are plenty of *those* about these days).

They fly slowly on account of the leather or cloth stuck on the ends and they are ludicrously easy to work with—albeit a little dull to watch.

---

[*] In passing-pattern terminology, an *Early Double* is a passing throw that is made one beat early, and from the wrong hand. It is given an extra spin so it takes one beat longer to arrive in your partner's hand—thus arriving on time like a reliable train. The converse is the *Late Double* which is thrown at the normal time, but sent to the "wrong" hand with an extra spin. This gives your partner time to spot it coming and make the relevant adjustments to their pattern. Once these throws have been mastered jugglers can jam and improvise their passing patterns which can morph into bewildering complexity from the audience's point of view.

A
B
C
D
E
F
G
H
I
J
K
L
M
N
O
P
Q
R
S
T
U
V
W
X
Y
Z

FLY AWAY PETER, FLY AWAY PAUL

MAGIC

Sometimes the simple ones are the best. This trick will completely baffle small children.

☆ Draw two little faces on the prints of your index fingers, make them look like Peter and Paul, or if you have lots of time to prepare you could make two little fingertip puppets instead.

Face your enthralled audience holding up the little faces as if making two simultaneous **UP YOURS** gestures to someone standing behind you. Now deliver the following little poem:

> *Two little dicky birds, sat on a wall,*
> *One named Peter, one named Paul.*
> *Fly away Peter, fly away Paul,*
> *Come back Peter, come back Paul.*

Now as you introduce the birds in line two you show them each little face close up.

In line three you move each hand in turn behind your shoulder and then swap from your middle to index finger before bringing your hand back to show that the little birds have vanished.

In the last line you reverse the operation to bring them back again.

So there's your happy ending and the kids can go to sleep—with luck!

Fly Fishing

OUTDOORPERSONSHIP

Every Trick In The Book has but a little to say on the excellent arts and crafts of **FLY FISHING**, since much has been said on the subject by better writers and practitioners of this noble sport.

There is one thing though:

☆ Casting a fly is *exactly* like cracking a **WHIP.**

This is the exact opposite of the advice on the subject from expert fishermen, for the simple reason that they are not experts in the art of cracking **WHIPS**.

The reason a fisherman will tell you casting a fly is unlike cracking a whip is that if the line is handled badly it is possible to snap the fly off the end of the line, and they assume that this happens in the same way that a whip cracks. What they do not realise is that it is also possible to snap the **FALL** of a whip with careless handling.

The action of casting a fly is very similar to the **WHIP MAN CRACK** yet the line and fly do not crack, because the fly is fluffier and heavier than the line behind it.

Fly Resurrection

ANIMALS

In this trick an apparently dead fly is miraculously brought back to life. It is a less-than-sensitive way of treating one of Nature's living creatures. Mind you, we swat enough of the things and at least this trick doesn't actually *kill* the fly.

The secret is that if you *freeze* a fly, it will stop moving entirely and behave as if actually dead. You can bring the poor animal back to life by warming it in your hands and breathing on it gently.

David Blaine has used this trick, in his presentation he removes an apparently dead fly from the windscreen of a parked car, swings it gently by the wing to show that it is "dead" and then brings it back to life by cupping in between his palms while breathing semi audible things at it while mentioning that "...this is really weird, but I just wanna try it..."

See also **DROWNED FLY**.

FLYING SAUCER

YO-YO

This trick is a pretty one, but its real purpose is to adjust the grip of the string on the **Yo-Yo**, which affects it's **SLEEPING** properties.

☆ Throw a **SPINNER** by chucking the **Yo-Yo** down at a diagonal angle, either to the left of the right. Catch the string with your free hand and hold the top half of the string horizontally.

The **Yo-Yo** will spin *on a horizontal plane* at the end of the string, like a **FLYING SAUCER**.

As the speed starts to bleed off you release the string and let the **Yo-Yo** return to your hand.

☆ If you threw the **Yo-Yo** to the right you will end up tightening the string, if you go to the left it will loosen.

FOOL'S MATE

GAMESMANSHIP

FOOL'S MATE is the trick of defeating an opponent in the game of Chess is an amazingly short space of time.

The true **FOOL'S MATE** (which is a win for black) goes like this:

> 1. f4 e5 (or f3 e5, makes no odds)
> 2. g4 Qh4 #

You are unlikely to pull this off in a real game of Chess, but it is the shortest possible route to a checkmate.

The most common **FOOL'S MATE** takes one move longer and is a win for white. With luck you just might be able to force it on a beginner:

> 1. e4 g5
> 2. Nc3 f6
> 3. Qh5 #

FOOT TO HEAD (& HEAD TO FOOT)

HAT TRICKS

If you're going to be a master of *Hat Juggling* this is an essential trick.

☆ Stand on one leg with the hat over the toe of the other foot and kick the hat up to a head catch using a single spin.

☆ To get the hat back onto the foot you simply karate chop the brim of the hat at the back of your head.

☆ With the hat back on your foot you can practice tossing it from foot to foot as well. Kick it up with a single spin, swap feet and catch it again.

There's no excuse, you just need to get these moves down solid.

FORCING A CARD

MAGIC

The generic card trick goes like this: get someone to choose a card and have it returned to the deck, destroyed, or marked in some indelible manner. Return the card to the deck (if it has not been destroyed) and then *reveal it in an interesting way*.

To pull this off it really helps if you knew what the card was going to be all along—your *interesting way* might, for example, have involved having the card signwritten onto the side of a heavy goods vehicle you have scheduled to do a drive-by in a couple of minutes time.

So, by cold reasoning we have arrived at the nub of the problem, you are going to have to **FORCE A CARD** on your victim right at the start of the trick. There are many ways of doing this.

☆ The easiest by far is to use a **SVENGALI DECK**—this being the **THUMB TIP** of card magic. Fan the pack one way to show that the cards are all different (but don't make a big thing out of it or they may wonder why you are bothering). Then fan it the other way, get them to pop in a finger and stop the cards. Allow them to change their mind if they want and go again. When they are quite sure they are happy get them to take a peek and show the rest of the audience while you look away and try to remember which bloody deck you are using (**SVENGALI DECKS** can be set up for any card, really keen rich magicians have 52 packs of the things).

But then you realise you don't have to remember because you have already set up the Big Finish.

They pop the thing back into the deck, you shuffle it like mad, wrap it up in brown paper, stick and Australian address and a stamp on it and pop it in a letter box. Moments later a courier arrives with a package for you. You open it, pull out the contents and ask: 'Is that your card?'

And of course it is!

The audience faint dead away and you are a hero.

☆ It's cool to be able to **FORCE A CARD** without having a specially prepared deck and there are a hundreds of ways of doing this. Magicians have been doing tricks that end with the line 'Is this your card?' for so long now that the human race is collectively starting to get a little sick and tired of it. Once upon a time playing cards were part of everyday life and the illusion that a magician could defeat the *whole point* of a pack of cards (i.e. you can't tell one from the other by looking at the back) was both mysterious and appealing.

Nowadays you'd be better off working out tricks with games consoles and mobile phones.

So let's just list a few:

The **CROSS-CUT FORCE** is the simplest and the **CLASSIC FORCE** is the most classic. You can also get some mileage out of the **RIFFLE FORCE**.

FORER EFFECT

PSYCHOLOGY

This effect is named after a psychologist called Bertram Forer who carried out some interesting experiments in human gullibility. You can carry out the experiment for yourself easily.

☆ Grab some trashy newspapers and extract some random phrases from the horoscope section and make a nice full-page document out of them—or just use the one printed here:

A
B
C
D
E
F
G
H
I
J
K
L
M
N
O
P
Q
R
S
T
U
V
W
X
Y
Z

You are likely to express yourself in dramatic, creative and assertive ways. You are also likely to enjoy the warmth of the physical Sun. You have great energy, courage and honesty. You are likely to be self-confident and maybe even a bit self-indulgent. You expect to be the centre of attention, and often are. You can be quite determined and usually get your way when you really want to. You also possess great integrity, and are a natural leader. Your challenge is to temper any tendency for arrogant or egotistical behaviour and to instead develop humility and compassion; to learn detachment in the gift of your affections, so that you radiate your abundant energy freely and enhance the life experience of others around you.

OK, now print off a dozen copies and assemble twelve subjects in a room, having earlier taken down their personal details, dates of birth and so on.

Explain that you have written up twelve character analyses based on their star signs and that you'd like them all to read their personal copy and mark them from one to five (from totally inaccurate to amazingly precise).

Amazingly, most people will give a score of four or five because they just *want* to believe what they are reading. This is the **FORER EFFECT**.

☆ Now just to ram your point home you can ask them to pass the readings around and read each other's so that they can see they are all the same.

Understanding just how gullible people are is the key to pulling of confidence tricks and magical illusions.

Always remember that there are 300* born every minute!

FORGING A SIGNATURE

ESPIONAGE

It's a great deal easier to pull off a decent forged signature if you do the work *upside-down*.

---

* Roughly five babies are born every second.

FORK AND APPLE TOSS

JUGGLING / OBJECT MANIPULATION

☆ Get a table fork and lay it on the *back* of your wrist with the tines pointing up your arm.

Hold an apple in the same hand.

☆ Toss the apple and fork up into the air. The apple should go high and the fork should do a three-quarter spin and get caught in the throwing hand.

Then you catch the apple on the fork—which is a lot easier than you might think.

FORK CATCH

JUGGLING

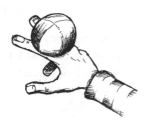

☆ A **FORK CATCH** is a catch made on the back of the hand between outstretched first and middle fingers.

You can juggle three ball, if you are so inclined, making every catch a **FORK CATCH**.

☆ A **FORK CATCH** can be used to make a nice punctuation point in a juggling routine. Juggle three balls and then stop with a ball in each hand and the third in a **FORK CATCH**.

☆ It's cool to juggle a Four Ball **FOUNTAIN** and make stops with **FORK CATCHES** on alternate sides—it makes you look very adept which is good for showoffs.

☆ Here's a nice two-ball move. Start with two balls in one hand, one in a normal grip and

A B C D E F G H I J K L M N O P Q R S T U V W X Y Z

the other in a **FORK CATCH**. Toss up both as a column **MULTIPLEX** then **SNATCH** the top ball and catch the bottom one in a **FORK CATCH**.

Got that?

☆ Now get back in the starting position but this time hold a *third* ball in your opposite hand.

Toss the two balls from the fork-hand as a *split* **MULTIPLEX**. The fork-ball goes straight up to a normal catch in the throwing hand, the hand-ball goes across to a **FORK CATCH** in the *opposite* hand.

Repeat mirrorwise to get back to the start.

☆ Now alternate the move form one side to the other and you are juggling a sort of **THREE BALL CASCADE**. With a little practice you can do this *very* fast. It looks great!

FOUNTAIN

JUGGLING

The simplest (and most usual) juggling pattern for *even* numbers of objects is called a **FOUNTAIN**. For odd numbers of objects you would, most likely, use a **CASCADE**.

☆ In a **FOUNTAIN** each of your hands independently juggles half of the objects in the pattern.

To juggle four balls in a *Four Ball* **FOUNTAIN** you juggle **TWO IN ONE HAND** with *both* hands, at the same time.

To juggle six, both hands need to be able to juggle *Three in One Hand* competently—You don't see this very often!

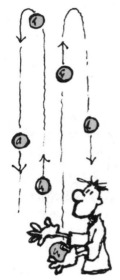

☆ Because both halves of the pattern are independent and unconnected, the **FOUNTAIN** can be juggled either sync or async (that is the hands can either throw together, or alternately). The async pattern is more common and feels more natural.

☆ When juggling a sync **FOUNTAIN** you can, with a little jiggery-pokery, engineer matters so that objects cross from one hand to the other, though you'll have to cheat things a little to avoid collisions.

If you make *every* pair of throws cross then you're doing what is known as a **WIMPY** pattern.

FOUR BALL BOUNCE

JUGGLING

There are many ways to juggle a **FOUR BALL BOUNCE**.

☆ Take two **BOUNCING BALLS** in each hand and juggle a two-ball **COLUMN BOUNCE** in each hand. You can juggle these synchronously or asynchronously—take your pick!

As with any **COLUMN BOUNCE**, the number of balls juggled is the number of columns, plus the number of hands. In this case 2+2=4.

☆ You can also juggle a **WIMPY** pattern.

Start with just two balls and practice making simultaneous crossing **PASSIVE BOUNCE** throws. You'll need to aim carefully so that the balls *just* miss. Both hands throw simultaneously, and the balls cross each other (and just miss) on the way down.

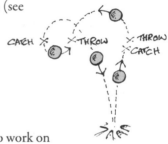

The **WIMPY** technique is often used by *Numbers Jugglers* when juggling even numbers of balls.

☆ A slightly more complex pattern is a 53 (see **TRIPLE SINGLES**) in which the 5's are thrown as crossing **PASSIVE BOUNCES** and the 3's as little airborne **CASCADE** throws. One hand throws 5's, the other throws 3's. It's a pretty tight pattern with a nasty little collision zone in the middle.

☆ Perhaps a little easier, and a great one to work on if you are going to learn a **FIVE BALL BOUNCE**, is the 55550—this is a **FIVE BALL CASCADE** with a **GAP** in it, hence it is also known as a **FIVE BALL GAP**. Every throw is a **PASSIVE BOUNCE** throw.

☆ You may find the 552 easier, it's the same pattern but you are **HOLDING THROUGH THE GAP**. The throwing sequence is a little weird. The throwing sequence is a little weird—it goes:

...right-left-(wait)-left-right-(wait)-right-left-(wait)-left-right-(wait)...

Which *feels* like: *left-left–right-right–left-left–right-right...*

☆ An exotic, but very learnable pattern is 633 juggled with **BOUNCING BALLS**. The 3's are air throws, and the 6's are bounces. Interestingly, two of the balls are *always* thrown as 3's—hence they never bounce. If you think about this you'll probably be able to guess why this pattern is described under **EGGS, JUGGLING WITH...**

...this is the *only* **BOUNCING BALL** pattern the author knows that can be juggled with eggs.

☆ It's also possible to juggle four balls in a bounce pattern with *just one hand!* See **FOUR IN ONE HAND BOUNCE** to find out how.

FOUR FOUR ONE (441)

JUGGLING

This pattern is terrific fun to juggle. It's a three-object pattern which we'll learn with balls though it works perfectly well with clubs too.

☆ If **SITESWAP NOTATION** means anything to you—juggle 441 and keep going, but a little explanation might help less mathematically literate readers. Here goes:

Start with two in the right and two in the left.

> Throw a ball straight up with the right hand (4).
> Throw a ball straight up with the left hand (4).
> **FEED** a ball from right to left (1).

We now continue by repeating those three moves mirrorwise.

> Throw a ball straight up with the left hand (4).
> Throw a ball straight up with the right hand (4).
> **FEED** a ball from left to right (1)...

...and that's it.

This is *almost* a *Square Juggling* pattern.

☆ Another neat *way of thinking* about this is that you are trying to juggle a Four Ball **FOUNTAIN** with just *three* balls—every time you find yourself with an empty hand (a **GAP**) you **FEED** a ball into it!

This curious logic has always worked for me!

A
B
C
D
E
F
G
H
I
J
K
L
M
N
O
P
Q
R
S
T
U
V
W
X
Y
Z

☆ By extension, you can juggle a **FIVE BALL CASCADE** with just *four* balls, which leads you to the pattern 5551 (the **FEEDS** always go one way when you do this).

☆ Moving on (for the advanced juggler) you can juggle a *Six Ball* **FOUNTAIN** with just *five* balls, once again **FEEDING** a ball into any hand that is empty. This creates the pattern 666661 which is just a tad easier than you might think!

See also **BOX, MACHINE, LUKE'S SHUFFLE.**

FOUR IN ONE HAND BOUNCE

JUGGLING

This amazing trick is attributed to *Radical Cheney.*

A quick reminder from the **COLUMN BOUNCE** theory class:

The number of balls you are juggling is the number of columns plus the number of hands.

It therefore follows that to juggle four **BOUNCING BALLS** in one hand you'll need to juggle in *three* columns—and so you do.

☆ Warm up by juggling a **THREE IN ONE HAND** bounce, using two columns that bounce *asynchronously* (OK, alternately). You'll need to develop a certain quickness of hand to extend this to four balls, so work on it for a while.

☆ To extend this to four we need three columns and your hand will make exchanges on a *right-middle-left-middle-right* basis. The columns themselves will rise and fall so that the outer two are in opposite time to the middle one (so the pattern *looks* a little like **RIGHT-MIDDLE-LEFT**).

This means that the outer balls are bouncing twice while the middle ball bounces once. You always need a very flat floor for double-bounce tricks.

The secret is to keep the whole thing tight and make sure that the outer columns stay in perfect time.

FOUR TRIANGLES FROM SIX MATCHES

MATCH TRICKS

That's the challenge: make **FOUR TRIANGLES FROM SIX MATCHES**!

☆ The rules are that each triangle should be equilateral with one entire match forming each edge.

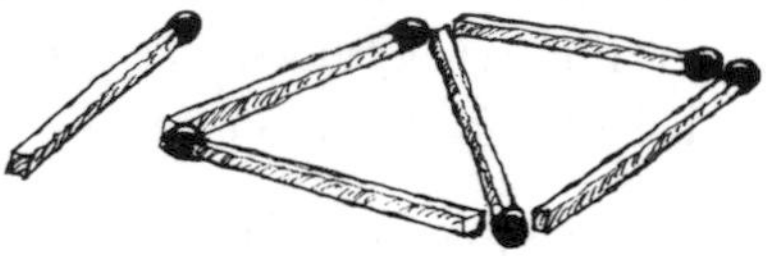

It's easy to make two triangles (you get one match left over) but making four seems impossible until you apply some lateral thinking.

The answer is a **TETRAHEDRON**.

FREE MOUNT

UNICYCLING

A **FREE MOUNT** is the action of getting onto a unicycle *without* any means of support. It is an essential skill, especially if you ever plan to ride a *Giraffe Unicycle*.

☆ To **FREE MOUNT** a standard unicycle, start by positioning yourself as if to do a *step-over* (see **HOW TO RIDE YOUR UNICYCLE**). The unicycle is in front of you, favourite foot on the down-pedal and saddle tucked under your bum.

A
B
C
D
E
F
G
H
I
J
K
L
M
N
O
P
Q
R
S
T
U
V
W
X
Y
Z

A B C D E F G H I J K L M N O P Q R S T U V W X Y Z

Launch yourself up as if doing a *step-over* but instead of stepping over you bring your top foot back hard into the top pedal, so that it kicks the unicycle back a little. Now ride off!

The little kick-back is important because it gets the wheel *under* your centre of gravity and sets you in the right attitude for riding off forwards.

☆ **FREE MOUNTING** a *Giraffe Unicycle* is a complex move. The technique used depends on the height of the machine. You have to climb up the thing as if it were a ladder, then get yourself on the saddle, and then find your balance—and all this before the thing falls over.

Do not attempt a **FREE MOUNT** until you are confident about **HOVERING** on your *Giraffe Unicycle*. You'll be wasting your time.

☆ With a five or six-foot *Giraffe Unicycle* you should be able to place your favourite foot on the bottom pedal while standing on the ground. Grab the saddle with one hand at the front and one at the back. Arrange the unicycle so that it is leaning slightly forwards and stand as close to it as you possible can.

Now stand up fast on the lower pedal, the machine will not scoot out from underneath you, but it will start to topple over. You therefore have a mere scantling of time in which to get your bum on the saddle, other foot on the top pedal, and *kick back* to lean the machine slightly forwards. You can now ride off or remain in a **HOVER**.

Chances are that you'll fail in the first few attempts, so it's wise to think about doing a controlled dismount. You let the unicycle fall forwards, keeping your foot on the lower pedal and hanging on to the saddle with your hand. This is important because you do not want to let the unicycle smash into the ground—that way you'll avoid causing expensive damage.

☆ **FREE MOUNTING** a higher machine requires extra technique and daring.

When it is not possible to get your foot on the bottom pedal (because it's just too *high*) you start by placing your not-so-favourite foot on the top of the tyre, jamming your foot against the frame of the unicycle. This acts as a sort of temporary wheel brake and will prevent the machine from scooting out. You then quickly step up, moving your favourite foot onto the bottom pedal (and taking over the braking job) then it's one more step up and onto the saddle as before.

This should be done quickly and you must start with the machine and your body in a nice tight line, with the centre of gravity ever so slightly forwards.

FREEDOM OF INFORMATION ACT

ESPIONAGE / TRICKS OF THE TRADE

The **FREEDOM OF INFORMATION ACT** of 2000 is an article of Law in the United Kingdom that was designed to solve a tricky conundrum, namely that all Government information has been traditionally held as secret unless specifically ordered into the public domain.

A
B
C
D
E
F
G
H
I
J
K
L
M
N
O
P
Q
R
S
T
U
V
W
X
Y
Z

It would have been impractical to change the law so that all of that information suddenly became public (unless specifically ordered to be secret) so instead a law was passed that gives anyone (in the UK) the right to request the disclosure of government information.

The Government, or a public authority that is part of the Government, is obliged within 20 days, to surrender that information *unless* it falls into a long list of exempted categories or costs more than £600 to retrieve.

Exemptions include such things as personal information, items related to National Security, things that the Government would rather you didn't know and so on.

It also includes things that you could find out from other sources, or items that the Government is intending to publish anyway.

In fact more or less anything can be excluded so it seems as if this law is a bit of a damp squib.

Not so!

The fact is that Government departments and public bodies are terrified of *seeming* to be unwilling to comply with this sort of legislation. So while you may be unable to actually get your hands on the information you requested you will have the satisfaction of watching those poor public servants wriggling on the hook.

These people have nice comfortable and secure jobs for as long as they fulfil their *Duties* and *Obligations*.

Duties and Obligations are littered aplenty in the long and rambling text of the Act.

So, when you have a problem with your local council and find yourself stonewalled, simply fire off a letter (or an email, the act does not specify and particular *form* for a request) demanding disclosure of some relevant information and mentioning the **Freedom of Information Act** and be amazed at how quickly they get back to you.

FRENCH DROP

MAGIC (VANISH)

The **FRENCH DROP** is probably the best known and most widely used method of vanishing a small object. It might be a good idea to learn a less well-known method like the **PALM RETENTION VANISH**.

☆ Hold the coin between the right thumb and the edge of your right forefinger. the hand is more or less vertical, but the small fingers should form a sort of shelf below the coin.

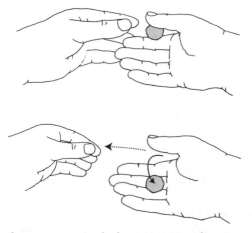

The other hand comes in to grab the coin, concealing it as it does so. As the fingers close the coin is allowed to drop onto the lower fingers of the right hand. There should be no perceptible movement in the right hand. The "taking" hand moves away, apparently with the coin inside and should command the attention of the **MARK**.

You must **PRACTICE IN FRONT OF A MIRROR** to make sure you are getting the misdirection right. Oh and do learn it both ways around (i.e right hand "takes" from left and left hand "takes" from right).

The **FRENCH DROP** is the vanish to use in the **DISAPPEARING BISCUIT TRICK**.

A
B
C
D
E
F
G
H
I
J
K
L
M
N
O
P
Q
R
S
T
U
V
W
X
Y
Z

A
B
C
D
E
F
G
H
I
J
K
L
M
N
O
P
Q
R
S
T
U
V
W
X
Y
Z

FREQUENCY TABLE

CODES & CIPHERS

When cracking a simple **SUBSTITUTION CIPHER** you can take advantage of the fact that some letters occur more frequently than others in normal English text. Here's a chart of the frequency of letters as they occur in the current draft of *Every Trick In The Book* which, as I write, is exactly 85,153 words long*. The most common letter is E, which occurs 40,622 times and the least common is Z which appears only 197 times.

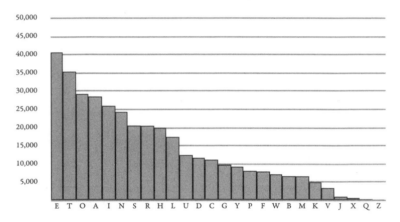

I'm quite pleased with the order in which the letters came out because it is generally agreed that a frequency table of English writing will *usually* start off in the order ETOAIN like this one does. It follows that I am probably writing in something that approximates English—which is fortunate for you (as the reader of my work).

The frequency table then *usually* proceeds SHRDLU, as opposed to my SRHLUD which is ever-so-slightly skewed. Read into that what you will.

☆ If you are trying to crack a simple **SUBSTITUTION CIPHER** you should start by drawing a copy of each symbol that occurs in the text and then counting up how many times it occurs. If your sample is long enough

---

* Of course it got a few words longer as I wrote that sentence.

you'll find that the most common symbol almost certainly represents the letter E. Here's an example:

ᚻᛗᚱᛗ ᛁᚻ ᛋᚠᚪᛗ ᛚᚠᚪᛗ ᚹᚱᛁᛏᛏᛗᛏ ᛁᛏ ᚱᚾᛏᛗᚻ

The most common symbol is the M symbol so we'll assume that it represents an E:

ᚻERE ᛁᚻ ᛋᚠᚪE ᛚᚠᚪE ᚹᚱᛁᛏᛏEᛏ ᛁᛏ ᚱᚾᛏEᚻ

I'm sure you can guess the first word now, and from that we can fill in a few more letters...

HERE ᛁᚻ ᛋᚠᚪE ᛚᚠᚪE ᚹᚱᛁᛏᛏEᛏ ᛁᛏ ᚱᚾᛏEᚻ

And it's a pretty easy step to guess the second word and fill in some more letters...

HERE IS SᚠᚪE ᛚᚠᚪE ᚹᚱᛁᛏᛏEᛏ IᛏRᚾᛏES

Now I know I made this one up, but doesn't that last word look like RUNES, rather like the symbols themselves?

HERE IS SᚠᚪE ᛚᚠᚪE ᚹᚱᛁᛏᛏEN IN RUNES

And the third to last word? Surely it is WRITTEN!

HERE IS SᚠᚪE ᛚᚠᚪE WRITTEN IN RUNES

Words three and four are still a little elusive but the second letter of each is the same and may well be one of the common letters (ETOAIN) but we've already used E, T, I and N so lets try guessing either an O or an A.

I leave the rest of the decryption as an exercise for the reader. You'll find a more extensive example later on in this book.

A
B
C
D
E
F
G
H
I
J
K
L
M
N
O
P
Q
R
S
T
U
V
W
X
Y
Z

☆ Now I fully expect the reader to be highly dubious when I claim that the principles of a **FREQUENCY TABLE** can also be applied to *numbers* that appear in documents.

This *is* actually true.

> *Benford's law*, also called the first-digit law, was made famous in 1938 by Physicist Frank Benford, who after observing sets of naturally occurring numbers, discovered a surprising pattern in the occurrence frequency of the digits one through nine as the first number in a list. In essence, the law states that in numbered lists providing real-life data (e.g., a journal of cash disbursements and receipts, contract payments, or credit card charges), the leading digit is one almost one third of the time. On the other hand, larger numbers occur as the leading digit with less frequency as they grow in magnitude to the point that nine is the first digit less than 5% of the time.

Statistically there should be more 1's than 2's, more 2's than 3's and so on though in actual fact the only thing that is *really* statistically significant is that there will be a great deal more 1's than anything else.

If you fill such a document with *random* numbers (i.e. ones you have made up) then the pattern disappears.

The clever people who audit accounts in order to seek out any *creative accounting* are hip to this secret and often check accounts in just this way. If they find no pattern they get very suspicious very quickly.

This pattern happens for subtle reasons that are beyond the scope of this book (but not, as it turns out, beyond that of *The True Nature of Things* to which I refer the more eager reader). What you must understand though is that the pattern works only when the numbers concerned are describing *quantities* of things (as is the case with a set of accounts). It would not manifest in a list of grid references marking interesting points in the British Isles, or the telephone directory for example.

By way of demonstrating this phenomenon to you the author has taken the liberty of processing the entire manuscript of this book, as it is at the time of writing this entry.

As you can see, *Every Trick In The Book* does indeed contains more 1's than any other digit and a keen statistical eye will also spot the *general trend* of diminishing frequency for the remaining digits, even though they do not progress in a constantly decreasing manner.

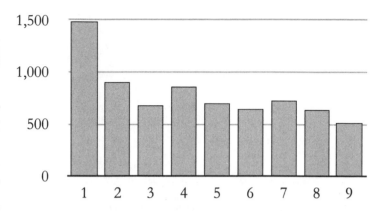

Since the digit 1 appears many more times than any other digit* you may take confidence in the indication that this book does actually contain some genuine information, rather than being *entirely* filled with things I have made up.

FRYING-PAN, EGG AND FIRE TORCH

JUGGLING

Here's an instant comedy routine for a street-performing club-juggler.

☆ Juggle a **FRYING PAN, EGG AND FIRE TORCH** then throw the egg way up high.

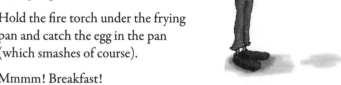

Hold the fire torch under the frying pan and catch the egg in the pan (which smashes of course).

Mmmm! Breakfast!

---

* 1,492 times to be precise, its nearest rival, 2, occurs only 905 times.

GAFFER TAPE

TRICKS OF THE TRADES

"What have *The Force* and **GAFFER TAPE** got in common?"

"They both have a light side, a dark side and they hold the Universe together."

GAFFER TAPE is possibly the greatest technological achievement of humankind. Nobody is quite sure whether it is a *tool* or a *material*, but you can fix *anything* with it.

It is so-named because it is primarily designed for use by the *Gaffer* in film making. The *Gaffer* is the head of the lighting department. The tape is remarkable because it is very sticky, yet can be easily removed and it has enormous tensile strength, yet can be easily torn by hand. It also comes in impressively generous rolls.

It has been said that "if you can't fix it with **GAFFER TAPE** then you haven't used enough."

In the United States of America this amazing stuff is often referred to as *Duct Tape* (because it is similar to the tape used to connect the big pipes that make up ducting) and also, by way of linguistic corruption and brand-namery, *Duck Tape*.

It would take a whole book to list everything that can be done with this incredible stuff so let me just list a few examples.

A B C D E F **G** H I J K L M N O P Q R S T U V W X Y Z

☆ When the outer tube on your **UNICYCLE** wears completely through at the low-spot and your inner tube pops you can make a quick repair. Fix the inner tube with a regular puncture repair kit and then wind six layers of **GAFFER TAPE** right around the wheel and tyre to cover over the hole. It will last this way for months.

☆ Lost the plug for your bath? Simply tear off a square of **GAFFER TAPE** and stick it over the hole. The stuff even works under water!

☆ Refused entry to a posh restaurant because you are not wearing a tie? Tear off a length of black **GAFFER TAPE** fold in the long edges and stick them down. Cut off the ends at forty-five degrees and hey presto! A cowboy-style tie. (I actually got *married* wearing one of these. It lasted for years—longer than the marriage in fact!)

☆ Taking **AERIAL PHOTOS WITH YOUR CAMERA**? Tape the poor camera up with **GAFFER TAPE** *before* you miss a catch and break it—it will stand much bigger knocks that way.

☆ Hole in your **BEANBAG**? **GAFFER TAPE**.

☆ Ripped car seat? **GAFFER TAPE**.

☆ Cable management? **GAFFER TAPE**.

☆ Quick but sturdy **MOEBIUS STRIP**? **GAFFER TAPE**.

☆ Rubber radiator hose split? **GAFFER TAPE**.

☆ Dog hairs on your clothes? Dab with **GAFFER TAPE**.

☆ Feelings of inadequacy? **GAFFER TAPE**.

GAFFER TAPE does have one drawback though, when you remove it there tend to be nasty little bits of white glue left behind which can look messy. There is, however, a very neat solution to this.

☆ Make a "dabber" from a fresh **GAFFER TAPE** and you'll find that it will lift the little gluey bits very easily.

GAP

JUGGLING

A **GAP** is a *hole* in a juggling pattern, a space that *could* take an object, but which is empty—either according to plan, or because a juggler has dropped something.

The skill of manipulating **GAPS** is almost as useful as the skill of manipulating objects.

When juggling a pattern with a "hole" in it there are various things you can do:

- you can either carry on juggling *as if* the missing object was still there, miming the missing ball if you like.

- you can **HOLD THROUGH THE GAP**, which means that the object that is in a hand immediately before the gap arrives *does not have to be thrown*. This results is some interesting patterns.

- when the Gap arrives in a hand you can **FEED** an object into it from the opposite hand. If you started juggling a *Four Ball Gap*, (4440—a rather dull pattern), and started feeding balls into the Gap you'd end up juggling 441—a rather cool pattern.

For examples of **GAP** manipulation see **FIVE BALL GAP, HOLDING THROUGH THE GAP**.

GARBAGE TRICK

JUGGLING

A **GARBAGE TRICK** is not necessarily rubbish.

A B C D E F G H I J K L M N O P Q R S T U V W X Y Z

The term refers to a trick in which a juggler does as many difficult things as possible at the same time. The great juggler *Francis Brunn* was famous for his awesome **GARBAGE TRICKS**, though I don't think he would appreciate the terminology.

So standing on a three-tier **ROLA BOLA** while juggling three rings in your right hand and spinning a ball on the finger of your left while balancing a sword on the end of your nose would be a nice **GARBAGE TRICK**.

GAS BOTTLE, FULL OR EMPTY?

TRAVELLER'S TIPS

Campers and truck-dwellers often rely on bottled gas for heating and cooking and, like pretty much everything one relies on in the field, gas has a habit of running out.

Two gases that are commonly bottled for mobile use: *propane* and *butane*. These gases liquify at fairly low pressures and the bottle you buy will contain gas in a liquid state just like the gas in a cheap cigarette lighter.

Serious travellers will use propane in preference to butane because it packs more heating punch per kilogram—though it costs about the same.*

Propane is more volatile than butane and liquifies at higher pressure, thus bottled propane is considered too dangerous for indoor use, which is why the bottles should always be kept outside in the open air.†

Neither propane nor butane are particularly *smelly* gases, but since gas leaks (which can cause explosions) are best detected by smell, the gas manufacturers add chemicals to the gas that can easily be detected by the human nose. These chemicals dissolve well in the liquid gas but they don't boil off quite as well as the propane or butane itself. Hence as your bottle slowly depletes the concentration of smelly stuff in the liquid gas gets stronger and stronger. When your bottle is about to run out the gas becomes very smelly indeed.

☆ So, when lighting your cooker, if you get a *very* strong whiff of gas, the chances are that your gas is about to run out.

The prudent traveller will always have a full bottle of gas in reserve in case they run out, but sometimes this will not be practical. At such times it may be desirable to check a bottle to see how much gas is left in it. Unlike cigarette lighters, which are typically made of transparent plastic, there is no way of seeing inside the bottle.

☆ HERE'S *The* TRICK: Grab the top of the bottle, quickly tilt it to an angle of about thirty degrees and stop it *dead*.

Any quantity of liquid gas inside the bottle will now slosh back and forth with a momentum you can *feel* as you try to hold the bottle steady. You'll find it pretty easy to judge the level of liquid gas from the force of the sloshing. It's rather like telling if an egg is **HARD BOILED OR FRESH**. If you don't feel any slooshing you're in trouble.

---

* Serious travellers prefer diesel to petrol for similar reasons despite diesel being more expensive than petrol and diesel engines being noisier, heavier and more expensive than petrol engines. The fact is that a diesel engine provides greater reliability, better fuel economy and longer life than a petrol engine. Diesel and propane are industrial fuels. Petrol and butane are domestic fuels.

† Statistically propane bottles are just about the most dangerous gas bottles around. More dangerous even than Acetylene bottles. This is mainly due to people not taking them seriously enough. Keep your propane outside—always.

GAS GUN

WEAPONS

A **GAS GUN** is a weapon in which a projectile is accelerated through a barrel by means of a controlled gas explosion, rather like the way in which the pistons in a petrol engine are powered by the detonation of a petrol-air mixture.

They are relatively easy to make and also relatively safe, as long as you restrict your projectiles to chunks of potato, and avoid shooting yourself in the face.

The usual design consists of a fat breech tube (3–4") with a strong screw top, such as you might be able to cobble together from plumbing parts. This is attached a length of narrower tube (1") which will form the barrel using a suitable adaptor component. Make sure you use high-pressure tube components, these are usually made from ABS plastic. PVC is far too weak and can shatter.

You can source suitable tubing from plumbing wholesalers, who will also sell you the plastic solvent glue to stick everything together with. Pay close attention to the instructions for the solvent, particularly noting that the joints will take about 24 hours to cure to full strength.

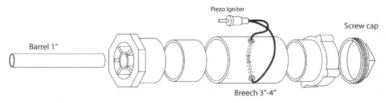

Next a piezo-electric spark generator is obtained. You'll find these in cigarette lighters or kitchen lighters. Two leads are connected to two electrodes glued firmly into the barrel terminating in two wires with a small gap between them. The trigger button secured to the outside.

To fire the weapon you first punch the end of the barrel into a potato and then you unscrew the cap and blow in a short burst of cigarette lighter gas. The trick is to get the mixture right—a short burst is best.

Point the weapon at the side of a barn and operate the trigger. If the mixture was right it will fire the chunk of potato with impressive force.

GEODESIC DOMES

GEOMETRY

GEODESIC DOMES are structures pioneered by a visionary called *Buckminster Fuller* who proposed them as a radical departure from conventional rectangular architecture.

They became very popular in the so-called Alternative Society of the late twentieth century which was doing its best to shake off the shackles of post-war conformity and which was enthusiastic about living in buildings that rejected the use of **RIGHT ANGLES**.

GEODESIC DOMES can either be constructed from triangular panels of stiff material, or more often by connecting rods together to form a lattice which can then be covered with fabric like a tent.

A *Geodesic* is a line that connects two points on the surface of a sphere by means of the shortest possible distance. This type of line is also known as a *Great Circle*.

There are many different designs for **GEODESIC DOMES** which vary both by *frequency* (the number of faces) and the fundamental geometrical

A
B
C
D
E
F
G
H
I
J
K
L
M
N
O
P
Q
R
S
T
U
V
W
X
Y
Z

A
B
C
D
E
F
G
H
I
J
K
L
M
N
O
P
Q
R
S
T
U
V
W
X
Y
Z

polyhedron that they are based on. The normal starting point for a design is either the **DODECAHEDRON** or the **ICOSAHEDRON**. These simple **PLATONIC SOLIDS** are built up into high-frequency domes by means of subdividing their faces into smaller faces by triangulation. As the frequency increases the dome more closely approaches a sphere in shape, but it also becomes less rigid. A high-frequency dome can have its side cave in under wind-loading like a stepped on ping-pong ball that has been.

As a structure for people to use a half-dome is not very useful because the walls slope in from the ground up. It's therefore more common to build structures that are two-thirds or three-quarters of the full sphere.

The trick of designing a **GEODESIC DOME** is the trick of working out the precise lengths of the edges of the triangles that will make up the structure. Depending on the frequency and type of dome there will typically be between two and five different side lengths involved. The mathematics can be complicated to work out (unless you are well-trained in such things) but once you know the relative lengths required for a particular type of dome you can scale them up to suit the size of the structure you have in mind and get to work. To a certain extent these structures build and align themselves which makes them a lot more fun to assemble than, say, a conventional roof for a regular house.

With this in mind the author has prepared some accurate figures and drawings which you may use as the basis of your own projects. One of the simplest ways of knocking up a geodesic

shelter would be to get hold of a large quantity of cardboard, cut triangles according to the given dimensions and tape the things together with **GAFFER TAPE**. You can make the cardboard waterproof by applying a a decent coat of gloss paint.

In each of the following designs the side lengths are given for a dome with a radius of *one unit*. To make a dome that is, say, ten feet across you first work out the radius (that's five feet) and then multiply all the side lengths given by that amount.

☆ We'll start with a plain old **ICOSAHEDRON**. It's not much use as a house, but it makes a great lampshade. To make one from sheet material you'll need 20 equilateral triangles and every edge must be 1.051462 times the radius you are aiming for. If you are making a framework instead you'll need 30 poles.

☆ To make a more interesting dome we can subdivide every triangle of the plain old **ICOSAHEDRON** into four smaller triangles. This produces a *2-frequency Icosahedron* which looks more hip. The down side is that in order to build the entire sphere from sheet material you are going to need 80 triangles. If you're making a framework you'll need 120 poles.

Either way it's starting to get complicated because there are two different edge lengths involved. Each of the original triangles from the regular **ICOSAHEDRON** is now made up from four smaller triangles. There is one central *equilateral* triangle with all sides measuring 0.618034 and three surrounding *isosceles* triangles with two shorter sides at 0.546533. Remember that those dimensions assume a dome radius of one unit.

If you are cutting poles you'll need 60 short ones and 60 long ones.

☆ The next stage is the *3-frequency Icosahedron* in which each of the original edges has been divided into three, so each of the original triangles is now made from 9 smaller ones. You'll need to make up 180 triangles to complete the entire sphere.

There are now three different edge lengths, each shown here as a fraction of the radius of the complete dome. If you're making the dome from poles you'll need to cut 270 as follows:

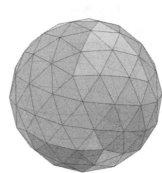

120	x 0.412411
90	x 0.403548
60	x 0.348615

A
B
C
D
E
F
G
H
I
J
K
L
M
N
O
P
Q
R
S
T
U
V
W
X
Y
Z

Here's one of the original icosahedron triangles with the three different length poles marked. Again, remember that the dimensions assume a dome radius of one unit.

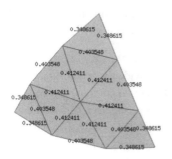

☆ Moving up to the *4-frequency Icosahedron* we get a 480 triangles,

... so this is not a dome for the fainthearted! The result is an extremely hip orb.

Each of the original triangles is now made up of 16 smaller triangles and there are five different edge lengths involved and if you are working from sheet material there are five different shapes of triangle that you'll need to cut out (counting left and right-handed versions).

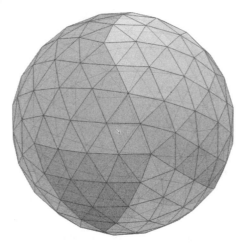

The dimensioned drawing shows how each of the original triangles from the **ICOSAHEDRON** is made up.

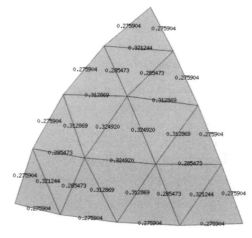

☆ You can also, if you feel so inclined, base your geodesic dome on the **DODECAHEDRON**. This fine shape has twelve faces which are all pentagons. Before we can do anything really useful with it we need to make it into a shape formed entirely of triangles. We do this by using every pentagon as the base of a pyramid of five triangles each of such a height that they reach out to the imaginary sphere touched by all the points of the original shape.

The result is called a *Striated Dodecahedron.*

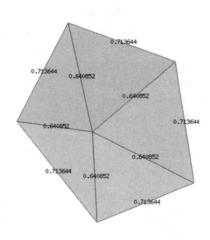

Every face of the original **DODECAHEDRON** is now formed from five isosceles triangles. The entire dome consists of 60 identical triangles each with two sides measuring 0.640852 and one measuring 0.713644.

If you're cutting poles you'll need 60 short ones and 30 long ones.

☆ Here's what happens if we double the frequency of the last dome:

The *2-frequency Striated Dodecahedron* has a total of 240 faces.

Each of the original pentagons from the Dodecahedron is now made up of 20 triangles. But since each pentagon had *already* been divided into five triangles the job is simpler than it seems.

There are just four different triangles, and five different edge lengths.

A
B
C
D
E
F
G
H
I
J
K
L
M
N
O
P
Q
R
S
T
U
V
W
X
Y
Z

A B C D E F G H I J K L M N O P Q R S T U V W X Y Z

If you are working with poles you will need the following quantities (for the whole sphere):

60	x	0.324735
60	x	0.376683
120	x	0.340340
120	x	0.362843
60	x	0.324735

All of those lengths must be multiplied up by the radius of your planned dome.

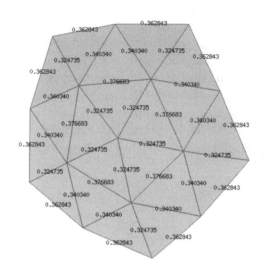

☆ This is a *3-frequency Striated Dodecahedron*. It has 540 faces. The lattice is mostly hexagonal in nature, punctuated by a few pentagonal vertices that are arranged like the corners of an **ICOSAHEDRON** around the sphere.

It's unlikely that you'll attempt to build one of these but the measurements have been supplied just in case!

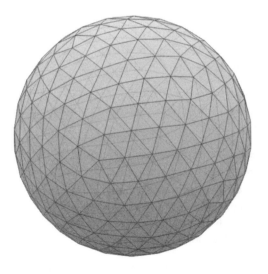

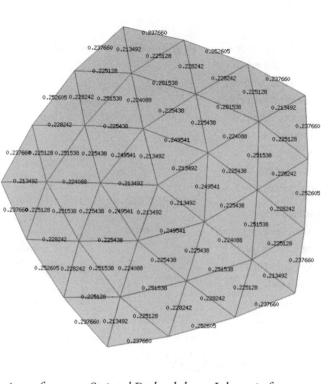

☆ Here is a *4-frequency Striated Dodecahderon*. It has 960 faces.

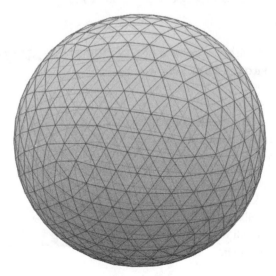

A
B
C
D
E
F
G
H
I
J
K
L
M
N
O
P
Q
R
S
T
U
V
W
X
Y
Z

This would be a pretty advanced project by any standards! Here is a breakdown of the edge lengths the 16 triangles that make up each of the triangles of the original striated **DODECA-HEDRON**. Five of these make up one pentagonal panel.

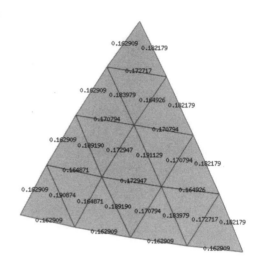

Note that two edges are formed from sections measuring 0.162909. These two edges meet at the occasional pentagonal vertices.

GETTING A CAT DOWN FROM A TREE

ANIMALS

If you are stuck with the problem of **GETTING A CAT DOWN FROM A TREE** here's the answer:

Do nothing.

Your cat is perfectly capable of getting back down any tree it can climb up. They just like to pretend that they can't.

The more time you spend going "Kitty, kitty, kitty!" and making offers of tempting food, the longer the cat will remain in the tree and the more pleased it will become with the attention you are lavishing on it.

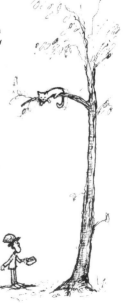

GETTING ON WITH HORSES

ANIMALS

Horses are curious creatures, they can easily be trained to charge a knight in heavy clanking armour at great speed towards rows of fierce soldiers with big pointy lances, but they will also chuck their rider over the nearest hedge if they spot a harmless discarded crisp packet fluttering on the ground. Horses are very big and strong, but also nervous creatures.

Big strong nervous creatures can be a problem, especially if they don't know you personally, so here are some basic tricks for getting on with them.

☆ Do not look a horse in the eye unless you want to make it wary of you.

☆ Try to keep your hands out of sight. Horses don't like hands because hands are what people use to *do things* to them.

☆ Blow up their noses gently giving the horse a chance to check out the smell of your breath. They like this.

☆ If you really must pat the poor animal give it good solid whacks. Light weight patting tickles them and they don't like it.

☆ Only a bloody fool would stand behind a mare who was looking after a foal.

GLASS HARMONICA

MUSIC

☆ Rub a wet finger around the rim of a wine glass and, if you get it just right, the glass will start to sing with a powerful, beautiful and ethereal note.

What's happening is that your finger is gripping, then slipping, then gripping and the slipping on the glass. This is happening at the resonant frequency of the glass, hence the glass rings like a bell.

A
B
C
D
E
F
G
H
I
J
K
L
M
N
O
P
Q
R
S
T
U
V
W
X
Y
Z

This trick has been known for over a thousand years, that is, for as long as we have had wine glasses to drink from. Musical instruments that rely on this type of friction to produce notes are called *friction idiophones*.

☆ A particular glass will always ring with the same note, as long as it is empty. But if you add wine (or water) to the glass the note will drop.

Fuller glasses make lower notes, emptier ones make higher notes. Generally the note the glass makes when rubbed with a wet finger is the same as the note it makes when tapped on the rim. For inexplicable reasons you'll find that better quality glasses make better music, so lead crystal is good, and pyrex bad.

Thus by careful preparation you can assemble a set of glasses that form a musical scale, like the keys of a piano, and which can be played like a xylophone.

In the 1800's this trick was taken very seriously and arrays of glasses were built into proper musical instruments of a kind that came to be known as the **GLASS HARMONICA**˙. One such machine was designed by Benjamin Franklin (no less) and is illustrated here from a publication of the period along with some curious lilies for reasons the author cannot comprehend.

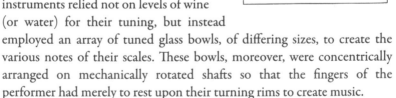

In their most perfected form these instruments relied not on levels of wine (or water) for their tuning, but instead employed an array of tuned glass bowls, of differing sizes, to create the various notes of their scales. These bowls, moreover, were concentrically arranged on mechanically rotated shafts so that the fingers of the performer had merely to rest upon their turning rims to create music.

˙ Also Glass Armonica, Hydrocrystalphone or Bowl Organ.

GLASS TURNING TRICK

BAR BET

This trick requires three glasses. It's one of those bets that you can't lose. It is particularly good because is is very repeatable—in fact that's the real fun of the trick.

1: Stand three glasses in a row the outer two should be upside down, and the middle one the right way up.

> 'OK,' you explain, 'I'm going to make three moves and I want you to watch very carefully. On each move I have to turn over *two* glasses. Here goes.'

2: Turn over the left two.

3: Turn over the outer two.

4: Turn over the left two.

> 'See how all three glasses are now the right way up? I bet you can't do the same thing.'

5: With that you turn the middle one upside down and it is the **MARK'S** turn. No matter how hard they try (even if you let them have more than three goes) they will never manage to get the glasses the right way up.

☆ HERE'S *The* TRICK: Position 5 is the *opposite* of position 1.

It is mathematically impossible for them to get the glasses the right way up again from here. When they realise they are stuck you can annoy them further by showing them just how easy it is.

> 'No, no, no!' You say. 'You're doing it *all* wrong, let me show you again!'

Quickly cheat back to the starting position and begin the whole trick from the start. Gets 'em every time!

☆ But before we get too carried away with our own cleverness it's worth taking another look at position 1. On reflection it should be obvious that the puzzle can be solved in just *one move* (by turning over the two end glasses). The same applies to positions 2 and 3. You see, the entire trick is a con from beginning to end!

GLOVE GUN

WEAPONS

This device is also known as a *Pug Gun* and it is actually illegal in certain jurisdictions. The **GLOVE GUN** is pretty powerful, though hardly lethal, and it can be made from objects 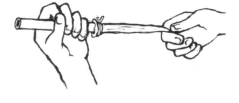 you'll find under your kitchen sink or in the garage.

☆ The main component is a short piece of plastic tube, you need something roughly half an inch (12mm) in diameter and two to four inches long. The barrel of a fat felt tip pen or marker is ideal.

Cut off one of the fingers of a washing up glove and join it to the tube by tying it securely. A **CONSTRICTOR KNOT** is ideal.

Find a projectile that fits neatly down the tube, pull the finger of the glove back as far as you dare and fire!

☆ Please note that, despite anything you may have learned from television and the movies, shooting people is *not* fun.

GOLD COLOUR

SIGNWRITING

Gold Colour is the name given by Signwriters for a shade of *Cream* which renders as an analogue for metallic gold leaf. The quality of true gold cannot be rendered in non-metallic enamel paints. Each signwriter will mix this colour differently but they will generally use a mixture mainly of white, with a dash of *Ochre* and a tinier dash of mid-chrome yellow. In modern computer terms the RGB colour #E6BE8A is a good match. This colour has been used by *Crayola Crayons* under the name "Gold" since 1958.

In heraldry the colour *Or* (French for "gold") may also be rendered in yellow, or for signwriting purposes Gold Colour.

In showground painting Gold Colour may be enhanced by overpainting it with pale yellow highlights to simulate metallicity.

Gold Colour looks particularly good on a blue field.

GOLDEN SECTION Φ

GEOMETRY

The **GOLDEN SECTION** (also known as the *Golden Ratio*) is a special mathematical ratio.

If you take a line of arbitrary length it is possible to divide it into two sections of differing lengths by placing a point on the line so that *the ratio of the whole length to the longer section is the same as the ratio of the longer section to the shorter section.*

The ratio you end up with is 1.61803398875* to 1. The mathematical symbol for this special number is Φ which is pronounced Phi.

---

* At least that is the value to eleven decimal places. In fact Phi like Pi is an irrational number which means that no matter how long you try to calculate it you just end up with a longer and longer number.

A
B
C
D
E
F
G
H
I
J
K
L
M
N
O
P
Q
R
S
T
U
V
W
X
Y
Z

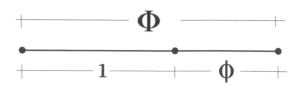

If you subtract 1 from you get 0.61803398875 which also has a special symbol, ϕ^* which is pronounced *Phee* and is known as the *Lesser Golden Ratio.*

A curious property of the Golden Section is that Φ is the inverse of ϕ, hence follows the remarkable result that the *inverse* of Φ is the same as Φ - 1

$$1 / \Phi = (\Phi - 1)$$

This sort of thing is of great interest to mathematicians and wizards. If it also appeals to *you* then you may be one (or the other).

If you are so gifted then you'll realise that the interesting nature of this number is giving us a glimpse of the mathematical beauty of the Universe, if you are not then you may as well stop reading this entry now and go and look up a fun trick to do in the pub instead.

There is a very neat formula for an exact value of Φ:

$$\Phi = (1+\sqrt{5})/2$$

The **GOLDEN SECTION** is often seen in architecture and the constructions of classical paintings where it may be used as the basis for a special rectangle: the *Golden Rectangle:*

The long side of the *Golden Rectangle* measures Φ and the short side measures 1. An interesting property of this shape is that if you extract a square of side 1 from it, the remaining small rectangle has the same proportions as the original. This is often the shape of canvasses and it is also the shape of the many windows in the Georgian houses in the City of Bath.

---

* This is simply a lower case ϕ, both letters being borrowed from the **GREEK ALPHABET**.

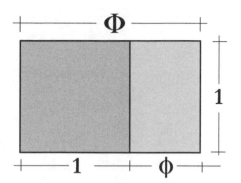

A
B
C
D
E
F
G
H
I
J
K
L
M
N
O
P
Q
R
S
T
U
V
W
X
Y
Z

You can construct a Golden rectangle using ruler and compasses as follows.

☆ Mark out a perfect square and divide it into halves. Place the point of a pair of compasses on one end of the square's "diameter" and set the tip to a radius that meets the far corner of the square. Now use this radius to intersect with the projected edge of the square and you have it!

☆ A very cool way of working out an approximation of the **GOLDEN SECTION** uses the *Fibonacci Sequence*, a series of numbers in which each value is the sum of the previous two. It goes:

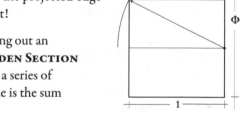

0, 1, 1, 2, 3, 5, 8, 13, 21, 34, 55, 89, 144, 233 and so on.

It turns out that the ratio of each number, divided by the previous one, gets closer and closer to Φ.

233/144 = 1.618055555... which is correct to four decimal places, more than adequate for most purposes.

☆ Here a Fibonacci Sequence has been used to create a spiral geo-metrical sequence that becomes a closer and closer approximation of a Golden Rectangle. Each segment of the spiral is actually a quarter *circle*.

A
B
C
D
E
F
G
H
I
J
K
L
M
N
O
P
Q
R
S
T
U
V
W
X
Y
Z

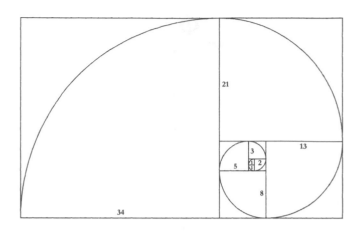

Even more remarkable is that you can start a Fibonacci-like series with *any* two numbers and it will still converge rapidly on a true value for Φ. Try it!

☆ A **PENTAGRAM** contains the **GOLDEN SECTION** and can be used as a construction to generate it.

☆ If you take three Golden Rectangles and arrange them so that their long axes lie on the three axes of cartesian space you can connect up the corners to generate an **ICOSAHEDRON.**

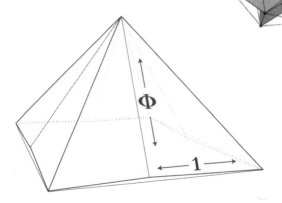

The half-sides of the Great Pyramid at Giza are proportioned almost exactly as Golden Rectangles cut into triangular halves by the diagonal. If you make a pyramid this way then the ratio of the entire circumference, to the height of the pyramid is *almost* exactly on 2π—just like the ratio between the radius of a sphere and its circumference. You can cheat this into a better match by making a slight fold inwards on each of the four sides (making them ever so slightly longer) so that the ratio comes out *exactly* right. Of course, if you did this you'd be able to see that the sides of the pyramid were slightly bent in—and so they are.

Thus the Great Pyramid displays considerable expertise in its design. It is, in fact, an incredibly sophisticated attempt to do a geometrical trick called *Squaring the Circle*.

The **GOLDEN SECTION** is *not* to be confused with the equally interesting **ROOT TWO RECTANGLE** but *is* very much related to the arcane symbol, the **PENTAGRAM**.

GOSHMAN PINCH

MAGIC / COIN TRICKS

This is a technique for **BACK PALMING** or concealing a coin in an apparently empty hand. It was allegedly invented by a chap called *Albert Goshman* though it is identical to the previously recorded method known as the *Tenkai Pinch*.

☆ The coin is pinched behind the hand between two fingers, usually the little finger and ring finger. The palm of the hand can then be shown, apparently empty.

This is an angle-sensitive illusion, but it has the advantage that the fingers *not* being used for the pinch may be splayed in a casual manner.

GRASS SCREAMER

HAND TRICKS / SURVIVAL

You are lost in the wilderness. For some reason your life depends on being able to mimic the sound of a gigantic bird unknown to science, or perhaps the wrenching scream of a dinosaur giving birth.

Perhaps you are in a movie and the plot demands such a skill, or perhaps you merely *imagine* yourself to be in such a movie. No matter. You have only your wit, your bare hands and a few blades of grass. What you *don't* have is much time.*

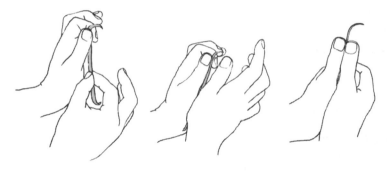

☆ Place your hands together as if praying and trap a blade of grass between the sides of your thumbs. Stretch the grass tight and bring it up to your mouth.

Blow hard through the gap between your thumbs. If all has been arranged properly you will be rewarded with an eerie and impressive wailing shriek.

And thus you survive the day.

---

* See Macguffin

GREASE YOUR BRUSHES

SIGNWRITING

Many years ago, a young man, who was determined to make a career in **SIGNWRITING**—and who had already discovered that you need the right sort of brushes (which are curiously named after birds)—went to a showman's yard that used to lie in the middle of Bristol in England. He was looking for some tips from an old-timer and had heard that there was a show painter living there called "Pete the Paint".

All the showmen were off doing the fairs and the yard was empty apart from an old chain-driven Scammel lorry, some broken parts of big rides and one extremely tatty little caravan.

He knocked on the broken caravan door and something stirred inside under a pile of rubbish.

'Hi, are you Pete the Paint, the signwriter?'

He was. The caravan was an unbelievable mess and it took him some time to find his boots.

"I'm a bit down on my luck right now, on account of the booze and having no money, d'you have a cigarette by any chance?" It had to be rolled for him on account of the shakes. He found his boots and his brush tin which he proudly displayed to his visitor as evidence of his signwriting credentials. A signwriter's brushes are their most expensive and important

A
B
C
D
E
F
G
H
I
J
K
L
M
N
O
P
Q
R
S
T
U
V
W
X
Y
Z

298 — EVERY TRICK *In The* BOOK

A
B
C
D
E
F
G
H
I
J
K
L
M
N
O
P
Q
R
S
T
U
V
W
X
Y
Z

tools. Pete's were horribly smeared in a thick greasy gunge that looked like a mixture of rancid butter and old sump oil.

'Always **Grease Your Brushes!**' Said Pete. 'Don't you grease yours? Anything will do, axle grease, lard, butter, even engine oil if that's all you can find! Keeps the moth's out and stops the paint drying in them.'

He reflected for a moment.

'Will you do me the kind favour of buying me a drink?'

The pub next to the yard was lavishly signwritten and ornately decorated.

Pete explained that he was actually working on a menu board in the pub and had just one bit to finish.

Inside the pub Pete settled down to a couple of pints of beer and in a few minutes his hands had stopped shaking. He laid down his brush tin and got out some paint.

'You're just an old soak Pete!' Said one of the locals. 'You can't do it any more! I remember you when you could actually paint, you're a shadow of your former self and it's all down to the booze.'

'I'll show you how I can paint! I'll bet you a beer.' said Pete.

He picked up two brushes, one in each hand and climbed his ladder and painted two perfectly mirrored baroque scrolls *simultaneously* with his left and right hand—and both in a single stroke.

Great Hailing Sign of Distress

CODES & CIPHERS

The **Great Hailing Sign of Distress** is the sign by which a Free Mason will communicate a need for urgent help and assistance. Any other Free Mason who observes this sign is obliged to lend such assistance as they can, up to, but not including, the loss of their own life —provided that the sign is being given by another Mason of course.

If you're stuck and out of diesel on the side of the M4 on a rainy night you may as well give it a try!

☆ Raise your hands as if being held up so that your arms form ninety degree angles. Now drop your hands to your sides in *three distinct steps* so that they end up at your sides.

☆ If you are stuck in a situation where you cannot move your arms (perhaps you have been handcuffed by the cops) you may use the verbal version of the Sign.

'Oh Lord, my God, is there no help for the Widow's son?'

Now just pray that one of the cops is a Mason*.

☆ Never use both versions together—that's a complete no-no and they'll spot you for a fake immediately. You'll probably be asked for a password, use the name of one of the **MASONIC HANDSHAKES**.

GREEK ALPHABET

CODES & CIPHERS / TYPOGRAPHY

The **GREEK ALPHABET** has been in constant use for three millennia by the Greeks and it also supplies a useful set of symbols for mathematicians and scientists. **SIGNWRITERS** and lettering artists should note that the letters are usually rendered similarly to **ROMAN LETTERS**, that is with serifs and the same general rules regarding the thick and thin strokes which normally appear where they would if the letter was being drawn with a wide-nibbed pen held in the right hand.

---

* In most of the British Police Forces one becomes a Mason on reaching the rank of Inspector.

A B C D E F **G** H I J K L M N O P Q R S T U V W X Y Z

A α *Alpha*

The shape of the lower case letter represents an ox, and the symbol often used in mathematics to represent an angular quantity. Also *alpha particles and waves* and *alpha waves* in brain function.

B β *Beta*

Used as a mathematical variable, also *beta testing* for computer software tests.

Γ γ *Gamma*

Often used to denote a photon in particle physics; hence Gamma radiation also gamma correction—a method of adjusting the tonal balance of images on computer screens.

Δ δ *Delta*

This letter, owing to its shape has given English the word *delta* to describe the mouth of a river that fans out as it empties into a lake or sea. In mathematics it refers to a *change* in something as in t to represent a change in time.

E ε *Epsilon*

This letter is popular with science fiction writers since it appears near the beginning of the **GREEK ALPHABET** and is therefore easy to remember, and while it is used a great deal in science, it does not appear much in common speech, hence it has mysterious overtones.

Z ζ *Zeta*

This letter brings to mind the *Riemann Zeta Function* which many people have heard of, but who know nothing whatsoever about. Suffice it to say that if the *Riemann Hypothesis* is ever proven to be true (it being one of the great unsolved problems in mathematics) mathematicians will party like it's 1999 all over again, and this despite the fact that everyone already *knows* that it is true. Odd bunch.

H η *Eta*

Used for various obscure scientific quantities, such as the *ideality* of a power transistor and the *metric tensor* in *Quantum Field Theory*.

Θ θ *Theta*

Commonly used to represent the angle at the business corner of a triangle.

I ι *Iota*

In the English phrase "not one *iota*" has come to mean "not in the slightest".

K κ *Kappa*

Used for *compressibility* in chemistry, and to represent *Einstein's constant of gravitation* in physics.

Λ λ *Lambda*

In computer science the lower case *lambda* is used to describe a particular kind of function, especially in the esoteric and wonderful language of LISP and its various derivatives.

M μ *Mu*

Most commonly seen in its lower case form as an abbreviation for *micro-* (one millionth part).

N ν *Nu*

Used for the frequency of a wave.

Ξ ξ *Xi*

A popular symbol for a random variable in mathematics.

O ο *Omicron*

On account of this letter's indistinguishability from the letter O it is not often used as a technical symbol. However it does sound very business-like and important and thus has been used as a name by various companies around to world who sell expensive things to businesslike and important people.

Π π *Pi*

One of the better-known Greek letters, which has it's own entry in *Every Trick In The Book*. See **Pi**.

P ρ *Rho*

This symbol is used for *Spearman's Rank Correlation Coefficient* which, in statistics, measures how sure we are that there is a relationship or *statistical dependence* between two variables. It varies between zero (no correlation) and one (utterly dependent). You can work out this sort of using either exotic mathematics or common sense

A
B
C
D
E
F
G
H
I
J
K
L
M
N
O
P
Q
R
S
T
U
V
W
X
Y
Z

Σ σ *Sigma*

This is best known, in its upper case form, as the sideways "M" that is *summation operator* in mathematics.

T τ *Tau*

The star *Tau Ceti* in the constellation *Cetus* was considered for some time to be very sun-like and searches for extra-terrestrial life have been focused here. The name of the SETI project (Search for Extra-Terrestrial Intelligence) is a deliberate pun on the star's name. Contemporary opinion on the likelihood of an earth-like planet in orbit around this star is "low to vanishingly remote".

ϒ υ *Upsilon*

This obscure letter is used by linguists as a term for the similarly obscure *labiodental approximant*.

Φ ϕ *Phi*

This letter is used to represent the **GOLDEN SECTION** which is $(1+\sqrt{5})\div 2$

X χ *Chi*

This letter, which is pronounced as "ch" has a Christian significance in that it is shorthand for *Christ*. hence the shortening of "Christmas" to "Xmas" (so it is not an *atheistic* or *secular* contraction as many people believe). The letter is often made into a special sort of ligature with Rho to form a symbol called a *Chi-Rho*, representing the first two letters of the Greek spelling of *Christ* and which is commonly seen in ecclesiastical design.

Ψ ψ *Psi*

This letter is most often seen as a symbol used by people working in the loose disciplines of *parascience* and *parapsychology* and was no doubt chosen for it's similarity to the *psy-* prefix of such words as *psychology*, *psychedelic*.

The character is also used to represent *pharmacology*.

Ω ω *Omega*

Best known for representing the *Ohm*, a unit of resistance in electronics.

GREENGROCER TRICK

OBJECT MANIPULATION / MAGIC

In the Good Old Days, when one was served in
shops (as opposed to rushing around with the
rabble loading carts and basket's oneself) or
indeed at open air markets (where the staff are
still good enough to serve you) it was customary
for greengrocers to deliver fruit and vegetables to your
brown paper bag with a dextrous flair and panache.

☆ The final potato, plum or apple is tossed into the air,
bounced from the inside of the elbow and into the open
brown paper bag, which is then "twizzled" by
grasping the two ears and swinging it like a child
going "over the top" on the swings at the park.

☆ A related trick is that of tossing an invisible
object from one hand into an open paper bag
held in the other. The bag-hand holds the mouth open with a finger
hidden behind that flicks that bag as the invisible object hits it creating
the very convincing illusion that something has landed in it.

GRIFTING

DEFINITION

A **GRIFTER** is a confidence trickster. It is an American word but is
increasingly used in British English because it sounds cool.

Like Dick Turpin, the notorious highwayman, **GRIFTING** has an air of
romance and glamour about it. However, in the the real world, both
highwaymen and confidence tricksters are in the business of being nasty to
other people in pusuit of their own personal gain.

They do have some amazingly cool tricks though and you'll find them
scattered through the pages of this book.

A B C D E F **G** H I J K L M N O P Q R S T U V W X Y Z

A
B
C
D
E
F
G
H
I
J
K
L
M
N
O
P
Q
R
S
T
U
V
W
X
Y
Z

GRIND

JUGGLING

A Grind is the action of holding one spinning object against another non-spinning object.

☆ In Diabolo work the juggler may make a catch on the stick instead of the string, this is called a Grind. The Diabolo needs to be spinning very fast so that the spin doesn't bleed off too much during the trick. The gyroscopic effect will keep the diabolo balanced.

☆ In *Ring Juggling* the juggler may catch a ring with another ring held flat in front of the body. You can actually catch two rings in one Grind like this.

☆ In Yo-Yo work the trick called Walking the Dog is a sort of Grind.

The Yo-Yo is made to Sleep at the end of the string and then does a gently Grind against the floor.

☆ You can take a *Hula Hoop* and toss it away from you with a lot of back-spin. It will clatter away from you **GRINDING** on the floor, before magically bouncing and rolling back to you.

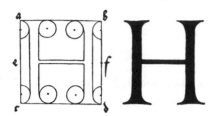

Half Hitch

KNOTS

Not to be confused with the **HALF KNOT**, a **HALF HITCH** is made when a rope is passed around a pole and then taken around the standing part with a *Single Hitch*.

☆ Take a rope and run it around a pole. lay the free end over the standing part and then poke it up through the *bight* (loop) you have just formed. This is obviously not very secure and most people would hardly consider it a proper knot. If we think of a knot as a word then a Half Hitch could be one of the letters that makes it up.

☆ A single **HALF HITCH** is horribly insecure, so usually you'll use a *Round Turn and Two half Hitches* to secure a rope in this way. Pass the rope around the one and a half times, then form two **HALF HITCHES** around the standing part.

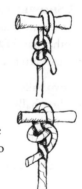

☆ Alternatively you can complete the job (especially if your are working with polypropylene rope) by poking the end of the rope *through* the strands of the standing part to make a sort of **LINESMAN'S HITCH**.

☆ A *slipped* **HALF HITCH**, while is a useful temporary fastening.

Pulling the loose end will immediately spill the knot.

HALF KNOT

KNOTS

The **HALF KNOT** is the first half of a **REEF KNOT**. It is often confused with the **HALF HITCH**. It is what you get if you tie an **OVERHAND KNOT** around something.

☆ Take a rope around a pole or the neck of a bag and wrap the ends around each other once.

You can then proceed to make a *Granny Knot*, a **REEF KNOT** or tie a **BOW**. It's up to you!

HALF SHOWER

JUGGLING

Here's a little bit of juggling theory.

☆ A **SHOWER** pattern, for any number of objects has one hand making throws through the air and the other hand **FEEDING** back. Here are the first few patterns in **SITESWAP NOTATION**.

3 1 - two balls
5 1 - three balls
7 1 - four balls
9 1 - five balls

I'm sure you can see the pattern that is emerging.

☆ Now if we consider, say four balls (7 1) there are also a series of patterns called **HALF SHOWERS** that fall between the **FOUR BALL** Shower and a balanced four-ball pattern (where both hands throw with the same weight) as follows:

7 1 - four-ball shower (very hard)
(6x,2x) - four-ball half shower (synchronous throws)

53 - four-ball half shower, also called *Triple Singles*, async.

(4x, 4x) - four-ball **WIMPY** pattern.

With five balls you get:

91 - five ball shower (unbelievably hard)
(8x, 2x) - sync half shower
73 - async half shower
(6x, 4x) - another sync shower
55 - the **FIVE BALL CASCADE!**

The point is that the more balls you are juggling, the more ways there are of doing a **HALF SHOWER**.

HANDLING POISONOUS SNAKES

ANIMALS

Well, the first thing to say about this is 'why bother?' These wild creatures are poisonous for a reason—*they would like you to leave them alone!*

Some snakes are very poisonous, a single bite can kill you in minutes, others are less so, like the Adder that lives in the British Isles, which is very unlikely to kill you unless you develop an allergic reaction to their venom.

Generally, the more poisonous the snake, the less likely you are to get bitten by it.

The ultra-lethal Puff Adder from West Africa, for example, has a bite so poisonous that you are almost bound to die, and yet even if you actually *tread* on one, you are unlikely to get bitten.

A
B
C
D
E
F
G
H
I
J
K
L
M
N
O
P
Q
R
S
T
U
V
W
X
Y
Z

The most feared snake in the world is the Black Mamba. It is also the fastest, capable of moving at 10–12 mph, which is *almost* as fast as you can run. Legend has it that the Black Mamba will actually attack and chase people before killing them with a single lethal bite. This isn't really true. What the snake will actually do is to treat you to a very aggressive display and rear up and stare you right in the face while hissing very loudly.

If you fail to take the hint at this stage you deserve to get bitten and die—the human gene pool will be better off for it.

☆ When catching a snake you should use a large piece of cloth. A cloth bag is best because you can end up with the snake in the bag. The first step is to immobilise the snake, which you can do by throwing the cloth over it. Be warned that throwing a piece of cloth over a moving snake is hard, since you'll be aiming at the curves of the snake which have the illusion of staying still, while the snake itself will have moved on by the time you get the cloth down.

This can be very dangerous!

You don't want to catch the tail and leave the head free! Aim a little ahead —not too far though!

☆ Assuming that you have trapped the poor animal, you now have to locate the head. The snake will now be very cross indeed so it will not be helping much. *Do not pussyfoot about!* Locate the head through the cloth and grab it firmly with your left hand.

Now reach under the cloth with your right hand and slide your hand up the neck until you get to the head.

Here comes the tricky bit.

Your thumb goes on top of the head, and the crook of your first finger goes under the jaw. Hold the snake *firmly* like this and it cannot bite you! The rest of the snake can still wriggle about in an alarming manner, but unless it is a very big animal you'll be able to keep it easily subdued by holding it with your left hand about two thirds of the way along its body.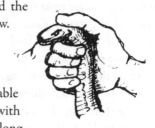

You're stuck now of course, because you haven't learned how to put it down again!

☆ The safest thing to do is to pop the snake in a cloth bag with a drawstring at its neck. (You do *have* a bag don't you?)

Open the bag and then more or less turn it inside-out and grab the snake's head (which you are holding in your right hand) with the left hand, *through* the cloth of the bag.

Pull the snake inside and tighten up the drawstring.

It's now safe.

Hangman's Noose

KNOTS

Every Trick In The Book does not recommend the use of this knot either for hanging yourself.

Or indeed anyone else.

That sort of thing is best left to the authorities.

It is occasionally useful for theatrical purposes or when you are trying to create a image of Gothic horror.

A
B
C
D
E
F
G
H
I
J
K
L
M
N
O
P
Q
R
S
T
U
V
W
X
Y
Z

Assuming you are right-handed, start with the standing part of the rope to your left and fold a loop some way from the end, then fold the free end back again so you have made a Z-shape. You hold the three legs of the Z in your left hand while whipping the free end around it. When you have covered most of the flattened Z there will be a little loop left which you can tuck the end though.

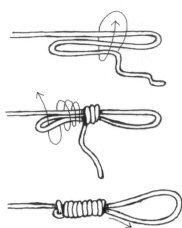

Finally pull on one leg of the noose to draw the loop tight up over the end.

This method of securing the loop is similar to the one used when doing the amazing trick of **PLAIN WHIPPING**.

It is often said that a "real" **HANGMAN'S NOOSE** should have 13 turns of whipping in it, but this isn't actually true., six or seven turns are usual, more tend to make the knot wobbly and unstable.

HARD BOILED OR FRESH?

KITCHEN TRICKS

☆ Spin an egg fast on a tabletop and let it go, now quickly stop it for a mere moment with your finger and let go again. If it starts spinning again it's fresh, otherwise it's hard-boiled.

The yolk of a fresh egg keeps spinning when you stop the shell from turning.

When you let go it starts the egg again as if it were a rubber band.

HAT BALL BOUNCE

JUGGLING / HAT TRICKS

Here's a nice comedy move. You'll need a **BOUNCING BALL** and a hat.

☆ Place the ball into the hat (it's best if your audience does not see this).

☆ Drop the hat to the floor. When it lands, the hat will stop and the ball will fly up out of it an impressive and surprising manner.

HAT HAND VANISH

MAGIC / HAT TRICKS

This is a silly trick with a hat, you can pop in into a *Hat Juggling* routine, or just use it as a comedy move.

☆ Hold a hat up in front of you, crown uppermost.

☆ Present a flat hand in a positive and showy manner, fingers pointing to the sky.

A B C D E F G H I J K L M N O P Q R S T U V W X Y Z

☆ Very positively bring the hand down over your hand, which curls into a ball as the hat descends—so that the hat appears to be a gateway into another dimension.

☆ Raise the hat as you uncurl your hand to reveal that it is still there.

☆ The comic duo *Hair Gag and Chisel* add a little rude innuendo to this trick. As Hair Gag bends down, Chisel places the hat's crown against his partner's bum, feeds his hand in (as a vet might) before removing it again with a look of comic disgust on his face.

HAT LINES

SHOWMANSHIP

Some people may wonder why the act of collecting money for a street show is sometimes called *Bottling* when in actual fact money is generally collected in a hat (which would suggest *hattling*). Wonder no more:

In days gone by, when street shows were more criminal in their nature than they are now, a busking performance would typically be carried out by a team of rogues from the wrong side of the river.

One would do the show itself, while others would work as lookouts, keeping a sharp eye out for the *rozzers* (cops). A child (or *urchin*) would be employed to collect the money by working their way through the crowd with the hat during the performance. *Radical Cheney* explains in *The True Nature of Things:*

> When any crowd gathered an opportunity arose for other miscreants to work the crowds, whether lifting from the pockets of the assembled or masquerading as part of the show itself and demanding monies for it. To forestall such trickery as this, the urchin that was *properly* employed for the task would be equipped with a hat, to be held on one hand, and a bottle to be held in the other. Within the bottle

would be trapped a large fly which would only remain for as long as a thumb was kept tight over the open neck. It is usually assumed that this device was intended to prevent the child from dipping the hat but the bottle had a more subtle purpose. Obtaining a bottle with a fly trapped *within it* was a task that took more time to prepare than it did to gather a crowd. Thus the bottle was in fact a *sign* that indicated the *bona fide* credentials of the carrier. The species most commonly used for this purpose was the large English fly *Calliphora Vomitoria* which is known in layman's speech, to this day, as the *Bluebottle*.

Which brings us to the actual subject in question: **HAT LINES**.

HAT LINES are things that you say to ease the passage of coins and banknotes from the wallets, purses and pockets of your audience into your hat. Without them the natural anxiousness of your audience regarding the simple act of giving away money will tend to overcome their desire to properly reward you for your entertainment.

The first thing to address on this subject is *how much*, you must make a joke of the issue and get everyone to laugh together about it *before* you do you finale trick and start passing the hat.

```
YOU: People often ask me how much they should give at the
end of the show!  I don't ask much, just open up your
wallet or purse, take out, say, two pounds—and give me
the rest.

YOU: If you're too shy to give to me the money yourself
then send out your son or daughter to drop some money in
the hat and kids, remember. If mummy and daddy don't give
you at least five pounds to give to the funny juggler
then it means that they don't really love you.
```

Failing to mention actual amounts of money this will cut your show's income by about 50%—you *must* mention actual amounts of cash if you actually intend to make a living as a busker.

Just before you perform your finale you may wish to say something along the following lines:

```
Oh, and if you do walk off without paying I warn you I
never forget a face. I'll find out your name, and your
address, and perform my show outside your house for the
rest of your life.
```

With the audience primed you can proceed with the Big Trick which should, of course, be suitably impressive.

> YOU: Thank you! I've had a great time doing this show for you and I hope you've enjoyed it, please *rush* forwards and place some money in the hat and remember, don't throw your money! Fold it up neatly and pop it in!

You'll generally find that the very first donations come from children whose parents have sent them to do the job.

> YOU: Look at this ladies and gentlemen, a whole *pound* from a small child. Think about it, if *they* can afford that much it's ten pounds minimum from the adults.

And then to the child:

> Now rush back and get me some more!!

If all this sounds very commercial and money-grabbing—well, it is!

Your job as a busker is to perform on the street for money, so you may as well be good at it.

The real point is that there are many ways of measuring the quality and entertainment value of a street performance but the amount of money you get in the hat at the end is as good an indicator as any.

In any case, think of it this way: the money you get in the hat is Magic Money.

Why? Because the people that gave it to you actually *wanted* to.

How often does that happen in normal life?

HEADSTAND

ACROBATICS

☆ In the classic **HEADSTAND** you balance, inverted, on the top of your head and both hands, the three points of contact with the ground being arranged in a triangle. Balance is maintained by sharing your weight between these three points. Your head will need to be cushioned if you are working on a hard floor.

A more elegant version of the **HEADSTAND** is the one used in Yoga.

☆ Kneel on the floor and place your forearms on the ground so that your hands overlap. Form a cup with your hands and place your head in it, now transfer your weight onto your head and forearms and lift yourself into a **HEADSTAND**. Note that you don't need any cushion for your head with this method.

Elegant isn't it?

HEADS I WIN, TAILS YOU LOSE

GRIFTING

This is a playground trick designed to fool only the greenest **MARK**, and is called out immediately before tossing a coin.

This carefully crafted double-negative means that they cannot win however the coin falls.

A very similar trick, that *will* fool a huge number of people is **I'LL TOSS YOU FOR IT!**

HEADS I WIN, TAILS I WIN
GRIFTING

You should try this only if you are very, very brave and very adept at **PALMING A COIN**. Actually you'll need to be able to palm *two* coins, side by side, and moreover you'll need to be able to catch a third from the air while they are so palmed without messing things up.

You are going to toss a coin while the **MARK** calls heads or tails. You catch the coin from the air with the throwing hand, smack it onto the back of your opposite hand and then reveal ... that they lost the toss.

This is just not British. It also requires a great deal of skill and confidence.

☆ You set the trick up thus: two coins are palmed side by side in the throwing hand, one shows heads and the other shows tails.

You then master the art of dropping one or the other onto the back of your opposite hand depending on the outcome you require. This will take a lot of practice. Once that part is mastered you add the third coin, which you must be able to toss with a confident and natural flick without showing the palmed coins.

Not only that, but you have to *catch* the coin as well and slide it out of the way into safe keeping as you slap your hand down onto the back of the opposite hand. Aim to trap it between the base of your thumb and the edge of your palm and with a little dexterity you can practically throw it there as you lift your hand up before slapping it down.

Once you have slapped down you calmly and deliberately announce, "You said heads, right?" And as they agree, drop the tails-coin onto the back of your hand and slide the covering hand away.

You're will still be left with two coins in the other hand, so a little **MISDIRECTION** is called for now—just to be on the safe side.

Toss the revealed tails-coin up from the back of your hand and **CLAW** catch it emphatically while announcing "I win!" and use this move as cover for stashing the coins in your other hand back into your pocket.

Now you know why they let the coin *fall to the ground* at football matches.

A
B
C
D
E
F
G
H
I
J
K
L
M
N
O
P
Q
R
S
T
U
V
W
X
Y
Z

HEAD UPSIDE-DOWN PUPPET

SILLINESS

Stick, or paint, two little eyes on your chin. Lie on the floor in front of a sofa and place your audience behind the sofa. Now tip your head right back and poke your chin up so that is all your audience can see and start saying stupid things and sticking your tongue out a lot.

The effect is truly bizarre and *very* funny—only you can't see it unless you are using *Muppetry* techniques. It looks like a tiny, but truly alive, little head with a big mouth.

HELICOPTER

FLYING MACHINES / JUGGLING

A **HELICOPTER** is best known as the type of flying machine that gave rise to the expression "It'll never fly!" because of the extraordinary complexity of making ones that actually work, and also because they are notoriously difficult to fly.

It is also the name of a rather cool **CLUB JUGGLING** trick.

☆ Juggle three clubs in a regular **CASCADE** and then, instead of making a throw, you place one club on top of your head with the knob pointing forwards. As you let go give the handle a little tap so that the club spins on your head. After 360° of spin the opposite hand reaches up and grabs it and the pattern resumes.

Not exactly elementary—but well worth learning for the effect.

See also **PAPER HELICOPTER**.

A
B
C
D
E
F
G
H
I
J
K
L
M
N
O
P
Q
R
S
T
U
V
W
X
Y
Z

HELIUM

FUN WITH SCIENCE / SILLINESS

HELIUM is the second-lightest element. The lightest being hydrogen.

HELIUM is an "inert gas" which means that it will not burn under any circumstances. It cannot be manufactured with earthling technology and is instead found in underground wells*.

Ever since the giant hydrogen-filled airship the *Hindenburg* crashed and burned, **HELIUM** has been the lighter-than-air gas of choice for filling balloons and airships.

This means that it is commonly available in convenient tanks.

☆ If you breath in a lung-full of **HELIUM** (which is completely harmless) then you will speak with a squeaky voice until it there is none left in your lungs.

Take care to keep breathing regular life-supporting air in between bouts of squeaky-talk because you could asphyxiate if you don't get enough oxygen.

☆ If you take a breath of helium and then blow bubbles with bubble mixture they will go up, and up, and up.

Breathing **SULPHUR HEXAFLUORIDE** will make you speak with a great big low gruff voice, but have a care! Study the appropriate entry in this book carefully before trying this out!

HEXAGON

GEOMETRY

A six-sided polygon is called a **HEXAGON**. If the shape has equal length sides and equal angles it is a *regular* hexagon.

---

* It's strange that the lightest element should be found deep underground, strange but true.

Regular hexagons are easy to construct using a ruler and pair of compasses. You *should* have been taught this at school but you may not have been paying attention.

☆ Draw a *circle* and then, without changing the setting of your compass you "walk" around the *circle*.

Draw a small mark at the top of the *circle* with the pencil end of the compass, and then mark off a point one 'radius' around. Then place the point of the compass on that mark and mark the next point.

If you're careful and precise you'll end up with the *circle* divided into exactly six parts. Draw in the sides of your hexagon by connecting these points.

If you have an enquiring mind you may wonder just why this construction works and how come the circumference of a *circle* is so conveniently divided thus into six parts—or you may just take it for granted.

See also **PENTAGON**.

_____

HOLDING THROUGH THE GAP
JUGGLING

☆ When you are juggling a pattern with a **GAP** in it one or more of the hands involved will occasionally have very little to do.

To explain the principle of **HOLDING THROUGH THE GAP** I will borrow the famous train-scheduling analogy first proposed by R. Cheney in his legendary dissertation on the relative capacities of different juggling patterns.

A B C D E F G H I J K L M N O P Q R S T U V W X Y Z

Cheney noticed that a juggling pattern was similar in many ways to a rail network, and that the time that objects spend in the hands of the juggler was analogous to the time spent by a train standing at a platform. A juggling pattern for a solo juggler would therefore resemble a network with just two platforms for trains to stop at, whereas a **FEED** for three club-passers would have six platforms, and so on.

The juggling pattern itself would therefore resemble a complicated, and very precise train timetable. In the **THREE BALL CASCADE** the Red Beanbag Special might be scheduled to leave *Left Hand Halt* at 10:31 and 4.2 seconds and arrive at *Right Hand Halt* at 10:31 and 5.3 seconds. It is, of course, very important that each object leaves on time, because another train is always about to pull in.

And so it goes. Each train has to leave the platform just before the next train arrives. *Cheney* describes the model thus:

> A novice's juggling pattern is therefore full of derailments, cancellations and collisions, much like the actual rail network that the working people of the United Kingdom rely on for their daily commute. The expert's juggling, on the other hand, runs more like the rail networks in Holland, Germany and Japan where the trains actually run on time and stay on the rails.

But what has this to do with **HOLDING THROUGH THE GAP?**

Well it is simply this: if a train has been cancelled and will *not* be arriving at a station then the train that is standing there can stand there for a little while longer.

So, translating from trains back into juggling: when a ball (or club, or ring) is *missing* from a juggling pattern the hands can occasionally *hold* a ball (or ring, or club) rather than throwing it. The result of this is a rail network with a lot less rains running (and therefore one that is easier to manage), or to put it another way, a juggling pattern with less stuff flying about in it (and therefore easier to juggle).

☆ It is common practice, when a **DROP** occurs in a passing pattern, to **HOLD THROUGH THE GAP** while one of the jugglers positions themselves so as to be able to pick up the fallen object.

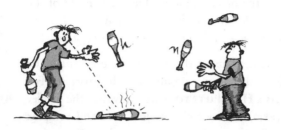

☆ If you **HOLD THROUGH THE GAP** in a two-person passing pattern you'll find that the jugglers take in turns to juggle. One juggles three for a moment or two while the other rests with two. Every time there is a pass they swap roles. This is handy because the juggler with just two objects can concentrate on locating the dropped object.

☆ If you **HOLD THROUGH THE GAP** in a **FIVE BALL CASCADE** you'll find that the pattern turns into 552—which is a nice easy way of juggling four balls.

For more on this see **FIVE BALL GAP**.

HOP THE FENCE

YO-YO

This is a simple, but cool **Yo-Yo** trick.

☆ Run the **Yo-Yo** down the string and let it rise again, but instead of catching it you flick it over your hand and let it go down again.

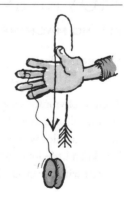

You can keep this going if you like.

A B C D E F G H I J K L M N O P Q R S T U V W X Y Z

HOT POTATO

JUGGLING

HOT POTATO is the name of a juggling style in which the juggler keeps the objects in a juggling pattern *out* of the hands as much as possible: minimum *dwell time*, maximum *airtime*—as if juggling burning hot potatoes!

Now juggling is all about rhythm and we can actually be specific about the precise timing of such a pattern. For three objects a **HOT POTATO** pattern involves the juggler throwing (6x,o)(o,6x) which may look odd and complex but it actually means that they are juggling **THREE IN ONE HAND** only letting the hands *take turns* to juggle the pattern.

☆ The **HOT POTATO** style is terrific fun, with clubs you'll be juggling triples or even quads and keeping all that stuff spinning high up above you.

The converse of **HOT POTATO** is the **SLOW CASCADE** in which the balls are held for as *long* as possible.

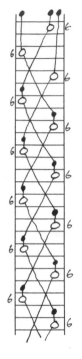

HOVERING

FLYING MACHINES / UNICYCLING / BICYCLES

HOVERING is the art of staying in one place without going anywhere. You can hover a helicopter or a unicycle, it's up to you.

There is obviously a slight difference in technique depending on the vehicle of your choice, but the really big difference is that, in training, a student helicopter pilot will be hovering at an altitude of about four feet (with the left skid a little low), while a unicyclist will have the wheel of the vehicle in contact with the ground.

HOVERING is an essential skill for both helicopter pilots and unicyclists, so let's get started.

☆ In a helicopter you have the benefit of an instructor who will tell you to focus on a point in the distance in front of you. You'll probably be broken in gently, first operating just the pedals, then just the cyclic and then the collective while the instructor operates the remaining controls. As you become familiar with the exercise you'll be allowed to operate two controls at once, and finally all three. You'll find that a small amount of left stick is required to counter the translational drift from the tail rotor, and you'll also discover that each control affects the others (adding a little collective will tend to yaw you to the right, which requires you to correct with the pedals and so on). Take it in nice easy steps. Nobody ever mastered this skill in their first lesson!

On a unicycle you will not have the benefit of an instructor and dual controls, so you will need to proceed more carefully, especially if you don't want to crash and burn.

☆ Start by riding forwards and bringing the vehicle to a complete stop. Rock back once, then ride on. Practice this with *both* feet. Do a stop and rock-back with the left foot, and then a stop and rock-back with the right.

☆ As you become more confident you can try double rock-backs: Ride forwards, stop, rock back, forward, back and then ride off again. Once again, practice this with both feet. When you can do that you are ready to learn the full hover.

☆ Position yourself in a door-way so that the *outside* of your arms are resting on the frame. Now hover! If you find yourself tipping over you can right yourself with the backs of your arms. As time goes on you'll find yourself using the door frame less and less.

Cyclists can also use **HOVERING** technology on their two-wheelers to stay

A
B
C
D
E
F
G
H
I
J
K
L
M
N
O
P
Q
R
S
T
U
V
W
X
Y
Z

upright at traffic lights, or at the beginning of a cycle race, without having to put a foot down. This can be useful if their feet are clipped to the pedals (as is common on racing machines).

It's the ultimate method of winning a slow cycling race, since you end up going precisely nowhere.

There are three methods:

☆ *Pure Balance:* It is possible, though ludicrously difficult, to stay upright on a bicycle without moving *at all.* There are no instructions for this, just try *really* hard—you just might manage it.

☆ *Fixed Wheel Hover*: Certain bikes (track bikes and *trick* bikes) have fixed rear sprockets rather than the usual freewheel set-up. This means that they can be pedaled *backwards* if you have a mind to.

To **HOVER** a fixed-wheel bike you bring it to a halt with the front wheel turned to about 45° either to the right or left. Choose one and stick to it.

On English roads, where we drive on the left, it's best to choose to point the wheel to the right for reasons I'll explain in a moment.

With the bike in this position you can correct a slight lean to the right by pedalling forwards a little to bring the machine *under* its own centre of gravity. If it leans to the left you can correct by pedalling backwards a touch. In practice you'll end up doing a little rocking motion just like a unicyclist.

☆ *Free Wheel Hover:* The technique here is the same as for the fixed wheel hover except that you cannot pedal the machine backwards. You therefore set up the balance with the front wheel pointing up the camber on the road, so that a little pedal pressure will move it to the right, and loss of pedal pressure will allow the wheel to roll back to the left.

That's why the best way to learn the fixed wheel hover is with the wheel pointing to the right—unless of course you are living in a country where people drive on the right hand side of the road.

HOW TO LIVE IN YOUR TRUCK (THE THREE RULES)

TRAVELLER'S TIPS

1: Do not disable your own vehicle.

2: Do *not* disable your own vehicle.

3: The ground you are parked on is not yours, so don't act as if it is.

You would be amazed at just how often the people who attempt to live the itinerant lifestyle manage to break these rules. Examples of disabling your own vehicle include: running out of fuel, flattening batteries, failing to carry a spare tyre, not having a jack, losing the keys, getting stuck in mud, ditches or sand, getting clamped or locked in behind gates, stacking several tons of tat* and firewood for the winter under the chassis, buying a caravan and not bothering to buy anything to tow it with, not knowing how to drive and even, believe it or not "lending the diesel injector pipes from my engine to a bloke called Dave".

As to the land you are parked on, well it really *isn't* yours, and even if it *was* you still wouldn't really be allowed to park on it because of all sorts of fiddly laws and stuff to do with planning permission and so on.

☆ HERE'S *The* TRICK: Be polite and cooperative and do your best to get on with landowners, *never* outstay your welcome and remember that the

---

* Tat: stuff you think you might need some day but never do.

whole point of having a house with an engine and wheels is that you can move it around from place to place as circumstances demand.

HOW TO RIDE YOUR UNICYCLE

UNICYCLING

> Nobody can ride a unicycle, it's just that some people have learned how to take an amazingly long time to fall off!—RADICAL CHENEY

Notwithstanding Cheney's remarks, you *can* ride your unicycle and you don't have to fall off.

LESSON ONE—"STEP OVERS"

Get your 20-inch machine and adjust the saddle so that your leg is almost, but not entirely, straight when the pedal is in the down position. Now work out which your favourite foot is. If you are right-handed it will probably be your left foot—but it could be your right if you are very slightly weird (like me). To work out which your favourite foot is you place a chair in front of you and step onto it. Now which foot did you use?

☆ Now stand the unicycle in front of you and arrange it so that your favourite pedal is at the bottom. Lean the machine back and stick the saddle under your bum and put your favourite foot on the down pedal.

Good. Now step over the machine. Your launch forward, lift you not-so-favourite foot over the high pedal and land it back down in front of the machine.

The most important thing (and I will go on about this) is to keep your weight on the bottom pedal. As long as you do this the machine will not scoot out from underneath you and crash you to the floor.

Well done! You have just managed a step-over.

Do a few more until you feel confident about this move and then we can tick off lesson one as done and dusted.

LESSON TWO—"GETTING ON"
Set up your machine between two chairs with their backs turned towards you and place the favourite pedal at the bottom. Grab both chair backs and arrange yourself as you did for lesson one: bum on saddle, favourite foot on the down-pedal.

Now say to yourself 'I will not take my weight off the bottom pedal.'

Haul yourself onto the machine, placing the least favourite foot on the top pedal and sit there all wobbly and insecure. Now would be a good time to remind yourself not to take your weight off the bottom pedal.

Hang about for a while trying to look cool. It will feel pretty impossible just sitting there so don't try to do much. Just relax, enjoy the view and get used to being there.

LESSON THREE—"GETTING OFF"
When you are fed up with trying to look cool you will need to get off. Remind yourself not to take your weight off the bottom pedal and carefully lean forward as you take your foot off the top pedal and return it to solid ground. Transfer your weight to the foot that is on the ground and then (and only then) you may take your weight off the bottom pedal.

You made it!

A
B
C
D
E
F
G
H
I
J
K
L
M
N
O
P
Q
R
S
T
U
V
W
X
Y
Z

Lesson Four—"Moving about a bit"

Ideally you'll find somewhere to work where there is a convenient handrail, but a plain old wall will do. You could also ask a friend to stand beside you so you have something to hold on to, but this next lesson takes a while and after your friend has run out of giggles they will probably get bored of helping you.

Arrange yourself and your unicycle so that you can climb on using the wall or handrail for support. I'll mention once again that the really big secret here is to keep your weight on the bottom pedal at all times, but you have probably worked that out by now and have bruises to show for it.

The aim of this lesson is to try and wobble that machine along the side of the wall or handrail so that your other foot ends up down. If you can do this you will have done two things:

- You'll have travelled a full half turn of the wheel.
- You'll have learnt how to transfer your weight from one foot to the other.

Make your way up and down the wall or handrail until you are reasonably confident about shifting from one foot down to the other foot down. It doesn't matter that you are horribly wobbly and slow—you are learning something. Take it in nice easy stages, you could be doing this for days!

You'll discover all sorts of new muscles that you never knew you had, and just how sore they can get in interesting ways but hey! This is good for you.

Lesson Five—"Launching into the Abyss"

Eventually, as a unicyclist, you are going to have to let go of any support and go for it. But HERE'S *The* TRICK: you do not have to fall off!

This is what you do: Park yourself and your machine against a wall with a nice big open space in front of you. You should have both feet on the pedals and your back to the wall. Breathe deeply, get brave and go!

Push yourself off and try to ride two pedals-worth into the void. Then step off! Stepping off is just like doing the step-over you learned in lesson one. You keep your weight on the down-pedal, while stepping off with the foot on the up-pedal. You also need to grab the back of the saddle with your hand to prevent the unicycle from dropping to the floor.

When you've managed that you can try three pedals-worth, then four, and so on.

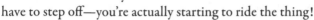

Pretty soon you'll manage a good six pedals across the void before you have to step off—you're actually starting to ride the thing!

A typical beginner will find that their route curves mysteriously to the right or left every single time. Don't worry about it, this is normal and there's very little you can do about it except to keep on trying.

You're really starting to get somewhere now. In no time at all you'll be able to ride for yards and yards. You may already be having fantasies about riding to work on your amazing machine.

LESSON SIX—"TURNING CORNERS"
As your skill develops you'll find you can ride in more or less a straight line for miles. But what about corners?

To a certain extent, turning corners will come naturally, but being an impatient beast you'll probably appreciate a tip or two.

Do this: ride with your arms outstretched as if you were playing aeroplanes. Now turn your upper body and look in the direction you want to turn while pushing down hard on the inside pedal.

Isn't that a nice trick?

OK, to hone your skills further go and look up **FREE MOUNTING**, and **HOVERING**.

HUNGARIAN PIG-DROVER'S CRACK

WHIPS

One presumes that the swine of Hungary are sullen creatures, since this crack goes off like a rifle-shot.

It's also pretty easy to learn.

☆ Grab a stock-whip or a bullwhip and swing it in an anti-clockwise circle around your body with your right hand so the line of the whip flies round like the hand of a clock.

Once the thing is flying nicely you can pull off the crack.

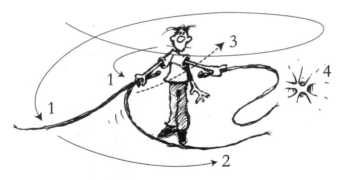

1: Wait until the whip-hand is at about twelve-o-clock and *stop dead*.

2: The body of the whip will carry on, curving into a nice bend.

Wait until the end of the whip reaches about nine-thirty...

3: Swing your whip-hand *past* the end, this is where you put the force in.

4: The big bend shrinks and travels to the end of the whip and turns over at about twice the speed of sound—*crack!*

With a little practice you can pop the whip on every single revolution.

HYDROGEN

FUN WITH SCIENCE / EXPLOSIVES

Hydrogen is the lightest element of all. It is also highly inflammable. You can use it to make bloody great big airships that sail elegantly through the skies before bursting into flames and killing all the passengers.

☆ You can make hydrogen (and oxygen) from water by taking two wires from the terminals of a battery and dunking them into water. Stick two jars upside down in the water, one over each terminal. You'll collect hydrogen bubbles in the jar over the negative terminal and oxygen bubbles in the other.

You can tell which is which because the hydrogen jar will be twice as full.

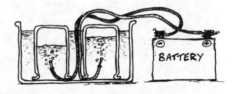

Water is H_2O which means it is made from two parts hydrogen to one part oxygen.

It helps if you chuck some salt in the water, but your wires will corrode quite quickly. It also helps if you chain a bunch of batteries together in series to get the voltage up a but, but *be careful!* You can get a very nasty belt off vehicle batteries especially if there is salty water about.

You think you can't, but trust me, you can!

Hydrogen burns with an all-but invisible flame and will leak out of just about anything because its molecules are so small.

☆ If you fill small balloons, or *Modelling Balloons* with hydrogen and burst them with a flame they will detonate with an unbelievably loud bang.

☆ If you fill them with a mixture of hydrogen and oxygen in the ratio 2:1 and do the same thing you had better be wearing earplugs.

A
B
C
D
E
F
G
H
I
J
K
L
M
N
O
P
Q
R
S
T
U
V
W
X
Y
Z

HYPNOTISING CHICKENS

ANIMALS / HYPNOTISM

A cataleptic cock set against a charming view of rustic Provençal buildings.

The following passage from *R. Cheney's* work is informative, but untypical of the great savant's style, being both sumptuously punctuated and notable for a plenitude of adjectives. This leads the author to believe that the passage may have been inspired by, or possibly translated from, the work of *Gaston Tissandier* who wrote in the late 19th century on matters of Popular Science—albeit in the French.

> We place a cock on a table of dark colour, rest its beak on the surface where it is firmly held, and with a piece of chalk slowly draw a white line in continuation from the beak, as shown in our engraving. If the crest is thick, it is necessary to draw it back, so that the animal may follow with his eyes the tracing of the line. When the line has reached a length of about two feet the cock has become cataleptic. He is absolutely motionless, his eyes are fixed, and he will remain from thirty to sixty seconds in the same posture he had at first only been held by force. His head remains resting on the table as shown in [the engraving]. This experiment, which we have successfully performed on different animals, can also be performed by drawing a straight line with a piece of chalk on a slate. M. Azam declares that the same result is also produced by drawing a black line on a table of

white wood. According to M. Balbiani, German students had formerly a great predilection for this experiment, which they always performed with marked success. Hens do not, when operated on, fall into a cataleptic condition so easily as cocks; but they may often be rendered motionless by holding their heads fixed in the same position for several minutes.

☆ Another method involves turning the bird upside-down, as before and then laying its head flat on its side the ground. Now draw an imaginary line with your finger, starting at the tip of the beak and running about four inches in the direction the beak is pointing. Run your finger back and forth along this line until the chicken goes into a trance.

☆ If you pick up a chicken and tuck it's head under a wing, and then rock it slowly the creature's diminutive brain will assume that it is night and furthermore that the rocking is the movement of a branch that it is roosting on. Thus the chicken will immediately go to sleep.

While you are handling chickens you may discover the extraordinary steadiness with which they hold their heads while you move their bodies about. It's almost as though the head is nailed to some invisible object.

You could, in theory, fashion a sort of *Steadycam* by taping a small video camera to the head of a chicken.

A B C D E F G H I J K L M N O P Q R S T U V W X Y Z

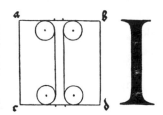

ICOSAHEDRON

GEOMETRY

The **ICOSAHEDRON** is one of the five **PLATONIC SOLIDS**. It has twelve vertices, thirty edges, and twenty faces—each of which is an equilateral triangle. Think of a Chinese lantern!

☆ The **ICOSAHEDRON** is the *dual* of the **DODECAHEDRON**. If you draw a point at the centre of each face and the connect the points together you can construct a **DODECAHEDRON** inside the original shape.

Similarly, if you connect up the midpoints of the faces of a **DODECAHEDRON**, you get back to the **ICOSAHEDRON**.

The **ICOSAHEDRON** is a popular starting point for designing **GEODESIC DOMES**.

There is an interesting relationship between the **ICOSAHEDRON** and the **GOLDEN SECTION** in that the vertices of an **ICOSAHEDRON** can be found by arranging three Golden Rectangles around the three axes of cartesian space.

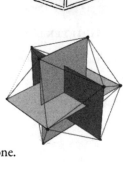

Lay one rectangle along the x-axis, another along the y-axis and a third along the z-axis and you're done.

A
B
C
D
E
F
G
H
I
J
K
L
M
N
O
P
Q
R
S
T
U
V
W
X
Y
Z

I'LL TOSS YOU FOR IT!

GRIFTING

Sometimes you may owe somebody money for something but not have the right change.

For example: You might owe someone five pounds but only have a ten pound note on you. So you could try:

```
YOU: I'll toss you for it!
```

The offer adds a little spice to the occasion, and in the long run it will work out fair, since there's an even chance of the coin landing either way.

However, unscrupulous **GRIFTERS** will work this game to their advantage if they get the chance.

☆ HERE'S *The* TRICK: This time the **GRIFTER** owes you twenty-five pounds but after rummaging through their pockets at some length they can (apparently) only find ten pound notes.

The **GRIFTER** hands over two ten pound notes and holds back the third.

```
GRIFTER: How about I toss you for it? It works out fair
in the end.
```

Naturally you may be a little resistant to the idea but the **GRIFTER** digs around some more and pulls out a coin and magically finds a five pound note at the same time.

```
Grifter: Come on, are you scared of a small bet?
```

The **GRIFTER** tosses the coin.

You call and, on average, you will lose because you are now betting for five pounds that *already* belongs to you.

Have a care!

IMPOSSIBLE PLAIT
KNOTS

If you take a piece of leather and slit it into three strips, leaving both ends intact, it can be formed into a plait.

The professional cyborg *Robert Llewellyn* first made his living by working leather into wristbands back in the hashish-fueled days when he lived in a **GEODESIC DOME** next door to *Radical Cheney's* comfortable shed. In his autobiography *Thin He Was and Filthy-Haired*, he mentions that:

> Both ends of the wristband were solid leather and the centre part was plaited.
> How did we do that? It is a secret of the leather-working brotherhood and I would
> die a horrible death if I were to divulge this Holy Knowledge.

This may be true. So let the Brotherhood of Leather-Workers join the angry ranks of Astrologers, Dowsers, Scryers, Magicians and Free Masons who would quell the pen of this author—and know that he fears them not. The secret of the **IMPOSSIBLE PLAIT** is revealed overleaf.

☆ Start with a piece of leather about three quarters of an inch wide and seven to eight inches long (check that it will fit nicely around your wrist).

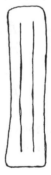

You could use an old leather belt if you're short of materials. Carefully mark it up as shown (ordinary biros make nice clear lines on leather) and then make two cuts along the strip to divide it into accurate thirds.

You should use a steel ruler and a surgical scalpel (or something as frighteningly sharp) to make the cuts.

You're ready for the magic part!

ABCDEFGHIJKLMNOPQRSTUVWXYZ

☆ Starting at the top you plait the rightmost strip into the middle, and then the leftmost strip into the middle. Now, while holding those strands in place with one hand, you feed the bottom of the work *through* the right-hand gap in the work from front to back.

☆ Make two more plaits: first the rightmost strip goes into the middle, then the leftmost strip goes into the middle.

The work will start to look a little tangled at the bottom but don't worry, it will come out right in the end!

Hold those the plaits in position with one hand and feed the bottom of the work through the *left* hand gap, again from front to back.

☆ Smooth out the work and you'll discover that two more plaits have been magically done *for you* as a natural result of poking the work through the gap. You now have a strip that has been plaited six times.

☆ If your piece is long enough and has room for another six plaits then you can add them now, just repeat the sequence of operations one more time:

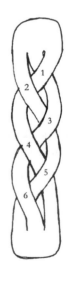

Two plaits starting from the right.
Feed through the right hand gap.
Two plaits starting from the right.
Feed through the left hand gap.

☆ You can add as many plaits as your piece of leather will allow, as long as you always add them in sixes.

IMPOSSIBLE WHEEL

UNICYCLING

"It's a bike, Jim—but not as we know it!"

The **IMPOSSIBLE WHEEL** is a wheel with an axle from which two stunt pegs, or two footplates, project and *nothing else*.

Stunt pegs being the special foot pegs that BMXers fix to their machines to allow them to do all sorts of tricks.

The machine is a lot easier to ride if instead of stunt pegs, you bolt footplates to the axle of a regular bicycle wheel. The plates can be made easily from folded metal plate.

☆ You ride one like this:

Roll the thing along the ground like a hoop, then run up behind it and jump on using a **SUICIDE MOUNT**: both feet land on both pegs simultaneously.

You can the ride the machine, for as long it it keeps rolling, by adjusting its position underneath you like somebody riding the back of a giant tortoise that's skidding about on sheet ice.

Riders typically roll along with their arms outstretched in front of them in an ungainly manner.

You can also maintain balance by means of **WHEEL BRAKING**, gripping and releasing as required.

The big problem is loss of momentum, which can be solved in two ways: you could (and people have) use a pair of ski poles to push yourself along —or you could set off downhill and try some *Gliding*.

A B C D E F G H I J K L M N O P Q R S T U V W X Y Z

Obviously this is a very advanced skill and you are going to get knocked about a bit while learning it.

☆ To make one, just borrow the front wheel of a BMX with stunt pegs, pop it out of the frame and screw the pegs back on.

☆ To learn to ride just cancel all social engagements for the next six months.

INSTANT KARAOKE MACHINE

FUN WITH SCIENCE

Karaoke (as I'm sure you know) is the tragic activity of singing along to the backing track of a popular song while pretending to be as good as the original recording artist.

This is rather like playing the "Air Guitar", except that it totally ruins the song for everybody—*even if their eyes are shut!*

The people whose job it is to provide the sound equipment for this activity generally have a collection of recordings of famous songs which have been re-mixed *without* the lead vocal. Their machines also provide auto-cueing via a television display so the singers can tell what the words are. Sadly there's nothing yet developed by science that can force them to sing the right *notes*.

Now it turns out that most popular songs are mixed in such a way that the lead vocal is fed to both stereo channels at equal volume, while the backing instruments are arranged in the soundscape by being panned either to the left or the right by the recording engineers to give breadth to the sound.

☆ So, if you place the two speakers from your stereo system right next to each other, and *reverse* the speaker wires on one channel something amazing will happen.

The parts of the sound corresponding to the lead vocal will tend to *cancel out* and the singer's voice will become muted.

You have created an **INSTANT KARAOKE MACHINE** from your own sound system.

Your appalling singing will not be drowned out by the original voice while the sound of the backing instruments will be largely unaffected.

You'll just have to remember the words.

☆ Conversely, if your mate's stereo system seems to be rendering the lead vocals rather more quietly than you'd expect (especially when your head is located on the mid-line between the speakers) it is highly likely that the speakers have been wired up incorrectly. Simply reversing the connections on one of the speakers should rectify the problem instantly and will earn you the respect due to one possessed of a keenly-honed scientific mind.

INVISIBLE EGG CRACKING

SILLINESS

☆ Get your victim to sit on a chair and make them close their eyes. Explain that you are going to crack an egg on their head. Cup one hand and place it palm-downwards on top of their head and smack it sharply with the other hand to create the sound and sensation of an egg cracking.

Now 'dribble' your fingers down through their hair and onto their face to complete the illusion. Yuk!

J*

J-Stroke

BOATS

The **J-Stroke** is a method of paddling a canoe with a single blade (such as those traditionally used with *Canadian Canoes*) without having to paddle on alternate sides of the boat.

Paddling on alternate sides is a great way of getting wet and a hopeless waste of energy— don't do it.

☆ The Canadian canoeist paddles on one side only, drawing the blade back through the water and then feathering it at the end of the stoke, pushing it gently away from the boat just before it leaves the water. This slight push compensates for the tendency of the boat to turn away from the paddle on each stroke.

As you practice the move you'll find that you can refine it into an effortless move and keep the boat travelling in a perfectly straight line.

After a couple of hundred strokes you'll swap the blade calmly over to the other side so as to use the muscles on both sides of your body evenly.

---

* The letter J is shown without a traditional construction because it is not a true Roman Letter.

A
B
C
D
E
F
G
H
I
J
K
L
M
N
O
P
Q
R
S
T
U
V
W
X
Y
Z

JUGGLING NOTATION

JUGGLING / MATHEMATICS

When this author learned to juggle way back in the last century there was no such thing as **JUGGLING NOTATION**—which was a shame because there was no way to record all the wonderful tricks and patterns that jugglers were busy coming up with.

In the old days, before the wave of circus skills mania that made juggling accessible to ordinary people, the more traditional jugglers considered their tricks and skills to be trade secrets, which was perfectly understandable since their livelihoods depended on being able to get bums on seats to watch their shows. Why *would* they want to share their hard-won skills with competitors? And so, despite the fact that jugglers have been around for centuries there was never anything that resembled musical notation to record or describe juggling tricks.

The juggling scene exploded into craze-driven creativity in the mid 1970's and people started juggling *just for fun* and quickly discovered that sharing their skills with others led to a new wave of creativity and excellence in this formerly secret craft.

It was therefore pretty much inevitable that **JUGGLING NOTATIONS** would appear on the scene.

Charlie V. Simpson[*] (a relative of *Radical Cheney*) invented **LADDER NOTATION** in the early 1980's. In this system a chart tracking the activity of the balls as they move from hand to hand is written from top to bottom as a sort of space-time diagram. It shows you where all the objects are at any given moment.

This was quickly followed by the more mathematical **SITESWAP NOTATION** which reduces a juggling pattern to a string of numbers. This is certainly the most popular system in use today.

---

[*] It is thought that the V is actually a Roman Numeral, suggesting that Simpson may have had four older brothers, all named *Charles*.

Then a clever man named *Martin Frost* invented **CAUSAL NOTATION** which tracks the paths of the *problems* that a juggler is dealing with. This may sound esoteric but it really does represent what is going through a juggler's mind as they work a pattern and is an excellent way of writing down **PASSING PATTERNS**—which are generally too complex to be represented in a useful way by the other systems.

These notations are useful tools for working out new tricks, in the same way that musical notation is a great aid to the composer, and they expose the elegant mathematics that is born out of the rules of juggling—which in itself has been the subject of serious scientific research.

Juggling tricks and patterns can also be recorded on video and one might reasonably assume that such recordings would be easy to learn tricks from —but while video recordings are *quite* useful, they only show the finished *effect* of a trick or pattern. In short they only show how a trick *looks*.

You might, again quite reasonably, think that by slowing down the playback of a complex trick you would be able to easily pick up the more subtle moves—but it turns out that this doesn't work too well in practice.

The thing that helps you to learn a trick is gaining an *understanding* of what your head needs to do to make the thing work, and what your *head* does is quite different to what the balls and hands are doing. And so this is where verbal, written and notated explanations score over video.

JUMPING ELASTIC BAND

MAGIC

This is an old classic
self-working trick.

It's a clever one
because it's very hard
to see how it works.

A nice brightly-coloured
elastic band is looped around the bases of the first two fingers.

You then close your fingers and hook the band over all four finger-ends. This is done subtly, with the back of your hand to the audience.

Now, by simply opening the fingers, the elastic band will "jump" to the last two fingers in a highly improbable manner.

To pile on the agony you can make the trick look even more impossible by lacing a second elastic band across the tips of all four fingers (pick a band with a contrasting colour to enhance the effect).

Amazingly, the trick still works!

JUMPING MATCH

MATCH TRICKS

In this classic illusion a match seems to move of its own volition.

☆ One match is held between thumb ar forefinger so that it points toward the little finger and rests on the shiny surface of your middle fingernail.

A second match is laid so that one end rests on this match at 90° and the other lies on the side of a finger from the other hand.

Ask your audience to watch very closely and suddenly the loose match will start to bounce and flick into the air as if by magic.

☆ HERE'S *The* TRICK: You are subtly sliding the fingernail of your right middle finger against the supporting match. You'll hear a tiny creaking sound if you do this right.

Each time the natural friction of the nail releases the held match will flick upwards with some force causing the loose match to jump around. It does look very spooky.

A
B
C
D
E
F
G
H
I
J
K
L
M
N
O
P
Q
R
S
T
U
V
W
X
Y
Z

KARATE CHOP BOUNCE

JUGGLING

Drop a **BOUNCING BALL** onto a hard floor, and as it bounces up give it a nice hard karate chop, just off centre. This puts a lot of spin on the ball which will bounce impressively from side to side—each time it hits the floor the spin reverses.

KEYHOLE CIPHER

CODES & CIPHERS

This is a sophisticated method of sending secret messages, and a quite a lot of fun into the bargain. It relies on a mechanical key, which both you and the message's recipient must have.

A
B
C
D
E
F
G
H
I
J
K
L
M
N
O
P
Q
R
S
T
U
V
W
X
Y
Z

☆ Take two sheets of paper, lay one on top of the other and carefully cut some square holes in it in. You should aim to make a nice random pattern. Keep one and give the other to the person you are sending messages to.

To code a message you lay the sheet over a blank sheet of paper and write your message as words or letters *through the holes*. Now remove the mask and fill in the rest of the page creatively so as to join up the words and letters of the message in a convincing manner. This will probably be a test of your creative writing, but can produce some interesting results!

The recipient decodes the message by laying their template over the rubbish you have written and reading off the original text. A message like:

The money is hidden under the third stone in the path.

... could end up as ...

What is the point of asking your parents for money when all they have to say is that you have some sort of hidden agenda? They just don't understand the trauma of wearing third rate trainers. I swear they are made of stone and that in the end they just make themselves look pathetic!

KICKED IN THE BALLS

MARTIAL ARTS

When exponents of the Martial Arts are sparring they try their best not to hurt each other (they save that for incidents outside the Dojo). But from time to time somebody will get **KICKED IN THE BALLS**.

As any person of the male persuasion will tell you, this can be both very painful and debilitating—so it is fortunate that the clever orientals have come up with a quick remedy!

Sit down immediately and pick up the foot on the side that hurts most as if doing a *Semi Lotus* position.

Now take a knuckle and screw it, hard, into a pressure point which is located exactly halfway along the inside edge of the arch of your foot. You know when you've hit the spot because it's just about the most sensitive place on the edge of the arch.

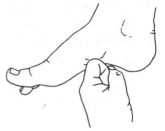

Screw that knuckle in so hard it hurts!

Ouch! Yes it does hurt, but you'll suddenly notice that the searing pain in your testicles has abated almost completely.

It's magic!

KICK-UP

JUGGLING

A **KICK-UP** is the magical skill of lifting a juggling club back into a juggling pattern using *just your foot!*

The **KICK-UP** was invented by *Rudi Wallenda*, who was a notoriously unreliable juggler in the 19th century. He toured with Lord George Sanger's circus and a famous argument ensued between Rudi and George Sanger himself which "*...quite upset the elephants...*" according to a contemporary witness.

Rudi had dropped repeatedly during the matinée performance and George said, in his characteristically brusque fashion:

> If you insist on dropped the things I suppose you will have to. But both the audience and I are heartily sick and tired of seeing you pick the d–mned things up and I for one am double-d–mned if I shall pay you for the privilege!

---

* Rudi Wallenda was the great-great grandfather of a clown I know. The Wallendas are a well-known circus family who used to work as the Flying Wallendas in the great old days of Circus.

A
B
C
D
E
F
G
H
I
J
K
L
M
N
O
P
Q
R
S
T
U
V
W
X
Y
Z

So, Rudi decided to solve the problem and went on to invent his own special method of lifting the clubs back into the air using his feet alone. And when you consider that a Victorian steel juggling club could weigh anything up to twenty-five pounds—this was no mean feat.

Presumably Lord George was pleased with the result because Rudi;'s name continues to appear on Sanger's circus posters right up to the turn of the 20th century.

The trick was developed into something of a performance in its own right and jugglers all over the world tried to copy it with varying degrees of success. It was performed in front of Queen Victoria in 1896 and after the show Her Majesty remarked:

> We were particularly impressed by the gentleman with such dextremity [sic] in his feet.

☆ HERE'S *The* TRICK: The **KICK-UP** *seems* impossible when you first try because it's very hard to see how the club can be lifted without it falling

off—but here's the crucial thing you need to know.

It's important to focus on the two points of contact between leg and club during the kick.

The neck of the club will contact the side of your foot and the knob will get trapped against your shin.

To practice this, place one club on your foot, and hold two more in your hands. Try to get the position

right and **KICK-UP** as you make a throw from the hand that will (hopefully) catch the kicked-up club.

☆ There's a variation called a *Step-Over* **KICK-UP** where the club is kicked up from the *inside* of the foot. It's a cool move, especially if done continuously, because the juggler makes a sort of sideways dance across the stage.

☆ Since **KICK-UPS** are used as a trick in their own right, as well as a way of recovering accidentally-dropped clubs, it's important to be able to get a club into the right position during the juggle.

☆ You can drop a club onto your foot in three distinct ways: a straight drop (tricky to catch it just right), a spinning drop (as if you were doing a **DIP**) or a helicopter drop.

The two spinning drops not only look good, they help to nudge the club nicely into position.

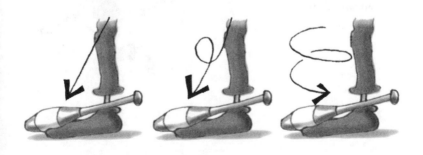

A B C D E F G H I J **K** L M N O P Q R S T U V W X Y Z

A
B
C
D
E
F
G
H
I
J
K
L
M
N
O
P
Q
R
S
T
U
V
W
X
Y
Z

☆ If you are passing clubs you can do a very simple **KICK-UP** by jumping 180 degrees, trapping the club between both feet, and then jumping up as you throw it to your partner with your feet.

☆ **KICK-UPS** are often used in *Numbers Juggling* to introduce extra clubs into a pattern.

Try juggling three clubs with a fourth positioned on your left foot.

Lead into a four-club **FOUNTAIN** with the right hand and immediately **KICK-UP** the fourth club to a left hand catch.

Don't worry.

This is advanced stuff!

KICK-UP MOUNT

UNICYCLING

This is another **FREE MOUNT** for a unicycle. I've written the instructions for the *left-footed* unicyclist (which you probably are).

You'll have to reflect the instructions in an imaginary mirror if you are *right-footed* (like me).

☆ Stand your machine up, facing forward and lay it down on its right side. The upper pedal (the left pedal) should be in the *down* position.

Place your right foot *under* the saddle and place your left foot on the left pedal. You're ready.

Transfer your weight to the left pedal while simultaneously kicking the unicycle up into your bum with your right foot.

As the saddle hits your thigh get your right foot onto the right pedal and ride off.

KNEE SITTING

ACROBATICS

This is the amazing trick of getting a load of people to stand in a circle close to each other (all facing either clockwise or counter-clockwise) and having them all sit down on each other's knees at once.

It's pretty easy to do with half a dozen people but it gets harder and harder to pull off as you add more people. It's not that the trick actually gets any more difficult—rather it is because somebody always gets the giggles and you all collapse in a heap.

KNUCKLE ROLL

OBJECT MANIPULATION

Also known as the *Coin Roll* this is the art of walking coins across your knuckles. It's a cool move but hard to learn—so you had better get started.*

☆ Get a nice big heavy coin. In the UK we have biggish fifty pence pieces and wonderful great big two pound coins, both are terrific choices.

You start with the coin gripped between your thumb and the side of your index finger. It's best to start in your favourite hand, probably the right hand.

---

* The first person I met who learned this used to work in an all-night garage which I used to visit in Dirty Dick Page's stolen cars in the wee small hours of the night back in the old days in Oxford. He was usually very bored but at least he got something out of the job. Dirty Dick got two years. I just got away with it.

Push the coin so that it flops over into the gap between your index and ring fingers. Now push it over again so that it drops into next gap along, until finally it arrives between your ring and little fingers.

Hard isn't it?

☆ From here you let the coin slide through the gap from where you push it back to the start with your thumb. When you're proficient you can carry it across balanced on your thumb.

☆ It could take you weeks to learn, but just make sure that you work in *both* hands. Jugglers all know that the easiest time to transfer newly learned skills from one side of your body to the other is *right after getting them down pat on one side*.

☆ Keen **KNUCKLE ROLLERS** can roll coins in both directions!

☆ Really keen ones can roll *two coins at once* across the same hand.

☆ Really really keen ones can do three.

And so it goes on.

A
B
C
D
E
F
G
H
I
J
K
L
M
N
O
P
Q
R
S
T
U
V
W
X
Y
Z

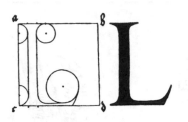 

LADDER NOTATION

JUGGLING

LADDER NOTATION is a form of **JUGGLING NOTATION** which works a little like musical notation. It is impossible to sight-read for obvious reasons.

The juggling pattern is written over a chart that looks like a ladder. The "rungs" of the ladder divide the passage of time into *beats*. Typically there is one throw on every *beat*. The objects being juggled are represented by lines that criss-cross the chart as they pass from left to right and back again. The throws are represented by open circles and the catches by filled-in circles.

The **THREE BALL CASCADE** shown here resembles a plait of three strands. Each ball spends two *beats* in the air and one in the hand as it is juggled. In **SITESWAP NOTATION** these throws are called 3's meaning simply that each object is thrown every three *beats*.

Curiously, if you attach three ribbons to three beanbags and juggle, you can plait them! To un-plait them juggle a **REVERSE CASCADE**.

See also **SITESWAP NOTATION**, **CAUSAL NOTATION**.

A
B
C
D
E
F
G
H
I
J
K
L
M
N
O
P
Q
R
S
T
U
V
W
X
Y
Z

LADDER TRICKS

CIRCUS SKILLS

Here are some cool things to do on a ladder.

☆ *Sliding down*:
When descending a ladder, instead of laboriously going from tread to tread in the normal fashion place the insteps of both feet against the outside of the rails of the ladder and slide down. You can slow your descent by adjusting the clench of your legs.

☆ *Ladder-Walking*
You can use a ladder like a pair of stilts. Ideally you will use a custom-made ladder for this which will be about six feet high and a good deal wider than a regular ladder, but you should be able to manage the trick with any short ladder.

With the ladder propped in front of you against thin air you boldly climb two or three rungs and then attempt a balance. A **SPOTTER** might be useful at this stage. The trick is to rock the ladder from side-to-side, hence lifting each foot off the ground in turn, which enables you to "walk" the ladder forwards or backwards as balance demands.

You should also be able to "hop" forwards and backwards.

Ladder-walking is used both by performance artists and by signwriters and painters eager to save themselves a trip down and up the job when moving along the work.

☆ *No-handed Ladder-Walking*
If you climb a little higher up your ladder and bravely tuck one leg *around* the ladder and onto a rung from the *far side* you will have a nice firm grip on the ladder with your legs alone, and hence you can let go with your

hands, which are now available for a little **Juggling** or some other **Garbage Trick** activity.

☆ *Free-Standing Ladder-Walking*

A Russian circus trick uses a ladder that is fitted with footplates on the tops of the rails. The performer stands on the foot-sized plates and, without the use of straps or any other attachments, rocks the ladder side-to-side and walks it.

Landing a Match on its Edge

BAR BET / MATCH TRICKS

☆ 'I bet I can throw up this paper match and have it land *on its edge*.'

Once the **Mark** has laid down the money or (promised a drink) you fold the match ninety degrees, toss it up, and drink or count your winnings.

Learning How to Learn Tricks

JUGGLING / PSYCHOLOGY

Jugglers are in the business of learning to do difficult things and they can save themselves a lot of time and trouble if they pay a little attention to the learning process itself, by **Learning How to Learn Tricks**.

To quote a famous book on the Art of Juggling:

> "Everything a juggler does, when they are juggling, is a *Trick*. What they do in their spare time is their own business."

By this the author was trying (and some would say *failing*) to make the point that jugglers do not juggle by pure conscious will, they juggle by

A
B
C
D
E
F
G
H
I
J
K
L
M
N
O
P
Q
R
S
T
U
V
W
X
Y
Z

means of doing **Tricks**. In this context a **Trick** means a move or a sequence or moves that has been rehearsed for so long that it can be done automatically or subconsciously.

The human mind consists of the conscious mind (which might decide to learn to juggle) and the subconscious mind (which will actually be doing the work). The conscious mind is a wonderful thing indeed, but it is not nearly as powerful as the subconscious. You cannot juggle by will alone, so you have to teach the subconscious to do what you want it to.

It will help you a great deal if you start to think of your subconscious mind as if it were *another person entirely*. Not only that, but this *other person* gets annoyed very easily when it does it will *not* do what you want.

☆ Let's suppose that you have set out to learn how to juggle five balls, or to ride a unicycle—both of which are difficult things to learn. Being a determined person you may decide to practice for long periods of time every single day. It's very natural, when setting out on such an ambitious route, to think that the more hours you put in, the quicker you will acquire the skills you are aiming for. To a certain extent this is true, but you can easily overdo things and find that the more work you put in, the slower you learn.

☆ The key is to make sure that your subconscious is having a good time. You can do this by making sure that you only practice for as long as it feels like *fun*.

☆ Always conclude a practice session on a high note. If you're working, say, with five balls, and you have just managed, after a good session, to get from the 10–12 throws stage by achieving a really good run of 25 throws —stop right there! Tell yourself out loud how well you are doing, put the balls down and resume work the following day.

☆ Your subconscious is very active while you are asleep, and it will often turn over the events of the previous day and try to make sense of them. That's why you often wake up in the morning, after an argument or a dispute, with the sudden thought *"I know what I should have said to that person!"*

Your subconscious has been turning the problem over all night and has come up with the right answer for you.

☆ A common mistake made by jugglers who get a little too determined and practice themselves into the ground is that of failing to take a short pause for breath after making a mistake.

Suppose you are learning five balls: you can manage about 10–15 throws before dropping. This is a stage that five-ball jugglers often reach and then get stuck at for days or even weeks. It's very common, when observing these people hard at work, to see that every time they drop a ball they quickly bend down, gather the balls together into the starting position and launch them up into the air again *without even pausing for breath!* They *think* that they are saving time this way but they are so, so wrong.

All they are doing is training their subconscious to make 10–15 throws and then drop. They are actually *reinforcing* this behaviour—which is the exact opposite of their intention.

When you drop, you should pause for a few moments while thinking, in a calm sort of manner, about what just went wrong.

Then try again: gathering up the balls and making a fresh attempt by changing your style is a small way. The most important thing is that the new new attempt must not feel like repeating the old one.

LEATHERMAN

SURVIVAL / TRAVELLER'S TIPS

LEATHERMAN is the brand name of the only real competitor to the **SWISS ARMY KNIFE**.

These pocketable toolkits are fantastically well-engineered from top-grade steel and come in many different versions. Unlike the **SWISS ARMY KNIFE** (which is an overgrown penknife) a **LEATHERMAN** is funda-mentally a pair of collapsible pliers with folding handles that allow it to close down to a conveniently carriable size, but within this mechanism is concealed an array of extra tools that can be folded out to perform other tasks.

Typically you will get:

> Pliers, wire-cutters, knife blades, screwdrivers (both flatblade and crosspoint), allen keys, rulers both metric and imperial, can openers, bottle openers and possibly a corkscrew.

Like the **SWISS ARMY KNIFE** the **LEATHERMAN** comes in many different flavours each with more or less features. It also comes in many different sizes. The bigger ones are superb general-purpose toolkits for people engaged in practical work. They need to be carried in a special belt-pouch. The smaller ones are also great but they are not quite as pocketable as a **SWISS ARMY KNIFE** preferring to live, like their big brothers, in a pouch on your belt.

LET GO OF MY EARS!

STAGE FIGHTING

Here's a great piece of comedy stage-fighting, it's easy to learn and great fun to do.

☆ Grab a partner and stand them in front of you. Now make two fists and press the fingers' sides against their ears. They grab the fists with their hands.

Now your *partner* jumps up and down screaming *"Let go of my ears!"* while you concentrate on keeping your hands over their ears.

This creates the effects that you are trying to pull their ears off while, in actual fact, *they* are doing most of the work.

☆ You can modify the move by placing one hand on the top of their head which they grab with both hands screaming *"let go of my hair!"* It's just as effective.

A
B
C
D
E
F
G
H
I
J
K
L
M
N
O
P
Q
R
S
T
U
V
W
X
Y
Z

LEVITATING POLYSTYRENE CUP

MAGIC

Take an empty polystyrene cup and wrap both hands around it as if trying to keep a hot drink warm on a cold day. Explain that cups are very very light, and that if you focus enough psychic energy you can make it float in the air for a little while.

Slowly open your fingers and the cup will float mysteriously between your fingers.

☆ HERE'S *The* TRICK: You have punctured the back of the cup with one of your thumbs!

Don't repeat it, just move right on the the **BALDUCCI LEVITATION**.

LEVITRON

FUN WITH SCIENCE

There are very few brand names mentioned in *Every Trick In The Book* but this one could not reasonably have been left out.

The **LEVITRON** is an awesome toy that was invented in the 1990's and which does something that had never been achieved before.

It combines the principle of a **GYROSCOPE** with the principle of magnetic repulsion to create a small spinning top which, once started, will hover improbably in mid air an inch or so above a base containing powerful magnets.

The little top hovers in the air with a gentle bob and wobble that just *looks* like magic.

☆ Setting up and spinning your **LEVITRON** is not easy.

The little top comes with a set of small washers of varying weights and needs to be tuned each time it is used.

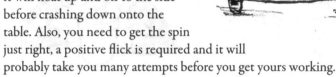

Too heavy and it will smack down onto the base plate, too light and it will float up and off to the side before crashing down onto the table. Also, you need to get the spin just right, a positive flick is required and it will probably take you many attempts before you get yours working.

When you do your patience will be more than rewarded: the **LEVITRON** is nothing short of incredible and it will spin happily for up to two minutes before losing momentum from the slight air resistance—at which point it will tip over suddenly and clatter to a stop.

Here's how it works:

The base unit contains a small array of powerful magnets which provide a field with a "dimple" in the middle which presents a slightly weaker field than that around it. The field is arranged so that one pole points upwards. The little top consists of a shaft pushed through a magnetic disk which has the corresponding pole pointing down. Thus, when the top is held over the base it is repelled from it.

If you were to simply held the top over the base and let go it would flip over in a moment and then become attracted to the base.

But if you spin the top the gyroscopic effect prevents it from tipping over. It's that simple!

☆ You can do some cool tricks with your **LEVITRON**: the author's favourite is to get an empty jam jar and scoop it around the **LEVITRON** while it's hovering. Then stand the jar on its base and screw on the lid. Somehow this makes the magic of the thing even more magical.

☆ Another good stunt is to get a heavy pair of steel scissors and snap them shut directly over, and very close to, the top. The steel in the scissors will interfere with the magnetic field enough to cause the thing to drop immediately onto the base—leaving onlookers with the idea that there was a string involved after all.

See also **SUPERMAGNET**.

LIFT CRACK

WHIPS

Here's an easy way to crack a whip.

☆ Lay your whip straight out in front of you with your whip hand down by your side. Move back until the whip lies straight.

Take one step forward. This puts a bend in the whip below your whip-hand.

Now smoothly raise your hand, arm at full length, from the down to the up position.

As the whip lifts it will crack. The bend you put in the whip by stepping forward has run all the way down to the thin end of the whip—where it escapes the only way it can—by breaking the sound barrier!

☆ You'll find that a **LION TAMER'S CRACK** follows very naturally from this move. Lay the whip behind you, take a step forwards, do the **LIFT CRACK** and then let the whip fall behind you.

As soon as it lies straight in the air pull it forward into a **LION TAMER'S CRACK**.

A
B
C
D
E
F
G
H
I
J
K
L
M
N
O
P
Q
R
S
T
U
V
W
X
Y
Z

A
B
C
D
E
F
G
H
I
J
K
L
M
N
O
P
Q
R
S
T
U
V
W
X
Y
Z

LINESMAN'S HITCH

KNOTS

☆ Take some rope and run it around a post or spar and make a single **HALF HITCH**, now use **GAFFER TAPE** or something similar and seize the end of the rope to the standing part.

Although it would be quicker to tie a **ROUND TURN AND TWO HALF HITCHES** this "knot" is neater and less bulky—and is preferable in many situations (perhaps you are using it to tie some thin stuff to the eye in the end of a cable that you are going to drag through a conduit and you don't want it to snag.

☆ If you don't have any tape and you are working with polypropylene rope (or any rope with a lay that you can easily open) then you can simply tuck the end *through* the strands of the standing part to create a kind of **BASTARD SPLICE**.

LINING AND STRIPING

SIGNWRITING

It has often been said of signwriters that the best indicator of their skill is their ability to execute neat block lettering. Well, that's pretty much true, but it is also true that **LINING AND STRIPING** is just about the hardest thing a signwriter is called on to do. A few **TRICKS** can help though.

☆ Get a proper lining brush. They are made from sable (if they are small) or ox hair (if they are large) and they have ridiculously long bristles. The width of the brush, as you lift it from your brush tin, will be about two thirds of the width of the line you are going to paint.

☆ Mix up some proper signwriting paint to a very nice consistency, you'll need quite a lot and you *do not* want to be messing about with its viscosity while you are working because you are going to be working *very fast*. Put the paint into a shallow dish (an enamel plate is good) and *do not* expose it to sunlight or wind while working. Paint that has been thinned with white spirit thickens to glue in mere seconds if you do.

☆ A good lining tip is to get an enormously long and very straight **Mahl Stick** and use it as a guide. I have used sticks up to six feet long for this sort of work.

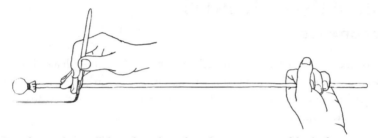

Lay the stick parallel to the job and park your ring and little fingertips on it, as if they were balancing on a horse. Now carefully lay the brush onto the job and paint the line while sliding your fingers along the stick.

☆ You *do not* watch the line as it appears behind the brush, you watch the heel of the brush instead. This is very, very important. As always in signwriting, the brush itself should be upright.

☆ Let the brush run at its own speed, as dictated by the paint.

So much for straight lines! How about curves?

☆ Well, there's no real trick here, you just have to do them, and in most cases you have to do them *without* the help of the stick. You need to be confident and positive. Remember that really good lining always shows that it has been done by hand, so some variation in line width and some subtle wobbles actually enhance the job. What will really mess it up is any sign that the lines have been worked over bit by bit, or that the brush was not running free and fast and smooth when the line was made.

☆ Don't worry too much about the corners, you can fault those in later with a small brush.

☆ Striping wheels on horse-drawn vehicles is a doddle though. Make up some very thin paint, jack up the wheel and spin it. I'm sure you can guess the rest.

☆ The old gipsy technique for striping wheels was to use a blade of grass, with the paint loaded into the V of the leaf, instead of a sable brush.

Good luck, you'll need it!

LINKING HANDS

ACROBATICS

Sometimes you need to pull somebody up—perhaps they have slipped over the edge of a cliff and need rescuing. Or maybe you are the *catcher* in an aerial trapeze act and you need to grab a partner with both hands in a truly secure manner.

What you *do not do* is to connect your hands so that the palms touch—if you do this then the grip will fail if either person loosens their fingers.

☆ Instead you grasp their wrist with your hand, while contrariwise they grip yours. This grip will hold even if one person faints dead away (perhaps from fear of heights!)

☆ You can link four hands in an Escherian[*] manner, like a **RECIPROCAL FRAME**, to form a sort of chair between two people. You grab your left wrist with your right hand, and your partner does the same, then you link together to form a little circle of four interlocked hands.

Because the grip is so strong you can carry a really heavy person like this.

---

[*] After M.C. Esher, the legendary engraver.

LINKING PAPERCLIPS

MAGIC

Here's a lovely self-working trick, you'll need a sheet of paper and a few paper-clips. Scrub that, make it a banknote— they both look and work better.

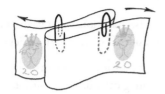

☆ Fold a sheet of paper as if posting an A4 sheet in a small envelope. That's two folds, concertina style.

Clip the top two sheets together at the edge, and then clip the bottom two sheets together.

Grab each end of the banknote and pull sharply; the paper clips will fly off having magically linked themselves together!

☆ You can link a series of paper clips into a chain by making more folds and using more paperclips. A banknote can be folded four times concertinawise and then linked with four clips.

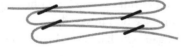

When performing this trick it's cool to have the person you are trying to impress stand a little way off with their hands ready to catch the linked paperclips as they fly off.

A
B
C
D
E
F
G
H
I
J
K
L
M
N
O
P
Q
R
S
T
U
V
W
X
Y
Z

A
B
C
D
E
F
G
H
I
J
K
L
M
N
O
P
Q
R
S
T
U
V
W
X
Y
Z

LINKING RINGS

MAGIC

These traditional magician's props are often called *Chinese Linking Rings*, presumably because the oriental tag adds an air of mystery to them.

The performer presents a set of unbroken metal rings which then appear to magically link and unlink in mysterious ways.

Rings come in different sizes (typically from 4 inch to 8 inch) and in sets of four rings upwards. The more rings, the more complex the routine.

While the trick is not self-working, it is pretty easy to learn and *very impressive*. You get a lot of bang for not much buck with linking rings. I suggest that the beginner obtains a set of four rings and learns the simple basic routine shown here before moving onto more elaborate presentations.

☆ HERE'S *The* TRICK: A set of four rings will consist of one solid ring, two pre-linked rings, and one ring with a small gap in it—this is the *key ring*. Needless to say, the aim of the game is never to let the audience see the gap, which isn't too hard to do.

You'll also need to make it appear that the two linked rings are actually separate at some point in your routine, but once more, this is pretty easy to do.

☆ Start by loading the four rings onto the fingers of your left hand, first the *key ring*, then the two linked rings, and finally the single ring.

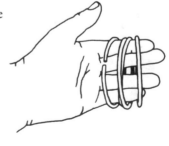

The audience will not see the gap in the *key ring* because it is concealed by your hand.

☆ Hand the solid ring to an audience member so that they can see it is entirely solid. Then take it back and explain that you have four identical rings by "pouring" the set one at a time off the fingers of your left hand and onto the fingers of the right hand. To do this you first drop the solid ring through the air, catching it on the fingers of the opposite hand, then follow this with the remaining three rings (first the joined pair, then the *key ring*).

As long as your fingers are reasonably close together they will not see that the middle two rings are linked.

You have now established, in the mind of your audience, that you have four separate rings.

☆ Now cheat the linked pair onto your right wrist, like a bracelet and arrange the remaining two rings so that you have the *key ring* in your left hand and the solid ring in your right.

Hold the *key ring* so that your left index finger covers the gap, tap it from behind with the solid ring a couple of times to show that the rings are solid.

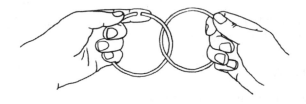

From this position you can quietly link the two rings by pushing the solid ring against the gap. Don't let the audience know immediately that they are linked instead, blow on them magically before tugging them hard to show that they have magically joined.

The idea here is to make them think that the rings linked when you blew on them, not when you were fiddling about a moment before.

☆ Drop the right ring and (quick as a flash) slip the rings off your right wrist to reveal that they, too, have magically joined.

You are now two "wows" into you short routine. Not only that, but you can pass the double ring to an audience member for them to examine.

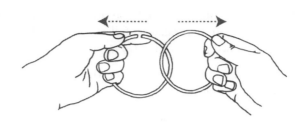

Now explain that the next trick is to pull the rings apart again. Hold them as you did before to link them, but this time you should cheat them *apart* while still leaving them overlapped.

Bring them up to your face, inviting your "assistant" to do the same. Blow on them magically and pull them smoothly apart.

Theirs will remain stuck together.

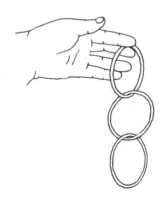

☆ Hook the solid ring over your right wrist and hang the *key* ring over your left hand, below your thumb, taking care to conceal the join.

Now take the two linked rings from your assistant in your left hand to, er, see if *you* can get them apart.

You'll fail of course, so take the solid ring of your right wrist to see if you can't *bash* them apart. This is misdirection of course, since while you're waving the single ring about in your right hand you are secretly linking the *key* ring to the two linked rings in your left hand.

☆ Bash the linked-rings with the single ring a couple of times and then drop the pair to reveal that you now have *three* linked rings in your left hand. The gap in the *key* ring is concealed by the grip of your fingers.

Next you will link all four rings. Taking the free ring in your right hand strike each of the three linked rings, from bottom to top, but as you strike the top ring you let the free ring link with the key ring, try to tug it off again, give up and present the chain of four.

The break in the *key* ring is concealed by the pinch of your left hand. To complete this short routine you should bring all four rings together and split off the *key* ring as you do so.

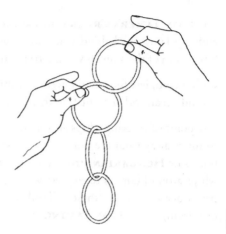

Finally, repeat the *pour* that you used at the start, dropping first the *key* ring, then the two linked rings from one hand to the other. The final (solid) ring is tossed from hand to hand and the show is done

Lion Poo is Cheaper than a Dog

GARDENER'S TRICKS

☆ If your garden is being dug up by cats using it as a toilet you could always get a dog, but dogs are expensive and not just for Christmas.

So go and get some **Lion Poo** instead.

You can buy it from safari parks and zoos. These people will do *anything,* for money having many mouths of all shapes and sizes to feed.

Sprinkle the stuff around the edges of your garden. The local cats will keep well away because they'll think there's a bloody great big lion hanging around somewhere!

A
B
C
D
E
F
G
H
I
J
K
L
M
N
O
P
Q
R
S
T
U
V
W
X
Y
Z

LION TAMER'S CRACK

WHIPS

The **LION TAMER'S CRACK** is so-named because the whip starts out (and ends up laid) out behind you—well away from the snickety claws and bitey teeth of the animals you are trying to control.

Only a complete fool would ever even think about actually *striking* a Lion (or indeed any other animal) with a whip.

The point of cracking whips around domestic animals is to persuade them to move away from the noise. This is useful when you want to get cattle, horses or **HUNGARIAN PIGS** to do your bidding. The point of cracking whips around lions is to *impress the audience* with your macho skills. Big predatory animals like these will only ever do what *they* want to do, whips or no whips—see **LION TAMING**.

The main use of the **LION TAMER'S CRACK,** in modern post-animal-circus days, is in target work, like cutting a cigarette from a volunteer's mouth, or slicing a piece of newspaper from the volunteer's hands into ever smaller pieces.

In actual fact the **WHIP MAN CRACK** is a far more accurate technique—though a lot less dramatic and harder to learn, so I guess the **LION TAMER'S CRACK** is here to stay.

☆ Lay the whip out behind you. Pull it forward and then back, over your shoulder (1). You are aiming to end up with the whip laid in the air behind you in a dead straight line (A). As you reach this point you push the handle forwards and down (2), keeping your eye fixed on the target point (B).

As the handle stops the whip keeps on going and creates the all important bend (some call it a *loop*) which runs down the whip at ever increasing speed (because the whip gets lighter and lighter as you move toward the **FALL**). Finally the bend reaches the **CRACK** and there is nowhere for all that energy to go, so the **CRACK** can easily break the sound barrier as it flicks over at anything up to 1000 miles an hour.

After the crack the whip will naturally tend to return to a position behind you, ready to start again.

See **WHIP MAN CRACK**, **FLY FISHING**, **ACCURACY WITH WHIPS**.

LION TAMING

ANIMALS

Contrary to popular belief (which is somewhat enhanced by the *style* in which lion-taming has traditionally been carried out) being horribly cruel to big cats is not a good way of getting them to do what you want. They love to bite and if you hurt them, they are going to hurt you. Moreover, big cats, like small cats, will *never* do what you want—they only do what *they* want.

Here is how to train these animals:

☆ Have your staff obtain a big cat and install it in a cage in your house. Do *not* visit the cat or even let it see you until you are ready to begin training.

Obtain a piece of ordinary wooden dowel about three feet long (a piece of broom handle will do). Now go and visit the cat every morning, taking with you a cup of coffee and a newspaper, or perhaps a copy of *Every Trick In The Book* (this is going to be a *very* boring and time-consuming process so you may as well have something to read).

Sit down quietly on a chair well away from the bars and quietly read but make sure that you are holding your stick in your hand *at all times*. Do not make eye contact with the lion, just ignore it.

A B C D E F G H I J K L M N O P Q R S T U V W X Y Z

The idea here is to persuade the lion that the stick is part of your body. Do not ever, ever let go of it.

After an hour or so you may leave.

Each day, when you visit your cat you should move the chair a little closer to the cage. You must understand that a lion (or any caged animal) knows *exactly* where the edge of their cage is and *exactly* when there is a chance of making a lunge to catch a hand or finger that has been stupidly poked through the bars. This is why the signs at zoos are so emphatic about these things. A lion will not pounce on a poking finger or hand until it *knows* it can catch it.

Eventually, after many days you will allow the stick to "carelessly" fall close enough to the bars for the lion to pounce and catch it. When this happens (which it surely will) the lion will pounce very aggressively but you must not show the slightest sign of fear or even acknowledge the fact that your stick is now having its head chewed off—except perhaps in a lazy kind of "Ooh, that scratches my itch!" sort of way.

If you panic and drop the stick you may as well go and buy a new lion because you have lost the game.

As the days proceed you get closer and closer to the lion who now believes that you are some sort of un-chewable super-being. No matter how hard they bite you you just don't seem to hurt! They are utterly convinced that the stick is part of your body. Now you start to use the stick to gently prod the animal about, scratch its itches and coerce it into moving about with gentle prods and pressure.

This familiarises the animal with the idea that you are in control and there is nothing to be done about it. You may also annoy the animal a little and persuade it to sit up on it's haunches and snarl while taking lazy swipes at the stick (which is exactly the same thing as getting a kitten to attack a dangled piece of string).

☆ By the time you finally enter the cage the animal will be quite accustomed to the uselessness of bothering to bite you, and you may swap the stick for a more showman-like whip. Just don't drop it or let the cat see it out of your hand.

☆ The other big trick, as in practically *all* animal training, is rewarding the animals with food. You will have noticed (if you have ever seen a big cat performance in the circus) that a cage, together with an access tunnel, is hastily erected in the ring at the start of the performance into which the lion-tamer goes. The gates at the ends of the access tunnel are then opened and the lion-tamer summons the beasts from a backstage pen.

Watch the enthusiasm (albeit somewhat *surly*) with which the cats slink down the tunnel and take their places in the ring in front to the performer. See also (at the end of the display of human mastery over savage beast) the urgency with which the big cats return down the access tunnel.

Why would the cats be so keen?

The answer is simple. They have been taught that *this is how they get their dinner*. For weeks and months they have been persuaded that the only way to get food placed in their cage is to go into an adjoining cage and play boring games with their unbiteable trainer for a few minutes knowing that when they return there will be food waiting for them.

And that, in a nutshell, is how you do *that*.

Lobster Claws

HAND TRICKS

☆ Hook your little finger over the back of your ring finger (it feels weird but it won't break) then hook the ring finger over the back of your middle finger, and so on until you run out of fingers.

Now do the other hand—isn't that weird?

LOONY WALKS

SILLINESS

☆ Stand close three abreast with two friends and walk in sync with each other making huge wide strides to the right and left. This is a totally pointless but hugely fun thing to do.

☆ The opposite version is fun too, in which the right step is made as far to the left as possible and vice versa.

☆ The great comic duo *Morecombe and Wise* famously used a similar step in a TV special in which, dressed up to the nines in top hats and tails, they descended an impressive staircase flanking the actress *Penelope Keith* while doing an elegant version of the **LOONY WALK.** They stepped down in time with each other making a dainty kick with each foot, across the other, before making each step.

☆ *Cab Calloway*, one of the best-known eccentric dancers of the twentieth century, famously used a walk where the right foot is placed around and *behind* the left (the hard way) and then the left foot is placed around and behind the right so that the walker actually goes backwards while appearing to walk forwards.

It's a truly great effect.

☆ Of course if moving backwards while appearing to move forwards is your goal you will simply have to learn the **MOONWALK**.

Some **LOONY WALKS** have, for bizarre reasons, been considered perfectly sensible (especially in military circles).

☆ The *Goose Step*—most famously the German Nazi's—is still used by particularly oppressive regimes when drilling their soldiers.

In this utterly **LOONY WALK** the poor soldiers are required to raise their legs to absurd heights while swinging the opposite arm across in front of their faces as if blocking a karate blow.

☆ The comedian *John Cleese* parodied the *Goose Step* with unbelievable and hilarious suppleness in the legendary *Ministry of Silly Walks* sketch from *Monty Python*.

☆ The *Slow March* should probably not be laughed at though, since it is used when drilling soldiers at funerals. The usual two beat march of a soldier is converted to a four-beat step by stopping the forward swing of each foot momentarily as it passes the opposite ankle.

☆ The most utterly **LOONY WALK** of all has to be the gait of the *speedwalker*. These bloody fools engage in the ridiculous sport of walking as

---

* Which, incidentally, Cab Calloway was performing years before Michael Jackson.

A
B
C
D
E
F
G
H
I
J
K
L
M
N
O
P
Q
R
S
T
U
V
W
X
Y
Z

fast as possible while never actually breaking into a run. In their efforts to gain more and more speed these people develop a movement that is utterly laughable. There is a very specific rule in this sport: the difference between walking and running is that when walking there is *always* one foot on contact with the ground, whereas in running there are often no feet on the ground.

The difference however is subtle and during races judges have to be placed along the entire track to make sure that nobody cheats (which they often do without even realising it).

MM

MACHINE
JUGGLING

Here's a great *Square Juggling* move that never fails to impress. It's easy to learn but hard to do *well* so work hard on it. Some people* call this move the *Factory*.

☆ Juggle One-Up Two-Up with three balls and then go into the **FAKE**, so that one hand (for the sake of argument we'll say the *left* hand) carries its ball, following the movement of the opposite ball precisely. I do mean precisely! We're going for maximum effect here.

OK, now keep that going and get the rhythm solid. Now take a *right turn* at the top of the carried ball's flight and carry it across the top of the pattern to the right-hand side at which point you *drop it* and, very rapidly, **SNATCH** the middle-ball which is at the top of its flight.

You now resume the **FAKE**.

☆ You can juggle this move continuously and it looks like a machine working magic with the balls.

---

* Like me for example.

You get big performance points if you can do this so that it looks as if it is happening *to you* rather than something you are doing to the balls.

See also **FAKE**, **YO-YO (BALL JUGGLING)**.

MAGIC

MAGIC

MAGIC, for the purposes of *Every Trick In The Book*, is the art of the performing Magician or, as they often call themselves, the performing *Illusionist*. By referring to themselves as such they make it plain that they are not performing *real magic*, they are *pretending to do so*.

Everybody knows this and yet the human mind, which adores to be gullible, is easily and willingly fooled.

When the Illusionist starts **SAWING THE LADY IN HALF** we all know perfectly well in our rational minds that this is not what is really happening. It's just a **TRICK**. Yet people who have seen the show will report that, as far as they could make out, what they saw was a genuine miracle.

Magicians make no pretence about this, except for a few; the famous magician *Uri Geller* being one such exception. All magicians of any standing have some sort of gimmick or special style and in Geller's case it was the ruse of performing close-up **MAGIC** (specifically bending spoons and other metal objects) while pretending that he was doing so, not by means of magical trickery, but by means of *actual psychokinetic powers*.

The Magician's Oath
Professional magicians will usually have sworn allegiance to a sort of professional guild, in the United Kingdom there is the *Magic Circle* and in other countries there are *Magic Rings*. When one joins such an organisation one has to make a solemn promise, the wording of which usually goes something like this:

> As a magician I promise not to reveal the secret of any illusion to a non-magician and I promise never to perform any illusion for any non-magician without first practicing the effect until I can perform it well enough to maintain the illusion of magic.

This oath is there for perfectly good reasons. If you perform, say, a nice little **PALM RETENTION VANISH** people will respect you for it, but they will also ask you how it's done. While it is very tempting to show them (and thus demonstrate just exactly how clever you are) you'll find that all the *respect* you earned with the actual trick will just melt away to nothing. The point is that people *want* to be intrigued and fooled by **MAGIC** and explaining it away destroys the illusion.

Similarly, performing a trick that you aren't very good at is just a shabby way of showing how it is *meant* to be done.

The oath sworn by magicians has the side-effect of creating a lucrative market for tricks which are bought and sold, in the **MAGIC** business, sometimes for very large amounts of money. In fact *most* of the money made in **MAGIC** is made by magic shops selling tricks to people who cannot do them very well.

It would be remiss of the author not to mention, at this point, the famous American magical duo *Penn & Teller* who have made it their business to reveal the secrets of magical illusions to the dismay of some of the magical establishment. However, while their performances are often based on revealing tricks, they will typically stymie their audience by using these revelations as a buildup to a more impressive trick that they *do not* reveal. "We showed you how we do that, but you'll never guess how we do *this!*"

The author would like to point out that he has never taken any such oath and is not a member of any Magic Circle or Ring.

The Types of Magical Illusion
Much of what we know of magic was born out of a fascination with Engineering in the Victorian era. Engineering was, after all achieving superhuman feats, so perhaps it could also be bent toward producing supernatural effects. Engineering was something of a gentleman's pursuit in those days and there were plenty of engineering workshops in the grounds of England's bigger houses—and hence we end up with the gentleman magician, working in formal evening dress and relying on complex mechanical contrivances to achieve illusions of actual Magic.

Classical **MAGIC** tricks can be broken down into a few distinct types:

A B C D E F G H I J K L M N O P Q R S T U V W X Y Z

PRODUCTION: A coin is produced from nowhere, or perhaps a rabbit is conjured from a hat.

VANISH: A coin vanishes from the magician's fingers, a lady enters a wardrobe on stage which is then revealed to be empty, or a entire Statue of Liberty seems to have disappeared.

TRANSFORMATION: Something appears to have changed into something else: the magician takes a frog and turns it into a princess. The logical mind will immediately realise that this is simply a combination of a VANISH and a PRODUCTION.

RESTORATION: Something is taken and destroyed, perhaps your pocket watch! And then the magician magically restores it to its former state.

TRANSPORTATION: Something appears to have moved from one place to another in an impossible way.

TRANSPOSITION: Two objects exchange places mysteriously.

LEVITATION: A human being or object seem to float mysteriously, not only in defiance of gravity but also at the will of the illusionist.

PENETRATION: One object passes through another in an impossible way. A knife is stuck through the artist's tongue. Steel rings link and unlink. A piece of rope passes through the magician's neck.

PREDICTION: The illusionist predicts something—often the card you are going to pick but sometimes something more interesting like the contents of your wallet.

These then are the basic things that amaze and enthrall people.

They are also things that people somehow *want* to believe in.

A very great deal of creative effort has been expended by magicians to build illusions around these basic components, with some truly incredible results.

MAGICIAN'S CHOICE

MAGIC / PSYCHOLOGY

This really *is* magic.

☆ **FORCE A CARD** on your victim, do the shuffle and mix those cards up really well. It would help (though it is not necessary) if you were to fumble and drop a few at this stage. We need to get some **MISDIRECTION** going as early as possible in the trick so it will help if it looks like you have messed things up a bit.

You now fan the cards, face towards you and make a show of trying to find their card. They must not see the faces.

    'Here it is!'

You slam a card face-down on the table. But just as they are about to turn it over you stop them.

    'Hold on, I was wrong, it's this one!'

Another card hits the table face down.

    'No wait a minute,'

You desperately fumble back and forth through the deck.

    'It's this one, oh. Or maybe this one.'

There are now four cards on the table, all face down.

    'I'm all mixed up, sorry. It's
    gone wrong.'

You stir the cards about in a confusing
manner and arrange them in a square.

    'Look, I'm sorry. I know
    that *one* of these cards is
    your card, at least I'm pretty sure, but I've messed the
    trick up. Now I want this to look good so there's only
    one thing for it.'

'What's that?' says the victim.

A
B
C
D
E
F
G
H
I
J
K
L
M
N
O
P
Q
R
S
T
U
V
W
X
Y
Z

> '*You* will have to choose the card.'

Now we get to the clever part. You know perfectly well which their card is, because it was the *second* card you put down, and you've kept an eye on where it is.

☆ HERE'S *The* TRICK: You are going to make it look like *they* are choosing one of the four cards, when actually *you* are going to do the choosing. This is easier than you might think, just proceed as follows and keep up the *pace* of the following monologue (so they will think it is a *dialogue*). If you start talking to someone while they are still thinking about the last thing that happened they will not catch on.

While making appropriate gestures you explain.

> 'there are two columns, like this and two rows like this.
> I'm going to ask you to choose a column, we'll keep one,
> and throw one away, which column?'

They indicate a column and *while they are indicating it* you say

> 'OK we'll throw that one away' or 'we'll keep that one
> and throw the other away'

depending on where the card is. Note that it's very important to use the phrase "throw that one away" in either case. Now say

> 'Now! There are two cards left. Pick a card!'

If they pick the right card you say

> 'Turn it over!'

and you are done—to the utter amazement of all around you.

If they pick the wrong card you repeat the magic phrase

> 'OK, so we throw that one away!'

And then you ask them to turn over their card—to the stunned disbelief of all present.

It's real magic! You will not only amaze the audience, you'll also amaze yourself.

Do *not* repeat this trick no matter how much they beg you.

MAGNETIC PENCIL

MAGIC

A pencil is held in a fist. The fingers open and it magically stays stuck to the palm of the hand.

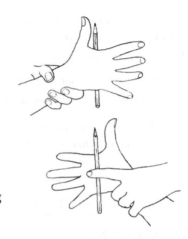

This is an angle-sensitive trick. There are various ways of pulling it off.

☆ The simplest is where you use the other hand to grasp the wrist of the hand holding the pencil a if to steady it. What the audience do not see is that the index finger of the supporting hand is holding the pencil in place.

☆ If you are wearing a watch you can use a *second* pencil, jammed under the watch-strap, to hold the pencil against your palm

☆ There's a nice variation in which you interlock the fingers of both hands and present the magically **MAGNETIC PENCIL** effect. the secret is that one of your middle fingers is secretly concealed *inside* your hands and is holding the pencil in place.

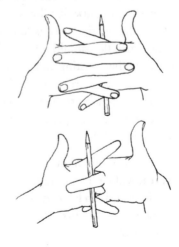

People are bad at counting fingers, a trick that is much used in animation—where cartoon characters traditionally have just three fingers on each hand, thus saving much work for the animators.

A
B
C
D
E
F
G
H
I
J
K
L
M
N
O
P
Q
R
S
T
U
V
W
X
Y
Z

MAGUFFIN

FILMING

☆ The **MAGUFFIN** is the thing that everyone is chasing each other about in a thriller or a spy movie. It could be a radioactive crystal, a necklace, a formula, or somebody's mojo.

The **MAGUFFIN** is not important in itself, it's just a plot device. By the end of the film we'll be far more interested in the girl.

☆ While we are on the subject of movies: have you ever noticed that nothing *good* ever happens in motels?

MAHL STICK

SIGNWRITING

Also known as a **DOLLY**, the **MAHL STICK** is an essential tool for the signwriter because it allows you to rest your hand *above* the work. This is important because the brush handle should always be pretty much vertical when writing and it's impossible to hold it that way while resting your hand on the job itself. It also helps to prevent the heel of your hand hitting wet paint as you move around the work.

☆ A really useful **MAHL STICK** will be at least three feet long and can be used as a guide when **LINING AND STRIPING**.

Typically it is made from a length of wooden dowel about half an inch in diameter with a small wooden ball fitted to the end. A piece of chamois leather is bound over the ball to provide a suitably soft end.

☆ Signwriting is a spectator sport; some wag will always come up to watch you at work on a shop front.

After a few minutes this tragic character will no longer be able to keep his peace.

Looking up and down the street he will first make sure that others are in earshot and then try:

```
WAG: Oi! Mate, you've
spelt it wrong!
```

Quickly throw him a quick look-of-death and then turn back to your work.

You now need wait only half a minute for one of the classic comebacks of all time.

The joker will speak up again, this time in a friendly sort of way:

```
WAG: What's the stick for mate?
```

You turn to him and then look slowly at the **MAHL STICK** as if it has just been teleported into your hand from another dimension.

```
YOU: I have no idea what the stick is for mate, it's just
that all the other signwriters have one and I didn't want
to look like a complete prat!
```

That's him sorted then.

A
B
C
D
E
F
G
H
I
J
K
L
M
N
O
P
Q
R
S
T
U
V
W
X
Y
Z

A
B
C
D
E
F
G
H
I
J
K
L
M
N
O
P
Q
R
S
T
U
V
W
X
Y
Z

MAKING A SAUSAGE WITH YOUR FINGERS

OPTICAL ILLUSIONS

☆ Point your two index fingers at each other and hold them one and a half inches apart, level with your eyes.

Now, while focusing on the wall opposite you, move your fingers towards your eyes, when they are just a few inches from your face a hovering pink sausage will appear to be floating in the air in front of you.

MAKING THE QUEEN SMILE (OR FROWN)

SILLINESS

You would have thought that she wouldn't need any help since she has all that money.

☆ Take any English banknote, crumple it up a bit and flatten it. Now turn it so that the Queen's face is facing you. Make a mountain fold that runs from the extreme right hand side of her mouth, directly through her right eye. Then do the same of the left. You don't want the folds to go to the edge of the note.

Finally make a valley fold that runs from below the chin and passes directly between her eyes and stops somewhere around the hairline.

Next make a gentle mountain fold just above the eyebrows, this is a not a crisp fold, more of a gently bump.

You're ready to go.

Hold the note with your left hand so that the thumb is just below the chin, this will hold the arrangement in place. Now arrange yourself so that the available light is pointing straight at the note (we don't want any obvious shadows.)

If you tip the note towards you the Queen will seem to frown (even more than usual) but if you tip it back she'll seem to smile. Practice getting the effect just right, but not too extreme.

To present the illusion you take a prepared note and show it to someone (tipped forwards a little) and remark that the Queen always looks so *grumpy*. Explain that you are about to cheer her up a little.

"By the power of hypnosis!" You say as you wave your free hand around in front of her. "I shall command you to be *happy!*"

As you say *happy* you pass your hand quickly over the note (as you tip it back) and her face will magically transform.

You can pile on the agony by waving your hand back and forth over her saying "Happy! Sad! Happy! Sad!"

I'm sure you get the idea.

MAKING THE STATUE OF LIBERTY VANISH

MAGIC

If, like the famous illusionist David Copperfield, you would like to make something as vast as the Statue of Liberty vanish then you had better know how to do it.

A
B
C
D
E
F
G
H
I
J
K
L
M
N
O
P
Q
R
S
T
U
V
W
X
Y
Z

☆ HERE'S *The* TRICK: Obviously you cannot *actually* make the thing vanish, because that would be ridiculous. Any fool can see that, except possibly your audience who will believe just about anything. And obviously you cannot *move* the thing because it is big and heavy and the job could take weeks—you have a minute at most to pull the feat off.

So the only sensible thing left is to *move the audience* instead—and that is indeed how it is done, not just for this trick, but for many similar vanishes (locomotives, aircraft, the moon and so on). The Statue of Liberty stands overlooking a large expanse of water, so why not set up your show on a specially built floating theatre on a hired boat?

Arrange matters so that the stage points towards the statue and place the seating facing it. Have two towers on each side of the stage between which you will hang a big drape to conceal the statue from view during the actual vanish (see COVERING THE JOIN).

Now go out and set up some big bright lights pointing at the statue and an identical set off to the side pointing at nothing. Then add a whole lot more lights so that there will be a lot of glare around the place to confuse people.

Bring in the audience and show them the amazing view of the statue and have a helicopter fly around it with a searchlight on just for added pizazz.

Now draw up the drape, while playing some loud music, and make some pretty serious-looking *abracadabra* type gestures while the entire venue is pulled around a few degrees (and make sure you give the helicopter pilot time to reposition the aircraft).

Now fire off some loud flashy pyros and drop the drapes to reveal that it has gone! The beauty of the floating stage is that it will move smoothly and silently. Oh, and don't forget to put it back afterwards!

MARK

DEFINITION

In GRIFTER talk a MARK is the person being conned. The MARK'S job is to lose the money you are going to gain.

Marking out a Sign

SIGNWRITING

When you are knocking out a quick sign you will usually end up trying to fit a word or phrase into a space of a particular size.

Signwriters like to work fast, so they have worked out a simple system for making sure that you don't run out of room for your letters. It's known as the "points system" and it works pretty well for any capital letters that are based on the **ROMAN LETTERS** (which means that it works for pretty much any type face).

☆ Each space between letters gets half a point.

☆ Letters get two points each, except "I" which gets one, "J" which gets one and a half and "M" and "W" which get three.

☆ Spaces between words get three points.

OK, so mark out the area into which you want to paint your letters by **SNAPPING A LINE** top and bottom, and then adding two vertical lines at each end with your marking-out pencil to enclose the area in which your letters are to sit. Measure the width of this with a tape and climb down your ladder to do some sums.

Let's suppose we want to write "TRICK BOOK SHOP" and we have 120 inches to fit it into. The phrase we are writing adds up to 25 points for the letters, 6 points for the spaces between words, and 5 points for the spaces between letters, which makes 36 points altogether. 120 divided by 36 is 3⅓.

So that's 3⅓ inches per point. This is a tricky measurement to make so you get a piece of card and mark off, from one corner, 3⅓, 6⅔ and 10 inches as little marks. Then hop back up the ladder and divide the area you are working on into the rectangles into which you are going to place the letters.

Note that the vertical lines you draw are done *by eye* not with a set square.

The beauty of the system is that you can also get on with the job of sketching the guide lines for the letter's themselves *without* having to worry about running out of room when you get to the far end of the job

A B C D E F G H I J K L **M** N O P Q R S T U V W X Y Z

(which will involve at least two trips down and up the ladder as you relocate it along the job).

Signwriting is all about cutting corners, that's the only way you'll make a living at it.

See also **SNAPPING A LINE**.

MARKED DECK

MAGIC / GRIFTING

A **MARKED DECK** is a specially prepared deck of cards designed so that the suit and value of a card can be read from the back. People like the *idea* of **MARKED DECKS** and they get bought in large numbers. The trouble is, they aren't really very useful.

The deck will usually carry very subtle marks worked into the design on the back of the card that will take some practice (and good eyesight) to read. Almost all commercially available marked decks carry their own special design on the back and they therefore look unusual to an experienced card-player. Needless to say, if you were to be caught using a **MARKED DECK** in a poker game you could find yourself in some very nasty trouble. Cheating at cards is Bad Thing To Do.

If you feel the need to use a **MARKED DECK** to perform tricks then you could probably do with some lessons in magic. I mean, what is the point of a trick in which you have to work out what a card is by looking at it's back? A proper magician would have known what the card was *before the trick even started!*

The whole *point* of a deck of cards is that you can't tell what a card is by looking at the back. If you can't live with that then you would do well to avoid card tricks and poker games all together.

If you take *my* advice you'll save your money and buy something more useful like a **TAPER DECK** or a **SVENGALI DECK**.

MARSHALLING AIRCRAFT

CODES & CIPHERS

Start engine number...	Apply brakes	Move toward me	Chocks removed
Slow down	Chocks inserted	Stop engines	Connect ground power
Place yourself facing me	Stop (side to side wave)	Turn left	FIRE!
Slow engines this side	Move back	Proceed to next marshaller	All clear

MARSHALLING AIRCRAFT is the art of giving signals to pilots so they know where to go and what to do. Come on, you know you want to!

A
B
C
D
E
F
G
H
I
J
K
L
M
N
O
P
Q
R
S
T
U
V
W
X
Y
Z

If you happen to be around when a helicopter is making a landing in a tight spot and you realise (as you should) that the pilot can only see out of the front of the aircraft, then it follows that you could be of great assistance if only you knew the right signs to make.

Well wonder no longer, here are the standard marshalling signals for regular aircraft:

There is another set of signals specially for helicopters (which is the type of aircraft you are more likely to happen on by chance).

Take off this
direction

Hover

Move to my right

Hook up
(winch / sling)

Release
(winch / sling)

Engage rotor

Move upwards

Move downwards

Land

Aviation is a pretty serious business, so you are cautioned against using these signals unless:

1: You can actually remember them.

2: You know what you are doing and you act in a responsible manner.

3: You realise that a helicopter pilot is, by definition, *not* an idiot and will know perfectly well if *you* are.

MASONIC HANDSHAKES

CODES & CIPHERS

It's well known that Masons use secret handshakes, but I bet you don't know how they are actually done.

Briefly, there are various ranks of freemasonry, and there are different handshakes that are used to communicate these ranks on meeting people.

A lowly *Entered Apprentice* will use a 'Grip' named 'Boaz' which is like an ordinary handshake except that their thumb will press against the first knuckle joint of the hand that is being shaken.

A slightly more senior *Fellow Craft* will use a 'Pass Grip' called 'Shibboleth' in which the thumb presses on the space between the first and second knuckle joints.

A
B
C
D
E
F
G
H
I
J
K
L
M
N
O
P
Q
R
S
T
U
V
W
X
Y
Z

A
B
C
D
E
F
G
H
I
J
K
L
M
N
O
P
Q
R
S
T
U
V
W
X
Y
Z

The *Fellow Craft* also has a 'Real Grip' called 'Jachin' in which the thumb presses on the second knuckle joint.

Good isn't it? It goes on: The 'Pass Grip' of a Master Mason is called 'Tubalcain' and (I bet you can guess) it involves pressing the thumb between the second and third knuckles.

Which brings us, finally to the 'Real Grip' of the Master Mason which is called (don't laugh) 'Ma-Ha-Bone'. It is also called the 'Strong Grip of the Master Mason' or the 'Lion's Paw'. Both hands are interlaced with the thumb and little finger attempting to circle the wrist.

Now I'm not suggesting that you actually *use* these powerful handshakes, but it's fun to pay close attention when you see world leaders meeting each other in front of the TV cameras.

See also **GREAT HAILING SIGN OF DISTRESS**.

MATCH PENETRATION

MAGIC / MATCH TRICKS

In this closeup illusion two matches appear to pass right through each other.

☆ You take two matches and hold each one between the tips of your index fingers and thumbs forming a finger-thumb-match loop in each hand.

You then move the two loops together and they magically link *as if the matches had penetrated each other.*

☆ HERE'S *The* TRICK: Squeeze the match in your favourite hand *very* hard between thumb and forefinger—so hard it hurts!

You'll find that if you release the grip on the match after a hard squeeze it will have embedded itself in your skin a little and one end or the other will *stick* to your finger or thumb—thus creating a gap that you can use to link the matches.

Make sure that the stuck match is pointing straight at the audience when you do this and they will not be able to see the subterfuge.

As soon as the matches are linked you close the gap again

You can safely link and unlink the matches several times, right under the noses of your onlookers. It really is an impressive illusion.

Obviously you need to **PRACTICE IN FRONT OF A MIRROR** to become really proficient at this trick.

A
B
C
D
E
F
G
H
I
J
K
L
M
N
O
P
Q
R
S
T
U
V
W
X
Y
Z

MEGALILTH

FUN WITH SCIENCE

Ancient people were able to raise massively heavy stones and place them on top of other stones to form intriguingly impressive monuments such as *Stonehenge*, the *Great Pyramid* and the thousands of *Dolmens* that litter the landscape of Brittany and Europe to this day.

The largest known stone to have been raised in prehistoric times is *Le Grand Menhir Brisé* which stood over 60 feet high and weighed over 260 tons. Today it lies shattered into four pieces at *Locmariaquer* in France. Some say it fell during an earthquake, others that it was struck by lightning—it may even have been torn down deliberately, but archæologists are quite sure that it did once stand.

Standing stones are often used as pointers to special places, or to form alignments with other features for the purposes of navigation or precisely locating things. The modern equivalents remain in the form of the trig points that you will find on the hills of England which are used to plot the baselines from which maps are drawn.

You need to stand right up close to these great stones to fully appreciate their extraordinary heaviness and the hopelessness of attempting to move them by any conceivable act of muscular strength with your frail, flimsy and fleshy human body. Nevertheless these stones were clearly raised by human beings—and all without the aid of diesel-powered machines.

Most will gaze in awe and wonder, 'Why?'

The Trickster, on the other hand, will gaze with a cannier eye and wonder, 'How?'

Here's the Problem: The stone you are trying to lift weighs, say, fifty tons. It's the weight that is the problem.

And so, as in martial arts disciplines like **TAI CHE NI**, we turn the *problem* to our *advantage*. We shall defeat the problem of the megalith's weight by adding *even more* weight, in the form of stones that we can move by hand. We shall then use the megalith as a sort of lever to raise itself.[*]

We begin with our fifty-ton megalith balanced on two stacks of stones (B and C) that lie close together below the megalith's centre of gravity. Slightly further out we place more stones that do not quite contact the underneath of the megalith (A and D).

Next we start to pile stones on top of the great stone, as far from the centre of gravity as we can manage. Each of these small blocks will be chosen to be of a weight that a single person can lift and move. After sufficient stones have been placed the megalith will topple sideways gently and rest on the stones we placed underneath to catch it.

We can now shore up the supports that it has swung free of and reverse the process, moving the counterbalancing stones across the top of the megalith from one side to the other. In due course the megalith will topple the other way and so the work continues.

Gradually, and in a very controllable fashion, the great megalith will be raised upwards. Each "topple" gaining us another inch or two of height.

The beauty of this scheme is that no great act of force is required at any time, in fact a stone of practically any size can be lifted by a single person —just rather slowly slowly.

---

[*] The technique here described was independently and more or less simultaneously discovered by *Wally Wallington* (a retired builder from the USA), *Radical Cheney* and others.

MEMORY TRICKS

PSYCHOLOGY

Your memory is a funny beast, but there's a very simple trick which will mean you can beat anyone at a memory game.

You see it's a little known fact that memory works in pictures. And the more gruesome, surreal or messy you make your mental pictures the better! Also it's great fun.

Next time you are in a car, try this game.

> YOU: Hey, shall we play the holiday game? You know the one where you have to remember what we all take on holiday?
>
> SISTER: Okay, I'll start. When I went on holiday I took with me my Barbie doll.
>
> BROTHER: When I went on holiday I took with me my Barbie doll and some green slime.
>
> AUNTIE: When I went on holiday I took with me my Barbie doll, some green slime, and some flowers.

Each person has to remember the whole sequence and then add another object.

... an hour later everyone else is starting to make mistakes, but ...

> YOU: When I went on holiday I took with me my Barbie doll, some green slime, some flowers, my goggles & snorkel, my pet cat, a map, some dirty socks, a gold coin ... and on and on

☆ HERE'S *The* TRICK: When someone adds a new object, picture it interpenetrating the previous object in the most vulgar, messy, smashed up way you can. Really look at it.

So in the example above you might have covered the Barbie doll in green slime, which spilt all over the place and floating in which you put some glowing flowers, which are reflected in the eyes of some goggles swinging overhead, being worn by a cat, wrapped up in an old map, and partially stuffed into an horrible smelly sock, from the toehole of which is glinting a gold coin ... and so on.

Imagine it as pictures, reinforce it each turn, and soon you'll be able to remember 100 objects like this.

Remember to choose vivid surreal and colourful imagery .

No problem!

MENTALISM

MIND READING / CODES & CIPHERS

This fine traditional trick works well in front of modern audiences though it can be especially funny if you slowly reveal the gag, instead of actually holding on to the pretence of telepathic prowess.

☆ The classic performance proceeds as follows: you dress yourself up as the *Great Mentalismo* in elaborate costume and assume the airs and graces befitting a psychic savant. You will need a competent assistant who can think fast and speak boldly and clearly.

You produce a genuine blindfold and have audience members assist you in checking that it really does render you incapable of sight.

Your assistant then approaches the audience and asks individuals to produce objects from their pockets which are held aloft one by one while you have to say what they are. Your assistant is responsible for announcing each object in the following general manner:

```
ASSISTANT: I have in my hand an object that you cannot
know or discern by eye since you are blindfolded—can you
tell me what it is yet?

After a moment of furious contemplation you will reply.
```

MENTALISMO: I'm getting an image of a great door through which only some may pass - is it a key?

The crowd are, or course, impressed and another object is obtained.

ASSISTANT: But can the Great Mentalismo now advise as to what I have now got in my hand?

MENTALISMO: I believe it is a magazine!

ASSISTANT: That is all well and very good, but your answer is a little opaque, will you now go on so we can understand exactly what magazine it is?

MENTALISMO: It is a copy of Vogue.

And so the performance proceeds.

☆ HERE'S *The* TRICK: The *hard* work is actually being done by the assistant whose job, as I mentioned before, relies on quick-thinking and a bold voice. The secret is simply that the name of the object is actually being *spelled out* in the assistants words by means of applying inflection or drawing out certain words. In the first speech, where a key was the object in question the assistant *actually* said:

I have in my hand an object that you cannot <u>*know*</u> or discern by <u>*eye*</u> since <u>*you*</u> are blindfolded. Can you tell me what it is yet?

Thus the first letters of the three words *know*, *eye* and *you* spell out KEY.

Now the style of inflection needs to be suitably prominent and drawing out the words is probably the best way to do this: the resulting speech will admittedly seem unnatural, but if it is combined with a suitably dramatic performance the audience will accept it as part of the show and not notice the trick. A good deal of practice will be required and it is handy to have pre-memorised words suitable for every letter of the alphabet to save thinking-time in performance.

The magazine was identified as follows:

But can the Great <u>*Mentalismo*</u> now <u>*advise*</u> as to what I have now <u>*got*</u> in my hand?

That is all well and <u>*very*</u> good, but your answer is a little <u>*opaque*</u>, will you now <u>*go*</u> on so we can <u>*understand*</u> <u>*exactly*</u> what magazine it is?

Which two lines spell out MAG and VOGUE respectively.

In traditional mentalism shows an alternative method was used, in which a code had to be learned that covered just about any object likely to be found in the pockets of the audience. A phrase like "quickly please" could refer to a watch as in "Can you tell me what I am holding in my hand quickly please?" Other phrases would refer to cigars, wallets, coins and so on. This was all well and good in the old days, but life is more rich and complex now and people carry some pretty bizarre things around with them. It could take years to develop and memorise a code to handle all eventualities.

Returning to our system: if you are going for a comic performance you should have your assistant seek out more and more elaborately spelt objects from the audience and start to really ham up the lines:

```
ASSISTANT: And now before me I have an object that I'd
like you to describe using the x-ray powers of your mind.

MENTALISMO: Is it perhaps a box of some sort?

ASSISTANT: Indeed it is, but I now wish to see if you can
tell me exactly what is contained in this small box.

MENTALISMO: I believe that the box contains insects.
```

And indeed it transpires that the audience member is carrying home a box of live crickets with which to feed their rare Amazonian Tree Frog named Buddy.

The joke is greatly enhanced by the fact that some members of the audience will start to catch on before others. The more exotic and hard-to-describe that the chosen objects are, the greater the fun.

MENTO AND DIET COKE

FUN WITH SCIENCE / EXPLOSIVES

☆ Add four Mentos (mint sweets, you'll find 'em) to a litre of Diet Coke. Stand well back *immediately* because the stuff goes off like a rocket and can spray coke several feet in the air.

A
B
C
D
E
F
G
H
I
J
K
L
M
N
O
P
Q
R
S
T
U
V
W
X
Y
Z

If you can work out a way of keeping the Mentos separate from the coke until the proper launch moment, it has been calculated that the force of the sudden production of huge quantities of gas might actually be able to power a small rocket fashioned from a bottle. Have fun trying and *do not try this indoors.*

It has to be Diet Coke by the way.

See also **FISSION POP BOMB**.

MILLS' MESS

JUGGLING

This pattern was invented by a chap named *Steve Mills* [*] in the days just before juggling went huge.

The **MILLS' MESS** is stunningly beautiful three-ball pattern. The hands do a wonderful little dance of crossing and uncrossing hands while the balls weave from side to side in a hypnotic manner. It's great to watch and lovely to do.

Here's how to learn it, we'll start by miming the six-throw sequence.

☆ Put *down* three balls and start working with empty hands.

1: Cross the left hand *over* the right, look at it and say *'Throw!'* as you uncross your hands.

2: Look at your right hand and say *'Throw!'* as you cross your left hand *under* the right.

3: Look at your left hand (which is crossed under your right) and say *'Throw!'*

We now repeat the same sequence on the left hand side.

4: Look at your right hand, which is crossed *over* the left, and say *'Throw!'* as you uncross your hands.

[*] So now you know why the apostrophe goes after the 's'.

5: Look at your left hand and say *'Throw!'* as you cross your right hand *under* the left.

6: Look at your right hand (which is crossed *under* your left) and say *'Throw!'*

...and you are back at the starting position.

Note that you are making three throws on the right-hand side, then three throws on the left hand side.

But what do the balls do? Well, they do exactly what they would do in a **THREE BALL CASCADE**, you see the **MILLS' MESS** is merely a *shape-distortion* of the cascade. Every right-hand throw goes to the left hand and vice versa. So if you are feeling brave you can now add the balls and get on with it!

Trouble is, this usually doesn't work for a beginner, the whole thing gets a bit too confusing and the trouble with juggling patterns is that you *cannot slow them down*, even while learning! What we need to do is to sidle up to the problem and catch it unawares. We need a trick to help us learn the pattern.

It turns out that the very simple pattern the **WINDMILL** can help.

☆ In the **WINDMILL** you make **UNDER THE HAND** throws with one hand, and **OVER THE TOP** throws with the other. The secret is to make direction-changes every *three* throws. You make the change with the hand that is doing the **OVER THE TOP** throws. This is a bit of a knack but you'll get it!

☆ The **MILLS' MESS** can be juggled with clubs, usually on single-spins. It's an advanced trick.

☆ The **MILLS' MESS** can be extended to more than three objects. The trick is to take a basic pattern, like a Four Ball **FOUNTAIN** or **FIVE BALL CASCADE** and apply the six-throw hand-crossing routine to it—three throws on the right, three throws on the left. The five-ball **MILLS' MESS** is particularly effective. Here's what three throws of a five-ball **MILLS' MESS** look like:

MIRRORS

FUN WITH SCIENCE

MIRRORS are magic.

Most of us believe that we understand what **MIRRORS** do pretty well, since they are everyday objects in this age of miracle and wonder—but do you *really* understand what a mirror does?

Here's the riddle:

> If a mirror reverses left and right, why does it not reverse up and down as well?

Tough question isn't it? There's an answer at the end of this entry.

☆ You are very used to seeing your reflection in the bathroom mirror and are familiar with the left-right flip as you shave your face or brush your hair. But have you ever noticed that if you place two mirrors at right angles to each other and stare into their corner you get a reflection that is the *right* way around?

☆ If you have ever stood between two mirrors that face each other you'll have experienced the *tunnel of mirrors* effect in which you see a reflection of a reflection of a reflection... ad infinitum—except that your head is in the way. To better experience this effect you should take a small piece of mirrored glass and scratch a small hole through the reflective material from the back. Now hold this up to your eye and direct your view directly at another mirror.

Mirror ⟶

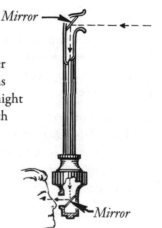

☆ With two mirrors and a little engineering you can fashion a *Periscope* which is a device that allows you to look over things or around corners. The two reflections cancel each other out (as a mathematician might say) and the result is a normal image in which up-down and left-right retain their normal orientations. *Periscopes* were invaluable military tools in the dark days of trench warfare when sticking your head into view was likely to result in a bullet to the face.

Mirror

☆ Mirrors were much-used in 19th century magic. One noted illusion was the **PEPPER'S GHOST** illusion.

☆ And the answer to the riddle? If a mirror reflects left and right, why not also up and down?

Well, in actual fact a mirror does not reflect left and right, neither does it reflect up and down. It reflects front and back.

Think about it!

MISDIRECTION

MAGIC TECHNIQUE

MISDIRECTION is the technique of drawing attention to what is *not* actually happening.

The human mind is easily distracted and can only think *consciously* about one thing at a time.

The trick of **MISDIRECTION** is the trick of supplying a strong stimulus to the **MARK** so that their mind is "looking away" from the real action.

For example, when Picking Pockets the basic technique is to prevent the Mark from feeling your hands dipping a pocket by applying a much stronger stimulus elsewhere.

A friendly clap on the shoulder can do the trick.

Also, when performing closeup magic like the **CUPS AND BALLS** you will be amazed how easy it is to make your audience look away from the action by simply directing your gaze away from it yourself, perhaps to engage an imaginary heckler.

More commonly, the artiste will make good use of the *Magic Wand*—here a cup is violently smacked with the stick in order to distract attention away from the dead rat.

You did see the rat didn't you?

See **TABLE TOP COIN VANISH** and **YOU DON'T WANT TO BE SMOKING THAT!** for two nice examples.

A flash and it's gone!

MOBILE PHONE AS A BUGGING DEVICE

ESPIONAGE

This is a pretty creepy thing to do, but then you may have your reasons!

☆ You need a mobile phone with decent battery life (several days is best) and with a number that nobody knows, the best way of doing that is to go and buy a new SIM card. You'll also need a cheap hands free kit, go for the type with an earpiece and a microphone on the cable.

Plug in the hands free kit and you'll find that you can now set your phone to answer automatically when called. You must also (this is very important) set the ringing volume to zero.

Make a site visit and conceal the phone somewhere in the room you want to bug, say your cheating lover's bedroom.

You can now phone the bug any time you like and miserably torture yourself by listening to conversations or *other activities* in the room.

MÖBIUS STRIP

MATHEMATICS / PAPER TRICKS

If you take a length of ribbon and join its ends together you will end up with a loop. The loop has an inside surface, an outside surface and two edges.

But if you take a length of ribbon and give one end a *half twist* before joining it to the other end you will end up with a **MÖBIUS STRIP**.

The **MÖBIUS STRIP** is a bizarre object with

A
B
C
D
E
F
G
H
I
J
K
L
M
N
O
P
Q
R
S
T
U
V
W
X
Y
Z

interesting and amusing *topological* properties. It was discovered* independently by *August Möbius* and *Johann Listing* in 1858.

Topology, in case you didn't know, is a special branch of mathematical science concerned with the way in which things can be arranged or fitted together in space.

Topology ignores distances, angles, curves and corners.

Instead it focuses on the connections between things.

A sphere and a cube are logically identical in topology—if you think about it they both simply amount to a basic closed three-dimensional surface with an inside and an outside.

On the other hand a doughnut (or torus) is topologically different to a sphere (no matter what shape and size it is) because the map of its surface connects to itself in a fundamentally different way.

Topology can tell the difference between a simple loop of string and an **OVERHAND KNOT** but it cannot tell you how thick the string is.

Topology knows that a normal piece of sheet material has *two* surfaces (front and back) and *one* edge—think of a sheet of paper.

Topology knows that a simple loop made from sheet material has *two* surfaces (inside and outside) and *two* separate edges (think of a bracelet and run your finger round the two edges).

Topology is therefore proud to announce the **MÖBIUS STRIP**—a loop made from sheet material that has just *one* surface and *one* edge. You are expected to be amazed and surprised by this peculiar mathematical oddity —you have been paying attention haven't you?

Is such a thing possible?

Well, yes it is!

---

* The use of the word discovered suggest that the Möbius Strip already existed in some way before these clever gentlemen knocked up their copies with sellotape scissors and paper. We might just as well say that the thing was invented simultaneously by these two men. Therein lies the great philosophical problem of mathematics: did we discover all this stuff or did we invent it? Does mathematics have any sort of existence outside the mind of the mathematician? And the answer to these riddles?—they're not sure.

Moreover it does behave in some weird and wonderful ways.

It is easy to make a **MÖBIUS STRIP** out of a piece of paper, but you can make an even better version from **GAFFER TAPE**.

☆ For the paper version, cut a strip of paper and then give one end a half twist before taping or gluing it back onto itself.

☆ To make one out of **GAFFER TAPE** take two almost equal lengths and fix them sticky side to sticky side, leaving a little but of stick exposed at one end. Give it a twist and join it up into a loop.

☆ If you examine the thing carefully you'll discover that the strip has only one side, and one edge! A good way to check this is to get a felt pen and colour the edge—you'll find that there is only one edge to colour—weird!

☆ If you cut the thing in half, by running down a pair of scissors down the centre line something odd happens.

Instead of falling into two pieces you get a new single strip with *two* half twists in it.

☆ If you cut this strip in half again you get two interlocking strips!

☆ Starting again with a *fresh* **MÖBIUS STRIP**, if you make a cut about a third of the way across and work your way around you'll end up with a thin version of the original strip (cut from the middle) while the two outside edges will combine into one long strip with two half-twists in it.

MONOCYCLE

UNICYCLING

A **MONOCYCLE** is *not* the same thing as a **UNICYCLE**. The monocyclist rides a machine in which the rider is *inside* the wheel.

While the engineers of the 19th century were re-inventing wheeled transport (after centuries of being stuck with the bloody horse) they came up with all sorts of weird and wonderful machines— **MONOCYCLES** being among them.

There is no doubt that a **MONOCYCLE** is potentially a beautiful and elegant machine but it has a couple of rather serious drawbacks:

☆ They only like going in straight lines.

☆ If you slam on the brakes too hard you end up going around and around like clothes in a washing machine *but you don't actually slow down.* This is referred to as *Gerbilling* in the trade.

MOONWALK

DANCE

The all-time absolute master of the **MOONWALK** is *Michael Jackson* who was once described by the legendary *Fred Astaire* as "one hell of a mover". The move is also known as the *Backslide* and is a *Glide Dancing* move.

In the **MOONWALK** the artist mimes the appearance of walking forwards whilst actually travelling backwards. This is an extension of the classic mime technique of *walking on the spot* in which the artist appears to walk forwards while actually staying still.

As with magic tricks the secret to perfecting the move is to **PRACTICE IN FRONT OF A MIRROR**.

☆ Begin by learning to walk forwards, in a natural manner, in a style that can be converted into a **MOONWALK**. The key is to develop a walk in which both feet stay in contact with the ground at all times, so as you swing one foot forward you must keep your toes touching the ground. It will take a little practice to make this look natural.

Now to reverse the walk you have to swap your weight onto the *wrong* foot, so that you are actually standing on the toes of one foot (A) while sliding the other foot (the one that is flat on the floor) *backwards.* Not only that but the rest of your body has to act as if it is supported by the foot that is sliding.

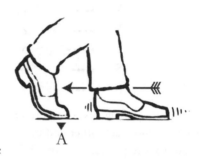

Your arms must swing as they would if your were walking normally—which feels very odd indeed.

However, if you practice hard and long (and in front of a big mirror like they have in dance studios) you'll be rewarded with an unusual and impressive skill.

MORSE CODE
CODES & CIPHERS

MORSE CODE is the old *dah-dit-dit-dah* method of passing signals by tapping telegraph keys, flashing lights, or transmitting a simple series of beeps over the airwaves. It was originally invented in the 1830's as a means of sending signals over the new-fangled electric telegraph.

Most people know that ••• --- ••• means "SOS" but few realise that when a Nokia phone beeps to tell you that you have an incoming text message it often says ••• -- ••• which means "SMS".

A	-	B	-••	C	-•-•
D	-••	E	•	F	••-•
G	--•	H	••••	I	••
J	•---	K	-•-	L	•-••
M	--	N	-•	O	---
P	•--•	Q	--•-	R	•-•
S	•••	T	-	U	••-
V	•••-	W	•--	X	-••-
Y	-•--	Z	--••	1	•----
2	••---	3	•••--	4	••••-
5	•••••	6	-••••	7	--•••
8	---••	9	----•	0	-----

The timing of signals is important if you are to avoid words and letters running into each other and becoming a meaningless binary clatter. It is customary to pronouce a dot "dit" and a dash "dah".

☆ A dah is equal to three dits.
☆ The space between dahs and dits within a letter is equal to one dit.
☆ The space between letters is equal to a dah.
☆ The space between words is equal to seven dits.

In addition to the letters and numbers above there are codes for simple punctuation.

Full stop	•-•-•-	*Comma*	--••--
Question Mark	•-•-•	*Apostrophe*	•----•
Exclamation	-•-•--	*Slash /*	-••-•
Parenthesis (	-••--•	*Parenthesis)*	-•--•-
Ampersand &	• •••	*Colon*	---•••
Semicolon	-•-•-•	*Equals =*	-•••-
Fraction Bar	-••-•	*Hyphen*	-••••-
Underscore	••--•-	*Quotation Mark*	•-••-•
Dollar Sign	•••-••-	*At @*	•--•-•

Note that the ampersand is sent as the letters ES. The @ sign is the new kid on the block. It was added to **Morse Code** in 2004 for obvious reasons.

☆ If you want to learn Morse Code you should know that it is very much easier to learn by speaking it out loud, in dah-dit style, than by treating it as a written language.

Basic proficiency in morse requires a speed of five to ten words a minute. Really skilled operators can manage about 40. The all time record (at the time of writing) is 75.2 words per minute.

MOTORCYCLE SURVIVAL TIPS

VEHICLES

There is no doubt that riding motorcycles is fun, that is right up the moment at which you mess up and end up seriously injured or killed. These machines are, without doubt, the most dangerous vehicles on the road. However nearly all motorcycle accidents can be put down to driver error.

Some of these tricks also apply to cars, and even bicycles.

Here's how to avoid getting hurt:

☆ The all-time classic motorcycle accident goes like this: the rider is travelling along a clear road with good visibility and is passing a T-junction at which a car is waiting to pull out. The rider is sure that the car has seen the motorcycle and proceeds without expecting a problem. Suddenly the car pulls out. The bike cannot stop in time and ploughs into the front of the car. The rider is likely to break both legs, if not be killed outright, by the impact. Hospital wards are littered with seriously injured riders who protest loudly that the accident was not their fault.

Well, while it is true that it is the car driver who has made a mistake and simply not noticed the bike bearing down on them, it is still the biker who ends up smashed to bits.

☆ HERE'S *The* TRICK: expect the car to pull out! Never, ever, ever assume that the car driver has seen you, even if they make full eye contact.

☆ The next most common accident goes like this: A rider, possibly in wet or otherwise adverse conditions, takes a corner a little faster than they would like and starts to throttle back on the bend, or even worse, apply the brakes. The bike loses traction and in the blink of an eye they have smashed down onto the deck and they are sliding along the tarmac.

☆ HERE'S *The* TRICK: Although you should never enter a bend at too high a speed, if you have done so, approach the corner aggressively rather than defensively. The bike will stick to the road far better if it is being powered around the bend and it will also lean over a lot further than most riders realise. It also helps if you throw your weight sideways into the bend (this keeps the wheels more upright during the bank). Hitting the brakes hard, especially the front brake, is a really bad idea.

☆ In heavy or stopped traffic it is very tempting to overtake great long lines of cars because you can. This is all very fine, but it's a good idea to realise that the car drivers are impatient and frustrated and almost certainly not watching their mirrors. It's very common, in traffic queues of this sort, for car drivers to make sudden decisions to turn off, change lanes or make U-turns. They will often do this without signalling. If you happen to be overtaking a car that suddenly decides to turn right, you run the risk of being bounced directly into the path of oncoming traffic.

☆ HERE'S *The* TRICK: Proceed on the assumption that nobody knows you are coming.

☆ Similarly, in slow-moving or stopped queues, there may also be pedestrians trying to cross the road who may take an opportunity (perhaps given by a generous truck or bus driver) to make their way across the road. Now, as any biker knows, you can see pedestrians through cars but you can't see through buses and trucks. Even worse, the pedestrian can't see you and won't be expecting you. If they suddenly appear in front of you it is highly likely that you'll hit them.

☆ HERE'S *The* TRICK: Always assume that there is a pedestrian in front of every slow-moving or stopped large vehicle and drive accordingly.

☆ Wet drain covers are extremely slippery. If you hit one while banking your front wheel will kick out from under you in an alarming manner.

☆ **HERE'S** *The* **TRICK**: Avoid cornering over wet drain covers. If your front wheel does kick out do not over-react because a fraction of a second later your back wheel will do the same thing—which tends to cancel out the effect of the loss of traction you just experienced with the front wheel

☆ Diesel fuel is often found lying on the road and is very slippery stuff, unlike petrol which evaporates to nothing is seconds. Usually the diesel will have been dropped from an over-filled tank and will have slooshed out when the guilty vehicle was negotiating a corner. Sometimes a diesel vehicle will have a leaking fuel system and will leave a small trail of fuel on the road, but a great big puddle where it had to stop for the traffic lights. In either case the fuel ends up being most concentrated where you could most do without it.

☆ **HERE'S** *The* **TRICK**: The adapt motorcyclist has a keen nose for the smell of diesel and watches out for it at junctions or on corners.

☆ Even without major fuel spills the amount of oil in the road builds up steadily during periods of dry weather and then floats to the surface during the first rain that follows.

☆ **HERE'S** *The* **TRICK**: Remember that roads are much more slippery during the first rain after a long dry spell.

☆ Most bikers have little or no idea about how long it takes to stop their machine from high speed.

☆ **HERE'S** *The* **TRICK**: Find out your braking distance. Select a nice clear straight road and make sure there are no other vehicles anywhere near you. Take your machine up to a high speed and then stop as fast as you dare.

Now turn round and take a look at how far you travelled while braking. Scary isn't it? Ok, now try again, and see if you can do better. With practice you'll learn to brake hard enough to lock the wheels, and how to ease off on the brakes to unlock them again. In a really hard controlled stop you might lock the front wheel three times. Needless to say, you should never lock the front wheel unless you are rolling in a dead straight line—otherwise you'll be on the road in the blink of an eye.

Whatever vehicle you drive, practice emergency stops often, both in wet and dry conditions, and you'll be a much safer rider for it. For one thing you'll

A
B
C
D
E
F
G
H
I
J
K
L
M
N
O
P
Q
R
S
T
U
V
W
X
Y
Z

know exactly how much clear road you need to keep in front of you, and for another you'll be able to stop much quicker when you really need to.

Finally, never let your vehicle drive you. It's very easy, on a sunny day, to go off into a daydream as you feel the warm wind on your face. Then suddenly something unexpected happens in front of you and you have no time to react. Instead always drive positively, even a little aggressively, so as to remain in control at all times.

Have fun and drive safely!

MOUTH TO HEAD

HAT TRICKS

Here's a great little *Hat Juggling* trick.

☆ Bite into the brim of a hat, so the crown points up. Now toss the hat up with a single-spin and catch it on your head.

MULTIPLEX

JUGGLING

A **MULTIPLEX** is the act of throwing more than one object from one hand at one time.

☆ A two-ball *split* **MULTIPLEX** is a throw in which two balls are thrown so that they end up being caught in opposite hands.

This is a useful throw when going from a **THREE BALL CASCADE** to a Four Ball **FOUNTAIN**. Start by juggling three balls with a fourth concealed in your right hand. When you want to make the change you too a two-ball split **MULTIPLEX** from the right hand, arranging matters so the the ball that will return to your right hand flies higher than the ball that's crossing to your left. Both balls will drop nicely into the four-ball pattern.

☆ A two-ball *column* **MULTIPLEX** is a throw that tosses two balls so that they both arrive in the *same* hand, usually one after the other.

You can use this to add extra balls to a **THREE BALL CASCADE** without actually changing the pattern. Try juggling a **THREE BALL CASCADE** with an extra ball, every third throw will be a column **MULTIPLEX** thrown from one hand to the other—it's a sort of cheat's way of juggling four balls.

If you can handle it you can try using five balls, so two throws out of three are **MULTIPLEXES**. Only real experts need try the awesome six-ball pattern in which each ball is replaced by a **MULTIPLEXED** pair.

☆ You can use a three-ball **MULTIPLEX** to do a **THREE BALL START**.

☆ The opposite of a **MULTIPLEX**, that is, *catching* more than one ball in the same hand at the same time—is called a *Squeeze*

See also **FIVE BALL SPLITS**.

MUSICAL BOTTLE

MUSIC

☆ Blow across the top of a beer bottle, as if you were playing a flute, and you'll find you get a note out of it. Try adding some water to the bottle to get a higher note.

So get eight bottles and set up a musical scale and play some tunes!

See also **GLASS HARMONICA**.

A
B
C
D
E
F
G
H
I
J
K
L
M
N
O
P
Q
R
S
T
U
V
W
X
Y
Z

MUSICAL SAW

MUSIC

There are few sounds as hauntingly beautiful as the sound of a well-bowed **MUSICAL SAW**. There are saws made and sold for just this purpose but you can manage perfectly well with a regular hand saw. Just pick one with a long blade (30 inches or better) and preferably a nice flexible one too.

The secret of creating the note from this instrument is that of forming an S-curve in the blade. Typically the musician will sit with the saw handle gripped between their legs and they'll hold the end of the blade with one hand, bending it into an S-shape.

☆ To learn how to make a note you should start with some small striking implement rather than a bow. Bend the saw into an S and try tapping it in different places along the blade. You'll find that, between the two curves in the blade, there is a *sweet spot* where a tap to the blade will cause a note to ring nicely. As you tighten up the blade you'll find that the note gets higher, loosen it and the note gets lower but get this—the sweet spot will move as you adjust the shape of the blade. As you tighten the blade it will move toward the tip, as you loosen it will move toward the handle.

To get the finest notes from your new instrument you'll need a violinist's bow (and some resin to keep the bow working properly). Tighten your bow, rub some resin onto it and get to work. The music made by bowing the sweet spot is ethereal. Playing tunes is pretty much like whistling once you have the knack of keeping the bow on the sweet spot and bending the saw to exactly the right note.

Nail up the Nose

STUNTS

It is a little-known fact that a person of average adult size can stick a four-inch nail up their nose—as long as they are careful. This trick will cause people of a nervous disposition to faint dead away in horror.

☆ Get a four-inch nail and polish it smooth with some fine abrasive paper and round off the sharp end so the thing ends up feeling nice to the touch —like a knitting needle. It's important that the nail is both smooth and sterile, so wash it carefully.

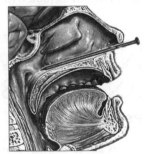

The nail passes into the nostril as far to the side as possible and parallel to the roof of your mouth. As it slides in it will rub against the *Inferior Turbinate*. This being the lower of three bony shelves inside the nose. It tickles! Needless to say, *do not force* the thing in, just slide it in gently all the way up to the head.

The tip of the nail will end up near the opening of the *Eustachian Tube* at the back of the nasal passage.

It will not skewer your brain.

Confident performers of this trick use a hammer to "drive" the nail into their head. Actually the nail slides in perfectly easily, but the hammer adds a nice touch of horror.

Never perform this trick with anything but a well-prepared nail that you have rehearsed with beforehand.

A B C D E F G H I J K L M N O P Q R S T U V W X Y Z

A
B
C
D
E
F
G
H
I
J
K
L
M
N
O
P
Q
R
S
T
U
V
W
X
Y
Z

NATO PHONETIC ALPHABET

CODES & CIPHER / LANGUAGE

This is the name of the words-for letters alphabet used by aircraft pilots, the Police and radio operators in the western world.

It is becoming increasingly popular with "ordinary" people these days since so much of our lives involves passing data over phone lines using your voice: your driving license number, your postcode, your unusual surname and so on. The operatives at the other end are usually trained to understand the code,

☆ It goes like this:

Alpha, Bravo, Charlie, Delta, Echo, Foxtrot, Golf, Hotel, India, Juliet, Kilo, Lima, Mike, November, Oscar, Papa, Quebec, Romeo, Sierra, Tango, Uniform, Victor, Whiskey, X-Ray, Yankee, Zulu.

This is *required learning* for tricksters, ranking slightly above **FINGER SPELLING** in usefulness (unless you are talking to deaf people of course).

NEVER GIVE A SUCKER AN EVEN BREAK

PSYCHOLOGY

This is a well-known quotation of *W.C. Fields* the legendary alcoholic, juggler and comedian.

NEVER GIVE A SUCKER AN EVEN BREAK sums up the fundamental principle of creating magical illusions, winning bets and scamming people so perfectly that *Every Trick In The Book* has nothing to add to it.

Never Show a Monkey Your Teeth

ANIMALS

Unless, of course, you *want* to send a very aggressive message to the animal.

Smiling at a monkey is a Bad Thing To Do.

Contrariwise, if the cute little thing seems to be smiling at *you*—take care!

You are probably about to get bitten.

And we don't want that do we?

Newspaper Balance

BALANCING

Take a whole sheet of a broadsheet newspaper and grab the diagonally opposite corners.

Tug sharply and you'll create a series of creases that will stiffen the paper enough to allow you to balance it on your nose or chin.

See also **Peacock Feather Balance**.

A
B
C
D
E
F
G
H
I
J
K
L
M
N
O
P
Q
R
S
T
U
V
W
X
Y
Z

NEWTONIAN SUPER-BOUNCE

FUN WITH SCIENCE

Who said science was boring? Remember, knowledge is power.

You need a nice big football (or basketball) and a **BEANBAG**.

☆ Place the **BEANBAG** on the very top of the big ball which is held about stomach-high.

☆ Carefully drop the two balls to the ground, so that when they hit the **BEANBAG** is still sat on the North Pole.

The little **BEANBAG** will bounce *really* high! It's like magic.

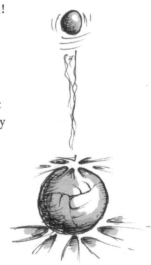

When two objects of different weights collide the energy of the impact is shared equally between them, so if one is a lot lighter than the other it follows that it must end up travelling a lot *faster*—all that energy has to go somewhere!

You can get a similar effect with a large and small coin on a smooth tabletop.

Slide the big coin so it collides with the small one and watch the titchy one go!

More on this below...

NEWTON'S COINS

OBJECT MANIPULATION

Oh there are so many fine things to do with coins on a smooth tabletop! This one is almost entirely pointless, but is is rather good fun.

☆ Get a few coins, pound coins are good, and lay three of four in a row on the table. Now smack a fourth one into one end by sliding it across the table top and it will stop dead—while the coin at the far and of the row flies off—just like a *Newton's Cradle*.

☆ Add more coins. Good isn't it?

☆ Now put a *really small* coin on the far end and it will ping off for miles!

Night Vision Cameras

FILMING / ESPIONAGE

Not a lot of people realise this, but ordinary digital video cameras pick up infra-red. You don't believe me? Turn it on and flash your TV remote at the lens—you'll see the infra-red LED light up and flicker as if it were white light.

So all you need to get is an infra-red light source and you can film badgers and burglars in the dark—without them seeing a thing.

A B C D E F G H I J K L M **N** O P Q R S T U V W X Y Z

NINETEEN TIMES TABLE

MATHEMATICS

OK, so a lot of people hate maths, chances are you do too, but after learning this trick you will hate maths *a little less* which has to be a Good Thing.

You know how to multiply by ten right? You just add a zero, so 10 times 13 is 130.

You know how to double a number don't you? Double 3 is 6, double 12 is 24 and so on.

Now this means you can easily multiply by twenty because all you have to do is double a number and then multiply it by ten.

13 * 20 = 260, and so on.

So here is how you multiply by 19:

Multiply the number by 20 and then take away the number you started with, so:

13 × 19 looks horrible but...

13 × 20 = 260!

Now take away the thirteen...

260 - 13 = 247

You're done.

NINE TIMES TABLE

MATHEMATICS / HAND TRICKS

OK, you should probably be able to guess the trick to this:

You multiply by 10 and then take away the number you're multiplying to get the answer.

So if we try 15 × 9, it's hard.
But 15 × 10 = 150, easy.

Now take away 15:
150 - 15 = 135, easy—and that's the answer.

☆ There's a *really* cool way of working out the first ten steps of the **Nine Times Table**. Hold your hands out in front of you, palms facing you, with all fingers outstretched. mentally number the fingers 1–10, starting with your left thumb and ending with your right thumb.

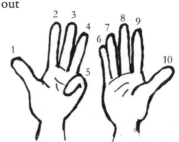

To multiply nine by any number from 1 to 10 you just fold down the finger for that number. So to do 5 × 9 we drop the little finger of the left hand.

Count the upright fingers on each side of the finger you folded down—in this case you get 4 on the left and 5 on the right. Stick those two numbers together you get 45!

Which is the right answer!

Ninja Rocks

TECHNICAL WIZARDRY / ESPIONAGE / CRIME

If you take a spark plug and crush the ceramic shaft with a heavy hammer (wear eye protection if you actually do this), you end up with small shards that are known to the bad boys as Ninja Rocks.

They have unbelievably hard and sharp edges and if thrown at a sheet of toughened glass with moderate force they will cause it to shatter, which is impressive because toughened glass is often resistant to heavy hammer blows.

Ninja Rocks are a favourite with despicable car thieves because they make light work of the otherwise difficult job of breaking through car windows.

On the other hand, modern double-glazed windows are also made of practically unbreakable glass, and lives have been lost in fires because of this, so carrying a small parcel of Ninja Rocks in your utility belt could, just possibly, make you a hero some day.

NUMB HAND TRICK

SILLINESS / HAND TRICKS

This is just bizarre. It works on about 80% of sober people but only 20% of drunken people—nobody knows why!

☆ Ask your subject to hold up their left hand against yours and then, with your right thumb and middle finger, you rub the back of their hand and the back of yours at the same time.

It feels *weird*.

Now get them to do the same thing. They will feel the same weird feeling.

It's a bizarre sensory feedback loop that makes you think your hand has gone numb.

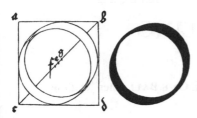

OCTAHEDRON

GEOMETRY

The **OCTAHEDRON** is the third **PLATONIC SOLID**. It is a polyhedron with six vertices, twelve edges and eight faces, each of which is an equilateral triangle.

Think of it as two pyramids stuck together base-to-base.

☆ The **OCTAHEDRON** is the *dual* of the **CUBE** which means that if you drew an imaginary dot in the centre of each face and connected them together you'd end up with a **CUBE**. Do the same thing to the **CUBE** and you get back to an **OCTAHEDRON**.

☆ The **OCTAHEDRON** can be *multiplied up* by means of triangulating the faces into smaller faces to create a series of **GEODESIC DOMES** although the **ICOSAHEDRON** and **DODECAHEDRON** are generally better shapes to start from.

☆ It is well known that identical **CUBES** will fill space leaving no gaps at all, less well known is the elegant fact that **OCTAHEDRA** and **TETRAHEDRA** of equal edge length will also fill in a similar manner. This arrangement can be used to make a strong three-dimensional lattice of equal struts.

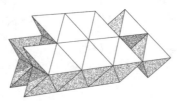

A
B
C
D
E
F
G
H
I
J
K
L
M
N
O
P
Q
R
S
T
U
V
W
X
Y
Z

ONE BALL JUGGLING

JUGGLING

There are a lot of things you can do with **ONE BALL** when juggling.

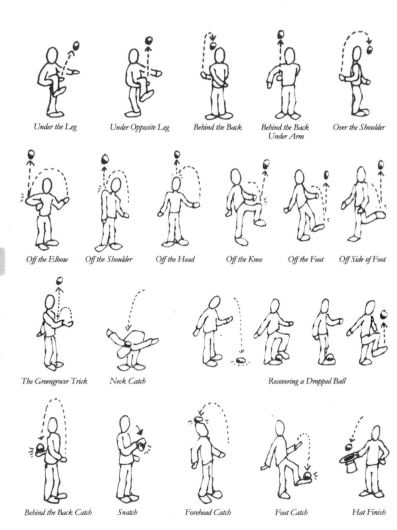

| Under the Leg | Under Opposite Leg | Behind the Back | Behind the Back Under Arm | Over the Shoulder |

| Off the Elbow | Off the Shoulder | Off the Head | Off the Knee | Off the Foot | Off Side of Foot |

| The Greengrocer Trick | Neck Catch | Recovering a Dropped Ball |

| Behind the Back Catch | Snatch | Forehead Catch | Foot Catch | Hat Finish |

ONE FINGER BOUNCE

JUGGLING / OBJECT MANIPULATION

☆ Get a **BOUNCING BALL**, preferably a silicone one, and bounce it against the floor like a basket ball player. Now take the bounces down really low so that the ball is bouncing just a few inches and use *just your index finger*.

You'll find that if you keep pushing the ball from the same imaginary spot it will become self-centring. When the ball rises a little off-centre the action of pushing it with your finger will catch the side of the ball (rather than the top) and will therefore impart a little spin on the ball which will tend to make it bounce back to the imaginary centre line.

☆ It gets better: get the bounce *really* low (just an inch or so) with a silicone ball and then just *push* it down at the floor.

You'll get an unbelievably high-frequency bounce that rings and rises in pitch as you push the ball all the way to the floor. It sounds like the **RULER BOING TRICK**.

OOBLECK

KITCHEN TRICKS / FUN WITH SCIENCE

This fictional substance was invented by the fine author *Dr. Seuss* in his book *Bartholomew and the Oobleck*. It is a green sticky substance that falls from the sky.

☆ You can make it in your own kitchen by mixing *custard powder* or cornflour (*corn starch* as the americans would have it) with a little water.

A B C D E F G H I J K L M N O P Q R S T U V W X Y Z

☆ If you add some green food colouring you will have created a Seuss-compliant product.

OOBLECK is technically known as a *non-newtonian fluid* with *dilatant* properties. Dilatant materials flow like liquids until they are stressed. Stressing the material causes it to act like a solid˙. You can stir **OOBLECK** slowly with a spoon and it will be perfectly runny, but if you bash it with the back of the spoon it will not splash—the spoon will just bounce off!

☆ Military designers have investigated using **OOBLECK** as the basis for clever armour which would move easily with the body, yet bullets would ricochet off it. This is plainly insane, covering yourself in **OOBLECK** and asking people to shoot at you is *not* a good idea.

☆ If you stir it hard the liquid will solidify and crack like chalky mud, only to liquify as soon as the pressure of the spoon is released. For some reason all of this is highly amusing and you can play with it for hours without getting bored.

☆ When the fun to be had with a cupful of **OOBLECK** has waned and subsided you could consider making a vast quantity of the stuff and placing it in a long foot-bath (like the ones on the way into the swimming pool).

You can now invite people to do the **OOBLECK** equivalent of **FIRE WALKING**.

By walking briskly and with "faith" over the goo you'll find that you can do a tolerable impersonation of Jesus—you will not sink in!

Any delay or prevarication and your feet will be engulfed. The harder you struggle, the harder it is to remove your feet.

Now that's a fun idea isn't it?

˙ Oobleck is often, incorrectly, called a thixotropic material. Actually thixotropic substances are solids but liquefy under stress—the opposite of a dilatant.

Orange Peel Flame Thrower

PYROTECHNICS

If you take a piece of orange peel and fold it in half while pointing the crease at a candle flame, tiny jets of extremely volatile oil will shoot out and burn with bright flames.

Origami Banknote Scam

GRIFTING

Here's a sweet (or very nasty, depending on your point of view) little scam that has earned **GRIFTERS** a lot of money over the years.

☆ The set-up is much like other street scams and will typically involve at least three people working together. You need an *Origami-Man*, a *lookout* (who is also there to act heavy if things go wrong) and at least one *plant* who will attract the **MARK** into the con by apparently buying into it and being generally enthusiastic about it.

The deal is this: somebody has set up a little stall and they are folding lucky cygnets, lotus flowers or some other simple good-luck charm from ten pound notes. The **ORIGAMI** is impressive and slick and the *plant* is having their own note folded as the **MARK** approaches.

"Isn't that beautiful?" they show you their little good-luck masterpiece.

"Take care of it," chimes in the *Origami-Man,* "keep it safe and when you finally unfold it to spend it on something—whatever you buy with it will bring you great good luck!"

What a sweet proposition! And all the *Origami-Man* wants for this service is two pounds for the work of folding your own note.

You hand him the fee and a crisp banknote and in a few moments it has been transformed into a beautiful work of **ORIGAMI**. You tuck it carefully into your pocket and leave with a smile on your face.

Poor fool!

When you finally unfold the thing you'll realise what has happened! Any fool should know that one of the basic principles of **ORIGAMI** is that you start with a *square* and that banknotes are generally made as 2:1 rectangles or something very close to those proportions. The lucky charm in your pocket was made from *half* a banknote. The *Origami-Man* had a stash of these prepared beforehand and did a simple switch as you handed him your whole note.

The profit on each transaction therefore, is your two pound fee, plus half the value of the note you proffered. Not bad for a couple of minute's work!

You have to hand it to the **GRIFTERS** though: the concept of a con which starts with cutting banknotes in half is devilish clever!

OVERHAND KNOT

KNOTS

The **OVERHAND KNOT**, to borrow some computerese, is the single *bit* of rope work. It's the simplest knot there is. Apart, that is, from the **BLACKWALL HITCH** and the *Slippery Hitch* which are not, mathematically-speaking, knots at all.

☆ Make a loop and put the end through it, pull tight. The main use of this knot is to prevent the cut end of a rope from unraveling.

☆ You can tie an **OVERHAND KNOT** by crossing your arms, picking up both two ends of a foot or so or cord, and then uncrossing your arms again!

☆ You can tie an **OVERHAND KNOT** with one hand as a trick.

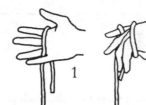  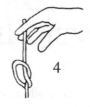

1: Hang the cord over your hand, trap the cord under your little finger.
2: Pick up the short end between your index and middle fingers.
3: Turn your hand sideways.
4: Drop the loop that's on your fingers *over* the end.

An **OVERHAND KNOT** appears in the cord!

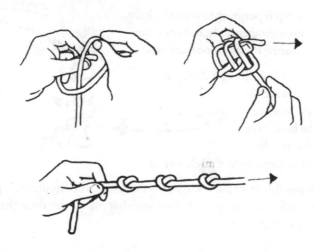

A
B
C
D
E
F
G
H
I
J
K
L
M
N
O
P
Q
R
S
T
U
V
W
X
Y
Z

☆ As a parlour trick you can tie a whole series of **OVERHAND KNOTS** in a cord in one movement.

Lay the end of your cord along the inside of your thumb and then start stacking loops of cord over the thumb.

Finally, pick up the end and pull it through the loops smoothly.

One **OVERHAND KNOT** will appear for each loop you stacked.

The **OVERHAND KNOT** is *not* the same knot as the **HALF HITCH** or the **HALF KNOT**, even though it looks very similar.

OVER HEAD CRACK

WHIPS

This is generally agreed to be one of the loudest ways to crakc a whip. A really huge amount of force can be fed in, and if you're not careful to direct it well you can snap the *crack* right off your whip.

Starting with the whip behind you, swing your whip around your head in an anti-clockwise circle (assuming you are *right-handed*).

When the whip is pointing to six-o'clock the whip arm stops momentarily, but the whip moves on creating the all-important *bend*.

The whip-arm then changes direction and strikes toward the two o'clock position, leading the bend over your head while the whip flies the target with a mighty crack.

Since it is possible to break a whip with this move, you should start gently, aiming for soft subsonic pops, before applying full power once the move has been mastered.

OVER THE SHOULDER

JUGGLING

An **OVER THE SHOULDER** throw is a sort of **BEHIND THE BACK** *self* throw (as opposed to a *crossing* throw—the hand throws to *itself*.)

☆ Whether thrown with a ball, club or ring the hand makes a backward scooping movement and the thrown object rises over the throwing shoulder to a normal catching position.

Note that, with a club or ring, the object flies with reverse spin.

☆ An **OVER THE SHOULDER** throw can be made with a club at the end of a **FLOURISH**.

☆ An impressive trick with balls is to make *two* simultaneous **OVER THE SHOULDER** throws.

You lead into the move by juggling a simple One-Up Two-Up.

See also **SLAP OVER**.

OVER THE TOP

JUGGLING

When you juggle a **THREE BALL CASCADE** each ball is thrown *under* the previously thrown ball.

☆ To juggle **OVER THE TOP** you change a throw so that it passes *over* the entire pattern, as if being lobbed over a hedge.

This is usually the first **TRICK** that a juggler learns after the basic cascade (Jugglers refer to any variation on a basic pattern as a *trick*).

A B C D E F G H I J K L M N O P Q R S T U V W X Y Z

☆ Once you can manage **OVER THE TOP** one way around, make sure you learn it the other way around!

Next learn all the combinations:

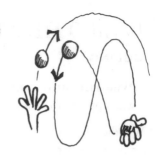

- every right
- every left
- same ball every time
- and finally *every* throw **OVER THE TOP**.

☆ When *every* throw goes **OVER THE TOP** you are juggling a pattern called the **REVERSE CASCADE** which is a *time-reversal* of a regular cascade.

OWL HOOT

MUSIC / HAND TRICKS / ESPIONAGE

For some reason people believe that making the sound of an Owl Hoot is a more surreptitious method of communicating with your comrades when sneaking around somebody's place at night than alternatives like "Psssst!" and "What did you say?" Obviously it is not, but it's a clever trick nevertheless.

It works by turning your hand into a sort of *Ocarina*. The hands are clasped together to for an airtight enclosure with both of your thumb pressed hard together at the tips, but leaving a narrow gap at the bases.

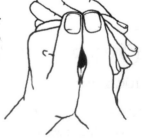

The sound is made like the note of a flute: by blowing air *across* the hole you have made between your thumbs.

☆ Wrap your lower lip *over* your lower teeth (as if miming a pensioner who has lost the bottom half of a set of dentures). Press your lower teeth *through* the covering lip against the joints of your thumbs just above the hole and blow!

If you get it right you'll be rewarded with a hoot. If not just keep moving things about little by little, blowing air over the hole from different directions and adjusting the shape of your hands.

Eventually you'll find the *sweet spot*— with luck before you pass out from hyper-ventilation.

The tone and volume of the hoot can be altered by opening and closing the back of the air pocket just like a trumpet player doing wah-wahs with a plate.

Oxygen Hangover Cure

ALTERNATIVE MEDICINE

The **Oxygen Hangover Cure** is well know among doctors, medical staff, pilots and divers who have bottles of this precious substance readily available—albeit unofficially.

It should be noted that oxygen can be toxic, particularly if it is supplied at greater than atmospheric pressure. It can also be dangerous when used by people with existing heart or lung problems.

In studies it was found that breathing pure oxygen for short periods reduces nausea, headaches and other symptoms of discomfort that characterise a hangover. It was not found, however, to improve mental or physical performance in any measurable way.

Still, feeling better is more than half the battle is it not?

PPP

PACKING AN AIR BED

TRICKS OF THE TRADES

☆ When packing an air bed, or any other inflatable object, you can reduce it down to a much smaller package by sucking all the air out with a vacuum cleaner. It's spookily effective!

This is the method used by operators of inflatable play equipment when they want to pack big structures down as small as possible.

PACKING KNOT

KNOTS

Way back in the twentieth century (which started out in black and white and moved to colour about half way through) shopkeepers would wrap up your goods for you in brown paper and string. They would do this with dazzling flair and panache and then finish the job off with a really clever knot—the **PACKING KNOT**.

The knot allows you to first tighten the string, and then secure it without losing a drop of tension, something that is difficult to do with regular knots. How often have you asked someone to "put their finger on the knot" while you finish it off?

☆ Typically the string would be kept on a bobbin hung over the serving counter. A length is pulled off and wrapped around the parcel. The end of the string is formed (around the standing part) into a **FIGURE OF EIGHT KNOT**.

A
B
C
D
E
F
G
H
I
J
K
L
M
N
O
P
Q
R
S
T
U
V
W
X
Y
Z

A B C D E F G H I J K L M N O P Q R S T U V W X Y Z

The string is then pulled tight and will briefly hold its tension.

A small loop is formed in the standing part and placed over the protruding end of the string. As this loop is pulled tight the knot locks permanently.

Finally the shopkeeper cuts off the string close to the knot (to conserve string). The job is done.

The only real disadvantage of this knot is that it is virtually impossible to untie—you have to cut your parcel open.

PALMING A COIN

MAGIC / COIN TRICKS

A coin magician must be familiar with the skill of **PALMING A COIN**. This is the trick of holding a coin securely in the palm of your hand with no help from the fingers at all. It's quite easy to hold a coin in this position, what is not so easy is the art of keeping the position of the rest of the hand looking natural.

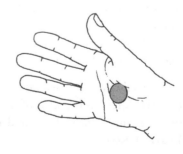

☆ The precise position of the palmed coin will vary according the its size and the exact geography of your particular palm, but in general one edge of the coin is trapped against what palmists would call your *Head Line* while the other is pushed into the fleshy mound at the base of your thumb.

☆ If you actually push the coin into this position with a finger from the opposite hand you'll find that you can wedge it in nice and tight and you'll end up being able to open you fingers and thumb very widely before the coin drops out.

☆ If you place a coin on your palm and then flip your hand over, so the palm points down, you can still trap the coin, but only by closing your fingers and thumb around it a little. Notwithstanding that, this move can look very natural and forms the basis of a perfectly decent coin vanish.

Place a coin on one palm and then toss it, with a flat hands, from one hand to the other a few times. Then execute one final toss with a little pizazz and close the receiving hand around it—except that you retain the coin in the throwing hand by palming it.

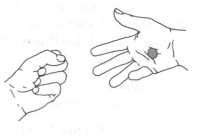

It greatly helps the trick if you *do something* with the hand that has palmed the coin before revealing that the coin has gone. Picking up a pint of beer and taking a sip is a good move at this stage.

☆ Since this is a hard trick to learn you had better get started on it right away; any time that your hand is idle you should keep it busy hanging onto a palmed coin, and practice *doing things* with the hand while the coin is secreted in it. Also practice *placing* the coin in the palmed position using the fingers of the same hand to nudge it into the trap.

See also **FINGER PALM, BACK PALM**.

PADDLE MOVE

MAGIC (TRANSFORMATION)

The **PADDLE MOVE** is an elementary illusion that requires only a small amount of dexterity. Children's magic sets often contain purpose-made paddles, but you can work with a swizzle stick or a lollipop stick if you like.

A B C D E F G H I J K L M N O P Q R S T U V W X Y Z

☆ The stick or paddle* is marked on one side with a symbol of some sort, say a little black dot and this is shown to the audience. The hand is then flipped over, as if to reveal the other side, but as the hand flips the paddle is rotated 180° between the fingers, so they end up seeing the *same side*. It's a cool move and impossible to spot. Having shown "both"

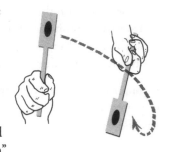

sides the end is gripped and the fingers make as if they have pulled the spot off, the paddle has been secretly flipped during the move so the spot has indeed vanished. The **PADDLE MOVE** is now repeated to show that both sides are blank.

☆ A nice finesse on this is to have previously marked the fingers with black dots so you can explain where the dots went.

☆ You can use a **PADDLE MOVE** to show that a coin has two heads, or two tails (or even both). Rest a coin on the tip of your index finger and clamp the edges with your thumb and middle finger.

Now start to turn the coin over by rolling it with your thumb across the index fingertip. Once the coin starts to move turn your entire hand over, as if "following" the coin, and it will end up showing the *same* face. Reverse the move to show the other side again.

See also **THAUMATROPE.**

---

* The word Paddle is the 150,000th word that has been typed into this manuscript. I know this because of the miracle of live word-counting that is built into the software I am using to assemble *Every Trick In The Book*. It is Tuesday the 20th of March 2007 and it snowed heavily yesterday. The current musical selection is So Lonely by the Police. I am located in my large and slowly deteriorating caravan which is located on the former site of a WWII airfield at Charmy Down, just outside Bath. The old control tower sits a couple of fields away in a dilapidated state and I confess I have my eye on it as a possible dwelling. It has taken me a great deal longer than I expected to reach this stage, though I have started the monstrous task of illustrating this work. As you might expect I'm reduced to a state of poverty but hey! You see this job isn't about money. I just happen to want to own a book called *Every Trick In The Book* and this is the only way I'm going to get my hands on it—unless someone else would care to write it for me?

PALM RETENTION VANISH

MAGIC

If you only learn one coin vanish—learn this one!

It's not as easy as the **FRENCH DROP** but it is *much* more effective. Learning it will take you a couple of hours of practice, and once mastered you will forever be able to vanish coins in a truly impressive manner.

The effect is this: you turn one hand palm up and place a coin into it with the other hand. Your fingers close around the coin...

...but by then it's already gone!

☆ Here's the move in three steps:

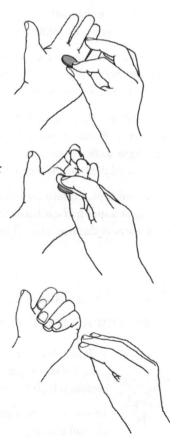

1: Hold a coin between the tip of the thumb and forefinger of one hand and place it into the palm of the opposite hand.

2: Close the fingers of the receiving hand around the coin. As the fingers close over it the free fingers of the other hand move forward to cover the coin as well. The audience do not see this, especially as the move is quite fast. As far as they can see the receiving hand has the coin.

3: Withdraw the "giving" hand with the coin. As you do so you should move the "receiving" hand toward the audience. This **MISDIRECTION** will be followed by the audience because they think the hand is holding the coin.

Once that's done you can drop the "giving" hand to your side and the illusion is complete. You can now, if you wish, open the hand to reveal that it is empty or use this as the first step in a more elaborate illusion like the **TABLE TOP VANISH**.

☆ To truly master this trick you must **PRACTICE IN FRONT OF A MIRROR**. An hour's work will produce great results. A couple of hours and you'll be a master.

When rehearsing the trick you should sit yourself down facing the mirror and practice actually putting the coin into the receiving hand until you are completely familiar with a natural action of actually doing what they *think* you are doing.

Once you have that smooth you can start retaining the coin to create the illusion that you are putting it into the other hand.

Once you have the trick down so well that there is no perceptible difference between your movements whether you are placing or retaining the coin you have cracked it!

☆ You can greatly enhance the illusion by getting a "flash" off the coin as you place it in the receiving hand. You can do this whenever there is a bright light source (such as a light or an open window) positioned in the same general direction as the person you are trying to impress.

As the coin is placed into the receiving hand you angle it so that the face is pointing at a spot halfway between the observer's eyes and the light source: this guarantees that the coin will look very bright as the fingers close over it.

PAPER HELICOPTER

PAPER TRICKS / FLYING MACHINES

 ☆ Take a sheet of paper and cut and fold it as shown here. The top is split into two rotors, and the bottom is folded in and secured with a paper clip.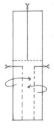

Toss it out of the window and watch it spiral down to a soft landing.

A
B
C
D
E
F
G
H
I
J
K
L
M
N
O
P
Q
R
S
T
U
V
W
X
Y
Z

PAPER PLANE

ORIGAMI

There are many ways of folding a paper aeroplane, but if it's performance and elegance you're after, there's only one. Strictly speaking this plane is not pure **ORIGAMI** because it does not start from a perfectly square sheet of paper, in fact it folds best from a sheet of A4, which is handy because this is the most commonly available paper in British Schools.

1: Start by making a valley fold that halves the paper along its long axis, flatten the work out again and then fold the top to corners onto that line.

2: Fold the pointed nose back.

3: Fold the corners into the centre aiming for the point marked X which is just short of the apex of the folded-back nose.

4: Lock the last two fold by turning over the small pointed tab, then fold the entire plane in half using a mountain fold through the axis of symmetry.

5: Fold down the wings. You can experiment with different wing profiles here.

6: Your aircraft is ready, you can trim it a little by turning up the back corners of the wings.

This is an extremely high-performance design for several reasons:

- The nose is blunt, which means it can stand repeated impacts and crash landings.

- Most of the weight is in the nose because of the first two folding steps.

- The nose is robust because it is locked into shape by the clever little tab you folded in step 4.

A B C D E F G H I J K L M N O P Q R S T U V W X Y Z

☆ Compare this with the traditional *Paper Dart* that has been flung about in classrooms since classrooms were first invented.

1: This aircraft starts as before with the two top corners being folded onto the centre line.

2: Next two long valley folds are made from the tip of the nose to the far corners.

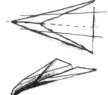

3: Finally the plane is folded in half down the centre and the wings folded down.

4: The aircraft is ready for flight. Note that the nose is very pointy and, after its first crash-landing the bent nose resembles Concorde having a bad day.

While this is probably the most well-known **PAPER PLANE** to school-kid science, there is little to recommend it. It typically flies on a spiral path because of the difficulty in trimming it to a stable attitude.

☆ If you want a *really* high-performance plane and you're prepared to fiddle around with scissors there are few planes better than the following:

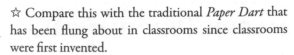

1: Start from an A5 sheet of paper, which you can easily make by taking an A4 sheet and cutting it in half. Make a valley fold about a fifth of the way down the sheet and turn it down.

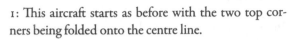

2: Make a valley fold halfway down the piece you just folded over, then fold it down again.

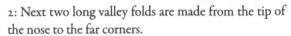

3: Fold in half inch strips down both sides.

4: Make a valley fold down the middle and fold the plane in half.

5: Using a pair of scissors cut a curve out of the aircraft. This will separate the wings from the tails. Use your artistic intuition here!

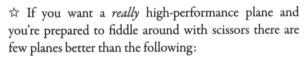

6: Open out the plane, note the nice tapered winglets! Chop any similar parts off the tail and fold up small elevators at the rear to trim the aircraft.

When properly trimmed this plane will out-perform pretty much any other paper plane design and it looks good as well. They are extremely stable in flight and tend to fly in nice straight lines. I threw one of these off the Empire State Building and as you might imagine it went for *miles!*

PARABOLA

MATHEMATICS / GEOMETRY

A **PARABOLA** is an interesting mathematical curve, for one thing it is the path that a thrown object—e.g. an arrow or cannonball—will follow under the influence of gravity (if we ignore air resistance). For another, it is the curve that determines the shape of a satellite dish.

☆ Mathematicians call a **PARABOLA** a *Conic Sec* because you can make one by taking a cone mad say, imaginary cheese and slicing it so that the sli parallel to the slope of the cone.

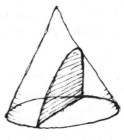

☆ You can also make one on graph paper by plotting the graph $y=ax^2$ where a is an arbitrary constant. High values of a make tall skinny curves and low values make lower flatter ones.

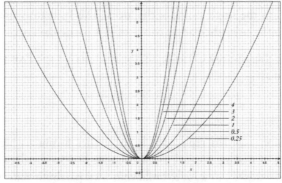

Parabolic curves for values of a from 0.25 to 4

A
B
C
D
E
F
G
H
I
J
K
L
M
N
O
P
Q
R
S
T
U
V
W
X
Y
Z

Before Galileo it was imagined that cannonballs headed off on a more or less straight path until they ran out of *impetus* whereupon they fell directly to earth. The theory of *impetus* was found to be flawed though it has to be said that the actual path of a cannonball through the air, when air resistance is taken into account, does deviate from a **PARABOLA** to a considerable degree. Thus the medieval estimates, as shown in early drawings, are not wholly inaccurate.

☆ A parabola is a mathematical curve, like an **ELLIPSE** or a *Circle*. A *circle* has a *centre*, and ellipse has two *foci*. Similarly it turns out that the **PARABOLA** has an associated point called a *focus*.

The focus is what makes the **PARABOLA** the ideal shape for the cross section of a satellite dish. If you form a **PARABOLA** from a reflective surface and point it at a distant light source then all of the rays that hit the curve will be reflected to the single point of the focus. This brilliantly useful fact is built right into the mathematical nature of this particular curve.

To calculate the position of the focus, the formula for the **PARABOLA** can be expressed as:

$$y = \frac{1}{4p} x^2$$

The expression *1/4p* has replaced *a* in the earlier formula which has the handy effect of making *p* equal to the distance *O-F* in the drawing. You'll need to know this if you want to build your own parabolic reflector.

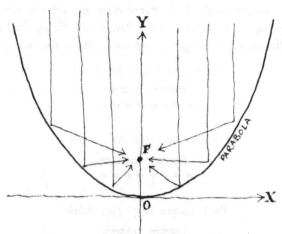

Rays of light are reflected toward the focus of the parabola.

The shape of these dishes is properly called a *paraboloid*.

☆ A paraboloid dish lined with silver paper and pointed at the sun will produce a dangerously high temperature at the focus.

☆ If a liquid is held in a circular container which is then spun about its axis, the surface will rise up at the edges and fall in the centre, the resulting shape will be a paraboloid.

Nature, it seems, loves the shape.

Paradiddle

MUSIC

A **Paradiddle** is a four-note 'sticking' pattern for drummers. It is one of the *Rudiments* of drumming, along with techniques like the *Flam*. If we count off right and left hand beats it goes:

It's fun to drum on a tabletop with your fingers. The sideways V's indicates notes that are to be emphasised.

A
B
C
D
E
F
G
H
I
J
K
L
M
N
O
P
Q
R
S
T
U
V
W
X
Y
Z

There are variations on the basic **Paradiddle**, in each one you alter the phrasing so that the four beats of the **Paradiddle** fill up the bars of the music in different ways, though the sequence remains the same.

The *Reverse Single Paradiddle.*

The *Inward Single Paradiddle.*

The *Outward Single Paradiddle.*

Then we have extended sequences like the *Double Paradiddle.*

The *Triple Paradiddle.*

The *Paradiddle-diddle.*

The *Flam* was mentioned earlier on, this is the act of striking a lighter extra note with the opposite hand to add breadth to a note. The extra note is played fractionally *before* the main note, which leads us to the

Flamadiddle or *Flam Paradiddle.*

You need to know this stuff!

PARKING A BIKE AGAINST A KERB

BICYCLES

In the Good Old Days when bicycles cost half a crown and were big black things with rod brakes, people would be seen **PARKING A BIKE AGAINST A KERB**.

But now that mountain bikes are made from titanium alloy, have NASA designed gear trains and cost thousands of pounds, it is fashionable to dismantle them and lock the resulting pile of spare parts to something immovable with heavy chains forged from depleted uranium.

For these troubles I blame relentless marketing* and crack cocaine, but the point is that the skill of **PARKING A BIKE AGAINST A KERB** is fast vanishing, so let me record it here for posterity.

☆ Nudge both wheels against the side of a highish kerb. Kick the inside pedal down and then gently reverse the bike until the pedal is exerting a little pressure on the kerb and lean the bike ever so slightly toward the pavement.

That's parked then. You may now pop into the shop and when you return ten seconds later the parking space will be free again since some little tea leaf (see **COCKNEY RHYMING SLANG**) has made off with your machine.

---

* The Mountain Bike was invented by marketing executives in the 1980's using the revolutionary technique of taking oxymoronically opposed concepts and welding them together into a product. In this case they combined the bicycle with its worst enemy—the mountain. The same period of history also delivered such unlikely combinations as Diet Coke and Designer Jeans.

PARTY POPPERS

PYROTECHNICS / EXPLOSIVES / SILLINESS

These are pretty fun things to start off with, but there are tricks that you can do with them.

☆ Open up a **PARTY POPPER**, remove the rolled-up paper streamers and replace with mayonnaise—messy!

☆ Or try a grape—it becomes a sort of fluffy cannonball.

☆ When you have a pile of spent poppers on the table try using them as spinning tops—they work really well. Hold between your finger and thumb and **SNAP YOUR FINGERS** to give the popper terrific spin. they'll balance on their little shafts and spin for ages.

☆ If you are feeling very adept at spinning your poppers you can try **SNAPPING YOUR FINGERS** while tossing one straight up—now catch it on the palm of your hand and keep it spinning there.

See also **CRACKERS**.

PASSIVE BOUNCE

JUGGLING

When juggling **BOUNCING BALLS** a typical throw starts in one hand, and then arrives in another after bouncing off the floor. There are two fundamentally different ways of making such a throw, the **ACTIVE BOUNCE** and the **PASSIVE BOUNCE**.

☆ In the **ACTIVE BOUNCE** the ball is forcibly thrown downwards so that it will return to at least the height it was thrown from. The force of the throw makes up for the natural loss of energy in the bounce.

☆ In the **PASSIVE BOUNCE** the ball is thrown upwards, usually only a little way, so that after the bounce it will rise to the height it was thrown from (despite the loss of energy in the bounce) on account of having fallen further.

Passive Bounce is easier to control and tends to produce gentle and slow juggling patterns, whereas Active Bounce is harder to control and delivers faster and more exciting patterns. You don't get anything for nothing!

The Passive Bounce is therefore the basic throw of the **BOUNCING BALL** juggler. Here's how to learn a Cascade of three balls, bouncing-style!

☆ Take one ball in one hand and lift it gently into a low throw, palm upwards. Allow it to drop to the floor and bounce across to the other hand. It's a nice gentle throw because you only have to lift the ball a little bit to make up for the small loss of energy in the bounce.

☆ Now take three balls and see if you can juggle them in a **CASCADE** using the **PASSIVE BOUNCE**. The pattern is *much* slower than a **THREE BALL CASCADE** juggled in the air.

Each throw is made by lifting a ball *over* the incoming ball—so this is, in a sense a **REVERSE CASCADE**. The paths of the balls cross on the way *down*. The **ACTIVE BOUNCE**, by the way, is the complete opposite.

People can, and do, juggle five, seven and even nine balls this way!

See also **ACTIVE BOUNCE, COLUMN BOUNCE, FIVE BALL BOUNCE**.

A
B
C
D
E
F
G
H
I
J
K
L
M
N
O
P
Q
R
S
T
U
V
W
X
Y
Z

A
B
C
D
E
F
G
H
I
J
K
L
M
N
O
P
Q
R
S
T
U
V
W
X
Y
Z

PATTING YOUR HEAD AND RUBBING YOUR STOMACH

SILLINESS

Here's a well-known old trick. It's silly, pointless and rather good fun.

☆ Can you pat your head with your right hand at the same time as rubbing your stomach with your left?

Use a big circular motion as if demonstrating that you have just eaten a fine meal.

☆ Once you can do this, you must master all of the variations as an exercise in *ambidexterity*. Begin by swapping hands.

Then try rubbing your head while patting your stomach in both right and left-handed mode.

☆ Once mastered you can challenge your friends to attempt this feat—and laugh at their hopeless ineptitude.

Children have been doing this to grown-ups for centuries.

PEACOCK FEATHER BALANCE

BALANCING

If you see a peacock's tail-feather lying about—grab it and keep it! Not only are they beautiful things, you can also do a very cool balancing trick with them.

☆ Place the feather on the tip of your nose and balance it. It is wonderfully easy to do.

☆ Now let the feather fall forwards until it is leaning at about thirty degrees—and walk forwards. You'll find it very easy to keep it at that angle.

☆ I've seen performers add in a fake sneeze, which can cause the feather to take off before being re-caught on the nose.

Magic!

See also **Newspaper Balance**.

Pen Rotation

BAR BETS / MANIPULATION

Bet someone that they can't do this.

☆ Get at pen and, while holding your hands in a praying position, grip the pen under your thumbs.

☆ The game is to move to a position where both hands are side by side, palms down and next to each other with the pen held up by the thumbs, in a single movement *without* letting go of the pen.

They will find it impossible, despite the fact that you will be able to do it right in front of them, time after time. It is wonderfully annoying.

☆ HERE'S *The* TRICK: This works like a Chinese metal puzzle in which one generally solves the problem by *putting the gaps together*. Only here you put the 'thumb-pits' (like armpits, but for thumbs) together and rotate them around the pen.

From the starting position tip your right hand upwards a little and your left hand downwards. Now, while keeping your thumb-pits pressed hard against the pen you'll find you can twist into the final position without ever letting go of the pen.

Very easily learnt!

A
B
C
D
E
F
G
H
I
J
K
L
M
N
O
P
Q
R
S
T
U
V
W
X
Y
Z

A
B
C
D
E
F
G
H
I
J
K
L
M
N
O
P
Q
R
S
T
U
V
W
X
Y
Z

PENALTY SHOOTOUT

GAMESMANSHIP / PSYCHOLOGY

To score a goal from a penalty the tried-and-tested technique is to blast the ball high into one of the corners of the net. If the goalie guesses which way the ball is going to go there's a chance of saving it. So the trick for the striker is to make sure the goalie goes the wrong way.

In serious games the striker will have decided which way to shoot *before* even placing the ball on the spot. Having made this crucial decision the ball is reverently placed on the ground. They move back a dozen paces or so, compose themselves, run forward and blast the ball hard at the goal. As a spectator you can impress your friends by announcing which way the ball is going *before* it gets kicked—and getting it right nine times out of ten. Here's how:

The striker is entirely focused on two things: which way they are going, and *not giving this vital information away*. Thus their brain is thinking "right, right, right—but don't let on!" If you watch the striker closely you'll notice, as they walk back from the ball, that one side of their body is more repressed than the other, their right arm may be swinging a little less freely than their left—and that's the giveaway: they're going *right!*

Of course once this becomes common knowledge (perhaps as a result of having been revealed in *Every Trick In The Book*) the world of football may experience a sort of arms race. Strikers may, in the future, be trained to give the *opposite* body-language signal, thus working to the time-honoured scheme that runs "he's thinking that I'm thinking that he's thinking that I'm thinking... but little does he realise that I *know* that he's thinking..." and so on.

Once *that* happens it's anybody's guess which way the ball is going.

That day has not yet come, so use this secret to your advantage. Perhaps you are a goalie? Or perhaps you are going to win a few bets at the pub during those Big Games—while the going is still good. And remember, **ALWAYS GET THE MONEY LAID ON THE TABLE** or you'll be wasting your time.

PENETRATING ASH TRICK

MAGIC (PENETRATION)

This is a very effective illusion.

☆ To prepare for the trick you need to get a nice big dab of cigarette ash on the end of your middle finger without anyone noticing. That's pretty easy to do if there is an ashtray handy.

☆ Ask someone to hold their hand out in front of them, palms down. Gently take hold of their hands as if moving them into an ideal position, explaining that you want to try something very strange and you need to choose a hand to work with. As you do this you transfer the ash from your middle finger to the palm of one of their hands.

☆ Make a show of "choosing" that ha ask them to close it into a tight fist.

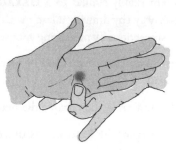

☆ Now take a dab of ash from the ashtray (with your middle finger again) and very deliberately transfer it to the back of their hand, rubbing it slowly and firmly as if trying to push it through their skin.

☆ After a few moments announce that you think the trick has worked and ask them to open their hand.

Stand back and bask in their amazement.

A
B
C
D
E
F
G
H
I
J
K
L
M
N
O
P
Q
R
S
T
U
V
W
X
Y
Z

This is a once-only trick—*do not* repeat it with the same audience. Move on to something else while the balance of the audiences minds are disturbed and susceptible. This could even be a good moment to pull off the **BALDUCCI LEVITATION**!

PENGUIN

JUGGLING

A **PENGUIN** catch is a catch made with the hand by the side and turned back and then out as far as it can go—as if imitating a penguin!

A **THREE BALL CASCADE** juggled entirely with **PENGUIN** catches is difficult—but a very impressive trick.

PENTAGON

GEOMETRY

A **PENTAGON** is a five-sided polygon.

It's remarkably similar to a **HEXAGON** which can be marked out in the classic way (by drawing a *circle* with a compass and then dividing the *circle* into six sections by measuring your way around with the compass).

There is an elegant method of marking out a pentagon with a ruler and compass.

☆ Draw a *circle*, then draw a diameter line horizontally with a ruler.

☆ Construct the **PERPENDICULAR BISECTOR** (OB) of the diameter.

☆ Bisect the line OB to create a halfway point, D.

☆ Bisect the angle ODP_1 and project a line to hit the line OP_1 at N.

☆ Raise a perpendicular line to hit the circumference at P_2.

☆ You now have the first two points of the pentagon and can set a compass to the radius $P_1 P_2$ and use that distance to "walk" around the *circle*, it will divide into exactly five equal parts. You can then draw a perfect **PENTAGON**.

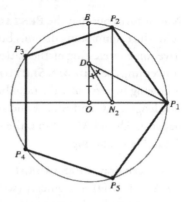

☆ If you draw in all the diagonals you will construct a perfect **PENTAGRAM**.

☆ A really cool and improbable *Paper Trick* is to take a strip of paper and tie it carefully into a flattened **OVERHAND KNOT**. You'll find that the knot takes the shape of a perfect **PENTAGON**.

PENTAGRAM

GEOMETRY / MATHEMATICS / OCCULT SCIENCE

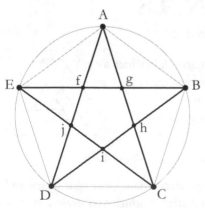

The **PENTAGRAM** is an familiar shape with magical overtones. You're probably used to seeing it in spooky films as a shape chalked on the floor and inscribed with curious symbols in an attempt (usually successful) to summon a demon or perhaps Old Nick himself. A **PENTAGRAM** is made by drawing a **PENTAGON** and then inscribing all of the diagonals. It's also known as a *Pentalpha,* a *Pentangle* and when used as a suit in a pack of **TAROT CARDS** it is called a *Pentacle.*

A
B
C
D
E
F
G
H
I
J
K
L
M
N
O
P
Q
R
S
T
U
V
W
X
Y
Z

Now it turns out that the **PENTAGRAM** is rubbish at summoning demons but it does have some interesting mathematical properties concerning the **GOLDEN SECTION** φ. The following In particular the ratio between the side lengths AC and Ah is φ and so is the ratio between Ah and Ag and so is the ratio between Ag and fg—amazing!

☆ You can draw a **PENTAGRAM** in five strokes (D-A-C-E-B-D) very quickly (with a little practice) and fun-loving people often add them to their signatures.

☆ If you are hell-bent on summoning pure evil from the depths of the underworld you'll need to draw a **PENTAGRAM** with the two points at the *top* and inscribe the thing with a picture of a goat and mark it around with strange symbols. This is referred to as the *Baphomet* design.

PENROSE TRIANGLE

OPTICAL ILLUSIONS / DRAWING

The **PENROSE TRIANGLE** is a drawing trick in which a strange perspective is presented in a simple drawing on a flat piece of paper. Three beams appear to be connected by three **RIGHT ANGLED** corners in a way that defies common sense.

It's pretty easy to sketch if you lay down the right guidelines.

Start by marking out three nested equilateral triangles in light pencil and then use this as guide for the second step in which you draw a sort of triangular swastika. The third step is to cut off the three corners and complete the outside lines. Finally a little judicious shading will enhance the illusion.

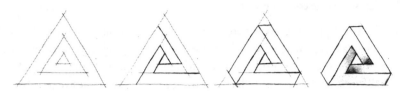

PEPPER'S GHOST

MAGIC

In 1864 Henry Dircks developed a method of presenting ghosts on the theatrical stage at the cost of some elaborate construction. Professor John H. Pepper improved on the technique by developing a more easily constructed apparatus what came to be known as **PEPPER'S GHOST**.

The principle is both simple and inspired. A sheet of glass is placed at 45° to the stage so that, by means of partial reflection, actors off to the side of the stage, when sufficiently lit, will appear as partially transparent entities on the main stage. Simply by turning the lights that illuminate them on and off, they can be made to appear and vanish at the whim of the director. When first shown to audiences in the late 19th century the effect caused a sensation.

Here an actor A stands behind a sheet of glass while a "ghost" B is hidden from view on a side stage and cannot be seen by a viewer sat on a chair C. When actors on the side stage are lit, their reflections will cause them to appear, partially transparently, as if on the main stage.

This type of arrangement has often been used in sideshow

booths, where the stage would be set up with a smal window to look through, to ensure that the viewer could not move to a position where the hidden side stage could be seen.

In theatrical productions, where a large side stage would not have been practical, a clever method was developed whereby the glass sheet stood at the front of the stage and leant forward towards the audience at a slight angle from where it could reflect hidden ghosts in the orchestra pit. This reflection would, of course, tilt the image of the "ghost" and the floor on which it walked forward a little, so the main stage, as is typical of theatre stages, would be "raked" to correct this aberration.

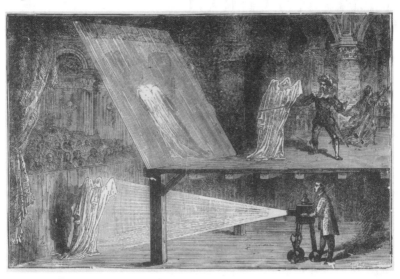

Stabbing a spectre through the heart with a sabre. This engraving is a little inaccurate, the stage would have been considerably "raked" to improve the illusion. Note also that the actor would not, of course, have been able to see the wraith.

Often a replica of the arrangent of objects on the main stage, such as tables and chairs and the like, would be carefully placed on the side stage so that the "ghosts" could seem to interact with them—thus strengthening the illusion.

And that is why we can see *through* ghosts, but not *into* them.

PERPENDICULAR BISECTOR

GEOMETRY

This a useful basic construction in geometry which you will, of course, remember perfectly well from school—if you were actually *paying attention!* The author confesses to have been drawing cartoons at the time, but caught up later.

The idea is to divide a line into two with a line at right angles to it. It's so amazingly useful that you have *no excuse* for not knowing how to do it.

Perpendicular means "at a right angle" and *bisector* means "chopper in half".

Draw a line and mark the two end-points. Set a compass to more than half the length of the line and, with the point at one end of the line mark a short arc above and below the middle of the line.

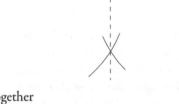

Repeat on the opposite end and your arcs will intersect directly above and below the *exact* middle of the line.

Connect these intersections together and you have constructed a **PERPENDICULAR BISECTOR.**

PERSPECTIVE DRAWING

DRAWING

Objects that are further away appear smaller, for example, railway lines seem to converge as they approach the horizon.

A B C D E F G H I J K L M N O P Q R S T U V W X Y Z

So **PERSPECTIVE DRAWING** is the art and craft of drawing things to create the illusion of depth and distance. Some of the geometric principles of perspective were understood as long ago as the 5th century BC but proper perspective did not feature much in Western art until the Middle Ages.

Here the great artist *Albrecht Dürer* (1471–1525) shows how the illusion of perspective can be achieved using a *Perspective Machine*, in this case to render a drawing of an attractive lady.

The machine consists of a wooden frame in which are stretched thin cords that correspond to a grid marked on the drawing paper. Albrecht keeps his eye properly aligned on the task with a sighting-stick which is made in the exact form of an Egyptian obelisk.

The engraving also conceals another non-mechanical perspective technique—the one that was actually used by the artist to construct the picture. Directly above the small jug on the window sill we see a small speck that represents a distant boat. If you project the horizontal lines of the two grids you'll find that they all converge where the mast of the boat cuts the line of the horizon.

This point is known as a *Vanishing Point*. The convergence of lines at this point is what gives the image the illusion of depth.

Accurate perspective drawing is a precise craft requiring careful measurements and a well set-up drawing board but the principles of **PERSPECTIVE DRAWING** can be used in freehand work. *William Hogarth* created a picture in 1822 which shows what can happen when the rules of perspective are ignored.

Whoever makes a DESIGN, *without the Knowledge of* PERSPECTIVE, *will be liable to such Absurdities as are shewn in this* Frontispiece.

Almost every element in the picture is wrong for one reason or another. Notice the sheep that increasing in size as they recede from us and the curious mounting of the inn sign. That sort of visual trickery would later be used to good effect by *M. C. Escher* in his drawings of the *Impossible Triangle*, the *Never-Ending Staircase* and other oddities.

HORIZON AND EYE LEVEL

To draw a convincing cartoon figure against a horizon you should place the eye level of the character at the same height as the horizon line. This is because the viewpoint of the imaginary observer would normally be at the same height as the eyes of the person in the picture.

If the person in the picture is a child their eyes will be lower down, so you position their eyes *below* the horizon, conversely a taller person's eyes would be *above* the horizon.

When drawing a crowd of people against a horizon you draw the people who are further away smaller but you keep their eyes level with the horizon. The exception is when you want them to appear taller or shorter, in which case you move them up or down a little.

Placing eyes on the horizon makes the characters looks as if they are at your eye-level. If you want to simulate a lower viewpoint (perhaps to make a character look more important by virtue of being taller than you are) then you'd raise their eyes above the horizon. Conversely. to look *down* on somebody, place them below the horizon.

ONE POINT PERSPECTIVE

This is the technique used by Dürer in the illustration of naked lady portraiture preceding: perspective rays converge on a single vanishing point on the horizon. We'll use this to create the classic picture of railway tracks vanishing into the distance.

Start by drawing a horizon line and then mark on it a *Vanishing Point*. Now draw two lines representing the tracks that fall off the bottom of the page and a couple more lines to define the tops and bottoms of the telegraph poles flanking the track.

Now draw in two vertical lines to indicate the positions of the first two telegraph poles. Add a diagonal line from the bottom of the closest pole to the top of the next one. This is a very important step because it's going to help you space the poles properly as they recede into the distance.

Copy the *angle* of that diagonal and run it up parallel from the bottom of the second pole until it hits the line representing the base of the line of poles. Construct a new pole exactly here and repeat the exercise. Notice how the poles get not only smaller but also closer together as they recede. As they approach the vanishing point they will become vanishingly small and impossible to draw.

The sleepers are handled in exactly the same way. This technique of using diagonals to space objects is a very important trick in **PERSPECTIVE DRAWING**, we'll see more of it shortly.

A
B
C
D
E
F
G
H
I
J
K
L
M
N
O
P
Q
R
S
T
U
V
W
X
Y
Z

TWO-POINT PERSPECTIVE

In *Two-Point Perspective* two vanishing points are used and one or both of these will probably lie *outside* the drawing area. Two point perspective is useful for creating convincing drawings of buildings and vehicles which are generally rectangular in nature and hence easy to draw.

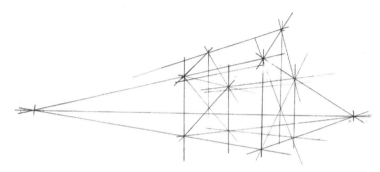

Start by marking out a drawing area on a large sheet of paper and place a horizon line on it. Now mark two vanishing points on this line. One point is the one to which east-west lines converge, the other is where north-south lines meet. Vertical lines will be drawn straight up and down.

The starting point is the nearest bottom corner of the house, everything else is worked from there.

Note that the right position for the ridge of the roof is determined by finding the centre of each end wall using intersecting diagonals—that's why the back walls have been marked in, even though they won't be seen in the final drawing. Adding windows and doors is pretty easy once you get the hang of it. You can even add a staircase up the side with every step in proper perspective. Notice how the tops of the steps are seen because they are below your imaginary eye level.

You should work in pencil because of all the construction lines you are going to make. Once you have the drawing marked out you can ink your masterpiece in and remove the construction lines.

THREE-POINT PERSPECTIVE

In *Three-Point Perspective* we use one vanishing point for north-south lines, one for east-west lines and a third for up-down lines. If the view is from above then vertical lines will converge at a low point called the *nadir* which represents the centre of the Earth. If the view is from below these lines will converge at the *zenith* which represents a point directly overhead at infinity.

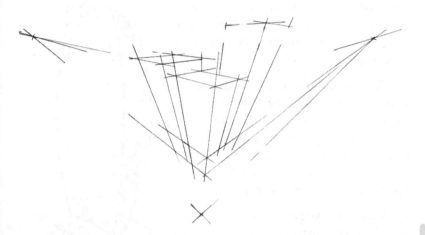

Three-point perspective is a good way of producing helicopter shots of skyscraper city scenes. Typically all three vanishing points will outside the drawing area by quite a long way, so you will either be working on a huge sheet of paper, or else you'll be using your judgement to make very careful estimates of the directions to your vanishing points.

FISH EYE PERSPECTIVE

The perspective techniques above are all *approximations* of the way things really look.

In actual fact the lines running toward vanishing points are really *curves* and we can only get away with simple straight line perspective tricks on small canvasses. If you want to model reality more closely you need to make the lines curved—a technique seen often in the work of background artists in cartoon animation. If you want to see some truly excellent examples of fish eye perspective drawing you should check out the work of the legendary engraver *M.C. Escher*.

Here's an sketch of a possible backdrop for an animated cartoon scene in which we want to give the impression of a high building. Note how the curved construction lines give a fish-eye lens effect.

If a picture like this was being used as an animation background the camera view would be smaller than the image and might start at the top of the picture and then travel down to the bottom, giving the impression of camera *tilt*—the action of tipping the camera up or down).

Circles IN PERSPECTIVE
A *circle*, when drawn in perspective is *always* a perfect ELLIPSE— it never makes an egg shape!

However, some caution must be used when drawing *circles* in perspective because the centre of the *circle* is *not* the same as the centre of the ellipse. So if we draw a clock face in one-point perspective we'll start by defining the enclosing

rectangle of the clock face properly distorted according to our vanishing point. Next we'll fit an ellipse into the box and then mark off the diagonals—where they cross is the perceptual centre of the *circle*.

PHANTOM PIANO

MUSIC

☆ Take the metal grill out of the grill pan in your cooker and tie two pieces of string to the corners. Wrap the strings a couple of times around each index finger and then stick your fingers in your ears.

I'm not joking!

Get someone to run a spoon along the wires and you'll hear the sound of a grand piano (as if being played by a kitten on the keys).

Try it!

PHANTOM STRANGLER

SILLINESS

Stand in a doorway, or between two curtains pulled around you like a cape and try to look like an innocent victim.

☆ Suddenly a mysterious hand reaches out from out of view and grabs you by the neck. After a brief struggle your vanish from view— the Phantom has struck again!

☆ A less well-known variation of this trick is even more effective. The hand, instead of reaching for your neck, grabs the top of your head from behind so that the fingers grasp your forehead. Because of the odd angle of approach people are more likely to think it is someone else's hand.

A
B
C
D
E
F
G
H
I
J
K
L
M
N
O
P
Q
R
S
T
U
V
W
X
Y
Z

A
B
C
D
E
F
G
H
I
J
K
L
M
N
O
P
Q
R
S
T
U
V
W
X
Y
Z

Pi

MATHEMATICS

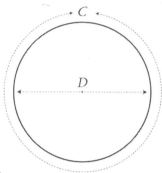

Pi is usually written using the Greek letter π. It is the ratio of a *circle's* circumference to its diameter. No matter what size of *circle* you draw the length of its circumference (C) is π times its diameter (D).

Pi is a very important number in mathematics and its value is approximately 3.14159. I say *approximately* because no matter how hard you try you cannot pin down the *exact* value with any decimal number.

A useful approximation of π is 22/7 which accurate to a 2 decimal places, 355/113 is a better one being accurate to 6 decimal places—and it's easy to remember.

Some useful formulæ using π follow:

☆ The circumference of a *circle* = πd
    - where *d* is the diameter.

☆ The diameter of a *circle* = c/π
    - where *c* is the circumference

☆ The area enclosed by a *circle* = πr2
    - where r is the radius.

☆ The area enclosed by an **ELLIPSE** = πab
    - where a and b are the lengths of the two radii.

☆ The area of the surface of a sphere = $4\pi r^2$.

☆ The volume of a sphere = $4/3\pi r^3$.

PICK A CARD, ANY CARD!

MAGIC

That's the line you usually hear when a magician is about to **FORCE A CARD** on you. After you have chosen a card, and examined it you'll be asked to return it to the deck in a random position and after a little more business the magician will reveal your choice in a magical and interesting way.

So far so good, but did you know that it's possible for the magician to reveal your choice *without* you ever taking the card and *without* ever showing it to you and *without* even meeting you?

☆ You are shown five cards and asked to pick out one mentally and remember it. The magician then explains that even though there is no way they can possibly know which card you picked they are going to remove it from the pile.

Tell you what, let's try it right here: look at these five cards and pick one out mentally.

Done that? Really concentrating on it?

☆ **HERE'S** *The* **TRICK**: I have magically predicted which card you would choose, and amazingly I did this way back when I was writing this part of *Every Trick In The Book* back in the year MMVI.

So go and look at the row of four cards opposite the title page at the beginning of this book.

The card you picked is missing!

You'll work it out!

478 — EVERY TRICK In The BOOK

PICKING POCKETS

GRIFTING

You may wish to go about **PICKING POCKETS** for various reasons. Fun and crime come to mind most easily. The author condones the use of pocket-picking skills for fun and entertainment but deplores their criminal use and pleads that knowledge of the methods used may help to protect you from *other* criminals.

Grifters refer to Picking Pockets as *Lifting*. The action of dropping your hand into an actual pocket is called *Dipping*.

☆ The purest technique involves some **MISDIRECTION**. It's called the *Bump and Lift*. The idea is simple, if you experience some sort of obvious physical contact with another person it will effectively *mask* any other more subtle contact they may be making, especially if they are making direct eye contact with you.

So if somebody lurches into you as a tube train jolts and looks you right in the eye—watch out in case their hand has just snuck into and out of one of your pockets and made the lift.

Similarly, if someone walking down the street trips and falls heavily against your shoulder, you are unlikely to notice their hand dipping your pocket at the same time.

The **MISDIRECTION** method is far more effective than you might think and is the one used by stage magicians to steal from people right in front of an audience.

☆ A popular street technique called the *Sandwich* involves two operators, code-named the *Stall* and the *Pick* in **GRIFTING** parlance.

The Stall walks in front of the **MARK** and the *Pick* walks behind. The Stall then stops suddenly in front of the **MARK** causing the *Pick* to bump into them from behind. The collision obscures any sensation of what is really going on, the Pick has just lifted the **MARK's** wallet. Then the *Pick* walks off with the proceeds while the Stall turns and apologises to the **MARK** which effectively removes any chance of the *Pick* getting caught.

Nasty isn't it?

☆ A variation on this theme has the *Stall* dropping a bag onto the pavement so that the contents spill out everywhere. The **MARK** being a compassionate sort of person will kneel down to help pick stuff up, especially if the *Stall* appears to be a vulnerable sort of person. If this happens to you, and especially if the *Stall* grabs your hand by way of thanks, pay close attention to what is happening behind you, because it's highly likely that the *Pick* has knelt down behind you and is rifling your bag or your pockets.

☆ Beware of anyone carrying their jacket or a bag in front of them at waist level, especially if they appear to be engrossed in a mobile phone conversation or reading a book. That bag or jacket may be concealing a furtive hand that is exploring your bag or pockets.

☆ Professional pickpockets are usually well-disguised adults but you should beware of children as well. There's a classic **MISDIRECTION** trick that is widely used.

You are sat at a café table when couple of doe-eyed children approach you and show you a piece of paper by holding it right in front of your eyes while making a beseeching looks at you. The piece of paper is probably held upside-down just to confuse you further.

The poor mites seem to be begging.

No they aren't! The little tow-rags just lifted your mobile phone right off the table in front of you (while blocking your view with the piece of paper).

Gets 'em every time!

A
B
C
D
E
F
G
H
I
J
K
L
M
N
O
P
Q
R
S
T
U
V
W
X
Y
Z

PICKING UP CIGARETTE ASH

TRICKS OF THE TRADES

If you have let a piece of cigarette ash fall onto an expensive Ottoman rug then you'll want to pick it up in a hurry before your host or hostess returns and catches you.

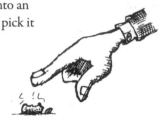

☆ Stick a bit of saliva onto your fingertip and touch the top of the ash, you'll find that it will stick to your finger and you can pick it up easily.

PIECE OF PAPER FROM THE FOURTH DIMENSION

PAPER TRICKS

Here's a strange little trick that takes advantage of the fact that our heads don't think in 3D very well.

☆ Cut a rectangle from a sheet of plain paper and make three halfway cuts in it near the middle as shown here. Grab both ends and put a 360° twist in it and lay it flat on the table. You end up with a weird conundrum.

It just seems impossible that this structure could have been formed from a sheet of paper. There must surely be some glue involved—but there isn't!

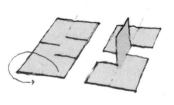

Let your audience touch the flap and flick it back and forth, but don't let them pick the whole thing up.

☆ There is a way to present this odd thing so as to make it even *more* strange. Make a hill fold down the centre, stand the thing on its legs with the flap pointing upwards and challenge anyone to say how you made it *without touching it*.

See also **MÖBIUS STRIP**.

PIGEON RACING TECHNIQUES
ANIMALS

You would have thought it amazing enough that pigeons can find their way home over vast distances—but people are never satisfied with the wonders of Nature: they have to *race* the poor creatures as well.

If you want your pigeons to get home before the Jones's then you could do a lot worse than harness the sex drive of the males and the maternal instincts of the females.

☆ A male pigeon can be crated next to an attractive female for a couple of days. When he seems sufficiently interested you may allow the couple a half hour's quality time before packing him into a truck bound for the Outer Hebrides. Have no doubt that he'll hurry home as quick as he can.

☆ A female pigeon, if she is sitting, will bust a gut to get home to her tragically cooling eggs.

PIG LATIN
LANGUAGE

This language is a type of *backslang* in which the first letter of each word (if it is a consonant) is moved to the end of the word and the suffix *-ay* is added. It is pretty much incomprehensible to those who have not practiced it a little.

Isthay anguaglay isay ypetay ofay ackslangbay inay ichwhay hetay isrtfay etterlay ofay eachay ordway (ifay itay isay ay onsonantcay) isay ovedmay otay hetay enday ofay hetay ordway anday hetay uffixsay -ayay isay addeday. Itay isay rettypay uchmay in-omprehensiblecay otay hosetay owhay avehay otnay ratisedpay itay ay ittlelay.

—good trickster-talk and easy to learn.

PILLOW ALARM CLOCK

PSYCHOLOGY / HYPNOTISM

☆ This may seem like an old wife's tale, but if you want to wake up at a certain time and have no alarm clock you could always try banging you head on the pillow five times to convince your subconscious to wake you up at five am. It really works.

Well, having said that, the author is of the opinion that when people fail to wake up in the morning it is because they didn't really want to in the first place. So before you set an alarm clock of any sort you might like to ask yourself just why this is necessary? Some people spend their whole lives doing things they don't really like and end up pretty miserable.

The fact is that your mind contains a very accurate clock and is perfectly capable of waking you up any time you really want to wake up. The trick of banging your head on the pillow is just a device for unlocking this ability. So if your reason for getting up at five is that you are catching a flight to somewhere lovely then you really shouldn't need an alarm clock!

PINCHING ELBOW SKIN

SILLINESS

☆ You can pinch the skin on the point of your elbow as hard as you like and it will not hurt.

PING PONG BALL ON THE NOSE

JUGGLING / OBJECT MANIPULATION

☆ The performer tosses a ping pong ball high into the air, it lands on their nose and is magically caught there in what appears to be an amazing feat of balancing.

The crowd cheers and the performer bows—but the ball stays stuck right where it is.

This usually gets a big laugh, especially if the ball is red and resembles a clown's nose.

☆ HERE'S *The* TRICK: The performer's nose and the ball have been given a thin coat of latex-based glue before the show started. You can use Copydex if you like. Although these glues are white when applied, a thin coat will dry transparently. The stuff bonds instantly on contact.

PINHOLE CAMERAS

FUN WITH SCIENCE

The **PINHOLE CAMERA** is an unbelievably simple sort of camera that has no lens! You can use this technology to make a real camera, to watch solar eclipses without burning out your eyes or to spy on people in a spectacular way.

☆ It works like this: if you make a light-proof box and make a tiny hole in it a faint image of the outside world will be projected onto the back wall of the box.

A B C D E F G H I J K L M N O P Q R S T U V W X Y Z

The boring and complicated way of doing this is to get a light—proof box and, in a darkroom, lay a sheet of photographic paper inside it and make a small pinprick on the opposite side. Now stick some tape over the hole and take it outside. Rest the box on something steady and point the hole at an interesting scene. Now peel

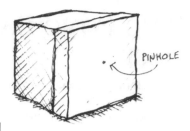

off the tape and wait for half a minute until you think enough light has got in to make an impression on the paper. Tape the hole shut again and go back to the darkroom and develop and print your picture. You should end up with a victorian-type photo!

That is all very well, but you probably don't have a darkroom, or photographic paper, or the know-how to complete the operation. After all, we are all living in the age of digital photography and this is all a bit yesteryear.

☆ You can however have a lot of fun if you make a big enough camera to actually *get inside!* For this you will need a bloody great big box and the chances are that you have one: *your own room!*

You need a room with a big white wall opposite the window. Got that? OK, now wait for a nice sunny day and block every scrap of light out of your room. Turn off the lights, hang a big thick rug over the window and block out any light leaking under the door. You need it pitch black.

Pitch black that is, except for *one tiny hole* through whatever is blocking the light from your window. Make that hole no more than a quarter of an inch in diameter and make sure that this is absolutely the only light getting inside.

Now sit there and let your eyes get used to the dark.

Now look carefully at the wall and you'll suddenly realise that you are looking at a full colour moving image of what is going on outside—only *upside down!* This is because rays of light that start high end up low after passing through the pinhole.

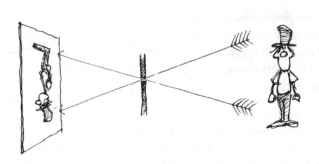

It's amazing!

☆ The next time you happen to be around when there is a solar eclipse you can make a nice pinhole camera to watch it with.

Get a big cardboard tube about six feet long and cover one end with a sheet of tinfoil and prick a tiny hole in it with a pin. Cover the other end with a sheet of tracing paper.

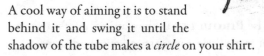

Mount the thing on a camera tripod and aim it at the sun, taking care not to stare into the sun yourself.

A cool way of aiming it is to stand behind it and swing it until the shadow of the tube makes a *circle* on your shirt.

You'll see an image of the sun, projected onto the paper, about half an inch across.

☆ The big problem with pinhole cameras is that, in order to get a nice sharp image, you need a small pinhole. Big holes make for blurry images and small holes make sharp ones. However a small hole produces a dim image because less light can get through. The only way out of this conundrum is to use a lens to focus the light passing through a larger aperture and this is why regular cameras have lenses.

A B C D E F G H I J K L M N O P Q R S T U V W X Y Z

Far-sighted people who need to
read some small print, but have
mislaid their reading glasses
can use a little **PINHOLE
CAMERA** technology.

By curling up the forefinger the near-
blind pentagenarian can form a tiny hole
in the crook of the finger. This is placed in front of and close to the eye;
through this hole the tiny letters will appear at once both very dim and
very sharp.

See also **CAMERA OBSCURA** to find out how to make a room-sized walk-
in camera with a reasonably bright image.

PIROUETTE

ACROBATICS

A **PIROUETTE** is a the dancer's move of making a 360° turn on the spot.
Skilled dancers can manage rapid double, triple or multiple **Pirouettes**
and then dance on, without seeming to get giddy! Actually they *do* get
giddy, but they are used to controlling and reducing the effects of
giddiness. It's a fun skill to learn.

☆ To turn an anti-clockwise **PIROUETTE** in the classic dancer's style you
start by standing with your feet a little way apart and raise both arms.

1: Now fold your left arm in front of your chest so both hands point to the right, in other words swing them the way you *don't* aim to turn in by way of winding yourself up. Meanwhile your left foot steps behind you, as if heading off the way you *do* want to go. This is the starting position.

2: Fix your gaze on a point straight ahead (this is called *spotting*) and lock onto that point. Now swing both arms hard to the left and as they reach the point at which they both point right pull them into your body *hard* and your torso will whip around very quickly.

3: As soon as your head can no longer *spot* the point you picked whip it around a full 360° to on your spot again..

4: As your whole body reaches the end of the turn extend your arms (which will slow you down) and stamp down with your right foot. Ta-daa!

Well, it won't be that neat the first few times you try it, but with practice you'll be a master.

As with juggling, don't forget to practice the move both ways around right from the start.

Plain Whipping

KNOTS

The title of this trick may be a little confusing since the broad scope of *Every Trick In The Book* means that "whipping" can refer both to the sort of cracking fun one can have with a bullwhip and to the act of binding things up with whipping twine.

This item concerns the binding-up sort of whipping.

☆ When repairing an ancient fishing rod, or perhaps when seizing the end of a rope to prevent fraying (or even when making repairs to a whip) one may find oneself binding something up in twine. To make a really neat job you proceed as follows.

A
B
C
D
E
F
G
H
I
J
K
L
M
N
O
P
Q
R
S
T
U
V
W
X
Y
Z

Start by selecting some nice twine and drawing it through a block of beeswax to make it waxy and grippy.

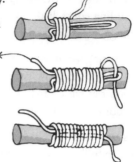

Now lay a loop of twine along the item you want to bind with the bend pointing in the direction you will be winding your binding. Then bind neatly in that direction.

When you're done tuck the end of your whipping twine through the loop you made and draw the end into the middle of the binding.

Finally, razor off the exposed ends and you're done—a perfect piece of **PLAIN WHIPPING** leaves no knots or ends visible and the grip of the wax should make it last for years.

☆ According to Clifford W. Ashley, author of the incredible *Ashley Book of Knots*, if you are seizing a piece of rope to prevent the end from unravelling, your whipping should be the same length as the diameter of the rope.

PLATE JUGGLING

JUGGLING

PLATE JUGGLING, like work with hats, canes and cigar boxes, harks back to the old days of Music Hall and Vaudeville when speciality acts would often create routines involving everyday objects.

Plates are obviously breakable items (like eggs) so any performance involving manipulation or juggling with them is enhanced by a sense of risk. The sense of risk is, of course, perfectly justified since a plate will almost certainly shatter if dropped, and you should also be mindful of the risk of personal injury if your hand happens to be in contact with a plate when it shatters—the shards can be very sharp indeed.

A basic **CASCADE** of three plates can be juggled in three different ways, each uses a different axis of spin.

1: You can juggle them as if you were cascading three juggling rings so that the axis of each plate runs from right to left. For the best effect in performance you would need to stand sideways to your audience.

2: You can juggle them with **DIP** throws, so that both you and the plates face the audience.

3: You can juggle them with *butterfly* throws, which is considerably harder and requires a great deal of confidence.

There are other things you can do with plates apart from actually juggling with them.

☆ A very nice plate manipulation is the *Plate Turnover*. Start by balancing a single plate on the upward-pointing fingers of one hand as a butler might when delivering a dainty dish. Now place your other hand as if it were about to karate-chop the back of the plate upwards.

Push upwards with the karate-hand so the plate turns over (like **FLIPPING BEER MATS**). Your Karate hand should follow the plate around.

The plate is caught, after a full spin, in the karate-chop hand. Now repeat the move and swap it back.

A
B
C
D
E
F
G
H
I
J
K
L
M
N
O
P
Q
R
S
T
U
V
W
X
Y
Z

With just a little practice this will become a fluid move and when you keep it going you'll have a very nice single-object juggling pattern.

☆ You can do a *Plate Turnover* in one hand as well.

Start with the plate sitting flat on the palm of your hand and push it upwards. Now, as it hovers turn the plate hand into karate-chop position, flip it over and catch it palm-upwards again. The plate should remain pretty much in contact with your hand throughout the move.

☆ The classic plate-juggling move is the *Three Plate Elbow Slide*. To learn this you should start with just one plate and get the *Elbow Slide* down pat.

Grab a plate in your left hand and then bend your right arm and raise your elbow to shoulder level, as if being measured for a suit. Place the plate on the flat of your right forearm-bicep, which should be as flat as a table. Ready?

Now drop your right elbow and the plate will slide off and fall—but catch it with your right hand. Cool move!

Practice this on both sides until it's solid.

☆ OK, now for three plates.

Start with two plates sitting on your elbows, while the third is held in your *right* hand.

Slide, drop (and catch) the plate on your left elbow and then immediately place the plate in your right hand onto your left elbow.

Now repeat the move on the other side.

Now keep going and you have a very nice juggling pattern running.

☆ You can also do **CURLS** with a plate in each hand. **CURLS** are always tricky moves, but they look great. Start with a plate held on the tips of the fingers of one hand (once more as a pretentious servant might). Pass your hand *under* your shoulder and then out and back, lifting it above the shoulder. The tricky bit is keeping it flat all the way. After much stretching the plate will have turned twice (720°) and will be back where it started.

☆ **CURLING** two plates, one in each hand, looks very impressive. Start curling one, and when you're halfway through the move start to curl the other.

PLATE SPINNING

CIRCUS SKILLS

Plastic plates, designed for children to do **PLATE SPINNING** tricks with, are commonplace these days. They vaguely resemble the plates you eat your dinner off. If you look under a normal china plate you'll see a circular ridge—the bit that is designed to sit on the table while the main body of

A
B
C
D
E
F
G
H
I
J
K
L
M
N
O
P
Q
R
S
T
U
V
W
X
Y
Z

the plate is held aloft a little, in case it is hot and damages the table.

☆ On the plastic spinning versions this ridge is very much enhanced to make it easy to spin. A stick is placed under the plate which flops to one side, hanging by the ridge. A quick twirling action of the stick gets the plate spinning and then the stick is cheated into the middle of the plate (which is conical) and the thing will spin for ages.

☆ Genuine spinning plates are made of china and also have a ridge that is a little more pronounced that on a normal plate, in the very centre of the base there is a slight dip which accepts the point of a stick. These plates are practically unobtainable.

☆ Instead you can use a regular plate and place a little tape on the base. Now secrete a needle in the end of your spinning stick.

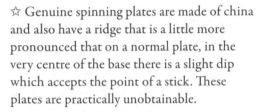

You'll find that you can place the plate on the stick, give it a quick spin and it will wobble and spin impressively for a very long time.

PLATONIC SOLIDS

GEOMETRY

It turns out, as was discovered by the ancient pioneers of mathematics, that there exist (in this particular universe) just *five* different regular *polyhedra*.[*] They were very significant in ancient Greek geometry and were known to Plato, hence they are often called the **PLATONIC SOLIDS**.

---

[*] For an impressive dissertation on just why this might so, see *The True Nature of Things*—a large, often rambling and out-of-print treatise on the state of the Universe by R. Cheney.

A *polyhedron* is a three-dimensional shape formed from flat faces and straight edges. A *regular* polyhedron is one in which all the edges are the same length and all the faces are the same shape, and all the shapes of the faces are regular polygons.

They are, in order of complexity, the **TETRAHEDRON**, the **CUBE**, the **OCTAHEDRON**, the **DODECAHEDRON** and the **ICOSAHEDRON**, having respectively 4, 6, 8, 12 and 20 faces each.

These polyhedra occur often in nature and also in the works of human beings. A basic understanding of them is a prerequisite to the design and construction of **GEODESIC DOMES** and they can be handy when making paper lamp shades and **TISSUE PAPER HOT AIR BALLOONS**.

POI

JUGGLING

> Poi is juggling for people who cannot count past two and who are scared of dropping things.—*Radical Cheney*

Notwithstanding Cheney's acrimony, **POI** has enjoyed something of a renaissance lately. In this form of juggling two balls are swung, one from each hand, at the end of two cords. Perfectly serviceable **POI** can be fashioned from long stripey socks with beanbags stuffed in the the end like oranges in the toes of Xmas stockings.

This art form originated in New Zealand. The word "Poi" is the Maori word for "ball".

A
B
C
D
E
F
G
H
I
J
K
L
M
N
O
P
Q
R
S
T
U
V
W
X
Y
Z

Like music (which has just eight notes, but an infinity of tunes) **Poi** has, at its core, a few simple movements which, when multiplied by the various planes you can swing objects in, combine to produce an infinity of possible movements.

Your task, if you want to learn **Poi**, is to train yourself with these basic principles. They are all simple, but they can be fiddly to learn and they do need to be practiced until they become instinctive. Let's go!

• Stand with your hands at your sides and swing your **Poi**, in unison, in circles like the wheels of a car going forwards.

• Now do the same thing but swing them like the wheels of a car going backwards.

• Now swing them in forward circles so that they are 180° out of phase, as one goes up the other goes down.

• Now do the same thing with backward circles.

That wasn't too hard was it? Take a break and congratulate yourself. The next exercise involves swinging the **Poi** in *opposite* directions.

• With your hands by your sides as before you swing the right hand forwards while the left swings backwards. This is a bit of a knack so take it steadily. Both Poi should peak and trough together.

• Got that? Good, now do it the other way around!

• Now see if you can manage to turn your **Poi** in opposite directions 180° out of phase—as one peaks the other troughs. And, of course, there are two ways of doing this: right-hand-forwards, left-hand-back and vice versa.

You'll probably find that exercise challenging at first and it's likely that your **Poi** will turn in unwanted directions and get all messy. So take your time, stay relaxed and familiarise your body with the moves gently. These simple exercises will teach you the basic *timings* of **Poi**. The next step is learning the *planes* in which you can move. So far you've been working in the forward plane, but another commonly used plane is the sideways plane.

• You can turn your **Poi** like two propellors on an aircraft.

• You can turn them like two propellors behind your body too.

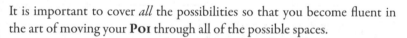

• Practice turning your **Poi** in the sideways planes using all of the combinations of direction and timing which boils down to the following list of exercises:

> *Both clockwise and in phase*
> *Both clockwise and out of phase,*
> *Both anti-clockwise and in phase,*
> *Both anti-clockwise and out of phase,*
> *Opposite directions in phase,*
> *Opposite directions out of phase.*

It is important to cover *all* the possibilities so that you become fluent in the art of moving your **Poi** through all of the possible spaces.

Now it's time to try moving your arms around!

• Try holding your arms outstretched, both fully forward, both fully backward and over your head and work through all of the previous exercises in all of these positions.

• Next you need to learn to work with the **Poi** turning in *different* positions, and also moving from one position to another—this is where the number of possibilities for movement multiplies up into *huge* numbers.

You might like to start by turning the right-hand **Poi** clockwise in front of your legs, while the left hand turns anti-clockwise *behind* them.

• Now swap them over, while they are turning so the left-hand **Poi** goes in front while the right hand one goes behind.

• Swap them on every *beat* and you'll end up with the **Poi** travelling in figures of eight around your thighs—very nice!

Learning to apply all of the variations of direction and timing to this simple move should keep you busy for a week or so! Adding in all the possible combinations of arm positions should keep you busy for a *month*.

• People often find it difficult, at first, to work the figure of eight move around their head —but there is an easy way to learn it. Just get the **Poi** running with your arms held low at your sides and slowly raise them to an overhead position—magic!

See also **Cross and Follow** (also known as the *Three Beat Weave*).

Polyethylene Pyrotechnics

PYROTECHNICS

This was a popular pastime among alternative folk in the 1970's though it is a trick rarely seen now for perfectly good reasons. It involves burning plastic which is a Bad Thing To Do. It is included in *Every Trick In The Book* in the vain hope of approaching some sort of completeness.

Cut a strip of polyethylene* sheet about a foot long and an inch or so wide. Hang it from something that will not catch fire at least eight feet from the ground and set fire to the end. It's best when it's dark.

---

* You probably call it Polythene—it's the same thing, the author is just being a pedant.

Droplets of molten polyethylene will fall from the strip as it burns, flying through the air incandescently and making buzzing and humming noises as they go. It's eerily beautiful if you can overcome your shame and guilt for pumping yet more crap into the air we all share.

In the 70's people would hang burning strips of polyethylene from helium balloons and let them float off over the heads of the crowds at rock festivals. The oohs and aahs of the masses conveniently drowning out the squeals of pain from those getting burnt by the fallout.

POPPING A BALL

JUGGLING

In the very old days of juggling (certainly before *you* were born) the skill of **POPPING A BALL** was highly regarded, indeed it was considered (by some sticks-in-the-mud) to be the *correct* way of throwing a ball.

It isn't, but it is a skill worth acquiring never the less.

☆ **POPPING A BALL** means throwing it without any wrist movement. The ball should seem to spring from your hand of its own accord.

This is actually not that hard to do, but it *is* hard to do well, so you'd better practice it a lot.

In actual juggling you use the technique of **POPPING A BALL** to create the illusion that the balls are juggling themselves while you stand behind them in a suitably gobsmacked manner.

For fun you can try juggling one ball in this style and the other two normally.

See also **ANTI-GRAVITY BALL, SLAP.**

A
B
C
D
E
F
G
H
I
J
K
L
M
N
O
P
Q
R
S
T
U
V
W
X
Y
Z

A
B
C
D
E
F
G
H
I
J
K
L
M
N
O
P
Q
R
S
T
U
V
W
X
Y
Z

PRACTICE IN FRONT OF A MIRROR

MAGIC

You've probably heard this advice again and again but taken no notice. This is totally normal and why most people can't pull of simple magic tricks effectively.

☆ Let's say you are trying to learn a simple retention **PALM RETENTION VANISH** with a coin. You'll note, if you look up that trick, that you are advised to **PRACTICE IN FRONT OF A MIRROR** and that is *exactly what you should do!*

Sit yourself down and start work. You should try *actually placing the coin in the receiving hand* to see what that looks like as well as doing the sleight whereby you *retain* the coin. Do one, then the other, then do it all again.

And again, and again.

After about forty minutes something very weird will happen: *you'll actually start to fool yourself!*

Once you get to that stage you are nearly there, about another ten minutes' work should do it. Then revisit the trick a couple more times over the next few days.

You now have a magic trick down and will actually be able to fool real people with it and blow their tiny minds.

So when it says **PRACTICE IN FRONT OF A MIRROR** you should do exactly that.

PHENOKISTOSCOPE

ANIMATION

This fine example of Victorian **ANIMATION** was created by *Eadweard Muybridge** , artist, photographer and pioneer of moving images and photographic **STEREOSCOPY**. Muybridge is probably best known for his studies of human beings and animals in which he captured rapid sequences of images in order to study the true nature of their walks and runs.

---

* Yes Eadweard! The author has no idea why the name is spelt thus. It's just conceivable that this will help you win points in a general knowledge quiz.

A
B
C
D
E
F
G
H
I
J
K
L
M
N
O
P
Q
R
S
T
U
V
W
X
Y
Z

This disc shows a lady and gentleman dancing a waltz in 13 frames. To view the animation you should make a copy of the image (and blow it up a little if you have a clever photocopier). Glue it to some card. Punch out the small hole in the middle and then carefully cut out the 13 radial slots.

Now poke the sharp end of a pencil into the hole from the back. Pinch the tip of the pencil to hold the card in place. You'll find that you can spin the card like a wheel.

Stand in front of a mirror, point the **PHENOKISTOSCOPE** at the mirror, look through the slots from behind and you'll see the couple dance. The images were made by tracing photographs, which is why the dance looks so lifelike.

The **PHENOKISTOSCOPE** was invented by a M. Plateau in the 19th century and in its original implementation it consisted of two discs, one containing the slots and the other the animation.

You can of course, make your own animations using the principle of the **PHENOKISTOSCOPE**, this Muybridge sequence of a horse galloping might be a good image to play with.

See also **ZOETROPE, PRAXINOSCOPE, THAUMATROPE**.

PRAXINOSCOPE

ANIMATION

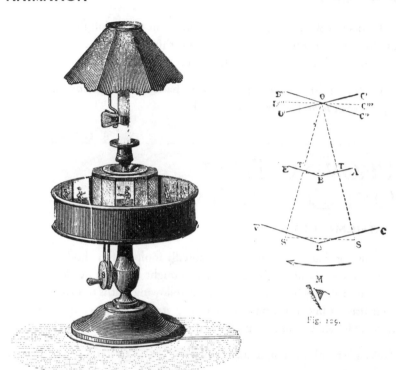

Fig. 129.

This animation machine is the invention of *M. Reynaud* and it is an im-proved version of the **ZOETROPE** using a set of prismatically arranged mirrors as a kind of optical shutter. Its advantage is that it produces a brighter image than the **ZOETROPE** because the images are not viewed through narrow slots and, as shown above, the device was typically fitted with a lamp to further brighten the display.

A
B
C
D
E
F
G
H
I
J
K
L
M
N
O
P
Q
R
S
T
U
V
W
X
Y
Z

A
B
C
D
E
F
G
H
I
J
K
L
M
N
O
P
Q
R
S
T
U
V
W
X
Y
Z

PRIEST

POACHING

A **PRIEST** is the name given to the thing you use to kill fish. If you are catching fish to eat then it is the done thing to kill them right away, quickly and cleanly. A short length of steel rod is ideal.

☆ Grab your fish and strike it hard at the back of the head once and it will rapidly *cease to be*. Do not be squeamish.

PROVING THAT ONE EQUALS TWO

MATHEMATICS

It turns out that you can use the supposedly foolproof methods of algebra to prove just about anything, and *you* thought that you needed *statistics* for that! You may be tempted to use the following maths to make a fool of your teacher but it will only work if they are not a very *good* teacher—if they are fooled by this they probably deserve to be.

☆ We start with the simple statement:

$a + b = c$

From this it follows that:

$2a - a + 2b - b = 2c - c$

...because *2a—a* is the same as *a* and likewise for b and c. Now if we do some simple algebraic jiggling to get all the 2's on one side we end up with...

$2a + 2b - 2c = a + b - c$

...or to put it more neatly...

$2(a + b - c) = a + b - c$

...and now we divide both sides by $a + b - c$ to end up with

$2 = 1$ Ta daa!

☆ **HERE'S** *The* **TRICK**: There are many variations of this trick and they all boil down to one thing. When we divided both sides of the equation by $a + b—c$ we were actually dividing both sides by *zero* which is a Bad Thing. It is such a Bad Thing that computers and calculators refuse to do it because it would blow their tiny minds. We know that $a + b—c$ is zero because it follows from the very first equation.

When you divide by zero the answer is always *infinity* no matter what number you started out with, hence both sides of the equation seem to be equal.

The trick doesn't really prove that algebra is wrong, it just shows that it can be inconsistent or *incomplete*, this was the subject of a very important mathematical theory by a man called Kurt Gödel.[*]

Prusik Knot

KNOTS / CLIMBING

The **Prusik Knot** was invented by one *Dr. Karl Prusik*, an Austrian mountaineer in the early twentieth century. It is used for climbing ropes.

You need a stout climbing rope, which you are to ascend—perhaps it has been thrown over the branch of a tree and you wish to ascend to affix a swing.

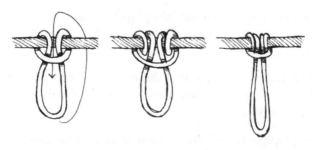

---

[*] If you want to find out more about this I suggest that you google Kurt Gödel or read an amazing book called Gödel, Esher, Bach: an Eternal Golden Braid by Douglas Hofstader.

Take some small stuff (that's narrow rope) and make a loop a foot or so long. Attach the loop to the climbing rope with a **COW HITCH** and then pass the hanging loop through the knot one more time (some people add a third tuck for extra security).

You'll need two **PRUSIK** loops and a climber's harness to climb your rope. The upper loop is carabinered to your harness, while the lower one is looped around your foot to form a sort of step.

The **PRUSIK KNOT** will not slip down the rope while it is under load, but it is easily slid up or down when there is no tension on it. Thus you may intrepidly ascend by first resting your weight on one loop and then the other as you slide the loops up the main rope.

See also **BLAKE'S HITCH**.

PUDDLE JUMPER

FLYING MACHINES

A **PUDDLE JUMPER** is one of those little propellors on a stick that you can make fly by rolling the shaft rapidly between the palms of your hands and letting go.

It consists of two pieces of wood. The propellor itself which provides the lift, and a shaft which provides some ballast and directional stability.

They can fly really very well indeed and you can whittle one from a piece of wood with a penknife in a few minutes. This is a nice thing to do while sat around a camp fire.

☆ A good propellor has a shallower angle of attack at the ends than it does in the middle. It's best to start with a squareish piece of straight-grained kindling and fashion the hole for the shaft before whittling the blade profile.

This drawing, which was published in a magazine called *Junior Model Planes* in 1945, will give you a few tips about the noble art of propellor carving.

Pump up the Bass

TECHNICAL WIZARDRY / SILLINESS

Some people just can't get enough *kick* to their music, so if you want to get really blasted, try holding a balloon to each ear. The bass-enhancing vibrational properties of the humble toy balloon will blow your brains out.

Which is probably what you want.

Punting

BOATS / OUTDOORPERSONSHIP / SILLINESS

Punting is the art of commanding and navigating a *Punt*. These charming flat-bottomed vessels were formerly used by *fowlers* and *anglers* to negotiate shallow and reedy water which they achieve by way of having a very shallow draft, and being propelled by a pole, rather than oars and paddles which can be troublesome in such waters. In more modern times the punt has become a leisure craft, particularly popular in the University towns of Oxford and Cambridge.

Handling a punt can be a tricky business, so the true trickster will have hired a vessel and practiced the art in advance of attempting to operate in a social or amorous situation.

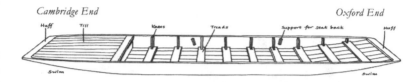

Cambridge End   *Oxford End*

Punts are driven from the stern by means of a pole, but there is dispute between Oxford and Cambridge regarding which end of the punt is which. In Cambridge the punter stands on the *till*, the small flat deck at one end of the boat, while a punter from Oxford will stand on the floor of the boat at the other end, so the till is at the front of the punt. Both will argue strenuously that their's is the correct method and a punter working from the Oxford end while negotiating the rive Cam will be quickly spotted for a foreigner. It is certainly more stable, and the feet get a better purchase from the Oxford End, but all would agree that the sacrifice of stability at the Cambridge end is compensated for by way of speed. When punts are raced, people from both towns will work from the Cambridge end.

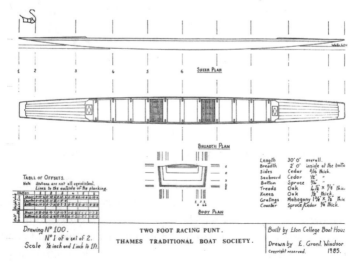

Indeed in this plan for a racing punt, designed at Eton, we see that the vessel is not only narrower than the punt used for social engagements, but it also has a till at both ends!

To pole a punt forwards (also known as *pricking*) one stands at one's preferred end and lifts the pole vertically and drops it into the water close to the side of the punt, until it hits bottom. The poles are usually 16 feet long and equipped with a pronged ferrule at the working end to save wear on the wood and provide good purchase. The beds of the popular rivers are usually quite pebbly providing the decent surface to work against, though the Cherwell in Oxford can be notoriously muddy and is very likely to be reluctant to release a pole after it has sunk through a couple of feet of mud. The punt is then pushed forward with the pole. When the pole reaches full extension the punter will pull it from the bed, giving it a hard twist if it is suspected that the pole is embedded in mud.

This is where the first embarrassing mistake is usually made and there are several ways things can go wrong here:

The pole is wedged firmly in the mud, the punter does not let go and is pulled from the boat into the water.

Sometimes the pole remains upright for a few moments and the punter is held aloft like a monkey on a palm tree before being casually delivered to the deep.

Alternatively, the punter lets go the pole and the boat drifts on helplessly as the crew attempt to retrieve the pole by hand-paddling—some boating stations equip each hired punt with a Canadian canoe paddle for these eventualities.

Assuming that the punter and pole are still united we now face the problem of steering the vessel. The pole itself is used as a rudder, and you will eventually learn that a punt can be steered with astonishing accuracy. Novices, however, are comically inept at steering their boats and proceed along the river colliding with each bank alternately and causing a huge nuisance for any other vessels on the river.

PYTHAGORAS' THEOREM

MATHEMATICS / GEOMETRY

In a right-angled triangle *the square on the hypotenuse is equal to the sums of the squares on the other two sides.*

So goes the mathematician's talk. We all learned it at school and then most of us promptly forgot it—the word *hypotenuse* probably didn't help, it means the "long side", the side opposite the right angle.

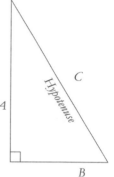

If we have a triangle with three sides, A, B and C, with the two sides A and B forming a **RIGHT ANGLE,** then we call C the hypotenuse.

PYTHAGORAS' THEOREM tells us that:

$$A^2 + B^2 = C^2$$

Which means that we can quickly work out the length of any side if we know the length of the other two sides, all we need is a calculator with a square root button!

☆ A typical maths question in a school exam might be:

> A painter leans a twelve foot ladder against a wall, the foot of the ladder is four feet from the base of the wall. How high does the ladder reach up the wall?

Well, in this case the ladder forms the hypotenuse, so it's C. The distance from the base of the wall is B, and the height to which the ladder reaches up the wall is A. So we know that:

$$A^2 + 4^2 = 12^2$$

Which works out to:

$$A^2 = 128$$

And the square root of 128 is 11.313708 (to six decimal places, which ought to be enough), so there's the answer!

☆ Here's another typical question:

> An explorer sets out from camp and walks ten miles north and then turns east an walks for three miles, how far is it back to camp?

This time we'll call the ten miles north A and the three miles east B (because North and East are at right angles to each other) and the distance back to camp is the hypotenuse, or C.

$10^2 + 3^2 = C^2$

$100 + 9 = C^2$

$109 = C^2$

The square root of 109 is 10.440306 (again to six decimal places) so there's the answer.

☆ Beware though, of a related trick question:

> An explorer left camp, walked 8 miles south then 4 miles east then 8 miles north and found himself back at his tent where there was a bear. What colour was the bear?

The only place on the planet where this could happen is at the North Pole, hence the bear was white. The point being that **PYTHAGORAS' THEOREM** works only on a plane, not on the curved surface of our planet.

☆ **PYTHAGORAS THEOREM** also has to do with things that mathematicians call *vectors.*

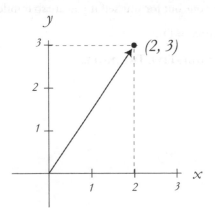

A
B
C
D
E
F
G
H
I
J
K
L
M
N
O
P
Q
R
S
T
U
V
W
X
Y
Z

A *vector* is simply a line pointing in a certain direction from the imaginary origin of a graph. If you draw a line from the origin to a point that lies two units along the x-axis (the horizontal axis) and three units up the y-axis (the vertical axis) then you have a vector that can be written as *(2, 3)*. The length of the vector, which we'll call D, can be calculated according to the equation:

$$X^2 + Y^2 = D^2$$

In our example that's

$$2^2 + 3^2 = D^2$$

So the distance D is the square root of 13 (that's 3.605551 to six decimal places).

☆ You can also have three dimensional vectors, which are lines from the origin that go to points expressed with X, Y and Z coordinates (X is normally to the right, Y is normally up, and Z is usually forwards, out of the sheet of paper or computer screen).

The length of a three dimensional vector is given by:

$$X^2 + Y^2 + Z^2 = D^2$$

A real-world example of this might be:

> A helicopter starts on the landing pad. After a while it has flown a thousand feet north, five hundred feet east and has lifted to an altitude of two thousand feet. How many feet is it from the landing pad?

You can work that one out for yourself if you are so minded. The sum is:

$$1000^2 + 500^2 + 2000^2 = D^2$$

See also **THREE-FOUR-FIVE TRIANGLE**.

QUEUE JUMPING

PSYCHOLOGY

It has recently been discovered, by means of a quasi-scientific survey, that people will allow you to walk straight to the front of a queue as long as you offer an excuse of some sort. Simply brazening it out is not good enough, so walking up to the front while pretending to talk on a mobile phone is a bad plan. Instead you offer an excuse. But HERE'S *The* TRICK:

any excuse.

"My wife's in labour."

"John has lost his keys."

"I don't speak English."

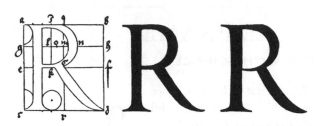 R R

RAVEN

MAGIC

A **RAVEN** is a magic *gimmick* which can be used to create some great effects. You can buy one from a magic supplier, or make one yourself. Technically it's what magicians call a *Pull* because it pulls items up your sleeve.

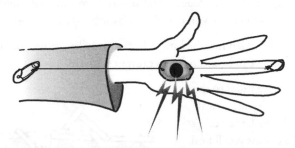

It consists of a length of elastic secured inside your sleeve with a safety pin. At the wrist end is a small padded pocket of cloth containing a **SUPERMAGNET** and at the finger end of the pocket is a loop of fishing line which you hook over the end of your finger, allowing the line to run under the end of your fingernail. When thus loaded it is invisible to the audience as long as the palm is held facing down.

☆ Place a magnetic coin in the palm of a volunteer's hand and wave the **RAVEN** hand over it a few times and let the magnet lift the coin. A slight bend in the finger is all it takes to have the coin vanish up your sleeve.

The volunteer will actually *feel* the coin vanish in a totally inexplicable manner.

And now you know the secret of yet another *David Blaine* trick.

A B C D E F G H I J K L M N O P Q R S T U V W X Y Z

A
B
C
D
E
F
G
H
I
J
K
L
M
N
O
P
Q
R
S
T
U
V
W
X
Y
Z

RECIPROCAL FRAMES

GEOMETRY / FUN WITH SCIENCE

If you take three poles and rest each on the other to form a sort of impossible triangle in the middle you end up with a **RECIPROCAL FRAME**. It is "reciprocal" because each beam in the circle *supports* the next while *being supported* by the last.

It's magic in the style of *lifting oneself up by the bootstraps.*

The poles tend to slip off each other, so you might lash them together or, if you're working with tabletop stuff such as pens and pencils, you could use elastic bands at the joints.

It's quite fun to work with matches at the bar while killing time, you'll find that the match heads can be arranged to prevent slippage.

If you now add more poles to the frame, working in a symmetrical manner to produce a lattice of triangles and hexagons you'll find that the resulting *Grillage* structure starts to lift itself off the ground and begins to form a low dome.

There is a significant difference between a normal **GEODESIC DOME** and a dome made in the form of a **RECIPROCAL FRAME**.

In **GEODESIC DOMES**, each element of the structure is either in pure tension or pure compression, whereas elements in **RECIPROCAL FRAMES** are subject to large bending forces which can be a problem.

On the positive side though, the joints are a lot easier to make!

The most brilliant thing about
RECIPROCAL FRAME domes
is that they can be built from the
top down!

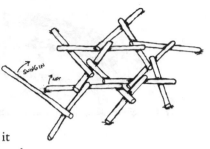

This is especially cool if you want
to construct a large span using,
say, scaffolding poles. Begin by
forming the crown hexagon, fixing it
together with swivel clamps. Then work
around it, snowflake style, adding
more elements.

For every two poles you add you need to do one small lift to complete the
Impossible Triangle joint.

In this way the entire dome is slowly raised.

Take heed though that the scaffolding
company will *hate* you for abusing
their poles in this manner.

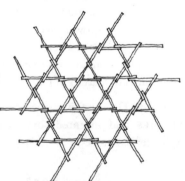

Typically, when the dome is struck and
packed away, you will find that most, if
not all, of the poles are bent.

Smaller spans can be made from a
simple tessellations for triangles and
hexagons, and although this pattern
is technically a planar one, the dome
will curve up on account of the overs
and unders of the poles—producing a
lens-like structure.

However, if you'd like to build a well-formed half-dome then you should
use replace some of the hexagons with pentagons to create something
more like a proper **GEODESIC**.

Replacing *every* other hexagon with a pentagon will result in a very useful,
strong and efficient structure.

A
B
C
D
E
F
G
H
I
J
K
L
M
N
O
P
Q
R
S
T
U
V
W
X
Y
Z

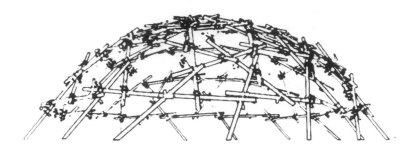

☆ **RECIPROCAL FRAMES** can be constructed from other arrangements, for example the square.

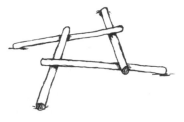

This is a very effective way to span a gap that is too long for any available beams to bridge, as might happen if you wanted to throw a cover over the four roofless walls of a derelict shed using, perhaps, locally found driftwood, as you do—on that sort of day out, by the sea when one's mind turns to matters of *Outdoorpersonship*, survival and the like.

Leonardo Da Vinci was one of the first people to design **RECIPROCAL FRAMES** and invented some very neat tessellations for his amazing "grillage" structures.

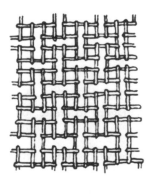

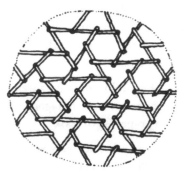

☆ An amazing application of **Reciprocal Frames** was in Leonardo's devilishly clever design for a temporary bridge, in which a large span is crossed by simple beams, none of which are long enough to span the water on their own.

Such a structure, once completed, could be used to suspend a roadway.

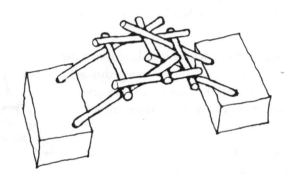

Reef Knot

KNOTS

This very popular knot has probably killed more people than all other knots combined. Why? Well because a lot of people know how to tie it, but very few know what it is *for*.

The **Reef Knot** is *lethal* if it is used to join ropes together which you will later suspend your life from. Even the often-maligned *Granny Knot* is a better bet for this purpose.

The real purpose of a **Reef Knot** is for *reefing* sails, that is rolling them up so they present less canvas (or indeed no canvas at all) to the wind.

It turns out that this knot is very good at holding cloth in a bundle and is perfectly secure when applied in this way.

It's also reasonably easy to untie. The **Reef Knot** is therefore useful for tying up the necks of sacks and bags.

A B C D E F G H I J K L M N O P Q R S T U V W X Y Z

☆ The **REEF KNOT** is formed from two **HALF KNOTS** each tied in the opposite directions.

People often remember this with the mnemonic *right-over-left, left-over-right.*

Despite being prominently featured in just about every dissertation on the subject of knots, and being the first knot taught to Boy Scouts this is one knot that you can perfectly well do without.

The reason that the **REEF KNOT** is so dangerous is that people often use it for joining two ropes together and when applied in this way the knot has a very nasty habit of *capsizing* into a **COW HITCH** formed by one rope around the other.

This disastrous knot has virtually no power to resist sliding to the end of the rope and falling off.

☆ The *Granny Knot* is what you get when both **HALF KNOTS** are tied in the *same* direction.

This is a less secure knot when it comes to tying up sacks or reefing sails but although it tends to slip, it rarely spills entirely.

☆ If you tie a **REEF KNOT** and make the second **HALF KNOT** from a loop made from one of the free ends, you get a *slipped* **REEF KNOT**, which is, of course, very easy to untie—just pull on the tail of the loop and the knot will fall apart.

☆ If you loop *both* ends you have tied a **BOW**—familiar to anyone who has been taught to tie up their own shoes.

There are better *Shoelace Knots* but this is almost certainly the one you use every day.

See also **SHEET BEND**.
(Especially if you are planning to join two ropes together).

REFUELLING INSECTS

ANIMALS

If you come across a wasp, butterfly or other insect that appears to be close to death and almost incapable of movement it may have simply run out of fuel.

Perhaps it has been flying around in your room for hours trying to find a way out and has completely run out of puff.

If you can knock a wasp off its feet so that it lies on its side wings vibrating feebly—you've probably got one in this state.

☆ Get a few grains of sugar and add a drop of water.

Place the sugar-water within tongue-licking range of the insect and watch.

After a couple of seconds they will start to lick the sugar (butterflies have the most *amazing* tongues) and they will take a tiny quantity on board.

Within a *minute* the creature will come back to life.

A
B
C
D
E
F
G
H
I
J
K
L
M
N
O
P
Q
R
S
T
U
V
W
X
Y
Z

A
B
C
D
E
F
G
H
I
J
K
L
M
N
O
P
Q
R
S
T
U
V
W
X
Y
Z

REMOTE CONTROL FOR CATS

ANIMALS

☆ A laser pointer makes an ideal **REMOTE CONTROL FOR CATS**. You can make a cat move at high speed and with great enthusiasm (in any direction you like) by teasing it with the little red spot.

☆ With two laser pointers and two cats you can even engineer collisions —I know of no other way to do this.

☆ By attaching a third laser pointer to your hat you can cause the creatures to run around in a sort of figure-of-eight **CASCADE** pattern.

REMOVING YOUR THUMB

HAND TRICKS

This trick has been amusing small children ever since their parents evolved the opposed thumb.

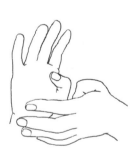

☆ Fold both of your thumbs to ninety degrees and place their joints together so the tip of one seems to continue from the base of the other.

To conceal this subterfuge you must **COVER THE JOIN** with the index finger belonging to the hand that is supplying the false tip of a thumb.

This requires a certain amount of dexterity and close attention to the viewing angles.

You can now slide the top of your thumb on and off at will to the horrified delight of your impressionable onlookers.

It will feel awkward at first, but once your hands get used to stretching into this position it will become a natural move.

REVENGE

MARTIAL ARTS

Revenge is supposed to be sweet and I suppose it is, if carried out with style and humour.

You are advised to think carefully before carrying out any of the suggestions below since you may incur some severe criminal penalties.

The Watercress Attack
The injured party uses their ex-partner's flat key to gain entry while the victim is away for the weekend, carrying with them a watering can and a large bag of watercress seeds which are spread liberally over the plush carpet. After watering the seeds and turning up the central heating they leave again.

The New York Chatline Ploy
The justifiably furious revengee gains access to the former significant other's dwelling and places a call to a seedy chatline in the Big Apple and leaves the phone on speakerphone ready for the victim's return. This is not a cheap call.

Prawn Pong
Fresh prawns are inserted secretly into the hollow interior of the victim's curtain poles. After a few days of decomposition a dreadful smell will pervade the entire house but it is almost impossible to find the source.

A
B
C
D
E
F
G
H
I
J
K
L
M
N
O
P
Q
R
S
T
U
V
W
X
Y
Z

REVERSE CASCADE

JUGGLING

In *Toss Juggling* the standard pattern for *odd numbers* of objects is called a **CASCADE**.

The most basic **CASCADE** is the **THREE BALL CASCADE**. The hands throw alternately and each ball is thrown so as to pass *under* the previous one. The balls travel in a figure of eight pattern. At the crossing point in the middle the balls are travelling upwards. The hands, meanwhile, are catching at the *outside* of the pattern and throwing on the *inside*.

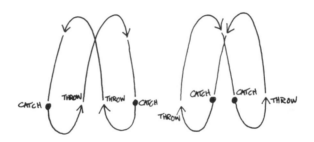

Normal and Reverse Cascades.

In a **REVERSE CASCADE** the balls effectively travel in the opposite direction. The shape of the pattern is the same, but now they move through the crossing point while they are travelling downwards. The hands are throwing on the outside and catching on the inside.

The pattern is a perfect time-reversal of the **THREE BALL CASCADE**.

☆ Juggling a **REVERSE CASCADE** is surprisingly easy and is often the first new pattern a novice juggler learns after mastering the **THREE BALL CASCADE**. All you have to do is throw *every* ball in the pattern **OVER THE TOP**—it's that simple!

☆ The time-reversal can be elegantly demonstrated by making a movie of a **THREE BALL CASCADE** and running it backwards (which is pretty easy to do these days). The result will be a **REVERSE CASCADE**.

☆ Club jugglers sometimes use the **REVERSE CASCADE**, though it's a hard trick to learn and while it is technically interesting the visual effect doesn't really justify the effort required. The pattern is usually juggled with normal spin, which isn't a true time-reversal because that would require *reverse* spin—and that would make the pattern even *harder* to do.

REVERSE PANEL

SIGNWRITING

White paint will not easily cover over a black base. So signwriters often have to undertake the laborious task of carrying out lettering *twice* in order to get clean white lettering that doesn't show through.

☆ That is, unless they use the **REVERSE PANEL** technique in which the board is painted white and then everything *but* the letters are painted in black.

This works well with block letters, but it is hardly practical with serif letters. It's also quite a challenge making elegant letter shapes when working this way around.

REVERSE RING CATCH

JUGGLING

Normally, when using *Juggling Rings* the catches are made by grabbing the vertical section of the closer side of the ring.

☆ A **REVERSE RING CATCH** is made by allowing the ring to fall *outside* the hand. The catching hand aims for the *far side* of the ring, allowing the near side to fall *outside* the arm.

A
B
C
D
E
F
G
H
I
J
K
L
M
N
O
P
Q
R
S
T
U
V
W
X
Y
Z

When you catch a ring like this it will be flipped as you bring it down and then throw it again, so you'll end up showing the *other side* of the ring to the audience (I'm assuming that you are working side-on).

This technique is used with **COLOUR-CHANGING RINGS** to produce a magical effect.

REVERSING A TRUCK UP TO A WALL

VEHICLES

This is a little secret taught to the author by a heavy goods vehicle driving instructor to solve the problem of knowing exactly where the back of your rig is when reversing up to a wall or a loading bay. It's a long way to the back of a big truck and *guestimation* is not really adequate.

MARK

☆ HERE'S *The* TRICK: You prepare your truck by parking it on level ground and placing a stone directly under the rear tail lights on the driver's side. Next you need an assistant with a small pot of white paint.

Now climb back into the cab and, while looking through the mirror, find a point on the side of your truck that lines up perfectly with the stone. Have your assistant mark the spot with a tiny dab of paint. If your truck is too posh for paint marks you can always use a piece of **GAFFER TAPE**.

Now when you reverse up to a wall you simply keep an eye on the mark's progress towards the base of the wall and you'll find that you can stop within an inch!

RIFFLE FORCE

MAGIC

The **RIFFLE FORCE** is a method of **FORCING A CARD** on a hapless volunteer in order to reveal it in an interesting way moments later.

☆ Make a *break* just above the card to be forced about halfway down the deck. You can keep the break open by pressing your little finger against it as you hold the pack in the left hand.

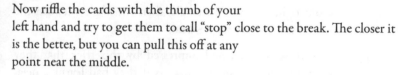

Make sure that the end of the deck facing the force is nicely squared off.

Now riffle the cards with the thumb of your left hand and try to get them to call "stop" close to the break. The closer it is the better, but you can pull this off at any point near the middle.

When they call out, you tilt the pack downward, frozen at that point in the riffle, and ask if they are sure. Make eye contact!

OK, now split the deck at the break and offer them the lower half so they can take off their card and examine it!

Gotcha!

A
B
C
D
E
F
G
H
I
J
K
L
M
N
O
P
Q
R
S
T
U
V
W
X
Y
Z

RIGHT ANGLE

GEOMETRY

A **RIGHT ANGLE** is a ninety degree angle, like the corner of a square. It's a very important angle that we take pretty much for granted.

It makes walls vertical, and floors flat, and allows us to make boxy things that stack easily.

If you're building stuff you'll almost certainly need to make perfect **RIGHT ANGLES** and that's why carpenters and builders have *Set Squares* which are simple devices designed to make it easy to mark out right angles.

☆ If you don't have a set square you can always use a piece of paper instead (with a little care) to mark off a neat right angle.

☆ The clever Egyptians, who were amazing builders of sometimes very huge things had a really cool and very simple way of marking out perfect right angles using ropes.

They used the **THREE-FOUR-FIVE TRIANGLE** technique: it turns out that if you get one piece of rope that is 3 somethings long, another that is 4 somethings long, and a third that is 5 somethings long (where *something* can be a foot, ten meters or a hundred yards)—and then you stretch the three ropes all out tight to make a triangle, then the angle between the two shorter sides is *exactly* a **RIGHT ANGLE.**

The Egyptians were so amazed and impressed by this trick that they assigned it an almost religious significance, as if they had learnt a deep secret of the Universe (which, of course, they had).

You'll find, if you look at their art, that the triangular loin cloths of the figures in their carvings are often 3-4-5 triangles.

☆ You can also make **RIGHT ANGLE** with a 5-12-13 triangle.

☆ Or you can use the construction for a **PERPENDICULAR BISECTOR** if you have ruler and compasses to hand.

RIGHT MIDDLE LEFT

JUGGLING

RIGHT MIDDLE LEFT is an easily learned three-object pattern, we'll assume you are juggling with balls.

It has an unusual throwing order: *right-right left-left...* and in **SITESWAP NOTATION** it is 423.

☆ Start with two in the right and one in the left.

Throw two throws of **TWO IN ONE HAND** with the right hand, starting with a column throw to the right, and following with a column throw in the middle.

Now throw two throws of **TWO IN ONE HAND** with the *left* hand, starting with a column throw on the left, and following with a column throw in the middle.

And so you continue, throwing *right-middle-left-middle...*

RINGING THE CHANGES

GRIFTING

RINGING THE CHANGES is a classic confidence trick in which the **GRIFTER** uses persuasion techniques in order to scam money from a shop assistant. It's a pretty despicable trick because the till will be light when it is reckoned up at closing time and the person operating it is likely to get into trouble from their employer. It's listed in *Every Trick In The Book* in the hope that the knowledge of how it is done will protect you from becoming a victim.

☆ The **GRIFTER** enters a shop and picks up between £11 and £12 of goods. This needs to be stuff they actually *want* or can sell on later—

A
B
C
D
E
F
G
H
I
J
K
L
M
N
O
P
Q
R
S
T
U
V
W
X
Y
Z

cigarettes are a popular choice. They go to the checkout and hand over a £20 note. The shop assistant will usually hand back a £5 note and some change. At this moment the **GRIFTER** *points to their change* and says, 'Hey, I gave you a twenty!'.

More often than not, when done confidently, the assistant will go 'Oh yes, I'm so sorry', and hand back an extra £10 note.

The **GRIFTER** actually ends up with *less* money than they started with, but they make a £10 profit in the goods they bought. Assuming that they knock the cigarettes out at the pub for, say, half price, they'll make around £5 per transaction. They will need a new £20 note for every scam.

If the trick fails because the shop assistant is on the ball they can simply pretend they have made an innocent mistake and leave with the goods.

☆ In another scam the **GRIFTER** seeks out a tired or inefficient shop assistant and walks up with about £3 worth of an assortment of goods, a £20 note and a handful of change that will make up the cost of the goods.

They hold out the note while the assistant enters the items into the till and as soon as the cash register opens they say 'Oh wait a sec, I've got the right change.' They fumble the £3 together while concealing the £20 note and hand the money over.

Just before the assistant closes the till they say 'Can I have the twenty back?'

Sometimes the assistant will simply hand back a £20 note and the **GRIFTER** leaves with a healthy profit. Other times the assistant will say either that they *already* gave it back, or that they never had it in the first place. A serious **GRIFTER** will argue this point and turn out their pockets to show that they don't have it any more and push the argument for as long as they think they can get away with it.

Sometimes this works and sometimes it doesn't but all they care about is not getting caught.

If things start to look really bad for them they'll suddenly *find* the £20 note, apologise and leave.

The really clever (and despicable) part of these scams is that it is very hard to *prove* that the **GRIFTER** was actually pulling a con.

Ripped Bank Note Trick

MAGIC / SILLINESS

Take a fresh £20 note, bring it up to your mouth as if kissing it and then mime ripping it in half quickly, while blowing hard on the paper. It will sound *exactly* as if you had ripped it in half.

Quickly fold it in half and repeat a couple of times.

Finally, slowly unroll the note to show that it is still intact.

Rizla ✠ Propellor

SILLINESS

Of all the tricks in this book, this was the most-suggested entry. The author has lost count of how many times people asked if he was planning to include "the one where you make a propellor from a cigarette paper."

The most popular brand of cigarette rolling papers in the UK is *Rizla croix* which first appeared in shops in 1866.

The name is short for *Riz Lacroix*. *Riz* means rice and croix is the French word for Cross. Hence we see the curious + in the name. The manufacturing company, originally in the paper-milling business, was founded by the Lacroix family in France.

The *Rizla Croix* logo is interesting, from a **SIGNWRITER'S** point of view, because it as very unusual piece of lettering. As well as containing the prominent 'croix' character the letters slope *backwards*, which is extremely rare in lettering. Moreover, the drop-shadow applied to them goes *up* and to the right (rather than the typical *down* and to the right).

A
B
C
D
E
F
G
H
I
J
K
L
M
N
O
P
Q
R
S
T
U
V
W
X
Y
Z

A
B
C
D
E
F
G
H
I
J
K
L
M
N
O
P
Q
R
S
T
U
V
W
X
Y
Z

This all, no doubt, was completely deliberate and was intended to ensure that the logo would stand out from the crowd—and the huge quantities of *Rizla Croix* papers sold suggests that this plan was a good one.

☆ Enough history! Take one of these fine rolling papers and lie it on the table so the central crease lies as a *valley fold* (see **ORIGAMI** for an explanation of this term) and fold up all four edges so that the thing resembles a tiny tea tray.

Don't worry about the corners, they never work out too neatly.

Now carefully lift up the device and touch your index finger to the centre of the underside of the "tray" and hold it there with a finger from your other hand.

Push your index finger through the air at about walking speed (some people do this by turning on the spot, and then release the steadying fingers.

With luck the paper will start to spin rapidly like a tiny propellor, and as long as you keep your finger moving through the air it will stay in place.

☆ The author has seen an expert Rizla+ propellor pilot keep four of these things spinning at once (two on each hand) in the style of a World War II Lancaster bomber.

It took the assistance of two "ground engineers" to help the pilot get the thing started.

Robot Bounce

JUGGLING

This is a nice simple three-ball *Square Juggling* move for **Bouncing Balls**. You'll need fairly well-developed mime skills to pull it off.

☆ Start by juggling a regular three-ball **Passive Bounce** to warm up.

Now instead of throwing the balls **Cascade** style you *lift* each ball to the opposite side of the pattern so that it drops perfectly vertically and then rises into the catching hand.

The trick is to make sure that the balls rise and fall in perfect straight lines, all of the sideways travel is in the hands which should move in a staccato and mechanical style.

☆ You can create a great effect by travelling this pattern sideways. To move to the right the throws are as follows:

The right hand, from a normal position, drops a ball *straight down*.

The left hand *carries* its ball right over and drops it into an imaginary column to the very far right.

The right hand makes a new column to the right of that..

The left hand makes a new column to the right of that.

And so you proceed.

It looks surreal.

A B C D E F G H I J K L M N O P Q R S T U V W X Y Z

A
B
C
D
E
F
G
H
I
J
K
L
M
N
O
P
Q
R
S
T
U
V
W
X
Y
Z

ROCK BALANCING

BALANCING

There are many things to do on the beach, but this is one of the more surreal activities you can indulge in in order to pass a few pleasant hours to the accompaniment of the crashing surf. You need a quiet mind, a steady hand and a beach upon which there are plenty of rocks.

☆ Seek out a large stable rock and then balance smaller rocks upon it. The trick is to seek out tall and pointy rocks and balance them on their finer points thus creating an improbable effect. You'll find that, with great care, you can *feel* rocks into the balance.

Although it will look as if the rock is balanced on a sharp point you will actually have sought out, by careful judgement, tiny tripods of connection between the rock being balanced and the one it is standing on. It is very important that the rocks are not ground together so as to produce rock dust, but rather gently "clattered" together into a stable balance.

This is a subtle and addictive skill which you'll acquire gradually as you work. One of the great advantages of balancing stones, as opposed to lighter objects, is that they are largely unaffected by wind on account of their weight.

At the end of your work you will be rewarded with a clear and mind and an impressive natural gallery of your work.

ROCKING THE BABY

YO-YO

☆ Throw a **SPINNER** (slam the **Yo-Yo** down so that it **SLEEPS**) and lift up your yo-hand so that the string falls just behind your thumb.

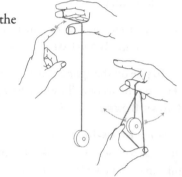

With the fingers of your free hand grab the *bight* of string between your yo-finger and thumb and pull it out to fashion a triangle through which you swing the **SLEEPING YO-YO** back and forth.

Finally drop the lot and flick the **Yo-Yo** back up into your yo-hand.

That's **ROCKING THE BABY.**

ROLA-BOLA

BALANCING

The **ROLA-BOLA** is a curious balancing device that you stand on. It can be highly entertaining to watch and skill-wise it is a little easier than a **UNICYCLE** to stay upright on.

☆ You need a short plank and a piece of sturdy tube about nine inches in diameter. The stuff they use for laying gas mains is pretty much ideal.

Some **ROLA-BOLA** artists stick small pieces of batten at the ends of the plank to stop it from rolling off completely.

The trick is to use a sideways slooshing motion to stay balanced—without letting the plank roll off the tube.

A
B
C
D
E
F
G
H
I
J
K
L
M
N
O
P
Q
R
S
T
U
V
W
X
Y
Z

A B C D E F G H I J K L M N O P Q **R** S T U V W X Y Z

☆ There are a couple of ways of getting on: a **SUICIDE MOUNT** is cool, but definitely not for beginners.

The normal method is to roll the plank off as far as it can go to one side as if making a jump-ramp for a bike, then place one foot over the roller and the other on the low end. Next you scoot the thing into a balance.

It'll take you a couple of days to get used to riding your **ROLA-BOLA** but, once learned, the skill will never leave you.

☆ Learn to juggle (or do something else that's clever) while on the **ROLA-BOLA** and you have a show!

☆ To pile on the agony you can use two planks, stacking the second above the first using a few **CIGAR BOXES** and ride that!

☆ Some **ROLA-BOLA** experts manage to go as many as four levels high like this and actually pile on each new plank *while they are riding*.

☆ A serious skill is that of riding the thing sideways! You can only manage a tiny "rock" in this position so your balance has to be good.

☆ You can, if you are so inclined, replace the tube with a ball! This requires you to rola- and bola in all *directions* and is horrendously difficult.

☆ For 1,000 points you can stack *two* **ROLA-BOLAS** on top of each other, at ninety degrees. It feels much like using a ball. This is *very advanced* and probably not worth the trouble of learning, except for your own satisfaction.

Whoah!

ROLLING A CANOE

BOATS

The trick of **ROLLING A CANOE** is an essential skill for slalom canoeists and people using canoe in very cold water.

The trick is often called the *Eskimo Roll* after the tough sea fishermen who invented the technique because bailing out of a capsized boat in the arctic would result in near certain death from exposure.

You'll need a boat with a spray deck—this is the waterproof gaiter that connects you to the boat in in a waterproof way. You'll also need to be totally proficient at bailing out of a boat safely, because your first attempts are doomed to fail.

To bail out you rip off the spray deck and then make a sort of forward roll to get your legs out of the cockpit.

Ideally you'll learn this trick in a nice warm swimming pool with a spotter at hand to save your life if things get messy.

The biggest problem you'll have is that of disorientation. It's all very well knowing what you have to do but once you capsize your boat you'll be upside-down and confused, you'll also be holding your breath which can make you panic and fumble.

A
B
C
D
E
F
G
H
I
J
K
L
M
N
O
P
Q
R
S
T
U
V
W
X
Y
Z

So, when you capsize, take a second to work out where you are, and most importantly, which way is up.

You should have previously rehearsed the method in an upright boat.

Get into the starting position by laying the blades on the water on one side of the canoe. Now sweep the leading blade out and away from the boat, then draw it in a big half-circle over your head, that's the stroke that will right the boat.

Now this isn't exactly what *really* happens when you roll a boat, but it's the best and simplest way of *thinking* about it,. Trust me on that one.

Here's how it works in practice: first you capsize, orient yourself and get the blades into position as you practiced in the upright boat. Now apply the stroke that moves the leading blade out and away from the boat. The paddle should be feathered so that it generates *lift* as it sweeps, the harder the blade is to pull the better you are doing.

As the blade sweeps you can start to lift the boat upright by forcing it to roll with your hips. When your head is nearly out of the water you can focus on pulling the blade back towards the boat. It feels like you are pulling it over your head (as you rehearsed before) because the boat is rolling.

The last part of the roll is achieved with a firm flick from the hips to drag the hull toward the blade and into an upright position.

This particular method of **ROLLING A CANOE** is known as the *Screw Roll* and is a commonly used roll in calm flat water.

In white water, where you are floating low in a foamy mixture of water and air, the screw roll is not ideal because the blade sweeps around just under the surface where it will not get much bite.

The *Storm Roll* is a solution to this. It works just like the screw roll except that the first sweep of the blade is straight *down* into deep water (where the paddle will get some purchase).

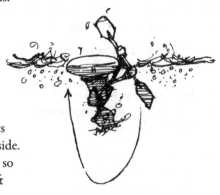

The leading blade starts out at the bow of the boat, and makes its way to the stern on the opposite side. You must get the feathering right so that the blade generates lots of lift throughout the sweep.

Another problem with capsizing in white water is that it is usually very shallow water, hence slalom canoeists wear crash helmets in case their heads end up banging on underwater rocks.

If you capsize in shallow water the best thing to do is to lie back on the rear deck of your boat.

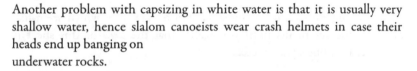

You can effect a roll from this position, the *Reverse Screw Roll*.

One arm is brought up over the head which places the paddle at the stern of the boat. The blade is then swept outwards, then over the head and finishes up near the bow of the boat.

It's exactly like a screw roll, but in reverse.

A
B
C
D
E
F
G
H
I
J
K
L
M
N
O
P
Q
R
S
T
U
V
W
X
Y
Z

ROOT TWO RECTANGLE

GEOMETRY

A Root Two Rectangle is a rectangle of such a shape that when it is folded or cut in half the two halves are of exactly the same proportions as the original.

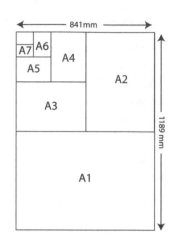

This only happens when the lengths of the sides are in the proportion $\sqrt{2}$ to 1.

The best-known practical use of this is in the European paper sizes named A0, A1, A2 and so on.

The most used of these is A4—the standard size on which letters are written and inkjet prints are inkjet printed. A6 is the postcard size.

A0 is the biggest size, it measures 841mm by 1189mm which seem like arbitrary measurements until you realise that the *area* of this sheet is almost exactly one square meter.

☆ It is easy to construct a **ROOT TWO RECTANGLE** with ruler and compass once you realise that the length of the diagonal of a unit square is exactly $\sqrt{2}$.

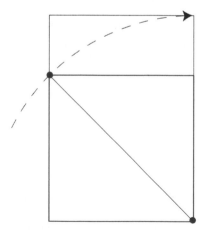

Mark out a perfect square and set your compass to the length of the diagonal.

Use that radius to mark a point on the extension of one side of the square to find the height of the **ROOT TWO RECTANGLE**.

See also **GOLDEN SECTION**.

ROMAN LETTERING

SIGNWRITING / TYPOGRAPHY

This has been staring you in your face for your entire life, but I bet you never noticed it. The fact is: we have not *one* but *two* distinct alphabets in written English.

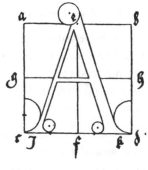

There are the CAPITAL LETTERS and the small letters, or as printers would have it *Upper Case* and *Lower Case** or as pedants would have it *Majuscule* and *Miniscule*.

Now it's perfectly true that a lot of the letters are quite similar in either flavour, but when you take a close look you'll find that a lot of them are very different indeed—you just never noticed! Here we go.

Here are the letters that are pretty much the same:

Cc Ii Jj Kk Mm Oo Pp Ss Uu Vv Ww Xx Yy Zz

Here are the letters that are *nearly* the same

Ff Ll Nn

And here are the letters that are *wildly different*:

Aa Bb Dd Ee Gg Hh Qq Rr

Our Capital Letters are descended from **ROMAN LETTERING** which were inherited from the great invaders themselves. Our Small Letters have a quite different pedigree and are a mishmash of different writing technologies from far back in the gloomy extremes of history.

Much **SIGNWRITING** is, traditionally, carried out in Capital Letters and a lot of signwriting is carried out in styles invented by the hands of signwriters themselves, rather than being executed in the mechanically perfect fonts so beloved by printers and users of computer publishing

---

* They used to keep hand-set type in two boxes, one stacked higher than the other!

A
B
C
D
E
F
G
H
I
J
K
L
M
N
O
P
Q
R
S
T
U
V
W
X
Y
Z

A
B
C
D
E
F
G
H
I
J
K
L
M
N
O
P
Q
R
S
T
U
V
W
X
Y
Z

systems. It is therefore important to be able to execute capital lettering in a style that looks pleasing and acceptable to the eye. Just about every typeface ever created in the Western world has been based on **ROMAN LETTERING**—so it would be a very useful exercise if you were to learn their rules of construction. Once mastered you'll never get the thick and thin bits of your letters muddled up again.

When the romans were carving their elegant letters into stonework they would first mark the job out using a flat brush, like a calligrapher's pen, which caused the thick and thin strokes to work themselves out naturally. They would then finish the job off with a chisel, adding the serifs as they went.

The classic roman letters are all based on squares and you cannot fail to have noticed that each alphabetical section of this book is introduced with a drawings showing the constructions for each letter. These constructions were worked out by the artist *Albrecht Dürer* in the sixteenth century.

☆ You'll learn an awful lot about laying out letters if you spend some time practicing making the letter shapes using a chisel-ended pencil or calligrapher's pen.

Take care to notice that the thick and thin strokes on the letter Z are the "wrong" way around.

The great typographer *Eric Gill* famously created the famous typeface *Gill Sans*, often wrongly thought of as the London Underground font*. This font took the bold and radical step of eliminating the serif that had been used for two thousand years.

ABCDEFGHIJKLMNOPQ RSTUVWXYZ

---

* Gill Sans was designed between 1928 and 1932 and was based on an earlier font called Johnston after its designer, Edward Johnston. Eric Gill also worked on the design. The Johnston font was commissioned in 1915 for use by the London Electric Railway Company (which later became the London Underground).

As you can see, the capital letters in Gill Sans follow pretty much all of the rules of proportion that make up the classic Roman style. They just do away with serifs and variations of stroke weight.

☆ If you want to write elegant *Block Lettering* (the signwriter's term for sans-serif work) then you'll need to be a master of Gill Sans.

ROMAN NUMERALS

CODES AND CIPHERS / TYPOGRAPHY

The Romans must have been terrible at maths, because their number system is an appalling mess. Nevertheless, **ROMAN NUMERALS** are used to mark important dates in a swanky sort of self-important way, and the accomplished trickster will be able to decode one at a single glance.

The number system is a curious mixture of addition and subtraction, where different letters represent different quantities. We'll start with I which represents *one*, harking back to the days of tally marks or finger-counting, where a single stroke or single finger meant one. The letter V represents *five* and possibly derives from a simple picture of a hand being held up to show all five fingers. Next comes X which means *ten* and this is supposed to represent two hands on account of it being formed from two V's. The letters L, C, D and M represent 50, 100, 500 and 1,000 respectively.

M	=	1,000
D	=	500
C	=	100
L	=	50
X	=	10
V	=	5
I	=	1

You start counting like this; I, II, III for 1, 2 and 3. Then you go IV for four (meaning *one less than five*). You then proceed V, VI, VII, VIII for 5, 6, 7 and 8 and IX for 9 (meaning *one less than ten*). 10, is of course X. You will *sometimes* see the number 4 written as IIII instead of IV.

There's a rule in roman numbers that the letters standing for powers of ten (M, C and X) can appear up to three times in a row, but the letters D, L and V, which stand for the "fives" can only appear *once*.

1955, the year in which *Radical Cheney* was born, is written MCMLV.

M	=	1,000	
CM	=	900	*(One hundred less than a thousand.)*
L	=	50	
V	=	5	

Here are few important dates:

MLXVI	1066, the year of the Battle of Hastings.
MMI	2001, a Space Odyssey
MCMXCIX	1999, year of the Great Party.

That last one was complicated. here it is broken down:

M	=	1,000	
CM	=	900	*(One hundred less than a thousand.)*
XC	=	90	*(Ten less than a hundred.)*
IX	=	9	*(One less than a ten.)*

If you are unusually bright you will have worked out already that, according to the rules stated above, the *largest* number you can write in **ROMAN NUMERALS** described so far would be MMMCMXCIX (3,999). To write higher numbers horizontal lines are written above the letters to indicate that their values are 1,000 times larger than usual. This means we can now write numbers up to 3,999,999, which looks like this:

$\overline{\text{MMMCMXC}}$MMMCMXCIX

An alternative style is to use lower case letters for the higher values.

mmmcmxcMMMCMXCIX

The obfuscation of this archaic system is demonstrated overleaf by listing all of the numbers from 1 to 500 alongside their corresponding Roman Numerals. Some of the numbers here require as many as eleven letters! As a test of their expertise, the reader is invited to work out the Roman version of the number 888 which requires twelve letters.

The longest possible **ROMAN NUMERAL** is 3,888,888 which is mmmdccclxxxvMMMDCCCLXXXVIII—a total of 27 letters long.

1	I	101	CI	201	CCI	301	CCCI	401	CDI
2	II	102	CII	202	CCII	302	CCCII	402	CDII
3	III	103	CIII	203	CCIII	303	CCCIII	403	CDIII
4	IV	104	CIV	204	CCIV	304	CCCIV	404	CDIV
5	V	105	CV	205	CCV	305	CCCV	405	CDV
6	VI	106	CVI	206	CCVI	306	CCCVI	406	CDVI
7	VII	107	CVII	207	CCVII	307	CCCVII	407	CDVII
8	VIII	108	CVIII	208	CCVIII	308	CCCVIII	408	CDVIII
9	IX	109	CIX	209	CCIX	309	CCCIX	409	CDIX
10	X	110	CX	210	CCX	310	CCCX	410	CDX
11	XI	111	CXI	211	CCXI	311	CCCXI	411	CDXI
12	XII	112	CXII	212	CCXII	312	CCCXII	412	CDXII
13	XIII	113	CXIII	213	CCXIII	313	CCCXIII	413	CDXIII
14	XIV	114	CXIV	214	CCXIV	314	CCCXIV	414	CDXIV
15	XV	115	CXV	215	CCXV	315	CCCXV	415	CDXV
16	XVI	116	CXVI	216	CCXVI	316	CCCXVI	416	CDXVI
17	XVII	117	CXVII	217	CCXVII	317	CCCXVII	417	CDXVII
18	XVIII	118	CXVIII	218	CCXVIII	318	CCCXVIII	418	CDXVIII
19	XIX	119	CXIX	219	CCXIX	319	CCCXIX	419	CDXIX
20	XX	120	CXX	220	CCXX	320	CCCXX	420	CDXX
21	XXI	121	CXXI	221	CCXXI	321	CCCXXI	421	CDXXI
22	XXII	122	CXXII	222	CCXXII	322	CCCXXII	422	CDXXII
23	XXIII	123	CXXIII	223	CCXXIII	323	CCCXXIII	423	CDXXIII
24	XXIV	124	CXXIV	224	CCXXIV	324	CCCXXIV	424	CDXXIV
25	XXV	125	CXXV	225	CCXXV	325	CCCXXV	425	CDXXV
26	XXVI	126	CXXVI	226	CCXXVI	326	CCCXXVI	426	CDXXVI
27	XXVII	127	CXXVII	227	CCXXVII	327	CCCXXVII	427	CDXXVII
28	XXVIII	128	CXXVIII	228	CCXXVIII	328	CCCXXVIII	428	CDXXVIII
29	XXIX	129	CXXIX	229	CCXXIX	329	CCCXXIX	429	CDXXIX
30	XXX	130	CXXX	230	CCXXX	330	CCCXXX	430	CDXXX
31	XXXI	131	CXXXI	231	CCXXXI	331	CCCXXXI	431	CDXXXI
32	XXXII	132	CXXXII	232	CCXXXII	332	CCCXXXII	432	CDXXXII
33	XXXIII	133	CXXXIII	233	CCXXXIII	333	CCCXXXIII	433	CDXXXIII
34	XXXIV	134	CXXXIV	234	CCXXXIV	334	CCCXXXIV	434	CDXXXIV
35	XXXV	135	CXXXV	235	CCXXXV	335	CCCXXXV	435	CDXXXV
36	XXXVI	136	CXXXVI	236	CCXXXVI	336	CCCXXXVI	436	CDXXXVI
37	XXXVII	137	CXXXVII	237	CCXXXVII	337	CCCXXXVII	437	CDXXXVII
38	XXXVIII	138	CXXXVIII	238	CCXXXVIII	338	CCCXXXVIII	438	CDXXXVIII
39	XXXIX	139	CXXXIX	239	CCXXXIX	339	CCCXXXIX	439	CDXXXIX
40	XL	140	CXL	240	CCXL	340	CCCXL	440	CDXL
41	XLI	141	CXLI	241	CCXLI	341	CCCXLI	441	CDXLI
42	XLII	142	CXLII	242	CCXLII	342	CCCXLII	442	CDXLII
43	XLIII	143	CXLIII	243	CCXLIII	343	CCCXLIII	443	CDXLIII
44	XLIV	144	CXLIV	244	CCXLIV	344	CCCXLIV	444	CDXLIV
45	XLV	145	CXLV	245	CCXLV	345	CCCXLV	445	CDXLV
46	XLVI	146	CXLVI	246	CCXLVI	346	CCCXLVI	446	CDXLVI
47	XLVII	147	CXLVII	247	CCXLVII	347	CCCXLVII	447	CDXLVII
48	XLVIII	148	CXLVIII	248	CCXLVIII	348	CCCXLVIII	448	CDXLVIII
49	XLIX	149	CXLIX	249	CCXLIX	349	CCCXLIX	449	CDXLIX
50	L	150	CL	250	CCL	350	CCCL	450	CDL
51	LI	151	CLI	251	CCLI	351	CCCLI	451	CDLI
52	LII	152	CLII	252	CCLII	352	CCCLII	452	CDLII
53	LIII	153	CLIII	253	CCLIII	353	CCCLIII	453	CDLIII
54	LIV	154	CLIV	254	CCLIV	354	CCCLIV	454	CDLIV
55	LV	155	CLV	255	CCLV	355	CCCLV	455	CDLV
56	LVI	156	CLVI	256	CCLVI	356	CCCLVI	456	CDLVI
57	LVII	157	CLVII	257	CCLVII	357	CCCLVII	457	CDLVII
58	LVIII	158	CLVIII	258	CCLVIII	358	CCCLVIII	458	CDLVIII
59	LIX	159	CLIX	259	CCLIX	359	CCCLIX	459	CDLIX
60	LX	160	CLX	260	CCLX	360	CCCLX	460	CDLX
61	LXI	161	CLXI	261	CCLXI	361	CCCLXI	461	CDLXI
62	LXII	162	CLXII	262	CCLXII	362	CCCLXII	462	CDLXII
63	LXIII	163	CLXIII	263	CCLXIII	363	CCCLXIII	463	CDLXIII
64	LXIV	164	CLXIV	264	CCLXIV	364	CCCLXIV	464	CDLXIV
65	LXV	165	CLXV	265	CCLXV	365	CCCLXV	465	CDLXV
66	LXVI	166	CLXVI	266	CCLXVI	366	CCCLXVI	466	CDLXVI
67	LXVII	167	CLXVII	267	CCLXVII	367	CCCLXVII	467	CDLXVII
68	LXVIII	168	CLXVIII	268	CCLXVIII	368	CCCLXVIII	468	CDLXVIII
69	LXIX	169	CLXIX	269	CCLXIX	369	CCCLXIX	469	CDLXIX
70	LXX	170	CLXX	270	CCLXX	370	CCCLXX	470	CDLXX
71	LXXI	171	CLXXI	271	CCLXXI	371	CCCLXXI	471	CDLXXI
72	LXXII	172	CLXXII	272	CCLXXII	372	CCCLXXII	472	CDLXXII
73	LXXIII	173	CLXXIII	273	CCLXXIII	373	CCCLXXIII	473	CDLXXIII
74	LXXIV	174	CLXXIV	274	CCLXXIV	374	CCCLXXIV	474	CDLXXIV
75	LXXV	175	CLXXV	275	CCLXXV	375	CCCLXXV	475	CDLXXV
76	LXXVI	176	CLXXVI	276	CCLXXVI	376	CCCLXXVI	476	CDLXXVI
77	LXXVII	177	CLXXVII	277	CCLXXVII	377	CCCLXXVII	477	CDLXXVII
78	LXXVIII	178	CLXXVIII	278	CCLXXVIII	378	CCCLXXVIII	478	CDLXXVIII
79	LXXIX	179	CLXXIX	279	CCLXXIX	379	CCCLXXIX	479	CDLXXIX
80	LXXX	180	CLXXX	280	CCLXXX	380	CCCLXXX	480	CDLXXX
81	LXXXI	181	CLXXXI	281	CCLXXXI	381	CCCLXXXI	481	CDLXXXI
82	LXXXII	182	CLXXXII	282	CCLXXXII	382	CCCLXXXII	482	CDLXXXII
83	LXXXIII	183	CLXXXIII	283	CCLXXXIII	383	CCCLXXXIII	483	CDLXXXIII
84	LXXXIV	184	CLXXXIV	284	CCLXXXIV	384	CCCLXXXIV	484	CDLXXXIV
85	LXXXV	185	CLXXXV	285	CCLXXXV	385	CCCLXXXV	485	CDLXXXV
86	LXXXVI	186	CLXXXVI	286	CCLXXXVI	386	CCCLXXXVI	486	CDLXXXVI
87	LXXXVII	187	CLXXXVII	287	CCLXXXVII	387	CCCLXXXVII	487	CDLXXXVII
88	LXXXVIII	188	CLXXXVIII	288	CCLXXXVIII	388	CCCLXXXVIII	488	CDLXXXVIII
89	LXXXIX	189	CLXXXIX	289	CCLXXXIX	389	CCCLXXXIX	489	CDLXXXIX
90	XC	190	CXC	290	CCXC	390	CCCXC	490	CDXC
91	XCI	191	CXCI	291	CCXCI	391	CCCXCI	491	CDXCI
92	XCII	192	CXCII	292	CCXCII	392	CCCXCII	492	CDXCII
93	XCIII	193	CXCIII	293	CCXCIII	393	CCCXCIII	493	CDXCIII
94	XCIV	194	CXCIV	294	CCXCIV	394	CCCXCIV	494	CDXCIV
95	XCV	195	CXCV	295	CCXCV	395	CCCXCV	495	CDXCV
96	XCVI	196	CXCVI	296	CCXCVI	396	CCCXCVI	496	CDXCVI
97	XCVII	197	CXCVII	297	CCXCVII	397	CCCXCVII	497	CDXCVII
98	XCVIII	198	CXCVIII	298	CCXCVIII	398	CCCXCVIII	498	CDXCVIII
99	XCIX	199	CXCIX	299	CCXCIX	399	CCCXCIX	499	CDXCIX
100	C	200	CC	300	CCC	400	CD	500	D

A B C D E F G H I J K L M N O P Q R S T U V W X Y Z

A
B
C
D
E
F
G
H
I
J
K
L
M
N
O
P
Q
R
S
T
U
V
W
X
Y
Z

ROTATING HEAD TRICK

MAGIC

Here is a great (if rather silly) illusion.

☆ Get a box big enough to go over your assistant's head (or *victim's* head if you prefer).

Cut a hole in the bottom for the neck and a hole in the front so you can see their face when they put it on.

You can decorate the thing if you like with dark red paint and baroque scrollwork to make it look showy.

☆ Sit your assistant down on a chair facing the audience and place the box over their head. Grab the box and make a show of slowly turning it around.

As the box turns your assistant should move with it, complaining of a stiff neck as they go. Turn the box a full 90 degrees and stop.

Now suddenly turn it another 180 degrees with great violence.

Your assistant should scream in pain at this point. Slow down and turn it the last 90 degrees—their head has turned full circle!

The trick is simply that once the box has turned 90 degrees the face of your assistant can no longer be seen, so while you turn the box the *hard way* they simply turn their head the *easy way* and the illusion is complete.

This is very funny when performed well.

Round Turn and Two half Hitches

KNOTS

☆ Take the free end of a rope and lead it around a pole.

Now make a second turn.

Finally, secure the end to the standing part with two **Half Hitches**.

This is a very common knot. It's easy to remember, secure and simple to tie.

It's also not too hard to untie especially if you *slip* the second **Half Hitch**.

Rule of Three

PSYCHOLOGY

☆ Surely you know this? The point is that the *third* time something happens it starts to get *funny*.

That's why so many jokes involve three characters; perhaps an Englishman, a Swede and a Belgian.

You can bet your last stick of chewing gum that it's the Belgian who will do the stupidest thing.

☆ With tiny children you can, say, toss them up high in the air and go 'Whee!' which is, of course, highly entertaining, but when you do it *three* times they will start to laugh, which more-or-less proves that the **Rule of Three** is hard-wired into the ancient reptilian core of our now hideously over-developed brains.

A B C D E F G H I J K L M N O P Q R S T U V W X Y Z

RULER TWANG TRICK

SILLINESS

This trick is pretty well known by school kids, but it's just possible that you have forgotten the happiest days of your life, or maybe you were so traumatised by the sheer boredom of it all that you have a serious memory block.

☆ Get a foot ruler and place it over the edge of a table so that about nine inches hangs over the edge.

Press down hard on the end to hold it in place with your left hand.

Twang the end of the ruler down so it vibrates with a dugga-dugga noise.

Now rotate it to shorten the amount overhanging the table, as the ruler turns the note will rise, in a loony tunes sort of way.

RUM, RAISINS AND PHEASANTS

POACHING

☆ Get a hypodermic syringe, raisins and some strong rum—*Wray & Nephew* is good.

Inject copious quantities of rum into the raisins (remembering to try a few yourself) and then stagger off to a place where pheasants hang about.

Scatter liberally on the ground and return an hour or so later.

The entire *nye** of poor birds will be drunk and incapable of flight (something they hardly excel in even at the best of times).

You, of course, will also be drunk, having found it far too fiddly to inject the *entire bottle* into your box of dried fruit. With luck you will be not quite as incapable as the poor birds. Bag up a few for the pot and head home before the gamekeeper catches you.

Alternatively, try some tricks from the old report below.

According to English law, next to the professional thief who takes forcible possession of property without the consent of its owner, there is no species of the genus lawbreaker, which displays more craftiness and less compunction in the shedding of human blood than the game poacher. Circumstances sometimes make him what he is, but in the majority of cases he is born to the mode of life he has adopted, and is as irreclaimable as the hardened thief of the slums. The professional poacher does not pursue his illegal calling for the love of sport, but, like the thief, he detests honest work, and derives unbounded satisfaction in being his own master.

Recently a representative of the fraternity favored the writer of this article with his views on poaching and the returns it yielded. He is fifty-three years of age and has always lived by poaching, excepting two years when he was employed as gamekeeper by Lord Stamford in the forest of Glenmore.

Attired in Scotch tweeds and heavy hobnailed boots, with a Tam o'Shanter for headgear, he presents the picture of a gamekeeper on duty. His face is slightly disfigured by a fierce poaching affray—the lower jaw projecting so far beyond the upper that he has difficulty when speaking in making himself intelligible. Four convictions are recorded against him in the police books, one of which carried with it one year's imprisonment without the option of a fine.

"My brother and myself," he said, "work together, and the partnership has lasted for twenty years. The engines, the terms by which the police designate our poaching instruments, include ferrets, dogs, snares, small nets for rabbit burrows, a larger size for winged game, and a double-barreled gun, which can be taken to pieces for concealment about the person.

"Our harvest time is from August till the end of the year, and during these months we have to work hard to make sufficient to keep us and our families for the rest of the year. Between the 9th and the morning of the 12th of August we have jointly made as much as 15s. per brace of grouse. It was, of course, the net that was used on such occasions for winged game, and it is the most destructive of all our 'engines.' The net is generally made of silk, and measures about 40 yards in length and 15 yards in breadth.

"The mode of working the net is very simple. When the moor or hill to be coursed is reached a lighted bull's-eye lamp of the smallest size is fastened on the head of a trained pointer dog. The ends of the net are fixed to poles 10 feet in length.

"When the poachers are ready to start the dog is unleashed and the men follow up, dragging the net along the ground. The zigzag movements of the dog are easily watched, and when he makes a sudden stoppage this is a certain signal that he is in the neighborhood of a covey of birds concealed in the heather or stubble. The poachers rapidly proceed to where the dog has taken up his position and make a semi-circle with the net. The dog leaps forward, the unsuspecting birds rise, and the chances are ten to one that they will rush into the upraised net.

"A covey numbers sometimes as many as a dozen birds, and in the early days of August, before the sportsmen invade the moors, I have seen us bagging twenty brace before the dawn of day. The risk of getting them to market is sometimes even greater than that of poaching for them. We confine ourselves almost entirely to winged game during August and September, beginning work about midnight and continuing, if not disturbed, till 5 in the morning. Sometimes we go by train a distance of twenty miles before beginning operations. Toward the end of September we abandon the moor and hill and concentrate our efforts on the low-lying grounds. We continue to work under cover of night and accompanied by a pair of dogs—'lurchers'—we usually select an inclosed turnip field. We stretch a net across the gate or entrance, the ends of which are held by both of us. The dogs never bark nor yelp, and at a signal bound into the field and drive the game into the net. Several fields in the course of the night are worked in the same way, and very often by this means we succeed in bagging a considerable number of rabbits and hares. Simultaneously with these night raids we do a great deal of ferreting during the day. The gamekeepers are subjected to the closest surveillance, and their movements watched by my sons and daughter. Should the keepers attend a marriage, funeral, ball, or any other local event, we utilize the opportunity thus afforded to the fullest extent. Ferreting is the easiest but not the safest method for rabbits. The ferret is put into the burrow, a net is placed on the exit, and if there is a rabbit within, the ferret, if properly muzzled, will drive it speedily into the net.

"The snare, though simply a piece of five-ply brass wire formed into a loop, requires more dexterity and ingenuity in 'setting' than any of the 'engines' used by the poacher. Perhaps in a stretch of ground a mile in extent there may be a hundred rabbit passes discoverable only to the experienced eye of the poacher. He sets the snares on the passes about four inches from the ground, when he 'rushes' the rabbits with a dog, and in the early morning when he goes to 'lift' the snares, he expects at least to have thirty or forty 'captures' out of 100 'set' wires.

"We seldom use a gun. It attracts too much attention, but in the dead of Winter I sometimes take a shot at a deer. We do not, however, sell the carcass, but retain it for home consumption. Venison does not net much to the poacher, and the risk in disposing of it is very great. Pheasants and black-winged game we frequently destroy with fermented barley. This is scattered on the ground, and the birds when they eat it become stupefied and are easily captured. The Summer months are a continual holiday, the monotony of which is occasionally broken by a day's salmon fishing."

The game laws are harshly enforced, particularly in the case of men of whom I am writing, who are taught from infancy that it is no crime to take a bird from the moor, a salmon from the river, and a stick from the wood.

---

* See Collective Nouns.

RUNAROUND

JUGGLING

There are a couple of amusing juggling patterns that are referred to as **RUNAROUNDS**.

☆ In the first, two jugglers share a **CASCADE** of three objects by running around each other while making alternate throws. The objects being juggled move just as they would in a regular solo pattern. The jugglers zoom around like crazy people each constantly **STEALING** the pattern from the other.

☆ Juggler B stands with a ball in each hand, juggler A stands behind.

☆ Juggler A throws a ball from their right hand, it passes up between B's hands and is caught in A's left hand.

☆ Juggler B throws with their left hand and juggler A reaches in and catches it.

☆ A and B have now swapped positions.

☆ Juggler B throws from their right hand, it passes up between A's hands and is caught in B's left hand.

☆ Juggler A throws with their left hand and juggler B reaches in and catches it.

☆ A and B are back where they started.

To learn this, start by making the throws *slowly* until it all makes sense and then wind it up to full juggling speed.

☆ An entirely different kind of **RUNAROUND** is done with three jugglers and six clubs. We'll call them A, B and C.

A always passes to B, B always passes to C and C always passes to A, but people run around while they are doing it.

A and B stand facing each other holding three clubs each. C stands to A's left.

At the start A starts passing a *Two Count** to B, while B starts throwing to C. Pretty soon A runs out of clubs and runs around to stand next to B, hopefully arriving just in time to receive C's first pass.

Every second throw is a pass, usually this means every right hand throw.

Shortly thereafter B runs out of clubs and runs over to stand at C's left shoulder, just in time to start receiving clubs from A.

Hilarity ensues.

☆ You may find it easier to rehearse this with just five clubs at first.

☆ Instead of passing the last club the jugglers have the option of *carrying* the club with them as they move into each new position. This allows for a very relaxed walk across the pattern.

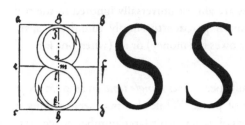

Salami Technique, The

GRIFTING

The **Salami Technique** is a notorious, effective, and *very* common method of stealing money.

The idea is simplicity itself: instead of stealing a *large* amount of cash in a single chunk, you steal hundreds, thousands or even millions of *tiny* bits of cash from hundreds, thousands or millions of different people. If you're careful nobody will notice, and even if a few do notice you can *still* get away with it because the individual amounts involved are so piffling—like the thinness of salami slices.

The classic rip-off works like this:

☆ In accounting, when tax is deducted or interest is added you can end up with accounts that hold amounts of money that do not work out precisely in pounds and pence, or dollars and cents. Since it looks messy to have amounts of money like £12.35670001 lying around in the books it is common practice to *round* such amounts up or down to the nearest penny or cent. There are complex and generally accepted rules, invented by clever statisticians, to make sure that when you do this to hundreds or thousands of accounts, the *total* amount of money in all the accounts works out to more or less what it would have been before. The usual rules go like this:

☆ If the amount after the second decimal place is more than half a penny, round it up to the next penny.

☆ If the amount is less than half a penny round it down.

☆ If the amount is exactly half a penny you round it up or down to the nearest *even* amount of pence.

These fair and reasonable rules are almost universally ignored in the real world. Instead it is *very* common practice to simply round any spare decimal digits *down* (when one owes the money) or *up* (when one is owed the money).

This scheme will earn about half a penny *every single time* an amount crops up that isn't a whole number of pence. While this may seem trifling it actually generates huge amounts of cash when a large number of accounts are being operated.

☆ Let me now describe, by way of an actual case history, a cunning **SALAMI TECHNIQUE** scam from my home town: the fine City of Bath in England.

In Bath there is a surfeit of cars and therefore a shortage of parking spaces. It has been calculated that two-thirds of the vehicular traffic in the City consists of people looking for places to park. These then, are the **MARKS**.

Now, wherever there *are* any parking spaces, there are parking machines: these machines don't actually park your car for you, they merely charge you for the privilege

Each machine is fitted with a digital clock which displays the time, or actually something *approximating* the time.

The person wishing to park approaches the machine, observes the incorrect time and inserts coins to buy some parking time.

The machine will take any coins fed into it, but it only awards extra time at 30p intervals, so you'll get exactly the same amount of parking time for 30p or 59p—that's the first trick and it's worth, on average 15p to the criminals (unless you manage to insert exactly the right amount of change, and when do you ever have exactly the right amount of change?)

Next, the digital clock on the machine displays the time *without* the seconds, and the ticket it issues (which you must display on your windscreen) is also printed without seconds.

This loses you an average of 30 seconds parking *every time you park*.

Finally, and this is the nasty bit, the clock is wrong.

The clocks are set by the maintenance people who operate as follows.

1: Set your wristwatch correctly.

2: Open up the door into the belly of the parking machine.

3: Set clock on parking machine so that the time it *displays* (without the seconds) is just one or two minutes *before* the time on wristwatch (again ignoring the seconds).

This is a very clever trick. Who is going to notice, let alone get bothered about, a clock that is one or two minutes slow?

This a real money-spinner. You see, when you buy your parking ticket it's already one or two minutes old—one or two minutes have *already* gone. You have, in short, been overcharged.

Parking in Bath costs 3p a minute and thousands and thousands of cars park every day. This multiplies up to a huge sum of money.

Mind you the evidence of the scam is in plain sight, on public display on the clocks of the parking machines, so it surely cannot be the deliberate policy of the local Council to commit so obvious a scam.

It is more likely, to be a scam operated by the bailiffs and debt-collectors who run the profitable business of collecting unpaid fines from people who have overstayed their tickets.

It's a dirty old world.

SAWING THE LADY IN HALF

MAGIC

The trick of **SAWING THE LADY IN HALF** * is based on a very simple principle—people are smaller than they look. Properly done this trick involves the use of a nicely painted box made in two halves, the head-end and the feet-end. The head-end has holes for the victim's head and hands to poke out through and the feet-end has holes for the feet.

---

* The author apologises for the rather sexist title which is, of course, traditional. It would be far more entertaining, in these enlightened times, if a lady was to saw a gentleman in half, especially if performed in the manner of an act of jealous revenge. Whether one could find a gentleman of sufficiently steely nerve to trust himself to the lady's saw is another matter.

A
B
C
D
E
F
G
H
I
J
K
L
M
N
O
P
Q
R
S
T
U
V
W
X
Y
Z

The two halves will be fixed
together with a pair of large
hinges with removable pins.

By pulling out one pin the two
halves can be swung open like
a door, by pulling out both
you can separate the two
halves entirely.

The lid of the head-end needs
to be able to open like a coffin.

To prevent the audience seeing into the separated halves there are two
slots, one in each half-box, just next to the join, and the illusionist will
have two boards (usually painted black) to drop into these slots.

Finally, each half needs to be on moveable stands so they can be separated
slickly and easily.

You need to make the boxes big enough to stash an entire human being *in
each half* but you need to make this less than obvious. As we have already
noted, people are smaller than they look, but you can help the illusion
along by doing a clever paint job on the boxes:

Paint the boxes in a nice bright colour (red is good) but then paint a two-
inch black edge around every face.

Finally add a nice stripe of yellow where the black and red areas meet and
stick some fancy scrollwork in the middle of the red bits. It *looks* as if you
have just decorated the box for show, but actually you have made it look
about four inches smaller in every dimension.

☆ To perform the trick you will need not one, but two assistants, and you
will have to have pre-arranged the whole thing, particularly with regard to
the shoes they are wearing. Prepare the trick by having volunteer *One*
conceal themselves in the foot-end.

Roll the entire rig onto the stage and ask for a volunteer, you will of
course, choose assistant *Two*. She lowers herself into the head end and the
lid is closed over her. Then you ask her to poke her feet out of the far end.
Assistant *One* does this.

It's traditional for the illusionist to tickle the feet at this stage, and for the unconnected head at the far end to laugh as if they were connected.

You pull out the huge comedy saw and run it down through the gap between the two ends making gruesome faces as you go.

It's traditional for the illusionist to repeat the foot-tickling after having sawn her in half—only this time the head has to say that it can no longer feel a thing.

Slide the two boards into their slots (ostensibly to conceal the hideous blood and guts from the audience) and swing the boxes apart.

The head then demands to be put back together again, so you pin the boxes back together, say some mumbo-jumbo, pull out the boards and lift the lid.

As the lady leaves the box the hidden assistant must pull their feet back though the holes—and that's it!

SCRATCHING A COIN FROM UNDER A GLASS

BAR BETS / OBJECT MANIPULATION

Here's an old one. Place a one pence coin under a glass which is supported on a tablecloth with two pound coins as shown.

You can make supports of two pence coins if you prefer.

The important thing is that the glass is high enough off the table to allow the one penny piece to slide out.

Now challenge someone to get out the coin without moving the glass or blowing or sliding anything under it.

HERE'S *The* TRICK: After your opponent has given up, simply scratch the tablecloth towards towards you with a fingernail. You don't need to move the tablecloth.

A
B
C
D
E
F
G
H
I
J
K
L
M
N
O
P
Q
R
S
T
U
V
W
X
Y
Z

SEALING A TIN OF PAINT

TRICKS OF THE TRADES

If you sometimes put away a partly-used tin of gloss paint and then get it out again a couple of years later you'll be used to finding the paint has skinned over, having dried a little inside the tin.

You'll be familiar with the inconvenience of breaking the skin before you can use the stuff again.

☆ The experienced painter has three tricks to stop this from happening.

Before replacing the lid drop in a dash of paint thinners. Next jam the lid on hard and bash around the rim with a hammer to make sure it's really seated properly as the slightest air leak will cause skinning.

Finally, just to ensure a perfect seal, turn the tin upside down for a moment so as to coat the join with wet paint.

That will pretty much guarantee a perfect seal.

SELF-SEALING ENVELOPES

FUN WITH SCIENCE

This doesn't work with every type of **SELF-SEALING ENVELOPE** but it works with most—and especially well if the envelope is slightly damp (so the paper feels soft and pliable rather than hard and crinkly.

☆ In dim light you peel the glue strips on the envelope apart slowly and steadily—you'll see a surreal blue glow.

Incredible!

See also **EXTRA STRONG MINTS**.

SELLOTAPE SIGNWRITING TRICK

SIGNWRITING

This is a cheap and cheesy method of banging out block letter signage by the mile.

It's not big and it's not clever but it is quick.

☆ Instead of **SNAPPING A LINE** for the top and bottom of each row of lettering you simply lay on a strip of Sellotape.

A
B
C
D
E
F
G
H
I
J
K
L
M
N
O
P
Q
R
S
T
U
V
W
X
Y
Z

A
B
C
D
E
F
G
H
I
J
K
L
M
N
O
P
Q
R
S
T
U
V
W
X
Y
Z

Now sellotape is *very* adhesive and there is a good chance that it will rip the top layer of paint off the board when you remove it. To prevent this you should de-tack it before applying it to the job by stretching it out and running it across the cloth of your jeans once before laying it down.

☆ Now you can get on with the lettering, and boy is it easy, especially I's which can be done in a single stroke. Bear in mind that O's and the pointy bits of N's should go slightly above and below the guide lines (see **ENTASIS**), so they will need to be faulted in after the tape is removed.

SEMAPHORE

CODES AND CIPHERS

SEMAPHORE, of one sort or another, has been in use since Roman times. It's a flag-waving code that works best when used from one skyline vantage point to another.

According to the *rules* the flags should be diagonally split into two colours: red and yellow are used at sea, blue and white are used on land.

SEMAPHORE has been overtaken by technology, first came the electric telegraph, then the telephone, the radio and finally the internet.

However, it's a cool thing to know and you can always amuse yourself by inserting rude messages into your *Club Swinging* routines. This was a popular trick in the legendary CAPTAIN BOB'S CIRCUS of the late twentieth century; as I recall from those heady days on the Island, the letter combination F.R.O. was often inserted elegantly into routines of otherwise high artistic merit.

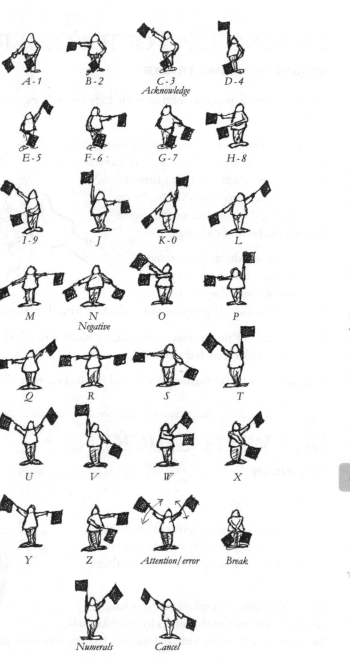

A-1   B-2   C-3 Acknowledge   D-4

E-5   F-6   G-7   H-8

I-9   J   K-0   L

M   N Negative   O   P

Q   R   S   T

U   V   W   X

Y   Z   Attention/error   Break

Numerals   Cancel

A B C D E F G H I J K L M N O P Q R S T U V W X Y Z

A
B
C
D
E
F
G
H
I
J
K
L
M
N
O
P
Q
R
S
T
U
V
W
X
Y
Z

SEWING UP YOUR FINGERS

SILLINESS / HAND TRICKS

This has been a popular routine with kids for as long as anyone can remember.

☆ The performer *mimes* the act of threading a needle with an invisible thread or hair picked from their head and then, starting with the little finger, they sew their fingers together one by one, making a big show of pushing the needle through the bone of each digit.

Finally they sew the thread through their lip, using this stitch as a pulley by means of which they can tug in the invisible thread and slap themselves in the face with their stitched hand.

☆ A variation of this routine *starts* with a stitch through the upper lip, and then a stitch through the eyebrow.

Tugging on the end of the invisible thread produces a sneer.

SEX WITH CHICKENS

SILLINESS

This is truly funny.

☆ After a meal out make a visit to the toilets taking a paper napkin with you. As you return tear the thing into tiny pieces and stash them all in your fist.

Back at the table you explain that you have just been propositioned in the toilets by a chicken who you went on to have sex with. Before they have time to work out what you mean by that bring your fist up to your face and cough hard through it producing a shower of "chicken feathers".

'It was quite nice actually!'

SHADOW PUPPETS

HAND TRICKS

In these days of energy-efficient light bulbs the shadows cast on bedroom walls are fluffy and blurred and no use for **SHADOW PUPPET** work.

But light a candle, for a special treat, and you can play the game of making creatures magically appear by careful handwork.

SHARPENING A KNIFE WITH A PLATE

SILLINESS

A nice trick for a trip to a restaurant.

You'll need a plain white plate that is devoid of markings for this one.

☆ Balance the plate on your knees against the edge of the table and then **MIME** giving it a good hard spin. Keep up the illusion of spin by wobbling it up and down on your knees as if it was mounted on a slightly eccentric bearing.

Take a steak knife and scrape it across the edge of the plate as if sharpening it. The noise is really quite convincing.

SHEEPSHANK

KNOTS

☆ Practical uses of the **SHEEPSHANK** knot include shortening a piece of rope (perhaps in the rigging of a ship) or isolating a weak or chafed section of rope.

When there is a load on a the knot you can cut right through it at the point marked X and it will not fail.

The "parlour method" of tying a **SHEEPSHANK** is an impressive trick.

Form three overlapping loops in the *bight* (centre) of a piece of rope, then pull the sides of the centre loop through the outer loops. With a little practice this can be accomplished in seconds almost by sleight of hand.

See also **Tom Fool Knot**.

SHEET BEND

KNOTS

The **SHEET BEND** is a knot for joining two ropes together, it's similar to a **BOWLINE** (which forms a loop in the end of a rope).

The word *bend* in knot-tying parlance is both a noun and a verb. *Bending* two ropes together means joining them with a knot, hence a *bend* is a knot intended for that purpose. The word *sheet* in sailing talk refers to a rope that is used to haul a sail about with. So a **SHEET BEND** is a knot for joining together ropes that you use to haul sails about with. See? We'll have you talking like a sailor in no time!

☆ The **SHEET BEND** is made by forming a loop in one rope, and an interlocking 'U' in the other. You can use the *rabbit story* to remember what to do if you like (see **BOWLINE**).

☆ The resulting knot is very secure, and also easy to untie. It's not quite as secure as the beautiful **CARRICK BEND** (which is the undisputed King of the Bends), but it is easier and quicker to tie.

☆ There is a very cool and quick way of forming a **SHEET BEND** which is described in the **BROKEN SHOELACE KNOT**.

A B C D E F G H I J K L M N O P Q R S T U V W X Y Z

A
B
C
D
E
F
G
H
I
J
K
L
M
N
O
P
Q
R
S
T
U
V
W
X
Y
Z

SHELL GAME

GRIFTING

The **SHELL GAME** (or *Thimblerig*) is a *very* old confidence trick that has been played out for profit by **GRIFTERS** since the Middle Ages. It is played out just like the **THREE CARD MONTE**, you cannot win the game. This is the criminal version of the **CUPS and BALLS** routine (and probably its origin).

THE EFFECT: The **GRIFTER** sets up a small table, or perhaps just a cardboard box, and lays out three walnut shells (or cups, or matchboxes or bottle tops or thimbles) and a pea (or another small ball). The ball is placed under one of the shells and they are shuffled, by sliding two at a time for three or four moves. An onlooker is asked to bet which shell the pea is under. Since it was pretty obvious where the pea ended up they guess correctly and seem to win. The game is played again and this time the onlooker makes an obviously stupid bet and loses. Now the **MARK**, who has been watching the game decides to have a go because they think they can do better—but they lose again and again and again.

☆ HERE'S *The* TRICK: The **GRIFTER** in this game is called the *Shell Man* or the *Operator*. The onlooker is actually a *Shill* (in fact everybody crowded around the table is either a *Shill* or a *Lookout*) and the job of a shill is to make the game look attractive to the **MARK**.

The simplest way of doing this is to have the pea drop out from under its shell and hold it in a simple **FINGER PALM** so that it isn't under any of the shells—then, no matter which one you pick, you'll be wrong! The *Shell Man* will then take your money with one hand (**MISDIRECTION**) while lifting a shell with their free hand as they drop the pea from its palmed position as if it was underneath all the time. You'll now be offered to play again for *Double or Quits*—which actually means you have to lay down even more money!

☆ Another technique used by the *Shell Man* is to secretly swap the pea from one shell to another during the shuffle. This is actually very easy to do and almost impossible for the **MARK** to detect.

The pea is now under one of the shells, but probably not where the **MARK** thinks it is. If they guess wrong the *Shell Man* simply reveals the real location and takes the money. If, by some amazing chance, the **MARK** guesses right then one of the *Shills* will immediately chime in with a higher bet on another shell. The *Shell Man* will say "Highest bets only! You can go next time!" then pay out to the *Shill* while making sure that the **MARK'S** stake remains on the table.

Just remember this: even if you know what's going on you are still going to lose because the *Shell Man* will never, ever, pay out a penny to the **MARK**. That's the only rule they ever play to—so don't be conned.

SHOTGUNNING

PSYCHOLOGY

SHOTGUNNING is a **COLD READING** technique used by psychics and sales people to give the impression that they have insight into their subject.

☆ The method relies on giving general statements that would apply to pretty much anyone but will *seem* specific to the person being read.

> "I'm seeing a younger person in your life, perhaps a child or a relative who has been in trouble lately and causing you some distress."

> "There has been a death in your family or a family close to you recently, perhaps heart disease or cancer?"

> "You felt misunderstood as a child and had difficulties at school or perhaps with a relative."

A B C D E F G H I J K L M N O P Q R S T U V W X Y Z

A
B
C
D
E
F
G
H
I
J
K
L
M
N
O
P
Q
R
S
T
U
V
W
X
Y
Z

"Some people in your family cause you a great deal of worry and concern but deep down you love them dearly."

"The spirits are with me now. Someone is calling, their name begins with a J or maybe a P…"

SHOTGUNNING is the standard method used by the writers of many newspaper Astrology columns to generate their predictions—you do realise that they just make their stuff up don't you?

SHOTGUNNING becomes **COLD READING** when statements like these are phrased as questions and used to encourage the subject to reveal more about themselves either by their verbal responses or body language.

See also **FORER EFFECT**.

SIGNWRITING BRUSHES

SIGNWRITING

Any craftsman can tell you that good tools matter. The same is true for signwriting. Get the right brushes. Signwriting brushes are longer than artists brushes generally are.

The chisels have every hair *exactly* the same length, whereas the points have long hairs on the outside and shorter hairs in the middle.

You'll only use points for very small serif lettering so they aren't nearly as useful as the chisels.

The brush you'll use most often will be your medium duck chisel—so you had better carry a spare.

Signwriting brushes are very expensive and almost unobtainable now since computerised plastic lettering took over all the boring work (and most signwriting is, let me assure you, very boring indeed). So you may have to source brushes from artists shops after all. Some of the synthetic materials are very good indeed, they just don't have any life or soul.

☆ Oh, and there is one other thing that you really need to know.

Always **GREASE YOUR BRUSHES!**

SHOWER

JUGGLING

For the *solo* juggler a **SHOWER** is a pattern in which one hand throws, and the other **FEEDS** back.

In the context of *Passing Patterns* a **SHOWER** is a *Two Count* passing pattern—one in which every second throw is a pass.

This usually means the right hand since people usually favour their right hands.

SILICONE BALLS ON A PARQUET FLOOR

JUGGLING

If you want just about the nicest **BOUNCING BALL** experience possible you need to get a proper set of **SILICONE BALLS** and find yourself a parquet floor. These floors are usually bonded to a concrete floor with a layer of pitch and consist of small polished wooden blocks laid in a herringbone pattern. They were very popular in schools in the 1960s and many survive to this day.

You won't get the highest bounce possible but the balls will bounce almost silently and you can create very smooth patterns on them.

Unlike the polished stone floors of airport terminals (which are also very good) a parquet floor is warm and will not chill the balls.

That might sound like a minor thing.

But it makes a big difference to your juggling.

A B C D E F G H I J K L M N O P Q R S T U V W X Y Z

A
B
C
D
E
F
G
H
I
J
K
L
M
N
O
P
Q
R
S
T
U
V
W
X
Y
Z

SINGLE STRING PLAIT

KNOTS

Take a length of cord and tie one end to something immovable like a door handle, the back of a chair, or your big toe.

Now make a **SLIPPED HALF HITCH** near the tied-off end.

You're ready to start.

Hold the end of the cord in your right hand and reach through the loop of the **SLIPPED HALF HITCH** with the fingers of your left hand and pull a small *bight* (loop) through, tightening up the loop of the half hitch around it.

Now reach through the *bight* and pull a new *bight* through—and keep going! Your hands will work in a see-saw motion and in no time at all the cord will have been plaited right up to the end.

Feed the end of the cord through the last loop and the whole thing is secure.

☆ To undo the plait you simply slip the end free and pull on it and the whole thing will unravel as if by magic. The plait works exactly like a chain stitch.

The **SINGLE STRING PLAIT** is useful for shortening rope to make it easier to store, it's also a nice decorative piece of rope work.

A
B
C
D
E
F
G
H
I
J
K
L
M
N
O
P
Q
R
S
T
U
V
W
X
Y
Z

SI STEBBINS ORDER

MAGIC

The **SI STEBBINS ORDER** is a simple way of ordering a pack of cards that allows you to perform some useful tricks.

You can cut a pack in **SI STEBBINS ORDER** without messing it up, but obviously you cannot shuffle it.

☆ Briefly, every card has a value three higher than the card before it, so the cards run in the order:

3 6 9 Q 2 5 8 J A 4 7 10 K —repeated four times.

The suits run in the order Clubs, Hearts, Spades, Diamonds (the mnemonic CHaSeD may help you here).

No matter how many times you cut the deck, the sequence will remain the same, albeit starting from a different place, so you can nonchalantly cut and recut the deck before starting a trick.

☆ Get someone to cut to a card in the pack.

☆ HERE'S *The* TRICK: Secretly glimpse the card above it and you should be able to work out what they chose.

☆ The ordering is also useful if you are trying to achieve a perfect **FARO SHUFFLE** because you'll be able to tell if your have cut to the 26th card by checking that both halves of the deck are showing the same value on the bottom.

A
B
C
D
E
F
G
H
I
J
K
L
M
N
O
P
Q
R
S
T
U
V
W
X
Y
Z

SITESWAP NOTATION

JUGGLING / MATHEMATICS

SITESWAP NOTATION is a terrifically clever method of describing juggling patterns which reduces the complex activity of juggling to a string of numbers. It has many interesting mathematical properties and has enabled jugglers to devise thousands of new juggling patterns.

It works like this:

Juggling proceeds in *Beats*, much like music. In a **THREE BALL CASCADE** (and in fact, most juggling patterns) the hands throw altern-ately* and there is one throw on every *Beat*.

It turns out that each ball in the **THREE BALL CASCADE** gets thrown every *three beats*.

In a Four Ball **FOUNTAIN** each ball gets thrown every *four beats*. In a **FIVE BALL CASCADE** each ball gets thrown every *five beats,* and so on.

In Siteswap notation we write down a series of throws as a series of numbers, so 333333333... is a **THREE BALL CASCADE** and 44444444... is a Four Ball **FOUNTAIN**.

Some patterns involve the hands making more complex sequences of throws for example 5353535353... is a pattern in which one hand acts like it is juggling five balls while the other acts like it is juggling three balls. The five-ball throws go about four times as high as the three-ball throws.

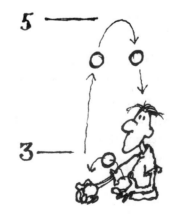

Instead of writing long sequences it is a convention to write just one loop of the pattern, 53.

Note that this is a four-ball pattern and the 4 is the *average* of five and three. It all works out very neatly because it turns out that for *every* Siteswap pattern, the number of objects being juggled is *always* the average of the numbers.

Note also that *even* numbers are always self throws, and odd numbers are crossing throws.

All you need to know now (as far as regular asynchronous patterns are concerned) is:-

0 is an empty hand
1 is a Feed (passing a ball directly from hand to hand)
2 is a hold, that is, not throwing a ball for a couple of *beats*.

So armed with this knowledge, here are a few simple and interesting patterns.

3   - a **THREE BALL CASCADE**.
31   - a **TWO BALL SHOWER**.
423   - an interesting and simple three-ball pattern.
53   - a four-ball pattern mentioned earlier.
501   - an unusual pattern for two balls.
534   - an interesting four ball pattern.
51   - a three ball shower.

☆ You can add (or subtract) the *length* of a sequence to any number in it and you'll still have a valid pattern (unless you end up with a negative number which is a Bad Thing To Do.

So we can start with 3, write it as 333 then add 3 to the first number to get 633 (which is a cool 4 object pattern). Similarly we can take 534 (which we mentioned earlier on) and subtract three from the last number to get 531 (a very nice three object pattern).

We could equally well have gone from 534 to 504 and then on to 501; all juggleable patterns.

Now all the rules so far have concerned patterns in which the hands throw alternately *(asynchronously)*.

Things change a bit when we go to *synchronous* patterns where the hands throw *at the same time*.

☆ Generally, in such patterns, the hands throw together *every other beat*.

Sometimes throws, and sometimes they don't. A popular synchronous pattern is the **Box** which is written as

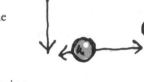

(4,2x) (2x,4)...

The parentheses denote pairs of throws being made at the same time.

The little x's indicate throws that cross, as opposed to the unadorned numbers that indicate throws that are caught by the same hand that threw them.

Interestingly the synchronous two-ball **Shower** uses the same weights of throws, just arranged a little differently as in:

(4x, 2x)...

Finally, let's take a quick look at **Multiplex** throws (where a hand throws more than one ball at a time. These are denoted by square brackets like this:

[3,2] 3 [3,2] 3...

Which is a **Three Ball Cascade** juggled with an extra ball held in one hand. Here's a sequence in which the extra ball is thrown into the pattern so that the juggler ends up doing a Four Ball **Fountain**.

[3,2] 3 [3,2] 3 **[4,3]** 4 4 4 4...

The bold type shows the **Multiplex** throw that turns the Cascade into the Fountain.

The reader who finds all this intolerably fascinating will find other books by the author that go into considerably more detail on this topic.

See also **Ladder Notation, Causal Notation**.

SIX BALL COLUMN BOUNCE

JUGGLING

This pattern is an easy way of juggling six balls.

You'll need a very smooth floor and six really good balls—get Silicone Balls.

According to Column Bounce technology you take the numbers of hands, add the number of columns and that's how many balls you are juggling.

So one way of doing six is to have four columns and two hands. This pattern is usually juggled synchronously (both hands throw together).

☆ Take three balls in each hand, imagine four columns ranged in front of you, take a deep breath and go!

Drop two balls into the two right-hand columns, let them fall and rise.

As they start to fall for the second time you drop two more balls in the two left-hand columns.

All four balls should hit the floor at the same time.

Now swing back and deliver the last two balls into the two right hand columns, exchanging them for the first two balls.

Now the patter proceeds much like **SPREADS**.

You drop two on the right, then tow on the left and so on.

Every balls bounces twice and on every bounce *four* balls hit the floor.

See also **FIVE BALL COLUMN BOUNCE**.

A
B
C
D
E
F
G
H
I
J
K
L
M
N
O
P
Q
R
S
T
U
V
W
X
Y
Z

A
B
C
D
E
F
G
H
I
J
K
L
M
N
O
P
Q
R
S
T
U
V
W
X
Y
Z

SLACKROPE WALKING

ROPE WALKING

Get hold of about twenty feet of rope—use stuff that is nice and thick and not too stretchy. Now tie it between two trees over some nice soft ground so that the dip in the rope is a couple of feet off the ground when you put your weight on it.

Now start work. It will take you at least a couple of weeks to start to get proficient at this—so take your time. It's like learning to ride a **UNICYCLE**; no amount of *thinking* about it will help, you need to train your body, not your mind.

Having said that, there are a few tips that will help you.

☆ Keep your gaze fixed on the anchor point at one end of the rope.

☆ Stand on one leg, both toe and heel resting on the rope. Keep the leg straight and balance from your *hips*.

☆ Hold something in your hands. If you're a juggler you could hold a set of juggling clubs. You'll find this helps enormously—until you try to juggle that is! The extra weight in your hands works like a *Balancing Pole*.

☆ Once you are managing to stand still for a little while you can try walking along the rope. Take this in very easy stages and bear in mind that the rope feels very different at the ends than it does in the middle.

☆ Walking *up* towards the end of the rope is a lot easier than walking *down* from the beginning.

☆ If you attempt a 180° turn you need to swap your gaze from one anchor point to the other *very* quickly.

☆ *Never* look down.

The real beauty of the slackrope is that you can rig it pretty much anywhere because the rope doesn't require tensioning like a tightrope does. It's even possible to sling a slackrope between two teams of strong men picked from an audience—so there's a complete street show that you can coil up and hang over your shoulder!

See also **BOUNCING ROPE**.

SLAP

JUGGLING

This trick was invented by *Radical Cheney*. Three balls are juggled as normal and one suddenly pings up high, apparently from nowhere!

☆ Learn the move with one ball first. You hold the ball in your hand, palm upwards, with the ball resting on your fingers. Now bring the ball-hand up *under* the heel of your opposite hand fairly hard and as the ball-hand stops the *twang* of your fingers will **POP** the ball very impressively.

It's a sort of sleight-of-hand throw. The ball goes up for miles but the hand hardly moves at all. It's good form to pull your hands *apart* as soon as the ball takes off, so it will seem to have been thrown from nowhere.

A
B
C
D
E
F
G
H
I
J
K
L
M
N
O
P
Q
R
S
T
U
V
W
X
Y
Z

A
B
C
D
E
F
G
H
I
J
K
L
M
N
O
P
Q
R
S
T
U
V
W
X
Y
Z

☆ OK, now juggle a **THREE BALL CASCADE** and make a slightly modified **UNDER THE HAND** throw. Instead of actually throwing under the hand you engineer the hand-collision we just learnt and **POP** the ball *way up* into the air. There should be an audible *slap* as the hands collide. Note that the hand not doing the throw is *holding* a ball during the move.

☆ You can make *every* throw a **SLAP** when you've mastered this.

SLAP OVER

JUGGLING

A **SLAP OVER** is a reverse-spin passing throw, much loved by high-speed club passers.

☆ The club to be passed is thrown almost **OVER THE SHOULDER** but actually never gets much higher than the juggler's elbow, passing just outside the wrist at high speed and spinning in the wrong direction!

It's sort of stretchy to throw!

SLAPPER

YO-YO

☆ Throw a **SLEEPER** with your **YO-YO** and let it sit for a second or two, then slap your yo-hand with your free hand and the **YO-YO** will zoom back up. It's nice effect.

☆ You can achieve a similar comedy effect by stamping a foot hard on the ground as you give the string a little tug.

SLAPSTICK

TOPIC

Slapstick is the name a style of comedy which is principally about fighting in an exaggerated and comic style. It often involves acrobatic comedy and liberal helpings of **CUSTARD PIES**. It was a common theme of the old silent movies featuring such greats as *Buster Keaton, Harold Lloyd, Charlie Chaplin* and *Laurel and Hardy*.

The term Slapstick refers to an actual device known as a slap-stick or *battachio* (in Italian) which consisted of two paddles of wood that produce a great deal of noise when struck against a  person, but does so without causing pain or injury. The *battachio* was used in *Commedia dell'Arte,* an old theatrical genre from which modern clown-ing evolved.

A rolled-up newspaper makes a good substitute, though the sound is more doffy than the note of a true slapstick.

SLEEPING

YO-YO

A **Yo-Yo** is said to be **SLEEPING** when it is spinning freely on the end of the string.

Some toy **Yo-Yos** will not sleep because they are cheap rubbish. Others have complex clutch-like devices built into them to make things "easier" for the performer, but a real **Yo-Yo** has a simple twisted loop of string that runs around an axle.

You can make the **Yo-Yo** sleep more easily by loosening the string (twist it *against* the wrap of the string) but it will also be harder to make it come back up again. Conversely, if you tighten the string it will sleep less easily, but will always want to come back to your hand.

Getting a nice long sleep out of your **Yo-Yo** is a basic skill and you should practice it until it is solid as a rock.

☆ Slam the **Yo-Yo** down hard and if you have a little "give" in your hand as it reaches the bottom it should sleep.

☆ To bring it back up just give the string a little tug and it should catch.

Basic tricks that require good sleeping skills are **WALKING THE DOG** and **AROUND THE WORLD**.

SLICING A BANANA

MAGIC / KITCHEN TRICKS

Anyone can slice a banana, but here's how to do it *without* peeling it first.

☆ Get a fine needle and work your way along the banana, poking in the needle and then scraping it up and down the inside of the banana skin. Each time you do this you'll create a slice *inside* the skin.

☆ When the banana is peeled it will be pre-sliced!

SLIPPED HALF HITCH

KNOTS

Form a loop in the middle of a piece of rope and push the standing part through it.

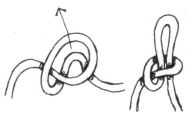

You have just made a **SLIPPED HALF HITCH**. Use it to hook the rope onto something, or perhaps to tie the **BROKEN SHOELACE KNOT**.

To untie the knot just grab
both ends and pull.

SLING

WEAPONS

The **SLING** is the hand-held equivalent of the awesome **TREBUCHET**.

With a small stone and a **SLING** a small boy can murder a giant, for so the Bible tells us. **SLINGS** are powerful, cheap, easy to carry and deadly. Ammunition, being simply small stones, is easy to find and this makes them pretty good weapons for revolutionaries and dissidents. Palestinian kids use them for lobbing rocks at Israeli soldiers—I'm not saying this is a *good thing*. It's just a fact.

A stone can leave a sling with frightening speed and howl through the air with a sound like a bullet turning end over end in a cowboy film. A blow to the head from a sling can easily be fatal. When learning you are advised to work alone and in a large clear area. At the time of writing the world record for a stone's throw with a sling is well over 400 yards.

☆ A standard **SLING** consists of a cord about four feet long with a pouch in the middle to hold the projectile. Sometimes, instead of a pouch an eye is spliced into the cord of just the right size to hold the projectile. the two cords are called the *retention cord* and the *release cord*. The retention cord is held in the hand throughout the throw, the release cord is dropped at the right moment in the swing so as to release the projectile.

A B C D E F G H I J K L M N O P Q R S T U V W X Y Z

A
B
C
D
E
F
G
H
I
J
K
L
M
N
O
P
Q
R
S
T
U
V
W
X
Y
Z

☆ The ideal projectile is something smaller than a golf ball and ellipsoid in shape—stones found in fast-running rivers can be ideal. The deadliest projectiles are small and made of lead.

☆ The standard throw is made overhand, like bowling a cricket ball. The weak hand holds the pouch of the loaded sling forwards and then drops it, the sling then falls behind the body, makes a loop behind the throwers head and is finally delivered forwards, with the release cord being dropped as it hits the top of the arc. Thus the sling turns through 720° during the shot. For added power the thrower can make a step forward during the throw.

A projectile can be delivered up to 200 feet in this way with lethal force and very accurately.

☆ For really long-range work you should use an underhand throw, swing the sling forwards and up and add power as it swings behind you, then drop the release cord so as to send the projectile upwards at about 45°. This method can deliver a hit over four hundred feet away!

Slings have been formidable weapons since the dawn of time and have been used by all the peoples of world save those in Australia—nobody knows why the antipodeans forsook the sling, perhaps the *boomerang* was the weapon of choice for the aborigines?

The ancient hilltop forts of England are designed to provide cover from attacking slingers as well as vantage points for pouring a rain of stone on the heads of the enemy. Huge caches of projectiles have been found in forts such at the one at Little Solsbury Hill, near Bath*.

SLOW CASCADE

JUGGLING

A **SLOW CASCADE** is the opposite of **HOT POTATO**—instead of keeping the objects in the air as much as possible, the juggler keeps them in the hands as much as possible.

Have you ever wondered why a beginner's juggling pattern is slow and lumpy whereas a more experienced juggler seems to run a smooth weave of movement? Well wonder now more—they are actually juggling different patterns.

☆ To juggle a **SLOW CASCADE** of three objects juggle **TWO IN ONE HAND** while holding a spare ball in the idle hand. Now swap the pattern from one hand to the other and then keep swapping on every throw. Feels slow and lumpy does it not?

In **SITESWAP NOTATION** you are juggling (4x, 2) (2, 4x) the 2's being long holds.

Human beings are rhythmical creatures and they tend to naturally lock on to integer-based rhythms which is why we have two-time, three-time, four-time and so on in music. Note that we don't spend much time on *two-and-a-half* time and other fractional rhythms.

This means that a beginner who has just learned to juggle a **SLOW CASCADE** cannot easily morph it into a true cascade by bringing the throw heights down gradually, they actually need to make a quantum jump from one pattern to the other.

* This is thought to be the site of the legendary Battle of Mons Badonicus where King Arthur is attributed with the defeat of the Saxons some time around 500AD.

A
B
C
D
E
F
G
H
I
J
K
L
M
N
O
P
Q
R
S
T
U
V
W
X
Y
Z

SMOKE RINGS

FUN WITH SCIENCE

We'll assume that you are entirely familiar with the idea that smoking is not big, clever, or cool and move right on.

A smoke ring is a toroidal vortex that is amazingly stable in air—they can last a while once formed.

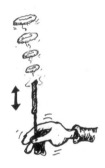

☆ Curiously, large smoke rings often travel slower than small ones, so it's possible to shoot a small ring through the middle of a large one.

☆ A really easy and safe way to make smoke rings is to take a stick of incense (or a joss stick if you prefer) and hold it vertically in still air. Now bob the stick up and down and you'll find that you can easily make dozens of tiny smoke rings. This will work with anything stick-like that is smouldering nicely—try using a charred twig from a camp fire.

☆ If you must work with cigarettes then please don't inhale, just fill your mouth with thick smoke and shape your lips as if you are about to whistle.

Now tap your cheek with a finger and you'll get nice little smoke rings flying out. Very cool.

☆ To blow a smoke ring *without* using a tapping finger you need to fill your mouth with smoke and push a little air out with your tongue while making a small out-breath. It's a hard move to get right and you'll need to practice a lot, which is obviously a *Bad Thing to Do* so we'll move right on.

See also **TOROIDAL BUBBLE**, **AIR CANNON**, **CIGARETTE PACKET SMOKE RING TRICK**.

A
B
C
D
E
F
G
H
I
J
K
L
M
N
O
P
Q
R
S
T
U
V
W
X
Y
Z

Snap Change

MAGIC

This little beauty is sometimes known as the "fastest trick in the world". It's also easy to learn.

The performer holds a single card and in an instant it has magically changed into another, in full view!

☆ Now in actual fact *two* cards are held up and shown to the audience, but pressed together this is unnoticeable. Typically you would place a low value card on top and something impressive like the Ace of Spades underneath.

The change is achieved by *snapping* the middle finger—which makes short work of moving the front card behind the back one.

Obviously this move is angle-sensitive, but it is very effective.

Snapping a Line

SIGNWRITING

SNAPPING A LINE is the preferred method of marking out the top and bottom lines for a piece of signwriting, unless of course you are using the **SELLOTAPE SIGNWRITING TRICK**.

This is done with a *Chalk Line* which is like a retractable tape measure except that string, not tape, is wound into the housing which is filled with chalk dust (usually blue in colour).

Pop a small pin into the board, hook the string

A
B
C
D
E
F
G
H
I
J
K
L
M
N
O
P
Q
R
S
T
U
V
W
X
Y
Z

onto it and then unwind to the other end of the job, pull the string tight and pluck it like a bass guitar string—snap! A perfect line appears.

On a shop front you'll need two lines, one at the top and one at the bottom. Here's a time-saving trick.

☆ Pop *two* pins in at the right hand end of the job one for the top line and one for the bottom. Hook the line onto the top pin and then climb down and move your ladder to the other end of the job. Pull the line tight while it is wrapped around the bottom pin and snap the baseline. Now flick the string off the bottom pin and repeat for the top line.

That's two more ladder-trips saved—we might even make some money today!

SNAPPING YOUR FINGERS

HAND TRICKS / MUSIC

Most of us know how to snap our fingers. You don't?

☆ It easiest to learn with the ring finger of your favourite hand (which is, more often than not, your *right* hand).

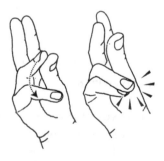

Pinch your ring finger and thumb together *hard* while resting your little finger against the base of your thumb. Now pinch *really* hard and then let your ring finger slide off the end of your thumb. *Snap!*

OK, it will sound a little dead for the first few tries but you'll get there.

Now most people learn this in both hands and feel pleased with themselves because they can now snap along to the groove sixties-style.

But the game does not end here.

☆ You can learn to snap *all* of your fingers with a little effort, which means that you can get four rapid snaps in succession from each hand—castanet-style!

☆ In the legendary film *The Blues Brothers* Jake and Elroy wile away a couple of tense moments, while they are waiting for the massed forces of Law and Order to take them down, by practicing a nice little **PARADIDDLE**-like move in which you make a fast little musical triplet by snapping a finger on each hand and then smacking the heels of your hands together. The three "notes" are played *very* close together.

☆ Rasta boys sometimes snap their fingers in an entirely different way. Place your thumb and middle finger together leaving the index finger loose.

Flick your entire hand downward and then stop suddenly, the momentum of your index finger will cause it to smack against your middle finger as your hand stops. It feels a little like cracking a whip.

SNATCH

JUGGLING

☆ A **SNATCH** is the action of catching a ball with the palm downward. It can be used to create a staccato moment in a juggling pattern. It's also useful when catching balls that are moving upwards, as in a **THREE BALL START**.

☆ Juggle a **THREE BALL CASCADE** and try catching balls with **SNATCHES**. It's good to work through the usual combinations:

- every right.
- every left.
- same ball every time.
- every ball.

Once you've done that you'll be an expert.

A B C D E F G H I J K L M N O P Q R S T U V W X Y Z

A
B
C
D
E
F
G
H
I
J
K
L
M
N
O
P
Q
R
S
T
U
V
W
X
Y
Z

SNOGGING AN INVISIBLE FRIEND

SILLINESS

Here's the classic teenager's trick of turning away from your onlookers and then wrapping your arms around yourself (as if to keep warm) as far as they will possibly go and then pretending to snog an invisible friend by having your hands roam around your back in a passionate manner.

Get the sight-lines right and it's very convincing, just make sure that your hands are acting like a member of the opposite sex, unless or course, you *want* people to think you are gay.

SOLAR SHOWER

TRAVELLERS TIPS

Get hold of about about 100 feet of black hose pipe (the hose from an old fire-reel would be perfect). Connect one end to a tap, and stick a shower rose on the other.

☆ On a nice sunny day you'll get hot water out of the other end, you can decide just how hot by turning the water up and down.

Just leave it running between showers otherwise it can get little *too* hot.

Regular green hose works too, but not nearly as well. Or you can just leave a watering can in the sun and hang it from its handle in a tree.

SOLAR OVEN

FUN WITH SCIENCE / PYROTECHNICS

Legend has it that the great Archimedes once came up with the idea of defending against attacking ships by reflecting the sun's rays onto them from dozens of highly polished shields. Where the multiple rays converged the wood from which the ships were made quickly burst into flame. This has since been confirmed as a practical technique by means of a modern experiment in which the reflected light from sixty such surfaces caused wood to ignite in just a few seconds.

☆ You should therefore be warned that converging reflected sunlight from a large number of mirrors onto a single spot can create, in empty air, the sort of temperatures that will melt skin from bone in a fraction of a second—be *very* careful!

Hang a kettle from a gypsy-style tripod in an open space on a sunny day and hand out a dozen small mirrors to your friends.

Get each of them to aim a reflected spot of sunlight onto the kettle and see how quickly you can boil it.

☆ Alternatively, attach each mirror to a stick poked into the ground and swivel them to get the same result.

Do not, under any circumstances, allow your hand into the hotspot— you'll be very sorry indeed.

Note that the sun moves across the sky quite quickly so your oven will not stay focused for long.

A
B
C
D
E
F
G
H
I
J
K
L
M
N
O
P
Q
R
S
T
U
V
W
X
Y
Z

A
B
C
D
E
F
G
H
I
J
K
L
M
N
O
P
Q
R
S
T
U
V
W
X
Y
Z

☆ If you can get hold of an old satellite dish (the larger the better) you can get a great result by covering the dish with aluminium foil and placing the item you wish to heat at the focus of the dish (which is where the receiver bit is normally placed).

When the dish is aimed at the sun the heat will be concentrated at this spot and make light work of any sausages that happen to be there.

It is quite common for satellite receivers to sustain damage as a result of the sun passing through the point that they are aimed at.

SPINNER

YO-YO

To throw a **SPINNER** you hold the **Yo-Yo** in your hand with the palm upwards, lift it high and slam it down towards the floor.

The **Yo-Yo** should run down the string at great speed and end up **SLEEPING** at the bottom.

It's very important to be able to throw a good **SPINNER** if you are going to learn more advanced tricks, some of which require huge momentum in the **Yo-Yo**.

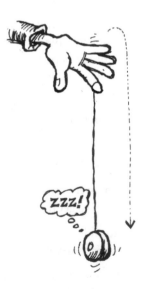

ZZZ!

SPINNING A GLASS

OBJECT MANIPULATION

This works best with a heavy tumbler or shot glass.

☆ Grip the rim of the glass with your fingertips and tilt it so that is is resting at an angle on the edge of its base. You'll need to experiment with the angle to get this right. Now give the glass a spin.

With care, and by adjusting the amount of tilt and spin, you can get it to teeter and totter for an amazingly long time before it finally cletters* to a stop. The movement of the glass can become what mathematicians call *chaotic* in that it may seem stable for a while but it can suddenly develop a serious teeter and fall over (and maybe break).

It's all very complex: no doubt some PhD student, even as I write, is working on an in-depth study of the dynamics of **SPINNING A GLASS**. No doubt this will be very time-consuming and involve many hours hard work at the bar.

SPINNING A HAT ON IT'S EDGE

HAT TRICKS

☆ Doff your hat so that you end up in a *Brim Grip*† and hold it up in front of you in your right hand.

---

* OK, so I just made that word up, but I'm sure you get the idea.

† In a *Brim Grip* your fingers are *outside* the hat as opposed to the *Crown Grip* in which your fingers are *inside* the hat.

A B C D E F G H I J K L M N O P Q R S T U V W X Y Z

Give it a quick spin clockwise and all your fingers out of the way except for your middle finger, which the hat will spin around on.

When it has made a full 360 degree spin, catch it again.

☆ With practice you can try 720 degree spins (two revolutions).

You can also spin a hat that is hanging down in a *Crown Grip*. Give it a fast little spin and get your thumb out of the way until it has gone around a full turn—at which point you catch it again.

You'll find that it helps to give the hat a slight upward toss as you make the spin.

SPINNING COINS

OBJECT MANIPULATION

All tricksters know how to spins coins properly, whether for calling heads or tails, betting on the length of the spin or just getting one gyrating across a table top or floor.

Here are some tips and techniques:

☆ *The Two-Handed Method:*
Hold a coin in an edge-balance with a finger from your left hand on a hard, smooth and flat table. Now give it a flick, just off centre, with your right hand. The coin will spin very fast anti-clockwise. Notice that it will tend to move in an arc away to the left, and then curve back towards you. With a little practice you can make it move like this reliably. Try tilting the coin a little before applying the spin.

☆ *The One-Handed Method:*
Hold the coin between the tips of your thumb and index (or middle)

finger of your right hand and **SNAP YOUR FINGERS**. You can impart a terrific spin this way. The coin will spin clockwise and tend to move in an arc to the right before curving back towards you.

One or two pound coins are particularly good spinners since they are heavy and compact.

☆ It's a fun game to see how many coins you can keep spinning at once (rather like a **PLATE SPINNING** routine).

Start with three or four and spin them all up. Take a little time between spins so that they will run out of puff one at a time instead of all at once.

Now as one coin starts to slow down you grab it and set it off again. On a good table you should have no trouble keeping four going (though collisions are often a problem).

Serious spinners can do seven easily.

☆ You can do a version of a two, three or four-object **SHOWER** pattern by taking advantage of the curved path the coins tend to follow when you let them go. Start with the two-coin **SHOWER**; spin one up, and as it curves away from your hand set the second one off and try to keep going.

See also **NEWTON'S COINS**.

SPLITTING NUNS

SILLINESS

This is a very long-term game to play with your friends. It is essential that it is carried out in a polite and well-mannered fashion. It was taught to me by my father—apparently it was all the rage in his university days.

☆ Nuns, as you can easily observe, tend to travel in pairs. The object of the game is to *split* a pair of nuns by the following methods for various point scores. The game is usually played over a long period of time (say a year).

A
B
C
D
E
F
G
H
I
J
K
L
M
N
O
P
Q
R
S
T
U
V
W
X
Y
Z

- walking between two nuns who are approaching you: *One Point*.
- allowing one nun to enter a doorway and then passing through the same door *before* the second nun: *Two Points*.
- One nun gets on a bus and buys a ticket, then you follow, and the second nun then misses the bus because there are no seats left: *50 Points*.

See also **URBAN GOLF**.

SPOON STUCK TO NOSE

SILLINESS

Get a cold spoon, breathe on it and press it onto your nose, handle pointing down.

It will hang there in a surreal and comical manner.

SPREADS

JUGGLING

This is a flashy way of juggling four objects.

☆ You juggle four objects using a synchronous **FOUNTAIN** so that both hands are juggling **TWO IN ONE HAND** in time with each other, but you make the pairs of throws first to the right and then to the left. You can work with any props you like but **BOUNCING BALLS** and clubs are the most dramatic to watch.

It's not an easy pattern by any means, but worth the effort of learning. The trick is to get the two halves of the pattern as *far apart as possible* as this creates great drama!

☆ With **BOUNCING BALLS** you can get the two halves of the pattern *ridiculously* far apart by letting the balls bounce *more than once.*

Obviously you will be using a sort of **COLUMN BOUNCE** technique.

☆ By extension there is a clever pattern called a **SIX BALL COLUMN BOUNCE** which *feels* like **SPREADS** but which uses, as the name suggests, six balls.

Curiously it is actually *easier* to juggle than a regular **FIVE BALL BOUNCE**.

Don't you just love tricks like that?

Yes you do!

SQUEALING FAN BELT

VEHICLES

If your fan belt is squealing it is probably loose and you should adjust its tension, or have a motor-mechanic do this for you, before your battery goes flat because your alternator is no longer generating enough power.

However, sometimes a perfectly well-adjusted fan belt will squeal and squeak just because it's settled into that mode, and this can be intensely annoying.

☆ HERE'S *The* TRICK: Pull out the dipstick from your engine and place just one tiny drop of oil onto one of the pulleys that the belt runs over and it will never squeal again.

A
B
C
D
E
F
G
H
I
J
K
L
M
N
O
P
Q
R
S
T
U
V
W
X
Y
Z

STAGE PUNCH

STAGE FIGHTING

The trick of faking a punch to the head, whether on stage or in film, is to take advantage of the *angles*.

☆ Mime a punch to your partner's face, but *miss* by punching short. They should mime receiving the blow by jerking their face away from the punch. Take care of the angles and get the timing right for a convincing effect.

☆ In the film world appropriate bone-crunching sound effects are added in post-production. The people that do this are known as *Foley Artists* (so now you know what *that* means). They routinely use everyday objects to create their sounds: the sound of a punch can be made by slapping a raw steak.

☆ If you are working live then you can add your own sound effect by smacking your spare hand hard on your chest to create a nice dull thud. Crack a handful of celery in the hand at the same time and you have foleyed a broken jaw.

See also **FAKE SLAP, LET GO OF MY EARS!**

STAR JUMP CLIMBING TRICK

CLIMBING / ACROBATICS

This trick is a favourite of street entertainers wanting to draw large crowds to watch their shows. It's long been known, among such artists, that two things that will draw a large crowd are **FIRE AND HEIGHT**. Thus a typical successful show will often end with the performer or performers juggling or manipulating fire while riding high unicycles, walking on slack ropes, or perhaps while one stands on the shoulders of another.

The **Star Jump Climbing Trick** can be used where two architectural columns stand a few feet apart. The climber needs supple ankles and grippy shoes to pull it off.

☆ They place one foot on one column a few inches off the ground, and then with great confidence, jump up and place the other foot on the other column. If there is enough grip and the columns are a suitable distance apart they'll be able to stand there quite happily.

Not only that, but by *jumping* in this position they can move themselves up between the columns a hop at a time until they reach an impressive height.

Don't make the mistake of going too high until you have learned how to descend as well, it's a bit of a knack.

A
B
C
D
E
F
G
H
I
J
K
L
M
N
O
P
Q
R
S
T
U
V
W
X
Y
Z

A
B
C
D
E
F
G
H
I
J
K
L
M
N
O
P
Q
R
S
T
U
V
W
X
Y
Z

STARTING A RELUCTANT DIESEL ENGINE

VEHICLES

This is a truly great trick and surprisingly few people know it.

Here's the scene: you have a diesel-engined truck and it's a cold and foggy January day and the battery is a little low. The engine is good, but it's cold and when you crank it the poor old lump of metal grinds slowly around and just can't quite manage to turn over fast enough to fire.

☆ HERE'S *The* TRICK: Stop turning that key and lift the engine cover. Now pop off the air cleaner to reveal the big round hole that leads into the inlet manifold.

Lick the palm of your hand and place it over that hole, completely blocking it. Now get someone to crank the engine. It will struggle for a second and then suddenly start to turn over very fast—at that moment you lift your hand away and nine times out of ten the engine will fire up and start. You are now an instant hero. People will openly weep.

```
THEM: How did you do that amazing thing?'

YOU: Simple! When I blocked the intake the engine had no
air to suck in because I created a vacuum. Since there
was no air in the engine, there was nothing to compress.
This meant very little resistance to stop it from turning
over and so it span up to a good speed. When I took my
hand off, the momentum of the engine carried on for long
enough to suck in some air - squeeze it down - and fire!
```

☆ You should always start a cold and heavy engine with the clutch fully depressed—that way the starter motor doesn't have to spin the gearbox over as well as the engine. You get a lot of drag from a cold gearbox.

☆ If the engine is being a real pig you can get a small ball of newspaper, set fire to it and drop it into the inlet manifold as you crank the damned thing.

Sounds like a terrible idea doesn't it? But it's fine. The heat should help the thing to fire and a little bit of newspaper ash will not harm anything.

STEAL

JUGGLING

In juggling a **STEAL** is the act of one juggler removing one object or even all the objects from another's pattern—while it is running.

☆ The easiest **STEAL** is from the front.

Get your partner to juggle a nice steady **THREE BALL CASCADE** and steal it off them by placing your hands into the pattern *above* their hands.

The most common problem is that of hand collisions.

☆ A *side-steal* is more audience-friendly. Stand to your partner's left and focus on balls heading for their left hand.

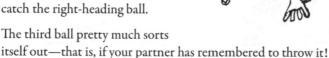

When you go in for the steal you grab one of these left-heading balls with your left hand, then immediately reach across to catch the right-heading ball.

The third ball pretty much sorts itself out—that is, if your partner has remembered to throw it!

Quite often the *stealee* is so dumbfounded by the proceedings that they just stop juggling.

If this happens, bash them on the head with a beanbag and try again.

☆ You can steal off each other continuously—see **RUNAROUND.**

A
B
C
D
E
F
G
H
I
J
K
L
M
N
O
P
Q
R
S
T
U
V
W
X
Y
Z

A
B
C
D
E
F
G
H
I
J
K
L
M
N
O
P
Q
R
S
T
U
V
W
X
Y
Z

STEPPING THROUGH A BROOM

ACROBATICS / SILLINESS

This is one of those "bet you can't do this" tricks with a clever solution.

☆ Get a nice big broom or just a nice big broom handle. Hold it in front of you with a hand at each end, palm downwards. That's the starting position.

The challenge is to end up with the broom *behind* you—without letting go—and without simply stepping over it the easy way.

This seems impossible unless you know the secret, and even then it's a bit of a contortion.

☆ HERE'S *The* TRICK: You lift your right leg and take it around the *outside* of your right arm before stepping down *behind* the broom.

Now take your left arm up, behind your head (yes, it's a stretch) and down. Finally step backwards over the broom with your left foot and you've won the bet.

See also **TEA TOWEL BEHIND THE BACK**.

A
B
C
D
E
F
G
H
I
J
K
L
M
N
O
P
Q
R
S
T
U
V
W
X
Y
Z

STEPPING THROUGH A POSTCARD

PAPER TRICKS

☆ Hand a pair of scissors and a piece of card (around postcard size) to the **MARK** and challenge them to cut a hole in the card and then *step through it!*

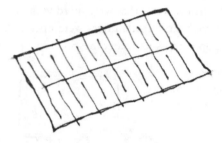

Fold the card in half, cut it carefully as shown above then open it up. The greater the number of zigs and zags, the larger the ring of card you end up with.

Needless to say you should have practiced this beforehand: you don't get points for merely understanding the *principle* of tricks—you have to be adept at putting them into *practice*.

STEREOSCOPY

FUN WITH SCIENCE / TECHNICAL WIZARDRY

STEREOSCOPY is the trick of creating 3D (three-dimensional) images in 2D media, such as the printed page or the computer screen. There are various ways of doing this and some cool tricks to learn.

People see the world around them in 3D, that is with *depth*. This is because the human being has two eyes, each of which sees the view ahead from a slightly different angle. This is known as *Binocular Vision*. The human brain uses the slight difference between the images seen by each eye to create the perception of depth.

A **STEREOSCOPIC** image is one designed to present two slightly different views of a scene, one to each eye. One type of stereoscopic image is the *Parallel Stereogram* which was invented by the great scientist *Charles Wheatstone* in the 1840's. Wheatstone was the first person to explain how binocular vision gave the impression of depth and went on to invent the *Stereoscope*, a device used to view stereograms.

The images themselves were made with cameras that were fitted with two lenses. They captured two images each time the shutters were operated. The resulting images were hugely popular in Victorian times.

A typical stereoscope of the period was a hand-held device on which the stereogram was mounted, the eyes being focused on the two images by means of two lenses.

It wasn't long before it was discovered that stereograms could be viewed *without* the aid of a mechanical device. All it took was a little practice.

This fine stereogram entitled *Stereograph as an Educator* from 1901 shows a woman improving herself with a stereoscope in the comfort of the drawing room.

The trick is to hold the stereogram up in front of you and gaze at infinity, as if focusing on the horizon.

You'll find that the two images, provided they are not *too* far apart, will align with each other, though they will be seen out of focus.

It is now possible, though not that easy at first, to focus the eyes on the stereogram while keeping the eyes pointed straight ahead.

Your brain will object and make you squint and squirm because it thinks that when the eyes are aimed at the horizon it should also *focus* on the horizon, but if you practice for a little while you'll pull off the trick and the image of the lady in the drawing room will suddenly spring into 3D.

The limitation of this technique is that the images in the stereogram cannot be further apart than the eyes which rather limits the size of picture you can look at.

This is because the trick of aiming your eyes so they *diverge* (as they would have to do with large pictures) is almost impossible to learn.

Enter then, the *Crossed-eye Stereogram*.

These are exactly like parallel stereograms except that the images have been swapped. The right eye's picture is on the left and vice versa. You need to learn the trick of *crossing* your eyes (as if looking at something really close) while focusing them on the images (which are a little further away).

The trick is to look at the image and then hold up your index finger about halfway between your eyes and the stereogram. Now focus on your finger and move it forward or back until you can arrange things so that the two images overlap. Once they match you must re-focus on the picture *without* uncrossing your eyes.

It is hard to master both parallel *and* crossed-eye viewing—just as it is hard to master a **THREE BALL CASCADE** when you have previously learned a **TWO BALL SHOWER**. Your brain just won't let you do it right. Chances are you'll master one or the other, but not both.

☆ You can make your own stereograms with an ordinary digital camera, computer and a colour printer, provided that whatever subject you are photographing is stationary when you photograph it.

Simply line up your shot, take a picture, then move the camera to the right one eyes-width and take the shot again.

Get the two pictures into your computer and then stitch them together so that one image sits to the side of the other. If you prefer parallel stereograms put the right hand image on the right, if you're more of a cross-eye viewer put it on the left.

Remember that, for parallel stereograms, the images should not be separated by more than the distance between your eyes.

Print the images out on a piece of paper and be amazed! Here is a typical view of the author's desk in the form of a parallel stereogram.

The skill of parallel-viewing is the one required of looking at *Autostereograms* or *Random Dot Stereograms*. These use a very clever technique to hide a three-dimensional picture in a single image.

Usually there are a couple of dots placed above or below the picture to aid you in aligning your eyes.

It's quite a knack learning to look at these things but after a little effort you should see it jump out into 3D.

This technique was first invented in 1979 and went on to become very popular in the 1990's mostly because of the *Magic Eye* series of books— much to the annoyance of the many people who just cannot get the knack of viewing them.

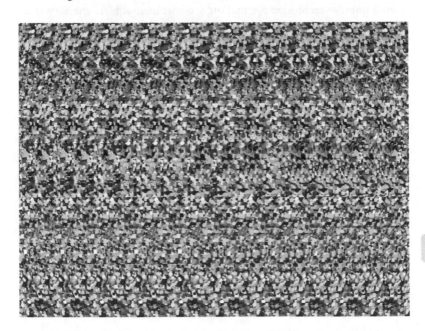

An autostereogram typically uses random dots or a repeating pattern as the basis of the image, but one anonymous and clever person managed to generate an amusing version based on simple plain text:

A B C D E F G H I J K L M N O P Q R S T U V W X Y Z

```
-----------------------------*----------------*------------------------------
here gold slim where gold slim where gold slim where gold slim where gold slim w
ly dog camel silly dog camel silly dog camel silly dog camel silly dog camel sil
eird dish goat weird dish goat weird dish goat weird dish goat weird dish goat w
cky bank mile lucky bank mile lucky bank mile lucky bank mile lucky bank mile lu
d stop rook brand stop rook bran stop crook bran stop crook bran stop crook bran
wasting ill ton wasting ill to wasting pill to wasting pill to wasting pill to w
 your host plant your host plan your ghost plan your ghost plan your ghost plan
s time pot stands time pot stand time spot stand time spot stand time spot stand
egg diet please egg diet please egg diet please egg diet please egg diet please
y a hit fool many a hit fool many a hit fool many a hit fool many a hit fool man
junkyard camels junkyard camels junkyard camels junkyard camels junkyard camels
dise fender paradise fender paradise fender paradise fender paradise fender para
ittles bitter skittles bitter skittles bitter skittles bitter skittles bitter sk
y lucky wow! very lucky wow! very lucky wow! very lucky wow! very lucky wow! ver
-----------------------------*----------------*------------------------------
```

Once you have amused yourself by discovering the secret hidden message you might care to examine the text carefully and see if you can work out exactly how it was done. A clever trickster should be able to construct their own secret messages this way.

A long-popular technique for making stereograms requires the viewer to wear specially coloured glasses. A stereo-pair of black and white photographs are taken and then they are printed on top of each other; one view is printed in red ink and the other in green. When viewed through red/green glasses, the right eye (with the red filter) sees only the green ink (which appears as black) and the left eye (with the green filter) sees only the red ink, which also appears as black.

☆ Before closing this entry, which is already very long by *Every Trick In The Book* standards, some mention must be made of *Long-Baseline* **STEREOSCOPY**, an amazing technique that reveals things that the eye just cannot see.

You have probably never noticed that your visual perception of depth is dulled by distance. It's easy to perceive the different depths of objects in the foreground, but much harder on objects in the far distance. This is because the differences between each eye's image become smaller and smaller as objects get further away.

To reveal the shapes of far-away things, like mountains, take two photos separated by a long distance, perhaps as much as 100 yards. After making your stereo image you'll be rewarded with an image that reveals the true shape in a way that you could never have seen with your own eyes.

You may have noticed that when using binoculars your sense of depth is increased on account of the wide separation of the lenses.

STICKING A GLASS TO THE WALL

SILLINESS / FUN WITH SCIENCE

☆ Chuck some lemonade at the wall, it sticks, big deal. But how about sticking it to the wall while it is still inside a bottle or a glass?

Now that would be amazing, if it were possible, and it turns out that it is!

☆ You need a bottle of pop, or a pint of something else in a straight glass. You also stick it into the *corner* of the wall, not onto the flat wall itself.

The bottle or glass needs to be carrying a little condensation on its surface, and the wall needs to be just right.

A plain papered wall, or painted plaster works best.

Simply push the glass into the corner, push down a little until you feel the wall *bite* it a little and let go.

If you were making a bet on this I hope you remembered how vital it is to **ALWAYS GET THE MONEY LAID ON THE TABLE**.

STICKY PENCIL TRICK

PSYCHOLOGY / HYPNOTISM

☆ Chose a willing subject and explain to them that this magic trick only works with lead pencils.

Pens or crayons just will not do.

This is not actually true, but it sets the victim up for a little hypnosis.

Hand them two pencils and ask them to push the flat ends together *hard* for about a minute.

Make sure it's really hard and tell them to keep the ends flat together.

A
B
C
D
E
F
G
H
I
J
K
L
M
N
O
P
Q
R
S
T
U
V
W
X
Y
Z

Now ask them to try and gently pull the pencils apart.

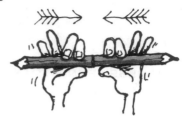

They will seem to stick together and then suddenly pop apart—it's a really convincing hypnotic illusion.

Enjoy!

STICKY FORK CATCH

JUGGLING

There's no actual cutlery *fork* involved here, we're using the term to describe the juggler's method of catching a ball so that it rests between two fingers.

This simple trick is a sleight-of-hand move in which a ball is bounced off the floor and then gets caught on the back of the juggler's hand.

What makes it surreal is the way that the ball seems to lock onto the hand as if it had hit fly-paper.

☆ Get a **BOUNCING BALL** and toss it ahead of your with terrific back-spin (or **ENGLISH** if you like).

Let it bounce up to a **FORK CATCH** in your throwing hand.

If you get this just right the ball will stop dead.

If it "burns" a little as it hits and tears the small hairs out of the back of your hand then you are doing it right.

STINGING NETTLES

GARDENER'S TRICKS, SURVIVAL

Stinging nettles were introduced into the British Isles by the Romans in order to make life difficult for the locals.

Well I'm a local and I take exception to this so here are a few useful things to know about Stinging Nettles:

☆ They do not sting when they are flowering.

☆ If you grasp a nettle firmly they don't sting—the spines are designed to attack things that merely brush past.

☆ If you sting the back of your hand lightly every day for a couple of weeks you'll build up an incredible resistance to them and find that you can walk through nettle beds with hardly an itch.

☆ They make a very nutritious base for a stew. Just use them as you would cabbage or spinach.

STRETCHY ARM

SILLINESS

Here's a trick that amuses children.

It uses some very simple **MISDIRECTION**.

A
B
C
D
E
F
G
H
I
J
K
L
M
N
O
P
Q
R
S
T
U
V
W
X
Y
Z

☆ You need to be wearing something with long sleeves, stand facing a small child and hunch up one shoulder discretely so that the sleeve of one arm covers your whole hand except for the fingertips while the other hand hangs normally—completely out of the sleeve.

> 'Oh no! One of my arms has shrunk!'

you say looking from one hand to the other. This, of course, is the **MISDIRECTION** as it draws attention away from your shoulders.

> 'Maybe I can stretch it back again!'

With your "normal" hand you grab the fingers of your "short" hand and tug them a few times. On each tug you allow your hand to drop a little more until it's back to normal. You declare:

> 'Thank goodness for that!'

> 'Again! Again!' says the child.

☆ The trick can be extended to the whole body.

If you are wearing suitable clothing you'll find that it's possible to hunch and compress your whole body to such an extent that you can lose several inches of height. Most of this height loss will occur in the spine, but another couple of inches can be lost in the neck and more in the knees. In this shortened state you and a short co-performer can start a dialogue. As the conversation proceeds you can slowly grow until the roles are reversed. Obviously a relevant script is required to turn this into a proper performance piece.

☆ The author, who happens to be an unusually tall person, finds most modern cars a little cramped when driving. He sometimes amuses his passengers by getting into a car and scrunching right down so he *looks* like he is comfortable and after a while he suddenly declares that either the car is getting smaller or he is getting bigger and slowly expands in the driving seat until his head is bent sideways by the roof. It is amazing to see how much a person can appear to grow in a small car.

STRETCHING ROPE TRICK

MAGIC

The magician presents three pieces of rope of obviously different lengths: one short, one medium and one long.

The six ends are all brought together and then each hand takes three ends. The hands pull apart and all three ropes are suddenly the same length.

The illusion of the ropes stretching to the same length happens in plain sight, which makes for a very effective trick. Entire street performances have been based on this one trick, so it's well worth learning.

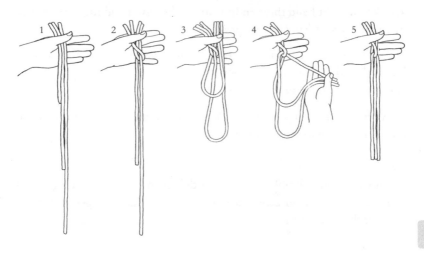

Take five feet of magician's rope (that's soft white rope to the uninitiated) and cut it exactly in half.

Take one piece and cut it a third of the way along.

You now have three lengths of rope, a short one, another double the length and a third three times the length of the smallest piece.

Take some white **GAFFER TAPE** and bind the ends.

☆ HERE'S *The* TRICK:

1: You start by showing your audience that you have three unequal lengths of rope: a short one, a middle one and a long one. As you show the three ropes you tuck them under the thumb of one hand so they hang down freely.

2: You explain that, for the purposes of the illusion you are going to tuck the end of the small rope up with the others. This is a crucial step. You lead the hanging short end *under* the hanging long rope and back under your thumb—all unseen by the audience who are out in front of you.

From this point on the trick is pretty much self-working.

3: Pick up other two free ends and tuck them under your thumb. You now have six ends held up between your thumb and forefinger.

4: Take the right hand three ends in your other hand and then, firmly and dramatically *stretch* the three ropes out.

5: As if by magic they all now seem to be the same length—except that we know that the short rope is looped around the long one. The join is conveniently hidden in your hand.

☆ After the stretch the performer peels off the medium sized rope from one hand and holds it up with the other.

   "That's one!"

Then with a little fumble it *seems* as if the second rope has been grabbed and shown whereas in actual fact the performer has swapped the single rope for the linked pair.

   "That's two"

Finally the medium piece is held up with the other hand.

   "That's three!"

After this demonstration all three ropes are scrunched up into a ball and blown on in a magical sort of way. One by one they are pulled out of the tangle to reveal that we're now back where we started with a short rope, a medium sized rope and a long one.

STRING THROUGH NECK

MAGIC

This is a pretty convincing illusion based on a simple sleight of hand.

☆ Make a loop from about five feet of string—thus it ends up stretching to two and a half feet between your fingers.

Hold it behind your neck with both thumbs. Look dead serious (Samurai warrior style is good) and bring your thumbs together in front of your face. With a big "Ha-wah!" (again samurai style is best) you pull your hands apart *hard* and the string appears to have passed right through your neck!

The secret is that while you were looking so serious and pulling all those stupid faces you dropped your thumb out of one loop and picked up the opposite loop with your index finger.

Stupid faces? No, clever **Misdirection!**

STUCK IN MUD, SAND OR SNOW

VEHICLES

☆ When your vehicle is stuck in mud, sand or snow with its wheels spinning there is one simple thing you can try before you start looking for a tow. Let your tyres down.

A
B
C
D
E
F
G
H
I
J
K
L
M
N
O
P
Q
R
S
T
U
V
W
X
Y
Z

Letting them down just a little (so they start to get splodgy) can help considerably. Letting them down to really low pressures (around 10–15 psi) can help *a lot*.

Be warned that your tyres may spin on the rim when they are at low pressure—which can cause two different problems depending on whether you have inner tubes fitted or not. You probably don't, since inner tubes are practically historical items but if you do have inner tubes the valve can get ripped out as the tyre spins.

If you are tubeless then the seal between the rim and the tyre may get broken when the tyre spins and the tyre could fall off the rim altogether.

Mind you, you're already stuck—so you might as well try it!

Once you get the vehicle moving you can avoid getting stuck again by following the great rule of off-road driving: drive as *slow* as possible, but as *fast* as necessary.

SUBSTITUTION CIPHER

CODES AND CIPHERS

The simplest code of all is the **SUBSTITUTION CIPHER** in which every occurrence of one letter is replaced by another.

It's not the best way of sending secret messages since you only have to take a glance at it to realise that you are seeing a coded message, and the text can be pretty easily decoded by applying the techniques described herein under the heading **FREQUENCY TABLE**.

☆ To encode and decode your messages you'll need a *key* which is a list of all the letters of the alphabet on one line and the letters they encode to on another. You can make up a key by simply scrambling the alphabet any way you like:

```
A B C D E F G H I J K L M N O P Q R S T U V W X Y Z
Y D E F G N B O P Q Z A C R S T H J K L M U V W X I
```

Using this key we can encode the *plaintext* HELLO into the *cipher* OGAAS and likewise decode it back again.

☆ It's a little cumbersome having to hulk a complete key around with you so a neat trick is to agree a *code-word* with your co-conspirator from which you can both quickly make up a key when required. Let's use the code-word TRICKY as an example. First write the alphabet down on a single line as before, and then, on the next line, write the code-word and then continue along the line writing down all the letters of the alphabet that you have *not already* written:

A B C D E F G H I J K L M N O P Q R S T U V W X Y Z
T R I C K Y A B D E F G H J L M N O P Q S U V W X Z

In this example HELLO would encrypt to BKGGL.

Obviously, if you choose a code-word in which letters repeat you'll still only use each letter once.

SUICIDE MOUNT

UNICYCLING

☆ Stand your unicycle in front of you with both pedals in the horizontal position.

Leap onto the machine so that both feet land on both pedals and your bum hits the saddle *all at the same time.* Now ride off immediately to hold your balance.

Don't miss for goodness' sake!

☆ The suicide mount is also used by riders of the **IMPOSSIBLE WHEEL**, albeit with the variation that your bum does not have to hit the saddle— because there isn't one.

It is the only way to mount one of these machines.

A
B
C
D
E
F
G
H
I
J
K
L
M
N
O
P
Q
R
S
T
U
V
W
X
Y
Z

A
B
C
D
E
F
G
H
I
J
K
L
M
N
O
P
Q
R
S
T
U
V
W
X
Y
Z

SULPHUR HEXAFLUORIDE

FUN WITH SCIENCE

This alarmingly-named substance is actually non-toxic.

☆ **SULPHUR HEXAFLUORIDE** is an odourless and colourless gas with a density of 6.3 grammes per litre at sea level. This is very heavy since the regular air that we breathe weighs just 1.2 grammes per litre.

Sound travels slower through heavier gasses, so if you breathe a little **SULPHUR HEXAFLUORIDE** into your lungs it will make you speak with a big low gruff voice. Similarly, if you breathe **HELIUM** (a light gas at just 0.18 grammes per litre) you will speak with a tiny little squeaky voice because sound travels faster in lighter gasses.

Breathing **SULPHUR HEXAFLUORIDE** is potentially dangerous because the gas, being so much heavier than air, can end up stuck in the bottom of your lungs and cause partial suffocation. You must therefore finish off the trick by breathing deeply while doing a **HEADSTAND** in order to let the gas escape.

SUITCASE WALK-AROUND

OBJECT MANIPULATION

Here's a nice bit of business with the suitcase you are using to carry your props. When done well it's a very funny move.

MOTIONLESS!

☆ Walk around the suitcase while holding it with the fingers of one hand. Aim to keep the suitcase *perfectly still* as you move around it. Your fingers will need to do a sort of *Cane Twirling* move to keep their grip.

SUNDIALS

FUN WITH SCIENCE

The great geomancer and part-time druid *Radical Cheney* is reputed to have said, *"if one is going to build a sundial, one may as well build one that tells the right time."* He then proceeded to embark on some elaborate geometrical calculations and constructed a device that was notable for telling, not *Greenwich Mean Time* but *Trebarwith Time*—which is about twenty minutes *layderon* in the Cornish manner of speech*.

By learning from Cheney's curious methods we can learn the correct way of telling the time from the shadow cast by the sun by an architectural device.

☆ The first thing to do is to establish the direction that points to the celestial north. The celestial north pole is somewhat like the cartographical north pole, except that it is a three-dimensional entity—it points *up* as well as north! Just how far up depends on your latitude. At 51° north (roughly where this book is being written) the direction to the celestial north pole is True North horizontaly, plus a vertical elevation of 39°. It can be a very fiddly line to find so the author recommends the use of a twenty foot scaffold pole on a nice starry night. The pole must be rigged so that one can view *Polaris* through the length of the tube. Polaris is the North Star, located on the end of the handle of the big saucepan that people once thought to resemble a bear. Due to the precession of the equinoxes, a cyclic wobble in the Earth's axis (taking about 25,700 years per wobble) the North Star is rarely at the exact true north of the heavens, but it has been pretty damn close for a while and will remain so for another few hundred years.

Interestingly, the temporary location of this unusually bright star at the north of the night sky has coincided with humankind's relatively recent ability to navigate the globe in small ships and 'discover' continents like the Americas and Australia. They were there all along of course, and inhabited by people, but not by *civilised* God-fearing people like us.

---

* If something is to happen *layderon* in Cornwall it will be happening *d'rekly.*

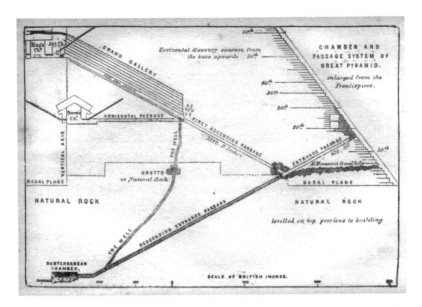

Another star that occasionally occupies this prestigious point in the heavens is *Thuban* also known as *Alpha Draconis*. It is sometimes (wrongly) thought that Thuban pointed true north at the time the Great Pyramid was being constructed at Giza (a date that is usually given as 2560BC). In fact it's closest approach was in 2795BC, a couple of hundred years earlier.

The Pyramid, it is alleged,* was aligned on a true north line by surveying a line pointed at Thuban by means of a Descending Passage dug into the bedrock of the Giza Plateau. As the huge structure was raised above ground the builders are supposed to have reflected the image of the star in

---

* Radical Cheney, the author of *The True Nature of Things*, objects to this widely-proposed and oft-quoted theory pointing out that the descending passage falls at an angle of 26° 18' 10" whereas the latitude of the Great Pyramid lies at 29° 58' 45" north. The result of this aberration is that the line of the passage misses the true celestial north pole by 3° 40' 35"—a metaphorical mile! He suggests that *Thuban* must have been off-centre by just this amount at the time of construction, in which case it would have been aligned with the passage briefly just once every twenty-four hours. Cheney explains, citing some fearsome astronomical calculations that Thuban would have passed through a true north line at precisely of 26° 18' 10" in 2205BC (which suggests that the passage was aligned 355 years *later* than commonly thought). He also points out that Thuban would only have been observable between August and January because during the remaining months its passage would have been obscured by daylight.

a pool of water lying at the junction between the Descending Passage and an *Ascending Passage*. Thus the baseline could be surveyed upwards into the rising stonework.

So as you work with your scaffold pole try to enjoy the feeling that you are doing something that has been done by clever people a *very long time ago!*

The end result of all this work is that you find a line that lies exactly parallel to the direction of the axis around which the earth spins.

Once you have found your north line you can go to bed and resume work in the light of day.

The work you need to do is to construct a *Gnomon*, this being the name of the sticky-up bit that will actually cast the shadow. You can either have it pointing up from a horizontal dial, or stick into a generally south-facing wall, or make it the axis of a celestial sphere. Hey, you could even just use the pole itself! Whatever you do, please make sure that your gnomon is *exactly* parallel to the line you discovered with the scaffold pole. If it isn't then your Sundial's accuracy will wax and wane with the seasons and you will end up being early, late or both.

Now you need to carve, paint or construct a marked surface for the shadow to be cast on. You'll be marking the hours of the day around it when you get to the calibration stage so consider how you are going to do this.

On a vertical wall it is probably best to get out your signwriting kit and paint the hours on. On a flat surface, like the ground or a plinth you could carve the hours, or place rocks in appropriate locations. If you are making a celestial sphere you'll need to build a circular belt from steel or copper and hang it around the gnomon like a wide belt.

Now here comes the really tricky part: you are, no doubt, used the idea that when it is twelve noon in London it is also twelve noon wherever you happen to be. This is not really the case, it's just a matter of convention. You see, noon is supposed to be the point in the day at which the sun is at its zenith in the sky, and this happens about half an hour *earlier* in the far east of England than it does in the far west. This is why East Anglian school children can be setting off for school in daylight, while the poor Cornish kids are stumbling off in the dark.

A
B
C
D
E
F
G
H
I
J
K
L
M
N
O
P
Q
R
S
T
U
V
W
X
Y
Z

The English invented a sort of time called Greenwich Mean Time which was based on the sun's position in the sky when observed from Greenwich, which is in London. The rest of us simply had to suffer the consequences. Then, as if to add insult to injury, a further nonsense was added with the invention of British Summer Time which kicks the clocks out by an hour in the summer, making everybody horribly miserable when the clocks go *back* in the autumn*, but ridiculously happy when the clocks go *forward* at the beginning of the summer—leading to the oft-enthused-about long summer evenings which we all enjoy so much.

It's a nightmare. I cannot understand why people can't just get up when it's getting light (as they have for the countless millennia before the State decided to mess with the clocks).

Anyway, the standardisation of time across the country means that you cannot easily plot out your hour-markers by geometry, but instead you are best off watching the shadow move for a whole day and making pencil marks every hour. Each hour will need to be marked with two numbers, one for BST and another for GMT. You can paint or carve these in a permanent fashion later on.

Once completed, your **SUNDIAL** will be a thing of usefulness and beauty for many years to come. It does not need batteries or winding and when the weather is poor you have the excuse that you had no idea what the time was—and *that* was why you never made it into work.

SUPERMAGNET

FUN WITH SCIENCE

"Any sufficiently advanced technology is indistinguishable from magic," said Arthur C. Clarke, and so it is with **SUPERMAGNETS**.

In the bad old days magnets were limp and useless things with about as much attractive power as wet wallpaper paste or a drunken lover.

---

* This psychological phenomenon is known as SAD, or Seasonally Adjusted Depression. An unhappy person, in the winter, might explain that they are downright miserable but *seasonally adjusted* they feel just peachy!

Technology, happily, has moved on.

You may now purchase **SUPERMAGNETS** which are made from the rare earth element *Neodymium*—the strongest permanent magnets known to modern science.

These magnets can be so powerful that even small ones must be packed in huge boxes before being shipped lest their magnetic fields destroy sensitive postal equipment.

Beware! If your finger should find it's way in between two inch-cube **SUPERMAGNETS** it will be crushed to jelly and it you will need well-tooled up engineers to separate them. They will destroy your watch, wipe data from credit cards and seriously mess up computers.

The vendors of the largest and most powerful **SUPERMAGNETS** advise that you actually *plan your route* before carrying one through a room in lest you find yourself attacked from all directions by flying metallic objects. Take one into a restaurant kitchen and you could die a loony-tunes death in an instant.

☆ They are so strong that you can actually *feel* magnetic north by holding one in your hand and turning in a circle.

☆ If you drop a **SUPERMAGNET** down a copper tube it will fall like a spoon sinking in treacle on account of the complex interplay between the magnetism and the induced electrical currents in the surrounding copper.

☆ Using four cubic **SUPERMAGNETS** and a flake of pure *pyrolitic graphite* you can achieve the incredible feat of levitation.

The first thing you have to do is to bind the four cubes into a two-by-two array. Two diagonally opposite magnets should have their north poles up and the other two should have their south poles up.

This is easier said than done. It is *extremely dangerous* to get your fingers muddled up in this process for reasons explained earlier.

What the magnets *want* to do is to snap together with great force, your job is to persuade them together in the manner explained—which they *do not* want to do. This is a feat of engineering that needs to be approached with care and forethought.

Having bolted, strapped or otherwise got the magnets together you lay the array flat on the workbench and hold your graphite flake about an inch above them. Now let go!

If you've seen anything more weird and amazing than that recently you must have been on drugs.

☆ Many modern coins are magnetic to some degree so if you can conceal a **SUPERMAGNET** in your sleeve you can perform an amazing feat of magic. Simply hold a coin in the palm of your hand and wave the magnetic sleeve over it and the coin will completely and utterly vanish to the utter befuddlement of your onlookers.

☆ Neodymium magnets are commonly available in the form of flat discs similar to coins. The north and south poles are at aligned as are the faces of the disc.

If you place one such magnet on the palm of your hand while holding another below your hand you'll find that you can cause the magnet on your palm to flip over simply by turning the coin below.

It's an impressive trick, but the movement of turning the lower magnet is hard to conceal.

A better presentation uses four magnets to do the turning: slide one inside your shirt sleeve and click another onto it on the outside.

Then do the same with another pair a couple of inches away making sure that the poles are opposite to the first pair. Now slide the sleeve of your jacket down to conceal them.

Finally, place a fifth magnet on the palm of your hand. As you move it over the hidden magnets you can get it to flip first one way and then the other.

The trick can be further enhanced by sticking the flip-magnet into some everyday object, like a matchbox.

See also **LEVITRON**.

SURFACE TENSION BALANCE

BAR BET

This trick is most commonly presented as a **BAR BET**.

☆ You can balance a credit card on
the edge of a beer glass pretty easily
by making sure that the curve of the
rim surrounds the centre of gravity
of the card.

Now challenge your **MARK** to place
one or more coins on the overhang
of the card without tipping it off.
Oh, and of course they can't touch
the glass either.

Anyone can see that a single coin is
likely to tip the card but let them try anyway.

When it's your turn you simply fill
the glass to the brim (which you
can do without touching it).

When the meniscus reaches
the card it will hold it in
place while the surface of
the water curves improbably
under the load.

You should be able to get
several coins onto the card before it
breaks free of the surface tension.

A
B
C
D
E
F
G
H
I
J
K
L
M
N
O
P
Q
R
S
T
U
V
W
X
Y
Z

A
B
C
D
E
F
G
H
I
J
K
L
M
N
O
P
Q
R
S
T
U
V
W
X
Y
Z

SURFACING WITHOUT YOUR AQUALUNG

SURVIVAL

Your air has run out at a depth of around one hundred feet, so how do you get back up?

Drop the bottles after taking a last breath of air and drop just enough weights to allow you to float slowly upwards.

As you rise through the water the air in your lungs will expand, so you must breathe out slowly all the way to the surface. Remember that a lung-full of air at that depth is the equivalent of many lung-fulls at the surface so you have plenty of time!

Float slowly upwards losing air all the way. The slow ascent is important if you are to avoid the bends.

SVENGALI DECK

MAGIC

The **SVENGALI DECK** is a trick deck of cards. You can get a Svengali deck from a magic supplier.

It works like this:

☆ Half of the cards in the deck are a random selection from a regular fifty two card deck. The other twenty six cards are all exactly the same card (for example, the eight of clubs). These identical cards are all trimmed very slightly shorter than the regular cards. The deck is arranged so that the twenty six identical cards are interleaved with the regular ones.

☆ This trick deck has some interesting properties. If you riffle the cards in one direction a spectator will think they are seeing a regular deck being riffled, but if you riffle it the other way it will look as if the entire deck is made up of the same card, say the eight of clubs.

☆ If you riffle it in the first way and ask a spectator to stick their finger in, during the riffle, and pull out the card below their finger they will *always* get an eight of clubs. This is a very reliable and self-working method of **FORCING** a card.

See also **TAPER DECK**.

SWANEE WHISTLE FROM A TWIG

MUSIC

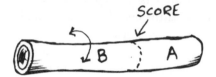

Take a smooth straight twig of maple about six inches long with no defects on it and cut both ends clean.

Now score a line around it with a pen knife, a little closer to one end than the other.

Gripping the short end A *hard* you should now twist and massage the long end B until the bark cracks free from the wood inside, forming a tube that will slide nicely up and down, lubricated by the sap of the twig.

Slide the bark up until it nearly falls off and place the instrument in front of your mouth.

Now blow (like a **MUSICAL BOTTLE**) and you can get a note out of it.

Pushing the little piston into the cylinder will cause the note to raise in pitch, so you should be able to conjure a tune out of this little instrument!

A B C D E F G H I J K L M N O P Q R **S** T U V W X Y Z

A
B
C
D
E
F
G
H
I
J
K
L
M
N
O
P
Q
R
S
T
U
V
W
X
Y
Z

SWAT TEAM HAND SIGNALS

CODES AND CIPHERS

The hand signals shown are the **SWAT TEAM HAND SIGNALS** for "Close Range Engagement (CRE) Operations".

This is the bit in the movie when brave guys with guns need to signal to each other without letting the bad guys know what they are up to. This sort of activity usually takes place in the third act of the movie, when everyone is madly chasing the **MAGUFFIN** and the line "We don't have much time!" is delivered at least once.

☆ SWAT, in case you didn't know, stands for *Special Weapons and Tactics*. SWAT teams are a feature of US Police departments. Their duties include serving arrest warrants against heavily armed criminals and dealing with hostage situations. They drive about in understated dark-coloured vans which are a bit like delivery trucks, but this cunning disguise is completely ruined by having SWAT written on the side in big letters.

The illustration that follows is reproduced from American Government literature *without* permission since, by law, all US Government documents are in the public domain unless specifically ordered to be made secret. The UK has traditionally held the opposite approach, in which all Government documents are automatically secret unless specifically ordered otherwise.

☆ **SWAT TEAM HAND SIGNALS** are useful in snowball fights or when paintballing with your friends.

☆ The skill of tossing clips of ammo, or spare snowballs, to your pals in a casual manner is also worth mastering.

One

Two

Three

Four

Five

Six

Seven

Eight

Nine

Ten

You

Me

Come

Listen or hear

Watch or see

Hurry ip

Stop

Freeze

Cover this area

Go here, move up

Enemy

Hostage

Sniper

Dog

Cell leader

Column formation

File formation

Line abreast formation

Wedge formation

Rally point

Pistol

Rifle

Shotgun

Ammunition

Vehicle

I understand

Do not understand

Crouch or go prone

Breacher

Gas

Door

Window

Point of entry

A
B
C
D
E
F
G
H
I
J
K
L
M
N
O
P
Q
R
S
T
U
V
W
X
Y
Z

A
B
C
D
E
F
G
H
I
J
K
L
M
N
O
P
Q
R
S
T
U
V
W
X
Y
Z

SWISS ARMY KNIFE

TRICKS OF THE TRADES / TRAVELLERS TIPS

☆ HERE'S *The* TRICK: Own one and carry it with you at all times.

Why? Well, the **SWISS ARMY KNIFE** is a toolkit in your pocket and while no *one* of the tools on the knife is quite as good as a single quality tool made for the purpose in question, *every* tool on the knife is adequate for the job it was made for and a damn sight better than your fingers alone.

These knives come in various shapes and sizes but the best deal is to buy the biggest, most fully-featured model in the range.

For this you will get (at least):

Pliers, two penknife blades (large and small), corkscrew, drill, three sizes of flatblade screwdriver (one small enough to handle spectacle repairs), crosspoint screwdriver (which fits just about any crosspoint screw), chisel, drill, metal file, metal saw (capable of **DEFEATING A PADLOCK**), wood saw, wire cutter, wire stripper, can opener, bottle opener, tweezers, magnifying glass, fish scaler, metric and imperial rulers, toothpick and a strange hooky tool that is fantastically useful though I do not know what it is really for.

The **SWISS ARMY KNIFE** packs a massive toolkit into an easily pocketable package of precision-made instruments each fashioned from top-grade stainless steel.

They are cheap to buy and they come with a lifetime guarantee, which means that if you break one, or wear one out, *they will give you a new one for nothing.*

☆ The genuine Swiss Army Knife to which I refer is made by *Victorinox*. Cheaper copies are available but they are all useless.

☆ Having a Swiss Army Knife in your pocket means that you can quickly do things that less well-equipped people around you can not. Having one but *not* having it in your pocket is a waste of money since the whole point of the thing is to solve problems when other tools are not available.

It follows therefore that you should only buy one if you are prepared to carry it with you *at all times*. A good incentive for this is the corkscrew, which ensures you a free glass (or swig) of wine anytime you find yourself with people who have thought of the booze, but who have forgotten to bring the means to open the bottle.

See also **LEATHERMAN**.

SYPHON

FUN WITH SCIENCE

Making a **SYPHON** is a hydraulic trick that can be achieved with any liquid and a length of hose which is magical in that it causes a liquid to flow *uphill*—something that is impossible in the normal course of events.

A common application of the **SYPHON** is that of removing petrol from a car's petrol tank. It's best to use a generous length of thin clear tube for this.

☆ Push one end of the tube deep into the petrol tank, you can tell when it is under the surface of the petrol by blowing down the tube and listening for bubbles.

Lay a couple of coils of the tube on the ground and have an open petrol can waiting. Now suck the tube until it flows down into the coils on the ground. Quickly remove the pipe from your mouth (a mouthful of petrol won't kill you but it tastes *horrible*) and place it in the container.

For the syphon to work the petrol can must be lower than the petrol in the tank, so leave it sat on the ground.

When the can is nearly full you lift it up, above the height of the car's petrol tank, and the petrol will stop flowing. Remove the tube from the can and put the lid on it.

Finally lift the tube up so that the remaining petrol in it flows back into the car's petrol tank and you're done.

If you're using a **SYPHON** to empty water out of a very large container there is an easier way to get it going: submerge the entire hose until it fills with water and then lift out one end with your thumb over it. This will keep the hose full of water while you move it to a position outside the container that is below the level of the water inside. Remove your thumb and the water will flow out as if by magic.

☆ Combine the principle of a **SYPHON** with that of capillary action to solve problems like puddles forming on a roof. Simply get a piece of old rope and put one end in the centre of the puddle and the other end lower down, possibly in a pot which needs watering.

Now every time it rains, instead of a puddle forming and rotting your covering, the water will travel along the rope, up over the edges, and down to water your plants!

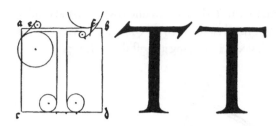

T-Shirt Folding

ORIGAMI / MARTIAL ARTS

While the **Rizla Propellor** was the most *requested* entry in this book, this amazing method of **T-Shirt Folding** is, in the author's opinion, the *best* trick in this book.

It has been categorised as ORIGAMI / MARTIAL ARTS because it achieves a supreme elegance of folding with minimum effort—in the blink of an eye.

Take a fresh T-shirt from the tumble dryer, imagine that you are facing north, and lay it on a table in front of you so that the neck lies *northeast*. Now consider how it will look when properly folded.

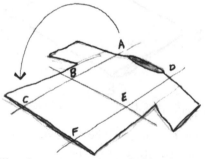

The only part you'll end up seeing is bounded by the points A, B, E and D —because there will be a fold along the line AC, another along the line DF and finally one across the line BE. We're going to make all these folds in one flowing movement.

With your *right hand* grab point A. With your left hand grab point B, making sure that you pinch so as to grab the back of the T-shirt as well as the front. Now lift point A *over* your left hand and pick up point C.

A
B
C
D
E
F
G
H
I
J
K
L
M
N
O
P
Q
R
S
T
U
V
W
X
Y
Z

A
B
C
D
E
F
G
H
I
J
K
L
M
N
O
P
Q
R
S
T
U
V
W
X
Y
Z

Your hands are now crossed: lift the T-shirt as you uncross your hands and it will look like this. Your right hand holds the AC corner, your left hand is holding the B corner. The left sleeve is hanging just off the table top.

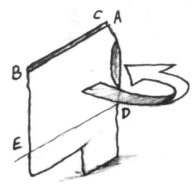

Drag the T-shirt toward you, letting the hanging sleeve drag on the tabletop and then drop it flat onto the table so the whole thing folds on the line DE.

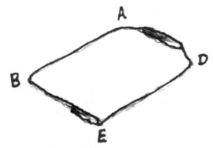

It will hit the table perfectly folded.

After a couple of practice runs you'll be doing the whole operation in one flowing movement and laundry days will be fun again

Amazing! After you have done this a couple of dozen times you'll be like a t-shirt folding machine.

☆ If you carefully unfold the thing you'll see just how neat and perfect this method is.

A
B
C
D
E
F
G
H
I
J
K
L
M
N
O
P
Q
R
S
T
U
V
W
X
Y
Z

TABLE BOUNCE

JUGGLING

☆ Throw a **BOUNCING BALL** hard under a table. It will bounce up, hit the bottom of the table and head back the way it came—right into your waiting hand.

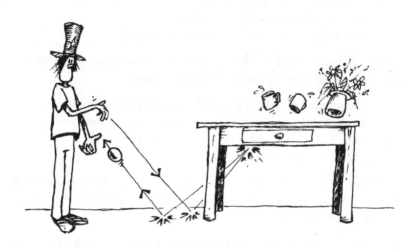

TAKING OFF A BRA

MATHEMATICS / SILLINESS

It's possible (if you are wearing a bra) to take it off without having to remove outer layers of clothing first. Many girls know how to do this and it makes an impressive party trick when performed in front of people who have not seen it before.

This is listed as a mathematical trick because it is evidence of the mathematical discipline of *Topology* being put to practical use.

To remove your *own* bra proceed as follows:

☆ First the catch is flicked open (see below) with the fingers of one hand either pushed down the back of the neck, or up from the waist.

Next the left hand reaches up the right sleeve, locates a shoulder strap and pulls it down over the right elbow, and then over the right hand.

Finally the right hand reaches up the left sleeve, grabs the opposite shoulder strap and pulls—*twang!* The bra is removed.

☆ The technique of "flicking the catch open" is one that all boys should practice before they embark on their lovemaking career, since male fingers can become tongue-tied and clumsy at important moments and can have great difficulty pulling, er, things off.

The thumb and middle finger are arranged as if for **SNAPPING YOUR FINGERS** in such a way that the snapping action will lift the hooks and eyes of the catch apart.

Note that, as with buttons on jackets, the catch is *always* the same way around, so the move only needs to be mastered in one orientation— though the wise trickster will ensure that they can manage the the trick with either hand and both from above and below. One can never be quite sure how one will be arranged with respect to ones partner when the opportunity strikes.

TAPER DECK

MAGIC

Unlike a *Marked Deck* (which is neither big nor clever) a **TAPER DECK** is both enormous and highly intelligent.

A **TAPER DECK** is a deck of playing cards wh
has been trimmed so that every card is a subtl
trapezoid instead of a rectangle. It contains
fifty two cards (plus two jokers) and is
generally made by taking a regular deck
and carefully guillotining off a tiny
triangular sliver from each side.

This means that it arrives in a regular box
with a familiar design. It looks normal and it is not easily
recognised as a trick deck (unlike the **SVENGALI DECK**).

The beauty of the **TAPER DECK** is that if you turn a single card around it
can be located easily by touch alone, and easily pulled out of the deck
without even having to look at the cards.

☆ In a classic **CARD TRICK** you **FORCE A CARD** and then reveal the
choice in an *interesting way.* With a **TAPER DECK** you don't have to bother
with the **FORCE**. You simply allow someone to choose literally any card, and
arrange matters so that it returns to the deck the wrong way around.

TABLE CLOTH TRICK

OBJECT MANIPULATION

Here's a classic move.

☆ A table is set with plates and crockery and perhaps a vase of flowers.
You grab the edge of the cloth and rip it out fast, leaving everything sat on
the table.

Do *not* assume that this is a self-working trick! Some table cloths have
nasty big seams in the edge that will send everything flying.

The trick is to take a nice wide grip on the cloth with both hands and pull
very hard and *downwards*. Don't make a wimpy pull and make sure that
you follow through so that the cloth is pulled completely clear in the
shortest possible time.

A
B
C
D
E
F
G
H
I
J
K
L
M
N
O
P
Q
R
S
T
U
V
W
X
Y
Z

Oh and you absolutely *must not* create any wrinkles in the cloth as you pull.

Good luck.

TABLE TOP COIN VANISH

MAGIC / COIN TRICKS

You need to be seated close up to a table that you can reach under, and opposite your audience to pull off this trick. It involves a very nice piece of **MISDIRECTION**.

☆ Produce a coin, preferably a 50p, £1 or £2 coin since doing coin tricks with lesser values always looks cheap.

Execute a simple vanish (try a **PALM RETENTION VANISH**) and move the (now empty) hand to the middle of the table in a dramatic sweep. This covers the fact that your other hand is reaching *under* the table with the coin.

☆ Mime the act of tapping the coin on the table while actually tapping the coin on the underside of the table.

Now mime *clacking* the coin down flat onto the table, while creating the sound from underneath.

Your audience is now utterly convinced that the coin is under your hand.

Ask them if it is heads or tails and, after they guess, you remove your hand to reveal that the coin has gone.

Sit back (to cover the fact that you are withdrawing your hand from under the table) and bask in their amazement.

Do *not* do it again. They'll catch on for sure.

TAI CHE NI

RUDE GESTURES / MARTIAL ARTS

The noted author, geomancer and philosopher *Radical Cheney* was, it is generally agreed, something between a genius and an enlightened master. He was also extremely unforgiving and prone to fits of rage. On being warned by his physician that these frequent bouts anger were bad for his heart he devised, as an outlet for his furies, his own martial art based on the calm and serene disciplines of Tai Chi.

He may have been influenced by a remark made by a French sentry in the film *Monty Python and the Holy Grail:* "I fart in your general direction!"

Tai Che Ni as it came to be named, is a dance in which slow-motion, curving and graceful moves terminate in elaborately formed rude gestures. These are aimed toward the opponent, who may actually be present, or merely imagined.

Tai Che Ni means *The Way of the Evil Breath*, the art of releasing the angry vapours and projecting them toward those who have caused them in the first place, thus deflecting and reflecting the damage and using the force of one's enemy against them.

A master of Tai Che Ni is immune to insults and slander by virtue of *T'zim T'yo* which means *immunity by perfect reflection.*

Generally the gestures are formed with the hands and fingers while the face provides fearsome grimaces to further the power of the attack. The facial expressions have names like *Bilious Dragon* or *Samurai with Sore Bottom* while the manual gestures have more westernised names like **Up Yours** and *Nah ne Nah Nah.*

TEA CHEST BASS

MUSIC

This instrument was a favourite of skiffle bands who also popularised the use of the washboard as a percussive instrument.

☆ A **TEA CHEST BASS** is constructed from a tea chest, which is a sort of cubical wooden packing case with a side length of about 30 inches. A tea chest is traditionally constructed from low-quality plywood with wooden reinforcement on the edges and metal corner brackets. A hole is drilled in the top surface and a length of cord with a stopper knot is led through the hole. The other end of the cord is tied to a length of broom handle which is otherwise unattached to the instrument.

The musician stands with one foot on the chest (to steady it) and tensions the cord by using the broom handle as a mast, guyed to the box with the cord.

By a combination of tensioning the pole and fretting the string with the left hand the musician can play low bass notes.

Obviously a good ear is required to hit the *right* notes.

TEA TOWEL BEHIND THE BACK

SILLINESS

Here's another impossible contortion you can bet on.

☆ Take a tea towel and hold each end in a fist in front of you. The challenge is to see if anyone can take a tea towel from that position and end up with it behind their back.

It's impossible of course!

Well, not quite.

Lift up your right hand and then wrap the tea towel *under* your right elbow with your left hand. Drop your right arm and you'll find the way from there pretty easily.

See also **STEPPING THROUGH A BROOM**.

TEARING NEWSPAPER

TRICKS OF THE TRADE

☆ Newspaper has a grain. It will tear easily in nice straight lines if you rip it horizontally, but you try to rip it vertically you'll have the devil's own job.

A B C D E F G H I J K L M N O P Q R S T U V W X Y Z

A
B
C
D
E
F
G
H
I
J
K
L
M
N
O
P
Q
R
S
T
U
V
W
X
Y
Z

TELEKINETIC CIGARETTE

MAGIC

Telekinesis is the art of moving objects by mind power alone.

Now you, dear reader, will surely realise that the only things you can *actually* move thus are parts of your own body, or occasionally, if you use the awesome power of *The Look*, your dog or small child.

In this illusion we cause a cigarette to roll across a tabletop using clever subterfuge. Your only problem, in these days of Health and Safety, is to find a venue where you may not only smoke, but where there is also a tabletop.

☆ Gather your audience around and place a cigarette on the tabletop so that it lies from right to left. As you wave your hand over it it will roll, first away from you, and then back toward you.

☆ HERE'S *The* TRICK:
You actually move the cigarette away from you by *blowing* on it ever so gently. You move it back toward you by blowing at your hand and *reflecting* the draught back onto the cigarette.

TETRAHEDRON

GEOMETRY

The **TETRAHEDRON** is one of the five **PLATONIC SOLIDS**, being the simplest regular polyhedron. It has four vertices (corners) six edges and four faces, each of which is an equilateral triangle.

☆ The **TETRAHEDRON** is the solution to the lateral-thinking puzzle concerning the problem of constructing **FOUR TRIANGLES FROM SIX MATCHES**.

☆ The **Tetrahedron** is its own *dual*. If you draw a point at the centre of each face and connect the points together you can form a new, smaller **Tetrahedron** inside the original.

☆ A **Tetrahedron** can be nested neatly inside a cube so that its edges are formed from diagonals across the faces of the cube. Its volume is exactly one third of the volume of the cube.

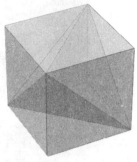

☆ The **Tetrahedron** is often confused with the *Pyramid*.

Thaumatrope

ANIMATION

This ancient animation device invention is something of a one-trick pony, since it is almost always seen performing the same illusion—magically placing a bird in a cage.

A disc is mounted between two lengths of string. On one side is depicted a bird cage, and on the other a bird. The strings are then twisted and by pulling hard on them the disc will quickly spin as if powered by two rubber bands.

The phenomenon of persistence of vision causes the viewer to see both images superimposed and thus the bird is placed in the cage.

A
B
C
D
E
F
G
H
I
J
K
L
M
N
O
P
Q
R
S
T
U
V
W
X
Y
Z

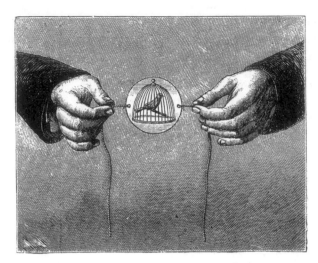

See also **ZOETROPE, PHENOKISTOSCOPE, PRAXINOSCOPE**.

THREE BALL CASCADE

JUGGLING

If you want to learn juggling then start here. If you have any sort of aptitude for juggling (and most people do) you'll manage three throws of this pattern after just a couple of hours work. Once you've done *that* you have my permission (for what it's worth) to call yourself a Juggler.

☆ The basic trick of three ball juggling is the *exchange*—a simple move learned with just two balls. It goes like this:

START WITH **ONE BALL** IN EACH HAND...

NOW CAREFULLY **THROW** THE **FIRST BALL**...

...AIM IT TOWARDS THE **OPPOSITE** HAND...

IT SHOULD RISE TO ABOUT **HEAD HEIGHT**

WHILE THE **FIRST BALL** IS IN THE AIR YOU THROW THE **SECOND**...

...IT SHOULD FLY **UNDER** THE FIRST BALL...

...THIS **CLEARS** YOUR HAND FOR THE **CATCH**!!

YOU'RE **NEARLY** DONE!! –THERE'S JUST **ONE MORE** THING...

IT'S **EASY** TO MAKE THE **MISTAKE** OF MISSING THE **SECOND** CATCH!

THIS **SIMPLE** MOVE IS KNOWN AS THE **EXCHANGE** – WELL DONE!!!

Let's go over that again:

1: Hold a ball in each hand.

2: Throw one ball about head height toward the other hand.

3: When it's about halfway across throw the other ball back.
This throw should pass under the first ball.
This is the moment of the exchange—you are swapping the ball the air for the one in your hand.

4: Catch the first ball.

5: Catch the second ball.

If you're lucky you'll pull off the exchange after just a couple of attempts. If not, don't worry! Check the tips below and try again.

☆ Some people have a nasty and hard-to-break habit of *passing* the second ball back rather than throwing it. Usually this is because they have previously learned the **Two Ball Shower** and the *passing* action has become habitual.

If this happens to you then you are going to have to break the habit— which is a fairly simple thing to do.

The best way out of this jam is to lead with the *other* hand. If you're right-handed make the first throw from your *left* hand. If you're left-handed, lead with your right. Also, as you make the throws, say out loud *"throw-throw!"* You'll find that your hands quite like being *told* what to do.

☆ Once you can do the exchange one way around (right-left), you should practice it the other way around (left-right). Work on the exchange until you can confidently do it both ways around. Then take a short break to let your new skill sink in.

If you can do all this in under half an hour you're doing just great.

If it takes an hour you're still doing fine.

If it takes longer than that you should leave off and try again tomorrow. Most juggling skills are learnt while you sleep—it's all to do with the subconscious, see **LEARNING HOW TO LEARN TRICKS**.

☆ With the exchange mastered, we can move on to actual three-ball juggling. Pick up three balls and place two in your favourite hand.

Note that each throw travels *under* the previous one.

Your mission is to make just *three* throws and hopefully, three catches.

Now this is a bit of a knack. Some will get it after just a few attempts, others take longer. Here are some helpful tips based on years of experience in teaching people how to juggle:

☆ Look forwards *through* the pattern rather than focusing on a particular ball.

☆ Make sure all three throws go to the same height—about head high.

☆ Some people find it hard to throw the third ball because they are too worried about catching the second ball. If this happens to you, try saying out loud, as you throw, *"One-Two-Three!"* If this still doesn't work then just practice making the throws and don't bother to catch a thing! Let them drop. Do this a few times and when the *throws* are working, go back to trying to make the catches.

☆ When you have mastered the three th you can move on to four throws, five thi six throws and so on. Note that it is a ve good idea, psychologically, to set definit targets that you can actually reach— rather than just juggling until you (literally) drop.

If you always end with a drop your subconscious may get the impression that you are *failing* all the time and the learning process will take longer. Juggling a few throws to a clean catch produces a sense of satisfaction that improves the speed at which the skill is acquired.

☆ Beginners sometimes find that the pattern "runs away" with them. The balls fly out forward and they end up chasing the pattern across the room. If this happens to you then you should *stand in front of a wall* while practicing.

☆ Beginners will also tend to juggle a higher and slower pattern than the more experienced juggler. The reason for this is that they are only moving one hand at a time—they do a *throw-and-catch* with the right hand, then a

A
B
C
D
E
F
G
H
I
J
K
L
M
N
O
P
Q
R
S
T
U
V
W
X
Y
Z

throw-and-catch with the left hand. There is no overlap of the hand movements.

The experienced juggler, if you look closely, will be throwing with the right hand *at the same time* as catching in the left (and vice versa). The hands are moving constantly. The slow, beginners pattern is known as a **SLOW CASCADE** by some technically-minded jugglers.

This is perfectly normal and you'll find that your pattern will settle down naturally in time and will eventually feel as smooth and effortless as walking.

☆ If your *real* ambition is to juggle with clubs then you need to get your **THREE BALL CASCADE** down solid before you start. The **SLOW CASCADE** is *not* a good starting point. Generally speaking, even the keenest novice jugglers will not start to work with clubs until they have a few weeks experience with balls.

☆ When you have the **THREE BALL CASCA:** solid* you can start to learn "tricks."

Obviously everything a juggler does is a "trick but what *they* mean by "trick" is some sort of variation or fiddly bit laid on top of the basic pattern. A good first trick to learn is that of throwing balls **OVER THE TOP**. Another is **UNDER THE HAND**.

It's worth noting that when a "trick" is repeated constantly in a juggling pattern you often end up with a totally new pattern. For example, you can combine **OVER THE TOP** and **UNDER THE HAND** throws to produce cool patterns like the **WINDMILL** and even the awesome **MILLS' MESS**.

---

* Jugglers often refer to tricks they have mastered as being "solid" when in actual fact they mean that it is being juggled so well it looks more like "liquid".

THREE BALL SHOWER

JUGGLING

The **Two Ball Shower** may be the most-learned juggling pattern (also a very easy one) but the **Three Ball Shower** is not for the faint-hearted—being considerably harder to juggle than a **Three Ball Cascade**.

☆ Start with two balls in your favourite hand and one in the other. Lead off with *two* high crossing throws from the favourite hand and then start **Feeding** balls back from the other hand. In **Siteswap Notation** the pattern is 51, which means that one hand is making **Five Ball Cascade** throws while the other **Feeds** back. The hands throw alternately.

Those **Five Ball Cascade** throws are what makes this a relatively advanced pattern.

☆ The classic **Three Ball Shower** is juggled with the hands working asynchronously—the hands taking it in turns to make their moves: first the right hand throws, then the left hand feeds, and so on.

You can also juggle a sort of **Three Ball Shower** with both hands throwing *synchronously* (at the same time). In this variation one hand throws 4's while the other throws 2's (almost horizontal throws) both throws being made at the same time. This results in a much lower pattern but is knacksome to "get" because your hands are doing fundamentally different things at the same time.

You should try and learn to juggle the pattern both ways around, and then develop the skill of making direction changes in mid-juggle. When you take this to the extreme of making a direction change after *every* throw you will find yourself juggling a clever little pattern called the **Box**.

☆ It's a tricky one to get, but once mastered you might be interested to know that you can convert this pattern into the wonderful **Box** by changing direction after *every* throw.

☆ Needless to say, in the interests of ambidexterity, you should learn both shower patterns *both* ways around, that is, in both right and left-handed versions.

☆ You can have a lot of fun with the regular 5 1 shower by making alternate throws **UNDER THE HAND**.

THREE BALL START

JUGGLING

The normal method of starting a three-ball pattern is to place two balls in your favourite hand and one in the other.

It's much more impressive to start with all three balls in one hand and throw a **MULTIPLEX** (all three balls go up at once) and pull them out of the air to start the juggle.

Here are a couple of neat ways of doing this:

☆ Throw a three ball *column* **MULTIPLEX**. The top ball goes high, the middle ball goes about half as high, and the bottom ball hardly lifts at all. You make the throw by lining the balls up in your hand and making a sort of scooping throw. This is a lot easier to do than explain.

The bottom ball is caught almost immediately by the *throwing* hand, the middle ball by the *opposite* hand, and the top ball is caught by the *throwing* hand (right after it has re-thrown the first ball you caught).

Try it. Honestly it is easier than you think.

☆ Alternatively arrange the three balls in a sort of upside-down triangle in your favourite hand. Throw them so the top two balls go high, and the bottom ball hardly lifts at all.

The throwing hand **SNATCHES** the bottom ball almost immediately, then re-throws it. The other two balls are caught simultaneously, one in each hand, as they fall.

Once again this is a lot easier than you might think.

☆ The last method also works very well if you throw the three balls **BEHIND THE BACK**.

THREE CARD MONTE

GRIFTING

The **THREE CARD MONTE**, also known as **FIND THE LADY**, is a confidence trick that has been played out on city streets by **GRIFTERS** for hundreds of years. It is very similar to the **SHELL GAME**—you will not win a penny.

The *Dealer* works with a *Lookout* whose job is to watch out for the cops. Unknown to the **MARK** the other two people gathered around the table are actually *Shills* whose job is to look like members of the public while actually enticing the **MARK** into the game.

The *Dealer* works with three cards on a table or box set up on the street. One of which is (let's say) a Queen, while the other two are non-face cards. The cards are shown to the player and then laid on the table face down and shuffled in the manner of a **CASCADE** a few times. The player lays down a bet and guesses where the Queen is. If they are right they win double their stake.

Of course, the only people likely to win are the *Shills* (unless the *Dealer* decides to let a **MARK** win a small amount to lure them into a bigger bet). There is deep trickery going on here and the **MARK** is bound to lose.

You'll notice, if you watch the game, that the cards are all bent slightly along their long axis, which makes them easy to pick up off a flat table. This is important because the *Dealer* needs to move the cards fast.

The *Dealer* may offer the **MARK** a *helping hand* after taking some money from them by folding down the top corner of the Queen before laying it down with the other cards and shuffling. The **MARK** will follow the marked card and bet on it—only to find that it is no longer the Queen.

☆ HERE'S The TRICK: The main technique used by the *Dealer* is called the *Throw* and it goes like this:

☆ The three cards are shown to the **MARK** in a very precise manner. The Queen is held between the thumb and forefinger of the right hand and a face card is held behind it between the thumb and middle finger. The other face card is held between the thumb and forefinger of the left hand.

'Watch the Lady!' says the *Dealer* as they toss (apparently) the Queen into the middle position on the table. In actual fact they toss the face card from *behind* it. This is quite undetectable, especially since they toss it down so fast that it slides across the table. The left hand then tosses its card *over* the card that just hit the table and then the right hand tosses the last card across that one. That card is, of course, the Queen.

The *Dealer* then continues to juggle the cards a round a few more times and then asks the **MARK** to make their guess. They'll lose of course!

☆ The folded corner trick is achieved by pre-folding the corners of all three cards. The corner of the Queen is bent to "help" the **MARK** and it ends up at the bottom corner of the Queen opposite the *Dealer's* thumb at the beginning of the trick. The *Dealer* then folds the concealed corner of the face-card lying behind the Queen and then, during the throw itself, the Queen's corner is unbent. Again, this is very easy to do with only a little practice.

GRIFTERS who play the **THREE CARD MONTE** are deadly serious about making money and don't think for a minute that you can win against them, even if you know what's going on.

THREE FLASHES

VEHICLES

I'm talking here about headlamp flashes, rather than the juggling sort of **FLASH**.

☆ If you are driving along the road in England and a vehicle coming the other way flashes its headlamps three times it means that there are cops up ahead on the road. It could be a speed trap, an accident or a road block, but whatever it was the person flashing you wants you to know and is trying to save you some trouble.

Now did you remember to renew that tax disc or not?

THREE-FOUR-FIVE TRIANGLE

GEOMETRY

If you construct a triangle with one side 3 units long, another 4 units long and another 5 units long it will be a perfect **RIGHT ANGLED** triangle. This is easy to confirm with **PYTHAGORAS' THEOREM** since $3^2+4^2 = 5^2$ (or to put in another way: $9+16 = 25$).

This is an amazing result, one of Nature's quirks if you like. It was well known to ancient people like the Egyptians who assigned it with a mystical significance.

It's also very useful when laying out large sites if you need to stake out perfectly rectangular areas, measure out three chains or ropes to these proportions and stretch them out to form perfect **RIGHT ANGLES** on the ground.

Another useful triangle is the 5-12-13 triangle, which also produces a perfect **RIGHT ANGLE**.

A B C D E F G H I J K L M N O P Q R S T U V W X Y Z

THREE IN ONE HAND BOUNCE

JUGGLING

Here are two entirely distinct ways of doing a **THREE IN ONE HAND** bounce, in one you juggle a one-handed three-ball **PASSIVE BOUNCE**, in the other you do a **COLUMN BOUNCE**.

☆ To do the **PASSIVE BOUNCE** you simply work both sides of a **REVERSE CASCADE** with a single hand—**HOT POTATO** style.

Did I say "simply"? Your hand will move like greased lightning. Make sure you learn this on both sides (in the interests of ambidexterity). Your hand will weave a figure-of-eight over the balls.

☆ The **COLUMN BOUNCE** is a more relaxed affair.

Start with a **TWO IN ONE HAND** bounce and the drop a third ball into a new column with your spare hand. You can drop the ball in so that both columns bounce together which results in a very slow and lazy pattern (both columns bounce twice between exchanges)—or you can drop the third ball in so that the columns bounce in alternate time (both columns bounce just once and your hand works twice as fast).

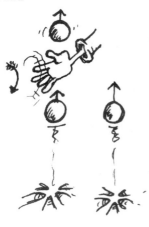

The alternately-timed pattern is the basis for the awesome **FOUR IN ONE HAND BOUNCE**.

THREE RING TOSS

JUGGLING

Here's a nice thing you can do with *Juggling Rings*.

☆ Pile three rings on top of each other and hold them *Frisbee* style, fan them a little. Your partner stands opposite, holding their hands up as if being robbed.

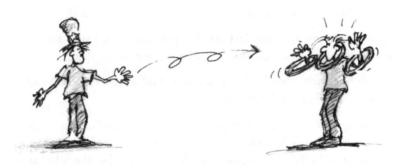

Throw all three rings, and they'll split as they fly, and if aimed right you can drop one over each of your partner's hands and one over the head. This is *much* easier than you might think—a great way to end a ring-passing routine.

THUMB TIP

MAGIC

Here's a *gimmick* that you need to know about.

The **THUMB TIP** can be used to create some truly amazing illusions that absolutely defy the imagination of the audience who simply cannot believe what they have just seen.

A
B
C
D
E
F
G
H
I
J
K
L
M
N
O
P
Q
R
S
T
U
V
W
X
Y
Z

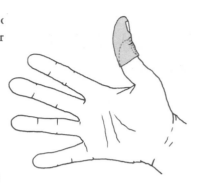

This simple device is a plastic model of thumb which you can wear over your real thumb. When it is worn it makes your thumb seem about twice as long as it should be, but curiously people don't seem to notice this, especially if you keep the thing moving and don't draw too much attention to it. You can stash a reasonably large object in the thumb without too much trouble.

It's good practice to keep the **THUMB TIP** pointing toward your audience whenever possible because this makes it almost impossible to detect.

There are hundreds of tricks that you can pull off with a little skill and a thumb tip. We'll just list three classics here.

☆ *Vanishing Silks:* This is a complete classic. The magician produces a large, usually red, silk and waves it about dramatically before draping it over their arm. As the silk is draped the thumb attached to the other arm dips into a pocket and returns with thumb tip in place. They then make a fist with their silk-hand and prod the thumb tip into it on the pretext of fashioning a "hole" in their hand.

The thumb tip remains in the fist.

They then stuff the silk into the hole, prodding it in with one finger after another.

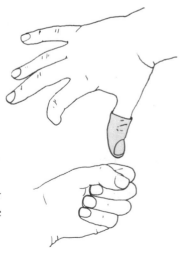

You've seen this a hundred times haven't you? You've wondered what all that stylised prodding was about haven't you? Well you're about to find out!

The last shred of the silk is rammed in hard with the *thumb* and the fist is held up high.

This last move is a piece of **MISDIRECTION** because what has *actually* happened is that the silk has been rammed into the thumb tip which is now back in place on the thumb of the hand you are *not* looking at.

The magician then slowly opens the fist to reveal that the silk has vanished! Nobody is watching the other hand dumping the thumb tip and its contents into a side pocket.

☆ *Cigarette through Jacket:* This is a favourite of street entertainers, especially of the Covent Garden variety. A jacket is borrowed from one member of the audience and a cigarette from another. The performer then lights the cigarette and smokes it hard to create a nice big fat red hot end. They drape the jacket over their left fist and fashion a hole in it by pushing a bulge of fabric down into the fist with their, erm, thumb!

I'm sure you can see what's going on here.

Then, to the horror of the person that lent them the jacket, they slowly and carefully stub the cigarette out, apparently in the jacket. The final stubbing-out is done with, erm, the thumb!

Finally they reveal the jacket as unharmed—this cigarette has vanished without a trace!

It's a good plan to load the thumb tip with a little bit of silver paper or a piece of damp cotton wool before doing this trick to save melting the plastic.

☆ *Vanishing and re-appearing salt:* I'm sure that you're starting to see the possibilities now so I'll keep this explanation short:

The performer makes a fist and pours a *lot* of salt into it and then rams it in hard with his thumb. The hand is revealed as empty—the salt having vanished completely!

They then re-make the fist and and feel inside with their opposite thumb. Something seems to have appeared! They tip their fist slowly over and all of the vanished salt pours out as if by magic!

THUMB WIND

YO-YO

This is a neat method of rewinding a **Yo-Yo** that has run out of puff.

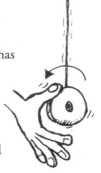

Hold your yo-hand high and grab the **Yo-Yo** in a firm grip with your free hand so that your thumb lies over the top of the thing. Now snap hard and see if you can spin the **Yo-Yo** hard enough to climb all the way back up the string.

THOUGHT EXPERIMENT

MATHEMATICS / TECHNICAL WIZARDRY

A **THOUGHT EXPERIMENT** is the method of testing a hypothesis by merely *thinking* about it. *Albert Einstein,* the noted patent clerk, managed to demonstrate that gravity was identical to an *acceleration* by this means, and then went onto demonstrate that light, which has no mass, would have its rays bent by the influence of a gravitational field by means of another similar mental exercise. A result that was amazing, mainly because it was later shown by practical experiment to be entirely correct.

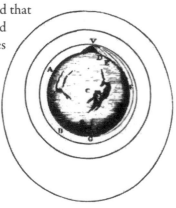

Here is how *Isaac Newton* demonstrated that the Moon could be held in orbit around the Earth by the same means that causes an object to fall to the ground—in other words, by the force *gravity,* the juggler's friend.

He reasoned that if one fired a cannonball horizontally from a mountain top it would fall in a curve toward the Earth. By progressively increasing the force of the cannon the projectile would fall further and further from the mountain. However, as the distance increased, so the Earth's surface would curve further and further away from the falling cannonball, and eventually, it would fall toward the Earth as fast as the Earth was receding beneath it, hence it would form an orbit.

A remarkable achievement!

THUNDER AND LIGHTNING

FUN WITH SCIENCE

As a storm approaches you'll notice that the flashes of lightning reach your eyes some time before the sound of thunder reaches your ears.

This is because sound travels relatively slowly, and light travels more or less instantaneously. The flash and the bag start at the same time, but the light rushes toward you at 983,571,056 feet per second while the sound dawdles along at 1,125 feet per second*, taking 4.67 seconds to travel a mile.

---

* This is the speed of sound in dry air at sea level at 20° Celsius. It equates to 343 meters per second. Sound travels faster in warmer air, less dense air, and more moist air.

As a rule of thumb you can approximate this to five seconds. So when you see a flash, start counting off seconds while you wait for the bang. Divide by five and that's roughly how far away the centre of the storm is in miles. If this distance seems to be rapidly reducing then it could just be that the electrical centre of the storm is going to end up right on top of you. Very close lightning strikes are the ones where the sound and light are synchronised.

Just before lightning strikes, massive electrical charge builds up and you can *feel* this if you are near *Ground Zero*. Your hair may stand on end, and TV screens may begin to crackle. It might be a good plan to disconnect sensitive electronic devices, like computers and TVs, from cables connecting them to the world, because these cables can carry the high-voltage electricity from a strike right into the guts of the machines. Telephones are also dodgy, since they are directly connected to cables that can often pick up strikes.

Bad places to be in an electrical storm are: on high open ground, under tall trees or inside the nacelle of a wind turbine (for servicing purposes). Good places to be are inside a building or inside a car, where the combination of the metal *Faraday Cage* of the vehicle's cabin, and the insulating properties of the tyres, render you pretty much immune even to a direct strike.

Roughly 2,000 people a year are injured by lightning, the mortality rate is about 10%.

TISSUE PAPER HOT AIR BALLOONS

FLYING MACHINES / PYROTECHNICS

Building and flying a **TISSUE PAPER HOT AIR BALLOON** is a remarkable feat of aviation, and it is a project that can be completed in single day with lift off at sunset—the very best time to fly.

You'll probably want to build your balloon to the same sort of shape as the real thing, so a short lesson in pattern-cutting is appropriate. The technique we're going to use is the same as that used by metalworkers to build elaborate prismatic shapes, like bases for sundials, from sheet material.

☆ Your finished aircraft should be about five to six feet tall. Smaller balloons will work, but they won't fly as well because there will be relatively less hot air to carry the weight of the envelope. Balloons can be unstable if they are either too tall and thin and also if they are too round.

We'll make the balloon from six panels, as if it was to have a hexagonal cross-section, but when it fills out with air it will round out nicely. This is a handy plan because it means that the *radius* of the balloon at any particular latitude is the same as the width of the panels at that point.

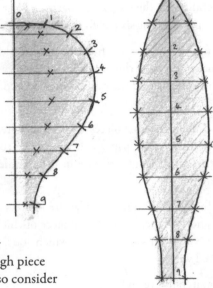

Start by making a full-size drawing of the profile of your balloon. Finding a large enough piece of paper could be a problem so consider chalking it out on a floor.

Now set a pair of compasses to a shortish distance and walk them down the profile, marking off equidistant points along the edge (shown here numbered 0–9). Then draw horizontal lines connecting these points to the axis of the balloon profile. Now mark the halfway point of each of the lines to create a shallower profile inside the original one.

Now you need a *lot* of tissue paper, you can buy this in newsagents or art shops, but it will come in small rectangles that will need to be stuck together to make six sheets, each large enough to make one of the six panels of your balloon.

Lie one of the sheets on the floor and carefully mark a centre line down it and then divide it by marking a set of points spaced exactly like the ones you made along the profile. Next mark off the width at each of those points, working from your original drawing. You should end up with a shape a little like a fish.

You can now cut out your panels, remembering to allow an extra inch or so on one side to allow for the width of the seam.

Carefully glue the six panels together. Now glue a nice round patch onto the top, where the six panels meet, and your envelope is done.

To support the burning fuel, and also to add a little ballast, you now need to make a circle of thin, but stiff, wire that will fit exactly into the opening at the bottom, fold the bottom inch or so of the envelope over it and glue it back.

Now add two cross-pieces of thinner wire. You can simply poke them through the tissue paper and wire-splice the ends onto themselves. Add another short length of wire in the middle to bind the two crosspieces together.

For fuel you'll find that regular fire lighters are very good. You should get two and fold them into a small piece of chicken mesh. Add a short length of wire with a hook on the end which you'll use to hang the burner on the crossed wires.

Your aircraft is ready!

☆ You should choose a calm evening, certainly with a wind-speed of less than 2 knots, and a clear area for the launch.

Do not attempt to inflate the balloon with a flame—it will simply ignite and burn before even taking off. Instead you should run a cable outside and plug a powerful blower-heater into it and use that instead. Blast hot air into the envelope until the balloon takes shape and starts to lift. It's best to have two helpers at this stage to hold onto the base of the balloon while you do the tricky stuff.

Carefully light your flamer and hang it from
the cross piece. Tell your helpers to let go
and carefully steady the balloon until it
wants to lift then release it very gently.

With luck, and as long as those flames don't
catch the thing alight, it should rise to three or
four hundred feet and will land, after exhausting
it's fuel, anything up to four miles away.

This is probably not the sort of thing you'd
want to be doing at harvest time or if there
are thatched cottages or barns in the
immediate area. They can also pose a
threat to cows so DO NOT do it an area
where these animals are grazing.

TOILET TRICKS

SILLINESS

Ever since there have been school kids and toilets for school kids, there
have been **TOILET TRICKS**. They are not big, they are not clever, but to
the immature mind they seem very funny indeed.

☆ Probably the most impressive is the *Bogroll
Flush* (so named on account of the English
habit of calling a toilet a "bog") in which the
kid's disgust of those mid-twentieth century
rolls of greaseproof paper masquerading as
toilet tissue was avenged thus:

The loose end of the roll is placed into the
toilet pan, then the toilet is flushed. When
executed by an expert the entire roll will
unravel into the sewer pipe from the force
of the water in just a few seconds.

A
B
C
D
E
F
G
H
I
J
K
L
M
N
O
P
Q
R
S
T
U
V
W
X
Y
Z

It was common practice, during the author's schooldays, to prime an entire row of cubicles and then flush each one in rapid succession in the vain hope that the massive expense to the school might prompt the authorities to consider using softer paper.

☆ Another common trick was that of locking a cubicle from the inside and then climbing out to give the impression that the cubicle was occupied. The doors on such cubicles often do not reach the floor, so a few pairs of stolen shoes from the changing rooms, carefully placed, will enhance the illusion.

☆ A really nasty trick is to lift the seat of a toilet and then cover the bowl with a carefully stretched sheet of cling-film, which will be virtually invisible one the seat is lowered again. The next visitor is bound to have some very serious problems.

One may also note, at the urinal, that some men pee while holding one hand against the wall in front of them. This is a child-learnt defence against a nasty bullying attack from their schooldays in which bigger boys would walk up behind a peeing victim and push them forwards into the trough. This is actually quite traumatic and is the reason that a lot of men "can't go" when others are around.

ᛏᚩᛚᚴᛁᛖᚾᛋ ᛞᚹᚪᚱᚠ ᚱᚢᚾᛖᛋ

ᚳᚩᛞᛖᛋ ᚪᚾᛞ ᚳᛁᛈᚻᛖᚱᛋ

ᚪᛒᚳᛞᛖᚠᚷᚻᛁᛁᚴᛚᛗᚾᚩᛈᛢᚱᛋᛏᚢᚢᚹᛉᚣᛣ

ᚦᛖᛋᛖ ᚪᚱᛖ ᛏᚻᛖ ᛞᚹᚪᚱᚠ ᚱᚢᚾᛖᛋ ᚪᛋ ᚢᛋᛖᛞ ᛒᚣ ᛁᚱᚱ ᛏᚩᛚᚴᛁᛖᚾ ᛁᚾ ᚻᛁᛋ ᛒᚩᚩᚴ ᚦᛖ ᚻᚩᛒᛒᛁᛏ : ᚦᛖᚣ ᚪᚱᛖ ᛒᚪᛋᛖᛞ ᚩᚾ ᚪᚾᚷᛚᚩ ᛋᚪᛉᚩᚾ ᚱᚢᚾᛖᛋ : ᚾᚩᛏᛖ ᚦᚪᛏ ᚦᛖ ᛚᛖᛏᛏᛖᚱᛋ **J** ᚪᚾᛞ **I** ᚪᛚᛋᚩ ᚦᛖ ᛚᛖᛏᛏᛖᚱᛋ **U** ᚪᚾᛞ **V** ᛋᚻᚪᚱᛖ ᚦᛖ ᛋᚪᛗᛖ ᚱᚢᚾᛖ : ᚦᛖᚱᛖ ᚪᚱᛖ ᚪᛚᛋᚩ ᛋᚩᛗᛖ ᛚᛖᛏᛏᛖᚱ ᚳᚩᛗᛒᛁᚾᚪᛏᛁᚩᚾᛋ ᛏᚻᚪᛏ ᚻᚪᚢᛖ ᛋᛈᛖᚳᛁᚪᛚ ᚱᚢᚾᛖᛋ ᚹᚻᛁᚳᚻ ᛁᛋ ᚹᚻᚣ ᚣᚩᚢ ᛗᚪᚣ ᛒᛖ ᚠᛁᚾᛞᛁᛝ ᚦᛁᛋ ᛥᚢᚠ ᚻᚪᚱᛞ ᛏᚩ ᚱᛖᚪᛞ

ᚦ TH

ᛦ ST

ᛝ NG

ᛐᚼᛁᛌ ᚦᛘᛘᛘ ᚱᚦᛏᛘᛌ ᛌᚾᚠᛐᛁᛌ ᚼᛘᛘᛐ ᚠᛘᚾᚱ ᛌᛘᛚᚱᛘᛏᛌ ᚼᛘᚦᛘ ᛁᚱᚦᛘ ᚠ
ᛚᚱᚾᛐᛚ ᚠᛒᛌᛘᚱᚾᛘᚱ ᛒᚾᛐ ᛁᚠᛐ ᚠᚱᚦᛘ ᛐᚼᛘ ᛌᚦᚱᛐ ᚠᚦ ᛚᛘᚠᛚᛐᛘ ᚦᛌᚦ
ᛚᛐᚦᛰ ᚱᚦᛐᛘ ᛚᛐᚠᛰᛌ ᚷᚦᛘᛘᛌ ᛌᚠ ᛒᛘ ᛐᛌᚱᛰ ᛚᚦᚱᛘᚦᛐᛚ ᛁᛐᛘᛘᛘᛘ :

TOM FOOL KNOT

KNOTS

The **TOM FOOL KNOT**, also known as a *Handcuff Knot*, is a trick knot that you can use to secure the hands of a victim. It is tied in seconds by sleight of hand and has been used to amuse children for generations.

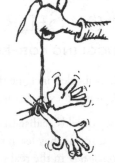

☆ Ask your victim to hold their hands out in front of them.

☆ Take a length of rope and form two loops that overlap. Pull the inner edges of each loop through the other loop to form two "butterfly wings".

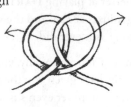

☆ Place these loops over the victims hands and then quickly pull the ends of the rope tight, which will draw the knot up to form a pair of handcuffs.

With a little practice you can form the knot in a couple of seconds.

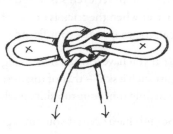

☆ The **SHEEPSHANK** can be tied with a similar technique using three loops instead of two.

A
B
C
D
E
F
G
H
I
J
K
L
M
N
O
P
Q
R
S
T
U
V
W
X
Y
Z

TOOTHBRUSH PROPELLOR

OBJECT MANIPULATION

☆ Get an ordinary toothbrush and a pen. Hold the pen out in front of you with your right hand and hang the toothbrush off it by its bristles, so that the bristles point to the left.

Now carefully swing the toothbrush clockwise. It will hang on as if by magic!

TOP SHIRT POCKET CATCH

JUGGLING / OBJECT MANIPULATION

Many jugglers imagine that their special skills might have applications in *real life*—as if they were some sort of superhero with amazing special powers.

They quickly realise that, in the main, the skills acquired as they learn to juggle are of *no use whatsoever* in the real world. They are not suddenly better at playing **DARTS**. They are not suddenly geniuses at *Pool* and the washing-up takes just as long as it ever did.

But, just occasionally, you'll find that your juggling skills have given you the power to pull off a trick that you never even suspected you could do. It's even better when the trick is one of those cool moves you can use to impress your friends!

☆ If you have learned how to juggle **BEHIND THE BACK** then you have just such a skill—that of tossing a small object behind your back and then catching it in your top shirt pocket.

Sounds hard? Not if you can juggle **BEHIND THE BACK**!

Try it: hold the pocket open with one hand and toss a lighter, coin or box of matches **BEHIND THE BACK** with the other hand so it lands in the pocket.

A decent juggler will get this trick down on the very first attempt.

TORN BANKNOTE CON

GRIFTING

Two **GRIFTERS** work together to pull this con. It requires a persuasive attitude and is best pulled off in places where the counter staff are busy and stressed—a busy café is a good choice.

☆ The **GRIFTERS** prepare for the con by taking a high-value note, say twenty pounds, and ripping off a corner. One of them takes the note and goes into the café and buys something cheap like a cup of tea.

Meanwhile the other takes a separate table and orders a coffee and a bun and then grabs the bill. They approach the counter and proffer the bill and no money from a busy member of staff. Almost immediately they ask for their change.

"But you didn't give me any money!"

"Yes I did, I gave you a twenty look!" They open their wallet. "I had a ten and a twenty, and look! There's only ten left in here."

"No you didn't!"

"Look, it was an old torn note—hey! Look here's the corner, it must have fallen off! Check your till, I honestly gave you a twenty—there should be one in there with a missing corner."

Reluctantly they check, and wouldn't you just know it, there's a twenty with the corner missing and the **GRIFTER's** corner matches it perfectly. If they have any trouble at this stage all they have to do is call for the manager who will assume that their staff member wasn't paying attention.

See also **RINGING THE CHANGES**.

A
B
C
D
E
F
G
H
I
J
K
L
M
N
O
P
Q
R
S
T
U
V
W
X
Y
Z

TOROIDAL BUBBLE

FUN WITH SCIENCE

Torus is the mathematical word for a doughnut-shape, so something *Toroidal* is something shaped like a dog's rubber ring.

A **TOROIDAL BUBBLE** is also known as a *Bubble Ring* and it's what happens when a pocket of air is propelled into water just-so.

It's very like a **SMOKE RING**.

Grab a pair of swimming goggles and hold onto something heavy (or wear some diving weights). Take a deep breath and allow yourself to sink to the bottom of the swimming pool and lie there on your back.

Fill your cheeks with air and then carefully open your mouth like a big fish gulping air, push your tongue hard forwards as your mouth opens and, with luck, the great big bubble of air you let out will form something almost exactly like a **SMOKE RING**!

The huge toroidal bubble will rise gently toward the surface to the amazement of all.

☆ Dolphins are known to make and play with bubble rings. They make them by puffing a little air out of their blowholes.

TOSSING GRAPES INTO YOUR MOUTH

JUGGLING

The essential skill of **TOSSING GRAPES INTO YOUR MOUTH** is required learning for tricksters. It is the eating method of first choice for cartoon characters.

The technique can also be applied to other edible items, such as peanuts, sweets and sugar lumps, but grapes are best to learn with because they don't hurt if they hit your teeth.

Learn the trick on your own with a whole bunch of grapes, nothing looks quite as tragic as a miss in public.

☆ It's fun to find similarly skilled friends and toss things into each other's mouths.

TOWING HITCH ON THE FRONT

VEHICLES

If you are towing a caravan or trailer you will need to master the skill of **REVERSING A TRUCK**, but no matter how good you get at this you'll find that there are some situations in which you'll have to unhitch and resort to moving the thing by hand in order to make that tricky corner.

That is, unless you have a **TOWING HITCH ON THE FRONT**.

A front-mounted towing hitch gives you amazing control over a trailer and you'll find that you can turn on a sixpence and perform very accurate manoeuvres. If you are really keen on setting up for this sort of work you'll also have a forward-facing mirror on the side of your cab opposite the driving seat so that you can see down the blind side of your trailer.

Showmen often use *drawbar trailers* which are almost impossible to reverse using a rear-mounted hitch.

A drawbar trailer is like the trailer from an articulated lorry but instead of having the front of the trailer resting on the "fifth wheel" of the tractor unit they are fitted with a "dolly" at the front end.

You make a dolly by chopping off the back end of a scrap truck and sticking an A-frame on the front.

When you try to reverse there are two points at which the rig bends so it's a bit like trying to balance two footballs on the end of your finger!

Unless, of course, you turn the tow-truck around and hitch the trailer to the front instead—then it's easy!

This is why circus and fairground tow-trucks have hitches on the front.

TRAPEZE (YO-YO)

YO-YO

☆ Do a **BREAKAWAY**, but as the **Yo-Yo** swings up you intercept the string with the index finger of your free hand. The **Yo-Yo** will loop over and, with a little care, you can make it drop right onto the waiting string and **SLEEP** there —ta daa!

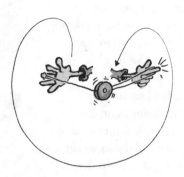

☆ To return the **Yo-Yo** to a less precarious position just give the string a a quick tug with your finger and it should hop off, orbit your finger and snap back into your yo-hand.

TRAPS

OUTDOORPERSONSHIP / SURVIVAL

In these enlightened times of Tesco supermarkets and political correctness a few things need to be said about capturing wild birds and animals, lest *Every Trick in the Book* become a banned volume.

If you are intending to eat the poor beast, then go ahead, but please be mindful not to pointlessly cruel to your fellow creatures.

If you are intending to capture the animal for research purposes, or perhaps to find a new friend in a pet, then it would be best not to harm the animal at all. For this reason we have little to say about devices involving fish hooks or *snares* which are inhumane and prone to cause a great deal of suffering.

We'll begin our exploration with the classic *Dead Drop* type of trap, in this case a *Figure Four Trap*.

A
B
C
D
E
F
G
H
I
J
K
L
M
N
O
P
Q
R
S
T
U
V
W
X
Y
Z

The device is pretty much self-explanatory. Three pieces of previously-prepared woodwork are knocked up in the workshop and it is then up to the trapper to locate a suitably heavy monolith out in the woods where the type of animal being hunted is common. A slight twitch on the bait and the stone comes crashing down with lethal results.

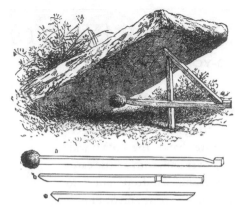

Other methods of killing your game involve setting up light artillery with woodsman-like trigger devices. These are very effective, but the relatively long range of the devices mean that they are too dangerous for use anywhere where people might be wandering about.

Also the legality of leaving a loaded firearm where anyone could find it is questionable. So you may choose to use some sort of bow instead, which while still dangerous, is considerably more law-abiding.

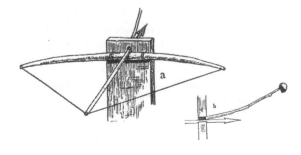

To catch a small bird alive you could do a lot worse than to employ the easily made *Brick Trap* in which a trapdoor brick is held aloft by a small prop attached to a forked twig on which the bird will usually perch in order to retrieve the bait you have used.

There is always a chance that the poor creature will be injured by the falling brick, so you may wish to construct a trap that is more or less guaranteed not to injure your prey. You could, for example, use the *Box Owl Trap* which is fashioned from a suitable wooden box.

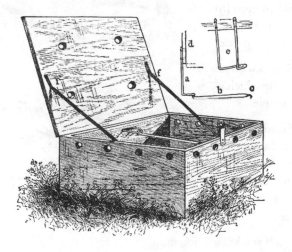

The lid is attached to the box by two elastic straps (f) and a cunning piece of bent wire (a) is attached to the lid and run through a slot in the back of the box. A small bar (b) keeps tension on the wire until it is disturbed by a bird entering the box to eat the bait you have scattered on the bottom.

A
B
C
D
E
F
G
H
I
J
K
L
M
N
O
P
Q
R
S
T
U
V
W
X
Y
Z

Ducks may be caught, quite humanely using a sort of open-air lobster pot.

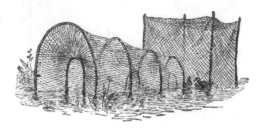

They are perfectly capable of entering such a device in search of bread or other delicacies, but far too stupid to find their way out again.

For small mammals there are few traps as humane, simple and ingenious as the *Self-Setting Trap* which consists of a simple box with one open and and a gate of wires that is easily pushed open from the outside, but impossible to open from the inside.

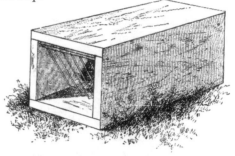

Pesky mice are suckers for the *Barrel Trap* which is brilliantly simple.

A sheet of card or paper is used to seal the open end of a barrel like a jam jar lid and a cross cut in it before giving the device a light dusting of tasty nibbles.

Be kind, and if you kill it—you must eat it!

See also **RUM RAISINS AND PHEASANTS**.

TRAY SPINNING

OBJECT MANIPULATION

TRAY SPINNING is the art of balancing a tray, or some other flat object, on the end of a finger while it spins in the horizontal plane. The skill is similar to that of **BALL SPINNING.**

☆ The tray is held flat from underneath by the outstretched fingers and thumb of your favourite hand. It is then tossed up with a flick to start it spinning.

Your spin-finger (usually the index or middle finger) catches the tray slightly off its point of balance and then rotates under the tray to build up momentum, while keeping the tray balanced. This can only be learned with practice, no amount of *thinking* about it will help. In this sense it's like learning to ride a **UNICYCLE.**

Practice a little every day and don't expect to learn it in an afternoon (see **LEARNING HOW TO LEARN TRICKS**).

☆ **TRAY SPINNING** can be easily and safely practiced in the home using small flat scatter cushions. It can also be done with a twice-folded bath towel: the centrifugal force of the spin will keep the towel flat in the air.

☆ Confident tray-spinners can manage a tray in each hand!

☆ Flamboyant pizza chefs use the **TRAY SPINNING** technique to stretch a round ball of dough into a large flat circular pizza base while turning the preparation of your meal into a lively show.

A
B
C
D
E
F
G
H
I
J
K
L
M
N
O
P
Q
R
S
T
U
V
W
X
Y
Z

A
B
C
D
E
F
G
H
I
J
K
L
M
N
O
P
Q
R
S
T
U
V
W
X
Y
Z

TREBLA

JUGGLING

A **TREBLA** is a reverse **ALBERT**—an **UNDER THE LEG** throw made *without* lifting your foot off the floor—thrown from front to back.

The throw rises over the shoulder to a catch in front of the body.

While technically possible with balls and rings, this trick is pretty much exclusively performed with clubs.

See **ALBERT**.

TREBUCHET

WEAPONS

The **TREBUCHET** was a medieval siege weapon of great accuracy and power, capable of slinging heavy projectiles over great distances without the use of explosives. It combines a counterweight and sling, gaining its lethal force as if **CRACKING A WHIP**. Here is how *Radical Cheney* describes the art of loading and firing this behemoth in his book *The True Nature of Things:*

> The Trebuchet once aligned on the enemy is made ready thus: the artillerymen first heave down on the mast by means of the two windlasses at D. It matters not if one man works harder than the other for they are heaving on opposite ends of a single line passing through a the block marked F which connected to another block I which runs on the *downhaul* rigged between K and L, where the more observant reader will see that the mast is whipped with stout rope to protect it from the flailing of the block that occurs when the weapon is released. The two blocks, I and F are held connected by means of the the *detente* or trigger-pin at the point marked E.

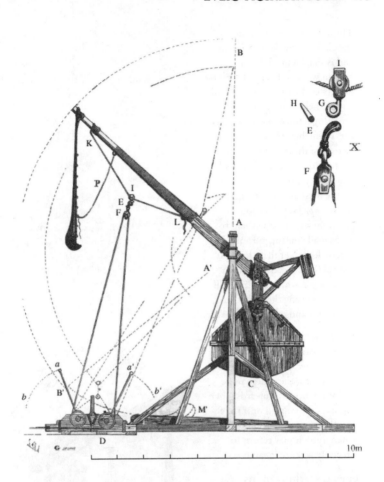

The charge itself, whether rock, steel balls set in clay, or a putrified corpse is laid in the *mainpognay* which now lies in the position marked M. The Trebuchet is then released on the command *Lancay!* by the the striking of the *detente* with a hammer, causing the tapered pin to fly from the steel ring G, which frees the mast.

---

* The author has not found the term *mainpognay* used in any other descriptions of the TREBUCHET save this one, from which we can infer either that Cheney made it up, or that he had a better source on which to base his account of the weapon. It would seem to derive from the French *main* (hand) and *poignet* (wrist).

A
B
C
D
E
F
G
H
I
J
K
L
M
N
O
P
Q
R
S
T
U
V
W
X
Y
Z

A
B
C
D
E
F
G
H
I
J
K
L
M
N
O
P
Q
R
S
T
U
V
W
X
Y
Z

The *mainpognay* which holds the charge is made from wicker and is shaped much like a human wrist and hand. It will be understood that the charge will remain held in it by the centrifugal force of the swing of the Trebuchet. However, the "wrist" of the *mainpognay* is restrained by a pair of sheets P that suspend from a short arm on the mast and may be tied to the *mainpognay* in various positions by knotting them to loops made for the purpose. The precise length of these lines is critical for it sets the point in the swing at which the line will tighten, causing the "wrist" to bend back and release the charge.

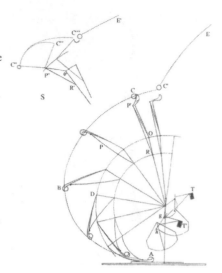

If the lines are not set correctly the artillerymen risk being killed by their own weapon. Nor is it unknown for the charge to be delivered directly upwards when the stays are tangled or if they have been set too short whereupon it may return to precisely whence it came.

Cheney is scathing in his accounts of other types of release mechanism declaring the *mainpognay* the only one worthy of use on the field of war.

The most common alternative is based on the **SLING** whereby a pouch, holding the charge, is attached to the end of the mast by two lines, one of which is permanently fixed, and the other

ends in a loop which is placed over a pin or hook projecting from the end of the mast. As the charge rises over the machine the loop slips off the hook, releasing the charge. But as Cheney points out:

> The free end of such a sling, once released, forms a lethal whip which is perfectly capable of slicing a man in half as it flails free of its load.

Adjustments to the aim of such a machine are made by bending the hook with hammers, a crude method which can easily cause the hook to weaken and fail altogether with disastrous results.

A well-made Trebuchet with a *contrepoids* (or counterweight) of a few tons can hurl a couple of hundredweight about a quarter of a mile. When manned by a good team of artillerymen, it can achieve up to six shots an hour.

See also **SLING**.

TREMBLING TROUSER

SILLINESS

The **TREMBLING TROUSER** is a comical trick in which a chap makes his trousers vibrate amusingly in order to express mirth and excitement.

This is not a good trick to perform in tight jeans, instead one needs to be wearing flannels or another gentleman's trouser.

☆ Grasp the absolute base of the seat of your trouser from behind, where the four seams meet. Tug backwards rapidly and repeatedly. Your entire trouser will vibrate to the great amusement of all.

A B C D E F G H I J K L M N O P Q R S T U V W X Y Z

A
B
C
D
E
F
G
H
I
J
K
L
M
N
O
P
Q
R
S
T
U
V
W
X
Y
Z

TRIGONOMETRY

MATHEMATICS / GEOMETRY

Carpenters, soldiers and builders often turn to **TRIGONOMETRY** when stuck for a measurement. It's a really useful trick to have up your sleeve.

A lot of people find Trigonometry hard—so here are a few tips.

Mathematicians long ago precisely worked out the relationship between the angle *theta* (written θ) and the movement, in terms of x and y coordinates, of a point P at the end of line one unit long swinging full *circle* around the origin. Even better, their modern descendants have stuck special buttons on your pocket calculator that do the clever bit for you. These buttons are labelled *sin, cos* and *tan* which are short for *Sine, Cosine* and *Tangent.*[*]

One way of understanding how *sines* and *cosines* work is to think of them as operating in a *circle*. So if you have moved a distance r at an angle of θ then

COSINE (or *cos* for short) means you can work out: "*How far East did we go?*"

The answer is *r times the cosine of theta* which is generally written down as:

$r * \cos \theta$

To do this sum on your calculator make sure that the machine is set to degrees and then type in the angle, hit the cosine button and then multiply that result by the radius *r*.

---

[*] There are other **TRIGONOMETRIC** functions with more exotic names like *secant, versin* and others but these are the most useful ones. Go look that stuff up in *Wikipedia*.

In the same way SINE (or sin for short) helps you work out:
"*How far North did we go?*"

The answer is *r times the sine of theta* which is generally written down as:

r * sin θ

To do this sum, enter *theta*, hit the *sine* button and then multiply the result by *r*.

The most useful sine, cosine and tangent formulæ are:

cos θ = x/r   hence   x = r * cos θ

sin θ = y/r   hence   y = r * sin θ

tan θ = y/x   hence   x = y/tan θ and   y = tan θ /x

TRIPLE SINGLES (53)

JUGGLING

This is a four-object juggling pattern, very popular with club jugglers.

☆ When working with clubs the one hand throws *triple-spins* and the other throws *single-spins*. Usually it's the right hand that makes the high throws. It's a pretty cool way of juggling four clubs, especially as it favours the strong hand. As a trick, jugglers often throw some or all of the high throws **BEHIND THE BACK**.

It's probably a good idea to learn it both ways around though, in the interest of cultivating ambidexterity.

☆ The pattern is also known by its **SITESWAP NOTATION**, 53 (one hand makes throws as if juggling a cascade of five objects, while the other acts as if it juggling three. The average of five and three is four—hence this is a four-object pattern.

☆ It's a simple change from a four-object **FOUNTAIN**, i.e. 4, into 53 (and back again) and you can have some rewarding fun trying the following routines (each starts with four throws of the **FOUNTAIN**).

44445344445344453444...
44445345345345345345...

If you can manage to throw a 7 (which would usually be a five-spin with clubs) then you can try this:

444453535375373333535353...

In plain English: start with a fountain, go into 53 for a few throws than lob a really high 7 and juggle three throws of a simple cascade underneath it while you wait for it to come down again.

This feels great and looks amazing.

TRISECTING AN ANGLE

GEOMETRY / OCCULT SCIENCE

It is possible, using *unmarked* ruler and compass, to perform the trick of **BISECTING AN ANGLE**. It is, however, *impossible* to perform the trick of **TRISECTING AN ANGLE** with the same tools. This was algebraically proven by *Pierre Laurent Wantzel* in 1836.

This has not prevented pseudo-scientists from continuing to attempt solutions to the present day. What people sometimes fail to realise is that the rule *'with only unmarked ruler and compass'* is a very precise mathematical limitation, and things can be very accurately proven about it.

"Why then," one might wonder, "is this such a big deal?"

Well, it is such a big deal because, during the early days of mathematics, many amazing discoveries were made about mathematics and geometry and the discoverers were so impressed with the power of their science that they suspected that the elegance of mathematics might be revealing to them the workings of the creator of the Universe. They further discovered that things that could be done with numbers could also be done by geometry, using ruler and compass to perform calculations graphically, as opposed to numerically. Reminders of this tradition remain with us even today, as seen in some of the imagery of the *Freemasons*.

However, despite the enthusiasm of the early mathematicians and geometers, the Universe was not so simple, and it was found that the problems of **TRISECTING AN ANGLE** and *Squaring the Circle* would not submit to the ruler and compass so easily. Indeed, some reasoned that anyone who could work out how to do these things would somehow stumble on the deeper secrets of creation. Others claimed to have done so, but chose to remain silent about the methods they claimed to have worked out, and so it went on.

☆ HERE'S *The* TRICK: So, for the trickster, here is a geometric method of **TRISECTING AN ANGLE** with ruler and compass (with a small cheat) that should be pretty easy to pass off—to all but the best-educated in such matters. We achieve the impossible by breaking the rules of the game and using a *marked* ruler—one on which two marks have been made—an arbitrary distance apart. This is against the rules of the game, but we will keep that as our secret. The clever bit is that it does not matter how the two marks are spaced. Any two marks will do.

---

* The image depicts: the Sun, the Moon, the seven planets, a mason's hammer or mallet, a book of knowledge, a set square, a pair of compasses & a trowel—the two remaining items in the engraving are both corruptions (by way of copying) of the same or similar tool: a plumb bob and line mounted on a device with a straight edge for calibrating true architecture according to the vertical and horizontal.

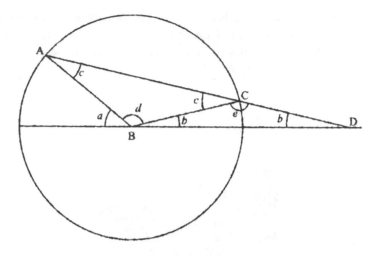

We start with the baseline passing through BD and a line BA that is at some arbitrary angle *a*, to the baseline. This is the angle we shall trisect, and the result appears as the angle b at the point CDB.

Here's how we proceed from the initial angle *a*:

1: We take a ruler with two evenly spaced marks on it and set our compass to the distance between them. This is the distance AB to which we set a compass and draw the *circle* around B.

2: Anchor the ruler at A, and slide it until one mark is on the *circle* at C and the other is on the baseline at D. Draw the line.

3: The angle *b* at CDB is one third of the angle *a* we started with.

The additional lines and angles marked are to support the proof which is given in this footnote[*].

The point is: *it works!*

---

[*] The thing to note is that the triangles ABC and BCD are both isosceles triangles. Since $e + c = 180°$, and $e + 2b = 180°$ we get $c = 2b$ from which $d = 180° - 4b$. Now since $a + d + b = 180°$, substituting $180° - 4b$ for d we get: $a + 180° - 4b + b = 180°$ so reducing we get $a - 3b = 0°$ therefore $a = 3b$. QED.

TRUCKER'S HITCH

KNOTS

This knot (also known as a *Dolly*) is the one that truck drivers traditionally use when *roping and sheeting*—that is to say loading goods onto a flatbed truck, optionally covering them with a tarpaulin sheet, and roping the load down.

The knot works like a block and tackle and can apply massive tension to the load. It's tied in the middle of a rope and unties very easily.

☆ Arrange the load on the truck and then cover it with a sheet. There are roping hooks all the way down the side of the truck, just underneath the edge. Take your rope and tie it to the first hook on the right hand side and throw the rope over the load. In times past, when the world was a slightly simpler place, the driver would have had a *driver's mate* who would be standing other side so the job would have proceeded a lot faster. Walk around to the other side and grab the rope about three feet above the hook.

1: Make a small bend in the rope with your right hand and lay it over the standing part of the rope which is hanging down over the load. Grab the standing part, just past the bend, with your left hand and loop it over the bend.

2: Wrap the standing part around the bend a second time, making sure that it goes *between* the previous loop and the standing part—it will jam in there nicely.

A
B
C
D
E
F
G
H
I
J
K
L
M
N
O
P
Q
R
S
T
U
V
W
X
Y
Z

A
B
C
D
E
F
G
H
I
J
K
L
M
N
O
P
Q
R
S
T
U
V
W
X
Y
Z

3: With your left hand twist the noose you have just formed in the direction shown. This is important, the twist will prevent the little loops from spilling under load.

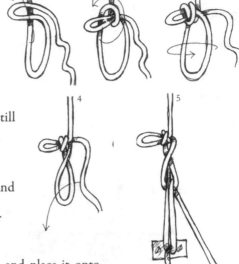

4: Your right hand will still be holding the knot you have made in the rope. Your left hand now reaches through noose and picks up a *bight* (loop) from the trailing part of the rope.

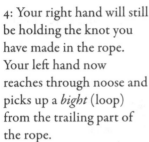

5: Pull this *bight* down and place it onto one of the hooks on the side of your truck. Grab the trailing part of the rope and pull hard. You'll be amazed at how much this tightens the rope.

6: When it is tight enough you wind the trailing part *twice* around the hook and throw the rope back over the load.

You can now let go and the knot will stay tight as you walk around to repeat the process on the other side. On a large truck you may have eight or nine of these incredible knots on each side.

When the load is secure you simply tie off the end with a nice solid slip knot and you are ready to roll.

When unloading you'll find that the knots simply fall out of the rope with a flick as you loosen them one by one.

☆ Once you have become totally familiar with this knot you'll be able to tie it in seconds.

TUBELESS TYRE-REFITTING AT MINUS 10°

VEHICLES

This trick is well-known by Icelandic 4×4 enthusiasts who like to take their vehicles for drives over the big glaciers in cold countries.

When driving on the ice they use very low tyre pressures to increase traction (see **STUCK IN MUD, SAND OR SNOW**) and from time to time a tyre will simply fall off the rim as it turns a corner or hits something. Refitting tubeless tyres can be tricky at the best of times, but in very cold conditions it can be all but impossible.

☆ HERE'S *The* TRICK: Jack up the affected wheel and grab a can of the stuff you use to refill gas lighters. Squirt this liberally into the gap between the tyre and the rim and then ignite it with a lighter.

There will be an explosive 'pop' and the tyre will snap back onto the rim.

Top it up with air and you're done.

TWO-BALL SHOWER

JUGGLING

The **TWO-BALL SHOWER** is a juggling pattern that is often juggled by children.

☆ Start with two balls, one in each hand. One hand throws to the other and the other **FEEDS** back—that is, it passes the balls across and *places* them in the receiving hand.

This is a trick often learned in the school playground, although easy to learn it's hardly real juggling!

A B C D E F G H I J K L M N O P Q R S T U V W X Y Z

When experts at the **Two Ball Shower** later try to
learn the **Three Ball Cascade** they usually have
serious problems because the ingrained habit of
Feeding balls with one hand while *throwing* with
the other is very hard to break.

In **SiteSwap Notation** this pattern is
represented by the numbers 3 1, the 3's are the throws,
the 1's are the **Feeds**.

Two in One Hand

JUGGLING

Juggling **Two in One Hand** with balls is about as easy as juggling a
Three Ball Cascade in *two* hands. It's just about the most useful
Trick a new juggler can learn.

There are lots of three-ball **Tricks** that rely on the **Two in One Hand**
technique to leave a hand free to do something impressive or improbable
like **Eating an Apple While Juggling**.

When you can juggle **Two in One Hand** in *either* hand you are ready to
move on to Four Ball Juggling.

There are three basic shapes you can use for a **Two in One Hand** pattern.

☆ *Rolling Out:* The hand throws on the inside and catches on the outside. The balls move away from the centre of your body while being juggled. This is the easiest shape.

☆ *Rolling In:* The hand throws on the outside and catches on the inside. This is a lot harder— but a worthwhile skill to learn.

☆ *Columns:* The two balls rise and fall each in their own column, with the hand giving attention to each in turn.

So go to it!

TWO UP

JUGGLING

☆ Take two balls, toss them straight up and catch them again. Easy!

☆ Take two balls and toss them up and catch them with your arms crossed. Cool.

☆ Take two balls, cross your arms, toss them up, uncross your hands and catch them. No problem.

☆ OK, here goes: Take two balls, cross your hands, toss them *so they cross* and catch them *without uncrossing your hands!*

Got you that time!

Get this, even *seven-ball* jugglers can rarely pull this off. It's like **PATTING YOUR HEAD AND RUBBING YOUR STOMACH**.

The trick, while impossibly difficult on a first attempt, takes just *ten minutes* to learn—so learn it, and use it to piss off people who are much better jugglers than you.

U*

ULTIMATE WHEEL

UNICYCLING

The **ULTIMATE WHEEL** is a unicycle
with the frame and seat removed. It
is considerably harder to ride than a
regular unicycle since it is more or
less completely unstable (if you
thought a regular unicycle was
unstable then you are in for a big
shock).

CONTACT

The point is that it *seems* as if there are only
two points of contact between rider and
machine—the two feet on the two pedals.
And two points, as anyone who knows
anything about the dynamics of
machinery like this will confirm,
is not enough to allow the rider to control it and keep it upright.

However, by allowing the wheel to flap against the inside of the rider's leg
when the foot is in the *down* position, we end up with three points of
contact, which is *just* enough.

☆ The trick of riding an **ULTIMATE WHEEL** is, therefore, to get it into
one almost-stable position (left foot down, wheel resting on left calf) and
then quickly move into another almost-stable position (right foot down,
wheel resting on right calf). And so the rider proceeds with the wheel
flapping from side to side as they pedal.

ULTIMATE WHEELS are typically made with the spokes and hub replaced by a single sheet of plywood, onto which the two pedals are directly mounted. For strength it is advisable to mount steel plates onto the wheel disc to which the pedals can be bolted securely. The plywood

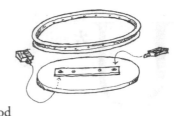

is then inserted into the wheel rim and screwed in place through the old spoke holes.

☆ It is possible to **SUICIDE MOUNT** an **ULTIMATE WHEEL**, though a kind of **KICKUP MOUNT** is more often used.

The wheel is laid on the ground on one side, and one foot placed next to its pedal. the other foot then lifts the wheel up, finds its own pedal, and off you go.

That's the theory anyway.

See also **IMPOSSIBLE WHEEL**.

UNDER THE HAND

JUGGLING

The first trick a new three-ball juggler usually learns is **OVER THE TOP**, the second is often **UNDER THE HAND**. When you have mastered both you can put them together to do a **WINDMILL**. Change the *direction* of your **WINDMILL** every three throws and you are juggling a **MILLS' MESS**.

Juggling, as you can see, is a deeply intertwingled art form but we're getting ahead of ourselves. Here's how to learn **UNDER THE HAND**.

☆ Juggle a **THREE BALL CASCADE** as normal and then throw one ball *under* the opposite wrist. It goes straight up and is caught as normal. The structure and timing of the cascade is not altered, only the *shape* of the pattern changes.

☆ It can be pretty hard to pull this off in a running **THREE BALL CAS-CADE,** so make your life easy and *start* the pattern with an **UNDER THE HAND** throw.

Place two balls in your right hand and one in the left. Throw the first ball from *under* the left wrist, then continue as normal.

☆ Practice this on both sides until it is solid.

☆ When you are having some success you should try all the regular combinations:

- Every right **UNDER THE HAND.**
- Every left.
- Same ball every time.
- *Every* ball.

☆ Note that when you throw **UNDER THE HAND** the hand you are throwing the ball *under* will dodge out of the way—all of its own accord. If you learn to accentuate this motion will have mastered a juggling trick called a **CHOP.**

UNDER THE LEG

JUGGLING

Juggling **UNDER THE LEG** is what is known as a *body move* — a trick in which the act of juggling is made even more impossible by contorting the juggling pattern around the body in awkward ways.

☆ When learning to juggle **UNDER THE LEG** the apprentice juggler should concentrate on *bringing the leg into the pattern*, rather than trying to wrap the pattern around the leg. A normal **UNDER THE LEG** throw from the right hand will travel under the right leg from the outside to the inside. An alternative throw, under the *opposite* leg, has the throw going under the *left* leg from inside to outside.

A B C D E F G H I J K L M N O P Q R S T U V W X Y Z

☆ **UNDER THE LEG** is actually *easier* to do with clubs than balls because clubs have nice long handles.

☆ To make a normal **UNDER THE LEG** throw the leg that is being thrown under has to be lifted off the ground.

☆ It follows that making *every* throw an **UNDER THE LEG** throw requires the juggler to dance on the spot like a complete idiot! This is an advanced and comical trick.

☆ With clubs you can juggle **UNDER THE LEG** *without* lifting your foot off the ground. This type of throw is called an **ALBERT** after *Albert Lucas*, a famous and very talented juggler.

☆ Juggling under the *opposite* leg without lifting your foot off the floor is known as a **TREBLA** throw (think reverse **ALBERT**).

UNICYCLING

TOPIC

Riding a **UNICYCLE** seems to be one of those all-but-impossible skills, especially if you have actually tried it, but the fact is that anyone can learn to ride one. Kids, annoyingly, can make real progress in a single afternoon. Older people take longer.

If you want to learn you'll need to beg, steal, or borrow a *Standard Unicycle* which is a machine with twenty inch wheels that looks pretty much like a BMX bike with all the really *useful* bits removed (see **HOW TO RIDE YOUR UNICYCLE***).

---

* **HOW TO RIDE YOUR UNICYCLE** is both an entry in this book *and* the title of small and reasonably-priced book by the author which explores the skills of unicycling in 32 spectacular pages.

Unicycles are not generally considered to be sensible forms of transport. They are very *wobbly*. They are rubbish on hills (both up and down). They have no brakes and they don't go very fast.

Having said that, certain obsessive people have achieved some amazing feats with unicycles, like riding all the way across America backwards, getting married on a matched pair, and juggling large numbers of objects while riding them.

The *Standard Unicycle*, as mentioned earlier, has a twenty-inch wheel. There are unicycles with larger wheels—which go much faster. There are chain-driven *Giraffe Unicycles*, which can be very high, and novelty unicycles with several wheels driving each other (though only one in contact with the ground of course).

If you want to do Juggling on a **UNICYCLE** you'll find it a lot easier on a *Giraffe Unicycle* because these tall machines, despite their awesomely impressive appearance are actually *easier* to stay upright on than the little ones.

Unicycling skills include **HOVERING** (staying in one place) **FREE-MOUNTING** (getting on without anything to lean on or climb up) *Wheel-Walking* (driving the thing with your feet on the tyre rather than the pedals) *Bunny-Hopping* (jumping up and down on the spot) and the lethal sport of *Gliding* (see **WHEEL BRAKING**).

A Unicycle, as I said, is a bike with all of the really useful bits removed, so that you end up with just a small frame, one wheel, two pedals and cranks and a saddle. It turns out that further bits can be removed to produce even more improbable vehicles *which can still be ridden,*

Take off the frame and saddle and you end up with the **ULTIMATE WHEEL**, which is actually rideable though it is not quite as *ultimate* as it claims to be. You can go one step further and remove the pedals and cranks and replace them with *stunt pegs* (BMX-speak for simple rods projecting from

A
B
C
D
E
F
G
H
I
J
K
L
M
N
O
P
Q
R
S
T
U
V
W
X
Y
Z

the axle that form foot-pegs) and you get the **IMPOSSIBLE WHEEL**
which is also poorly named because it isn't (impossible, that is).

The unicycle was first discovered (and shortly thereafter actually *ridden*)
sometime in the 1870's. Note that it was *discovered*, rather than *invented*.
This happened because of a defect in the design of the two-wheeled cycles
of the time—the *Penny Farthings* or, as they are more properly called,
Ordinary Bicycles.

This *Double Hollow Fork "Challenge"* bicycle was manufactured by Singer
& Co. of Coventry* in 1880. It retailed at £15 ¹⁰/- for the 31" leg version,
with an additional charge of 5/- for every additional leg-inch.† It was state-
of-the-art, expensive and lethal—just like every other Penny Farthing.

The problem was this: notice that the rider sits just behind the centre of the
front wheel. Now try to imagine what will happen if that woefully

---

* Yes—that is indeed Singer & Co. of Coventry, the famous sewing machine manufacturers.

† Quick lesson in Old Money: £12 5/6d means 12 pounds, 5 shillings and 6 pence. The little "d"
stands for denarii which is the Roman word for the ancient equivalent of a penny. The £ sign itself
is a stylised letter "L" and is short for livre—the French word for pound. Thus the acronym LSD
was often used to refer to Pounds Shillings and Pence—no really! There were 20 shillings to a
pound and 12 pence to a shilling. So altogether there were 240 pence in a pound. Where a price
came out as an exact number of shillings (i.e. no pence) it was written with a dash instead of a
zero for the pence i.e. £12 5/-. Complicated? You bet! It gets worse: it was customary, before
decimalisation in the 1970's to price really expensive items in *Guineas* instead of pounds shillings
and pence. One Guinea was 21 shillings (£1 1/-) this was a simple way of charging very rich
people a little more.

ineffective front brake is jammed on really hard—the bike will simply rotate forward, lifting the back wheel off the ground, and smashing the rider's head into the road. About 10,000 people were killed in this way in the early days of cycling. You didn't even need to use the front brake to have this accident, simply attempting to slow the vehicle down on a hill descent by pushing backwards on the pedals can have the same effect.

But it wasn't long before somebody discovered a cool trick: They could lift the back wheel from the road and *still* manage to stay upright.

It was a small step to realising that the rear wheel could be removed *completely* and you'd still have a rideable machine. Moreover it would be considerably lighter than a regular bike. Thus the unicycle was born. They had handlebars where the modern unicycle has a saddle and they were much-used in cycle racing events as well as being a popular prop for trick riders.

In 1885 the chain-driven *Safety Bicycle* was invented by *John Starley* who christened his machine the *Rover Safety Bicycle.* It didn't kill people nearly as fast as the old Ordinary and the design remains virtually the same to this day.

"ROVER" SAFETY BICYCLE

Unicycles are not to be confused with Monocycles though they often are.

---

* Later on production moved into motorcycles and finally cars, and that's where the legendary *Rover* name comes from.

A B C D E F G H I J K L M N O P Q R S T **U** V W X Y Z

UPGRADING ON AIRCRAFT

TRICKS OF THE TRADES

The ideal scenario, when boarding an aircraft is that of *turning left* on entry, since that is the direction in which the fist class cabins lie. This is, however very expensive.

If you are tall, like that author, and by tall I mean well over six feet, or if you are large, and by large I mean over sixteen stone, you can get upgraded if you follow these instructions.

☆ Wait until the plane has pushed back and is taxiing to the end of the runway. Pay close attention to the safety briefing and when it has finished call one of the cabin crew over.

'Excuse me, I was just reading my safety card and I notice that I cannot actually achieve the *brace position* because the seat in front of me is too close!'

You should then demonstrate the problem.

According to safety regulations you should be upgraded to business, or even first class, just don't expect good service for the rest of the flight.

UPSIDE DOWN GLASS TRICK

BAR TRICKS / FUN WITH SCIENCE

This is a good one, a trifle mean, but a good one nevertheless.

☆ A large glass is filled absolutely to the brim with water. Now take a flat and thin object, like a piece of card and place it over the liquid. You can now, very carefully and with a little support from your fingers, turn the glass upside down and place it on the table or bar top. This will only work on a non-absorbent surface.

Slide out the card and you have a full glass sitting upside down. Now just leave it there for the staff to clear up.

What are they going to do about that?

UPSIDE DOWN WATER TRICK

OBJECT MANIPULATION

☆ Get a bucket full of water and carefully swing it back and forth. Note how the surface of the water can be kept level with the rim of the bucket so that none is spilt.

Now bravely swing the thing through a full 360° over your head and see if you can avoid spilling a drop. It's not that hard.

☆ Armed with this new skill you should now start practicing with a beer glass filled to about seven eighth's capacity with water. You should have little trouble rotating it at arm's length. See just how slow you can go!

☆ Next learn the side-flip: put the glass on the table and extend your right hand toward it as if picking the glass up normally. Before you grab the glass turn your hand 180° anti-clockwise (so your thumb and forefinger arc at the *bottom*)—now pick it up.

From this position you swing the glass, with a twist of the wrist, 360° clockwise—just like swinging the bucket, but in miniature. Then see if you can swing it back again. Practice the move until you can do it as slowly as possible without losing a drop.

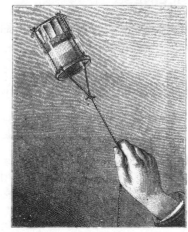

☆ As with all juggling tricks you should learn this every which way and in both hands. Once mastered you can start to work with *real beer!*

☆ When you get very confident and can happily work with two glasses at once, you'll find that you can apply moves borrowed from *Club Swinging* and **POI** such as the **CROSS & FOLLOW** and the **CURL**.

UP YOURS

RUDE GESTURES

☆ We're all familiar with the view of the back of someone's fist with the middle finger raised.

☆ It's considerably more comical if the fist starts off with the finger held down. Then the other hand winds it slowly up and back down again with an imaginary crank.

☆ Alternatively, offer your enemy a straight **UP YOURS** with the remark *"that's for you!"* followed by the same gesture aimed horizontally *"and that's for your dog!"*

URBAN GOLF

SILLINESS

This game is an extension of the schoolboy's pass-time of kicking a stone all the way home.

☆ Two players, at the starting point, equip themselves each with a **BEANBAG** or similar non-destructive object and agree on a target.

"The fountain at Laura Place!" Declares one to the other at the door of the Bell on Walcot Street. And so battle commences.

Unlike true golf, no whacking implement is used, instead the players simply lob their missiles as far as they can down the street, and the one who manages to get theirs to the fountain in the fewest number of *lobs* is the winner of that particular "hole".

The rules concerning the nature of a lob are exacting: the lob commences with the beanbag in hand and the player is not allowed to take a single step or loosen their grip during the move. A grip-change or a step counts as one lob—it's a little like *French Cricket* in that regard.

However there are no other limitations on lobs, so tossing a beanbag onto the roof of a passing car (in the hope that it will drop off at a suitable corner further down the fairway) is perfectly allowable.

Train and bus journeys may also be taken during play, though the beanbag must be lobbed on board (one lob) and left motionless for the duration of the journey before being lobbed off again at the end. In this way a game of **URBAN GOLF** may start in, say the fine city of Bath, and end, after only a few lobs, in Trafalgar Square, London.

See also **SPLITTING NUNS**.

A B C D E F G H I J K L M N O P Q R S T U V W X Y Z

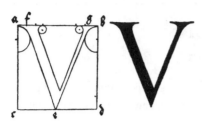

V

VANISHING FOOT TRICK

MAGIC / HAT TRICKS

Here's an old classic.

☆ Hold a towel in front of you so that it hangs down to the floor. Lift it up slowly to reveal your feet. Now lower it and raise it again and one leg has vanished!

All you have to do is to stand on one leg.

OK, so it's pretty lame, but it's funny!

☆ You can do more or less the same thing with a Hat, and it's a sweet little trick to throw into a *Hat Juggling* routine—though it is very angle-sensitive.

For this effect you slide a hat, crown towards the audience, down your leg from the knee to the floor. As you raise it, bend your leg so that by the time the hat gets to your knee your lower leg seems to have vanished.

Done to a small audience at the correct angle this can be very amusing.

See also **HAT HAND VANISH**.

VIDEO FEEDBACK

FUN WITH SCIENCE / FILMING

We're all pretty familiar with audio feedback, especially if we are fans of heavy metal music, but did you know that you can do the same thing with video?

☆ Plug a video camera's output into your TV and point the camera at the screen. Zoom in, twist the camera, mess around.

You can produce some truly amazing effects this way. Some are stable, some are chaotic, but most are controllable if you are careful.

Hit record on the camera and grab some of this stuff to cut into the title sequence of your latest movie!

☆ Truly extraordinary effects can be obtained if you can find a video projector and some glow-in-the-dark juggling props like light balls, fire torches or sparklers.

You'll also need a tripod for the camera, it won't work if it is hand-held.

Erect a screen, something large and white like a bed sheet will do, then set up the projector so that its image fills the screen.

Erect the camera and tripod next to the projector and adjust the zoom so it is seeing pretty much whatever the projector is chucking out and then simply plug the output of the camera into the input of the projector, turn out the lights and you're ready.

Place a juggler, dancer or sparkler-twirler in front of the screen and an incredible array of psychedelic effects will be at your fingertips, ready to manipulate and create oohs and aahs in your audience.

As with TV feedback you may need to tweak the focus and orientation of the camera before things start getting magic.

VULCAN SALUTE

HAND TRICKS

☆ Make your hand flat and then open the gap between your middle and ring finger.

Some people can do this and others can't but you know why? The people who can have *practiced* it—so get on and learn it˙.

It's not that useful, unless you want to impress Trekkies, but it's a nice piece of dexterity worth learning for its own sake.

☆ There is a variation in which the middle and ring fingers stay together and the other fingers splay.

If you do one after the other it looks pretty cool.

If you want to annoy Vulcan lovers then you could buy an English-Klingon dictionary and learn the language. There are hundreds of Klingon speakers today and one American linguistics professor even brought up his son bilingual in English and Klingon.

It takes all sorts.

Heghlu'meH QaQ jajvam!

˙ This is quite unlike the skill of rolling up your tongue which you either you have or you don't, genetically speaking.

W*

WALKING THE DOG

YO-YO

☆ Chuck your **Yo-Yo** down hard so that you get a nice long **SLEEP** at the end of the string.

Now gently let it **GRIND** against the floor so that it travels forwards as you keep the string taught above it.

As the momentum drops off flick the **Yo-Yo** back up into your hand.

You have just been **WALKING THE DOG**.

WASHING CLOTHES ON THE ROAD

TRAVELLER'S TIPS

People of an itinerant disposition are sometimes known as *Hedge Monkeys* but at least with this trick they are less likely to be called *Soap Dodgers*.

---

* No traditional construction for W is shown beccause W is not a Roman letter.

☆ Get a great big container (perhaps a shiny new dustbin) and fill it with dirty clothes, hot water, and washing powder. Stick a secure lid on it and place it as for up to the back of your truck as you can.

Now drive 100 miles.

On reaching your destination the dirt will have been *vibrated* out of your laundry and all you have to do is rinse it out and hang it out to dry.

See also **WHERE TO STOW FRAGILE ITEMS IN YOUR TRUCK**.

WASHING-UP IN THE WILD

TRAVELLER'S TIPS

When washing up the dishes by the side of a stream, miles from civilisation, it is totally unacceptable to use conventional domestic household chemicals which will pollute the water in unfriendly ways.

☆ Wood ash makes great detergent, stick it in the pan and add a little water and get slooshing. That baked-on grease will just fly off.

☆ If you need a pan scourer you have only to grab a sod of turf from the bank and rip it out with its roots. The root fibres will combine with the abrasive soil itself to provide the ideal tool. It will feel a little odd at first to be smearing mud all over your pan, but when you rinse it off it will be as clean as a whistle.

WALL BOUNCE

JUGGLING

☆ If you throw a **BOUNCING BALL** at the floor just short of a vertical wall it will bounce up, glance off the wall and pick up terrific spin.

It will then arc back towards you and when it hits the floor it will head back towards the wall. Successive bounces will alternate forward and backwards, just like the **KARATE CHOP BOUNCE**—the spin reverses each time it hits the floor.

☆ If you throw the ball from a position *very* close to the wall and make it hit at a really shallow angle something extraordinary happens: the ball will do a complex sequence of five bounces and end up flying back towards you at high speed.

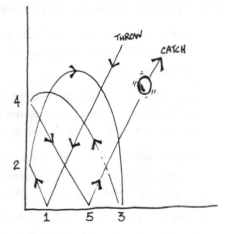

You can chuck three balls at the wall like this in a rapid sequence and they will all cavort magically through their five bounces (very rarely hitting each other) and finally pop back out into your waiting hand—one, two, three! Hey, try five!

The most amazing part of the trick, from a scientific point of view, is that the balls actually *pick up speed* on bounce number four.

This might seem unlikely but it's true! The reason is that the ball has been spinning terrificly fast, but finally leaves the floor with practically none. The spin energy has been converted into raw speed.

A
B
C
D
E
F
G
H
I
J
K
L
M
N
O
P
Q
R
S
T
U
V
W
X
Y
Z

WATER BOMB

WEAPONS / ORIGAMI

The **WATER BOMB** is a fine weapon for attacks on people or property, especially on hot days. There are various ways of constructing them.

☆ You can use regular party balloons, filled from a tap and inflated to about a third of their usual size. Just be careful that the things don't go off and cause a friendly fire incident.

☆ You can buy balloons specially made for the purpose, which are smaller than regular balloons and naturally fill to a good throwing weight.

☆ Condoms, though expensive, can make excellent water bombs, and they are especially horrific weapons when used against girls (for obvious and squeamish reasons).

If you are of an appropriate age you can obtain huge numbers of condoms for nothing by persuading well-meaning adults to arrange a sex education workshop in which dozens of the things will be handed out for free.

☆ Silicone rubber gloves are used widely in the modern workplace because mechanics and medical people can no longer be insured to touch anything yukky in today's insurance-governed society.

They come in boxes of up to a hundred because they are use-once-and-throwaway items. Nobody will miss a couple of dozen and they make terrific water bombs.

☆ Zen water-bombers will want to make the classic **ORIGAMI** water bomb. As strange as it might seem, a simple piece of paper can be folder into a perfectly good water container.

Here's how you do it.

Begin by taking a sheet of paper and square it. You do this by folding a diagonal over from one corner so show the line of the square and then marking that line tearing off the excess.

See **ROOT TWO RECTANGLE**.

1: Make two diagonal *valley* folds and one central *hill* folds

2: Lift the two ends of the hill fold together to make a fan shape.

3: Take two top corners and fold them down to the apex of the fan.

4: Fold the two sides of the little diamond you have just formed and fold them into the middle.

5: Here's the clever bit! Lift up the little triangular tab at the bottom and fold it in half with a hill fold and then tuck it into the hold in the triangular piece above it.

6: Repeat with the tab on the other side.

7: Turn the work over and perform steps 4–6 on the other side.

When you're done you'll end up with a little kite shaped piece of paper. If you examine it closely you'll see that there is a tiny hole in the top.

Blow *hard* into this hole and your origami will magically inflate into a cube.

The side length of the cube is one quarter of the size of the square you started out with.

You fill the thing by holding it carefully under a slow-running tap so the water pours into the hole. It will hold water for a long time before it becomes completely soggy and falls apart, but that's not a problem because you will have thrown it at someone long before that happens.

With practice you can fold a paper water bomb in about half a minute.

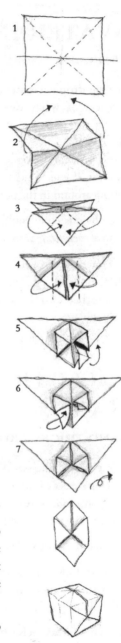

A
B
C
D
E
F
G
H
I
J
K
L
M
N
O
P
Q
R
S
T
U
V
W
X
Y
Z

A
B
C
D
E
F
G
H
I
J
K
L
M
N
O
P
Q
R
S
T
U
V
W
X
Y
Z

WATER IN PETROL TANKS

VEHICLES

Having drops of water in your petrol tanks is a bad thing because tiny droplets of water can become lodged in the very fine jets of your carburettor and cause running or starting problems. This is a problem with older vehicles because the small amounts of water that have condensed inside the tank over the years may have built up into an appreciable amount. If you could see into your tank you'd see some dirty brown blobs rolling around in the bottom.

The obvious cure would be to remove the tank, turn it upside down, and remove *everything* from it before refitting it and filling it with fresh fuel.

☆ However, a simpler method is to add a little methanol to your tank. Methanol and water mix, whereas petrol and water do not. The water will be absorbed into the fuel and will run through the engine without causing any problems.

WELL DONE, MEDIUM OR RARE?

HAND TRICKS / KITCHEN TRICKS

This trick is much-used by chefs to train their underlings in the art of cooking steaks to various degrees. Note that you can never really tell what's going on *inside* a steak, it is possible to char the outside while the inside is still raw. The way to test is by pressing the steak and feeling how firm it is.

Your hand can provide a sort of comparison gauge for this test.

Make an O.K. sign with your right hand, and then with your left index finger simply touch the fleshy part of the base of your right thumb—this will feel fairly soft.

That's how steak feels when it's cooked *Rare*.

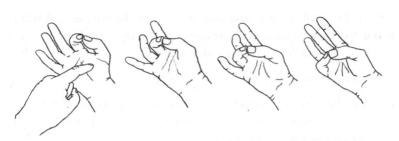

Now make the OK sign with your middle finger—that's *Medium Rare.*

Ring finger—*Medium.*

Little finger *Well done.*

This is why the more muscular and burly chefs tend to overcook steaks.

WHEEL BRAKING

UNICYCLING

WHEEL BRAKING is a method of controlling a **UNICYCLE** or an **IMPOSSIBLE WHEEL** in which the forward speed of the vehicle is kept in balance by gripping or applying friction to the wheel with your legs or feet. It is often used when making fast hill descents on **UNICYCLES**—a very dangerous but exhilarating activity.

☆ It is very difficult to ride a **UNICYCLE** down a steep hill because, as the speed picks up, it becomes virtually impossible to keep your feet on the pedals. Certain suicidal **UNICYCLISTS** discovered that if they took their

A
B
C
D
E
F
G
H
I
J
K
L
M
N
O
P
Q
R
S
T
U
V
W
X
Y
Z

A B C D E F G H I J K L M N O P Q R S T U V W X Y Z

feet off the pedals entirely and placed them on the tyre, as if **WHEEL-WALKING** they could actually remain upright on a machine that was achieving speeds as high as thirty miles per hour.

This activity is sometimes referred to a *Gliding*.

To learn this skill you would be advised to work on the flat at first, building up as much speed as you can and then doing a short *Glide* as you bring the machine gracefully to a stop.

☆ This skill will stand you in good stead if you are ever ambitious enough to attempt the **IMPOSSIBLE WHEEL** which is controlled pretty much by **WHEEL BRAKING** alone.

WHERE TO STOW FRAGILE ITEMS IN YOUR TRUCK

TRAVELLERS TIPS

The least bouncy place in your truck is the point exactly halfway between the front and rear axles and as low down as possible.

That's where you place delicate items.

You'll be amazed at just how steady that point is.

If you *want* something to get bounced around a lot (see **WASHING CLOTHES ON THE ROAD**) you stick it as far to the rear as possible.

WHICH COIN DID I TOUCH?

MIND-READING

This is a very, *very* cool **BAR BET**.

☆ You lay out three coins in a line and explain to the **MARK** that you are going to look away while they point to one of the coins. Then you will turn back and tell them which coin they pointed at.

Again and again you get the right answer.

This trick is almost infinitely repeatable and always completely baffling to your unsuspecting victim.

☆ HERE'S *The* TRICK: The very nature of the trick demands that it *must* have spectators—otherwise the **MARK** could deny that you pointed to the right coin. That's what you use to pull it off.

One of the people watching is a *shill* and they are signalling the **MARK'S** choice to you every time you turn around.

There are so many ways of signalling that I hardly need to describe them, but here are a few ideas.

One classic is for the secret helper to place their beer glass either off to the right, off to the left or in the centre of their beer mat.

Or they can take a new sip of beer each time the trick repeats.

Or they can scratch a cheek or nose.

Or glance in a particular direction to indicate the coin.

Once you have rehearsed the trick with your shill you can do it anytime you like.

☆ A popular variation of this trick uses nine coins arranged three by three. The shill signals the coin by placing their beer glass in an appropriate position on a beer mat.

A B C D E F G H I J K L M N O P Q R S T U V W X Y Z

WHICH HAND IS THE FROG IN?

SILLINESS

This trick is of great value when you are in one of those dreadful situations where your friend wants *you* to make up your mind where to go or what to do—and you'd really rather prefer that *they* made the decision.

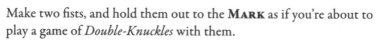

Since loggerheads of this kind can be aggravating and contentious, the true trickster manipulates their opponent by injecting some comedy into the situation.

Make two fists, and hold them out to the **MARK** as if you're about to play a game of *Double-Knuckles* with them.

    YOU: Which hand is the frog in?

As you say this you make small jumping moves with one hand, as if holding a captured frog. If they choose correctly, which they can hardly fail to do, then they have to make the decision.

Everyone will be mightily amused*.

There are several variations to be mined from this rich seam of comedy:

    YOU: Which hand is the Meerkat in?

One hand is elevated to form a Meerkat puppet scanning the horizon.

    YOU: Which hand are the drugs in?

A fist is brought surreptitiously to the nose and casually snorted.

    YOU: Which hand are the sleeping pills in?

The hand slumps into a faint.

... and so on.

---

* Unless you previously prepared by drawing a small frog on the palm of the *other* hand, in which case they lose. Though they may have *wanted* to lose, so have a care.

WHIPS

TOPIC

The **WHIP** is the weapon of choice for a trickster. They are also fearsome, elegant and startlingly impressive devices.

WHIPS are capable of inflicting severe pain, but unless they catch an eye or an ear they will do little real damage.

In the bad old days when people were flogged to death it was generally *shock* that killed them rather than their actual injuries.

Having said that you *don't* want to catch yourself with your own whip.

It really hurts!

The two most useful types of whip are the *bull whip* and the *stock whip*. Both have wooden handles at the thick end which are wrapped in plaited leather. In a bull whip this plait continues straight on, tapering slowly to the knot that attaches the **FALL**, or *rat tail*, which is an unplaited section leading finally to the **CRACK**, or *cracker*, which is the sacrificial piece of twine at the business end of the weapon.

The stock whip is similar except for a leather hinge at the end of the handle. Stock whips are designed to be used on horseback and are easier to control when they are being held by a rider. It is generally held that bull whips are more accurate than stock whips.

When using whips to control animals the idea is *not* to hit them.

Apart from being very non-PC this would be entirely unproductive.

A
B
C
D
E
F
G
H
I
J
K
L
M
N
O
P
Q
R
S
T
U
V
W
X
Y
Z

Instead you crack the things to scare the living daylights out of them, which is perfectly OK.

Some people think that whips crack because the end bangs into itself. This is not the case. A whip cracks because the end is travelling through the air faster than the speed of sound, which is 770 miles per hour.

So, quicker than, say, you can run.

A whip will *pop* when it is travelling slower that that.

There are many different ways of cracking a whip, but technically they all work pretty much the same way. You create a bend or *wave* in the whip and then send the wave hurtling off in some direction. At first the wave is carried by a thick part of the whip, but as it moves along the whip gets thinner. Since there is a certain amount of momentum energy in the wave, and since momentum (scientifically speaking) is *speed* multiplied by *weight,* it follows that as the whip gets thinner (and hence lighter) the only way the wave can hold the momentum is to go *faster*.

And so it does.

Eventually the wave reaches the end of the whip which peters out into nothing. At this point all of the momentum given to the whip by the burly whip-cracker (way back at the *fat end*) is focused on the couple of inches of very thin and light cord that makes up the **CRACK** (down at the thin end).

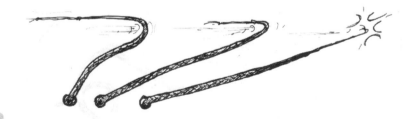

The **CRACK** accelerates to fantastic speed and creates a little sonic boom that can, if it goes off close to your head, leave your ears ringing.

It is also perfectly possible, if your cracking technique is not right, to put a lot of energy into an attempted crack which misfires and can cause severe damage to the whip itself.

It's not uncommon for whips to snap at the top of the **FALL** from bad technique.

When learning a new technique you should proceed slowly and be satisfied with subsonic *pops* until your technique is good enough to apply some real force.

Since the whip is moving so fast it can be used to cut things as it cracks, a trick that requires great **ACCURACY WITH WHIPS**.

If the thing you are cutting happens to be a banana (and why not?) and if the **CRACK** is indeed supersonic when it hits it, you'll find that the banana is not only sliced neatly, but has also been turned to jelly for an inch or so on either side of the cut; this being a result of the tremendous supersonic shock wave that has just run through it.

If you own a whip you are advised *not* to let others handle it. For one thing they are quite likely to hurt themselves and for another, if they mess up they are likely to break it. In both of those regards **WHIPS** are very like **MOTORCYCLES**.

The classic beginner's accident goes as follows. The novice (remembering attempts to crack a length of cord from their school days) holds the whip in their right hand and quickly lifts and then drops it, as if smacking a bottom.

What they haven't bargained for are the special properties of a tapered whip.

Instead of cracking in front of them, as expected, the whip rises to head height and cracks right next to it—or may well hit them in the face, or the ear, or the eye...

Don't lend your whip—especially to beginners.

A
B
C
D
E
F
G
H
I
J
K
L
M
N
O
P
Q
R
S
T
U
V
W
X
Y
Z

WHIP MAN CRACK

WHIPS

The **WHIP MAN CRACK** is the most elegant and accurate way I know of cracking a whip. It was shown to me by the legendary *Whip Man* of New Zealand, one *Peter Jack*. Peter makes beautiful whips which are much sought-after by artistes and bondage freaks the world over. He also controls whips with a Zen-like mastery.

He made a series of cuts into a piece of spaghetti I held in may hand, each taking off another eighth of an inch—using a twelve foot whip! He then proceeded to cut the stalk of an apple that was hanging from a tree in his garden after passing the whip through a small gap between the branches from the *far side* of the tree!

The **WHIP MAN CRACK** as I have taken the liberty of calling it, can be very frustrating to learn because it is such a pure technique.

It goes like this:

☆ Lay your whip out behind you and then push it forwards.

Er, that's it!

☆ You can keep this going with minute arm movements. Push the whip forwards, let it pop and then it will return behind you and you can repeat the move.

The action of the arm is as if gently hammering a nail into the wall, your thumb should lay on top of the handle, guiding each stroke to the target.

It's all about getting a very smooth action and looking after the bend (or loop as some would have it) in the whip.

This really is *Zen and the art of Whip Cracking*.

WHISTLE AND HUM

SILLINESS

☆ It turns out that if you **WHISTLE AND HUM** *at the same time* you can make a noise rather like a large jet engine in the cruise.

Try it!

WHO THREW THAT?

SILLINESS

This is a very funny bar stunt.

☆ Take a beer mat and tear out a V shape. Push the slot onto your nose so the beer mat just hangs there. Turn to your friends with a serious look on your face and say:

"Who Threw That?"

WIMPY

JUGGLING

CASCADES, FOUNTAINS and **SHOWERS** are the names of *the* classic juggling patterns. They share nice watery names which reflect the elegant way in which well-juggled objects can be made to flow through the air.

Cascades work only for *odd* numbers of objects.
Fountains work only for *even* numbers while
Showers can work for any number.

To this triplet of techniques we can add a horribly-named sibling, the Wimpy pattern, which works only for even numbers of objects.

☆ In a Wimpy pattern both hands throw together (in "sync" as jugglers would say) and every throw is a crossing throw. They are the nearest thing you can get to a Cascade when working with even numbers.

Collisions are the obvious problem; if both hands throw across at the same time and to the same height then logic dictates that the objects being thrown will meet in the middle. A little cheating is required and by making the throws from one hand slightly higher than the throws from the other this can be avoided.

Visual purists sometimes juggle the arch from one hand slightly in front of the arch from the other so they can keep the heights identical. Fans of symmetry will alternate this arrangement: first the right passes in front of the left, then the left in front of the right. This is obsessive behaviour.

☆ Wimpy patterns are often used in *Numbers Juggling* (when working with an even number of objects) because jugglers tend to find it easier to juggle patterns in which both sides of the pattern are connected rather than independent. It is also a little easier to make a crossing throw than a *self* throw at the fast hand-speeds required for juggling large numbers of objects.

☆ Wimpy patterns are also used by jugglers working with Bouncing Balls when they want to juggle even numbers. The skill acquired by way of mastering the five-ball Passive Bounce can easily be applied to six balls if a Wimpy pattern is used.

WINCH ON A 4X4

VEHICLES / TRAVELLER'S TIPS

S.U.V. is an American acronym for a Sports Utility Vehicle, Brits call them 4×4's, Either way, these are vehicles designed for seriously punishing off-road useage which most of them never see.

Serious off-roaders will aspire to fitting a winch so that when they get utterly stuck in the mud they can tie a cable to a tree and wind themselves out of trouble. Ideally you would fit a winch on *both ends* of the vehicle but winches are expensive so you'll often see vehicles fitted with just one.

☆ HERE'S *The* TRICK: fit the winch to the *back* of the vehicle. It may look cool on the front but it's not going to do you a lot of good. When you are totally bogged down this is Nature's way of saying "don't go that way!"

A
B
C
D
E
F
G
H
I
J
K
L
M
N
O
P
Q
R
S
T
U
V
W
X
Y
Z

Just like **FALLING THROUGH THE ICE**, you should immediately head back in the direction you came from, and for that you will need a winch on the back of your vehicle.

WINDING FINGER TRICK

PSYCHOLOGY / HYPNOTISM

This trick is used by some hypnotherapists as a test of a subject's suggestibility—but it's also a good fun trick to play on people.

☆ Get your "subject" to clasp their hands together, fingers interlocked, and then raise their two index fingers up, and hold them an inch or so apart.

> YOU: Hold your fingers
> like that ...
> ... and see how they
> will be magically drawn
> together.

☆ Now wind your index finger in a tight little circle in front of their fingers as if winding up the propellor on an elastic band powered model plane. Or, some people make the winding motion in the horizontal plane going around the fingers.

In 80% of cases the subject will be unable to keep their fingers apart.

You would do best *not* to say, 'you will not be able to keep your fingers apart,' since that would be an invitation to a *polarity responder* to try and break the magic spell you have just woven over them.

WINDING UP YOUR THUMB

SILLINESS / HAND TRICKS

☆ Place your hand on the table with our thumb over the edge.

'OK I'm going to give it ten turns,' and you turn your thumb ten times as if winding up an elastic-band powered plane.

'Er, can you help here? Just hold my hand down a second please, yeah stick yours on top and press hard. I'm gonna give it just three more winds.' Crank it slowly three more times.

'OK, now when I say just let go OK? One! Two! Three! Now!'

As they let go your hand should wriggle and clatter about violently as if having an *elasto-leptic* fit before running out of power and lying limp again.

Silly, but very amusing!

WINDMILL

JUGGLING

☆ Juggle a **THREE BALL CASCADE** with every right hand throw going **OVER THE TOP** and every left hand throw **UNDER THE HAND**. This is called the **WINDMILL** for obvious reasons, it's also known as a *False Shower* on account of the circular path that the balls take.

Work on getting a nice round shape to the pattern.

☆ Don't forget to learn it both ways around.

☆ Direction changes are fun, try a few throws of a right-handed **WINDMILL** and then a few throws of a left-handed **WINDMILL**.

☆ A **WINDMILL** with a direction change every *three* throws can turn into a **MILLS' MESS** which is a very sophisticated pattern and one you *really* want to learn. Trust me.

WINE BOTTLE, OPENING WITHOUT A CORKSCREW

TECHNICAL WIZARDRY

It is cruel fate that sometimes presents one with a bottle of wine but not the means to open it. The well-prepared drinker therefore carries, at all times, a **SWISS ARMY KNIFE**.

However, there are times when even the finest trickster will have forgotten this vital piece of kit.

☆ A bottle of wine can be opened by pushing the cork *into* the bottle using a suitable instrument such as a cigarette lighter, a pen or even a key. Once loosened, the cork will try to float back into the neck when the bottle is turned upside down. A vigourous shake should persuade the first glassful of wine to emerge.

☆ It has been known for extremely strong (and desperate) drinkers to open a bottle by pushing the cork into it with a sturdy *finger*.

The act of opening a bottle of Champagne with a sabre, or other sword, is known as *Sabrage*. You will need some expensive champagne and a large and heavy sabre or other similar sword.

☆ Remove the foil and the wire from a champagne bottle and hold it in your left hand at arm's length so that the cork is pointing to the right and slightly downwards.

☆ Draw your weapon and strike the bottle hard on the neck just below the lip below the cork. The sabre will slide along the neck and strike hard and strike the lip below the cork. The end of the bottle, complete with the cork, will break cleanly away from the rest of the bottle and the champagne will gush out as the pressure is released, taking with it any tiny particles of glass that may be present. Turn the bottle upright and pour—ladies first!

Modern science is unable to explain how it is possible to open a bottle of wine with a shoe or indeed how it came to pass that somebody was once too drunk to remember to bring a corkscrew, yet managed to invent this very useful trick.

☆ Remove a foot from your shoe and replace it with a bottle of wine. Strip off anything covering the cork.

Now hold the bottle firmly in the shoe and smack the heel *hard* against a solid wall. You can be brave —it takes a lot to smash the bottle!

After just a very few taps the cork will have worked itself out of the neck.

WOBBLY PENCIL TRICK

SILLINESS / MAGIC

Hold a pencil between thumb and forefinger about a third of the way down and give it a wobble, by holding the pencil loosely you can create the illusion that it is made of bendy rubber—and very convincingly too!

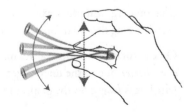

A B C D E F G H I J K L M N O P Q R S T U V **W** X Y Z

A
B
C
D
E
F
G
H
I
J
K
L
M
N
O
P
Q
R
S
T
U
V
W
X
Y
Z

WOBBLY TABLE THEOREM

TECHNICAL WIZARDRY / MATHEMATICS

As this book was going to press the author was advised by *Tarim* of a mathematical discovery regarding wobbly tables.

Unlike a tripod, which will always stand steady on an uneven surface, our friend the table has *four* legs, and on an uneven floor it will tend to rest on two legs while rocking between the third and fourth. This can be extremely annoying if you are eating a delicious roasted dinner in one of England's older stone-floored pubs.

The usual solution is to obtain a deck of beer mats with which to wedge up one of the floating legs—but mathematics, and more specifically *Tarim's Theorem*, offers us a better solution.

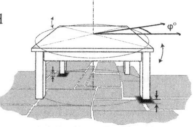

To understand this we will engage is a simple **THOUGHT EXPERIMENT**:

Imagine a four-legged table was constructed so as to have three fixed legs of equal length while the fourth is constructed to be telescopic so it can extend and retract as circumstances require. Now if such a table was placed on an uneven floor we know that the three solid legs would always contact the ground no matter what the surface was like. The fourth would extend or retract as required so it too would also contact the ground. If we rotated such a table around its centre on such a floor we would find that at some angles the telescopic leg would be shorter, but at others it would be longer than the fixed legs. As mathematicians we could now draw a graph of the extension and retraction of the telescopic leg, with the x-axis denoting the angle of rotation and the y-axis denoting the extension or retraction of the fourth leg.

On careful consideration of the matter it is easy to see that if the leg is ever *shorter* due to the uneven ground there must be another angle at which it is *longer*. So the graph of its extension must pass through the x-axis at *at least two points* (it has to go from shorter to longer so it must, conversely, also go from longer to shorter).

So the **WOBBLY TABLE THEOREM** will save us a trip to the bar to beg for beer mats because we now know that you can always arrange to have four feet of a table in solid contact with the ground by turning the table on its axis until we find one of the *sweet spots* where all four legs are in contact with the floor.

WRAP

WHIPS

A **WRAP** is the action of wrapping a whip around a person or thing.

☆ Only Indiana Jones wannabees would dream of **WRAPPING** a whip around a branch and then swinging off it. These things are expensive! Use a piece of rope for goodness sake!

☆ You can use a whip to retrieve a dropped juggling club from a **GIRAFFE UNICYCLE** though. Lay the **FALL** of the whip next to the club, then cheat it under the nose *twice*. You now have the club in a small loop. A quick flick will send it flying upwards into your waiting hand.

☆ A popular **WRAP** involves a tough-looking whip person and a mild-mannered and vulnerable volunteer— usually a gorgeous girl.

First you need to master the sideways **WHIP MAN CRACK**.

Here are a few tips:

A
B
C
D
E
F
G
H
I
J
K
L
M
N
O
P
Q
R
S
T
U
V
W
X
Y
Z

Lay the whip out behind you pointing away from the target. Pull forwards to get the whip going and then turn the handle so it points towards the target. This turning action puts a bend in the whip which will crack at the point you were aiming at.

Notice how the whip will carry on after the crack—but with greatly reduced force. This is how you wrap it around your victim. A right-handed whip-cracker should aim to the right of the victim.

Make sure you have this trick solid before trying it with a real human being.

Stand the girl at about half the whip's range and lay the whip out behind you. Pull it hard so that it misses her (by a little) and makes a sideways

WHIP MAN CRACK

somewhere behind her. The excess energy of the whip will carry it on so that it wraps a few coils around her.

If you are right-handed you'll crack it to her right and she'll get wrapped in counter-clockwise coils.

The energy of the whip is pretty much dissipated after the crack (make it a loud one) so she won't get hurt.

☆ For extra style points you then pull her toward you with the whip, steal a kiss and push her away again—she should pirouette off clockwise with her hands over her head.

☆ Obviously, in these enlightened times, the whole thing becomes *much* funnier if the whip is wielded by a sassy girl and the volunteer is a tough but obviously terrified bloke.

You can also do a solo **WRAP**.

☆ Swing a whip around your head and then allow your hand to fall low and stop. This causes the whip to wrap itself a full turn around you.

Raise your hand again and follow the whip one turn and it will unwrap .

Finish off with a nice positive forward stroke and you'll get a nice crack at the end of the move.

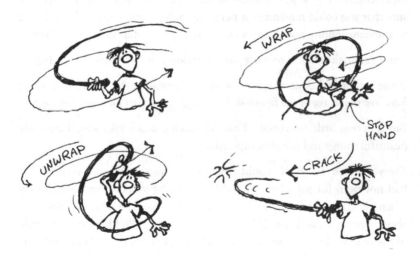

This looks very brave and scary, but it's perfectly safe.

A
B
C
D
E
F
G
H
I
J
K
L
M
N
O
P
Q
R
S
T
U
V
W
X
Y
Z

WRITING THINGS DOWN RIGHT AWAY

PSYCHOLOGY

☆ When you are engaged in a creative activity like, say writing a book, you'll find that creative ideas can pop into your head at pretty much any time of day or night. Some of these ideas can be really rather good. The trouble is, that they can pop back out of your head just as mysteriously as they popped in—leaving you desperately wondering just what that truly great idea was.

So what you have to do is write the ideas down *right away!*

☆ Sometimes people record their dreams for self-analysis purposes or as a source of creative ideas for stories, poems and songs. You'll surely have experienced the strange sensation of having a vivid dream and being quite sure that you could remember it perfectly well—until you tried to relate it to someone. Funny how dreams vanish like mist under the morning Sun.

Once again, the trick is to write this stuff down immediately on waking.

If the author had done that on one fateful morning, the World might not have lost the secret of the famously lost juggling pattern *Dancey's Devilment.*

Buy a decent little notebook (I use Moleskine notebooks which are truly beautiful things and not that expensive).

Every Trick In The Book would have been a thin and flimsy volume if it had not been for my obsessive habit of writing ideas down immediately when they occurred to me. The great writer Roald Dahl was obsessive about writing ideas down. If he had not actually pulled his car to the side of the road in the pouring rain one night and written down "a boy inherits a chocolate factory" his most famous book might never have been written.

Not that I'm comparing myself to Dahl.

Actually I'm more like Charlie Bucket.

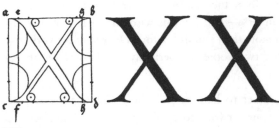

XEROGRAPHY

SILLINESS / MATHEMATICS

You wouldn't have thought that there was much you could do with the humble photocopier trickwise—and indeed short of xeroxing your bum there really isn't.

However, *Every Trick In The Book* required material for the X section (if only to be able to show the classical construction for the letter at the head of the page) so *something* had to be found.

☆ Obtain a photograph of a friend and place in on the scanner table of a photocopier and hit the Copy button.

Now timing is everything here, you need to slide the picture across the glass *as it is being scanned*. With a little practice you can produce hall of mirrors style images in this way.

☆ Alternatively, if you are feeling brave, you can ram your face against the glass and move it, while making grimaces, during the scan. The result is a combination of the old face-pressed-on-the-window gag and a hall of mirrors distortion.

☆ On the general subject of photocopying: have you ever tried to reduce your master copy of the gig flyer from A4 to half size so you can get two copies on a sheet and got it horribly wrong?

Thought so.

You probably typed 50% into the reduce size option and ended up with something way too small—so small that *four* will fit on the A4 sheet.

A
B
C
D
E
F
G
H
I
J
K
L
M
N
O
P
Q
R
S
T
U
V
W
X
Y

☆ HERE'S *The* TRICK: To reduce an A4 master to half its area, you *actually* need to type in 71%—and for this wisdom you'll probably just hate mathematics even more than you did before. Once your artwork is so reduced you'll find that two copies fit perfectly side-by-side on an A4 sheet.

In fact, to reduce *any* sheet to half its area the magic number is 71%. Conversely to enlarge your artwork to double its area the number you need is 141%.

See **ROOT TWO RECTANGLE**.

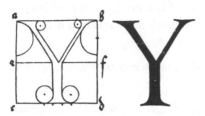

YEAST TABLETS AND BEER

EXPLOSIVES

☆ You must never *ever* surreptitiously drop a yeast tablet into a pint of Guinness, or any other beer for that matter. The resulting unstoppable foamy slow-motion explosion of beery goo will cause *severe* distress and annoyance.

And you know how emotional people can get when they are drinking!

YO-YO

TOPIC

A **Yo-Yo** as you know perfectly well, is a toy that seems to create an unstoppable craze every few years and then vanishes back into near obscurity only to re-emerge at a later time in history.

There are also some toss-juggling tricks that mimic the real **Yo-Yo**. You can read about those at the end of this section.

During the last **Yo-Yo** craze vast fortunes were made as the toy industry quickly jumped on the bandwagon before suddenly finding themselves stuck with vast mountains of unsold stock that will sit gathering dust until the phenomenon repeats. Predicting the onset of these crazes is like waiting for earthquakes in San Francisco when all people can ever really say is that a Big One is probably overdue.

☆ Serious artists will have a top-quality **Yo-Yo** and will carry a bag full of spare strings because the stuff wears out. Their machine will certainly

A
B
C
D
E
F
G
H
I
J
K
L
M
N
O
P
Q
R
S
T
U
V
W
X
Y
Z

A
B
C
D
E
F
G
H
I
J
K
L
M
N
O
P
Q
R
S
T
U
V
W
X
Y
Z

be capable of **SLEEPING** at the bottom of the string (essential for most tricks) and may even have some sort of clutch mechanism in it to make this work better.

It is beyond the scope of this book to discuss the merits of various brands, just get a good one.

The string on a **Yo-Yo** is actually a single cord that is folded in half and twisted on itself like a two-ply rope. This creates a natural loop in the bottom of the string that goes around the axle.

The **Yo-Yo** can **SLEEP** because the loop only grips the axle lightly. You can tighten or loosen the loop by twisting or untwisting the string.

This can be done manually or more cleverly by using the trick called the **FLYING SAUCER**.

The correct length of string depends on your height.

☆ The loose end of the string is tied into a small loop that can be pulled through itself to form a loop that is placed around your "yo-finger" which is the first finger of your favourite hand.

☆ Winding the string can be a little tricky since it will tend to spin on the axle. So trap a piece of string against the body of the **Yo-Yo** before winding it up.

Now hold the fully wound **Yo-Yo** in your hand, palm down and with the string at the top. You're ready to go.

☆ Begin by letting the **Yo-Yo** fall and see what happens. It will hit the bottom of the string and stop there slowly spinning to a stop.

☆ Rewind it and set it off again, but give the string a little tug and you can encourage it to hop up and wind itself up again. In a few minutes you'll be happily yo-ing away and wondering what the fuss is all about.

The fuss, my friend, is about **TRICKS**. There are hundreds. Start off by learning the **SPINNER**, **SLEEPING**, **WALKING THE DOG**, **AROUND THE WORLD**, **ROCKING THE BABY** and when you're feeling really up there you can move onto more complex combination tricks.

YO-YO
(BALL JUGGLING TRICKS)

JUGGLING

A number of **BALL JUGGLING** tricks mimic the action of a **YO-YO**.

☆ Grab three balls and juggle **TWO IN ONE HAND** in columns (that is side- by-side).

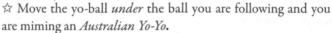

Now with your spare hand move the spare ball in time with and exactly above, one of the two-in-one-hand balls. Announce that you are doing a **YO-YO**.

It's a very similar move to the **FAKE**.

☆ Move the yo-ball *under* the ball you are following and you are miming an *Australian Yo-Yo*.

☆ A great illusion can be created with **BOUNCING BALLS** if your mime skills are up to it.

Juggle a **TWO IN ONE HAND** as a **COLUMN BOUNCE** with a spare ball in your spare hand. Now, as you make the exchanges use the spare ball as a yo-ball and lift it *above* the ball that is being exchanged into the pattern. Make sure it moves precisely in synch.

OK, now swap the trick from one side to the other as you juggle, so that on each exchange there are *three* balls directly above each other, all moving in perfect time. The top ball is the yo-ball, then

A
B
C
D
E
F
G
H
I
J
K
L
M
N
O
P
Q
R
S
T
U
V
W
X
Y
Z

under that is the ball being swapped *into* the juggle and finally there is the ball that is being swapped out.

Improvise on this theme and you'll find you can create some awesome **Yo-Yo** like illusions—people will almost believe that there is string involved.

YOU CUT AND I'LL CHOOSE

PSYCHOLOGY / TECHNICAL WIZARDRY

When dividing valuable booty between two or more people it is always handy to have a set of accurate weighing scales to hand, but circumstances may not provide them.

This is when the principle of **YOU CUT AND I'LL CHOOSE** is an invaluable method of ensuring rapier-keen fairness.

The only possible improvement on the scheme is the more chivalrous offer of *I'll cut and you choose!*

If, say, the remainder of a delicious cake is to be shared by two friends it is important that the cut is made fairly lest they become enemies on account of their love of cake temporarily eclipsing their love of each other. Thus one companion may offer **YOU CUT AND I'LL CHOOSE** (or the converse) as a solution.

Radical Cheney made both observations and practical experiment on this subject which were recorded in his magnum opus *"The True Nature of Things"* (which, as I may have mentioned elsewhere, has long been out of print).

> The precision of the divisor in the matter of just apportionment of half shares when the choice is given to the second party has been studied and found to exhibit an accuracy of division comparable to the best practices of the most diligent scientists and engineers who typically conduct measurements with such devices as precision rulers and calibrated balance scales and theodolites and so forth. A divisor unaided by such contrivances and working instead only with the natural tools of optical observation and mindful consideration was found typically to deliver divisions accurate to the hundredth part or better.

One remarkable event was observed in which two gentlemen wished to share the remains of an oriental intoxicant of not inconsiderable value that lay before them in the form of one irregular mass containing the bulk of the matter and a smaller collection of crumbs and dust and débris the whole amounting to a little less than an ounce. Both men had partaken freely of the spoil by way of smoking it for several hours and their manner of speech indicated an extreme degree of narcotic hypnosis from the effects of the stimulants contained in aromatic material.

The offer of division made the first party embarked on the task of separation into halves with a keenness of eye and steadiness of hand that was astounding in comparison to the more relaxed and euphoric behaviour exhibited but minutes before. The division complete, the second swiftly made his choice and I took the opportunity to gain their permission to examine the results for the benefit of Science. I was astonished to discover from careful tests with a pharmaceutical beam balance of rare precision that the shares differed one from the other by less than the thousandth part. Moreover, the gentleman with the benefit of choice, notwithstanding his hallucinatory state of mind, had correctly picked the marginally larger share on a single glance despite the obstructions of a room both darkened and considerably obscured by smoke. I returned from my laboratory naturally eager to convey the anecdote of my discoveries to my companions but I found them in a state of insensible hysteria and quite unable to recollect the transaction that had so recently taken place.

A
B
C
D
E
F
G
H
I
J
K
L
M
N
O
P
Q
R
S
T
U
V
W
X
Y
Z

YOU DON'T WANT TO BE SMOKING THAT!

MAGIC

☆ You see someone smoking a fag. Walk up and very positively swipe it out of their mouth and then throw it to the floor where you stub it out with your foot.

> YOU: You don't want to be smoking that!

Now, just before the big fella punches your lights out, you reveal that you have actually retained the cigarette in your hand.

This is an unbelievably easy piece of **MISDIRECTION** because the nicotine-addled brain of your victim will simply follow the movement of the cigarette to the floor and assume that it is under your foot as you scrunch it out. Be careful though! People can get pretty upset about this sort of thing.

YOU STEER WHILE I PEDAL!

BICYCLES

This has to be the most sociable and sensible way of sharing one pushbike between two riders.

☆ You sit on the saddle and steer the machine.

☆ I sit on the handlebars, facing backwards, and pedal the thing.

Obviously there is a certain amount of trust involved in this operation, but at least we end up face-to-face, which is nice if we happen to be in love. It's much more comfortable than a *Backie* anyway.

YOU'VE GOT DIRT ON YOUR SHIRT!

SILLINESS

If you ever, *ever* get caught out by this one again you may as well burn your copy of *Every Trick In The Book* because you are not capable of learning *anything*.

☆ "Hey, you've got a bit of dirt on your shirt!"

Your protagonist points to your shirt.

You look down.

They tap the bottom of your nose with their finger and exclaim "gotcha!" and laugh at your wonderful stupidity.

Some people *never* learn and you can get them time and time again with the same stupid trick.

It gets better and better with repetition, so if you find a pliable victim just keep on working the trick.

But please help this author to keep up the illusion that this book has an intelligent readership and don't get caught out yourself!

A
B
C
D
E
F
G
H
I
J
K
L
M
N
O
P
Q
R
S
T
U
V
W
X
Y
Z

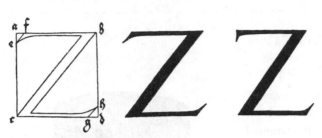

Zen Wrestling

MARTIAL ARTS

Zen Wrestling, also known as *Push Hands* is the only form of combat I know of in which the largest and strongest person can be pitted against the smallest and weakest—and it's still a fair fight.

Stand a couple of feet away from your opponent, face to face. Raise your hands and place them against your opponent's hands, palm to palm.

The fight can now begin. Your hands must say in contact with your opponent's, and no other contact is allowed.

The first person to move their feet is the loser.

It's a brilliant game, mostly played in the mind and the eyes.

A
B
C
D
E
F
G
H
I
J
K
L
M
N
O
P
Q
R
S
T
U
V
W
X
Y
Z

A
B
C
D
E
F
G
H
I
J
K
L
M
N
O
P
Q
R
S
T
U
V
W
X
Y
Z

ZOETROPE

ANIMATION

Also known as the *Zootrope* this popular animation device consisted of a drum mounted on a bearing so that it could spin about its vertical axis. A series of slots in the drum, when looked through, form a kind of shutter system allowing the viewer to see the successive frames of an animation through them.

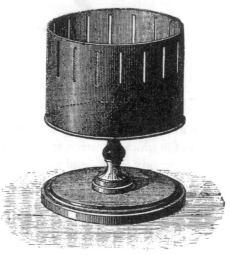

Animations were supplied on strips of card that could be placed inside the drum, so a single machine would be capable of displaying several different shows.

The modern trickster will obtain an old record player and fashion a drum from a biscuit tin with slots appropriately cut.

A selection of the sort of images that amused children in the 19th century are shown opposite—which the trickster will duly copy and mount in their own machine.

See also **THAUMOTROPE, PHENOKISTOSCOPE, PRAXINOSCOPE.**

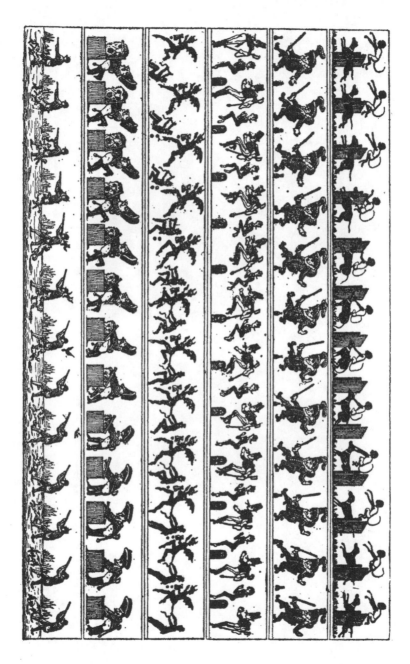

INDEX

About the Author

Charlie Dancey was born in 1955 when the cars were all black and the Beatles had yet to be invented. After brief careers, first as as a truck-driver and then as a signwriter, he discovered juggling and nothing was ever the same again. For many years he worked as a street-entertainer which, curiously, does not involve entertaining streets, so much as the people who walk along them. He is best known in the circus world as the taller and balder half of the comic juggling duo *Haggis & Charlie*.

In 1993 he delivered the *Encyclopædia of Ball Juggling* to a world of hungry circus freaks eager to gobble down new tricks. The book was a great success and was followed by the *Compendium of Club Juggling* and *How to Ride your Unicycle*.

It turns out that jugglers and unicyclists also have a passion for tricks of all kinds and Charlie Dancey is no exception. *Every Trick in the Book* was the next logical step. It is an autobiographical work in the sense that anyone reading it will quickly get an idea of what the author finds entertaining and amusing.

Now that *Every Trick in the Book* has finally gone to press, Dancey hopes to devote more time to other unfinished projects such as his electrically-powered bicycle trailer and the long-awaited juggling machine that reads and performs siteswaps from punched paper tape.

It should come as no surprise that Charlie lives in Glastonbury, England.

```
AMPETRONICUSTINAMPETRONICUSTINAMPETRONICUSTINAMPETRONICUSTINAMP
APKWJXCLIESDSLIAPKWJXCLIESDSLIAPKWJXLIESEDSLIAPKWJXLIESEDSLIAPK
HTEBCIOMWUIINKSHTEBCIOMWUIINKSHTEBCIOMWUINLKSHTEBCIOMWUINLKSHTE
VMONSKUWRFABIOAVMONSKUWRFABIOAVMONSKUWRFABIOAMONSOKUWRFABIOAMON
INPERIBADONASDUINPERIBADONASDUINPERBADONEASDUINPERBADONEASDUINP
MOSTICANIFRUNTEMOSTICANIFRUNTEMOSTICANIFRUNTEMOSTICANIFRUNTEMOS
SULNIFICANSOMASSULNIFICANSOMASSULNIFICANSOMASSULNIFICANSOMASSUL
```